Maya 4.5

SAVVY™

Maya® 4.5

JOHN KUNDERT-GIBBS | PETER LEE

WITH DARIUSH DERAKHSHANI | MARK BAMFORTH

KEITH REICHER | MARCEL DE JONG

SAN FRANCISCO | LONDON

ALIAS | WAVEFRONT
APPROVED

SYBEX®

Associate Publisher: Dan Brodnitz
Acquisitions Editor: Mariann Barsolo
Developmental Editor: Pete Gaughan
Editor: Pat Coleman
Production Editor: Elizabeth Campbell
Technical Editors: Keith Reicher, Dariush Derakhshani
Compositor: Happenstance Type-O-Rama
CD Coordinator: Dan Mummert
CD Technician: Kevin Ly
Proofreaders: Amey Garber, Emily Hsuan, Laurie O'Connell, Nancy Riddiough
Indexer: Ted Laux
Cover and Interior Design: Caryl Gorska, Gorska Design
Cover Photographer: William Helsel, Stone

An earlier version of this book was published under the title Mastering Maya 3 © 2001 SYBEX Inc.

LIBRARY OF CONGRESS CARD NUMBER: 2002113566

ISBN: 0-7821-4109-9

Dear Reader,

Thank you for choosing *Maya 4.5 Savvy*. This book is part of a new wave of Sybex graphics books, all written by outstanding authors—artists and professional teachers who really know their stuff, and have a clear vision of the audience they're writing for.

With each title, we're working hard to set a new standard for the industry. From the paper we print on, to the designers we work with, to the visual examples our authors provide, our goal is to bring you the best 3D graphics books available.

I hope you see all that reflected in these pages. I'd be very interested in hearing your feedback on how we're doing. To let us know what you think about this, or any other Sybex book, please visit us at www.sybex.com. Once there, go to the product page, click on Submit a Review, and fill out the questionnaire. Your input is greatly appreciated.

Best regards,

Daniel A. Brodnitz
Associate Publisher
Sybex Inc.

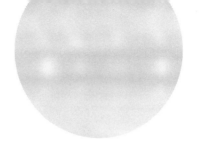

Dedication

To Kristin, Joshua, and Kenlee.

—JLKG

To John, David, and my parents.

—PL

Acknowledgments

It both amazes and inspires us how many people devote their time to work on a book the size of *Maya 4.5 Savvy*. Although there are always more people to thank than we can possibly fit within the confines of this page, we would be remiss if we didn't thank the people who gave the most to this project. ■ First, we would like to thank those who contributed to or edited various portions of this book. Perry Harovas, for his inspiration in creating the original *Mastering Maya Complete 2* and for his interviews with Jill Ramsay and Shai Hinitz; the following contributors for their work on various chapters: Dariush Derakhshani, Chapters 3, 15, 19, and 24; Mark Bamforth, Chapters 4–6 and 8–13; Keith Reicher, Chapter 1–2 and 16–18; Rebecca Johnson, Chapter 14; Josh Tomlinson, Chapter 20; Uma Havaligi, Chapter 21; Wil Whaley, Chapters 22 and 23. Additional thanks to Keith and Dariush for their technical edit of the entire book. ■ A special thanks to Marcel de Jong for his expertise on Fluid effects and writing the tutorials for Chapter 25. ■ We would also like to thank Danny Williams, Jonathan Fischoff, James D. Lee, Charmie Tate, Andrew Shearer, Hae Young Moon, Kyoung Soo Kim, Rebecca Johnson, Deborah Wright, Uma Havaligi, Jong Chan Sohn, Soo Hyun Ahn David De Vos, Matt Welch, Mark Penleson, Bob Meniert, and John Pedone whose work appears in the color section. ■ As always, the great staff at Sybex made work on this book go smoothly. We would especially like to thank Mariann Barsolo, Pete Gaughan, Dan Brodnitz, Bonnie Bills, Elizabeth Campbell, Pat Coleman, Maureen Forys, Dan Mummert, Kevin Ly, and proofreaders Amey Garber, Emily Hsuan, Laurie O'Connell, and Nancy Riddiough. ■ Without the generous support and freedom our employers have given us, we could never have completed this book. A special thanks to President James Barker, Provost Doris Helms, and the faculty, staff, and students of Clemson University and to its Digital Production Arts program for their support and help. Thanks to Alan, Rudy, and Melissa and all the folks at Sight Effects for their insights and knowledge. ■ As always, our loved ones have helped and supported us throughout production of this book, and thus deserve our undying gratitude. John Kundert-Gibbs wishes to especially thank his parents, Lee and Joan Gibbs, and his family, Kristin, Joshua, and Kenlee Kundert-Gibbs. Dariush Derakhshani would like to thank his family and friends for their love, all the teachers of and in his life, and his fiancée Randi, who puts up with all the humming computer gear all over their place.

About the Authors

John Kundert-Gibbs is director of the Digital Production Arts program at Clemson University, which is preparing the film, television, and games technical directors of the future. Author of several publications on Maya, computer graphics, and dramatic literature, he directs students in producing animated shorts, creates effects for live-action projects, and designs electronic media for theatrical productions. He is co-author of such works as *Mastering Maya 3* and *Maya: Secrets of the Pros* and has a B.A. in physics from Princeton University and a Ph.D. in dramatic literature from Ohio State University.

Peter Lee is director at Storydale Inc. in Seoul, South Korea. He has worked in Canada on projects such as Columbia Tristar's *The Nuttiest Nutcracker*, New Line Cinema's *Jason X*, and Jon Nappa's *The Super Snoopers;* co-authored Sybex's *Maya* books; and taught computer animation at ITDC, University of Toronto. At Storydale, he has lead projects such as cinematic for Dong Seo Game Channel's *The Three Kingdoms III* and Joycast's PS2 game *Wingz.* He occasionally lectures at Yonsei and Hongik universities and is currently working on the Korean translation of Sybex's *Maya: Secrets of the Pros.*

About the Contributors

Dariush Derakhshani is a senior CGI effects animator with Sight Effects in Venice, California, working on award-winning national television commercials. He has won the Bronze Plaque from the Columbus Film Festival and has shared honors from the AICP and London International Advertising Awards. He has worked as a CGI animator and compositor on a variety of projects from films to television and was a Supervising Technical Director for the *South Park* television series. He enjoys splitting his time between teaching at a variety of schools, including USC Film School's MFA Animation program, and writing. His works have appeared on `thescratchpost.com` and on various sites of the `digitalmedianet.com`, and he is the Senior Editor of `taintmagazine.com`. He has a B.A. in architecture and in theatre from Lehigh University, an M.F.A. in animation from USC Film School, and flat feet.

Mark Bamforth has been working with 3D applications for 9 years and programming for 19. His animated short *Space Station Fly-Through* was screened at Siggraph 2000. He is currently working on an animated children's series as a programmer/animator at Xvivo LLC.

Keith Reicher is a layout animator for PDI/Dreamworks and holds an M.F.A. in computer graphics from Pratt Institute. He is the creator of the 3D animated short *Benjamin Task,* taking on the roles of writer, modeler, animator, and music composer. His interest in visual effects and animation began with the first *Star Wars* movie. He is currently working on *Shrek 2* and *Madagascar.*

Marcel de Jong worked as an Industrial Designer for years before he became a Visual Effects consultant on features, and a Product Specialist teaching and consulting in Maya for studios such as DreamQuest Images, Disney Feature Animation, Warner Digital, and Digital Domain. As an Industrial Designer he designed products that were published in ID magazine, Popular Science, and Popular Mechanics. Winner of several Design Excellence Awards such as IDEA, Marcel was also the co-founder of Gnomon Inc., School of Visual Effects, founded in 1997 and located in Hollywood, California. He majored in Marketing at the University of Texas and in Industrial Design at Art Center in Pasadena. Today all of his time is spent creating content, consulting, and demonstrating for Alias|Wavefront.

Perry Harovas is a partner at Xvivo LLC, an animation company that produces visual effects for features and television, as well as character animation and medical visualization.

CONTENTS AT A GLANCE

Contents

Foreword

I first met John Kundert-Gibbs on the floor of a trade show in 1999. He was the Maya instructor at the University of North Carolina at Asheville, and I was coordinating Alias|Wavefront's academic programs. He was filled with enthusiasm for our product and was even more excited about sharing his knowledge with his students. John wanted to teach the world to animate, and he wanted to do it with Maya.

Fast forward a few years, and you'll find John at Clemson University, still as devoted to his mission of sharing the power of Maya with his students. John has also brought his knowledge and his passion to writing several successful Maya books. Peter Lee shares John's enthusiasms, and their partnership has resulted in *Maya 4.5 Savvy*, the evolution of their combined experience as teachers, Maya users, and editors. The result is a book that is both technical and accessible to the artist.

There is one thing you should know before you go further: 3D animation is addictive. Peter, John, and I have all witnessed the effects of Maya on the user: late nights at the computer; obsession over minute details; red eyes; and the introduction into your day-to-day speech of a vocabulary that many of your friends and family will not understand. You've started a learning process that you may not want to stop, so be forewarned. I'm confident, though, that you are in good hands.

Maya 4.5 Savvy offers you the knowledge of educators, professional animators, and artists packed into a truly exhaustive study of Maya. This book will be a staple in the library of any student of Maya and will be useful whether you've just launched Maya Personal Learning Edition for the first time or have been working with Maya in a professional capacity. This book addresses all of the features of Maya 4.5 and is a must-have if you are truly dedicated to the study of Maya. *Maya 4.5 Savvy* covers both Maya Complete and Maya Unlimited features.

For these reasons, we are proud to recognize *Maya 4.5 Savvy* as the first Alias|Wavefront Approved publication. This book's wealth of information will assist you in unlocking your potential when using the most powerful 3D animation software on the market—Maya 4.5.

What you'll be able to do in Maya is limited only by your imagination and your skill. This book is a great step towards building your skills, which prompts the question: "Can you imagine?"

Danielle Lamothe
Product Manager—Education
Alias|Wavefront

Introduction

Welcome to Maya 4.5 Savvy! If you're new to Maya and this series of books (formerly the *Mastering Maya* series), *Savvy* will lead you through the wonderful, deep riches that are Alias|Wavefront's 3D animation universe, Maya. If you have already used one or more of our earlier books, you'll want to know that this new version (with new layout and design) has been updated to include all the latest features and improvements Maya 4.5.

Whether you are new to Maya (and even to 3D animation) or have spent years working with Maya and other 3D software, *Maya 4.5 Savvy* will help you work with more challenging scenes and create better images and animations than you have before. Whether you work through the examples in this book step by step or use the book as a reference guide, you will find new techniques, shortcuts, and software capabilities that will help you get the most out of the investment in time and money you have put into Maya.

Regardless of whether you work in the trenches of a large animation and effects house or are starting up a studio of one, the knowledge you gain by reading this book will help you realize your visions more fully and more rapidly. Digest the book, experiment with the software as you go, play, and above all take joy in what you're creating with Maya. After all, there aren't many people who have the privilege of realizing their dreams and visions!

What You Will Learn from This Book

Maya is an enormously rich, full-featured 3D graphics and animation package that uses the tremendous power of today's computers to produce amazing images and animations. Maya's new Fluids engine, for example (available in Maya Unlimited), lets you create complex, realistic fire, smoke, water, and even ocean effects that are jaw-droppingly gorgeous and easy to set up. While Maya has amazing power and depth, it presents this in a user interface that is both logical and consistent enough for you to learn quickly and flexible enough to adapt to the needs of your particular workflow.

Maya 4.5 Savvy is a comprehensive, practical guide to every major aspect of the program. Rather than work through what every radio button or check box does without grounding this knowledge in practice, this book presents Maya's tools in a hands-on manner, showing not only what everything does, but why you would want to use a tool in a specific way. Additionally, through a number of real-world projects, you will learn how to use Maya efficiently for your creative needs, so you won't have to figure out an optimal workflow on your own.

You'll begin with a tour of the user interface and its tools for optimizing your workflow. Then you'll learn the basics of computer modeling and the major types of modeling in Maya: NURBS, polygon, and subdivision surfaces. You'll next work through different modes of animation, including keyframe, dynamics, and Maya's Trax nonlinear animation. After this, you'll learn how to texture, light, and render scenes out to take best advantage of Maya's rendering engine. Next, you'll discover how to create MEL (Maya Embedded Language) scripts to automate your workflow. Finally, you'll learn about Maya's advanced tools: Paint Effects, particle dynamics, and fluid dynamics.

Who Should Read This Book

This book is intended for a range of Maya users, from beginners to experts. There is something in *Maya 4.5 Savvy* for everyone, but we expect most readers will be in the advanced beginner to intermediate range. We assume that most people who invest in a professional-quality 3D graphics program (and the hardware on which to run it) are serious about 3D animation. We assume you have already done some work with 3D modeling, animation, and rendering and are now ready to hone your skills and take advantage of the breakthroughs that Maya makes available. You may be working in a production environment already, in a training or educational program, or in a related field and preparing to make the jump to 3D modeling and animation. Or you might be a person who has always been interested in 3D animation and with the advent of Maya's free new PLE (Personal Learning Edition) have decided to take the plunge and learn the best tool around. In any case, whether you're a neophyte or a guru, you will certainly learn something here, whether it's how to use the Maya interface or some cool new way to perform a complex task.

If you're a relative beginner or feel your background in the fundamentals of Maya and 3D animation has a few holes in it, start from the beginning and work through the first sections of the book. Here you will learn how the Maya interface works and how to create a human model from the ground up, texture it, add a skeletal control system to it, and animate and render it. You will also learn how to create a living environment, a pet dog, and everyday objects for your character to interact with.

Users at the intermediate level will find plenty of interest beyond the fundamentals. A chapter introduces the MEL scripting language, giving you the key to unlocking Maya's full automation power. As you'll see, you don't need to learn the entire language to customize your workspace and automate repetitive tasks to make your workflow more efficient. The last several chapters provide an introduction to the Paint Effects 3D modeling and painting tool and an in-depth look at Maya's particle dynamics and fluid effects.

No matter what your background or level of experience, you can find valuable information in practically every chapter, including exciting projects, tips, and techniques that will improve your work and/or workflow. As an added attraction, we have collected 16 pages of wonderful Maya art, including the results of projects from this book and images from professional studio projects. All this material should inspire you to create better, more challenging work than you might have believed yourself capable of.

How to Use This Book

Maya 4.5 Savvy is not just a reference manual. As working animators and 3D artists, we knew from the beginning that simply explaining the settings of menus and dialog boxes would not be an effective way for you to learn how to use the software—or for us to share insights and experiences. We knew that "hands-on" would be the best approach for learning this complex software—and for retaining that knowledge the next time you need the information. Therefore, we've built each chapter around examples and tutorials that let you try out each new feature as you're studying it.

To implement this approach, we've created a fully integrated book and CD-ROM. The companion CD contains working files—Maya scene files, sketches, TIF images, and MEL scripts—that will get you started with each exercise, as well as rendered images and animations you can use to check your progress as you go. (The CD also contains some illustrations that are best viewed in color, along with some bonus material.)

Many of the exercises are intended to create production-quality work, but most can be done by anyone with a little 3D experience—and of course some patience and persistence! A few exercises are intended for more advanced users and are identified that way.

Several of the more ambitious projects in the book (such as creating and texturing a human model) span several chapters, allowing you to build up knowledge in a step-by-step manner. Even so, you do not need to read the chapters through from beginning to end: we have provided intermediate scene files that will allow you to "step into" the process at any point. As with any how-to book, you can focus on the subjects that interest you or the tasks you need to accomplish first, particularly if you are already an experienced animator. However, should you find the book hard to put down once you start reading it, we won't complain!

How This Book Is Organized

Depending on your interests and skill level, you can either study each chapter from beginning to end or start with what you need to know first. Here's a quick guide to what each part and chapter covers.

Part I: Maya Fundamentals introduces Maya and its tools with the following topics:

Chapter 1: The Maya Interface introduces the elements that make up models, windows, menus, and other parts of Maya, with short examples of how to use these elements.

Chapter 2: Your First Maya Animation uses a hands-on example—building and launching a rocket ship—to solidify understanding of the basic elements of Maya: modeling, texturing, lighting, animation, dynamics, and rendering. This provides a good foundation if you aren't accustomed to using Maya.

Chapter 3: Techniques for Speeding Up Workflow introduces Maya tools that allow you to work quickly and efficiently, saving screen real estate, organizing your work, and using tricks to speed up tool selection and repetitive tasks.

Part II: Modeling provides a detailed exploration of Maya's modeling techniques:

Chapter 4: Modeling Basics uses relatively simple objects to introduce basic modeling concepts and Maya's way of implementing them. The example projects are a great way to learn about construction history and other aspects of Maya's modeling tool kit.

Chapter 5: NURBS Modeling opens up the world of NURBS modeling, showing what elements make up a NURBS curve or surface, how to edit them, and finally how to apply these concepts by modeling an aftershave bottle and a human face.

Chapter 6: Polygons and Subdivision Surfaces explores the basic ingredients for creating and editing polygons and subdivision surfaces. Various techniques are employed to create a hand in polygons; then another project deals with completing the human head from the previous chapter as a subdivision surface.

Chapter 7: Working with Artisan gives you a guided tour of Artisan. You'll learn why it's such a useful set of tools and what you can do with it, including modeling, texturing, and dynamics work.

Chapter 8: Organic Modeling follows up on all the work you've done so far. In this chapter, we show you how to take a dog from a sketch to a finished NURBS patch model, and we finish building the human character using subdivision surfaces.

Part III: Animation shows how to add motion to the models you've created:

Chapter 9: Animating in Maya is where you'll learn all you need to know to get started creating, controlling, and editing animation in Maya. The hands-on project will teach you how to animate fingers by using Set Driven Keys.

Chapter 10: Paths and Bones introduces you to setting up skeletons correctly and shows how to animate cameras and objects quickly with motion paths. The hands-on project sets up the human character for animation.

Chapter 11: Deformers shows how to use the many deformers in Maya to aid in modeling and animating efficiently. You will also discover how to create facial animation, learning in that process how to create proper facial expressions and phonemes.

Chapter 12: Binding introduces you to the two different skinning processes available in Maya for binding a character to skeletons. The hands-on tutorials takes you through binding the human character and the puppy model created in earlier chapters.

Chapter 13: Character Animation Exercises introduces and explains walk cycles, both two-legged and four-legged, going through the fundamentals of animation in the process. In addition to a walk cycle, we teach you how to animate a run cycle and catch and throw a ball.

Chapter 14: Animation Using the Trax Editor shows how to create Maya characters and then use the Trax Editor to create poses and "clips" of animations for these characters that can be used as often as needed to create everything from walk cycles to facial animations and lip synching.

Chapter 15: Working with Rigid Body Dynamics shows you how to animate using Maya's dynamics engine instead of traditional keyframing techniques. You'll learn what rigid bodies are and how to control them, and you'll put them to use in real-world examples such as animating a pair of dice being tossed. You will learn how to use fields and forces for different results and how to "bake" the animation when you are done.

Part IV: Rendering takes you through the details of producing rendered images and animations:

Chapter 16: Rendering Basics explores the way Maya defines a rendered image and how to use IPR (Interactive Photorealistic Renderer), image planes, and Depth of Field. You will also learn how to set up multiple-pass renders that allow changes to be made quickly and without rerendering the entire animation.

Chapter 17: Shading and Texturing Surfaces shows you how to texture surfaces correctly the first time using the Hypershade and how to create a number of effects using various networks of render nodes. Polygon texturing and UV mapping are also extensively covered. As hands-on exercises, we texture the dog model and the clothing and skin of the human model from previous chapters.

Chapter 18: Lighting examines the Maya lighting system, the shadow types available, how to add effects to lights, and proper studio lighting of your subjects. You will learn how to balance speed and quality with Depth Mapped shadows and when to use raytraced shadows, as well as how to create fog, light color, glow, and halo effects.

Part VI: Advanced Maya Effects extends your Maya skills to automating workflow with MEL and working with advanced tools such as Paint Effects, particles, soft bodies, and fluids.

Chapter 19: Paint Effects takes you into the world of Maya's tube-based scene-generating tool. You will learn what's possible with Paint Effects and what the hundreds of attributes mean to help you understand and use Paint Effects to its fullest potential. The tutorial that ends the chapter takes you step by step through adding real hair to the human model built earlier in the book.

Chapter 20: MEL discusses how Maya Embedded Language can work for you, from basic "one click" automation of common tasks to creating, debugging, and editing full-blown MEL scripts and graphical user interfaces.

Chapter 21: Particle Basics introduces you to Maya's dynamic particles engine. You will learn what particles are, how and when to use them, and how to control them. Throughout the chapter are a number of practical examples that are built upon in the next chapters.

Chapter 22: Particle Rendering shows you the different ways to render particles, explains the differences between hardware and software rendering, and explains why each type of particle render has its own place in your rendering pipeline.

Chapter 23: Using Particle Expressions, Ramps, and Volumes expands our understanding and control of particles, as it shows how to add expressions and ramps to grow and move the particles, as well as to define their radii and other particle attributes, and how to control what happens to particles as they age and die.

Chapter 24: Dynamics of Soft Bodies takes the particle and rigid body knowledge you gained in the previous chapters and puts it to use in soft-body simulation. We cover Goal Weights, springs, constraints, and more. The chapter concludes with two great uses of soft bodies: simulated water ripples from a fountain and a water tentacle out of science fiction.

Chapter 25: Fluid Effects introduces Maya Unlimited's new volume fluids simulation engine. We take a quick look at the complex theory behind this new tool and then show how to use—and adjust—Maya's built-in preset scenes and make your own, to create astoundingly complex effects such as stormy oceans, rain dripping down a window, clouds that can be flown through, and smoke that billows and curls realistically.

Finally, the **Appendix** provides some food for thought as Perry Harovas interviews Jill Ramsay, Alias|Wavefront's Director of Brush Technologies and project manager for Fluid Effects, and Maya Product Manager Shai Hinitz. Jill Ramsay discusses the evolution of this new technology and provides insight into how major new modules for Maya are added, tested, and updated. Shai Hinitz discusses the inclusion of Mental Ray for Maya in the Unlimited and Complete versions of Maya 4.5.

Hardware and Software Considerations

Because computer hardware is a quickly moving target, and Maya now runs on four distinct operating systems (Windows 2000/XP, Irix, Linux, and Mac OSX), specifying which particular hardware components will work with Maya is something of a challenge. Fortunately, Alias|Wavefront has a "qualified hardware" page on their website that describes the latest hardware to be qualified to work with Maya for each operating system. Go to this URL:

www.aliaswavefront.com/en/Community/Jump/qual_charts2.jhtml

Click the Maya Qual Charts link, and then choose your operating system from the list provided.

Although you can find specific hardware recommendations on these web pages, we can make some general statements about what constitutes a good platform on which to run Maya. First, be sure to get a fast processor (or a dual-processor machine if you can afford it); Maya eats through CPU cycles like crazy, so a fast processor is important. Second, you need lots of RAM (memory) to run Maya; 512MB is a minimum, but 1–2GB is ideal, especially if you are working with large scene files. Third, if you expect to interact well with your Maya scenes, a powerful GPU (Graphics Processing Unit, or video card) is a must; although Maya will putt along with a poor graphics card, screen redraws will be slow with complex scenes, which gets frustrating quickly. A large hard disk is also important, but most computers these days come with huge drives anyway. Some suggested setups might be as follows (current at the time of writing):

- Windows or Linux
  - AMD Athlon XP 2000+; 1GB RAM; nVidia Geforce 4 Ti 4600; 80GB hard disk
- Intel Pentium IV 2.4Ghz; 1GB RAM; nVidia Geforce 4 Ti 4600; 80GB hard disk
- Mac OSX
  - PowerMac G4 dual 1.25Ghz; 1GB RAM; nVidia Geforce 4 Ti (4600); 80GB hard disk, third-party three-button mouse
- Irix
  - Silicon Graphics Octane 2; dual 600Mhz; 1GB RAM; built-in graphics; 40GB hard disk

Fortunately for us users, computer hardware is so fast these days that even laptop computers can now run Maya well. (Indeed, we used laptop computers running Maya while working on this book.) Additionally, even hardware that is not officially supported by Alias|Wavefront can often run Maya—just remember that you will not be able to get technical support if your system does not meet their qualifications chart.

The CD-ROM accompanying this book has been tested on Windows, Mac, and Linux machines and should work with most configurations of these systems.

The Book's CD

The CD-ROM in the back of this book provides all the sample images, movies, code, and files that you need to work through the projects in *Maya 4.5 Savvy*, as well as Maya Personal Learning Edition 4.5.

Maya Personal Learning Edition 4.5

If you don't already have a version of Maya, you may want to install the Maya Personal Learning Edition 4.5 software, which you can find on the CD at the back of this book. Maya PLE 4.5 is a special version of Maya that gives you free access to Maya Complete for non-commercial use. Maya PLE 4.5 works on Windows 2000/XP Professional and Mac OS X. Please see the back of the book for more information.

The Next Step

By the time you finish *Maya 4.5 Savvy*, you'll be well on your way to mastery of Maya. Several chapters provide suggestions for further reading related to animation and 3D graphics and to some of the most important websites in the field. Be sure to check these websites, as well as the Sybex website (www.sybex.com), for updates on Maya and for bonus materials and further information.

As you work through this book and begin exploring Maya on your own, you'll probably think of topics you'd like to see us cover in future editions of this book, as well as other improvements we might make. You can use www.sybex.com to provide feedback; or you can send feedback directly to:

John Kundert-Gibbs
Kundert@clemson.edu

We welcome your input and look forward to hearing from you!

Now it's up to you to make the most of the tools that Maya offers. Have fun, work hard, and remember that the most important tool you have as an artist is your imagination—so get out there and make yourself proud!

PART I

Maya Fundamentals

Maya *(from the Sanskrit word for "world of illusion") is a program designed to produce groundbreaking, photorealistic models and animations. Built into this program are an abundance of tools and "subtools" that can overwhelm even the most wizened old 3D artist. To make all of Maya's tools work together in a logical, consistent, and intuitive manner is a monumental task that continues with version 4.5 of the program. Still, the basic structure of the Maya interface is not only solid enough for most users to quickly learn and use, it is so intuitive that several other 3D software manufacturers are busy copying much of Maya's look.*

In Part I of this book, you will learn the fundamentals of interacting with Maya's user interface. If you are already familiar with the Maya interface, you might want to skim these chapters; however, we will cover several aspects of the program that have changed in version 4.5, so a little time spent leafing through these pages might help you get up to speed with the new release. If you are new to Maya, reading these three chapters should help you better understand how you can work effectively with Maya and the Maya interface. After working through this section, you should be well prepared for the more advanced parts of this book.

CHAPTER 1

The Maya Interface

Three-dimensional modeling and animation are challenging tasks. Trying to get your vision of a universe transferred into pixels is part science, part art, and a great deal of perseverance. Fortunately, the engineers at Alias|Wavefront have spent a great deal of time and energy making Maya as helpful and transparent to use as a complex program can be. Still, with a program as large as Maya, a good introduction to its components can be helpful in getting the most from your work as quickly as possible. This chapter explores Maya's user interface, examining each element of the work environment in turn. After reading through the chapter, you should have a good understanding of the major parts of Maya's GUI (graphical user interface) and know how to use these parts in your modeling and animation work.

- ■ **Introducing Maya 4.5**

- ■ **What's behind the Maya interface?**

- ■ **Scene windows and scene objects**

- ■ **Window layouts**

- ■ **The hotbox**

- ■ **Menus and shelves**

- ■ **The Outliner and the Hypergraph**

- ■ **The Channel Box and the Attribute Editor**

- ■ **The Timeline**

- ■ **The Command line, the Feedback line, and the Script Editor**

What's Behind the Maya Interface?

What makes Maya different? First, interacting with it is a straightforward process, for several reasons. All scene windows, plus the Hypershade and the Hypergraph windows, are easily navigated via the same keyboard and mouse combinations for zooming, tracking, and rotating (rotating only works in perspective camera views). Because navigating works the same way in all windows, you have to learn only one set of commands to get around Maya's world. Moving objects around a Maya scene window is similarly intuitive: select the Move, Scale, or Rotate (or any other) tool, grab a manipulator handle (or the center box, to move on all axes simultaneously), and alter the object. To try out an example, you can create a new scene in Maya, add a ball (by clicking the sphere object on the "shelf" located above the scene window, or by choosing Create → NURBS Primitives → Sphere). Now rotate around the ball by holding down the Alt key and clicking the left mouse button. This type of rotation is known as *camera* or *scene* rotation. To rotate the ball itself, choose the Rotate tool from the Tool Box, located on the left of the scene window, (or simply press the E key on the keyboard), select any of the manipulator rings around the ball, and then rotate it by dragging with the left mouse button, as in Figure 1.1. To move an object, select the Move tool (or press the W key). To scale, select the Scale tool (or press the R key).

THREE-BUTTON MOUSE CONVENTIONS IN MAYA

Maya makes extensive use of all three mouse buttons. This book—as well as the Maya manuals—uses a shorthand notation to describe the basic mouse operations:

Click or **LM click** means to click (press and release) with the left mouse button.

Drag or **LM drag** means to click the left mouse button, hold it down, and drag.

Shift+click means to LM click, hold down the Shift key, and click another item.

Choose means to either click or hold down the left mouse button and choose an item from a menu.

MM drag means to click and drag with the middle mouse button.

RM choose means to hold the right mouse button down (in a specified area) and choose an item from the pop-up contextual menu.

Rotate (Tumble) view means to rotate the (perspective) camera; that is, hold down the Alt key and the left mouse button, and then drag in the perspective window to rotate the view.

Move view means to move (any) camera; that is, hold down the Alt key and the middle mouse button, and then drag in any scene window to move the view.

Scale view means to scale—or zoom—(any) camera; that is, hold down the Alt key and the left and middle mouse buttons, and then drag in any scene window to scale (or zoom) the view in or out.

Another powerful difference between Maya and other packages lies in how you interact with Maya's user interface. You can almost always accomplish a task in two or more ways—called *workflows*—in Maya. For example, if you prefer not to use menus on top of the screen, you can use Maya's hotbox (which you can customize) to access all menus or any grouping therein by merely pressing and holding the space bar, as in Figure 1.2. (The Cloth and Maya Live menus shown in Figure 1.2 are available only in Maya Unlimited; Maya Complete users won't see them.)

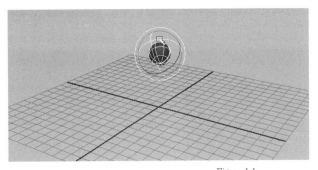

Figure 1.1

Rotating a sphere in Maya

You can also, as mentioned earlier, create items via the buttons on the shelf or, equivalently, via menu commands. Most impressive, however, is that Maya will let you decide how you interact with it. If you are not satisfied with Maya's interface, you can alter it in many ways, including creating marking menus, shelf buttons, and hot keys. Although all these can contain extremely complex instructions, you can create them rather quickly (especially the shelf buttons).

For more on how to tune Maya's GUI for your own work, see Chapter 3, "Techniques for Speeding Up Workflow," or Chapter 20, "MEL."

Figure 1.2

The Maya hotbox

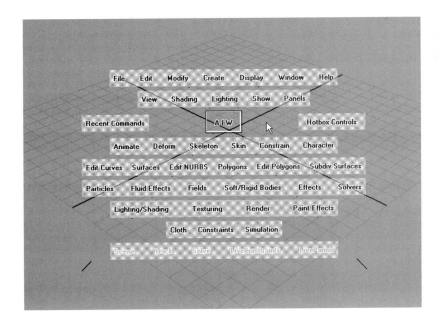

Finally, Maya's plug-in architecture (its API, or application programming interface) and especially its built-in scripting language, MEL, are open and comprehensive. Because of Maya's API, plug-ins (such as the built-in Artisan and FX) fit seamlessly into the program, so much so that it is often difficult to determine where the main program stops and the plug-in begins. Although the API is fairly complex and is best left to knowledgeable programmers, MEL (Maya Embedded Language) is a reasonably simple scripting language that gives just about anyone with a bit of programming experience access to nearly all of Maya's powerful features in the graphical user environment. Not only can you create specialized, time-saving scripts with MEL, you can also create entire windows or even a whole new GUI for the program (because Maya's entire GUI is built on MEL scripts in the first place). For example, a technical director can create a custom interface for their artists, allowing them to deal with character animation without knowing anything about the low-level details of the construction and "stringing" (or animation setup) of a character.

As should be obvious from these features, Maya provides an up-to-date, intuitive environment that you can customize. Whether you have a shop of one person or one hundred, Maya's adjustable interface will get you building complex animations far more quickly than other—even more expensive—packages. Let's now take a more thorough tour through the Maya interface, looking at several important areas of the GUI.

WHAT'S NEW IN MAYA 4.5

Although the Maya interface might at first glance appear much as it did in version 4, a number of new features and improvements make Maya easier to learn and use than ever before. Here are some highlights:

- Two items have been added to the Modify → Snap Align Objects menu: Align Tool and Snap Together Tool.

- New options in the Tool Settings windows are Discrete Move, Rotate, and Scale (which allow you to specify the amount in increments that an object is moved, rotated, or scaled).

- You can now display a smooth wire-framed object in 3D views by choosing Shading → Smooth Wireframe from the scene window's panel.

- Choose Create → Annotation to type and display names for objects in scene windows.

- You can now add notes within the Attribute Editor (choose Window → Attribute Editor) in order to detail information about specific objects.

- Learning Movies, found in the Help menu, are a series of MPEG movies that demonstrate essential Maya skills.

Interface Elements

Although Maya is composed of many elements, they can be grouped into about eight categories. We will quickly examine each category in turn.

Scene Windows

The scene windows are your primary interface with the objects (and lights and cameras) you create. Opening a new Maya scene opens the default configuration, which is one large scene window (the default perspective camera), alongside the Channel Box, similar to what is shown in Figure 1.3.

> If you prefer, you can toggle the Channel Box with the Attribute Editor (rather than floating the Attribute Editor in a separate window). To toggle the two windows, choose Window → Settings/Preferences → Preferences, and click the Open Attribute Editor In Main Maya Window radio button.

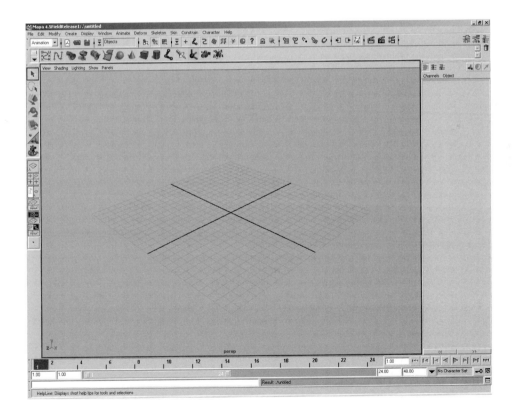

Figure 1.3

The Maya user interface

Once the default window is open, you can activate the perspective view window by clicking anywhere inside it. When you select this (or any) window, its borders turn blue. At this point, you can rotate, scale, or translate the view to adjust what you see in this window (for specifics on how to do this, see the earlier sidebar on mouse conventions). The default scene window is called the *persp* (for perspective) view and is simply the view from the default perspective camera that Maya builds upon opening a new scene.

You can build other perspective cameras by choosing Create → Cameras → Camera. To view the scene through this new camera, choose Panels → Perspective → camera1.

In addition to the default perspective camera, Maya also creates three *orthographic* views—top, side, and front—that you can also see (in what's called a "four-view" window) by selecting the perspective window and then quickly pressing and releasing the space bar, as shown in Figure 1.4.

Figure 1.4

The four-view display

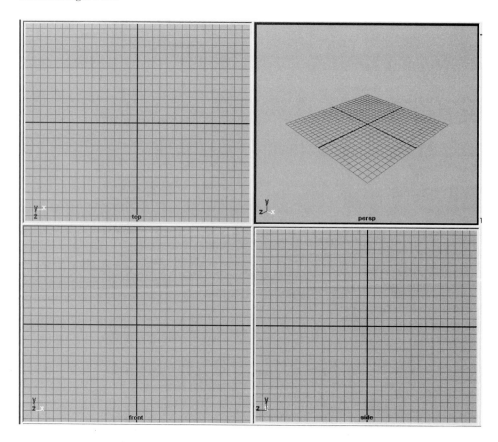

To fill the screen with one of the orthographic views, click in it (to select this window), and press and release the space bar again. Being able to switch quickly between view layouts and window sizes greatly speeds up your workflow in Maya, because no extensive menu selection process is required.

To switch views in Maya without losing your current selection, MM or RM click in the view you want to activate (for example, the front view), and then press the space bar.

ORTHOGRAPHIC AND PERSPECTIVE VIEWS

An orthographic view is a nonperspective view from a 90-degree (or orthogonal) angle. Because these are not perspective views, they do not reduce the size of objects as they move away from the camera. A perspective view of a row of columns, for example, would show the back column as smaller than the column nearest the camera. An orthographic view, on the other hand, will show all columns as the same size, scale is not reduced (perspective) in this view. You can think of an orthographic view as similar to a blueprint drawing; a perspective view is similar to a camera picture.

Perspective View   Orthographic View

Quick Layout Buttons

Another quick way to switch between view layouts is to use the Quick Layout buttons. The Quick Layout buttons (see Figure 1.5) are in the Tool Box (more on the Tool Box later), which is to the left of the Maya workspace. Simply LM click any of the first six buttons for a different view layout. To change a button, RM click it to display the Saved Layouts pop-up menu and choose from a variety of view layouts.

The appearance of the seventh button, the Panel/Layout button, depends on the view layout you chose from the first six buttons. For example, if you click the first Quick Layout button, which, by default, is the Single Perspective View, the Panel/Layout button has one arrow. If you chose the Four View button, four arrows appear on the Panel/Layout button. You can change a specific panel by LM clicking any of the arrows and choosing from the pop-up menu. RM clicking will give you options to change the layout configuration such as Single Pane or Two Panes Side By Side.

After you configure the Panel/Layout button to your liking, you might want to save the layout. RM click the Panel/Layout button and choose Save Current Layout from the pop-up menu. A small window will open, asking for you to name your layout. Type **My Layout** (or anything you please) and click OK. To access your saved layout, RM click any of the first six Quick Layout buttons to open the Saved Layouts pop-up menu (as you did before) and choose it from the menu.

Figure 1.5

The Quick Layout buttons

Moving in Scene Windows

Moving around scene windows is fairly straightforward, once you learn the keyboard and mouse combinations for doing so. Additionally, because you move in all scene windows (plus the Hypergraph and the Hypershade windows) using these same commands, once you learn how to move in one window, you can move in all. Because the perspective window has the most options (you can rotate, or tumble, the view as well as zoom and translate), let's quickly look at how to maneuver in the default perspective window.

Open a new scene in Maya; then hold down the Alt key and the left mouse button and drag the mouse around. The scene should spin around as you drag the mouse.

If the scene does not rotate as you drag (you might see the cursor become a circle with a line through it), you could be in an orthographic view, which does not allow rotations. To move to a perspective view, either press the space bar to display the four-view layout or LM click the four-view Quick Layout button in the Tool Box; then click in the perspective window (top right) and press the space bar again.

To translate a scene (move up/down or left/right), hold down the Alt key once again, hold down the middle mouse button (MMB), and drag the mouse. You will see the scene move around with the mouse movements. (Notice that the camera is actually moving opposite to your mouse movements: as you drag right, the camera moves left, so the objects appear to move right. You can see this clearly if you make cameras visible and look at the camera in a different view as you drag.)

To scale your view (zoom the camera in and out), hold down the Alt key once again, hold down both the left and middle mouse buttons, and drag. As you drag right, the scene grows larger (you're zooming in); as you drag left, the scene grows smaller (you're zooming out). To quickly zoom into a specific area of your scene, hold down the Alt and Ctrl keys, and then drag (with the left mouse button only) a box around the area of the scene, starting on the left side. When you release the mouse, the scene zooms in, covering the area you outlined. If you drag the mouse from right to left, the scene zooms out so that the entire scene window you start with fits into the box you drag (the smaller your box, the farther out you zoom). If you now open the Hypergraph or the Hypershade (choose Window → Hypergraph or Window → Rendering Editors → Hypershade), you can use the same key/mouse combinations to scale or move around either of these windows. You will notice, however, that you cannot rotate either of these views, because this would accomplish nothing useful.

You can think of the Alt key as the "scene movement key." Whenever you hold down the Alt key, you are in scene manipulation mode, rather than in object manipulation (or some other) mode. The consistent use of the Alt key for movement is just one more example of the thought that has gone into the Maya interface.

Scene Objects

Scene *objects* (primitives, curves, cameras, and lights) are the fundamental building blocks from which you create a Maya scene or animation. The procedure for creating and manipulating any object is generally the same: create the object (most often by using the Create menu), choose a manipulation tool (such as Translate or Rotate), and alter the object. You can also adjust the pivot point (or "center") of an object, and you can manipulate the individual components of geometric objects.

Creating Scene Objects

Because you create most scene objects in much the same fashion, we'll go through a few representative examples here, rather than discuss how to create all possible objects in Maya. If you have specific questions about creating a type of object that is not covered here, you can always check Maya's online documentation (accessed via the Help menu).

Maya's built-in help files are a great (and easy-to-use) resource. To access them, choose Help → Library (or a specific aspect of the program). You can also press F1 to access the main help library. After opening the Maya Library window (which opens in a web browser because it is an HTML document), you can search for a term, browse through a complete index of all Maya documents (the index alone is nearly 2MB of data!), or read any of the Maya manuals in electronic form.

To create a primitive (a sphere or a cone, for example), you choose the type of primitive you want to create from the Create menu. For a simple three-dimensional object (such as a torus or a cube), you can choose from polygonal, NURBS, or Subdivision Surface primitives. Using the NURBS option, you can also select a two-dimensional (nonsurface) square or circle. When you create an object, you can either use the last saved settings or open the Creation Options window and adjust the object's settings before creating it.

You create NURBS (or Non-Uniform Rational B-Spline) objects via a series of curves (or "isoparms") that are mathematically derived from several points (control vertices, or CVs). NURBS surfaces are more complex to calculate, but they can be warped and twisted more before they show excessive unnatural creasing. Polygonal surfaces, on the other hand, are created by placing many small triangular or rectangular surfaces together. Polys are simpler to calculate—at least for simple surfaces—but tend to show their constituent blocks if they are bent or distorted too much—especially if the surfaces are created with a minimal number of polygons, or facets. Subdivision Surfaces offers the best of both, providing the smoothness of NURBS with the benefits of intricate polygonal modeling. NURBS and Subdivision Surfaces tend to be better suited to organic forms (such as bodies), and polygonal surfaces generally work better for more mechanical objects (such as space ships); but this is by no means a hard-and-fast rule.

Figure 1.6

The NURBS Cylinder Options window

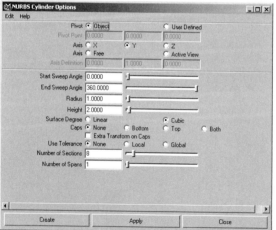

As an example, let's create a default polygonal sphere, and then use the option box to create a NURBS cylinder. To create the poly sphere, simply choose Create → Polygon Primitives → Sphere. On releasing the mouse, you should see a sphere appear at the center of Maya's default grid. If you look closely, you will see that the sphere consists of many rectangular objects (more accurately called quadrilaterals) that butt up against one another, forming the sphere. Now move the sphere aside (press the W key and move the sphere away from the center of the grid) and create a NURBS cylinder with nondefault options. To access the option window of the NURBS cylinder, choose Create → NURBS Primitives → Cylinder ❐ (choosing the ❐ symbol— the *option box*—in a Maya menu item always opens an options window). Upon releasing the mouse button, you should see the window shown in Figure 1.6.

In this window, you can define any of the following:

- The pivot point

- The axis the cylinder will use as its long axis

- The start and end angles of the cylinder

- The radius

- The height (a higher number will make a taller cylinder)

- The number of sections (horizontal pieces) and spans (vertical pieces) the cylinder has

For the purposes of this little example, try setting the End Sweep Angle to 270 (this will create a three-quarters cylinder), Set the Radius to 1 and the Height to 4 (making the cylinder taller), and set the Caps option to Both (creating a cap on both the top and bottom of the cylinder). When you click the Create button at the bottom, you should get the object shown in Figure 1.7.

You can almost always reset an object's creation settings to their default values by choosing Edit → Reset Settings in the options window.

To see the object smooth shaded with textures (instead of a wireframe), press the 6 key on your keyboard (not the numeric keypad). To view an object at a smoother interactive resolution, press the 3 key (pressing these keys will not affect how the object renders, only how it is displayed). Figure 1.7 uses these settings to display the cylinder.

Figure 1.7

A cylinder created using custom options

Creating a camera object is as simple as creating a primitive object. Choose Create → Cameras and choose Camera, Camera And Aim, or Camera, Aim, and Up from the submenu. A new perspective camera is created. (Perspective cameras are initially called camera1, camera2, and so on until you save them with more specific names.) To adjust the camera's options as you create it, choose the option box (⬚), and change the camera's settings. Although all the settings in the camera options window are a bit much for an introductory chapter, most are fairly self-explanatory to anyone familiar with photography or 3D animation. The following are some notable options:

- You can make any new camera orthographic (as opposed to perspective).

- You have control over near and far clipping planes (where the camera stops "seeing" objects that are too far away or too close).

- You can choose to have an aim point or an aim point and an up vector on the camera (allowing you to manipulate where the camera is looking, for example, via a manipulator handle outside the camera itself).

Try creating a camera with an aim (choose Create → Cameras). When you create this camera, shown in Figure 1.8, it automatically has a second manipulator handle for a new view node that you can move (by pressing the W key and dragging the handle around), and the camera follows the manipulator handle. For more on camera options and other rendering basics, see Chapter 16, "Rendering Basics."

Figure 1.8

A camera with an aim

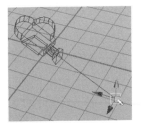

To create lights, choose Create → Lights and select a type of light. When creating lights, you can choose from the following:

- Ambient (a light that fills all space evenly, such as indirect sunlight in a room)
- Directional (parallel light rays from one source, mimicking direct sunlight)
- Point (radial light such as that from a bare light bulb)
- Spot (light as from a theatrical spot light)
- Area (light emitted from a rectangular area that imitates a block light source such as a window)
- Volume (a light that illuminates within the space of a given boundary)

For example, create a spotlight (choose Create → Lights → Spot Light ❏) with the following options: Intensity 1.5, Cone Angle 50, Penumbra Angle 10, and Color a light blue (click the default white color chip to display the color picker; then choose a light blue color). The penumbra controls how quickly your spotlight "fades out" around its edges: a value of 0 means that the spotlight goes from full intensity to 0 at its edges (not a very natural look); a value of 10 or 20 degrees makes the spotlight fade out from full intensity to 0 over that number of degrees. If your spotlight were aimed at a simple plane, the rendered image would look something like the light on the right in Figure 1.9 (the one on the left is a spotlight with a penumbra of 0).

To see how an area light works, create a sphere, stretch it out, and add an area light (be sure its direction vector is pointing at the sphere). Stretch the area light out, and in the Attribute Editor set the light's decay rate to Quadratic. As you move the light (very) close to the sphere, you will see an oblong of light appear on the sphere, shown in Figure 1.10, matching the points where the light is closest to the sphere. Use the IPR renderer (click the IPR icon in the status bar) to see the light's effect change as you adjust its attributes.

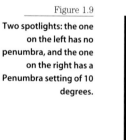

Figure 1.9

Two spotlights: the one on the left has no penumbra, and the one on the right has a Penumbra setting of 10 degrees.

Figure 1.10

A new area light shining on a distorted sphere

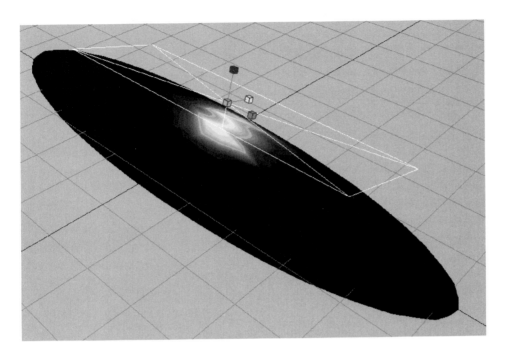

For more on creating and using lights, see Chapter 18.

You can also create either CV (control vertex) or EP (Edit Point) curves by using the Create menu (choose Create → CV Curve Tool or Create → EP Curve Tool). The CV Curve tool creates a CV with each click of the mouse. The EP Curve tool creates edit points as you click the mouse button. There is really no difference between a CV curve and an EP curve except in the way that they are created. Each type of curve tool is useful under certain circumstances—the basic rule of thumb is that for smoother curves, you use the CV Curve tool, and for more tightly controlled curves you use the EP Curve tool. Figure 1.11 shows a CV curve (on the left) and an EP curve (on the right) created with identical mouse clicks. Since the CV curve does not pass through each point that you define, the resulting curve is smoother than the EP curve. The extremes of the EP curve are much more pronounced because the curve *is* forced to pass through exact points.

For more on creating and using curves, see Chapter 5, "NURBS Modeling."

Figure 1.11

A curve produced with the CV Curve tool on the left, and one produced with the EP Curve tool on the right

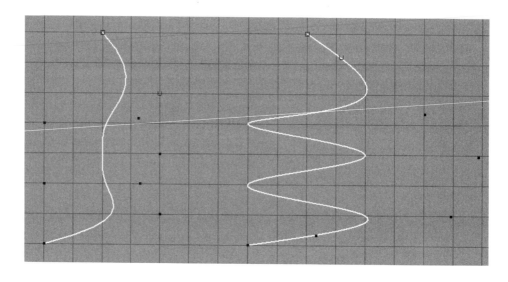

Figure 1.11

A curve produced with the CV Curve tool on the left, and one produced with the EP Curve tool on the right

To create, say, a CV curve, choose Create → CV Curve Tool (or click the CV Curve Tool button on Shelf 1), and then click several times in the scene window. You can also drag the points around as you create them, and you can erase points by pressing the Delete or Backspace key or by pressing the Z key to undo the last action. When you are satisfied with the curve, press the Enter key to construct the curve.

Moving Scene Objects

After you create an object, you will probably want to move, rotate, and/or scale it. Because the procedures are the same for all objects (and lights, cameras, and curves), let's just use a cylinder as an example here. Create a new cylinder with default options (choose Create → NURBS Primitives → Cylinder ❏; then choose Edit → Reset Settings, and click the Create button). To move this cylinder, press the W key on the keyboard—you should now see the *Move tool manipulator handles* that allow you to move the cylinder on any or all axes, as shown in Figure 1.12.

Figure 1.12

A cylinder with Move tool manipulator handles

If you do not see the manipulator handles, be sure the cylinder is highlighted by clicking (or click+dragging) it.

To move the cylinder on the X axis only, click and drag the red arrow; to move on the Y axis, click and drag the green arrow; to move on the Z axis, click and drag the blue arrow. To move the object freely in all directions, click and drag the yellow box at the center of the manipulator handles. Try moving the object up a little on the Y axis and to the right on the X axis.

All manipulator handle colors are consistent with the axis marker, on the bottom-left of a scene window—X is red, Y is green, and Z is blue. This consistency lets you know which axis you are adjusting, no matter from what angle you are viewing the scene.

To scale the cylinder, press the R key, and then scale the object on the X (red), Y (green), or Z (blue) axis—or click and drag the yellow box at the center of the manipulator to scale all axes simultaneously. Try scaling the cylinder up on the Y axis and then out in all directions, until you get something like Figure 1.13.

To rotate the cylinder, press the E key, and then rotate around the X (red), Y (green), or Z (blue) axes—or click the yellow circle on the outside to rotate on all axes at once (rotating on all axes at once is difficult to control and therefore not advisable). Try rotating clockwise on the Z axis and then counterclockwise on the X axis, as in Figure 1.14.

> The shortcut keys for manipulator controls are arranged so that they follow the top row of a QWERTY keyboard—Q for select, Ctrl+Q for lasso select, W for move, E for rotate, R for scale, T for the Manipulator tool, and Y for the Last Used tool (such as the CV Curve tool, for example). This layout makes the manipulator tools easy to access, and it's easy to remember their shortcut keys.

Finally, it is possible to move the pivot point of your cylinder (or any object) so that it is not in the object's center. To move the pivot point, press the Insert key on your keyboard (turning the manipulator handle into the pivot-point handle); then move the handle to where you want the object's center of rotation, movement, or scaling. Try moving the pivot point of the cylinder to its bottom, as shown in Figure 1.15, so that any further rotation will occur from that point.

After you move the pivot point, you must return the manipulator to its "normal" state by pressing the Insert key once again.

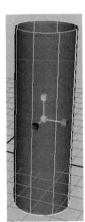

Figure 1.13

A moved and scaled cylinder

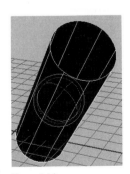

Figure 1.14

The cylinder, rotated

Figure 1.15

The cylinder, with its pivot point moved to the bottom

Figure 1.16

The Tool Box

The Tool Box

In addition to using the shortcut keys to access the manipulator controls, you can access them from the Tool Box (Figure 1.16), which is to the left of the Maya workspace. Here you will find the Select tool, Lasso tool, Move tool, Rotate tool, Scale tool, Show Manipulator tool, and the last selected tool. The Lasso tool is a selection tool that works by dragging a lasso around the objects or components you want to select. The last selected tool depends on (you guessed it) the last tool that was selected from a menu or a shelf.

Objects versus Components

All geometric objects are made up of component elements. In object mode, clicking or dragging any part of an object selects the entire object. In component mode, however, you can choose specific pieces of an object to manipulate. Using the cylinder from the previous section as an example (just create a default cylinder if you've deleted it), select the object (so it turns green) while in object mode and choose the Select By Component Type button in the Status line (or just press the F8 key) to change to component mode. You will now see the CVs that make up the cylinder, as shown in Figure 1.17—if you had created a polygonal cylinder, you would see the points defining the edges of the polygonal facets.

As shown in the following illustration, the Select By Component Type button is on the Status line, just to the right of the word *Objects*. The leftmost of these three buttons is Select By Hierarchy; the middle button is Select By Object; the right button is Select By Component Type.

You can adjust components of an object just as you adjust an object itself by using the Move, Rotate, and Scale tools. Try selecting the top row of CVs on the cylinder (LM drag a square around them or use the Lasso tool to draw a selection around them), and then moving them up some, scaling them out on the X and Z axes, and rotating them a bit, as shown in Figure 1.18.

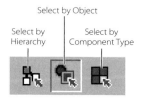

To select several components (CVs, facets, vertices, and so on) at once, you can drag a selection marquee around them (a selection marquee is the square box that you see when you drag in a Maya scene window). For more control, use the Lasso tool. To add more components, hold down the Shift key and the Ctrl key and drag (or click) more points. (If the points are already selected, Shift alone+clicking or dragging will deselect them.) Remember that you can always maneuver around the scene window (hold down the Alt key as you drag the mouse) to make selection easier.

If you now switch back to object mode, you will once again be able to choose and manipulate the entire object. Modeling (and even animating) is often a dance between object-mode and component-mode manipulation of your objects, and remembering that the F8 key switches between these two modes can be a real time-saver.

Figure 1.17

The cylinder, with CVs displayed in component mode

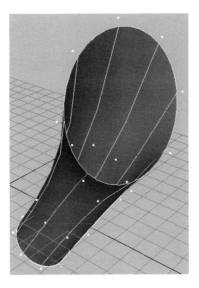

Figure 1.18

The cylinder, with several CV components manipulated

Selecting by Component Type

One of the trickier aspects of Maya (at least for some) is selecting the proper component of an object when in component mode. You can select many types of components, including CVs, hulls, faces, edges, and so forth (and there are usually several options in each of these choices), but you can make these selections in only two ways. One way is more thorough; the other is better suited to quick selections of the most common component types.

Figure 1.19

Options available when RM clicking a NURBS sphere

The quicker, easier method for selecting specific component types is to use a contextual menu while your mouse is over an object. To try this, create a sphere in an empty scene, and then, with your mouse over the sphere, hold down the right mouse button. You will be presented with several options (shown in Figure 1.19) for component masking, plus a menu of actions you can perform on the object (such as templating or untemplating it).

By selecting Control Vertex (for example) from this pop-up menu, you can easily move into component-selection mode for CVs and begin manipulating your CVs. To return to object mode, press the F8 key twice.

Although the contextual menu method is quick and easy, it does not give you access to all the component types. To choose a component

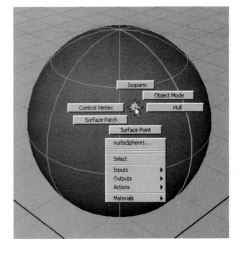

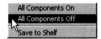

type that's not listed in the pop-up menu, you need to use the Status line. To the right of the Object/Component text field and Hierarchy/Object/Component icons is a set of eight icons, each representing a class of components you can enable or disable in your selection process. To the left of these icons is a black triangle; clicking this triangle enables or disables all components for selection. The component types you enable here are then available when you drag your mouse over an object in component mode.

> If you turn off all components, you will not be able to select anything in the scene window—including objects in object mode! This is a good place to look first if you discover you cannot choose any objects in a scene.

Holding down the right mouse button on any of the icons displays a menu of subtypes that you can either enable (check) or disable (uncheck) for component selection. Enabling or disabling component types is known as *selection masking*, and it's a great way to simplify the task of selecting a specific object or component in a complex scene. If you are not familiar with components or selection masking, try playing around with these options in Maya before continuing.

Window Layouts

In addition to the default window layout (the perspective view plus either the Channel Box or the Attribute Editor), Maya provides many other built-in layouts, and—as is consistent with the Maya interface philosophy—if you want, you can create your own.

Built-in Layouts

Maya offers two types of built-in layouts: generic layouts and saved layouts. Generic layouts are just basic layout elements (such as a four-view layout), and saved layouts are useful combinations of the basic elements prebuilt into layouts for different purposes. To begin with, let's look at how to access a generic layout. You can use the Quick Layout buttons in the Tool Box to select views and switch between layouts, as we did earlier in this chapter. But you can also use the Panels menu located in the scene windows. Choose Panels → Layouts (accessed either via the Panels menu in the scene panel, as shown in Figure 1.20, or from the hotbox) displays several layout choices for your scene windows.

Figure 1.20

The menu choices for generic layouts

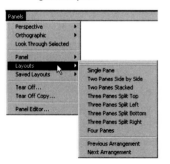

Choosing Four Panes places the active view (often the perspective view) in the upper-left quadrant of a four-view layout. (Note that this is different from the layout you get by pressing the space bar, as the perspective view—or whichever view you have active—ends up in the top-right quadrant when using the space bar, but the top left in this case). The Three Panes Split Top, Left Bottom, or Right views place the active window on the top (or left, bottom, or right) half of the screen and then split this view into two; the other half of the screen has a single view window. The Two Panes Side By Side or Two Panes Stacked layouts are similar, except that they don't split the active view in half (thus the active view and one other view share the screen space evenly, either top-and-bottom or left-and-right). There is also a single view, which is the same as selecting a view and pressing the space bar to make it fill the entire screen.

Figure 1.21

The Saved Layouts menu

While the generic views can be useful (especially for building your own layouts—discussed below), the saved layouts are more commonly used because they fulfill specific needs. To access the saved layouts, choose Panels → Saved Layouts, as in Figure 1.21, and then select a saved layout to use.

You are already familiar with Single Perspective View and Four View. Rather than look at each saved layout in a list, let's examine just a few—once you understand a couple of the saved layouts, the rest are fairly self-explanatory. Persp/Graph/Hypergraph is a three panel layout with the top half split between the perspective view and the Hypergraph, while the bottom half of the screen is occupied by the Graph Editor. This view was created from the generic Three Panes Split Top layout by changing each panel to the Perspective, Hypergraph, and Graph Editor views and then saving the layout. The Hypershade/Outliner/Persp view is a Three Panes Split Bottom, with the Hypershade occupying the top half of the screen and the Outliner and perspective view splitting the bottom half. Another useful layout is the Persp/Relationship Editor layout, which stacks the perspective view on top of the Relationship Editor. If you have Maya Unlimited and the Maya Live plug-in active, there are several layouts specifically for use with Maya Live toward the bottom of the menu, including Maya Live Setup, Track, Solve, and Manual MatchMove.

Building Your Own Layout

If the prebuilt Maya layouts don't quite fit your needs, never fear: the final choice in the Saved Layouts menu (Edit Layouts) lets you create and save your own layout for later use. You can even erase any or all of the prebuilt layouts from the menu.

> Don't erase a saved layout unless you are sure that neither you nor anyone else working on your machine is interested in using that layout any further. To get the layout back, you'll either have to reconstruct it manually or reinstall Maya.

As an example of how to create your own layout for later use, let's create a layout with the perspective view filling half the screen on the top and with the bottom being split between the Hypershade and the Hypergraph. (This can be a useful layout if you need to connect several materials to several objects at a time, because selecting the objects in the perspective window can become tedious.) As with most things in Maya, you have a choice about how to create your new layout: you can either start from a generic layout or modify a prebuilt layout. Although starting from a prebuilt layout is often simpler, we will start from a generic layout in order to describe the entire procedure. Follow these steps:

1. Choose Panels → Layouts → Three Panes Split Bottom.

2. Make sure the top half of the window is occupied by the perspective view (if not, select the top half and then choose Panels → Perspective → Persp).

3. Select the lower-left quadrant and choose Panels → Panel → Hypershade. This should turn the lower-left window into a view of the Hypershade.

4. Select the lower-right quadrant and choose Panels → Panel → Hypergraph, turning this corner into a view of the Hypergraph, as seen in Figure 1.22.

5. To save the new layout, choose Panels → Saved Layouts → Edit Layouts, which displays the Panel Editor.

6. If necessary, click the Layouts tab.

7. In the Layouts tab, click the New Layout button, rename the layout from its default name (Panel Configuration) to something more memorable, such as Persp/Hypergraph/Hypershade, and press the Enter key to change the name.

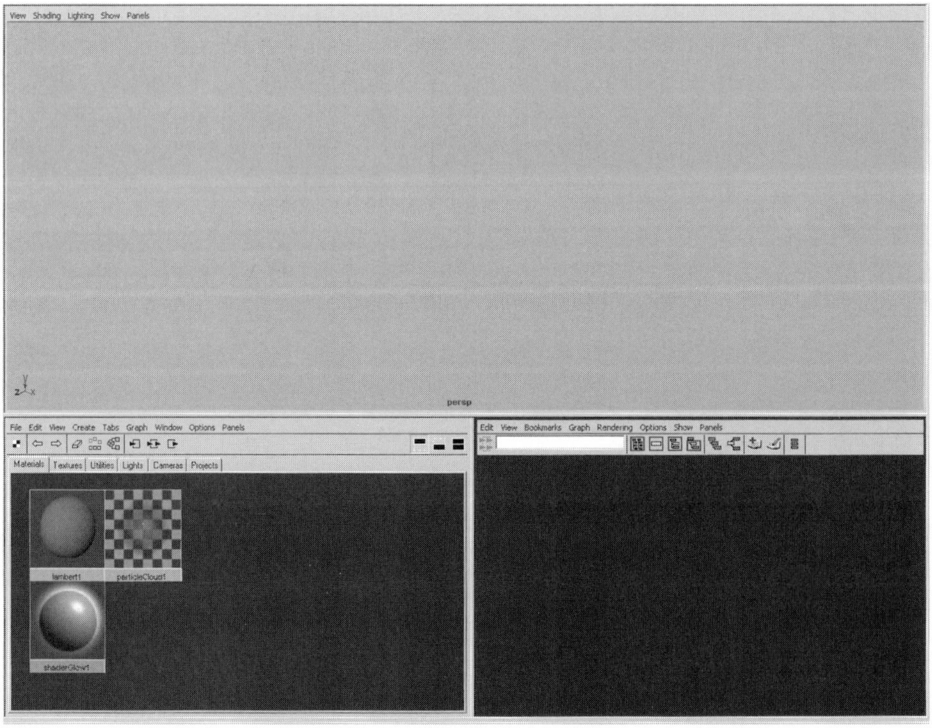

Figure 1.22

The lower-left panel shows the Hypershade.

When you close the window, your new layout will be placed at the bottom of the Saved Layouts menu (as shown in Figure 1.23). If you later choose to discard this new layout, return to the Edit Layouts menu, select the new layout, and press the Delete button.

You can actually build a custom configuration directly inside the Edit Layouts menu, by using the Panels and Edit Layouts tabs. This method is more difficult than the one outlined here, however, so our recommendation is to stick with the method we just described.

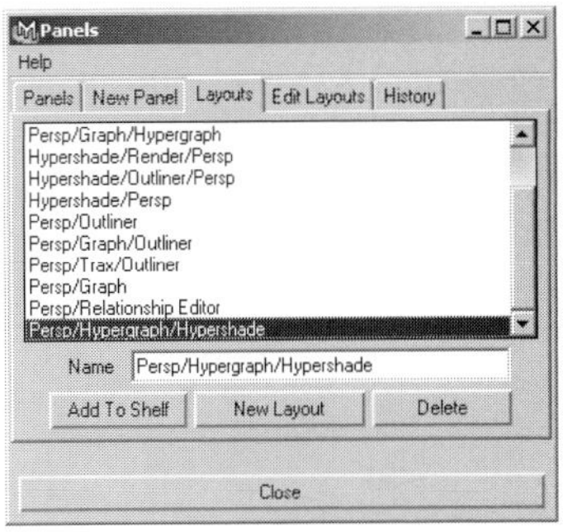

The Hotbox

The hotbox in Maya is a tool for displaying all the menus relevant to your work at a given moment, without taking up any screen real estate when it's not in use. Although you can do everything you want in Maya without ever using the hotbox, once you get used to the way the hotbox conserves space and puts nearly all of Maya's tools in easy reach, you'll wonder how you ever got along without it. To access the hotbox, just press (and hold) the space bar. In its default configuration, you will see something like Figure 1.24.

The top row of the hotbox always shows the general menus (the menus that are available in all menu sets), such as the File, Edit, Modify, and Create menus. The second row replicates the menu set of the active panel (in this case, the perspective view), with menu items such as View, Lighting, and Panels. The third row has a Recent Commands menu (showing the last 15 commands you issued) and a Hotbox Controls menu, which allows you to fine-tune how the hotbox and general menus display information. The bottom row of menus is, in this case, the Modeling menu set, with special menus for editing curves, surfaces, and polygons. In the center of the hotbox (where the A|W logo sits) is a quick way to change views from perspective to front to side to top, as well as an options menu for how the hotbox displays. Access to all these menus is the same: click (and hold—the hotbox menus will not remain open when you release the mouse button) the left mouse button over the menu; then drag inside the new submenu that appears (called a *marking menu*) to select the item you want, as in Figure 1.25, releasing the mouse when it is over your selection.

Figure 1.23

The new layout is added to the bottom of the list.

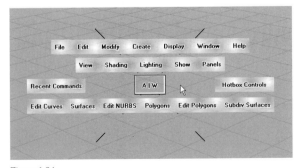

Figure 1.24

The hotbox in its default configuration

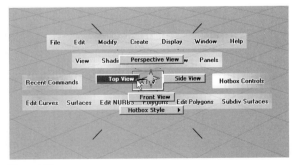

Figure 1.25

Selecting the top view using the hotbox

In addition to the menus you can see, four regions, called zones (defined by the four lines extending from the hotbox at 45-degree angles), have special functions. You use the top zone to quickly select from several saved layouts. You use the right zone to toggle elements of Maya's GUI on or off. (We'll discuss customizing your workspace in Chapter 3). You use the bottom zone to change the selected window to any of several useful views (such as the Hypergraph or the Hypershade). You use the left zone to toggle between object and component mode (mimicking the F8 key) and to toggle on and off several masking modes.

Although you can use the hotbox in its default configuration, it is more useful (if a bit more cluttered) when you turn on all menu sets (Modeling, Rendering, and so on). In the Hotbox Controls menu, choose Show All, which displays all menu sets, as shown in Figure 1.26.

In this configuration, you have access to nearly all of Maya's tools in one place, and it's all available at the press of the space bar. If you are not familiar with using the hotbox, try forcing yourself to use it for all your menu choices for a couple of hours of work; you'll likely find that you soon prefer using the hotbox over the standard menu selection method.

Menus

Although we have discussed menu sets on and off throughout this chapter, let's take a moment to look at how Maya's menus are organized. The top row of menus (or the top row in the hotbox) is split into two parts: the menus that are always present (the constant menus) and those that change according to the mode of the program (the mode menus, such as the Animation menu set, for example). Always present are File, Edit, Modify, Create, Display, Window, and Help. To change the variable menus, choose the menu set you want from the Status line (just below the menus—or under hotbox controls in the hotbox). You can choose from Modeling, Animation, Dynamics, and Rendering sets. If you have Maya Unlimited, you will also see an entry for Live.

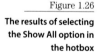

Figure 1.26

The results of selecting the Show All option in the hotbox

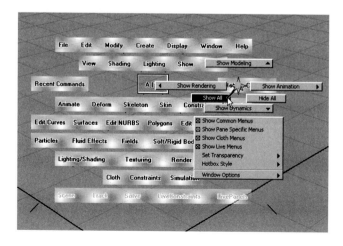

In addition to the general menus, nearly every view window in Maya has a built-in menu. The perspective view, for example, has the following menus: View, Shading, Lighting, Show, and Panels. (You use the Show menu to display and hide different types of objects.) The Hypergraph view contains these menus: Edit, View, Bookmarks, Graph, Rendering, Options, Show, and Help. For perspective and orthographic views, you can either access their menus from the top of the window pane or use the second row of menus in the hotbox. For views such as the Hypergraph or the Hypershade, clicking and holding the right mouse button displays the menus (or you can use the menu across the top of the window). There are also menus for the Channel Box and the Attribute Editor. Many of the options windows now have menus with Edit and Help options.

Generally speaking, most windows in Maya have their own menu set, which explains why Maya doesn't use just one menu bar across the top of the screen: there are at least 100 individual menus, and there would be no space to place all these menus across one screen. Attempting to nest all these menus, on the other hand, might have taken 10 or more levels to fit all the menus into one menu bar, making the task of choosing any individual menu item both laborious and baffling. Given the complexity of the task, organizing Maya's windows into contextual subsets was both a necessity and a more elegant solution to the problem.

Even so, it is often difficult to locate a menu item you have not used in a while. Fortunately Maya provides a menu search function. Choose Help → Find Menu, enter the text of the menu (a partial name is fine), and press Enter. For example, if you enter **sm** in the text box, the menu search will find all occurrences of *smooth*, *smoothness*, *smart*, and *smoke*. This is a handy feature and worth trying out.

Shelves

Although we have not touched on shelves much in this chapter, they are a convenient way to group your most frequently used commands and tools. The shelf (Figure 1.27) is one of the most noticeable features of Maya's GUI, and it appears just below the Status line. Several icons, organized into tabs called Shelf1, Shelf2, and so on, perform useful commands. For example, to create a NURBS sphere, you merely click the blue Sphere button; to create a spotlight, click the Spotlight button; to create a CV curve, click the CV Curve Tool button (the leftmost button on the right side of the shelf). Most useful are the two widgets just to the left of the shelf icons. By clicking the top one (a gray tab icon), you can quickly navigate to any tab (useful if you have created dozens of tabs). Clicking the bottom widget opens a menu of common shelf commands, plus access to the Shelf Editor.

Figure 1.27

The shelf

You can customize shelves and shelf icons to suit your needs. For more on how to do this, see Chapter 3 or Chapter 16.

Having these buttons available on a shelf makes the process of creating each item much more straightforward than having to find them in a hierarchical menu set.

The Outliner and the Hypergraph

Although we will cover the inner workings of the Outliner and the Hypergraph later in this book, let's take a quick look at these two scene management windows. The basic purpose of the Outliner and the Hypergraph is the same: to allow you to see an abstract (or outline) of the scene. The way the two display a scene's outline, however, is very different.

Figure 1.28

The Outliner, showing a leg object childed to a body object

If you have used a 3D animation program in the past, you are probably familiar with a scene management tool such as the Outliner, shown in Figure 1.28. From top to bottom, the Outliner (choose Window → Outliner) lists all objects in your scene, including cameras (note that the orthographic views—top, side, and front—are just cameras listed in the Outliner), lights, curves, and geometric objects. If you have objects that are parented to one another (a leg, for example, is parented to a body so that they move together), the Outliner indicate this relationship by displaying a plus sign to the left of the parent object (the body in this case). Clicking the plus sign displays the child object (the leg), which, because it is the child object, is tabbed in under the parent. The Outliner menu contains several options, which will be discussed further in Chapter 3.

The Hypergraph, by contrast, is probably like nothing you've seen before. It is, essentially, a linked (or hyperlinked) outline of your scene, showing not only your scene elements, but how they are connected. Although the Hypergraph may at first appear bewildering, its fashion of laying out a scene can prove invaluable. Figure 1.29 shows how the scene shown in the Outliner, in Figure 1.28, would look in the Hypergraph.

Figure 1.29

The Hypergraph with leg and body

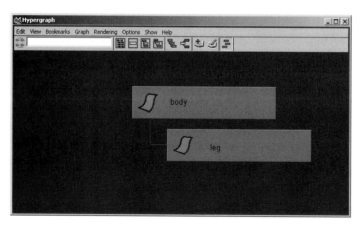

If you're interested, you can learn much more about the Hypergraph and the Outliner in Chapter 3.

The Channel Box and the Attribute Editor

The Channel Box (to the right of the main scene window) and the Attribute Editor are related windows that give you access to just about every aspect of the objects and materials in your scene. The Attribute Editor (accessed by pressing Ctrl+A) gives you access to all of an object's attributes, and the Channel Box displays a more simplified view of only the object's *keyable* (or animatable) attributes. Because these two panels are counterparts, it makes sense for them to be grouped together, and you can set the two to toggle (the Attribute Editor replacing the Channel Box on the right side of the window), Choose Window → Settings/Preferences → Preferences, and then, in the Interface section, click the Open Attribute Editor In Main Maya Window radio button.

The Channel Box is so named because elements that can be animated in a 3D program have often been termed "channels." To animate a ball going up and down, you animate its Y-axis channel (by setting several keyframes over time). Although Maya uses the term *attribute* for anything that could potentially be keyable in a scene, those that have actually been set to keyable are placed in the Channel Box.

As you'll see throughout this book, the Attribute Editor and the Channel Box are your keys to controlling all of an object's attributes, including numeric inputs for translation, rotation, scale, and visibility, as well as its construction history, such as spans of CVs and the radius of a circular object. The Attribute Editor, in addition (via its tabbed windows), allows you to access materials, tessellation criteria for NURBS objects, and other features. To toggle between the Channel Box and the Attribute Editor, press Ctrl+A.

Materials? Tessellation? If you're new to 3D animation, don't worry about absorbing all the jargon right away. The following chapters introduce all the essential concepts in a logical and straightforward way.

If you click the name (not the text box, but the actual name—see Figure 1.30) of an attribute in the Channel Box and then MM drag in the scene window, you will get a "virtual slider" that controls the number next to the channel name, as shown in Figure 1.30. This is a powerful, time-saving feature in Maya.

Figure 1.30

**Creating and using a
virtual slider**

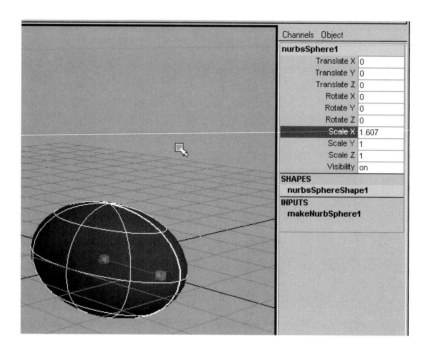

The Timeline

The Timeline, just below the main scene window(s) and shown in Figure 1.31, is the key to animation in Maya.

By default, the numbers on the Timeline are set to frames (and by default, frames per second is set to film rate—24—so 24 frames equals one second of animation). To the right of the Time Slider is the current time marker (probably set to 1.00). To change the current time in your animation, you can either drag the time marker in the Time Slider or double-click the Current Time field and enter a number (such as 5). You will then see the time marker move to that frame. Larger numbers (such as frame 20) are, of course, later in the animation. Below the Time Slider is the Range Slider (the gray bar with a 1 on one end and a 24 on the other) that lets you control the range of the time slider within a larger animation. To change the position of the Time Slider while maintaining the same range (24 frames by default), drag the Range Slider by its middle. To change the starting point of the range, drag the left square left or right. To change the ending point, drag the right square to the left or right, as shown in Figure 1.32.

Figure 1.31

The Timeline

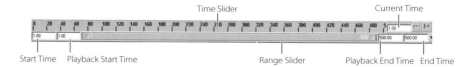

Figure 1.32

Drag the right square to change the ending point of the Time Slider.

To the left of the Range Slider are two numeric fields. The leftmost field sets the animation start frame (often people set this number to 0 for the first frame instead of 1). The field to its right sets the starting frame of the time range (changing this number is equivalent to dragging the left square of the Range Slider). To the right of the Range Slider are two more fields; the left field sets the ending time of the animation range (equivalent to dragging the right square on the Range Slider), and the right field controls the end point of the animation (set to 48 frames as a default).

To change the settings for the Time Slider, open the Animation Timeline and Playback Preferences in the Preferences window(either click the Animation Preferences button, to the right of the key icon at the bottom right of the screen or choose Window → Settings/ Preferences → Preferences and then choose the Settings/Timeline category). In the Preferences window, shown in Figure 1.33, you can control the height of the Timeline (useful when sound files are imported), set playback speed to Play Every Frame, Real-time, Half, or Twice (Play Every Frame is required for playback of dynamics), and even adjust animation beginning and end points. In the Settings section, you can change your slider units from the default film (24fps) to PAL, NTSC, seconds, minutes, or even hours.

To play back an animation, you can either use the VCR-like controls to the right of the Time Line, or you can press Alt+V to start and stop the animation and Alt+Shift+V to reset the animation to its starting frame.

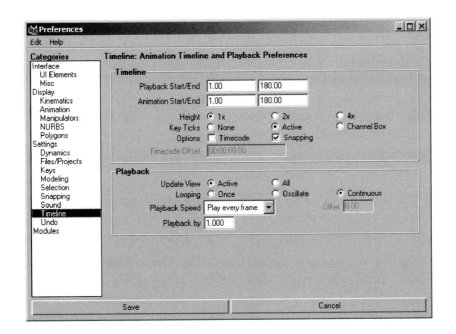

Figure 1.33

The Animation Timeline and Playback Preferences in the Preferences window

The Command Line, the Feedback Line, and the Script Editor

At the bottom of the Maya screen is the Command/Feedback line. The two halves of this line function in tandem and are simply the last lines of the Script Editor's input and history windows, respectively. Therefore, let's first take a quick look at Maya's Script Editor. Although most of your interaction with Maya is via the GUI, most of what you actually tell Maya to do is passed to it via MEL. The selections and other actions you make in the GUI are recorded as MEL commands. Creating a NURBS sphere, for example, is simply the command sphere followed by several optional flags. To access the Script Editor, either click the Script Editor icon just to the right of the Feedback line (at the bottom right of the screen), or choose Window → General Editors → Script Editor. The Script Editor, shown in Figure 1.34, is split into two halves. The top, which is the history window, probably has several lines of code in it (these would be the last commands you issued to Maya). The input window at the bottom awaits any MEL commands you might want to give to Maya.

Figure 1.34

The Script Editor window

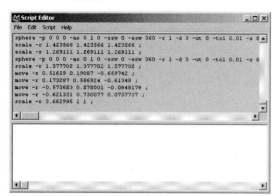

For information on how to use MEL commands with the Script Editor, see Chapter 20.

To see how the Script Editor works, type **sphere** (in lowercase letters) in the input window and press the Enter key on the *numeric keypad* (not the alpha keyboard). You should see the line

```
// Result: nurbsSphere1 makeNurbsSphere1 //
```

appear in the history window (telling you what Maya has done to complete your command), and a sphere will appear at the origin of your scene.

You can press Ctrl+Enter (on the main keyboard) to execute your command.

Because the Command line is just the last input line in the Script Editor, you don't have to open the Script Editor for a simple command. Try closing the Script Editor and then, in the Command line, type **cone** (all lowercase letters), and press Enter. A cone should appear in your scene, and the Feedback line (to the right of the Command line) should now read

```
Result: nurbsCone1 makeNurbsCone1
```

This lets you know what actions Maya has taken to complete your command.

To "focus" on the Command line when you are in a scene window (so you don't have to click in the Command line field with your mouse), press the ` (reverse apostrophe) key on your keyboard.

Summary

This quick tour has shown that, while Maya is a deep and complex program, a great deal of thought has gone into making the interface intuitive. Consistent interface elements (such as using the Alt key and mouse drags to move around many different windows), grouping tools, and even placing clues about your orientation in space and the type of tool you're using directly in the scene windows—all these features work together to ease the new user's entrance into this complex environment.

More important, you can customize the interface, from its smallest to its largest detail, so that you can tailor the program to meet your needs. As you grow more comfortable with using Maya, you will want to optimize its interface to allow you to work more quickly with less clutter. In Chapter 3, we will explore exactly this issue, looking into built-in options, creating buttons and menus of your own, and making the best use of some of Maya's organizational windows (such as the Outliner and the Hypergraph). If you are new to Maya, spend a bit of time playing with the interface after reading this chapter. Otherwise, move on to the next chapter and put your understanding of the Maya interface to good use while creating a complete animation from scratch!

CHAPTER 2

Your First Maya Animation

Now that you have an overview of how Maya works, let's put this knowledge to practical use. In this chapter, you'll get to try out modeling, keyframing, texturing, and using Maya's built-in dynamics, all in one animation that shows off the power of Maya's interface and renderer. You'll also get a chance to practice the basics of maneuvering around a Maya scene, and you'll start to see how adjusting various options can lead to different results.

Although we won't deal with theory or do a lot of explaining in this chapter (that's what the rest of the book is for!), you should get a good idea about many of the major parts of Maya if you follow along.

If you are familiar with other 3D animation packages, going through this chapter should get you ready to use Maya proficiently. If you are new to the whole world of 3D animation, the animation in this chapter will be challenging yet rewarding. Don't get discouraged if things don't turn out perfectly the first time you try. Just remember to save your project often, and under different names, and you can always go back a step or two and try again.

But enough talk—let's do some animating!

- ▪ **Setting the scene: modeling**

- ▪ **Texturing your models using the Hypershade**

- ▪ **Lighting the scene**

- ▪ **Animating the rocket**

- ▪ **Creating a follow camera**

- ▪ **Rendering the animation**

- ▪ **Advanced topic: adding exhaust**

Setting the Scene: Modeling

In this chapter, we're going to build, texture, light, and animate a little rocket ship that takes off, loses power after a couple of seconds, and crashes back to earth.

Although this modeling and animation project is a bit simplified, it is definitely a real-world example of what you can do in Maya. Remember that you can return to this project as you progress through the book, refining your work. Given a bit of time and practice, you should be able to get this project looking good—even if you've never done 3D work before! To give you an idea of what you're working toward, take a look at Figure 2.1, which shows a still shot from the completed animation. (To get the full effect, see the Color Gallery and the 02rocket.mov movie on the CD.)

SAVING MAYA PROJECT AND SCENE FILES

Your project consists of several folders (or directories) of information about the scene (which is where your scene file is stored), any rendering jobs, source images, output images, textures, and so forth. Whenever you first create a new scene in Maya, there are *two* steps to saving: first, save your project (which contains all the proper places for Maya to store your project's information), and then save the actual scene file.

You might want to browse for your new project's file location. With the New Project window open, click the Browse button next to the Location text field, and use the standard file browser to choose the location of your project.

Maya is based on the Unix operating system, which means you *must never* use spaces in your filenames—even if you're running the Windows version of Maya. If you do, Maya displays an error message when you try to open your scene later, and you won't be able to access your earlier work! The Windows operating system will allow you to save according to its filename conventions, but Maya's file system will have problems recognizing names with spaces.

It is a good idea to append a number to the name of every scene (for example, rocket001). Maya does this automatically when you turn on the Incremental Save option. Choose File → Save Scene ❏. (The ❏ symbol in Maya is known as an *option box*. More on this a little later.) When the Save Scene Options window opens, click the Incremental Save check box. As you work, you will want to save your scene often, in case you run into any problems. With Incremental Save turned on, each time you save, Maya will create a new file, numbered sequentially (rocket002, rocket003, and so on). If you are concerned about disk space on your hard drive, you can limit the number of incremental saves since new backup files are created each time you save. In the Save Scene Options window, click the Limit Incremental Saves check box. The default limit is 20 increments, which is usually enough to save the last four or five versions, so type 5 in the Number Of Increments box. Once the limit is reached, Maya deletes the oldest incremental file and replaces it with the most recently saved one.

Figure 2.1

The rocket taking off

As described in the Introduction, the companion CD is designed to be an integral part of this book. It contains working files for all the exercises, along with finished versions of many projects. For this chapter's project, you'll find the complete animation, along with the 02rocket.ma project file.

The first step to almost any animation in Maya is to build your scene elements; therefore, we'll build the rocket (and ground) as our first step. To build our little ship, we'll use just a couple of the many modeling techniques Maya has available.

1. First, we need to create a project and save our file in this project so that it has a home. Open Maya by double-clicking its desktop icon. Now, from the File menu, choose File → Project → New. In the New Project option window, click the Use Defaults button, type a name for your project (something such as rocketProject) in the Name text box, and click Accept to accept these choices. You now have your project saved in your default directory on your hard drive. You also need to save your scene. To do that, choose File → Save Scene As, and then choose an appropriate name for the file (such as rocket1).

2. After you save your project and file, change your scene window from the default perspective view to a "four view" of the scene by first clicking in the scene (large) window and then pressing and releasing the spacebar quickly. (You can also simply LM click the Four View Quick Layout button in the Tool Box.) Your scene window should change to four smaller panes, each labeled for its view (top, side, front, and persp—perspective). Select the side view by clicking your mouse inside this pane; then press and release the spacebar quickly again so that the side view fills the entire viewing pane (see Figure 2.2).

Figure 2.2

The side view pane

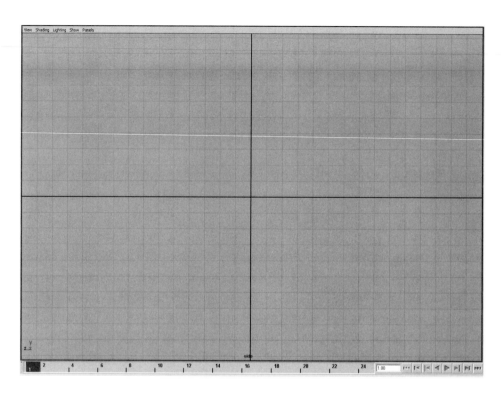

To create the body of the rocket, we'll use an EP (Edit Point) curve tool to define four points that make up the rocket's outline and then "revolve" this curve into a surface.

3. Select the EP Curve tool (choose Create → EP Curve Tool); your cursor should turn into a cross, indicating that you're now using the EP Curve tool. Because we want the first (top) point of the curve to lie directly on the X axis (the thick vertical line at the center of the pane), we need to turn on the Snap To Grids feature before we create the first point on the curve. Click the Snap To Grids button on the Status line (the topmost toolbar).

You can also use a keyboard shortcut to enable grid snapping: hold down the X key on the keyboard while clicking, and each point you click will snap to the nearest grid intersection.

4. A little below the top of the window, where the Y axis meets one of the other grid lines, click once (with your left mouse button) to create your first point. Now turn off the Snap To Grids feature (click it again), and create three more points, approximately like Figure 2.3. If you hold down the mouse button when you click to create a point, you can move that point around until you like its positioning; you can also press the backspace key to remove the last point you made. When you are satisfied with the shape of the ship, press the Enter key to save the points (the line will turn green).

5. The next step is to create a surface from our outline. Be sure Modeling is showing on the Status line (at the far left top of the screen). If it is not, choose Modeling from the pop-up menu there. Now revolve the curve by choosing Surfaces → Revolve ❑.

Selecting the option box with your mouse opens a window in which you can change the options of your command—in this case, the Revolve command.

6. In the Revolve option window, choose Edit → Reset Settings and then set the segments to 16 (instead of the default 8). Click the Revolve button. You should now see your curve transformed into a squat rocket ship body! To shade your rocket ship, press the 3 key (on the main keyboard, not the numeric keypad) and the 6 key—the 3 key changes your view to high-resolution, while the 6 key turns on smooth shading mode (instead of wireframe). Figure 2.4 shows the revolved rocket in high-resolution, smooth shading mode.

Most option windows close when you click the *item-name* button (in this case, Revolve). To keep the window open (to create other objects, for instance), click the Apply button instead of the Revolve (or other) button.

7. Rename your object (shown in the Channel Box, at the right of the main window) from revolvedSurface1 to something more appropriate, such as body: click once on the object's name (revolvedSurface1) at the top of the Channel Box and type your new name, replacing the old one. Press Enter and save your work now.

If you don't see the object name listed (and a Channels menu directly above it), click the Show The Channel Box button (above where the Channel Box would be). This should change your view to the Channel Box view. If you still don't see the object name, make sure your object is selected.

> If something goes wrong on this or any step in the project, remember that you can always press the Z (undo) key to move back one or more steps in your work.

8. Now we need to build our rocket engine exhaust nozzle. We'll create this from a revolved curve that we'll drag up into the rocket, leaving only its broad base visible. We'll use the same method we learned to create the rocket itself: choose the EP Curve tool (or press the Y key, which will reselect the last used tool), and then click several points to form the outline curve (see Figure 2.5) that you'll revolve into an exhaust nozzle shape. To make the size (scale) of the curve easier to see, try creating the exhaust nozzle directly below the rocket body.

9. When you are satisfied with the look of your curve, press the Enter key and, while the curve is still selected (green), choose Surfaces → Revolve to revolve it into a nozzle. (Note that we don't have to use the options this time; this revolve operation will use the same options you set for the rocket body last time.) Press the 3 key to smooth out the view of the engine nozzle; then rename the object (in the Channel Box) from revolved-Surface2 to nozzle and save your work.

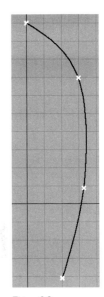

Figure 2.3

An outline of the rocket ship

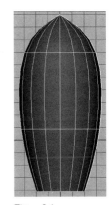

Figure 2.4

The revolved rocket

Figure 2.5

The curve for the exhaust cone

MAYA SHORTCUT KEYS

The QWERTY keys (across the top left of your keyboard) are shortcut keys. Memorize these keys now—using shortcut keys is one secret to getting work done in Maya quickly! (If you tend to share your computer, such as in a school lab environment, the default Maya Hotkeys may have been altered. To restore them to their defaults, choose Window → Settings/Preferences → Hotkeys and press the Restore Defaults button.) The function for the QWERTY keys is as follows:

Q Places Maya into Select mode (in which you can only select, not modify, scene elements). (Ctrl+Q places Maya into Lasso Select mode (also for selection only).

W Places Maya in Move mode.

E Places Maya in Rotate mode.

R Places Maya in Scale mode (not Rotate mode!).

T Places Maya in Manipulator mode. (We won't deal with this tool in this chapter.)

Y Places Maya in whatever mode—besides Move, Scale, and Rotate—was last chosen (the EP Curve tool, in our work).

You can also adjust the display of objects in the scene using the 1–7 keys on your alpha keyboard (not the numeric keypad).

1 Changes the display of any selected object into low-resolution display (which increases interactivity with the program, but the objects look blocky).

2 Changes the display of any selected object into medium-resolution display.

3 Changes the display of any selected object into high-resolution display (which looks much better, but can slow response).

4 Changes the display of all objects in the scene (not just selected objects) to wireframe display (faster interactivity and the ability to see through objects).

5 Changes the display of all objects in the scene to smooth-shaded display (basic coloring is visible).

6 Changes the display of all objects in the scene to texture-shaded display (the basic look of a texture is visible on objects).

7 Changes the display of all objects in the scene to textured-shaded and lit display (so the basic effect of lights can be seen).

10. We now need to move the nozzle into the base of the rocket. Choose the nozzle (if it's not green, click or drag a selection marquee on the nozzle—be sure not to highlight the rocket body or the original curve you used to revolve the nozzle); then press the W key to enter Move mode. You should see several colored arrows (above the nozzle) around a yellow box. Click and drag up on the green arrow until the nozzle is where you want it , as shown in Figure 2.6.

11. Now let's create a cockpit for our ship from a default sphere. Click the sphere (ball) button on your tool shelf, or choose Create → NURBS Primitives → Sphere (remember to press the 3 key to display the sphere in hi-res mode). You won't be able to see the sphere, because it is currently inside the rocket body, so change to Move mode (press the W key) and move the sphere to the right of the rocket body. Now change to Scale mode (press the R key) and stretch the sphere up until it is about twice as tall as it is thick. Finally, change back to Move mode (press the W key) and move the sphere into position near the front end of the rocket body (see Figure 2.7). Be sure to change the name of the object (in the Channel Box) from nurbsSphere1 to cockpit, and save your work.

12. No 1950s-era space ship would be complete without some fancy fins. We'll create one fin using a default cone and then adjust its points to make it look more like a fin. Choose Create → Polygon Primitives → Cone ❑, choose Edit → Reset Settings, set the Subdivisions Along Height option to 5 (instead of 1), and click Create; then name the cone fin1. Set Maya to Move mode, and then move the cone out so it is below the cockpit. Now change to Rotate mode (press the E key) and rotate the cone so it points away from the side of the ship. To do this, grab the outermost (yellow) ring of the Rotate tool and MM drag to the right, as illustrated in Figure 2.8.

13. The fin is almost correctly placed, but it's currently much too small. Change to Scale mode (press the R key), and scale the whole cone out (click the yellow box in the center, and then MM drag to the right) until it is the right size. We're getting closer, but now the cone has been scaled out in all directions. To fix this, change to four-view mode (press the spacebar quickly), and, in front or top view, click the red (X axis) scale box at the end of the scale manipulator and scale the fin so it is thin in that dimension (see Figure 2.9).

14. Now that the cone/fin is thin, return to the side view (click in the side view, and then press and release the spacebar). Highlight the fin so it is green; then press the F8 key to go into Component mode. Drag a selection marquee around the point at the tip (it will turn yellow), press W (Move mode), and then move that point down so it is about as low as the exhaust nozzle—don't worry that it looks very angular right now. Next, draw a selection marquee around the second row of points in from the tip (be sure to select

Figure 2.6

Move the nozzle up to the bottom edge of the rocket.

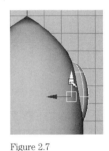

Figure 2.7

Putting the cockpit in place

Figure 2.8

The cone, moved and rotated

Figure 2.9

The cone, scaled

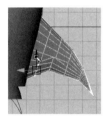

Figure 2.10

**A curved fin in Compo-
nent mode**

only this row), and move them down some as well. Finally, choose the bottom set of points on the next three rows in (toward the body), and move them up a bit. You should now have a curved fin, as in Figure 2.10. Save your work.

15. When you like the shape of the fin, press the F8 key again to return to Object mode. Although the fin is nice, it could use some smoothing. Be sure the fin is still selected (green), and then choose Polygons → Smooth to smooth out the angles between polygon facets. At this point, you might want to move the fin in toward the body more so that the fin sticks partway into the body.

We have one fin; now we need to make two more. Rather than model these new fins, let's make Maya do the work. First, we need to move the pivot point of the fin (the point around which it rotates) to 0 on the X and Z axes, and then we'll just tell Maya to make two duplicates and rotate them.

16. Click the fin to highlight it and make sure you are in Move mode (click the Move tool in the Tool Box or press W on your keyboard). Now, press the Insert key on your keyboard. The arrows of the manipulator handles will disappear, and you will see the pivot point in the center yellow box. Click the blue handle (it may be difficult to see), and drag it to the center line. To more accurately center the pivot point, hold down the X key while dragging, forcing the pivot point to snap to the grid. When the pivot point has been moved, press the Insert key again to return to normal Move mode. You may find it easier to move the cone's pivot point if you shift to wireframe display mode momentarily. To do so, just press the 4 key on your keyboard (not on the numeric keypad).

17. Now choose Edit → Duplicate ❐. In the option window, set Rotate Y (the middle box) to 120 (120 degrees, or one-third of a circle), set Number Of Copies to 2, and click Duplicate. You will now have three fins spaced evenly around the body of the ship—Maya even names the other fins fin2 and fin3 for you!

18. As a last step, we need to make some ground for our rocket to take off from. Choose Create → NURBS Primitives → Plane ❐, choose Edit → Reset Settings, and then set the Width and Length to 100 (so the ground is very big). Click Create, and then rename the plane ground. You'll notice that the plane is right in the middle of the rocket. Using the Move tool, move the plane down until it is a significant distance below the ship (as in Figure 2.11)—don't let the rocket body, fins, or nozzle touch the plane, or you will have big problems later in this chapter!

To alter the size of the plane, you can either scale it using the Scale tool or click the makeNurbsPlane text in the Channel Box and change the width setting.

19. Now that we have all our pieces, we need to get rid of the construction history for each of them and then erase the curves that generated them (otherwise we'll have problems later in the animation process). First, select everything in the scene (or RM choose Select All in the scene window); then choose Edit → Delete By Type → History. Now find the curves you used to build the body and nozzle of the rocket. (You can choose any component of the rocket and then use the Right and Left arrow keys to "scroll" through all the components—or you can use the Outliner or Hypergraph to find the curves.) When you each curve is selected, press the Backspace or Delete key to delete them all.

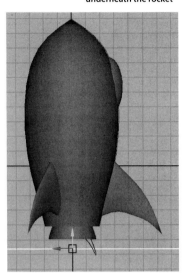

Figure 2.11

Moving the ground underneath the rocket

As a last step, we need to make all our rocket components into one object (we'll call it rocket) and move the pivot point of our rocket down to the ground plane (the reason for this will be apparent as we animate the ship).

20. Drag a selection marquee around the ship and all its components (be sure not to include the ground, though!); then hold down the Ctrl key and press G. This creates a new group (called group1) that contains all the pieces of the rocket we have modeled. Rename this group to rocket. If you accidentally highlight the ground plane with the rocket components, hold down the Shift key and click anywhere on the plane to deselect it.

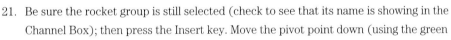
In the future, if you click any component of the rocket (the body, say) and press the Up arrow key, Maya automatically chooses the rocket group for you. This technique is known as "pick walking."

Figure 2.12

Moving the rocket pivot point down

21. Be sure the rocket group is still selected (check to see that its name is showing in the Channel Box); then press the Insert key. Move the pivot point down (using the green handle) until it is below the bottom of the nozzle (see Figure 2.12). Moving the pivot point will be important when we animate the scale of the ship (otherwise, the ship will scale around its middle, instead of its bottom). Be sure to press the Insert key again after you move the pivot point. Save your work.

22. Let's take a look at our handiwork. Change to perspective view in the scene panel (remember the spacebar trick), change to Shaded mode (press the 6 key), and then rotate around your ship by holding down the Alt key and the left mouse (LM) button and dragging around the scene window. Your rocket should look like that in Figure 2.13.

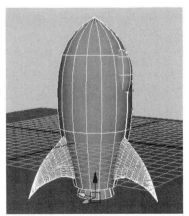

Figure 2.13

Perspective view of the rocket

If your results are different from those you see in the book, you might want to return to the area that is different and rework it until you are satisfied with the results.

Save your work and take a break—good job so far!

Texturing Your Models Using the Hypershade

You might find the model you've created so far a bit... well... gray. Let's remedy that situation now by adding *materials* to the model elements, giving them a bit more color and interest. Materials in Maya are the general container for a shading network, which gives an object its color, transparency, reflectivity, and so forth. Normally, you create a material and then edit the material's settings or add textures (images or procedural textures) to get the look you want. Think of materials in Maya as your own virtual paint can.

To create these materials, we'll use the Hypershade. Follow these steps:

1. Select the cockpit and then choose Window → Rendering Editors → Hypershade to open the Hypershade window.

2. To the left of the Hypershade is the Create Bar panel. (If you don't see it, click the checker icon in the upper-left corner of the screen, or choose Options → Create Bar → Show Create Bar.) To create a new material, click the button at the top of the panel and choose Create Materials. Simply click the Phong material, and a new material will appear in the window on the right called the Hypershade panel. Name the new material cockpit-Phong by holding down the Ctrl key, double-clicking the default name (Phong1), and then typing the new name, as in Figure 2.14.

Figure 2.14

Creating a new material for the cockpit

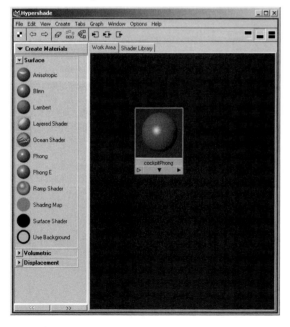

3. To assign this new material to the cockpit, just MM drag the material ball onto the cockpit in the scene window. Because the Phong material is still gray, you won't see much difference yet.

4. To adjust the color of the new material, double-click it in the Hypershade. This opens the Attribute Editor (shown in Figure 2.15) with several options you can control for color and other attributes.

5. All we're interested in for the cockpit is its color. Click the gray rectangle next to the word *color*, and, in the color picker that pops up, choose a very dark blue (almost black) color. You can watch the cockpit itself change as you adjust the color. When you get a color you like, click the Accept button.

6. Let's make another Phong material for the body of the rocket. Once again, click the Phong icon in the Create Bar panel on the left side of the Hypershade window, and then rename this new material bodyPhong. Now MM drag the material ball onto the body of the rocket.

7. In the Attribute Editor, adjust the color of the new material to a very pale blue-gray (the color of brushed aluminum). To make this work right, you'll need to set the saturation of your color very low (we set it to 0.075).

8. When you accept the color, you'll probably notice that the specular highlights (the shiny areas) on the rocket body are big and ugly. Fortunately, we can compensate for this. In the Specular Shading area of the Attribute Editor, set the Cosine Power (the size of the highlight) to a large number, such as 75, and set the Specular color to a darker gray (drag the slider to the left). When you finish, you should have a more pleasing highlight.

9. To create the ground shade (we don't want a specular high-light on the ground!), let's use the Lambert shader, which does not create highlights. Create a new Lambert material by clicking the Lambert icon in the Create Bar panel and renaming it groundLambert. Then MM drag the new material onto the ground plane, assigning it to the plane. (You may need to go into perspective view to see the ground plane.)

10. In the Attribute Editor, set the color of the ground plane to a dusty orange-yellow (a desert dirt color).

11. The last two materials we'll make will be a bit more interesting. First, let's create a material with a procedural texture for the nozzle. Create a new Phong shader, name it nozzlePhong, and assign it to the nozzle.

12. Instead of assigning a color to the new material, click the little checkerboard next to it (to the right of the slider) to open the Create Render Node window. Click the Checker button to apply a checkered pattern to your material, as shown in Figure 2.16.

Figure 2.15

Attributes for the Phong shader

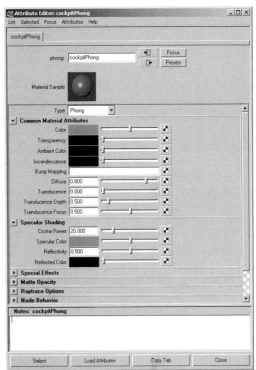

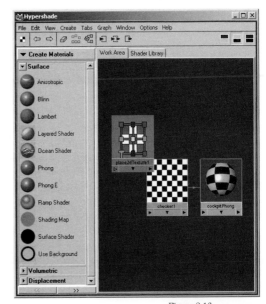

Figure 2.16

Giving the object a checkered material

13. Although this texture as it currently is might be all right for playing checkers, it's not what we're after. In the Attribute Editor, make both of the colors in the checker pattern a shade of gray (drag the sliders next to the color swatches). Finally, decrease the Contrast setting to about 0.7. These changes will make the pattern much subtler.

14. Now click the place2Dtexture1 tab (at the top of the Attribute Editor) and set the Repeat UV to 16 and 0.5, respectively. This will give the nozzle the ringed appearance (seen in Figure 2.17) common to rocket nozzles.

15. Finally, let's create the fin material, using a ramp to get our effect. First, create a new Phong material (called finPhong), and assign it to all three fins—you will probably have to rotate the scene panel in order to see all three fins so you can do this.

16. In the Attribute Editor, click the checkered box next to Color again to open the Create Render Node window. Choose Ramp from the list of 2D textures. You should see a Ramp Attributes window with a default ramp, and all the fins should have the colors applied to them.

17. Although the smooth transitions of the default ramp are nice, they're not what we need for our fins. From the Interpolation pop-up menu, choose None. This turns off the smooth interpolation of the colors, making the ramp a series of color bars.

18. To change the ramp colors, select the ramp node (the circle to the left of the color bar) and then click the Selected Color swatch to open the color picker. To create a new color node, just click in the color swatch where you want that new node. To move a color up or down, drag the circle on the left of the color bar. Finally, to remove a color, click the box to the right of the color bar. You can use whatever colors you like for the ramp, but when you are finished, you should have something like Figure 2.18, which is also on the CD in a color version.

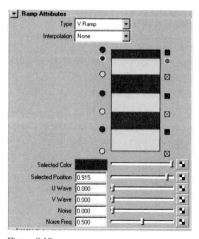

Figure 2.17

A ringed nozzle

Figure 2.18

The finished ramp

We now have a fully textured ship and ground plane. Although none of these materials is terribly complex, they give the ship some color and add to the cartoonish feel of the world we're creating. To be able to see our ship when we render it, we'll next need to add some lights to the scene.

Lighting the Scene

To light this scene, we'll add four lights: one ambient light to shade the whole scene and three spotlights. This lighting setup will give the scene a night-time quality, which is a bit more fun than one big light for the sun. Additionally, we'll make two of the lights "track" (or aim toward) the ship at all times. Follow these steps:

1. First, let's create our ambient light. Choose Create → Lights → Ambient Light □. In the option window, set the intensity to 0.2, click the color swatch and set the color to a pale blue, and then click Create.

2. To see how the scene is lit so far, press the 7 key on your keyboard to go into Lighted mode (the scene should be almost dark). Press the 5 key to return to Smooth-Shaded mode.

3. Now let's create our spotlights. Choose Create → Lights → Spot Light □. In the option window, choose Edit → Reset Settings, and then set the penumbra angle to 10 (this fades the edge of the spotlight); then click Create. Rename this light frontSpot (if the Channel Box isn't open, click the Show The Channel Box button at the far right of the Status line to toggle it back on). Press the W key to get into Move mode, and then move the light up and away from the ship, toward the camera. Be sure the light is above the rocket by a significant amount; otherwise, it won't light the ground below the ship (which gives depth and solidity to the scene).

> To move your lights, you will need to use the top and side views (press the spacebar to see these views) and scale these views out by holding down the Alt key, along with the left and middle mouse buttons, and dragging to the left in each window pane.

4. Because we want this spotlight to aim at the ship at all times, let's add an Aim constraint to it. First, click any part of the ship; then press the Up arrow key (be sure the Channel Box says rocket in its title area). Then, holding down the Shift key, click (or drag around) the light, highlighting it as well. Finally, from the Animation menu set (choose Animation from the top-left pop-up menu), choose Constrain → Aim □. Choose Edit → Reset Settings, and then change the three aim vector text boxes to read 0, 0, and –1. Click the Apply button and verify that the spotlight is pointing toward the rocket (the cone should open toward the rocket body). If the spotlight is "looking" in another direction, try the following settings until one works: 0,0,1; 1,0,0; or –1,0,0. (The aim vector of

a spotlight—like that of the camera we'll add shortly—is determined by where you place the lights in relation to the rocket. Because your rocket might be aligned along a different axis, you will have to try these settings until you discover the proper axis for your scene.) After you determine the proper aim vector, as shown in Figure 2.19, the spotlight will be locked onto the rocket, wherever it goes.

5. We now need to create another light, this one off to the right side of the ship. Create a new spotlight (choose Lights → Create Spot Light), call it rightSideSpot, and move it off to the right of (and above) the ship.

6. We want this light to follow the ship as well, so we'll do the same trick again: first, select the rocket (remember to press the Up arrow key), and then Shift+select the rightSideSpot light. Finally, choose Constrain → Aim to force the light to point at the ship. You should not need to open the option box this time, because the proper aim vector should be set now. If your light is not aiming in the right direction, undo the last step, open the Aim constraint option box, and repeat the end of step 4, earlier.

7. Finally, let's create our last spotlight (which will stay pointed at the launch area). Once again, create a spotlight; then name the new light leftSideSpot, and move it to the left and above the rocket. Figure 2.20 shows all three spotlights as they would look in the top view.

8. Because we won't be auto-aiming the light, we'll need to aim it manually. In the top view (with the light still selected), from the panel menu at the top of the top view panel, choose Panel → Look Through Selected to change the view to show what the light sees (nothing at this point). Rotate the view until the rocket is centered in the view as in Figure 2.21 (hold down the Alt key and drag with the left mouse button). To return to top view, choose Panel → Orthographic → Top.

Figure 2.19

The spotlight aimed properly

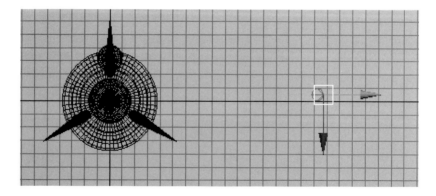

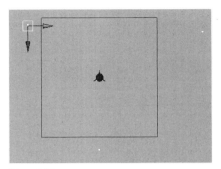

Figure 2.20

The left-side spotlight placed

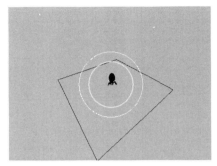

Figure 2.21

A view of the rocket through the light

9. To see how your scene is lit, press the 7 key again. It should be well (and evenly) lit across the ship and the ground near it. If not, try moving your lights around, or increasing their intensity.

10. Save your work and take a break. Good job so far!

> It is often difficult to see how well lit your scene is using the flat (openGL) renderer. To get a better view of your scene, either click the Render The Current Frame button in the right part of the Status line or choose Render → Render Current Frame from the Rendering menu set (the top-left pop-up menu). This will create a quick little rendering of your scene.

Animating the Scene

If things haven't been interesting enough so far, we're really going to have fun here: we'll animate our little ship and use some of the power of Maya's dynamics engine to launch it and bring it back to earth.

Keyframed Animation

First we need to create a keyframe animation of the ship about to take off. *Keyframe* is an old animation term for important moments in an animation (key frames). In digital animation, you tell the computer which frames are important (the keyframes), and the computer "in-betweens" the rest of the frames between these key frames, creating an animation.

For our simple animation, we'll animate only the scale of the ship as it squashes, getting ready for takeoff, and then stretches as it "leaps" off the ground. This is classic cartoon

Figure 2.22

**Choose Key Selected
from the pop-up menu.**

anticipation and overshoot—you'll recognize the effect from any old Tex Avery cartoons you run across. Follow these steps:

1. To create our first keyframe, first be sure you're on the first frame of the animation (use the VCR-like controls at the bottom-right of the screen to rewind, and check to see that the Timeline marker is at 1).

2. Next, select the rocket (be sure it's the whole rocket group, and not just the body); then, in the Channel Box, drag your mouse over the text of the three scale channels (scales X, Y, and Z), highlighting them. Then, with the mouse over the selected channels, use the right mouse button to choose (RM choose) Key Selected from the pop-up menu (see Figure 2.22). The channels for scale should turn orange (green on Irix), indicating that they're now keyframed.

3. After you create your first keyframe manually, Maya can automatically keyframe your channels. Check to be sure the auto-keyframe option is on by verifying that the Auto Keyframe Toggle icon at the bottom-right of the screen (below the VCR-like time controls) is red. If it's not, simply click it to turn it red.

4. By default, our animation runs for 24 frames, or one second. (Maya defaults to 24 frames per second—film speed.) So we need to lengthen our animation. In the number field for the end time (to the right of the Range Slider), set the frame range to 100 frames—a bit over four seconds.

    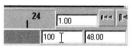

5. Move the time marker (the gray bar in the Time Slider) out to 48 frames (2 seconds) by dragging it across the Time Slider—or just click about where the 48th frame would be. Be sure your rocket is still selected, and then enter Scale mode (press the R key) and scale down the Y (green) axis so that the rocket becomes shorter (a scale of about 0.7 on the Y axis channel should do). You may notice that this simply shrinks the rocket; we also need to scale out the X and Z axes to make the rocket appear to maintain a consistent volume as it squashes. Although we could do this via the X and Z scale handles, it is easier to do so in the Channel Box itself. Click in the scale X text box, and then enter a value of 1.4. Do the same in the scale Z box. Your rocket should now look squashed, as in Figure 2.23, rather than simply shrunk.

6. We now need to hold this squashed look for some frames (a *hold keyframe*). Move the time marker to frame 60, select the scale X, Y, and Z channels again, and RM choose Key Selected. (Alternatively, you could reenter the numbers you had before, forcing Maya to create a new keyframe via the auto-keyframe option.)

7. At this point, it's a good idea to play back your animation to see how it looks so far. Click the Rewind button on the VCR-like controls (or press Alt+Shift+V); then click the Play

button (or press Alt+V) to play the animation. The rocket should squash down and then hold its appearance—and then the animation loops and repeats itself.

8. Now let's make the rocket stretch out, as if stretching to take off from the ground (don't worry for now that it's not moving up). Move to frame 70 and set the X, Y, and Z scales to 0.7, 1.4, and 0.7, respectively. (The rocket should look stretched out now.)

9. We need another hold keyframe (with the rocket stretched out), so move to frame 78, choose the scale channels, and RM choose Key Selected once again.

10. Now move to frame 90 (close to four seconds), and reset all the scale channels to 1—the ship will now return to its original shape at 90 frames. When you play back the animation, you should see the rocket squash, preparing for takeoff, then stretch up (as it takes off—don't worry, we'll take care of that next!), and finally return to its original shape. If you don't like how the animation runs, you can Shift+click any keyframe in the Timeline (highlighting it in red), and then drag that keyframe left or right on the Timeline, thereby adjusting the speed of the animation between each keyframe.

Figure 2.23

Squash your rocket ship.

Using Dynamics for Animation

We've completed the keyframing for this animation project. Now let's make Maya do the rest of the work. We'll make the ship rise into the air by giving it a force (or impulse) and then drag it back down using gravity. Finally, we'll make the ground and rocket collide. To do all this, we'll use what is known as *rigid body dynamics* to tell Maya what forces act on our object (the rocket). As explained in Chapter 15, "Working with Rigid Body Dynamics," Maya (specifically, its *dynamics engine*) will use our input to do all the calculations necessary for realistic movement. Follow these steps:

1. First, we need to make both the rocket and ground rigid bodies, so they'll react to each other and forces we apply to them. Select the ground plane, and then change to the Dynamics menu set (from the pop-up menu at the top left of your screen). Choose Soft/Rigid Bodies → Create Passive Rigid Body ❒. (Be sure not to select Active!) In the option window, set the Static and Dynamic Friction to 0.5, and set the Bounciness to 0.2. Click Create to create the rigid body.

2. Now let's make the rocket a rigid body. Select any of the rocket's body parts and press the Up arrow key (be sure rocket is the name selected in the Channel Box). Choose Soft/Rigid Bodies → Create Passive Rigid Body ❐. In the Rigid Options window, as in Figure 2.24, set the rocket's mass to 1000, set the Impulse Y to 5000, and set the Impulse Position Y to 12 (this forces the impulse to be above the rocket's body, so it won't spin around when you launch the rocket). Click Create.

    If you get an error message when you try to create the rocket's rigid body, check (using the Hypergraph or the Outliner) to be sure you have erased the two curves for the nozzle and body of the rocket. If you haven't, do so—this should take care of any error messages.

3. With the rocket still selected, choose Fields → Gravity ❐. In the option window, set the magnitude of gravity to 25 (this setting is far heavier than Earth's gravity, but it makes the animation look better!), check to be sure the Y direction of gravity is set to –1 and that X and Z are 0, and then click Create. Because the rocket was selected when you created the gravity field, it will be "attached" to gravity (that is, affected by it).

4. If you play back the animation now, you will see that it looks just the same as before. That's because our rocket is still a passive rigid body (meaning that nothing can affect it). What we have to do is keyframe the rocket to be an active rigid body just at the frame where it should take off. Select the rocket, and then move to frame 62. Under the Shapes/RigidBody2 node (in the Channel Box), you should see a channel called Active (toward the bottom) that is set to off. Click once on the text (the word Active), and then RM choose Key Selected to set a keyframe. Now move to frame 63, click in the Off text box, and type the word on. This will set a keyframe, setting the active state of the rocket's rigid body to on, so it can now be affected by forces.

Figure 2.24

The Rigid Options window

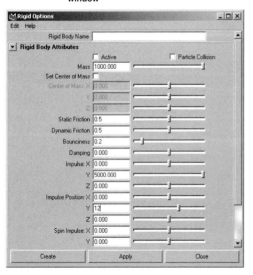

5. Before you play back the animation, you'll want it to run longer. Set the playback length to 1000 instead of 100. (Type 1000 in the Playback End Time box, just to the right of the Range Slider.) The frame range should now go from 1 to 1000. Rewind and play back the animation (which is *extremely* important; otherwise Maya will become confused about its calculations and you will see some very strange results). You should now see the rocket zoom off into parts unknown. If the rocket gets stuck in the ground, you've got a *rigid body interpenetration error*, a problem you'll learn more about in Chapter 15. To fix it, move the ground down a bit and run the animation again. (Don't forget to rewind!)

6. To make our ship stop going up and up, we need to turn off our impulse. Go to frame 104 (with the rocket still selected), select the channel for Impulse Y, and RM choose Key Selected. Move to frame 105, and type 0 in the Impulse Y number field (setting the impulse to 0 from this point on). When you play back the animation, the rocket should rise out of sight and then, about frame 450, crash back down into the ground, bouncing around until it comes to rest.

> To see the animation better, try zooming your camera back (press Alt, and with the left and middle mouse buttons, drag left) —this is called scaling the view. Also, if you don't like the way the rocket bounces off the ground, you can set the ground's bounciness lower (or higher), and you can change the rocket's impulse setting from 5000 at the start to some other similar number (such as 5001). This small change will make the bounces go in very different ways.

You should now have a complete rocket animation, using keyframes for part of it and making Maya do the calculations for the rest. Next, we'll discuss how to make a new camera and have it aim at the ship at all times; then we'll talk about how to render out the whole animation.

Save your work and take a break. Good job!

Creating a Follow Camera

As you might have noticed, the default perspective camera's view of this animation leaves something to be desired. What we need is a camera that follows the rocket into the air and back again—we need to aim our camera at the ship, just as we did with the lights.

Aiming a camera at an object would *not* be a good idea if we wanted realistic animation. It is generally better to keyframe the camera to follow the object's motion, because this introduces "human" errors into the camera tracking (making the motion look like a person operating a camera instead of a computer operating one). For our cartoonish animation, having a camera follow the rocket is acceptable; however, if you want, you can keyframe the motion instead.

1. Create a new camera (choose Create → Cameras → Camera) and name it followCamera. Using the four view panes, move the camera down the X axis (to the right in the top view), and then move it up a bit off the ground plane—do not rotate the camera at this point!

2. Select the rocket, and then Shift-select the new camera. In the Animation menu set, choose Constrain → Aim to force the camera to point at the rocket.

3. To look through your new view, choose a panel (the top view, say), and, with *only* the followCamera selected, choose Panels → Look Through Selected. Make this your sole

viewing pane (press the spacebar), and then play back the animation. You should see the camera follow the rocket up into the air and then back down again.

4. Save your work.

If the camera is too close to the action or too far away, just zoom your view (Alt+LM and RM buttons and drag) to get a better view.

Rendering the Animation

Although watching the animation play in your scene window is great, it's probably a bit bumpy (especially if you have a slower machine). You can render a cleaner view of your animation in two ways: playblasting and final rendering (batch rendering). Although a final rendering gives high-quality results, it takes a great deal of time to produce these results. Playblasting, on the other hand, produces a rougher (smooth-shaded) look, but goes as fast as your video card can spit out images. Thus, for a quick look at the animation, playblasting is a far better choice than a final rendering.

Figure 2.25

The playblasted animation in its own window

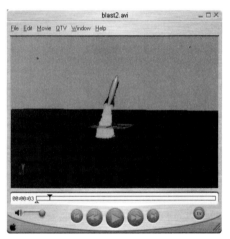

Playblasting the animation is one step: choose Window → Playblast and watch as Maya creates an animation for you, using the basic shading mode of your computer. Once the animation is complete, you can view it in its own little movie window, as in Figure 2.25. You'll learn more about playblasting in Chapter 9, "Animating in Maya."

Rendering the final product is a bit more complex and takes much longer. Essentially, a final (batch) rendering creates a high-quality "snapshot" of each frame of the animation, using all the lighting, material, and animation information your scene can provide. The results of a final rendering can be excellent, but it is a fairly slow process, because your computer has to do many calculations for every pixel of every image. Thus, you will only want to proceed with these steps when you're sure you're happy with your animation.

1. Choose Window → Rendering Editors → Render Globals or click the Render Globals button in the Status line to open the Render Globals option window. In the Image File Output section, type a name (such as **rocketRender**) in the File Name Prefix File box. Set the Frame/Animation Extension to name.#.ext, set the end frame to about 700 (you want to be sure it's a large enough number that the rocket has come to rest first), set the Frame Padding to 4 (this adds zeros before your frame number, so the frame will be numbered render.0001, render.0002, and so forth, instead of render.1, render.2, and so on), and set the active Camera to followCamera (otherwise Maya will use the default persp camera, and you will waste your rendering time).

2. Twirl down the Resolution arrow, and set the Render Resolution to 320×240.

3. Twirl down the Anti-aliasing Quality arrow, and set the Presets field to Intermediate Quality (this makes for a fairly fast render time, but with decent quality).

4. After you change your settings, close the Render Globals window, and open the Rendering menu set (the top-left pop-up menu). Choose Render → Batch Render.

5. Maya will render out all 700 frames of the animation (which will take some time). You can view the progress of each frame in the Feedback line (at the bottom-right of the screen), or, to view the current frame that is rendering, choose Render → Show Batch Render. To cancel the render at any time, choose Render → Cancel Batch Render.

6. When the rendering job is finished, you can view it using the FCheck utility. In Irix, type **fcheck** in a shell window; in Windows, choose Run (from the Start menu), and type **fcheck** in the text field or select **fcheck** from the Maya folder by browsing the Programs folder in the Start menu. A window will open, letting you navigate to your images folder (it should find this for you automatically). Choose the first frame of your animation and click OK. FCheck cycles all frames into memory and then plays back the animation at full speed.

Congratulations! You have modeled, textured, lit, animated, and rendered an animation in Maya. If patting yourself on the back isn't your style, you can move on to the next section, where you will learn how to create a particle exhaust trail for the rocket. If this was enough practice for a start, just skip right on to the next chapter and save particles until the end of the book.

Advanced Topic: Adding Exhaust

If you've worked extensively with other animation packages, what we've done so far may seem fairly straightforward. In that case, you're probably ready to explore another area of Maya dynamics, namely particles. We'll use a particle emitter to create a shower of particles and then texture them to look like smoke and flames. To make it appear that the "exhaust" is powering the rocket, we'll turn the emitter on and off (via keyframes) at the appropriate moments.

1. First, we need to create our emitter. In the Dynamics menu set (top-left pop-up menu), choose Particles → Create Emitter ❏. In the option window, name the emitter exhaustEmitter, set the emitter type to Directional, set Rate to 0, and, under the Distance/Direction section, set Spread to 0.3 and DirectionY to –1 (so the emitter points downward). Twirl down the Basic Emission Speed Attributes arrow and set the Speed to 60. Finally, click Create. You now have a particle emitter, which needs to be attached to the nozzle of the rocket.

2. To attach the emitter to the nozzle, first move the emitter (which should still be selected) down into the base of the nozzle. With the emitter still selected, Shift-select the nozzle and press the P key, making the nozzle the parent of the emitter (so that the emitter will travel along with the rocket as it moves).

3. If you play back the animation right now, the particle emitter will shoot out no particles, because its rate is set to 0 particles per second. Just before the rocket takes off (frame 63), we need to turn on the "engine"—our particles. Go to frame 59, select the Rate channel for the emitter, and RM choose Key Selected to set a keyframe at 0 for this frame.

4. Now go to frame 60 and set a rate of 500 so there are suddenly many particles shooting out from the ship. If you play back the animation now, a shower of particles (points by default; we'll fix that in a moment) will shoot out from the exhaust nozzle, as shown in Figure 2.26.

5. Now we need to turn off our rocket. Go to frame 104 and set a keyframe for the Rate at 200 (select the Rate text, and type 200). Now, at frame 105 (where the impulse turns off as well), set a new keyframe for Rate at 0. When you now play back the animation, the particles will stop coming out of the rocket at frame 105—however, the particles hang around forever (they never die). We need to give our particles a life span so they will die off like good flames should.

> For more on controlling how particles live and die, see Chapter 21, "Particle Basics," Chapter 22, "Particle Rendering," and Chapter 23, "Using Particle Expressions, Ramps, and Volumes."

Figure 2.26

Particles being emitted from the nozzle

6. With the emitter still selected, press Ctrl+A to open the Attribute Editor. Once in the Attribute Editor, click the particleShape1 tab at the top; then, in the Lifespan Attributes section, choose Random Range for the Lifespan Mode. Leave the Lifespan at 1 (second), but change the Lifespan Random to about 0.3. Setting these two attributes this way makes each particle live 1 second, plus or minus 0.3 seconds (or in a range from 0.7 to 1.3 seconds). When you now play back the animation, you should see the particles die out approximately a second after they are created (thus the trail of particles follows the rocket up as it takes off). Save your work.

7. Now that we have a good trail of particles to work with, let's change the rendering type from points to something more interesting. In the Attribute Editor (with the particleShape1 node still selected), under the Render Attributes section, set the Render Type to Cloud (s/w—for software rendered). Next, click the Current Render Type button to add the attributes that belong with the cloud render type.

8. In the new fields, make the radius 1.5, the Surface Shading 1, and the Threshold 0.5. When you play back the animation (which will now run significantly slower), you should see that the exhaust particles are now spheres. To see what they would look like in a real rendering, click the Render The Current Frame button in the Status line or choose Render → Render Current Frame (from the Rendering menu set).

9. Now we're closing in on a good exhaust cloud. The last piece of the puzzle is to create a texture for the particles. Play the animation to a frame where the particles are showing; then open the Hypershade (choose Window → Rendering Editors → Hypershade). To create a cloud texture, we need to create a volumetric texture. To do so, click the arrow next to Volumetric in the Create Bar panel to open the volume materials. Click the particleCloud material (the light blue ball), which will then appear in the right-hand window of the Hypershade (Figure 2.27), and then rename the material exhaustVM.

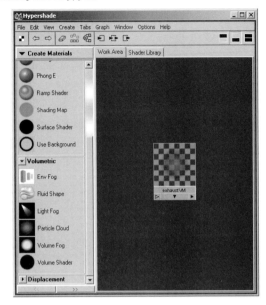

Figure 2.27

A new particle cloud shader

10. Select the exhaust particles, right-click the material (in the Hypershade), and RM choose Assign Material To Selection. Move over to the Attribute Editor, and set the color of the material to a bright yellow. Set the Transparency to a light gray (by moving the slider to the right), and set the Glow Intensity to 0.5. Test render your current frame—the exhaust should now glow a bright yellow as it is emitted from the nozzle. If you're not satisfied with the look of the exhaust, try adjusting some of the material settings or the render attributes of the particleShape1 node. Save your work again.

When you are satisfied with the look of your exhaust, you can render out the entire animation sequence (see the "Rendering the Animation" section earlier) to see how things look with your exhaust plume. To compare your work with ours, you can take a look at 02rocket.mov on the CD-ROM.

Summary

Congratulations! You have completed a real-world animation project your first time out. If your work does not look the way you would like it, that's all right: it can take quite a while to get an animation package producing just what you had in mind. No matter how you did, you can always return to this project as you continue through this book.

You may find that after a few more chapters, you'd like to give this project another try. In that case, use this chapter as a reference, not a guide. In other words, try to do the work by yourself, and read the directions here only when you get stuck. In this way, you'll make the project your own, and you'll learn even more from it.

Whether you tried this rocket animation with years of digital 3D experience under your belt or it was your first foray into the wonderful world of 3D, you should be able to see how powerful the Maya environment can be. Now that you have an idea of what Maya can do, it's time to learn more about why and how Maya does what it does. Throughout this book, we'll give you a great deal more explanation about what we're doing than we did in this chapter, but you'll still be working on real-world projects, refining both your understanding of and skill with Maya. You've taken your first step into the world of Maya—now use this book as your guide to a journey through your new and exciting world.

CHAPTER 3

Techniques for Speeding Up Workflow

In Chapter 1, we examined many of Maya's interface features. Here, we will look at ways in which you can adjust the default Maya interface to optimize the ways you interact with the program. From adjusting basic interface options to using hotkeys, shelves, and marking menus, and on to proper use of the Outliner, Hypergraph, and other windows, this chapter will show you how to customize Maya to do what you want quickly and easily. Finally, we will end with a quick demonstration of how to use Maya's tools to perform a modeling task with a minimum of pain and effort.

This chapter features these topics:

- **Adjusting interface options**
- **Using the hotbox instead of menu sets**
- **Shelves**
- **Hotkeys**
- **Marking menus**
- **Working in layers**
- **Object annotation**
- **The Outliner, Hypergraph, Connection Editor, and Hypershade**
- **Hands On: Building an arm**

Adjusting Interface Options

The first and most obvious place to start customizing Maya's interface to optimize your work is via the general interface options. Changing these options can make the interface cleaner—allowing you to work with fewer distractions—and also allot more space to the main scene view.

To adjust most interface options and preferences, choose Window → Settings/Preferences → Preferences. In the Preferences window, most UI preferences are (fittingly enough) under the Interface section of the Categories list, to the left of the window, as shown in Figure 3.1.

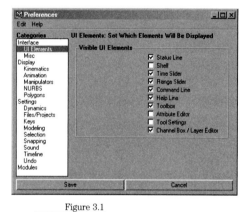

Figure 3.1

The Preferences window for UI elements

If you choose the Interface category, you can turn off the title bar and main menu bar. Doing so removes the blue border at the top of the screen (which contains the title of the scene) and the menu set at the top of the main window, saving about 30 or 40 pixels of space for your scene window and cleaning up the interface look a bit. You can also tell Maya to either remember or forget where you position your windows, whether menus should appear in panel windows, whether the focus (the cursor) will stay on the command line after you execute a MEL command from it, and whether the Attribute Editor appears in a separate, floating window or replaces the Channel Box when Ctrl+A is pressed.

You can also turn off the main menu bar and/or pane menus under the Hotbox Controls menu in the hotbox: display the hotbox and choose Window Options → Show Main (or Panel) Menu Bar.

You can use the Interface/UI Elements category to turn on or off all components of the window (except the main scene window). If, for example, you are only modeling for a while, you could turn off the time and range sliders, freeing more space for your scene. In the Interface/Misc category, you can specify how the main scene window first appears when you open a new Maya scene (it defaults to Single Perspective view), as well as how existing files are opened and saved and how help is displayed in your Internet browser.

In the Performance Settings window (choose Window → Settings/Preferences → Performance Settings), you can adjust the settings for Stitching, Trim Display, Flexors, Blend Shapes, and a number of other options. You can set these calculation-intensive Maya elements to be on or off by default, or you can set them to work on an interactive basis, in which Maya ceases trying to update calculations while you work in the scene window (during mouse actions). Under the Dependency Graph Evaluation section at the top, you can tell Maya to update scenes while you drag with the mouse (set as the default), after you release the mouse button, or only on demand (when you press a button in the scene window). For complex scenes, adjusting some or all of these settings can significantly increase the speed with which you can interact with a Maya scene.

Using the Hotbox Instead of Menu Sets

As we discussed in Chapter 1, using the hotbox instead of dealing with all the Maya menu sets can really speed your work, as well as clean up your Maya environment, giving you more room to work. Many professionals turn off all menu bars (main and panel) and solely use the hotbox to choose menu functions, since the hotbox contains all the menus. To turn off display for the menus, either use the Preferences menu (as described in the previous section) or clear the Main and Panel menus under the Hotbox Controls menu (choose Hotbox → Hotbox Controls → Window Options → Show Main (Panel) Menu Bar). After you turn off Main and Panel menus, just press and hold the spacebar to display the hotbox and access menus. You can display any or all menu sets in the hotbox, depending on your choices under the Hotbox Controls menu. Generally speaking, advanced users tend to display all menu sets simultaneously (Animation, Modeling, Dynamics, Rendering, and Maya Live, Cloth and Fur, if those are available), making the hotbox fairly complex to look at, but once you find all the menus, it's only a one-step procedure to access any menu.

> For more on how to use the hotbox and how to set its options, see Chapter 1, "The Maya Interface."

Shelves

Although we briefly discussed shelves in Chapter 1, they might have appeared to be only marginally useful. What makes shelves really useful is not what appears on them by default, but the new buttons you can easily add to any shelf. You can, for example, make any menu item a shelf button or even place MEL scripts on the shelf, allowing you to perform complex tasks at the click of your mouse. Additionally, because you can create and use multiple shelves, you can make a shelf specific to a task. For example, you can devote one shelf to MEL scripts, and another to common tasks for a specific project. To create a new shelf, choose Window → Settings/Preferences → Shelves, select the Shelves tab, and click the New Shelf button.

To switch to a new shelf (Shelf2, for example), simply click its tab on the shelf bar, or select the shelf from the pop-up shelf menu (the gray "folder" button to the left of the shelf), as shown in Figure 3.2. (You can also customize shelf settings using the drop-down menu, the black triangle just below the shelf menu tab.) To create a new shelf button from a menu item, hold down the Ctrl, Alt, and Shift keys (all together), and choose the menu item from the menu bar (*not* the hotbox). A new button will appear on the active shelf, and clicking this button will be the same as selecting the menu item you chose.

Remember, you must create shelf buttons from the main menu bar or a panel's menu bar and not the hotbox. Because many users turn off these menu bars, it is a bit of a pain to create new shelf buttons—you first have to reactivate the menu bar, then create the button, and finally turn off the menu bar again.

Figure 3.2

Selecting a shelf using the Shelf pop-up menu

Figure 3.3

**The new cylinder
button**

To delete any shelf button, just MM drag it to the trash can at the top right of the shelf bar. To move an item to a different place on the shelf, simply MM drag it to the place where you want it. Other shelf items adjust to the new placement.

As an example, let's create a button that automatically creates a NURBS cylinder and place it just next to the NURBS sphere button on Shelf1. First, be sure Shelf1 is selected by making sure its tab is foremost (or click the Folder button, as described earlier). Next, hold down the Ctrl, Alt, and Shift keys and, from the main menu bar, choose Create → Nurbs Primitives → Cylinder. A new button icon should appear at the far right of Shelf1 (as in Figure 3.3). Finally, just MM drag the new button between the sphere and cone icons on the shelf. Voilà, one more primitive you can now create without resorting to the menu bar!

> You can also create a NURBS cylinder button that automatically displays the options window. Just hold down Ctrl+Alt+Shift and choose Create → Nurbs Primitives → Cylinder ❑.

You can create as many of these buttons as you want (though you might have to scroll through the list if you create too many on one shelf) and/or delete any of the default buttons Maya provides for you, thus customizing your shelves to contain buttons that are the most useful to you. It's handy to place buttons for items such as the Hypergraph and Hypershade on Shelf1 for easy access.

You can also turn MEL scripts into shelf buttons by merely MM dragging the script's text onto the shelf. To see how this works, let's create a simple example. Open the Script Editor (click the Script Editor icon at the bottom right of the screen, or choose Window → General Editors → Script Editor). In the input (bottom) section of the window, type the following:

```
sphere -n ball -r 2;
```

Highlight this text (drag over it, or triple-click the line) and MM drag the text up to the shelf to display a new button. Now, whenever you click this new button, a new NURBS sphere named ball, with a radius of 2, will appear at the origin of your scene. Even this simple example makes it clear how powerful a little MEL scripting can be; clicking one button not only creates a sphere but names it and gives it the radius you want. You could even build a whole shelf for geometric primitives, with a group of buttons for each primitive type, each button having a different option set.

Hotkeys

After using Maya for a short time, you should be familiar with many of its default hotkeys, which are simply shortcuts to commands (or command modifiers) that are accessible by a keystroke. Accessing the Move tool, for example, is a simple matter of pressing the W key. As with most of Maya's interface, you are not limited to what's built in. You can design your own hotkeys, modify hotkeys, or even delete the Maya default hotkeys.

Maya is case sensitive, so when you assign hotkeys, take note of whether they're defined as capital or lowercase letters. To represent a G key press alone on your keyboard, you'll see a *g* in dialog boxes; Pressing shift plus the G key will appear as G. In this book, as in most computer books, shortcuts are represented as capitals because that's what appears on most keyboards. Capitalized keys, such as a capital G, will be specifically written as Shift+G in this book. Thus "the Alt+G hotkey" means the Alt and G keys, without the Shift key, while Shift+Alt+G will mean a capital G press with the Alt key depressed as well.

As an example of how to create a hotkey, let's make a keyboard shortcut to display the Hypergraph. First, open the hotkeys option window (choose Window → Settings/Preferences → Hotkeys). Scroll down until you reach the Window Menu set, and find and highlight Hypergraph-Window, as shown in Figure 3.4.

First, we need to find a key that is not currently mapped to any other hotkey. Under Assign New Hotkey, in the Key text field, type a lowercase **g**, be sure the Press radio button is enabled, and check the Alt box (which means the hotkey will be Alt plus the G key, not just the G key). If the key is not queried automatically (telling you the key is or is not assigned), click the Query button to see if any hotkey currently uses this combination. You should see a message just above the Query button telling you that no command is currently mapped to this key (if one is, try another key/modifier combination). To enable the new hotkey, click the Assign button; you should now see (in the Current Hotkeys section) that "Alt+g" has been assigned to the Hypergraph command. Click the Save button to save your changes. To test the new button, close the Hotkey Editor window, and press Alt+G in the scene window. The Hypergraph should pop right up for you!

Figure 3.4

The Hotkey Editor

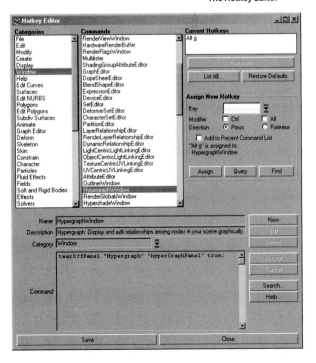

Marking Menus

In addition to creating shelves and hotkeys, you can also create entire contextual menus (called *marking menus*) that appear either in the hotbox or when you press a hotkey combination.

For example, let's create a marking menu that creates a sphere using one of four options: radius = 1, radius = 2, radius = 3, radius = 4. First, open the Marking Menus options window (choose Window → Settings/Preferences → Marking Menus). In this window, you will see listed several marking menus that have already been created for Maya, including the region menus that appear to the north, east, south, and west in the hotbox, similar to what is shown in Figure 3.5 (for more on this, see Chapter 1).

For our purposes, we want to create a new marking menu, so click the Create Marking Menu button to display the Create Marking Menu window, which has several blank boxes that we will use to create our own marking menu, shown in Figure 3.6.

First, give the marking menu a name, such as CreateSpheres. Because we will create a marking menu with four options, it is logical to use the top, right, bottom, and left boxes as our menu positions. You can assign a command to a menu item in several ways:

- You can MM drag a shelf button that you have made (or one of the default buttons, such as the cone button) onto a menu box.

- You can MM drag MEL scripts or commands to the menu item.

- You can RM click a menu item and choose Edit Menu Item (the option we will use here).

Starting at the top center box, shown in Figure 3.7, RM choose Edit Menu Item, and in the window that pops up, type **Sphere radius 1** in the Label field, and type `sphere -r 1;` in the Command(s) field (be sure the `sphere` command is in lowercase!). Finally, click Save And Close to save your changes.

Now move to the right center (east) box, RM choose Edit Menu Item, and repeat the previous steps, but this time label the button **Sphere radius 2**, and make the MEL command `sphere -r 2;`. Move to the south and west boxes, and repeat the steps, making the south box create a sphere of radius 3, and the west box create a sphere of radius 4. When you are finished, your Create Marking Menu window should look like that in Figure 3.8.

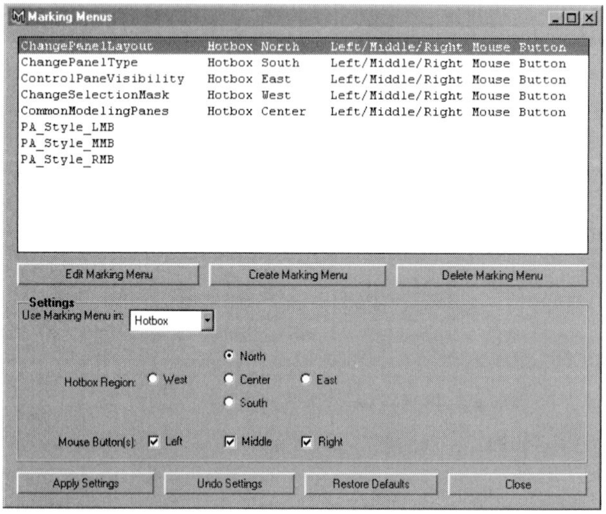

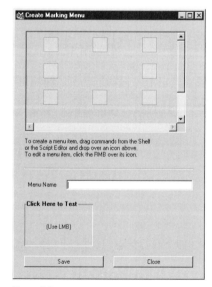

Figure 3.5

The Marking Menus option window

Figure 3.6

The Create Marking Menu window

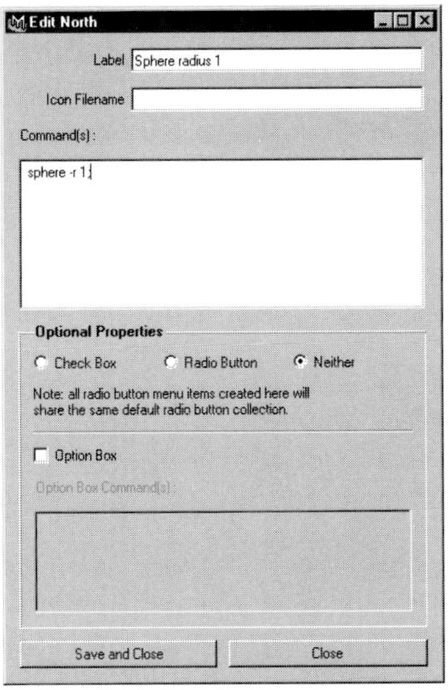

Figure 3.7

Editing the "north" marking menu box

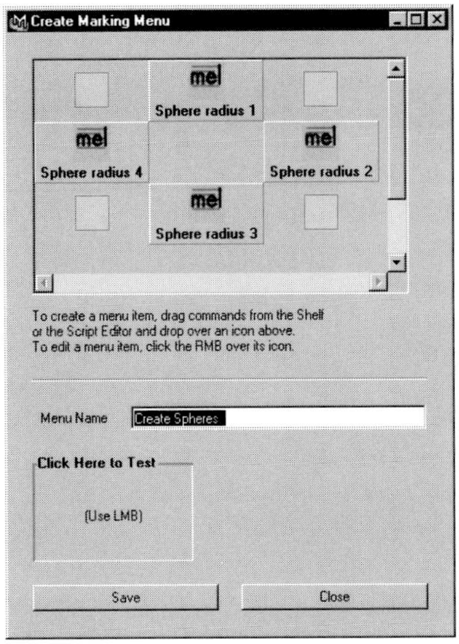

Figure 3.8

The completed marking menu

To test the buttons, click in the Click Here To Test box. You should see all your menu options appear, as in Figure 3.9, and if you choose an option, an appropriately sized sphere should appear in your scene window.

Once you have your menu working as you want, click Save and then Close to return to the Marking Menus options window. Your new CreateSpheres menu should now appear at the bottom of the list, highlighted (if it's not highlighted, do so). We now have our menu, but we can't access it from the scene window. To do so, we need to choose whether we want the menu to be part of the hotbox or accessible via a keystroke. This time, let's create a marking menu that will appear when we press a special key: under Settings, choose Hotkey Editor from the pop-up menu and then click the Apply Settings button. To the right of the CreateSpheres item in the list at the top of the window, there should now be the message "Accessible in Hotkey Editor," meaning that we can now make a hotkey for our new menu.

Close the Marking Menus options window and open the Hotkeys Editor window (Window → Settings/Preferences → Hotkeys). Scroll all the way to the bottom of the Categories list and click on the User item. You should see CreateSpheres (Press) and CreateSpheres (Release) in the Commands pane.

Figure 3.9

Testing the new marking menu

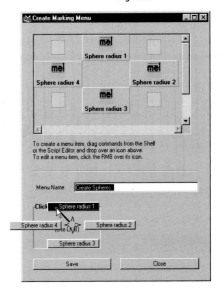

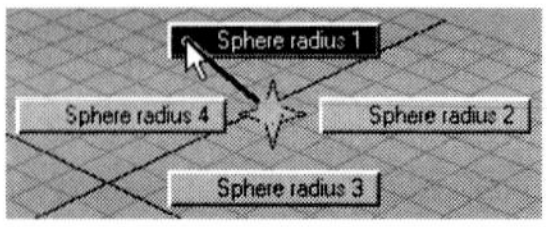

Figure 3.10

The marking menu, ready for action

The press and release states are important to a marking menu: while you are pressing the hotkey (the press state), the menu will appear; when the key is released (the release state), the menu disappears. If you forget to define a release state for your menu, it will not disappear when you release the hotkey!

Now we just follow the steps we used in the last section to define a hotkey. First, select the Press item, CreateSphere, and then query a key—Ctrl+R should be open for your use. When you have found an open key combination, be sure your Action radio button is set to Press; then click the Assign button. You should see a menu asking if you want to create a release state as well for your hotkey—answer yes. When the key is assigned, you should see that CreateSphere (Press) is now set to Ctrl+R Press in the Current Hotkeys pane, while CreateSphere (Release) is set to Ctrl+R Release.

To test your new marking menu, hold down Ctrl+R, and press the left mouse button. As Figure 3.10 shows, you should see your marking menu, ready for use!

Many steps are involved in creating a marking menu, so you probably wouldn't create one for a quick, simple task. But consider the power a marking menu gives you: it's a complete new menu with multiple items (and even subitems) that you can access anywhere in the scene window at the click of a key. Marking menus are relatively easy to create and a great idea for tasks you repeat often—especially if they have multiple options.

> This discussion of customizing shelves, hotkeys, and marking menus is basic. Because MEL scripts are the most efficient tool for customizing these interface elements, you'll find a much more thorough discussion of these topics in Chapter 20, "MEL."

Working in Layers

Working in layers can be particularly useful when you are modeling a multiple-part, complex object (for example, the inner workings of a mechanical clock or a complex creature such as a human or a dog). By placing groups of objects in layers (fingers in one layer, hand in another, arm in another), you can easily hide, display, template, or otherwise adjust large groups of objects at once, rather than tediously selecting each object and then changing it—or, even worse, being unable to select one object that is hidden behind another.

The Layer Editor (Figure 3.11) is a quick visual reference for working in layers, so if you have it turned off, turn it back on again (choose Window → Settings/Preferences → Preferences; then choose Interface/UI Elements and click the Channel Box/Layer Editor check mark). The Layer Editor should appear just below your Channel Box to the right of the work panels, and it has two modes, Display and Render, that you can select from the drop-down menu at the top of the Layer Editor.

Display Layers are the layers that allow you to organize the objects in your scene. With these layers you'll be able to easily navigate within your scene by toggling layers of objects' display properties. Render Layers allow you to place objects on different layers (unassociated with

Figure 3.11

The Layer Editor

Display Layers) when they are rendered. Render Layers help immensely in organizing rendered elements for compositing and assembly, but they do not help in organizing how the scene is arranged in your work panels. We'll deal with Display Layers here, since they are most helpful in speeding up and organizing your workflow, so make sure your Layer Editor is set to Display.

To create a new layer, just click the Layer icon (the icon in the top-right corner of the Layer Editor that looks like three sheets of paper). You can also choose Layers → Create Layer from the Layer Editor menu bar.

Once the layer is created, you can double-click the layer's name (layer1) to open a dialog box in which you can rename the layer and select a color for its display. Once your new layer is created and named, make a couple of simple objects (such as a sphere and a cylinder). Select your objects, click the layer, and choose Layers → Add Selected Objects To Current Layer. You can also RM click the selected layer's name to access the command Add Selected Objects from the context menu that pops up. The objects you selected are now part of the new layer. Return to the scene window, deselect your objects, and (using RM click on the layer name for the Layer pop-up menu) choose Select Objects. Now your objects are selected, because they are a part of this new layer.

Figure 3.12

The layer Relationship Editor

To get a better view of your new layer, choose Membership from the Layer pop-up menu. This displays the Relationship Editor, shown in Figure 3.12, with all layers on the left side and all objects on the right side.

When you click a layer name, all objects in that layer are highlighted on the right (highlighting signifies inclusion in the layer). You can then click any object on the right side, toggling its inclusion in the layer. Each object node can belong to only one layer. Therefore, if you highlight your sphere in another layer (for example), it will be unselected from its original layer. Keep in mind, however, that an object's child node can be assigned to a different layer without affecting the membership of the parent node(s). So always try to assign an object's topmost node to a layer, since that also assigns all its children as well. You can quickly change the layer you are working on and which objects are included in each layer by using this window. Try placing one object in one layer and another in a second layer.

> You can also adjust each layer's attributes by choosing Layer Attributes from the Layer pop-up menu.

To quickly hide or show all objects in a layer, check the box to the farthest left of the layer name (which should currently display V). This button toggles the visibility of that layer, but does not toggle the visibility attribute of the objects in the layer. The button to the right of the visibility toggle switches the layer's working state from Standard to Template to Reference. By default, the layer is in Standard state, allowing you full access to selecting and manipulating

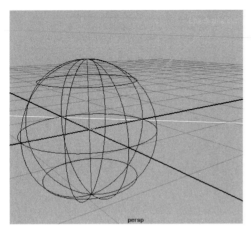

Figure 3.13

An annotated sphere

the objects within that layer. The Template state turns the objects into templates (they cannot be selected or moved, and they turn a darkish gray). The Reference state makes the layer a reference layer, once again making all objects in it unselectable, but keeping their display properties.

Working in layers for a simple scene like our example might seem a waste of time, but as we move on to more ambitious projects, you'll see how useful it is to select, hide, template, or otherwise alter several objects in a complex scene. If you have not used layers before, try modeling an intricate object that has many overlapping pieces, such as a stapler, and you'll appreciate how much layers can speed up your workflow.

For more information on layers, see Chapter 4, "Modeling Basics."

Object Annotation

With Maya 4.5 comes the ability to tag individual objects with annotations to label them with names, notes, and so on. To annotate an object, select it and choose Create → Annotation. A small window will pop up and ask for your notation. After you enter your text and click OK, Maya creates a tag of that text that attaches to your object. Select the text and move it where you want it. The arrow points directly to the center of the object, but you can move it by selecting the locator at the end of the arrow and moving it, as shown in Figure 3.13.

You can edit the annotation's text by selecting the text and opening the Attribute Editor. To delete the annotation object, select it and press the Delete key, just as you would to delete any other Maya object.

Annotation is handy, especially when you're working on the same scene file as another person or when you want to remind yourself to pay attention to a particular object or task when you next return to the scene. Having an organized and efficient scene file is important to a pleasant work experience, and annotations are a good step.

The Outliner

You can view all the information in your scene in two basic ways:

- By using the Outliner
- By using the Hypergraph

Although the Hypergraph is the more flexible and powerful of the two tools, the Outliner is usually easier for a new Maya user. You can use the Outliner to perform several tasks in a more straightforward fashion than doing so with the Hypergraph. Conceptually, the Outliner is exactly what its name implies: an outline of the scene on which you are working.

To open the Outliner, choose Window → Outliner from the main menu set (or hotbox). If you created a default sphere and it is selected, the Outliner window looks like that shown in Figure 3.14.

The first four items in the Outliner are the four default cameras (plus any other cameras you might have created). Listed next are geometric objects (such as the sphere). Finally, sets (groupings of objects, such as the default light and object sets) are listed. Any highlighted objects (in gray) are selected in the scene, and vice versa. You can rename any object listed in the Outliner by double-clicking its name. You can also display the Attribute Editor and focus it on any object in the Outliner by double-clicking its icon.

Several viewing options are available in the Outliner, accessed either via the Outliner's menu or by holding down the right mouse button anywhere inside the Outliner window. Among the more important options are displaying only specific types of objects, such as geometry (choose Show → Objects → Geometry), displaying shape nodes for objects, or displaying all objects, rather than just the DAG (Directed Acyclic Graph—a technical term for the nodes that represent the common objects you see in the scene) objects. If, for example, you turn on Show Shapes, a plus sign appears to the left of any object in the scene that has a shape node (as a sphere or other geometric object would have). By clicking the plus sign, you can expand the outline to see the shape node; in the case of our sphere, clicking the plus sign displays the nurbsSphereShape1 node, as shown in Figure 3.15.

You can use the Outliner in several ways, but three are probably the most appropriate:

- To get a quick look at the scene as a whole
- To manipulate object hierarchy
- To access objects in a complex scene without having to select the object in a work panel

Getting an overview of the scene is the function of any good outline (from the outline of a term paper to the schematic outline of an electrical circuit). Because you can show or hide any type of object in the Outliner, you can, for example, display only the lights in a scene. In this way, you can quickly see the number of lights, and, by double-clicking the light icons, you can just as quickly display the Attribute Editor to examine or adjust their options.

Second, the Outliner is a good tool for quickly assessing and manipulating the hierarchy of an object. All the objects listed in the Outliner are shown with their hierarchies intact, meaning that an object's child (a second object that has been grouped as the child of this object) appears under the plus sign, just as its shape node would (mentioned in the previous example). Using the Outliner in this way is not only good for getting a quick idea of how objects relate to one another in your scene, but also for manipulating those relationships. By simply MM dragging an object onto another in the Outliner, you can make that object a child of the target object or remove it from its current hierarchy.

Figure 3.14

The Outliner with a sphere selected

Figure 3.15

The Outliner showing the shape node

> Hierarchies allow you to group objects, giving them parent to child relationships. When one object becomes the child of another, it inherits the positions, rotations, and scaling of its parent object.

The third main use for the Outliner—allowing quick selection—flows from the first two uses. Because the Outliner provides easy access to any or all objects in the scene, you can rapidly choose, alter (via the Attribute Editor), or rename objects in a convenient list form, rather than having to hunt through a scene to find them, never knowing for sure if you have forgotten an object. In complex scenes, the ability to choose objects becomes even more important. Consider an object such as a Christmas tree that has a hundred ornamental lights on it. The tree itself might consist of two or three dozen objects (branches, base, and so on), and the hundred lights are intertwined in the tree, making them difficult to select for modification. In the Outliner, however, this job is easy. First, you choose to display only light objects (choose Show → Objects → Lights), and then you move down the outline of the scene, selecting and adjusting lights at will. As should be apparent, interacting with your scene in this way can be a real lifesaver.

However, it becomes important to name your objects properly as you create them. A list of oddly named or default named objects in the Outliner will most likely be as confusing as trying to dig through the scene's work panels to find an object. Seeing the Outliner filled with objects that can be identified easily by their names saves a lot of time and effort, especially in large or complicated scenes.

Maya also lets you split the Outliner window vertically, so you can see two different and independent places of the Outliner in a large scene. To split a window, simply place the cursor over the bottom of the Outliner window and drag the mouse up into the window somewhere. To move the divider, drag it up and down. To remove the split, drag the divider down off the bottom of the window.

The Hypergraph

You can use the Hypergraph to perform many of the same functions as the Outliner, but the Hypergraph has a completely different interface design. This tool is worth studying at length in a chapter on interface optimization; use of the Hypergraph can radically reduce the time you spend hunting through the scene and other windows, thus speeding your workflow.

Although the Hypergraph might seem confusing at first glance, once you understand that its interface was designed to parallel Maya's scene window interface—and once you see the many ways in which the Hypergraph can function—you will wonder how you ever got along without it. Even if you consider yourself an experienced Hypergraph user, you might find that this section will reveal a few tips and tricks you didn't previously know.

What Is the Hypergraph?

The Hypergraph is a hypertext-like view of your scene (thus the name). If you have worked with an HTML-authoring tool, you will recognize the weblike appearance of linked objects in the Hypergraph. Every element visible in a scene is represented by a text box, and any linked objects have a line that connects them, showing their relationship in the scene. Passing your cursor over the line, you'll see which elements of each object are connected.

Besides displaying the relationships between objects and elements in a scene, the Hypergraph also lets you create or modify those relationships. For example, you can parent two objects together or break an input connection directly in the Hypergraph, rather than having to open the scene window or the Relationship Editor. Moreover, the types of objects visible in a scene depend on the filtering choices you've made using the Hypergraph's Options → Display menu.

In essence, the Hypergraph *is* your scene; with it and the Channel Box, you can do almost everything you can do in a scene window, and more. The difference is that the Hypergraph is represented as text boxes instead of the objects you see in the scene windows. Although the Outliner is probably more familiar, the Hypergraph is more aligned with Maya's general interface philosophy, and, more important, it allows quick tracking and focusing across hundreds of scene elements, so it can be much more efficient than the Outliner in complex scenes.

Getting to Know the Hypergraph

Because the Hypergraph provides so much information, some effort is required before most people to feel comfortable using it. We will therefore work through the Hypergraph piece by piece in the following pages, using examples to clarify certain concepts, but mostly just showing how the interface works. By the time you finish this section, you should feel comfortable enough with the Hypergraph to begin using it in your work (if you don't already).

Navigating the Hypergraph

Open a new scene in Maya, and create two objects—say a sphere and a cone. Now open the Hypergraph, by choosing Window → Hypergraph from the main menu set. In the Hypergraph window, you should see icons for the objects you created, as shown in Figure 3.16.

Because you will probably access the Hypergraph many times while working in Maya, it is a good idea to create a button on your shelf for it or to use the hotkey (Alt+G) we created earlier in this chapter. To create a shelf button, from the menu bar (not the hotbox), choose Window → Hypergraph while holding down the Ctrl, Alt, and Shift keys. A new button appears on the shelf for the Hypergraph.

Figure 3.16

The Hypergraph, showing a sphere and a cone

If you compare Figure 3.16 with a view of the same scene in the Outliner, you can see that the Hypergraph is actually less complex (it doesn't show the cameras or default sets), but it is organized in a side-to-side manner, rather than top-to-bottom.

You will also notice that when an object is selected in a scene, the corresponding box in the Hypergraph turns yellow; if the object is not selected, its box remains gray (similar to the default shading color of all objects in Maya). Clicking an object box (or node) in the Hypergraph is the same as selecting the object in the scene window: the box turns yellow (indicating it is selected), and the object in the scene is highlighted in green. It is worth noting that you can choose to display only certain objects in the Hypergraph (choose Show → Objects → NurbsObjects, for example) or to display object components such as shape nodes (choose Options → Display → Shape Nodes).

The Hypergraph really shines in its ability to navigate (zoom or track) any of the scene windows in Maya. To zoom, hold down the Alt key and the left and middle mouse buttons—dragging to the left zooms out, and dragging to the right zooms in. To track across (or up and down) the Hypergraph window, hold down the Alt key and the middle mouse button, and then drag the mouse. By tracking and zooming, you can quickly move through even a large scene, finding nodes of interest. Additionally, you can use two hotkeys to frame the window around a selected object or around all objects in the Hypergraph. To focus the window on one or more selected objects (highlighted in green or white in the scene window), press the F key. To expand the view to fit all graphed objects, press the A key. If you try this with our example scene (with the cone selected), pressing F fills the Hypergraph window with the cone node; pressing A expands the view to fit both the sphere and the cone.

The A and F keys work in any scene window. Pressing F focuses the window on the selected object(s), and pressing A makes the entire scene fit in the window.

If your scene is complex, and you find yourself consistently hunting for a particular object (or group of objects) in the Hypergraph, you can save yourself a great deal of time by bookmarking any or all views you are likely to need at a later point. Although our example scene is too simple to warrant using bookmarks, let's see how the process works by creating three bookmarks: one focusing on the sphere, one focusing on the cone, and the third showing both objects. First, highlight the cone and press the F key (or just zoom and track until the cone box fills the Hypergraph window). Then choose Bookmarks → Create Bookmark ❐ from the Hypergraph menu set. Choosing the option box opens a window in which you can name the bookmark. (If you don't open the option box, Maya chooses a default name for you.) In this case, type **cone** and click the OK button. You now have a bookmark for this view arrangement, which you can return to at any time. Next, select the sphere object, press the F key, and then create a bookmark for it (name it **sphere**). Finally, create a bookmark for the complete view of the scene (press the A key to jump to a complete view of the scene) and name it **all**.

To test your bookmarks, zoom and track the window to a completely different view, and then choose Bookmarks → Cone (or Ball or All) from the Hypergraph menu set. The view should jump back to the one you defined for that bookmark. To edit your bookmarks (add a new bookmark, delete a bookmark, or rename a bookmark), choose Bookmarks → Bookmark Editor, select the bookmark you want to edit, and choose the appropriate action from the Bookmark Editor's Edit menu.

You can also create bookmarks for different types of views (with the Hypergraph in different modes—as discussed later in this chapter). This functionality can really save time, because you can avoid having to continually reset the Hypergraph's view modes as you switch between different aspects of your project.

One other nice feature of the Hypergraph is that it shows you when an object is keyframed, by changing its box shape in the window from a rectangle to a parallelogram. If you keyframe the ball shape, for example, its Hypergraph representation changes to give you a visual indication that it is now a keyframed node, as shown in Figure 3.17.

Working in the Hypergraph

Besides viewing selected objects in the Hypergraph, you can select any object simply by clicking its box. To select the sphere in our example, click its box, turning it yellow (and selecting it in the scene window as well). To select multiple objects, you can either Shift+select them or drag a selection marquee around the boxes representing all the objects you want to select. To deselect one selected object, Shift+click it. To deselect all objects in the scene, click anywhere in the Hypergraph window outside a text box. To rename an object in the Hypergraph, Ctrl+double-click the name in the box, type the new name, and press Enter. For example, you can rename the sphere **ball** and the cone **hat** in our practice scene.

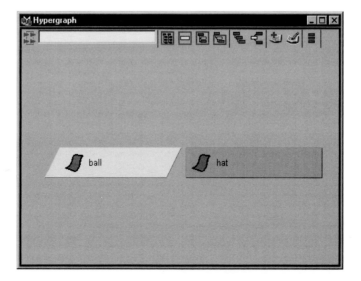

Figure 3.17

The Hypergraph with the ball node keyframed

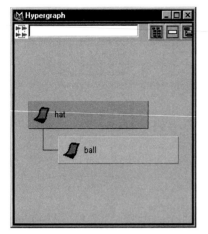

Figure 3.18

**The ball as the child of
the hat**

In the Hypergraph, *parenting* one object to another (the child object will then follow its parent's movements, rotations, and scaling) is just a matter of MM dragging the child object on top of its parent-to-be. In our example, MM drag the ball (sphere) onto the hat (cone). As Figure 3.18 shows, the ball will now appear beneath the hat—with a line connecting the two—showing that it is now the child of the hat.

If you now select the hat, you will notice that the ball also becomes highlighted (in the scene window) and that any transformation you apply to the hat is automatically applied to the ball. To unparent (disconnect) the two objects, MM drag the ball into an empty space in the Hypergraph window. The objects will once again appear side by side (with no interconnecting line), indicating that they are independent of each other.

Nodes and the Hypergraph

The underlying structure of a Maya scene is based on nodes and attributes. A *node* is the fundamental element of a scene, and most of the time an object in a Maya scene window (or in a shader network or the like) has several nodes. An *attribute* is a behavior (or characteristic) of a node, and each node can have many attributes, including custom attributes that you create. Some common nodes are the nurbsSphere1 and makeNurbsSphere1 nodes created when you make a default NURBS sphere. The attributes of the nurbsSphere1 node include translateX, Y, and Z, rotateX, Y, and Z, scaleX, Y, and Z, and Visibility. Attributes of the makeNurbsSphere1 node include radius, start and endSweep, and spans.

Nodes are connected either by default when you create, say, a geometry object (which has a shape and a transform node connected together) or when you manually connect two objects (for example, by parenting one object to another or by attaching a new texture to a material group). Most attributes that are of the same data type (for example, floats or vectors) can be attached to each other across two nodes.

If you are not used to working with Maya, the entire concept of nodes may seem rather frightening. Although the theory might seem difficult, nodes and attributes are fairly easy to understand in practice: nodes are anything that can be shown in the Hypergraph (or a bold-faced name in the Channel Box, or a tab at the top of the Attribute Editor), and attributes are what appear in the Channel Box or Attribute Editor when a node is selected.

In the Hypergraph, all you see are nodes, and changing Hypergraph display modes just changes which nodes you are looking at.

To see how changing display modes changes the nodes you see in a scene, let's again look at our simple example scene (the ball and hat). From the Hypergraph menu set (or by holding down the right mouse button inside the Hypergraph window), choose Options → Display → Shape Nodes. Now that shape nodes can be seen in the Hypergraph, you will see the ballShape and hatShape nodes, as in Figure 3.19, which are separate from the ball and hat nodes. (The ball and hat nodes are called *transform* nodes and are in control of where the object is, its rotation, and its scaling; the shape nodes are in charge of what the object looks like.)

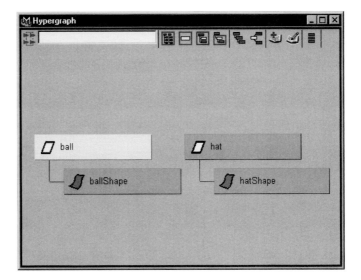

Figure 3.19

The ball and hat with shape nodes showing

You can also show all nodes (many of which are normally invisible) that lead into and out of an object node, revealing the hidden depths of what Maya is doing when you create a "simple" object. Select the ball node and choose Graph → Up And Downstream Connections from the Hypergraph menu set (or click the Up And Downstream Connections button at the top of the menu bar). You will then see all the input and output nodes connected to your ball, as shown in Figure 3.20.

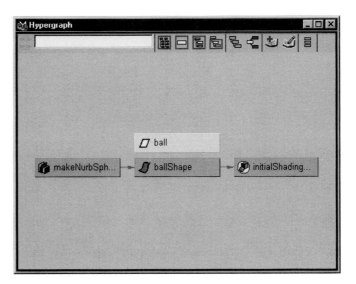

Figure 3.20

The ball node, showing upstream and downstream connections

In this layout, the ball transform node sits atop the others, and the bottom three nodes show the flow of information for this object: the makeNurbsSphere1 node (where you control radius, U and V isoparms, and so forth) outputs to the ballShape node, which then outputs to the initialShadingGroup node, where the ball is given a texture and made visible.

No objects in Maya are visible in a render unless they are attached to a shading group. Although the underlying structure of an object is contained in its shape and transform nodes, it is only in the shading group that the object is given a color and texture—therefore, without its connection to a shading group, you could not see the object in the rendered image.

If you want to dig even deeper, choose the initialShadingGroup node, and display the up and downstream connections again. This time, as Figure 3.21 shows, you will see the shapes (plus a lambert shader—the default one) that feed into the initial shading group, plus the shading group's output to the renderer and lights. To return to your original view, choose Graph → Scene Hierarchy, or choose one of the bookmarks you previously saved (a nice time-saver!).

Figure 3.21

The InitialShading-Group with up and downstream connections showing

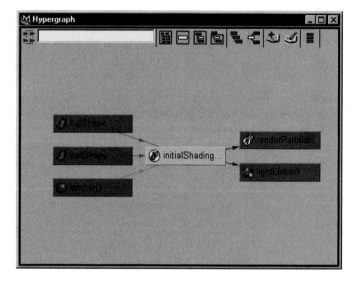

Because Maya is constructed on nodes, and the Hypergraph can show just about any node grouping (based on your filtering choices), you should begin to see how valuable a tool the Hypergraph can be as you work through the stages of your animation process. From modeling to texturing to lighting to animation, the Hypergraph is flexible enough to display the data you need—and even *only* the data you need, should you wish—for each stage of your work. Just keep in mind that the Hypergraph shows nodes and that Maya is built on nodes, so all you have to do is figure out which nodes you want to see for any given stage of your animation process, and you can get the Hypergraph to display them for you.

KNOW YOUR NODES

Although there are a great number of nodes in Maya, they tend to fall under one of these general categories:

- Transform nodes (containing items such as Translate X or Rotate Y)
- Shape nodes (containing items such as the makeObject inputs)
- Invisible nodes (such as default cameras)
- Underworld nodes (nodes that are created, for example, when a curve is drawn on a surface)
- Material nodes (such as lambert or phongE)
- Texture nodes (colors, procedural textures, or image files used to alter the behavior of a material node)
- Texture placement nodes (used to place textures on objects)
- Light nodes (lights, such as a spotlight)
- Utility nodes (which provide a utility to a shader network, such as the multiply/divide node)

Menus and Buttons: Where the Action Is!

Although the Hypergraph's default view is useful, it is just a first step to viewing your scene in the Hypergraph. By using the Hypergraph's menu choices (the most common of which are repeated in buttons across the top of the Hypergraph, shown in Figure 3.23), you can make the Hypergraph show just what you need in an organized, concise manner.

THE EDIT MENU

You can use the Edit menu to control the display of selected items (or edit those items) in several ways. First, you can rename an object—this is the same as Ctrl+double-clicking the object's name. You can also collapse or expand a hierarchy; for example, if the ball has its shape node showing, you can collapse the shape node, hiding it beneath the ball's transform node. A red triangle reminds you that there are collapsed nodes beneath the visible node, as shown in Figure 3.22. To expand the nodes again, choose Edit → Expand.

You can also collapse and expand nodes by simply double-clicking the top node of the group you want to hide or reveal.

If you have several groups of collapsed nodes beneath a parent node (for example, if you have several child objects, all of which have collapsed subnodes), you can expand all nodes at once by choosing Edit → Expand All. The Show Selected option displays items that are selected in the scene window (or Outliner) but have been filtered out of the Hypergraph display. For example, if you have turned off display of NURBS objects in the Hypergraph, but choose a NURBS sphere in the scene window, you can force the Hypergraph to show it by choosing the Show Selected menu item. The Attributes menu item opens the Attribute Editor for the selected item (the same as selecting the item and pressing Ctrl+A). Finally, you can choose to clear your Hypergraph view, if you feel your view has become too complex.

Figure 3.22

The downward arrow shows that the ball node has hidden children

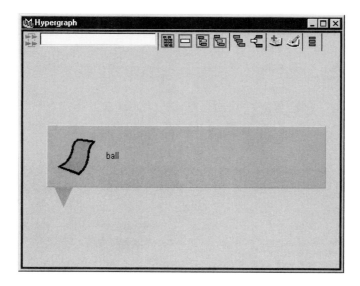

The Edit menu also provides a couple of options for use with the freeform layout, which we will discuss shortly.

THE VIEW MENU

You can use the items on the View menu to change the Hypergraph to the last view you used—or the next, if you have moved backward and forward in views. This command can be useful if you move a great distance through the Hypergraph in a complex scene and want to return to where you were. The Previous and Next View commands function in a similar manner to bookmarks but change according to the Hypergraph view. You can also frame your selection (this has the same effect as pressing the F key), frame all (the same as pressing the A key), frame the hierarchy, or frame a branch of the hierarchy.

You can access these four framing options (Frame All, Frame Selection, Frame Hierarchy, and Frame Branch) by clicking the four leftmost buttons in the Hypergraph toolbar, which is located at the top of the Hypergraph window, as shown in Figure 3.23.

Figure 3.23

The Hypergraph buttons

Framing a hierarchy focuses on the selected object plus any other objects in that hierarchy. Framing a branch frames the selected object plus any objects *below* it in the hierarchy. If the ball is the child of the hat in our example scene, selecting the ball and then framing the hierarchy focuses the window on the hat and ball nodes; framing the branch focuses the window only on the ball (and any child nodes it might have).

THE BOOKMARK MENU

You use the Bookmark menu to create and edit bookmarks for any layout or view you want to save in the Hypergraph. We discussed bookmarks earlier in the chapter, so here we need only note that two buttons on the Hypergraph toolbar are related to the Bookmark menu: the Add Bookmark button (a book with a red plus on it) and the Edit Bookmark button (a lifted leaf with a book below it). Clicking the Add Bookmark button simply adds a bookmark for the current view; clicking the Edit Bookmark button opens the Bookmark Editor window, in which you can rename, delete, or add bookmarks.

THE GRAPH MENU

The Graph menu controls the general parameters of what the Hypergraph shows. You can graph the upstream connections for an object (all nodes that feed into the selected object), the downstream connections for an object (all nodes that the selected object feeds information into), and both the up and downstream connections for that object. Because choosing one of these options changes the view from the default scene hierarchy, you can also choose the Scene Hierarchy view to return to the scene hierarchy after you choose an upstream/downstream graph.

The Graph Up And Downstream Connections and Scene Hierarchy menu items are also available as buttons on the Hypergraph toolbar, as shown in Figure 3.24.

Scene Hierarchy ——————— ——— Up and Downstream Connections

Figure 3.24

The Hypergraph buttons

If your graph gets behind your scene window (an unlikely event, but possible), you can force the Hypergraph to rebuild itself by choosing Graph → Rebuild. By using this command, you can be sure the Hypergraph is up-to-date. Finally, you can use the Layout command in the Graph menu to change (or reset) the arrangement of items when you are looking at upstream or downstream connections. Arranging these nodes might allow you to make more sense of them or to move unwanted nodes off screen while you work.

When you graph the up and/or downstream connections in the Hypergraph, you are displaying what is known as a dependency graph. Put simply, a *dependency graph* shows the connections between nodes (such as shading network elements) in a Maya scene, allowing you to see the flow of information from one node to another—in other words, how each node depends on the others to which it is connected.

THE RENDERING MENU

You use the Rendering menu to focus the Hypergraph on materials, textures, shading groups, lights, and images. You can also choose Rendering → Create Render Node to create a render node directly in the Hypergraph, rather than having to use the Hypershade or the Multilister to do so.

Although the Rendering menu set in the Hypergraph is perhaps less useful than the Hypershade window, it is still convenient to have all shading information accessible in the same window as the scene hierarchy, especially when you just want to take a quick peek at a shading item rather than work with it extensively.

THE OPTIONS MENU

The Options menu gives you control over how the Hypergraph displays nonstandard (invisible, shape, or underworld) nodes and also how the Hypergraph as a whole is laid out. Of the Options submenus (Display, Orientation, Layout, Transitions, and Update), the one you will probably use the most is Display. The Display submenu lets you choose which types of nodes and connections will be displayed in the Hypergraph window. As you have already seen, you can show shape nodes (which control the structural options of an object); you can also display invisible nodes (such as the cameras or any objects you have hidden) and underworld nodes (these are nodes generated by objects such as surface curves, which have their transform nodes in a local rather than a global space). You can also turn on or off the display of expression, constraint, or deformer connections. For example, Figure 3.25 shows that if you aim-constrain the ball to the hat in our example scene (choose Constrain → Aim), you can display the connections Maya makes between the ball, the hat, and the new aimConstraint node.

You can also display a background image for the Hypergraph window if you are in freeform layout mode by choosing Options → Display → Background Image (in freeform) from the Display submenu.

Figure 3.25

The Hypergraph displaying constraint connections

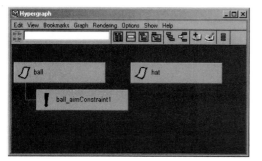

The Orientation submenu of the Display menu lets you toggle between horizontal (the default layout) and vertical layout modes. If you like working in an Outliner-like fashion (with nodes stacked on top of each other), you might prefer the vertical orientation mode. The Layout submenu allows you to choose automatic (default) or freeform layout mode. The freeform layout mode lets you move nodes around into any shape you want, and the automatic mode places the nodes in a predetermined order next to one another. The Transitions submenu lets you create an animated transition between views when you choose View → Previous or View → Next View. By default, the view changes instantaneously, but by checking the Animate Transitions box (and then choosing how many frames the transitions will be), you can force the Hypergraph window to scroll from one view to the other. Although they are cute, transitions are more of a time-waster than anything useful—unless you need to figure out where one view is in relation to another. The Update submenu lets you choose when to update the Hypergraph window; you can choose to update on a selection, on a node creation, on both (the default), or on neither.

THE SHOW MENU

The Show menu lets you make specific choices about the objects you want to see in the Hypergraph window. Under Show → Objects, you can show (or hide) geometry, lights, sets, and cameras, to name just a few. You can display all objects by choosing Show → Show All. You can select several objects (in the scene window or in the Hypergraph), and then show only those and other objects with the same type as your selected objects (choose Show → Show Selected Type(s)). You can also invert the types of objects you display (choose Show → Invert Shown). If, for example, you are working on a scene with 10 lights and 20 geometry objects, you can display only the lights while you work on lighting the scene and then invert the selection filter to show all your other objects while you tweak your models or animate the scene.

Making and Breaking Connections in the Hypergraph

One of the most interesting features of the Hypergraph is its ability to make and break data connections between nodes. To see how this works, take our example scene (the ball and hat), and add a lattice deformer to the ball (select the ball node, and then choose Deform → Create Lattice from the Animation menu set). Select the ball node again, and choose Graph → Up And Downstream Connections. In this new view, you will see connecting arrows between the nodes that make up the lattice-ball group. By passing your cursor over one of these arrows, you can see the output/input data connections between nodes, as shown in Figure 3.26.

To break one of these connections, click one of the arrows (highlighting it yellow) and then press the Delete key. You can, for example, break the deformer connection between the lattice and the ball if you highlight the arrow that shows the ffd1LatticeShape.latticeOutput to ffd1.deformedLatticePoints connection (shown in Figure 3.26). If you alter the deformer (scale it, say), you will immediately see the ball return to its original shape when you delete the connection.

> As should be obvious, it is dangerous to go around deleting connections between nodes—especially if you don't know what you're doing. This is not to say you shouldn't experiment; just save your file before you start deleting connections. If you can't get what you want, you can at least return to a good version of your project.

Figure 3.26

The Hypergraph showing deformer input/output connections

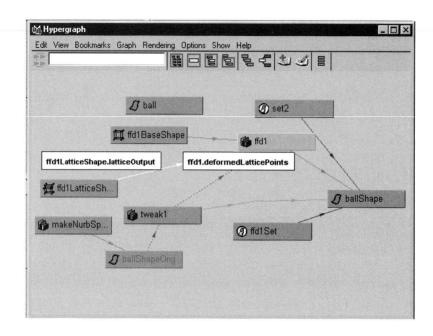

To make a connection between nodes, just Shift + MM drag one node on top of another (the node that will output a value will be the one you drag; the one that will accept an input value will be the node you drag onto). When you complete the drag operation, the Connection Editor opens, allowing you to choose which attributes to connect. If, as in Figure 3.27, you MM drag ffd1Lattice onto the ball node, you might connect the lattice's visibility attribute to the ball's visibility (click each of these attributes on the right and left of the Connection Editor to connect them). Then, when you hide the lattice, the ball will hide as well. To confirm that the connection has been made, you will see a new arrow in the Hypergraph showing the connected attributes.

Figure 3.27

The Connection Editor showing connected visibilities

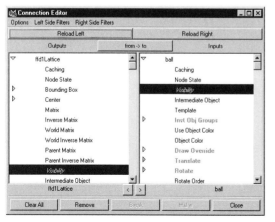

In general, most people use the make-break connection ability of the Hypergraph (and Hypershade)) primarily to make and break connections between shader nodes in a shader network, such as the luminance output of a texture being fed into the transparency of a material node. Although the connected attributes differ between types of scene elements, the method of making and breaking connections is the same as described earlier.

THE INS AND OUTS OF THE CONNECTION EDITOR

The Connection Editor is an extremely useful Maya feature. Essentially, it lets you connect any output of one node to any matching (that is, of the same data type) input of another node. The Connection Editor can do some amazing things, connecting even the most bizarre attributes (as long as their data types match). This ability to manipulate connections at such a low level gives you creative control over anything from ramp texture colors to object rotation order based on another object's position (or that of another node on the same object), visibility, node state, or whatever else you can dream up. In shader networks, the output color of one node (such as a fractal map) is often automatically input into the input color of another node (such as a phongE texture) when you create a texture map. With the Connection Editor, you can also plug the output color of one node into the bump map node—a node that controls how "bumpy" a surface looks—of a texture (which is the same as MM dragging the node onto the bump map channel of the texture), or even control the intensity (or height) of a different bump map based on the output of this node.

Although the number of attributes available to connect via the Connection Editor can be a bit overwhelming, the window's controls are fairly straightforward. Let's take a look at how the Connection Editor works.

Using the Connection Editor

To make a connection, first load the left and right sides of the Connection Editor (choose Window → General Editors → Connection Editor) with the two nodes you want to connect (or, alternatively, Shift + MM drag one node onto another in the Attribute Editor to automatically open and load the Connection Editor). Then click the output attribute you want to use and, from the list of attributes with matching data types (not grayed out), choose the input node.

Some data types, such as color, have arrows next to them, allowing you to access their component attributes—in the case of color, it is the red, green, and blue components. Thus, while color (a vector) may not be a match (and is thus grayed out) for the X scale of an object, you *can* connect the red component of color to the object's X scale. Depending on the direction of this connection, the object's redness is controlled by its X scale, or the object's scale is controlled by its redness.

The Connection Editor Controls

The controls in the Connection Editor's window are easy to use. The buttons at the top enable you to reload the left or right side of the window (thus changing which node is loaded on each side of the window). By clicking the "from -> to" button, you can change the direction of the input/output of the two nodes (making it "to <- from").

The Right Side Filters and Left Side Filters menus let you display only those attributes of interest—this can be a great way to reduce the clutter of available attributes to a more manageable number.

Under the Options menu, you can change the default behavior of the Connection Editor—which is to make and break connections automatically as you click the attributes in the left and right windows—to a manual mode. If you select manual mode, you must click the (now-enabled) Make and Break buttons at the bottom of the window to create (or disconnect) the connection between two attributes.

Clicking the Clear All button removes all connections, and clicking the Remove button removes the loaded nodes.

continued

continues

Finally, the two arrow keys just below the left and right windows allow you to step through all nodes on an object (for example, the shape to the transform node of a geometric object), saving you a trip back to the Hypergraph to highlight a new node, and then reload it into the Connection Editor. To disconnect the two attributes, click a connected attribute on one side of the window to unhighlight it.

The possibilities for using the Connection Editor are so many and varied that the best advice is just to open a new project, create some objects and shader networks, and play with different connections, so you can get a feel for the different ways you can control one node via another. This way, when you are faced with what might appear to be a difficult problem in a "real world" situation, you might see that some clever use of the Connection Editor will do the trick nicely.

Freeform Layout Mode

You can modify the Hypergraph in one last way to make the data in it even more understandable: the freeform layout. This layout mode allows you to place your nodes anywhere you want in relation to each other (above, beside, around, and so forth). This can be a real help when you build a complex character such as a human, because you can arrange the nodes for the hands, say, where the hands of a figure would be. You can even import an image as a background plate for the Hypergraph window (perhaps a sketch of your figure) to serve as a reference in the freeform layout mode.

To enter freeform layout mode, either choose Options → Layout → Freeform Layout or click the Freeform Layout toggle button on the toolbar in the Hypergraph (the button farthest to the right). Once you are in freeform layout mode, you can drag nodes anywhere in the Hypergraph window that you want, perhaps shapes or figures. To load a background image for your new layout, choose View → Load Background Image and browse to find your image. You can also reset your freeform layout to its default arrangement by choosing Edit → Reset Freeform Layout. Thus, no matter how much mess you make of your node arrangement, you can always return to a clean view at the click of a button.

As an example of using the freeform layout, let's build a human figure in the Hypergraph. (We won't actually build a character in the scene window, but if you have one you've already built, feel free to use that figure instead of our random assortment of primitives.) First create 20 or 30 scene primitives. If you want, you can lay them out in the scene window in the form of a person, or you can just arrange them in the Hypergraph. In the Hypergraph, be sure you are in freeform layout mode, and then drag nodes up to the head region (renaming areas such as "skull," "nose," "right eye," and so on), the body, the arms, and the legs. When you're finished, you should have a graph like that in Figure 3.28, which looks something like a person, where every node is intuitively related to its

Figure 3.28

Freeform layout representing a person

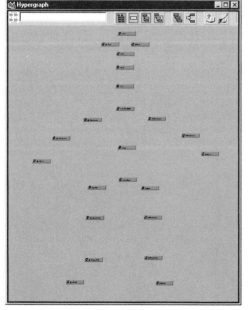

(supposed) function in the scene window. Obviously, arranging nodes like this in a complex scene can save you a great deal of time when it comes to finding a particular node (the right eye, for example) that you want to manipulate.

The Hypershade

Although you can still use the Multilister (choose Window → Rendering Editors → Multilister) from version 1 of Maya, the Hypershade (introduced in version 2) is now the de facto standard for working with materials and other render-related objects. Using a similar convention to the Hypergraph, the Hypershade not only shows you interactive previews of what a material or texture will look like, it shows how the elements of a shader network are connected, giving you a great deal of information in an intuitive interface. As with the Hypergraph, you can zoom and track the Hypershade like any Maya scene window, and you can use the F key (frame selected) and A key (frame all) to quickly focus on any element(s) you want, making it easier to navigate scenes with large numbers of shading groups.

To open the Hypershade, choose Window → Rendering Editors → Hypershade. You'll see the display shown in Figure 3.29. On the left is the Create Bar, which is the column that contains graphic icons of Render nodes (such as materials and textures) that you can create. On the right is a Hypergraph-like window with all materials listed—in a new scene, there will only be two materials listed, the lambert1 shader (the default shader for geometry) and the particleCloud1 shader (the default shader for software-rendered particles).

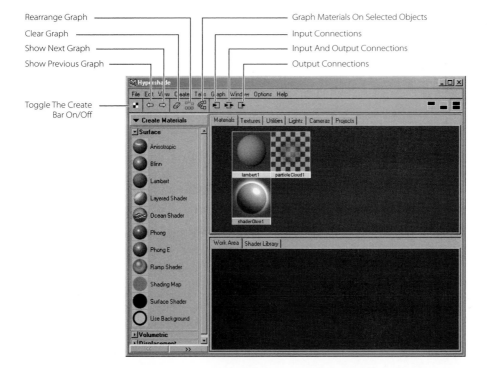

Figure 3.29

The Hypershade, in its default state

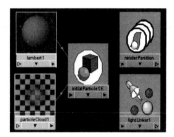

Figure 3.30

The Hypershade graph of the particle material

You can split the window on the right side into a double panel, the top displaying the materials in the scene, and the bottom displaying the work area, where you can edit the connections between Render nodes much like editing objects in the Hypergraph window. To toggle the double-panel view, simply click one of the three buttons in the upper-right corner of the window from Show Top Tabs Only to Show Bottom Tabs Only to Show Top And Bottom Tabs. You can also toggle the Create Bar on and off by choosing Options → Create Bar → Show Create Bar to give you more room to work.

To select a material, simply click it; yellow highlight will indicate that it is selected. You can then view that material's input connections, its output connections, or both by clicking the appropriate button at the top of the Hypershade window, as shown in Figure 3.29—or by choosing Graph and the connection type from the Hypershade menu. The particle cloud, shown in Figure 3.30, has several inputs and outputs that appear if you click the Input And Output Connections button.

> An upstream connection is any Hypershade node that "feeds into" the selected node (its output is fed into the currently selected node; it is upstream in the data flow). A downstream connection is any node that the currently selected node feeds data into—thus, it is downstream from the selected node in the data flow.

To get back to a general view of materials, choose Materials from the pop-up menu at the top left of the Hypershade window. You can also view shading groups, utilities, lights, cameras, and so on by choosing the item from this pop-up menu.

In addition to looking at materials, textures, and such, you can also create them directly in the Hypershade in one of two ways. To create a material, click the button at the top of the Create Bar and select Create Materials, if it's not selected already. Select the material and click it to create a material node that will show up in the window on the right. For example, if you click the PhongE button in the Create Bar, you will see a phongE material node appear in the Hypershade window.

To assign this new material, you can just MM drag it on top of any object in your scene window. (Or select your object and then RM choose Assign Material To Selection with the cursor over the material; this is a good way to assign the material to several objects at once.) To change the material's attributes (color or transparency, for example), double-click the material ball to display the Attribute Editor, and then make any changes you want to the material. The ball in the Hypershade, as well as any objects that have this material assigned to them, will automatically update with your changes. The other way to create a new material is simply to choose Create Material from the menu in the Hypershade; for example, choose Create → Materials → phongE. This produces a new material in the Hypershade window, just as clicking the material button in the Create Bar does.

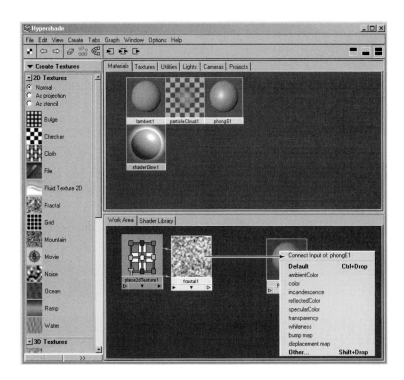

Figure 3.31

MM dragging a fractal texture onto a phongE material

To assign a texture to your new material, you can again choose to create the material via menu commands (choose Create → 2D Textures → Fractal, for example), or select the Create Textures Bar, click the Fractal button, and then MM drag the texture swatch onto the material icon in the Hypershade, as shown in Figure 3.31.

Once you finish dragging, a menu will open, letting you select which element of the material (that is, which input) you want to assign the fractal (or other) texture to. The most common choice is simply Color, so choose that. The Hypershade window will be updated to show that the fractal1 texture is connected as input to the phongE material ball (coming from the left is input; going to the right is output), as in Figure 3.32. This ball and any other objects with the phongE material in your scene will update to show the new texture.

Although the Hypershade can play many other functions besides the basics we covered here, the centralized power of being able to create, modify, connect, and disconnect individual material attributes, textures, and so forth should be obvious from this quick tour. It is worth the effort to get to know the new Hypershade, as it will save you a great deal of time and effort later in your work with Maya's shader networks.

Figure 3.32

A fractal texture being applied to a phongE material node

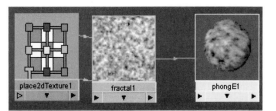

For more on rendering with the Hypershade, see Chapter 16, "Rendering Basics."

Hands On: Building an Arm

Let's take all the interface/optimization information we've gathered thus far and put it to use in a practical example. Over the next few pages, we'll model an arm and then "string" it to bend at the elbow, using an Inverse Kinematics (IK) chain. (You'll learn more about IK modeling in Chapter 13, "Character Animation Exercises.") Throughout this example, we'll put our understanding of Maya's interface to good use, making our modeling task easier.

1. Open a new scene in Maya.

2. Either sketch out a top and side view of an arm and scan them into your computer, or use the sketches included on the CD-ROM (`ArmTop.tif` and `ArmSide.tif`).

3. Because we will use these sketches to make our model, they need to be loaded into Maya's top and side views so that we can reference them as we build our arm. In the top panel, choose View → Image Plane → Import Image to open a file selection dialog box. Find your file and click Open to bring it into Maya as an image plane for the top panel. The top panel will now display that image in its view, outlined in yellow indicating that it is selected. Press Ctrl+A to open the Attribute Editor and take a look at some of the options. You can resize how the image fits in the window or change the image file by selecting a new image file under the Image Name attribute. Whenever you want to access these attributes, in the panel window choose View → Image Plane → Image Plane Attributes and select the image plane. Just repeat this procedure for the side panel, and when you're finished, your four views should look like Figure 3.33.

To keep from accidentally selecting one of these planes as we continue to work, let's put them on their own layer and make that a reference (unselectable) layer. From the Layer bar, click the Create A New Layer button, rename this layer ImagePlanes, select both image planes, and choose Assign Selected from the Layer menu. To make the layer a reference layer, choose Reference from the pop-up layer menu.

WORKING FROM SKETCHES

Sketching your image before you model is *always* a good idea—even if you have no skill at drawing. It is much easier to see what you're creating by quickly drawing it on paper than it is to try to create an object in 3D space out of your head. You will find that sketching an object before modeling it, far from taking extra time, will save you a great deal of time and give you better-looking results as well.

When you sketch an object for use as a background image for modeling, it is important that your two views (top and side here) are exactly the same size. Graph paper is useful in these circumstances, as it is easy to see the exact measurements of your image on this type of paper.

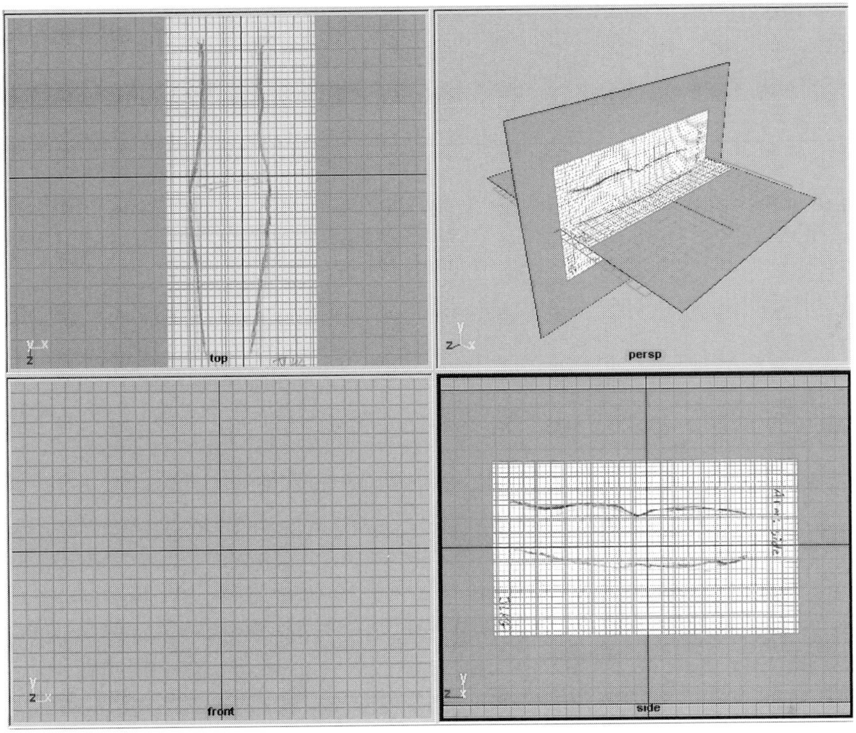

Figure 3.33

The arm sketches as image planes

There are several good modeling techniques to use from this point on, but we will use a common, fairly painless technique that produces good results quickly: lofting a series of circles into a shape.

> *Lofting* creates a shape in something like the way a wooden ship hull is laid (or lofted) over a skeleton of wood that defines the shape the hull will have once the lofting process is complete.

First, create a new layer (click the Create A New Layer button in the Layer Editor) and name it Circles—we will assign our circles to this layer to keep them separate from our eventual lofted surface. Next, expand one of the views (the top, say) to fill the screen (activate the panel by clicking in that pane, and then press the spacebar quickly). Choose Create → Nurbs Primitives → Circle ❑, and in the options window, change the Normal Axis setting to the Z axis. (From our angle, the circle will now appear as a line, as it is lined up with the arm's axis). Click the Save button (to save the settings) and close the window. We could create our circles by going to the menu each time, as we just did, but let's speed up our workflow by quickly making a button on the shelf to make our circles. Hold down the Ctrl, Alt, and Shift keys and, from the main menu bar (this won't work from the hotbox!), choose Create → Nurbs Primitives → Circle; a new button should appear on your shelf, and clicking that button will create a circle.

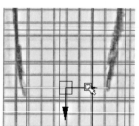

Figure 3.34

The first circle, moved and scaled to the proportions of the arm sketch

Now we're ready to build our arm. In the top view (don't worry about the side view yet), click the Circle button, move the new circle down to the bottom of the arm, and scale it to the same size as the bottom of the sketched arm, as shown in Figure 3.34. Remember that you can zoom your view in to see how accurately you're placing the circles.

To build the outline of the arm, create several circles and position and scale them to fit the sketch of the arm in the top view. Be sure to place more circles around the elbow area, because that area will eventually bend (as any good elbow should) and therefore needs more definition. When you are finished, your "arm" should look similar to that in Figure 3.35.

If you find the background image too dark or distracting, select the image plane by choosing View → Image Plane → Image Plane Attributes and reduce the alpha gain of the image plane to about 0.5. Because the alpha channel here corresponds to how opaque the image is, this adjustment fades the image back a bit, giving you a clearer view of the circles you are creating. You may also select the image plane by selecting the camera, opening the attribute editor, and selecting the imagePlane1 tab.

When you finish with the top view, you will need to switch to the side view, this time scaling and moving the circles so that they fit from this view as well. (Don't move them along the X axis, however, because this will destroy the work you've done in the top view.) Your completed side view should look similar to Figure 3.36.

If you find you need a new circle to help build the shape in the side view, add one—just be sure to go back to the top view and adjust it there!

We now have the outline of our arm finished—it's time to create the arm itself! We need to select all the circles that will make up our arm and then loft them. But don't just drag a selection marquee around the circles: the loft tool depends on the order in which you select your circles, so we need to be careful about the order in which we select them. Starting at either end (the top or bottom of the arm), Shift+click each circle in order until all are selected. Before we loft these circles, assign them to the Circles layer for later use (choose Assign Selected from the Circles layer menu). Now let's see how we did: loft the circles into a surface (choose Surfaces → Loft). You should see an armlike tube appear in your perspective window, as Figure 3.37 shows. Because of the image planes, it's a bit difficult to see the arm. To quickly get rid of the image planes now (because you won't need them from now on), go to the ImagePlane layer's pop-up menu and clear the Visible box.

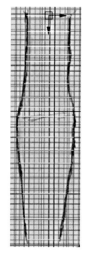

Figure 3.35

Circles complete the top of the arm

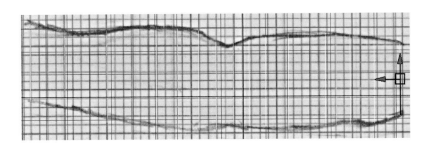

Figure 3.36

Side view of the completed arm

You will probably find that the arm doesn't look realistic yet. Fortunately, because Maya remembers construction history, you can go back and tweak the position, scale, and rotation of the circles (using the same techniques we used to create the circles earlier) to get the arm to look the way you want it. When you like your arm, turn off the circle layer's visibility so that you can see the surface more clearly, as in Figure 3.38.

Figure 3.37

The arm, lofted

Figure 3.38

The completed arm

Templating the lofted surface (choose Display → Object Display → Template) so you can't accidentally select it is a real time saver. To "untemplate" the object when you are finished with adjustments, select the lofted surface in the Outliner or Hypergraph, and choose Display → Object Display → Untemplate again. Or you can simply create a layer, assign the lofted surface to that layer, and then make the layer a reference or template layer.

Now we need to string our arm with an IK chain so that we can move it around like a natural arm. Make the side view fill your workspace, and then choose the IK Joint tool from the shelf (or choose Skeleton → Joint Tool). Starting at the top (shoulder), click (or drag) the tool where the shoulder joint should be, click again where the elbow should be, and finally click where the wrist would be, as in Figure 3.39. If you don't like where your joint is, undo the last click (press the Z key) and try again. When you are satisfied with the look of the joints, press the Enter key to confirm the new joint.

Figure 3.39

Arm with skeleton joint

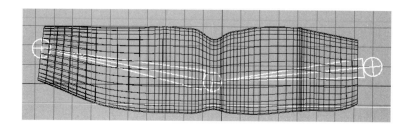

Be sure not to make all three joints follow a straight line, though. Maya's IK solver uses the direction of the joint's initial bend to determine which direction it will bend later. If you make the joints straight, Maya won't know which direction to bend the arm, and you will get bizarre results.

We could now manipulate the joints using the rotate tool, but it is generally easier to create an IK chain to make the moving simpler. To do so, choose the IK Handle tool on the shelf (or choose Skeleton → IK Handle Tool) and click first on the shoulder joint and then on the wrist joint. (Skip the elbow joint so that the kinematics chain will go through the elbow, allowing it to bend with the wrist movements.) You should now see a green line connecting the shoulder and wrist joints. If you want, you can now move the joint around by drag-selecting the wrist IK handle and moving the arm—however, only the joint moves at present; we need to attach the arm to our new joint.

> If you move the joint around before attaching the arm to it, be sure to undo (press Z) back to the original position before attaching the arm.

The final step, attaching the arm surface to the arm joint, is a process of selecting the joint and surface and binding them together. First, select the root joint of the arm skeleton (the shoulder joint), and then Shift-select the arm surface. Finally, choose Skin → Bind Skin → Smooth Bind to bind the two together. To see your beautiful new arm at work, drag-select the wrist joint and use the move tool to move the wrist around. The skeleton (and arm surface) should follow the wrist where you drag it, as in Figure 3.40.

Figure 3.40

The arm, bent

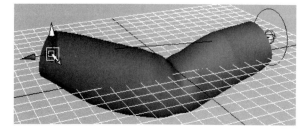

You may notice that the elbow doesn't bend properly (it folds too much). You can use the Artisan tool to adjust the joint goal weights of the arm to make the bend far more realistic looking. For more on how to do this, see Chapter 7, "Working with Artisan."

Summary

In this chapter, we went over many elements in Maya that you can either adjust or use as-is to get the most out of your work. Looking at general options, shortcuts, organizational windows such as the Hypergraph, the Hypershade, the Outliner, and the Connection Editor, as well as working in layers, we saw how much you can adjust Maya's default interface to improve your workflow. The final working example—building a movable arm—took many of the workflow lessons we learned in this and the previous chapters and put them to real-world use. We created a shortcut button, worked in layers, and used hotkeys to choose the scale, move, and rotate tools, all of which increased the speed with which we completed a reasonably complex task.

Even if much of what you have read in this chapter is a bit confusing to you now, try to remember, as you begin working on more complex projects, the little tricks and shortcuts we discussed here. With a bit of practice, many of the techniques discussed in this chapter will become second nature to you, and your Maya skills and products will reflect this.

PART II

Modeling

This part *of the book will take you through all the modeling methods in Maya. Before you can texture, animate, or render anything, you must build visible surfaces. In the following five chapters, you will learn how to do that by creating and editing primitives, curves, NURBS, polygons, and subdivision surfaces. By progressing through exercises that build a living room, a hand, a puppy dog, and a full human character, you will begin to master the techniques to build any object you can imagine inside Maya.*

Of special interest to advanced users will be the discussion of subdivision surfaces and the accompanying tutorials. Subdivision surface modeling has developed into an attractive and convincing alternative to the more traditional modeling methods, and we accordingly cover it in depth.

CHAPTER 4

Modeling Basics

This chapter introduces the basics of modeling. The first section is devoted to the concepts you will need to become familiar with before plunging fully into the modeling tools and actions in Maya 4.5. A good understanding of the general principles of modeling will enable you to use your time wisely and efficiently as you work.

In the following pages you will have an opportunity to try out some of Maya's modeling aids as you learn some modeling fundamentals, and then you will create some furniture using Maya's primitives. You will begin to master:

- **What is modeling?**

- **Modeling tools**

- **Modeling with primitives**

- **Hands On: Creating a living room scene with primitives**

What Is Modeling?

Let's begin with a working definition of what modeling is in computer animation: 3D modeling is the process of creating three-dimensional surfaces using a computer, for the purpose of rendering them into a picture or a sequence of pictures. In fields such as the automobile industry or engineering, digital models are actually built with specific products in mind—their purpose is to create a physical model or prototype that will ultimately become a working automobile or a building. Rendering is only a stage they go through in order to get to their ultimate destination. For 3D artists working in computer animation, however, the ultimate destination is pictures that exist in TV, videos, or celluloid—all 2D environments.

This difference gives rise to an important principle that determines how we build models for computer animation: *the only thing that really matters in modeling is the picture(s) people will see.* Modeling anything that will not be seen, in other words, is a waste of time.

Creating an Illusion

Digital space is a world of facades. If only the back and right walls of a room (as in Figure 4.1) will be seen, it makes no sense to build the front or the left side. For the computer animator, modeling is all about creating illusions for the eye to feast on—build only what the eye (the camera) will see. This is why careful preproduction planning is so crucial and why well-organized production teams create detailed storyboards before they commit to building anything.

ARE YOU A MODELER?

A professional sculptor or an architect usually has a much easier time modeling on the computer than a person with no such background, just as a painter or a photographer finds it easier to do texturing or lighting in a digital environment. Many skills that are used in these fields transfer immediately into the computer environment, and other skills soon follow, as you become familiar with your surroundings.

But don't be discouraged if you want to become a modeler but have no such background. Computer animation is a different world, and the computer, a different tool. You must learn skills that are specific to digital modeling. View digital modeling as a separate and independent artistic medium—as different as painting is from sculpting, for example, each with its own sets of rules and technical skills. You must feel as comfortable with the computer as a painter is with a brush or a sculptor with clay. And just as some painters know nothing about sculpting but still are great painters, so can you be a great 3D modeler without being a sculptor or an architect.

Good Models and Bad Models

Good models look good when rendered, and bad
models look bad. It's that simple. The catch, of
course, is that producing models that look good
takes a lot of time and care, and producing great-
looking models always takes a lot of sweat and
effort. Tight schedules and deadlines often
make this a difficult—if not an impossible—task.

Other less-obvious factors in the production
environment also determine whether a model is
good or bad, and these are just as important as
the model's appearance. The two criteria for good
modeling most frequently used in animation are
how computationally *heavy* or *light* a model is
and how well it can be set up for animation.

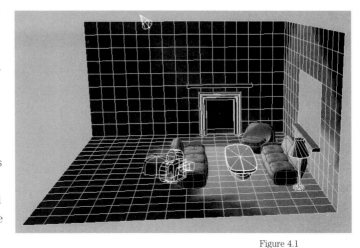

Figure 4.1

**The living room we'll
begin creating in this
chapter**

Improperly built models often end up being heavy, meaning they are built with too much
geometry and can cause numerous problems for the animators or a loss of precious production time in rendering. A heavy model makes the computer's CPU work harder than it would
otherwise need to. A light model, in contrast, does not have a lot of geometry for the computer to calculate and thus allows the animator to act more interactively with it, producing
better animation in shorter time. It generally renders faster too.

If a model is going to be deformed in a certain way—in other words, to bend and stretch
as it animates—the modeler needs to build with that in mind, including the necessary points
where they will deform properly. Generally, you need to insert extra isoparms around
joint areas such as elbows, knees, or fingers. The isoparms should also run along the way
the surface will stretch or crease. In some cases, not having points in certain areas is
actually better. For example, creating different facial shapes for lip-synching takes a lot
of time, and if the face has a lot of CVs or vertices, the work becomes exponentially more
time-consuming. Compare the faces in Figure 4.2: which would be easier to work with
when creating different facial shapes?

Modeling Methods

In Maya, you can model in many ways: you can model with NURBS, polygons, and/or subdivision surfaces. How do you decide which method best serves your modeling needs? It's really
a matter of personal taste and what's available in the software. This question is all the more
significant because increasingly in recent versions of Maya, subdivision surfaces have truly
become a legitimate way to model and animate.

Figure 4.2

A face created using subdivision surfaces (left) and one created using NURBS surfaces (right)

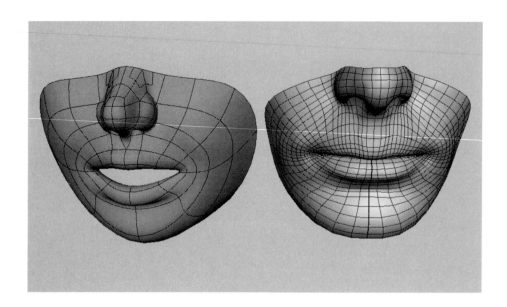

The conventional wisdom is that NURBS models are good for smooth, organic, deformable surfaces, whereas polygons are good for sharp-edged, rigid structures. This is an oversimplification, and although different situations might ideally call for the use of one or both methods, you can accomplish almost anything you want with either approach—there are die-hard enthusiasts on both sides. The advantage of NURBS surfaces is that they are smooth, whereas polygons are faceted. On the other hand, polygons allow arbitrary topology, whereas NURBS are restricted to four-sided patches.

> *Topology* is a mathematical concept that deals with those properties of objects that are not affected by changes in size or shape. In Maya, topology refers to the way points interconnect to create a surface.

What is revolutionary about the subdivision surfaces in Maya is that they combine the strengths of both NURBS and polygons, minus their weaknesses. They are smooth like NURBS, but they can also be built on arbitrary topology similar to polygons. You can create one smooth and continuous subdivision surface in building almost any organic model, bypassing the sometimes tricky situation you can run into with NURBS patches of trying to keep tangency along the seams. In Figure 4.3, the NURBS patches on the left are smooth, but they can't be joined in the middle. The polygon surface shown in the center is joined but is faceted. The subdivision surface on the right is joined at both the middle and smooth.

Does this mean that subdivision surfaces are better than NURBS surfaces or polygons? That we should use them over the other two methods? Not necessarily. As you can see from Figure 4.3, clearly you should work with polygons if you want to create a diamond. To build a wine bottle, you would want to work with NURBS. For complex organic models, such as a human head, subdivision surfaces seem to be a good choice. The models you'll be building in this and the following chapters will generally incorporate all three methods: build the rough shapes with NURBS, tweak as polygonal surfaces, and then insert finer details as subdivision surfaces. Chapter 5, "NURBS Modeling," is an in-depth lesson in NURBS modeling, and Chapter 6, "Polygons and Subdivision Surfaces," provides a similar look at polygon and subdivision surface modeling.

Modeling Tools

Let's now look at some of Maya's modeling features. Maya has a vast array of tools that can aid in modeling. Here are some of the more basic and useful functions we will cover in this chapter:

- Templates
- Layers
- Isolated selection
- Pick-masking
- Snapping
- Freezing transformations
- Construction history

Figure 4.3

The advantage of using subdivision surfaces

Templates

In Maya, templates are mainly used as guides for modeling. Objects that become templates remain visible but cannot be selected like other objects. The standard way to turn an object into a template is to select the object and then choose Display → Object Display → Template. You can also open the Attribute Editor (press Ctrl+A), choose Display, and toggle on Template.

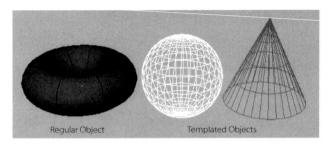

Regular Object   Templated Objects

Because you cannot select the templated object in the usual way by dragging, in order to untemplate it, you must either select it in the Outliner or the Hypergraph Editor, or use a selection mask (see "Pick-Masking" later in the chapter), and then toggle it back by choosing Display → Object Display → Untemplate.

You can also template objects by using the Layer Editor. A layer also has templating capability, and it is generally the more efficient way to template objects because it can handle groups. You access layers through the buttons above the Channel Box (see Figure 4.4). You have three options for viewing them—layer only, Channel Box only, or both together.

Templating using layers is a bit different from templating using the method just described. You can select a regular template using Selection Mask for templates, but not the layers templated using layers—they can be selected only from the Layer Editor or the Outliner.

The Layer Editor

Chapter 3, "Techniques for Speeding Up Workflow," introduced the Layer Editor, an extremely useful tool for modeling. Originally created for Alias Power Animator, it came back in its original form in Maya 2 and has become even better with each new version of Maya. A layer creates an exclusive collection of objects that can be selected, hidden, or templated together. Essentially, a layer acts as a directory or a folder for objects to aid in organization and work efficiency.

Figure 4.4

The Channel Box with the Layer Editor visible

Be sure you are familiar with the basic techniques presented in Chapter 3 for working with the Layer Editor:

- To display the Layer Editor if it has been turned off, choose Display → UI Elements → Channel Box/Layer Editor. If the Channel Box is showing but not the Layer Editor, click the second or the third button in the top-left corner of the Channel Box to display it.

- To create a new layer, choose Layers → Create Layer from the Layer Editor's menu, or click the New Layer button—it's to the right and just below the menu.

- To add an object or a group of objects to a layer, first select the layer in the Channel Box interface by left-clicking its name. A yellow box should appear around it. Then select your objects. Next, click the Layers drop-down menu and select Add Selected Objects To Current Layer. You can also access this menu by right-clicking the layer's name.

- To move an object from one layer to another, simply select the object and assign it to the other layer.

Figure 4.5

Layer visibility options

You can also move objects between layers using the Relationship Editor; and by using the Layer Editor, you can hide a layer's objects, template them, or reference them. The middle box on the left side of each new layer displays *T* for Template or *R* for Reference. The box on the left contains a letter *V* when the layer is visible and is blank when it is not, as in Figure 4.5. Objects in a Reference layer are just like regular objects in that they can be used for snapping (see the section "Snapping" later in this chapter) and can be shaded, but they cannot be selected. Removing a layer does not delete its member objects, but only the layer itself.

Use the Layer Colors palette to identify groups of objects as belonging to a layer. Double-click the layer's name in the Layer Editor to open the Layer Colors palette and assign a color. Using different colors can not only make things much easier to work with for complex scenes; it can also make the scene a bit more interesting, as in Figure 4.6 (also available in the Color Gallery on the accompanying CD). Colors assigned to objects are visible only when the object is neither templated nor referenced and when Maya's shading level is set to Wireframe or Wireframe With Shaded.

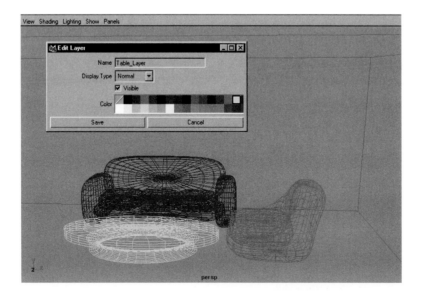

Figure 4.6

Using the Layer Colors palette

Isolate Select

At times, you will want to display only the objects or parts of an object that you want displayed within a view panel. Select objects (or their CVs or faces) that you want to isolate for viewing; then, in the view panel menu, choose Show → Isolate Select → View Selected. Figure 4.7 shows the results. You can also add or remove objects for viewing inside the panel with the other menu options such as Add Selected Objects and Remove Selected Objects. This feature can be a lifesaver when working with heavy, complex models, especially with dense polygonal surfaces. Remember, Isolate Select affects only the screen display and only the specific viewing panel in which View Selected is turned on.

Pick-Masking

One of the most elegant features of the Maya interface is its ability to limit selection to specific types of objects, components, or hierarchical elements. This function is also known as creating a *pick mask* or *selection mask*. (Maya uses the terms interchangeably.) You can RM choose an object to pick-mask elements which specifically apply to that object, or you can use the buttons on the Status line to pick only the elements you want to select.

> When you point to the buttons on the Status line, Maya identifies them. RM clicking a button displays a submenu that lists the elements that button will select. You can turn off the elements you do not want selected.

When you RM choose an object you are working on, Maya automatically figures out which marking menu selections should become available for that specific object type and gives you the appropriate choices. For a curve, you get a set of items that is different from the items displayed for a NURBS surface, as you can see in Figure 4.8.

Figure 4.7

Using the Isolate Select function

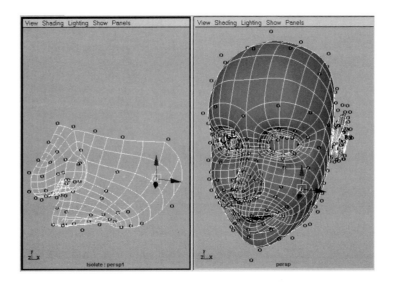

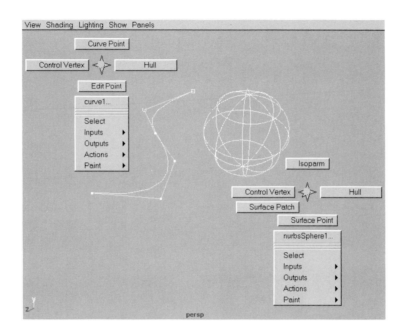

Figure 4.8

Pick-masking displays a different marking menu for a curve than for a NURBS surface.

The really cool thing about this feature is that depending on the pick mask you choose, Maya adjusts the display of control vertices, edit points, and hulls so that you select only what you want to select, and Maya hides the rest. For example, if you pick-mask Control Vertex from the curve's marking menu, Maya automatically goes into the Component Selection mode and displays only the CVs for you to select. Or if you pick-mask Hull, Maya shows only hulls. Figure 4.9 illustrates the difference.

If you want to select individual NURBS patches the way you select a polygon face, you can use the NURBS surface selection mask called Surface Patch. It allows you to select individual NURBS patches the way you select a polygon face. This selection option is used with another command, Edit NURBS → Duplicate NURBS Patches. See the Hands On tutorial in Chapter 5 for an example of its usage.

Another useful addition to the Status line is the Highlight Selection Mode button. In Component mode, this button hides all the nonselected components to give you a clearer view of your edits.

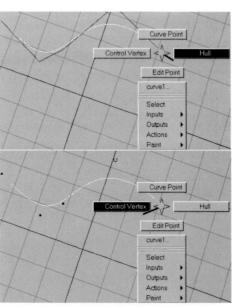

Figure 4.9

Pick-masking to display a curve's hull (top) and its control vertices

Figure 4.10

The Status line, configured to show component buttons, object buttons, or hier- archy buttons

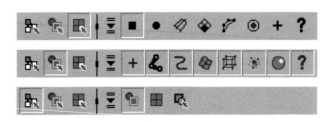

You can create various selection masks using the Status line in three different levels, as shown in Figure 4.10:

- You can limit your selection by *component types* such as CVs, Edit Points, Faces, Edges, and so on.

- You can also create Selection Masks to pick only *object types* such as Curves, Surfaces, Joints, and so on.

- And finally, you can limit selection by *hierarchy types*, such as pick-masking only the root or leaf level of a hierarchy. When you are in Hierarchy mode, you can also create a pick mask to select only templated objects as well. Component selection masks will not work in this mode because Maya allows only root or leaf nodes to be selected.

When several elements are active in the selection mask, Maya has a *priority list* that causes certain elements to be selected before others. Maya's default selection mask is set to select by object type with all the object types turned on; so dragging over a NURBS surface and a joint at the same time should select both objects. But because Maya's default selection prior- ity list has "joints" before "NURBS surfaces," Maya selects the joint and leaves the NURBS surface unselected. To display the selection priority list, choose Window → Settings/Preferences → Preferences, and the choose Settings → Selection to open the Preferences window shown in Figure 4.11. It is strongly recommended that you not change the default priority list or turn it off unless you have a good reason. The priority list was defined with careful deliberation, and you will find as you work your way through the various stages of a production in Maya that the default priorities make a lot of sense and are efficient.

Snapping

You use the snapping tools (see Figure 4.12) to transform an object or a component to snap to grids, curves, points, view planes, or surfaces. These elements become targets, or magnets, when activated. You can access these tools in the order they are listed in the Status line as snapping toggle buttons.

You also can use Maya's default hotkeys for snapping to grids, curves, or points. By default, Maya defines the following hotkeys:

- Press X and click or drag to snap to grid.
- Press C and click or drag to snap to curve.
- Press V and click or drag to snap to a point.

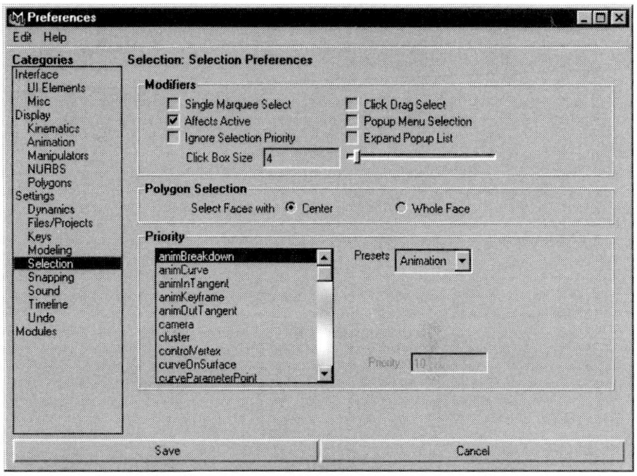

Let's briefly try out these tools. Create two curves as shown in Figure 4.13. Choose Create → CV Curve Tool and X+click the grid. Click eight times and press Enter to complete the first curve, on the left. Press Y to access the CV Curve Tool again and draw the second curve, on the right.

RM choose to pick-mask CVs over the first curve, and do the same for the second. Then select the first CV at the bottom, select the Move Tool by pressing the W key and V+drag with the left mouse button to

the first CV of the first curve. It should snap to the CV as in Figure 4.14. Now try to C+drag the last CV of the second curve to the first curve. It's not snapping, because snapping to a curve is distance sensitive. Drag the selected CV over to the first curve, making sure it's right over the curve. Now C+drag the CV back and forth. It should stay on and along the curve, as in Figure 4.14. Snap-to-curve also snaps to curves on surface, polygon edges and surface isoparms. To snap a component or an object to a curve independent of its distance to the curve, simply drag using the middle mouse button.

Maya also has point-to-point snap capabilities. Choose Modify → Snap Align Objects to display the options Point To Point, 2 Points To 2 Points, and 3 Points To 3 Points. The object containing the first selected point or set of points snaps to the second selected point or set of points. These points can be CVs or vertices, but it is the object controlled by the selected points that moves, not the points themselves.

Figure 4.11

The selection priority list in the Preferences window

Figure 4.12

The snapping tools

You can also snap the manipulator to stay locked on one of the manipulator handles when you are in the Perspective view, restricting the manipulator's movements to XY, XZ, or YZ handles, just as if you were in an orthographic window. Just Ctrl+click the manipulator handle where you want the snap, and the square plane at the center of the manipulator facing the camera will rotate to face the manipulator handle. The constraint applies only when you drag the manipulator center, not one of the axis handles. To release the constraint, Ctrl+click the center of the manipulator (this actually snaps the manipulator to move along the camera view plane).

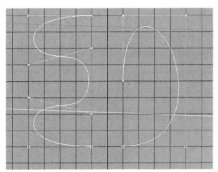

Figure 4.13

Two curves, snapped to a grid

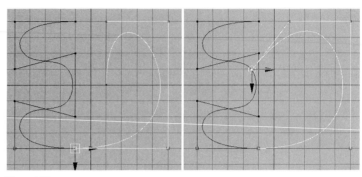

Figure 4.14

Snapping a CV to a point and a curve

Making an Object Live

Yet another way to snap objects or components is to make an object *live*. A live object acts as a construction aid in modeling, a magnet for other points. Any point you move snaps to the live object's surface. You can apply this useful modeling aid to any single object.

To do this, choose Create → NURBS Primitives → Sphere, and then choose Modify → Make Live, or click the Make Live button, the one with only the magnet icon, on the Status line. You'll see that the sphere has turned green, and if you are in Shaded mode, the sphere is no longer shaded. It has become *live*, a magnet for other elements, and while it is in that mode it cannot be selected. Choose Create → EP Curve Tool and try clicking a few times in the perspective window. All the edit points snap to the sphere surface. Press Enter to complete the curve and try translating it. The manipulator now shows only X and Y handles, as in Figure 4.15, which are actually U and V handles that move the curve along the parameters of the sphere surface.

Toggle the Make Live button off, and open the Outliner window. The new curve is not displayed because a curve becomes a part of the object it was drawn on when it is drawn on a NURBS surface using Make Live. To see the curve in the Outliner, right-click its entry and choose Show Shapes from the menu that pops up. A plus sign appears to the left of the sphere's entry, indicating that it is now expandable. Expand the sphere's entry until the new curve becomes visible. To bring a copy of the new curve into XYZ 3D space, make sure it is selected and choose Edit Curves → Duplicate Surface Curves. Any changes made to the curve drawn using Make Live also affect the duplicated curve. This has to do with Maya's construction history, which we'll discuss later in this chapter.

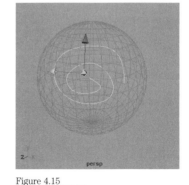

Figure 4.15

Because this sphere is live, the curve's edit points snap to its surface.

Using the Construction Plane

Maya also has a special *construction plane* under the Create menu. It does not render and, with the default setting, is displayed as a 24-unit plane in the XY axis, but it's actually infinite in size, like the ground plane in the perspective window. It exists primarily to be made live and aid in the construction of curves as an alternate ground plane. To appreciate how the construction plane differs from a regular NURBS plane in the way it behaves as a *live* object, try the following short exercise.

Start a new scene. Choose Create → CV Curve Tool, and X+click to snap the CVs for a curve on the ground plane. Do not press Enter yet. Choose Create → Construction Plane ❑, click Apply with everything at default, set the Pole Axis to YZ, and click Apply again. Close the option box. You should see the planes intersecting, as shown in Figure 4.16.

Select the hotbox (press the space bar), and choose North Zone → Persp/Outliner. In the Outliner, select plane1 and then choose Modify → Make Live. Continue to X+click CVs on plane1 as shown in Figure 4.17, until the curve being created comes to the grid next to the intersection point of the two construction planes. Since plane1 is now live, the CVs snap to its grid. Only construction planes allow the CVs to continue to build in this way. When working at object level, you have to move the curve's manipulator's center, not one of its axis handles, to make it snap to a live plane.

In the Outliner, select plane2 and then choose Modify → Make Live. Start X+clicking the CVs on plane2 until the curve being created comes to the grid above the ground plane. Toggle off the Modify → Make Live option and finish X+clicking the CVs once again on the ground plane, as shown in Figure 4.18. Press Enter to complete the curve!

Figure 4.16

A CV curve with construction planes

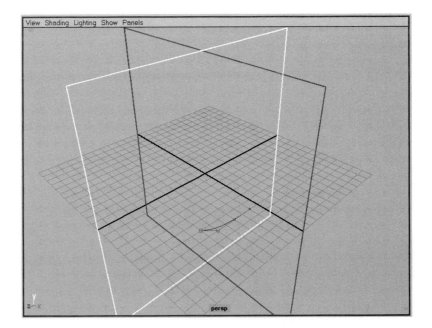

Figure 4.17

The CV curve on the first construction plane

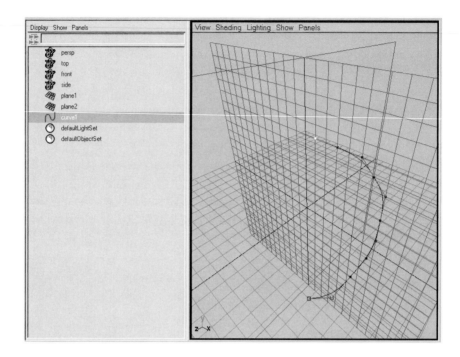

Figure 4.18

The CV curve completed with construction planes

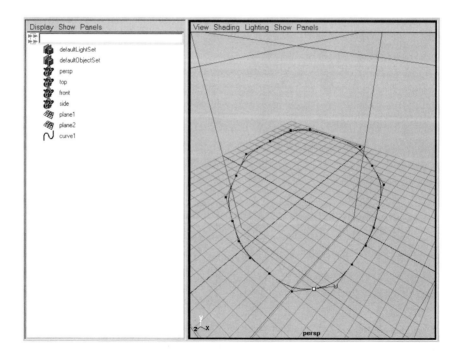

Freeze Transformations

When you create any object, it is initially placed at the origin, or (0,0,0), in the world space. As you work with the object, transforming it in various ways through translation, rotation, and scaling, there may be times when you want the point where you've placed the object to become its local origin, or (0,0,0), even though it is not the world space origin. To do this, select the object, and then choose Modify → Freeze Transformations.

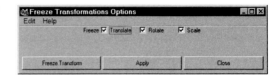

Figure 4.19

The Freeze Transformations Options window

But what if you wanted to freeze only the translation values of an object and leave its rotate and scale values intact? Maya has an option window for Freeze Transformations that allows you to do precisely this. You can choose to freeze only the Translate, Rotate, or Scale values of an object. Figure 4.19 shows the Freeze Transformations Options window.

How Maya Handles Construction History

One of Maya's more powerful features is its handling of construction history. Its procedural structure allows construction history to be maintained, which means you have more control and greater freedom to explore alternative modeling possibilities. Because it makes the scene complex, however, in certain situations you might want to turn off the construction history. You can do this by toggling the History button off in the Status line.

You can also delete a specific object's construction history by choosing Edit → Delete By Type → History. You will see more examples of construction history in the next chapter's tutorial.

Modeling with Primitives

Finally, we are ready to begin modeling! Although Maya provides many ways to do what we need to do, often the fastest and easiest way to get the job done is to use *primitives*—ready-to-use basic shapes such as those shown in Figure 4.20. Maya has a wealth of NURBS and polygon primitives: spheres, cubes, cylinders, cones, planes, and toruses. Maya also has a NURBS circle and square, which are made of curves.

Figure 4.20

Examples of primitives

Although they are all different in form, many of these primitives are created using similar variables, an example of which we will see a bit later. By starting with the primitives, you can immediately create simple objects, which you can then manipulate in various ways to produce more complex surfaces easily and quickly.

Building a Staircase

Let's begin exploring primitives by building a spiral staircase. In the following example, we will start with a cube to represent an individual step in the staircase, and then copy it many times.

1. Start a new scene, and choose Create → Polygon Primitives → Cube.

2. Manipulate the cube as follows: in the Channel Box, type –6, 0, and 0.5 for Translate X, Y, and Z respectively, and enter 5, 0.5, 1 for Scale X, Y, and Z. You should now see the cube placed as it is in Figure 4.21.

> In the Channel Box, the default naming convention is set to Nice. For example, you read "Translate X" in the first line of the Channel Box. If you are a beginner, this is helpful, because everything is clearly stated. But you can also change this to Short format by RM choosing Channel Names and selecting the Short setting. The first line should now read "tx," which looks cleaner and gives a bit more space for the modeling windows.

3. Keeping the cube selected, choose Edit → Duplicate Options. Set the numbers in the dialog box as follows: Translate 0, 0.5, –1; Rotate 0, –10, 0; Number of Copies, 35; Geometry Type, **Instance**.

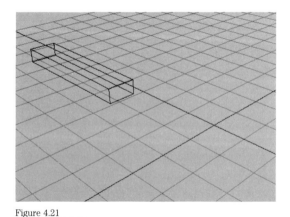

Figure 4.21

A cube primitive, offset and scaled

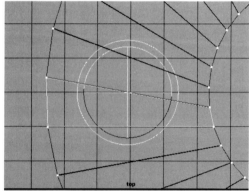

Figure 4.22

Top view of the staircase steps

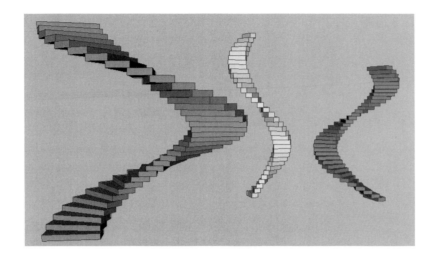

Figure 4.23

Some spiral staircases

4. Click the Duplicate button, and voilà! You should now have a spiral staircase. Note that the duplicates here are *instances*, which means any manipulation to the shape of the original cube is applied to the duplicates as well. Instances are also computationally much lighter (less taxing on the CPU) than copied duplicates. Go to the Top View, RM choose Vertex over the original cube, select the four vertices at the top side of the cube, and then rotate and translate them until they overlap the duplicated cube at the bottom side as shown in Figure 4.22.

5. You can also get different shapes for the spiral staircase, as shown in Figure 4.23, by selecting all the vertices of the original cube and translating them in X and Z.

A Look Inside a Primitive: Torus

The torus is a good example of Maya's primitives, so let's look at its properties in detail. A torus is basically a revolved circle, a donut-shaped surface that is closed on both U and V parameters.

Choose Create → NURBS Primitives → Torus, and in the Channel Box, under INPUTS, click makeNurbTorus1. You will see the various variables that form the shape of the torus (see Figure 4.24).

Try doing the same with some other primitives, such as the cylinder and the sphere. Many of the torus primitive's properties have exactly the same counterparts in the other primitives—you should go over those variables with the other primitives as well in order to see the various possible shapes they can form with different settings. When working with primitives, it is good practice to ensure that sections and spans are finalized before pulling any CVs because changing them afterward will produce unpredictable results.

makeNurbTorus1	
Radius	1
Start Sweep	0
End Sweep	360
Degree	Cubic
Sections	8
Spans	4
Height Ratio	0.5
Minor Sweep	360

Figure 4.24

Default input variables for a torus

Figure 4.25

**Different settings for a
torus can produce radi-
cally different results.**

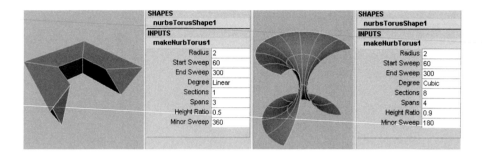

Now let's experiment with some torus settings. Click Radius; then, inside the modeling window, MM drag slowly and see what happens to the torus. The radius measures the distance from the center of the geometry to its circumference. In the case of a torus, the radius measures the center of the circle revolving around it, which effectively means the Radius setting controls the size of the torus.

Start Sweep and End Sweep determine in degrees where the torus starts and where it stops revolving along V.

For the Degree section, click Cubic to display the drop-down menu that contains Linear as the other degree choice—this setting will give sharp edges to the torus as shown by the torus on the left side in Figure 4.25. Sections subdivide the torus along V, and Spans subdivide it along U.

Height Ratio is the ratio between height and radius; this setting effectively determines the thickness of the torus.

And finally, Minor Sweep determines in degrees the amount of surface (along U) the circle revolving around the torus will have, as shown by the torus on the right side in Figure 4.25.

Primitives are useful not because of what they are, but because of what they can become, because of the way they can help create the final surfaces you want, as you will see in the next section.

Hands On: Creating a Living Room Scene with Primitives

In this tutorial, we will start building a living room scene with primitives. Remember the principle, build only what the camera will see? The first thing you need to do, then, is to visualize what you want to see at the end. Picture the camera capturing a living room at an angle, with a sofa set, a table, a lamp, and a dog by the window! (You'll find the rendered image in the Color Gallery on the CD. It's called `livingroom.tif`.)

We'll get to the lamp and the dog later, but for now, we can build the rest with three simple primitives that Maya provides us with.

1. Create a new scene. Drop a sphere into the scene: either click the sphere icon in Shelf1 or choose Create → NURBS Primitives → Sphere. Go into Side View, pick-mask Control Vertex, and drag to select the top two rows of CVs (see Figure 4.26). Press W to use the Move tool.

2. Snap the CVs to the first grid above the ground level by X+dragging the Y handle to that grid. Make sure you are not dragging the center of the manipulator; if you do so, all the CVs will snap to one point. If the grid isn't displayed, choose Display → Grid to make it visible. Repeat the same action with the two bottom rows of CVs to the grid below ground level, as shown in Figure 4.27.

3. Go to the Top View, and again snap the edge rows of CVs to the unit grids on each side of the sphere. Your sphere should look like that in Figure 4.28.

4. Choose Edit → Duplicate Options, and then choose Edit → Reset Settings. This will help ensure that the sphere is cloned in a predictable manner.

5. Duplicate the sphere, which now looks more like a cube with round edges, several times (choose Edit → Duplicate), scaling, translating, and rotating it to make the sofa, as shown in Figure 4.29. Make sure you keep at least one unmodified duplicate of the original to copy from in later steps.

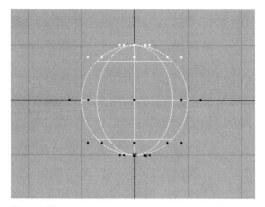

Figure 4.26

Side view of sphere with CVs

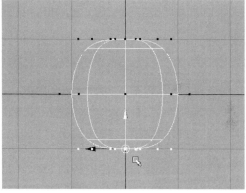

Figure 4.27

A sphere with CVs snapped

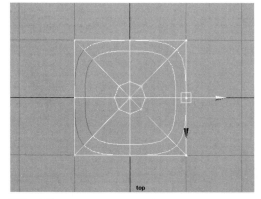

Figure 4.28

Top view of the sphere with CVs snapped

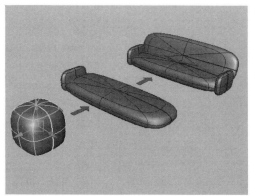

Figure 4.29

A cube transformed into a sofa

When you are building several objects, it is good form to build each object at the origin and then move it out of the center when it is finished. As long as you do not freeze its transformation or change the pivot, you can always transform it back to its original position for further modifications.

6. For the cushions, copy the sphere, pull the top row of CVs (which looks like a single point) down just a bit, scale and translate it to be on the sofa, and make two more copies to cover the whole sofa. When the sofa is done, make sure it is resting on the ground plane, select all its elements, and choose Edit → Group. This makes it a lot easier work with the sofa as one entity. You can hide the sofa for now while you move on to the table and the chair. Choose Display → Hide → Hide Selection.

7. For the table, choose Create → NURBS Primitives → Cylinder ❒, set Caps to Top. and click Create. This will become the table top. Move it to one side for now. For the table base, choose Create → NURBS Primitives → Torus, and (in the Channel Box under makeNurbTorus1) set the Height Ratio to 0.2 and Minor Sweep to 190 degrees. Translate the cylinder to the top of the torus, and scale and translate each object to form the table shape you see in Figure 4.30. Group the cylinder and the torus; then translate them to the ground level.

8. Choose Display → Show → Show Last Hidden to make the sofa visible again. Place the sofa and the table roughly in the positions shown in Figure 4.30.

Figure 4.30

Positions of the sofa and table

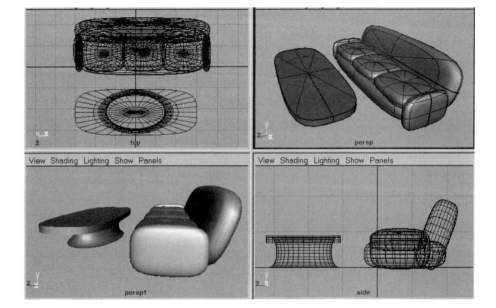

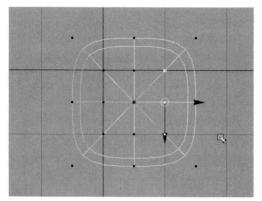

Figure 4.31
Sphere, top view

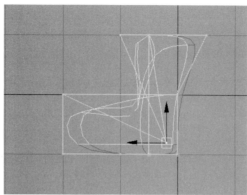

Figure 4.32
Side view

9. To select a group node in the modeling window, select one object in the group and press the Up arrow key. If there are branches in the group hierarchy, press the Up arrow key until you reach the root level.

10. The chair is a bit trickier. Copy the sphere, and hide all the rest. Translate the sphere to (0.5, 0, 0.5) using the Channel Box. Switch to Top View, and snap the middle CVs to the grid for each side of the sphere as shown in Figure 4.31.

11. In the side view, grab the two rows of CVs at the bottom-right corner and snap them to the Y axis. Grab the rows of CVs at the left side and snap them to the second grid to the left. Grab the CVs at the top-left corner and drag them down as shown in Figure 4.32.

12. In the Perspective view (see Figure 4.33), select the CVs as shown and push them back in Z a little. You can also select the CVs at the chair's side and scale them out to make the chair look rounder. If you are having a hard time seeing the right CVs, toggle the hulls to be visible by choosing Display → NURBS Components → Hulls.

Figure 4.33
Perspective view

13. To finish, copy one of the cushions from the sofa and put it on the chair. Group the chair and the cushion. Choose Display → Show → All. Create three planes by choosing Create → NURBS Primitives → Plane for the floor and the two walls, and then arrange the "furniture" as you see fit. Figure 4.34 is the final textured and lit living room. We will come back to this scene later to add more interesting pieces.

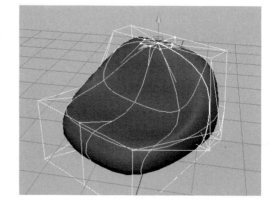

Summary

This chapter introduced the basic concepts of modeling and the tools that Maya provides to aid you in creating and editing surfaces. You also learned how to use primitives to build more complex objects such as a staircase or pieces of furniture.

In the next two chapters, we will delve in more depth into three major types of modeling: NURBS modeling, polygon modeling, and subdivision surfaces modeling.

Figure 4.34

The final living room

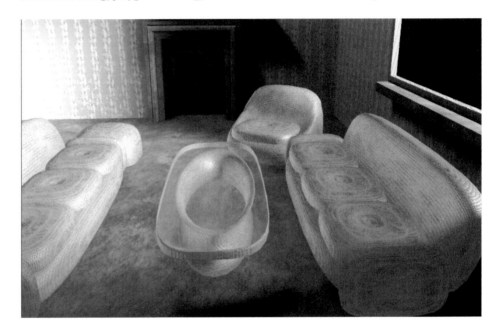

CHAPTER 5

NURBS Modeling

This chapter covers modeling with NURBS curves and surfaces. It begins with an explanation of the basic theory and concepts involved in modeling curves. The goal is simply to give you a basic understanding of what you are doing as you work with NURBS in Maya. If you are familiar with these concepts, you might want to skim this section. The chapter then introduces the tools that Maya provides for working with curves and for creating and editing surfaces. It concludes by demonstrating these tools in two hands-on exercises; one creates an aftershave bottle, and the other creates a human head.

The second hands-on exercise is quite advanced, in the sense that the operations are more involved and the instructions are not as detailed as in basic tutorials; it assumes that you have more working familiarity with Maya's interface and basic techniques. Although it will take time to work through this and other advanced tutorials in this book, you should by all means go through them, because that's where all the really fun stuff happens, where the artist in you can come to the fore. Topics include:

- **Curve and surface concepts**
- **Creating curves**
- **Editing curves**
- **Creating surfaces**
- **Editing surfaces**
- **Hands On: Aftershave bottle**
- **Hands On: Building a character I (advanced)**

Curve and Surface Concepts

Part of the genius of Maya is that it makes the highly complex mathematics of modeling and animation almost completely transparent to the user. You don't need to know much about what Maya is doing behind the scenes when you use its tools. Not everyone wants to know what *NURBS*, *B-splines*, or *parameterization* means. When you are striving for artistic expression, you probably don't want to delve into mathematical concepts. These concepts may seem like unwelcome relatives at a hip party—you invite them in and exchange pleasantries ("How are you? How are the kids?") but want nothing to do with them afterward!

Nevertheless, these and other "techno-words" are built into the fabric of computer animation. Maya is, after all, computer software. The better grounded you are in these "esoteric" concepts, the deeper and further you will be able to go in mastering your art. But be assured that as dry (or exciting!) as things may get in the following sections, nothing overly technical will be thrown at you.

> If you find it difficult to understand some of the concepts in the next few sections, just skip them for now. You can come back later when those topics have become more relevant.

Curves Are Equations

The curve you draw in the computer is actually a curve segment or a continuous series of segments. One segment is called a *span*. A curve span is a digital representation on the screen of a mathematical concept called a parametric equation. Because the equation describes a position in 3D space, it always has three variables (x, y, z), and the power of the variable with the highest degree in the equation determines the classification of the curve. Hence, a first-degree curve is a linear equation, which is a straight line. A second-degree curve is a quadratic equation, or an arc. A third-degree curve is a cubic equation, which can actually twist in 3D space. Two higher-degree curves, fifth- and seventh-degree curves, can actually twist twice in one span. Maya has all these degree options in its curve-creation tools, but for most practical purposes, the cubic curve is almost always used. In Maya, the default curve is cubic (see Figure 5.1).

Figure 5.1

The anatomy of a cubic curve

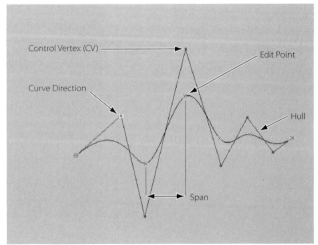

Control Vertex (CV)

Curve Direction

Edit Point

Hull

Span

Curves Are Also Splines

A Control Vertex (CV) is a point in 3D space that determines the shape of the curve it is attached to by defining and influencing its equation. The CVs and the curve segments they control are collectively known as *splines*.

Historically, a spline was a plank of wood bent to form part of a ship's hull by forcing it between pairs of posts, known as "ducks." The placement of these ducks determined the shape of the plank's curve, just as the placement of CVs determines the shape of a curve in computer graphics.

There are different methods for calculating how the CV positions are interpreted into curve shapes, and these methods—types of equations or formulas—distinguish the splines further into Bezier curves, B-splines, or NURBS. NURBS, the focus of our attention in this chapter, stands for *Non-Uniform Rational B-Splines*. (Don't worry about understanding the meaning of all the components of this daunting acronym. The important thing to understand is how a NURBS curve behaves.)

The advantage a NURBS curve has over the other types of splines lies essentially in the way it can be cut and joined. Regular splines cannot be cut and joined at arbitrary points along the curve, only at their control points. A NURBS curve, however, can be cut and joined anywhere, because any point on the curve can be calculated and located. This advantage carries over into surfaces as well. NURBS surfaces can be attached to other NURBS surfaces with different numbers of spans, or *isoparms*, for this reason.

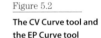

Figure 5.2

The CV Curve tool and the EP Curve tool

Curve segments join to form one continuous line at Edit Points (EPs), which are also called *knots*. Maya has a CV Curve tool and an EP Curve tool for creating curves. The two tools create curves differently, but both create NURBS curves (see Figure 5.2).

Surfaces and Parameterization

Curves cannot be rendered; only surfaces can be rendered. In modeling, curves help create surfaces. At the end of the day, no matter how many curves you create, only surfaces matter. Any discussion about surfaces, however, needs to include the concept of *parameterization*—yes, here comes another unwelcome relative.

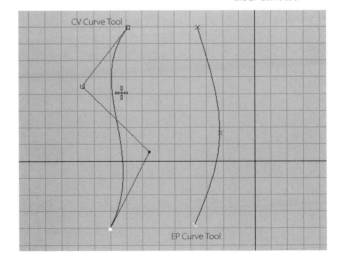

To best understand parameterization of surfaces, we need to examine curves first. Parameterization of a curve is the calculation of where knots (Edit Points) are placed along the curve, enabling any point on the curve to be assigned a parameter value. The variable representing this value is defined as U, and the curve is given a direction as a result.

To see this at work, create a default curve made of four spans: either seven clicks of CVs or five clicks of EPs. Now pick-mask Curve Point, and try dragging along the curve. At the top of the Maya window, you should see the curve parameter value changing as you drag. The start of the curve is assigned a parameter value, U[0]. The second edit point of the curve is assigned the value U[1], the third edit point, U[2], and so on. The halfway point between the fourth edit point of the curve and the last edit point is assigned a value of U[3.5], as shown in Figure 5.3. Any point on the curve can be similarly assigned a parameter value this way. This method of calculating the point values along the curve is called *uniform parameterization*.

Figure 5.3

Uniform parameterization

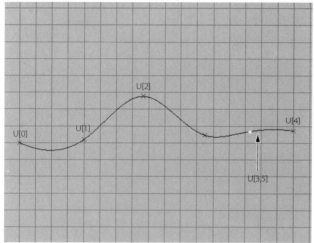

Another calculation method in Maya is called *chord-length parameterization,* and the way it assigns the U value to a point on the curve is more complicated. We needn't go into exactly how the calculation is done, but the value assignment depends on the distances between successive Edit Points of the curve, not on the number of Edit Points. Two curves with the same number of Edit Points but drawn differently will end up with different parameter values at those Edit Points. You can see the difference between chord-length and uniform parameterization in Figure 5.4. The curve in Figure 5.4 is drawn in exactly the same way as the curve in Figure 5.3, but the values assigned to the points on the curve are different, because the curve in Figure 5.4 is a chord-length curve. Notice that the third edit point of this curve has a value of U[8.5012].

How does all this relate to surfaces? A surface is an area in 3D space defined by the parameterization of two variables, U and V. The area is calculated in

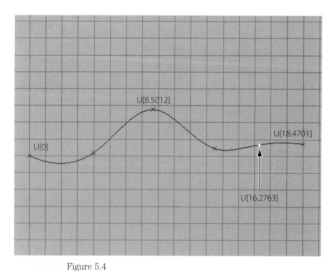

Figure 5.4

A chord-length parameterization curve with values at different points

such way that at any point on the surface, a *UV* coordinate can be given, and the area is given *UV* directions. This is exactly the same situation as with the curves, except now you have the *V* parameterization as well. It's important to understand the difference between the UV coordinate system and the XYZ world space coordinates. The latter system identifies any point in Maya's 3D world space, whereas the former deals only with a 2D surface area.

Uniform parameterization produces more predictable values for curves and surfaces than chord-length and is therefore the preferred choice for modeling in general and the default setting in Maya. The advantage of chord-length parameterization is in texturing: it allows more evenly distributed textures on uneven surfaces than the uniform method. The bottles shown in Figure 5.5 are revolved from curves that have exactly the same CV placements, except that the one on the left uses chord-length and the other is uniform.

You will generally want to use uniform surfaces over chord-length surfaces. As you will see in Chapter 17, "Shading and Texturing Surfaces," Maya provides a Fix Texture Warp option in the Attribute Editor for all NURBS surfaces that distributes UV textures using the chord-length method. Nonetheless, the concept is worth knowing about, because it is still part of Maya. Many command options mention chord-length.

Figure 5.5

The bottle on the left was rendered using chord-length parameterization; the bottle on the right, with uniform.

Surface Normals

In addition to having UV directions, a surface also has a front side and a back side, determined by its *normals*. A normal is essentially a vector shooting out perpendicularly from a point on the front side of a surface. In other words, a normal is the direction that surface point is directly facing. The concept of surface normals is important for using certain modeling tools, as well as for texturing and rendering, and you should become comfortable with it.

You can use the "right-hand rule" illustrated in Figure 5.6 to determine which side of a surface is front, or which way the normals are pointing. If the thumb points to the increasing *U* direction, and the index finger points to the increasing *V* direction, the middle finger bent perpendicularly to these two fingers is the direction of the surface normals. You can see the surface normals of a surface while in Shaded mode by selecting the surface and then choosing Display → NURBS Components → Normals (Shaded Mode).

Figure 5.6

Using the right-hand rule to determine surface normals

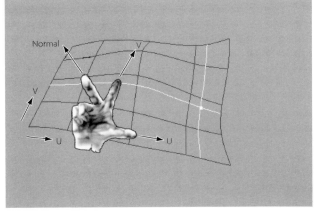

Figure 5.7

**The anatomy
of a surface**

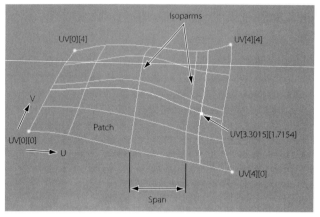

Surfaces, like curves, are made up of spans, or rather they span a given number of span areas. The area covered by one *UV* span is called a *patch*. The flowing lines separating the patches are called *isoparms*. These are the surface equivalents of knots, or Edit Points. Figure 5.7 illustrates the terminology of surfaces.

Pick-masking the isoparm element allows you to select any flowing *isoparametric* curve that has either a *U* or a *V* value on the surface, just like selecting a curve point on a curve. With surfaces, you can also pick-mask Surface Point, which enables you to select any point on the surface with a *UV* parameter value. Or you can pick-mask Surface Patch, which enables you to select patches like polygon faces.

When you select a surface point and choose Edit NURBS → Insert Isoparms, both *U* and *V* isoparms are inserted.

Open, Closed, and Periodic Curves and Surfaces

A curve or surface can be open, closed, or periodic. If a curve's form is open, its start knot and end knot are not together. In a closed curve, it's the start knot and end knot occupy the same position, called the seam, and tangency can be broken at this point. A periodic curve is distinguished from a closed curve in that none of its CVs occupy the same position as the knots. It has a seam, but tangency is unbroken. Surfaces are always open in at least in one direction. The only exception is the torus, which is periodic on both U and V.

Creating Curves

Maya has several tools for creating curves and also a Text tool. As mentioned, Maya can create curves either with Edit Points or with CVs.

Generally, if the curve needs to pass through a specific point, the EP Curve tool is a better choice, because the Edit Points actually lie on the curve. The CV Curve tool is preferred in most other situations because it is better at controlling the curve shape.

Using the CV Curve Tool

In front view, choose Create → CV Curve Tool ❏. In the resulting option window, you can see that the default settings are Cubic and Uniform. Leave everything at the default setting, and X+click near the origin. Draw the curve on the left in Figure 5.8. Oops! The last CV placement was a mistake. No problem. Because you haven't pressed Enter yet to complete the action, you can still control the CV's placement after you create it. Just MM click and X+drag the CV back to where it should be placed, like the curve on the right.

Once you complete the curve, you can revolve it to create a wine bottle like the ones shown in Figure 5.5.

You can also edit CVs or EPs while you are creating a curve by pressing the Insert key. With this method, you can select multiple points for repositioning. To continue creating the curve, just press the Insert key again.

Using the Pencil Curve Tool

Pencil is another great curve-creation tool in the Create menu, especially if you have access to a digitizing tablet. It may look as if it is producing a thousand Edit Points when you are using it, but with a simple rebuild command, Edit Curves → Rebuild Curve, you can get an elegantly simple curve. Rebuild Curve ❐ has a Number Of Spans setting for Uniform Rebuild Type that you can adjust.

Each time you release the mouse, the Pencil tool completes building the curve. As a result, you will often end up with several separate curves. Again, you can easily attach these curves using Edit Curves → Attach Curves. In Figure 5.9, raw curves on the left have been rebuilt and attached to create the curve on the right.

> When using the Pencil tool, it's far better to end up with several separate curves that better represent what you wanted to draw than to try to draw everything as one curve.

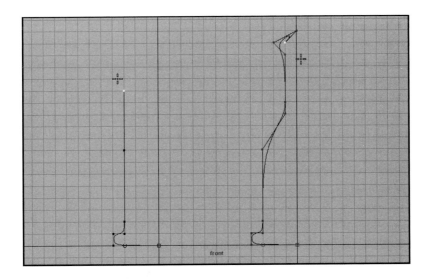

Figure 5.8

Using the CV Curve tool. you can easily correct mistakes.

Figure 5.9

The raw curves on the left have been rebuilt and attached to form the curve on the right.

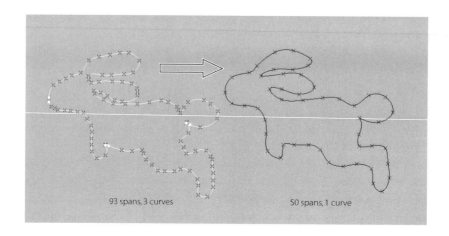

93 spans, 3 curves   50 spans, 1 curve

Using the Arc Tools

In contrast to the free form of the Pencil tool, the Arc tools let you create circular arcs of various angles. There are two types: the simple two-point circular arc, and the three-point circular arc, which has one more control point than the other tool. Figure 5.10 illustrates both types.

Once you create, for example, a three-point circular arc, you can still manipulate the arc's Edit Points. First, choose Modify → Transformation Tools → Show Manipulator Tool (or press the T key), and then, in the Channel Box, under Inputs, choose makeThreePointCircularArc. The three points should be visible now.

Duplicating Surface Curves

Figure 5.10

A two-point circular arc (left) and a three-point circular arc (right)

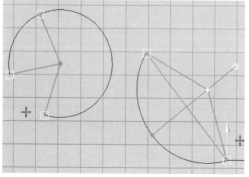

Yet another curve creation method is Duplicate Surface Curves, which is actually not part of the Create menu but appears on the Edit Curves menu. It can be an efficient and powerful curve generator, especially with its ability to duplicate all the isoparms of a surface. To try this tool for yourself, create a default cylinder, pick-mask Isoparm, select an isoparm anywhere on the surface, and choose Edit Curves → Duplicate Surface Curves. Figure 5.11 shows the result: a curve with the same number of spans as the cylinder has been duplicated.

Now translate the duplicated curve out of the cylinder. Select the cylinder, and choose Edit Curves → Duplicate Surface Curves. This time, as shown in Figure 5.12, all the isoparms of the cylinder are duplicated. You can set the options so that only *U* or *V* will duplicate. The default is both.

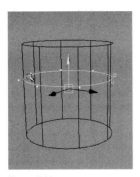

Figure 5.11

A curve duplicated from
a cylinder

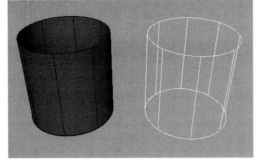

Figure 5.12

Selecting the cylinder before duplicating surface curves duplicates all its surface isoparms.

The span of the duplicated curves will be the same as the cylinder's, but the number of
curves being duplicated will match the number of isoparms being displayed on the screen—if
the cylinder's NURBS smoothness is set to fine, you will get more curves than if the smoothness is set to rough.

Editing Curves

Once you create the curves you need, Maya provides various actions and tools to edit them.
In this section, we'll go through attaching and detaching curves, aligning curves and surfaces,
rebuilding curves, inserting knots, adding points to a curve, cutting and filleting curves, and
offsetting curves.

Attaching and Detaching Curves

The Attach Curves option requires that you select
two curves or curve points. For most situations,
Maya can automatically figure out which ends of the
curves are being attached, and you only need to
select curves as objects. If the ends being attached
are not correct, you can select curve points to force
the proper ends to attach. To select curve points,
pick-mask Curve Point, and then drag the curve
point to the curve end you want, as shown in
Figure 5.13.

Figure 5.13

Attaching two sepa-
rate curves to form a
new curve

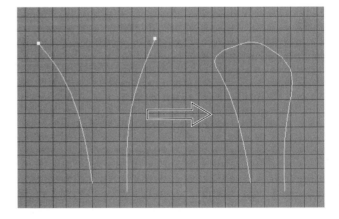

When selecting curve points on two or more curves, first select the curve point on one curve,
then pick-mask Curve Point on the other curve, and Shift+click the second curve point. The
first selection stays selected.

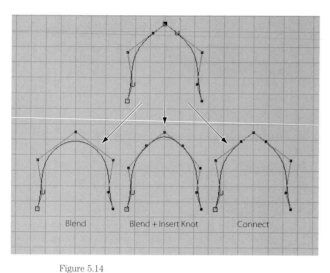

Figure 5.14

Three ways of attaching two curves

When both of the correct end curve points are selected, choose Edit Curves → Attach Curves ❑. Blend is the default attachment method, and Blend Bias 0.5 specifies that both curves meet halfway. This setting is ideal when you need to maintain symmetry. When the Blend Bias is set to 0, the first selected curve attaches itself to the second curve.

If you find the curve shapes are changing too much when you attach them, try clicking Insert Knot in the option window. If you absolutely need the curves to maintain their original shape, you can change the Attach Method setting to Connect. For this to work properly, however, the curve ends have to be touching already. Figure 5.14 shows the effect of these different attachment methods.

When attaching curves or surfaces, make sure the Keep Original option (the default setting) is toggled on if the construction history is on. Odd behavior can occur if it is toggled off and the attached object is modified later.

Detaching connected curves is simple. You just select curve points, Edit Points, or both, as shown in the three curves in Figure 5.15, and then choose Edit Curves → Detach Curves. These commands also works on multiple curves.

Curve and Surface Alignment and Continuity

Figure 5.15

Detaching curve segments

When two separate curves or surface ends are not touching, they are said to be *discontinuous*. When they are touching, there are three possible levels of continuity between them: *position continuity, tangent continuity,* or *curvature continuity*. In creating a smooth continuous surface out of patches, you need at least tangent continuity between the connected patches. In this section, you'll work with two example curves to understand the concept of these degrees of continuity.

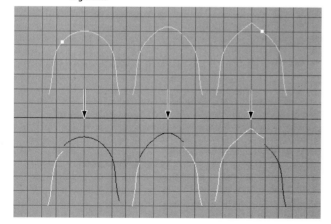

To set up the example curves, start by creating a new scene and switching to the front viewport. Starting with the curve on the left, create two CV curves as shown in Figure 5.16, using X+click to snap them to the grid. Select the curve on the left and press Ctrl+A to open the Attributes Editor. Under the curveShape1 tab, expand the options for Component Display. Turn on Disp CV and Disp Hull. Do the same for the curve on the right, and close the Attributes Editor. Make copies and translate them aside.

Position continuity, also called zero-order continuity (C0), occurs when the two end CVs are placed in the same 3D space. Select the two copied curves, and choose Edit Curves → Align Curves ❑. Set Continuity to Position, and modify Boundary to Both. Then click Align to see the result shown in Figure 5.17.

Tangent continuity, also called first-order continuity (C1), occurs when the tangents at the ends of the two curves have the same slope in addition to position continuity. Practically speaking, this occurs when the two end CVs of the curves align. Select the two original curves, change Continuity to Tangent in the option window, and click Align to see the result shown on the left in Figure 5.18.

Curvature continuity, also called second-order continuity (C2), occurs when in addition to having tangent continuity, the curves "curve" away from their end points in the same way. Another way of saying this is that the radii of the curvatures of the two curves are the same. Practically speaking, this means that in the curve being modified, the third CV from the end

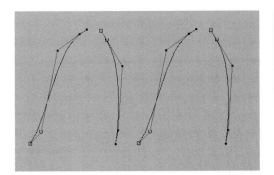

Figure 5.16

Two curves and their copies

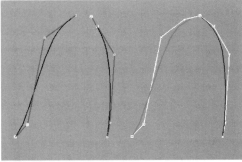

Figure 5.17

Curves aligned with position continuity

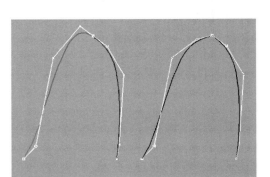

Figure 5.18

Position alignment (right) and tangent alignment (left)

Figure 5.19

Tangent alignment (left) and curvature alignment (right)

point, in addition to the second CV, is also translated to accommodate the curvature change. Select the copied curves again, the curves with point continuity alignment, change Continuity to Curvature, and then click Align again. Notice, as shown on the right in Figure 5.19, the changes in the positions of the second and third CVs from the end. Few tools in Maya give options for curvature continuity: Align is one, and the other is Project Tangent, which is not covered in this book.

The default setting for Align Curves and Surfaces (they are the same action) is Modify Position First, which means the first curve selected will move in its entirety to align itself. After you perform the Align, experiment with the various settings in the Inputs section of the Channel Box to get a better idea of how the Align Curves tool works.

Rebuilding Curves

The Rebuild Curves tool allows you to rebuild curves in various ways. Rebuilding curves is important for creating good surfaces. When you work with curves for a while, they can end up with unnecessary CVs or CVs bunched up unevenly. You can clean them with the Rebuild Curves tool. Remember that from cleanly built (or rebuilt) curves come clean surfaces. To try this tool, create a curve using the Pencil Curve tool. With the curve still selected, choose Edit Curves → Rebuild Curve ❒.

When the Rebuild Type is set to Uniform, which is the default setting, you must specify the number of spans. The default is set at four spans, but the number you need to use will depend on the complexity of the required shape.

The Reduce setting simplifies the curve according to the Global or Local Tolerance level you set, as illustrated in Figure 5.20. The Match Knots setting requires two curves to be selected: it reparameterizes the first curve to match the number of knots in the second curve. The No Multiple Knots setting gets rid of multiple knots, which are sometimes created when curves are attached or knots inserted. A multiple knot occurs when more than one knot, or edit point, occupies the same position on a curve. The Curvature setting redistributes and inserts more Edit Points in areas of higher curvature according to a Tolerance level, just like the Reduce setting. To change the Global Tolerance setting for the Reduce or Curvature options, choose Window → Settings/Preferences → Preferences and click Settings to open the Tolerance section.

Figure 5.20

Curves rebuilt with different local tolerances and thus different numbers of spans

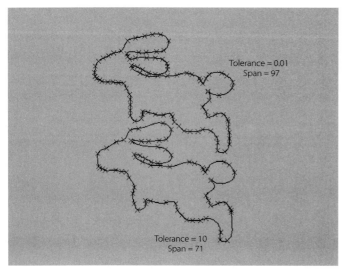

Tolerance = 0.01
Span = 97

Tolerance = 10
Span = 71

Let's cover one more option: the Keep CV option allows you to rebuild the parameter of the curve while keeping the CVs in their original position. When you insert knots, as described next, the span of the curve increases and more CVs are created, but the parameterized values of points along the curve stay the same as before the insertion. The Keep CV option recalculates the curve parameters to include the inserted knot, while keeping the CVs in the same position.

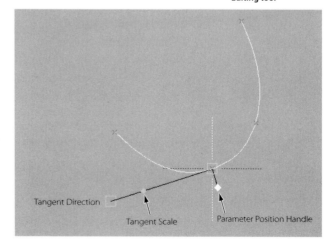

Inserting Knots

The Insert Knot command allows you to add more Edit Points or CVs to further edit a curve. To use Insert Knot, select a curve point on the curve where you want the extra edit point created, and then choose Edit Curves → Insert Knot. Note that another CV is created as well. A useful option for Insert Knot, also available for Insert Isoparms for surfaces, is the Between Selections option. Select two Edit Points; then choose Edit Curves → Insert Knot ❑, click the Between Selections option, and click Insert. As shown in Figure 5.21, another edit point is added exactly halfway between the two selected Edit Points. If you select two curve points with this option, these two curve points will also turn into Edit Points, along with the new edit point you've inserted in the middle.

Adding Points to a Curve

Once the curve is created and you want to add more curve to it, you can choose Edit Curves → Add Points Tool. If you want to add points not from the last CV but from the start of the curve,

Figure 5.22

Manipulating a curve with the Curve Editing tool

select the curve, and then choose Edit Curves → Reverse Curve Direction. If you want to add Edit Points instead of CVs, just RM choose the curve and pick-mask Edit Point. Then, when you select Add Points Tool, it will be set to add Edit Points and not CVs. Make sure you click an existing Edit Point before you begin adding new ones, preferably at the end of the curve. Note the difference between Insert Knot and Add Points: the former adds more points inside an existing curve, whereas the latter actually creates a longer curve segment.

Tangent Direction

Tangent Scale

Parameter Position Handle

Using the Curve Editing Tool

Usually you can manipulate a curve by translating the CVs. But at times you may want an edit point to stay in position while the CVs around it move to change the curve shape. The Curve Editor is useful in such situation.

Create a curve, and then choose Edit Curves → Curve Editing Tool. Grab the Parameter position handle (as shown in Figure 5.22) and move it along the curve while keeping V pressed to snap the editor to Edit Points. Once it's on the edit point you want, you can modify the curve tangent direction and scale around the edit point without moving the edit point itself.

Cutting Curves

Choosing Edit Curves → Cut Curve is another way to edit curves. It detaches multiple curves where they intersect. The default option setting for Find Intersections is In 2D and 3D, which finds the intersections for the curves even if they are not actually touching in 3D space, but only seem to touch in one of the active 2D views. In Figure 5.23, a group of circles that were created from a cylinder have been cut by a large circle, with the cutting done in the Side view panel. Notice how the large circle isn't touching any of the cut curves in the actual 3D space.

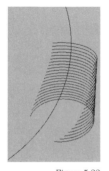

Figure 5.23

A group of circles that have been cut with a large circle

Filleting Curves

Curve Fillet (choose Edit Curves → Curve Fillet) creates a fillet from two intersecting curves. Unlike Cut Curve, which can be projected from a 2D view, the fillet curves actually have to be touching. The default setting creates a circular fillet from the two curves. Where the lines are intersecting, sometimes the fillet occurs at the wrong corner. In such a case, you need to cut the curves first and then select the curves you want to fillet. The Trim and Join settings in the option window can also save you a lot of time by trimming the curves and attaching the segments into one curve. See Figure 5.24.

Figure 5.24

Curves cut and filleted

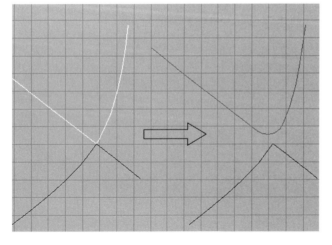

Offsetting Curves

Offsetting a curve (choose Edit Curves → Offset) duplicates a curve with an offset distance that you set in the option window. There is an important difference between offsetting a curve and copying and scaling a curve. When a curve is duplicated and uniformly scaled, it maintains the curve shape, whereas a curve created from the offset maintains the distance between it and the original curve, though not necessarily the original shape. Figure 5.25 illustrates the difference.

Creating Surfaces

Once the curves are prepared, you can create surfaces from them in various ways. In this section,
we'll look at the surface creation actions and tools in
Maya's Surfaces menu, as well as the Text tool
under the Create menu, because it is closely related
to the Bevel tool.

Revolve

The Revolve tool on the Surfaces menu revolves
selected curves around a designated axis, which you
set in the option window. The default revolve axis is
vertical, or Y. The other settings are X, Z, and Free.

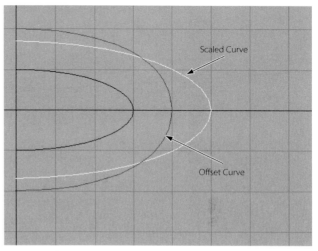

Figure 5.25

**Scaling and offsetting
a curve**

The last option makes available the Axis boxes, which use the translation values of the Show
Manipulator axis handle. This allows you to change the revolve axis interactively after creating a surface, by manipulating the Show Manipulator tool.

For a simple example, let's build a lamp to go into the living room we built in the previous
chapter. Follow these steps:

1. Start a new scene and select CV Curve Tool. Draw curves in the front view as in Figure 5.26.
   To ensure that later steps will work properly, choose Create → Locator. In the Channel Box,
   translate it to (–6, 38, 0). Use the locator's position as a guide for placing the lampshade's
   first CV, and count three grid units up to place each of the remaining three CVs.

Figure 5.26

**A curve profile for the
lamp we'll create**

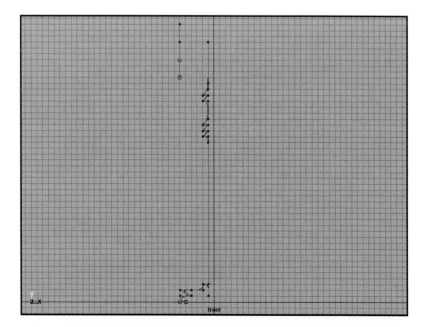

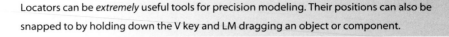

Locators can be *extremely* useful tools for precision modeling. Their positions can also be snapped to by holding down the V key and LM dragging an object or component.

2. With the curves selected, choose Surfaces → Revolve. The default setting works fine for our purpose, and we see a revolved lamp. But wait, the lamp cover seems a bit lacking in design. Let's see if we can make it look a bit more stylish, like the lamp in Figure 5.27.

3. Select the lamp cover profile curve, and choose Modify → Center Pivot. Press the Insert key to go into Move/Rotate/Scale Pivot mode. V+LM drag its pivot to the locator. Press Insert again to toggle back into regular Translate mode.

4. Select the lamp cover surface, and once again choose Modify → Center Pivot. In the Channel Box, scale it to (1, –1, 1). A curve's pivot center is crucial to how a revolved surface will appear when the profile curve is transformed after the revolve has taken place. Remember that Maya always places a curve's pivot center at 0, 0, 0 upon creation.

5. Select the lamp cover profile curve again, go to Channel Box Input, and click revolve2. Change Degree to Linear, and change Sections to 12. Go to the Channel Box and translate it (1, 2, –2), rotate it (–25, –25, –25), and scale it (1, 2, 1).

6. Put a simple sphere inside the lamp cover and deform it like a light bulb, and the model is ready for texturing. The Color Gallery on the CD-ROM shows the finished version. We can add this lamp to the living room later, so save the file as Lamp for future use.

Figure 5.27

The finished lamp

Lofting

Lofting is without a doubt the most often used function in surface creation and, hence, the most important. The Loft command creates a surface using selected curves, isoparms, or trimmed edges. The settings for Maya's Loft command are simple, and you need not change the default settings for most occasions. You can loft any combination of curves, isoparms, and even trimmed edges. One thing you must always be careful about, however, is the order of the curves you select for lofting. The first curve selected defines the U direction of the lofted surface, and since the surface is lofted in the same order the curves are selected, the way you select the curves is important. Sometimes you will encounter a situation like that illustrated on the left in Figure 5.28; if you marquee-select a group of curves and loft them, the resulting surface is not what you want. In such a case, you can either select the curves one by one in the proper order or move them in the Outliner, as we've done on the right in Figure 5.28, so that the order in which they are listed matches the order in which you want the lofting to occur.

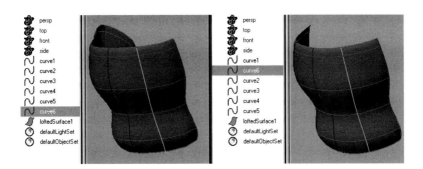

Figure 5.28

Using the Outliner, you can place curves in the correct order for lofting.

If the curves being lofted are uniform and have the same number of spans, the resulting lofted surface will retain the same uniform parameterization and the number of U spans as the curves. If the curve spans are different, you will generally end up with a surface that has many more U spans. The number of V spans of the surface will equal the number of the curves being lofted minus 1, assuming you are using the default settings.

The Loft command has an option called Section Spans, which can increase the number of spans between curves being lofted. This can be a time-saver when you want to create a surface with several sections but have only two or three curves to work with.

An excellent example to use for lofting is the torus primitive. Create a default torus, and while it's still selected, choose Edit Curves → Duplicate Surface Curves ▢, click V, and click Duplicate. Select only the torus and delete it. You are left with eight circles to loft. Select all of them, and loft with the default setting by choosing Surfaces → Loft. You end up with seven-eighths of a torus, as shown on the left in Figure 5.29. Select the surface and check the Attribute Editor. Notice that it has seven spans in V, its Form V is Open, and from the top view, its span direction for V is clockwise.

Undo with Z until you have only the curves again. This time, select the circles individually counterclockwise, and in the Loft option window, click the Close setting. Choose Surfaces → Loft again, and you should get a complete torus, as on the right in Figure 5.29. Notice that now the V span is 8, its Form V is Periodic, and its span direction for V is counterclockwise.

Extrude

The Extrude command extrudes a surface from selected curves, curves on surface, or isoparms. Extruding isn't complicated, but it can get confusing because there are so many buttons you can click in the Extrude option window.

Extruding usually involves two or more curves, curves on a surface, or even isoparms. The first curves are the Profile curves that will be extruded, and the last one is the Path curve that will

Figure 5.29

Open loft and periodic loft of a torus

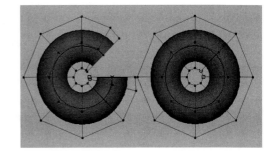

guide the extrusion. The Extrude command provides several settings that control the shape of the surface being extruded:

- The Tube setting in the option window turns the profile curve with the path.
- The Flat setting lets the profile curve maintain its own orientation as it moves along the path.
- The Distance setting requires only one curve, and it activates the Extrude Length slider. With Distance, you can determine the direction of the extrusion with either the Specify setting, in which different axis choices are listed, or the Profile normal, in which the extrusion goes along the direction of the profile curve's normal.
- The Result Position option lets you either bring the path to the profile curve, which is the At Profile setting, or take the profile to the path, which is the At Path setting.

The following example illustrates a general method that should work well as a way to create extrusions. Let's say you want to build a frame for the fireplace in the living room from Chapter 4. Start a new scene. With the EP Curve tool set to Linear, create the fireplace frame path using a construction plane as shown in Figure 5.30. Then, in the top view, create the profile curve for the frame.

Select the profile, move its center to one of the ends of the path curve, select the frame path, and choose Surfaces → Extrude with everything at the default setting. You should now have a frame shape like the one in Figure 5.31. You can adjust the shape of the surface by manipulating the curves.

Figure 5.30

The frame profile and the frame path curves

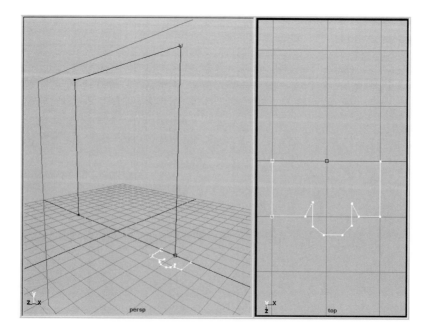

Working with Planars, Text, and Bevel

An object is *planar* if can be wholly mapped to a plane; that is, if it is a 2D object in 3D space, if it has length and width, but doesn't have depth. A true planar object, then, cannot be twisted in three directions. As soon as it is twisted, it ceases to be planar. Using a planar surface is an efficient way to create trimmed surfaces from closed curves, assuming these curves themselves are planar. Planars are especially useful when it comes to creating text in Maya; in fact, there is actually a Trim option setting for creating text, which creates planar surfaces.

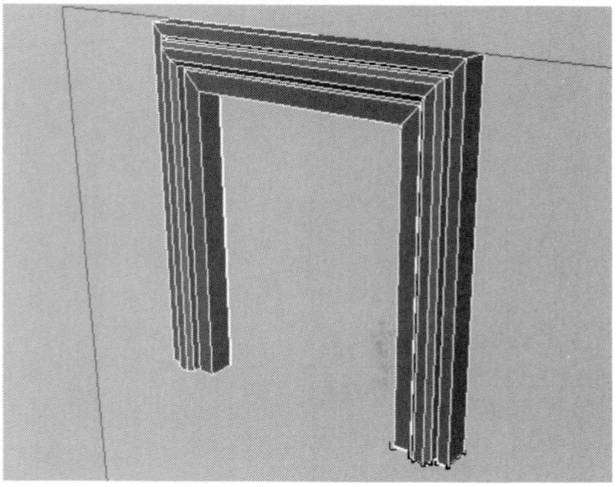

Figure 5.31

The finished frame shape

For a quick example of a planar, create a circle and apply a default planar on it by choosing Surfaces → Planar to get a trimmed surface. Pick-mask on the circle and try moving a CV up and down. The trimmed circle surface will disappear and come into existence only when the CV is perfectly on the ground plane.

To better understand planar objects, let's create a simple letter *M*. Start a new scene, choose Create → Text ❑, and type **M** in the Text field (we are being economical here). Although the Trim option is available here for creating a planar surface, we will create it another way. Leave everything at its default and click Create. A planar curve outline of the letter *M* is created. Open the Perspective window to see the planar curve letter in 3D. You should see the picture a) in Figure 5.32.

Bevel is almost the opposite of planar in that it usually creates depth in flat objects. It is a flexible and powerful function that can take a curve, an isoparm, or even a trimmed edge and create bevels, or sloping edges.

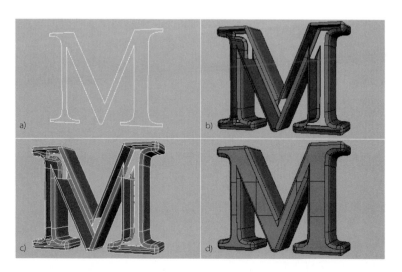

Figure 5.32

Creating the letter *M*: (a) as a planar curve; (b) with a default bevel; (c) with bevel properties adjusted; and (d) with a planar surface added

Let's bevel the planar outline of the letter *M* you created in the previous section. Select the M curve and choose Surfaces → Bevel ☐. The options here are not complicated, but they can be a bit confusing because of the orientation: Top Side bevels the back of the letter, Bottom Side bevels the front, and Both bevels front and back.

When you create text in Maya, it faces front. If you have trouble relating Top to back, Bottom to front, and Height to extrusion depth, just imagine the letters lying face down on the ground.

You can make the bevel corners Straight or Circular, and you can have the bevel edges straight, arc in (Concave) with sharp definitions, or arc out (Convex) smoothly. You can leave the Bevel Width, Depth, and Height at default settings—we'll be interactively adjusting them afterward—click Bevel, and you should the picture b) in Figure 5.32.

If you want to change the default settings for corners and edges, go to Channel Box, Input section and click bevel1 to get at those settings. Press T to activate Show Manipulator for Bevel history. You should see three blue dots connected with lines. If you don't see these, go to the Input section and click bevel1 again, and they should appear.

These blue dots are handles with which you can manipulate Bevel Width, Depth (the depth of the bevels, or the sloping edges), or Height (the depth of the actual extrusion of the text curve). Manipulate them until you are satisfied with the shape of the letter *M*; then pick-mask Isoparm and select the front edge of the bevel surface, as in the picture c) in Figure 5.32. Choose Surfaces → Planar, and you should see the front side of the *M* now covered, as in d). You can use the letter to decorate the living room later. Save the file.

Boundary

The Boundary function is most easily described when compared to lofted curves. When two curves are lofted, the result is a four-sided surface, two of whose opposing edges are defined by the curves. The other two edges are automatically calculated to be straight lines going from one curve to the other. When more than two curves are being lofted, the other two edges can become curved, but these too are interpolations between the curves being lofted. A boundary function, in contrast, enables the four sides of a surface to be created from four curves, thus giving you more control over precisely how the surface edges should be defined.

Figure 5.33

The four curves on the left define the boundary of the surface on the right.

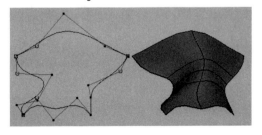

To see how boundaries work, start a new scene. Create four different curves with two or three spans each. Place them so that their ends intersect, like the curves on the left in Figure 5.33. You can select the curves in any order you want or drag-select them all together, but the first selected curve determines the *UV* parameterization of the boundary surface, because the surface *U* parameters are determined by the curve's own *U* parameters. If the *UV* direction for the boundary is important, keep that in mind when you are building the first curve.

Once the curves are selected, choose Surfaces → Boundary with the default settings. You should end up with a surface that has three or four *UV* spans, like the one on the right in Figure 5.33. Save this file; you can use the same curves for working with birails in the next section.

As shown in Figure 5.34, the Boundary function can also create surfaces with only three curves. This type of surface created with the boundary is not really a surface with three edges, but rather a surface with one zero-length edge. The selection order is significant in this case because the pinched zero-length edge (also called the *degenerate surface*) occurs between the first two curves selected. This is important when the surface patch needs to be attached to another surface patch.

Maya also provides a Square tool, which works much like Boundary in that it takes three or four curves and produces a surface patch. The way it creates tangency, however, is more complex, and Square is considered an advanced tool.

Birails are functions much like boundaries in that they work to determine the four sides of a surface. Essentially, birails extrude one or more profile curves along two rail curves, or paths. The parameters of the profile curve(s) define the *V* parameters of the birailed surface, and the two rail curves define the *U* parameters of the surface.

Let's see how birailing works. Get the curves you built for testing the boundary function. Choose Surfaces → Birail → Birail 1 Tool. (We'll look at the options a bit later.) Maya asks you to select the profile curve; select one of the curves. Now you are instructed to select the two rail curves; select the two curves adjacent to the first selected curve. The birail surface is created.

You can try this again with different selection orders and see how the surface differs in each case and how it also differs from the boundary surface. The fourth curve of the boundary is basically ignored, being replaced by the profile curve. Let's look at the other birail tools.

Click Birail 2 Tool, and again leave all the settings at their defaults. You are instructed to select two profile curves now. Select the two parallel curves, and then select the two rail curves. A birail is created. Notice how this surface looks much like the boundary surface? That is because the same four curves are used to create the surface.

For the Birail 3+ Tool, we need another curve to act as a profile curve. It would be good to build a curve with two or three spans like the other curves,

Figure 5.34

Surfaces created with the Boundary function from three curves, selected in different orders

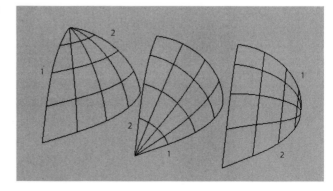

and you should make sure the newly added profile curve is touching the rail curves. You should have something like the curves shown in Figure 5.35.

The Birail 3+ tool works a bit differently—you select all the profile curves first, press Enter, and then select the two rail curves. The birailed surface appears. Birail 3+ is basically a high-level loft, with the U parameter surface edges following the rail curves, and you can control the inner areas of a surface with the Birail 3+ tool that you cannot control with Boundary or the other birail tools.

Let's look briefly at a few option settings. All three types of Birails have Non-proportional or Proportional settings under Transform Control. The Non-proportional setting modifies only the parts of the profile curve that change when it birails, whereas the Proportional setting maintains the shape of the profile curve—thus the name proportional. If the rail curves grow wider, the nonproportional setting stretches the profile only sideways, but the proportional setting enlarges the entire profile.

The Rebuild option also allows the curves for the birail to have their own rebuild options, which may in some situations give us much lighter surfaces. For the rebuild settings, see the "Rebuilding Curves" section earlier in this chapter.

Editing Surfaces

Once a surface is created, you often need to manipulate it to produce its final form. Maya's many surface-editing tools and actions generally behave in exactly the same way as their curve counterparts, which we discussed earlier; so we'll go through most of them quickly. Some others require a closer look, such as the Trim tool. We will also focus more on modeling techniques using these tools.

Figure 5.35

Three profile curves and the rail curves

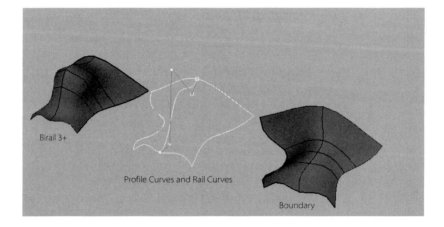

Attach and Detach Surfaces

These actions work exactly the same as their curve counterparts. With curves, you pick-mask curve points, whereas with these surface actions you pick-mask isoparms.

Start a new scene. Choose Create → NURBS Primitives → Cone. Focus in on it by pressing F, and select its isoparm about halfway up. Now choose Edit NURBS → Detach Surfaces

with the default settings. Select the top half and move it up a bit. Now, to get the results in our example, select the bottom half, and then Shift+select the top half. Choose Edit NURBS → Attach Surfaces and translate the resulting surface to the side. You should see something like picture a) in Figure 5.36. Now grab the top part of the original cone again and try transforming it in various ways while observing the effect this has on the new surface. Figure 5.36 shows more examples of the various effects produced on the new surface.

Figure 5.36

A detached cone and reattached surfaces

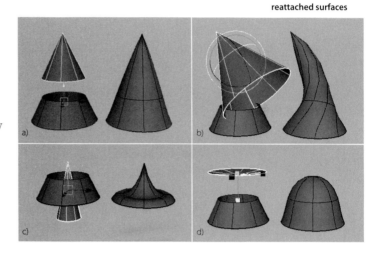

The Surface Editing Tool

The Surface Editing tool is similar to the Curve Editing tool. You'll find it by choosing Edit NURBS → Surface Editing, and like its curve counterpart, it provides a good alternative to surface modeling with CVs. You can move the editor along the surface without disturbing it

using the Manipulator positioner, and you can deform the surface by dragging the Move manipulator or using the Tangent manipulators, as shown in Figure 5.37.

Figure 5.37

The Surface Editing tool deforming a plane

Inserting Isoparms and Aligning Surfaces

The Insert Isoparms command (choose Edit NURBS → Insert Isoparms) is the surface equivalent of Insert Knots for curves. But in contrast to selecting Edit Points, selecting isoparms can be a bit tricky at times. Isoparms must be selected when the option

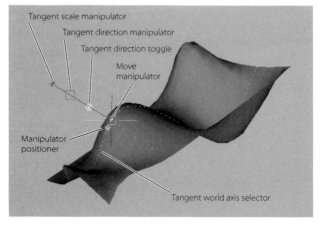

window is set for Between Selections. (Make sure you are not click-dragging, but just clicking, or you may end up highlighting an isoparametric curve between the isoparms, in which case they will be inserted as isoparms as well.)

> You can also check the Help line just below the Command line to see if what is highlighted has a neatly rounded parameter value (assuming it is a uniform surface). If it does, you have usually selected an isoparm.

Align Surfaces (choose Edit NURBS → Align Surfaces) is the surface equivalent of Align Curves. Both commands use the same option window. In most situations, simply attaching or stitching (see Chapter 8, "Organic Modeling") creates the continuity you want, but if you specifically want surface curvature continuity, use Align Surface first.

Extend and Offset Surfaces

Extend Surfaces and Offset Surfaces are both Maya 4.5 Unlimited actions. The first action extends a surface's edge(s) according to a set distance. It can either extrapolate the direction to the way the surface was curving at the edge or simply go off in a tangential direction.

Figure 5.38

You can use the torus shown here to test the effects of extending and offsetting surfaces.

To try this option, first create a torus. Go to the Inputs, click makeNurbTorus1, and set its variables as shown in Figure 5.38. You should see a quarter-formed torus. With the torus still selected, choose Edit NURBS → Extend Surfaces. Open the Attribute Editor, select the extendSurface tab, and set Extend Side to Both and Extend Direction to V.

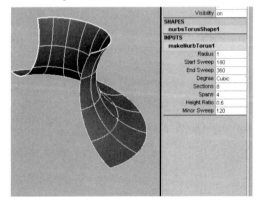

The Offset Surfaces option (choose Edit NURBS → Offset Surfaces) is the surface equivalent of Offset Curves, with simpler settings. In its option window, the Surface Fit setting calculates the distance of the offset from the surface, whereas the CV Fit setting calculates the distance of the offset from the CVs. Select the extended torus, and apply Offset Surface. Go into the Inputs window, click Distance, and then, in the modeling window, MM drag to interactively adjust the distance of the offset. A good distance is –0.2. You should see something like the picture in Figure 5.39.

> It's often better to use editing functions at default settings and then interactively change the settings by using the Attribute Editor or the Channel Box with Show Manipulator.

Offsetting can be used with lofting. Try offsetting a curve from one of the top edges, lower it a bit, and use it with the two surface-edge isoparms to create a loft between the two surfaces. Repeat for the bottom edges, and you should see something like Figure 5.40.

Trim and Round

Trimming is a way to cut surfaces into desired surface shapes using curves on surfaces (see the following section). Trimming indiscriminately can produce heavy models because it can create a lot of unnecessary isoparms, and that is always a factor to keep in mind when using the Trim functions, but at the same time, a well-applied trim can save a lot of work in producing the models you want.

Using the Project Curve On Surface Command

In order to trim a surface, you need "curves on surface" first. This is Maya's term for curves that are mapped to the UV parameters of the surface they are on, rather than to the XYZ coordinates of world space. You can project curves, curves on surface, isoparms, or trimmed edges to a designated surface and create curves on that surface. Let's look at this with an extended example.

Let's try building a spherical opening protruding from a wall. We will use projections, trimming, and filleting to do this.

1. Create a NURBS sphere, scale it uniformly to 2, and rotate it 90 degrees in X.

2. Create a NURBS circle, which should appear right inside the sphere.

3. Go to top view, select both objects, and choose Edit NURBS → Project Curve On Surface, with the default setting.

4. Go back to the Perspective window, and you should see two curves on surface on the sphere (as in the image on the left in Figure 5.41).

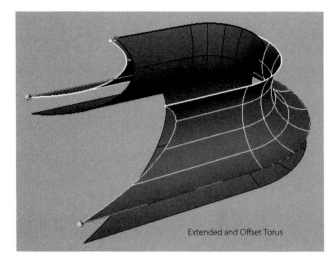

Figure 5.39

The torus extended and offset

Figure 5.40

The torus extended, offset, and lofted

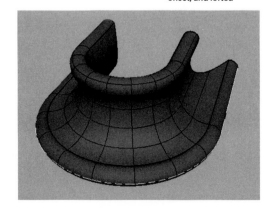

The Trim Tool

Now you're ready to try trimming:

1. Select the bottom curve on surface (you should be able to just select it like a regular object) and delete it.

2. Choose Edit NURBS → Trim Tool.

3. Select the sphere, and it should turn white. Click the middle of the sphere (do not click within the projected circle) to designate that as the part of the sphere you want to keep. Press Enter. You should see a trimmed hole as in the image on the right in Figure 5.41.

4. Select the sphere and scale it up to (3, 3, 3). Notice that the hole on sphere is keeping its size. When you move the circle, the hole follows it.

5. If you moved the circle, undo it. Select the sphere and choose Edit → Delete By Type → History to erase the procedural relationship between the circle and the trimmed hole.

Untrimming Surfaces

Oops! We made a mistake: we wanted to make a hole at the front of the sphere, not at the top—but since we deleted the history, we can't move the hole. How do we fix this situation? Curves on surface can be deleted like objects, but not trimmed edges. To untrim surfaces, choose Edit NURBS → Untrim Surfaces. You can choose to delete only the last trim or use the default setting, Untrim All. Select the sphere and apply Untrim Surfaces.

Projecting with Surface Normal

Project Curve On Surface has another option we haven't used yet—projecting based on surface normals. To try this, open the Project Curve On Surface option window. The default setting is Active View, which means the curve is projected onto the surface from the camera of whatever view is active. The other option is Surface Normal, which determines the projection of the curve by the normals projecting from the surface. Here the projection is actually done the opposite way. Delete the curve on top of the sphere that was created in the previous example. Click Surface Normal, keep the option window open, select the circle (use the Outliner since the circle is in the middle of the sphere), move it to (0, 0, 4), rotate it (–60, 0, 0), and scale it (3, 3, 7). With the circle still selected, select the sphere and click the Project button. You'll see the results shown in Figure 5.42. Notice that you see only one curve on surface created near the circle and not on the other side. That is because the normals on the other side are not seeing the circle. Trim the sphere, and delete the circle.

Curves on surface (left), trimmed sphere (right)

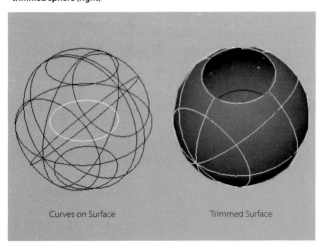

Curves on Surface   Trimmed Surface

Intersect Surfaces

As well as projecting curves and isoparms, Maya can
also create curves on surfaces when NURBS surfaces
intersect. Choosing Edit NURBS → Intersect Surfaces
with default settings creates curves on surfaces on both
intersecting surfaces. To try this tool, create a NURBS
plane, rotate it 90 degrees in X, translate it –1 in Z, and
scale it uniformly to 30. Go to its Input settings in the
Channel Box, select makeNurbPlane1, and set both
Patches U and Patches V to 5. This will be the wall.
Drag-select both the sphere and the plane, and choose
Edit NURBS → Intersect Surfaces. You should see
curves on surface on both surfaces. Select the plane
and trim out the circle. Trim the sphere as well, and
you should see something like Figure 5.43.

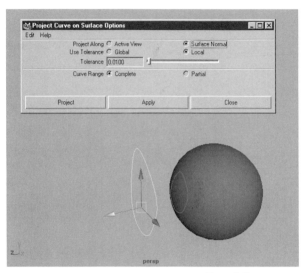

Figure 5.42

Projecting a curve
based on surface
normals

Fillet and Round

Two more Maya Unlimited features, Fillet and Round, are similar functions, but Round is
considered a more advanced tool. Let's try both, starting with Fillet. Drag-select the plane
and the sphere. Choose Edit NURBS → Surface Fillet → Circular Fillet. The default setting
works well here. In other situations, you might have to go into Input and fiddle around with
Primary or Secondary Radius to get the fillet to curve correctly. The result should look like
the upper image in Figure 5.44. The option window also has a Create Curve On Surface setting for further trimming.

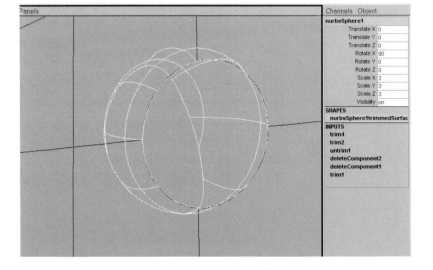

Figure 5.43

The sphere and
the trimmed wall
intersecting

Figure 5.44

**Filleting and round-
ing, and the final
opening in the wall**

Now, to try out Round, undo the Fillet action. To use Round, you must have two edges. Choose Edit NURBS → Round Tool, and select the trimmed edges. You should see the yellow Round radius manipulator indicating the fillet radius. You can interactively

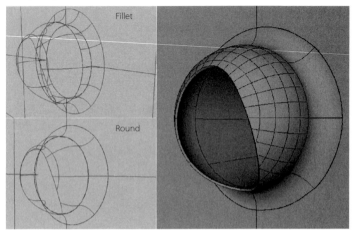

change the radius by grabbing the end handles of the manipulator. The default is 1, which is fine for this example. Press Enter, and you'll see the fillet created once again, as in the lower image in Figure 5.44. But with Round, the surfaces are also trimmed so that the fillet actually joins the trimmed edges of the surfaces. You can offset the sphere and loft the trimmed edges of the spheres to get some thickness, and you can create a tunnel into the wall, as in the picture on the right in Figure 5.44.

Trim Convert

Trim Convert is an option in Maya Unlimited for Rebuild Surfaces. It can rebuild single-region trimmed surfaces as non-trim surfaces. This means the trimmed half sphere in Figure 5.44 can be trim converted, while the wall cannot, because it has a hole inside it. Select the trimmed sphere, choose Edit NURBS → Rebuild Surfaces ❐, set the options shown in Figure 5.45, and apply. The sphere becomes a regular NURBS surface again. You can proceed to attach the sphere with the round surface if you want.

Figure 5.45

**Using the Trim Convert
option**

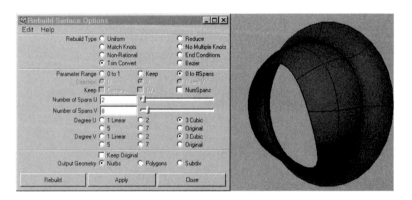

Hands On: Aftershave Bottle

Our discussion of NURBS modeling has covered a lot of ground. An extended hands-on exercise will help you see how to use these tools effectively together. Let's try building an aftershave bottle.

1. Start a new scene. Begin with Edit Points building straight lines. Make sure you are in top view, and X+click the Edit Points as shown in Figure 5.46.

2. Select two adjacent curves, and choose Edit Curves → Curve Fillet with the Trim option turned on. Do the same for the other three corners (as in Figure 5.47). If the curve fillet fails, change the curve direction of one of the curves by choosing Edit Curves → Reverse Curve Direction and try again. If the angle of intersection for the curves is too wide, Maya will also have trouble calculating the fillet.

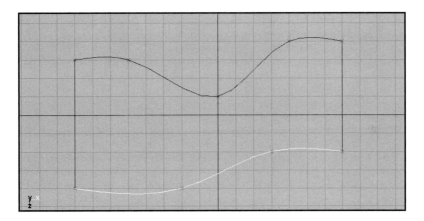

Figure 5.46

Curves in top view

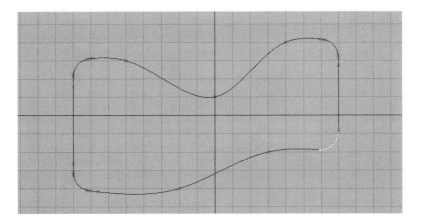

Figure 5.47

Curves filleted and attached

3. Attach the resulting eight curves (choose Edit Curves → Attach Curves) with the options set to Connect Attach Method and Remove Multiple Knots.. Rebuild the curve with the options set to Uniform and Keep CVs. The curve should now have a parameter range of 32 spans or something similar. Edit the CVs until you're satisfied with the shape.

4. Using the marking menu, get into the Persp/Outliner view. Although there is now only one curve, you will notice a lot of invisible nodes because of the construction history. Since we no longer need them, select the curve and choose Edit → Delete By Type → History.

5. Select the curve, choose Edit Curves → Offset → Offset Curve ❑, set the Offset Distance to 0.5, and reduce the Max Subdivision Density to 0. This is important in keeping the same number of curve spans for the offset. Click Offset, and check the Attribute Editor (Ctrl+A) to make sure the new curve has the same number of spans as the original curve. Translate the curve up in Y to 1. Now duplicate the curves as shown in Figure 5.48.

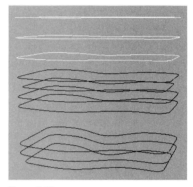

Figure 5.48

Duplicated curves

Make sure you choose Edit Reset → Settings from the Loft Options box (choose Surfaces → Loft ❑) before proceeding with the next step.

6. Select the curves (in proper order), and then choose Surfaces → Loft. Delete all the curves. Duplicate the lofted surface, and enter –1 for Scale Y in the Channel Box. Translate it up, and you should see something like image a) in Figure 5.49.

7. Pick-mask Control Vertex over the top surface, and, in the front view, translate the points down in Y and closer together. You should have something like image b) in Figure 5.49.

8. Select the edge isoparms, choose Edit NURBS → Attach Surfaces ❑, check Keep Originals, and click Attach. You now have the body of the aftershave bottle. Select the top edge isoparm of the surface, choose Edit Curves → Offset → Offset Curve ❑, set Offset Distance to –0.5, set Max Subdivision Density to 0, and click Offset. An offset curve is created as in Figure 5.50. Loft between the surface edge isoparm and the offset curve. Then select the offset curve again, and apply Surfaces → Planar with the default settings. You should have the surface's top covered as in Figure 5.50.

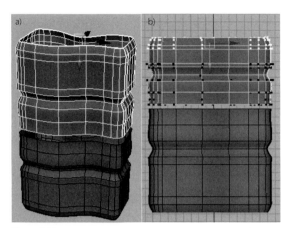

Figure 5.49

A lofted surface, (a) before and (b) after moving CVs

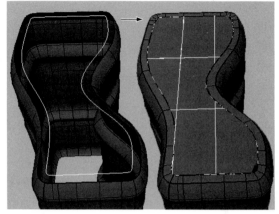

Figure 5.50

An offset curve with its top surface covered

9. Attach the lofted surfaces. Put a cylinder and a sphere at the top as the bottle cap. You might want to squash the bottom of the sphere a bit. The modeling part is done. You can find the finished version in the Color Gallery on the CD-ROM.

Hands On: Building a Character I (Advanced)

We will be creating a character in several tutorials throughout this book. There is no one standard way to create characters; the approach in this book is only one of many possibilities. In this tutorial, we will cover the NURBS part of building the character's head. Building a realistic human head used to be more difficult, but with the arrival of subdivision surfaces, that task become considerably easier.

The face we'll create appears as `face_reference.tif` in the Chapter 5 folder on the CD-ROM.

1. Start with a sphere, with 14 sections and about 16 spans. Cut out the front—the front will be the mouth, and the back will be the top of the head. Shape the sphere into a rough figure of a human head as in Figure 5.51.

> It's always a good idea to have a sketch or a picture as reference when building models, a front view and a side view.

2. Select v isoparms number 10 and 11. Choose Edit NURBS → Insert Isoparms ❏. Choose the Between Selections option with # Isoparms To Insert set to 1. Do the same for v Isoparms number 3 and 4. Select the newly created isoparms, and choose Edit NURBS → Detach Surfaces to cut the head in half down the middle. Refine the head more, pulling

out the chin and roughly sculpting the mouth. Insert isoparms where you need them, and delete rows of CVs where you do not need them. You want the following minimum number of isoparms or patches for the face as in Figure 5.52: three rows and columns of patches for the eye area, and three isoparms (or two patches) each for the mouth corner and mouth bottom. Duplicate curves from the mouth edge and loft as in Figure 5.52 to create the oral cavity. Attach the oral cavity to the face.

Figure 5.51

A rough human head—a sphere

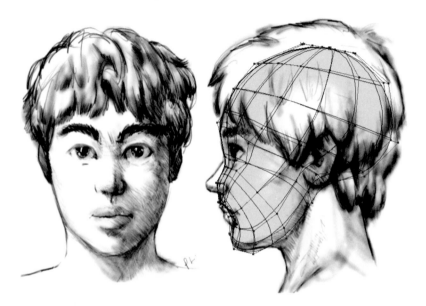

Figure 5.52

A more refined head—a half sphere

It's always better to start with a minimum number of CVs and insert more isoparms as needed, rather than starting with too many and having to delete them later. Remember, it only takes three points (isoparms) to curve a surface. This is a simple rule that is often overlooked in modeling.

3. If you want to see the other half of the face as you are modeling, duplicate the half face, and then make the scale value of the resulting surface negative along the X axis so that it becomes a mirror image of the face. Open the Connection Editor. Select the first face's shape node (select the geometry and then press the Down arrow key) and load it into the Output window. Load the second face's shape node into the Input window. Connect World Space to Create as shown in Figure 5.53. Now the second face on the right deforms when the CVs of the first face on the left are moved.

4. Pick-mask Surface Patch to select the nine patches for the eye area, and then duplicate the patch by choosing Edit NURBS → Duplicate NURBS Patches. Attach the duplicated patches so they form a single surface, and delete its history. Place a sphere where the eyeball will go, and project a curve to form an outline of the eye on the sphere as in the first picture of Figure 5.54. Duplicate several curves from the curve on surface and loft to get the eye area as in (b). Cut the new surface into four pieces, and then rebuild them in U so that they are 3 spans each, as in (c). Loft between the edges of the duplicated patch and the edges of the four cut pieces, as in (d).

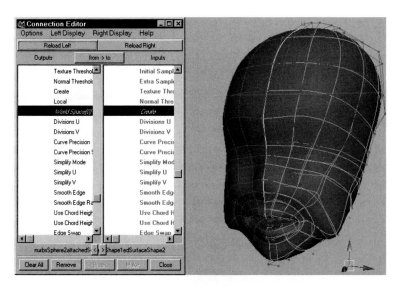

Figure 5.53

Linking two faces in the Connection Editor

Figure 5.54

Modeling the area of the eye

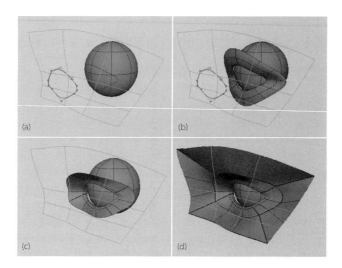

5. The NURBS part of the eye area is done. Refining the eye area, as well as the nose and the neck areas, will continue in Chapter 8. The eyes can be as simple as a plain sphere or a bit more sculpted like the one in Figure 5.55. There are two spheres, the inner one deformed for realistic pupils, and the outer one transparent and used for specularity only.

Figure 5.55

Modeling the eyeball

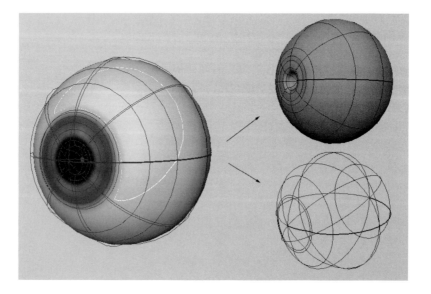

6. The method for building the ear is similar to that for building the eye area. Select the four surface patches on the head as in the first image of Figure 5.56, and then choose Edit NURBS → Duplicate NURBS Patches to duplicate the area where the ear will be attached. Place a sphere with eight spans and sections near it as in (b). Later, once converted to polygons, the eight sections of the sphere will be connected to the eight-span area of the head. Cut the sphere in half, and start sculpting it into an ear shape as seen in (c). Insert more isoparms along V as needed, but keep U sections the same number. Otherwise, you will have problems connecting the ear to the head later. Once the ear is sculpted (d), you could cut it into four pieces the way we did with the eye area and loft with the duplicated patch, but in the case of the ear, we'll keep it simple and connect it to the head as a polygon in Chapter 8.

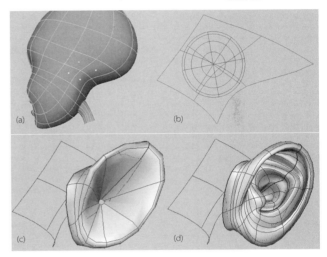

Figure 5.56

Modeling the area of the ear

The NURBS part of the modeling is done. Save the scene with all the parts. In Chapter 8, we will come back and work with polygons and subdivision surfaces to finish creating the head.

Summary

This chapter covered a lot of material. You learned to create and manipulate NURBS curves and surfaces and saw examples of building things with them. We also started an advanced tutorial on building a human face, which takes a lot of practice. The next chapter will also be quite substantial, introducing the world of polygons. Then we will come back to modeling with NURBS again in Chapter 8. We'll build a puppy dog in patches and then continue our character modeling.

CHAPTER 6

Polygons and Subdivision Surfaces

Polygons are still the preferred modeling and animation choice for many gaming companies. If you are interested in that field, you should be particularly interested in this chapter. Because subdivision surfaces are so closely related to polygons, they are presented in the latter part of this chapter as well.

We'll begin with some polygon terms and concepts, and then we'll discuss how to create and edit them. We'll then introduce subdivision surface modeling concepts and show how to work with them. The chapter ends with a pair of tutorial exercises, the first building a polygon hand and the second continuing our character modeling tutorial begun in the previous chapter.

This chapter covers the following topics:

- **Polygon faces, solids, and shells**

- **Techniques for creating and displaying polygons**

- **Polygon selection and editing tools**

- **Working with subdivision surfaces**

- **Hands On: Building a hand**

- **Hands On: Building a character II (advanced)**

Polygon Concepts and Terms

The word *polygon* is derived from a Greek word meaning "many angled." In mathematics, a polygon is defined as a closed figure formed by a finite number of coplanar segments that are not parallel and intersect exactly two other segments only at their endpoints.

As far as we are concerned, polygons are triangles, rectangles, pentagons, and other many-sided line drawings. Each endpoint is called a *vertex*, each line is called an *edge*, and the area inside is called the *face*. Figure 6.1 shows these and other terms used with polygons.

Polygon Faces

Faces have a front side and a back side, like NURBS surfaces. The basic polygon surface is the triangular face. The front side of a triangular face has only one normal vector, because triangles are, by definition, planar. Quadrangular polygons (quads) are four-sided faces and may or may not be planar. You also can create faces that have five or more sides, called *n*-sided faces, but as a general rule, polygon surfaces should be kept as triangles or quads.

A triangular face is the building block of all modeling. Every type of surface geometry is eventually converted into triangular faces (a process known as *tessellation*) before it is rendered.

Figure 6.1

The anatomy of a polygon surface

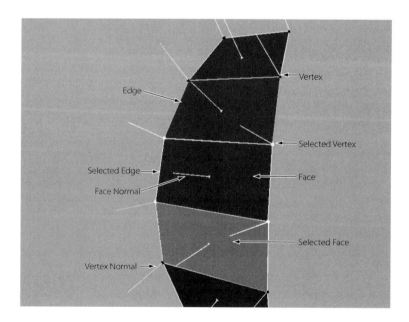

Polygon faces are usually connected (attached to each other), sharing common vertices and edges, but they can be *extracted* with their own unshared edges and vertices while still being part of the polygon surface. Unshared edges are also called *border edges*, and they cannot become *soft edges* (see the Reverse and Soften/ Harden commands in the "Editing Polygons" section). Figure 6.2 illustrates the difference between shared and unshared edges.

Polygon Solids, Shells, and UV Values

Polygons are classified as either solids or shells. A polygon *solid* is made up of connected faces that form an enclosed volume; each edge is shared by two faces. A polygon *shell* is a collection of connected faces with some edges open as border edges. A polygon object can have more than one shell, as illustrated in Figure 6.3.

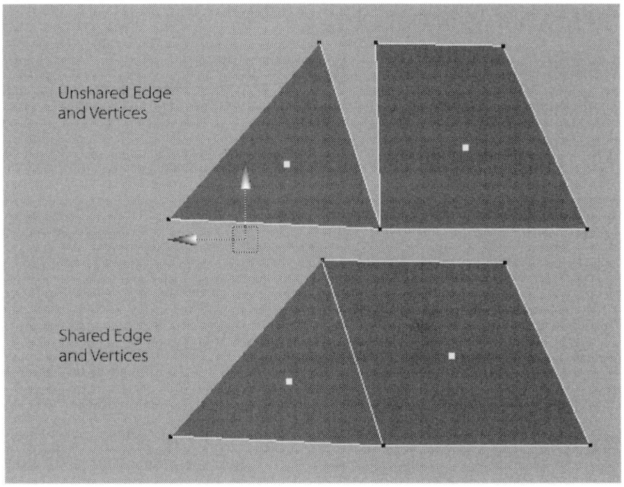

Figure 6.2

Shared and unshared edges

By default, UV values are assigned to faces when they are created. As explained in Chapter 5, "NURBS Modeling," a surface in 3D space is defined by the parameterization of the variables *U* and *V*. A UV coordinate can be given at any point inside the area, and the area is given *UV* directions. UVs are needed for texturing purposes. Polygon UVs are difficult to distinguish from the regular vertex points, but they turn bright green when they are selected. We will come back to UVs when we deal with texturing polygons in Chapter 17, "Shading and Texturing Surfaces."

Figure 6.3

A polygon solid and shells

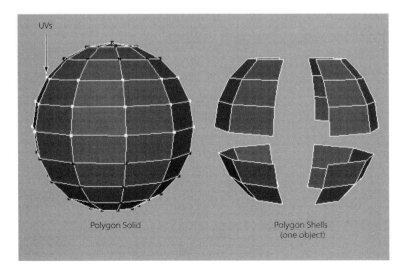

Non-manifold Surfaces

When working with polygons, you will sometimes end up creating surfaces that have an edge without a face, an edge shared by three or more faces, faces with opposite normals, or faces that are shared by a single vertex and no edge. Illustrated in Figure 6.4, these are called *non-manifold* surfaces, and they are considered poor polygon surfaces, because they can lead to some unpredictable results. Be careful not to create these topologies, and get rid of them when they do occur.

> Maya has an option in its Polygons → Cleanup command to get rid of non-manifold geometry.

Creating Polygons

You can create polygons by clicking on vertices to generate edges, much as you create curves. Two or more edges create a face, which contains face normals and vertex normals. You can also create polygon primitives or convert NURBS into polygons.

Using Polygon Primitives

As with NURBS, Maya provides several default polygon primitives you can use as starting points for creating more complex polygonal surfaces. When you choose Create → Polygon Primitives, you'll see a list of primitives much like the NURBS primitives.

Figure 6.4

Examples of non-manifold surfaces

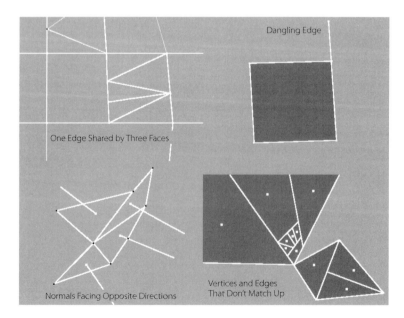

The polygon cube, cylinder, and cone surfaces are all one-piece solids, unlike their NURBS counterparts, which are made up of several pieces.

As an example, choose Create → Polygon Primitives → Sphere ❑. In the option window that appears next, the Subdivisions Around Axis attribute is equivalent to the Sections attribute of the NURBS sphere, and Subdivisions Along Height is the same as the Spans attribute of a NURBS sphere. The Texture setting, which is turned on by default, maps UV values to the sphere being created. Click Create.

You can try editing the sphere's radius and subdivision attributes in the Channel Box's Input section or in the Attribute Editor's polySphere tab. The examples in Figure 6.5 show spheres with different settings.

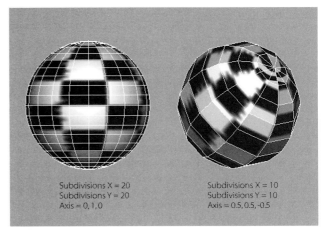

Subdivisions X = 20
Subdivisions Y = 20
Axis = 0, 1, 0

Subdivisions X = 10
Subdivisions Y = 10
Axis = 0.5, 0.5, -0.5

Figure 6.5

Two spheres created with different settings

Creating Faces

We can use Create Polygon to draw faces. Let's try a quick example:

1. In the side view, choose Polygons → Create Polygon Tool ❑.

2. Set all the options to their default values by clicking the Reset Tool button, and then change the Limit Points setting to 3.

3. Click in the modeling window in a counterclockwise direction as shown in Figure 6.6. The third click creates a triangular face.

4. Change the Limit Points setting to –1 (the default). Then click again, as shown in Figure 6.7. Press Enter after the fourth click to create a quadrangular face.

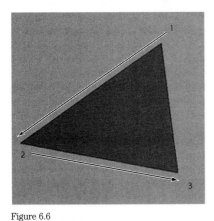

Figure 6.6

Creating a triangular face

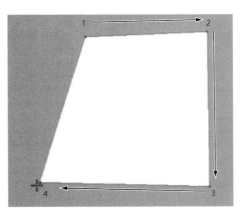

Figure 6.7

Creating a quadrangular face

> If you leave the Limit Points setting at its default of –1, you can just press Enter to complete the action after you've entered the desired number of vertices.

5. Choose Display → Custom Polygon Display ❐. Click the All button at the top of the dialog box to set the display for both faces. Check the Normals box in the Face section and the Vertices box in the Show Item Numbers section. Click Apply, click Close, and switch to perspective view. You will see that the normal directions for the faces are opposite, as well as the directions of their vertex numbers, as in Figure 6.8.

Figure 6.8

Normals in opposite directions

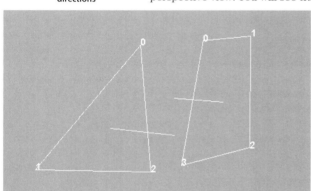

The direction in which you create vertices determines the direction of the normal: you create the front side of a face by clicking counterclockwise.

Faces that are not triangular may or may not be planar. If you want to make sure the faces you are building remain planar, you can select the Ensure Planarity option for the Create Polygon and Append To Polygon tools. This option forces the face being built to remain planar.

Adding Faces

The Append To Polygon tool is the same as the Create Polygon tool, except that it adds faces to existing faces rather than creating new ones. Let's add some faces to our triangular face:

1. Switch to side view and choose Polygons → Append To Polygon Tool.

2. Click the triangular face to select it. You can tell it's selected because the border edges appear thicker. By default, to select a face, you need to click or marquee its center. If you want to be able to select a face by clicking anywhere in it, choose Window → Settings/Preferences → Preferences, go to Settings, and in the Selection section, change the Polygon selection from Center to Whole Face.

3. Select the edge on the left side, and you will see pink arrows going clockwise around the triangular face. Also, a bright green dot appears at the zero vertex. That is where the appending begins.

4. Click two more times, as shown in Figure 6.9, and then press Enter. You now have a quadrangular face attached to the original face. Notice that the vertex numbers are 3 and 4. You can continue to add faces this way.

You can set the Append To Polygon tool to continue adding faces by setting the Limit Points option to 4. You can try this with the quadrangular face, as illustrated in Figure 6.10. The second click creates another quadrangular face, and you are still in the Append mode. You can build polygonal strips in one round of clicking this way, as illustrated. You also can create a triangular face by pressing Enter after the first vertex placement, but that will exit Append mode. Another technique, illustrated on the right in Figure 6.10, is to click one edge and then click another adjoining edge to create a face that is attached to those two faces and continue to attach the face to more edges as you go. Follow the direction of the pink arrows to create the extra faces. You can reposition a vertex while you are creating it, just as you can with curves (see Chapter 5), by MM clicking or pressing the Insert key.

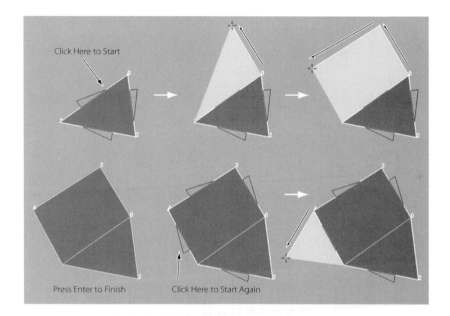

Figure 6.9

Appending faces

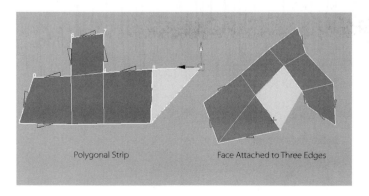

Figure 6.10

Polygonal strips and attaching faces to edges

Creating Faces with Holes

With the Create Polygon or Append To Polygon tool, you can easily create polygon faces with holes. After you position the desired number of vertices with the default tool settings, do not press Enter. Instead, press Ctrl, and then place vertices inside the surface area. With the third vertex, a hole is created inside the surface, as shown in the upper right of Figure 6.11. If you want to create another hole, Ctrl+click to start again. When you're finished placing the holes, press Enter to complete the action. You cannot apply the Split Polygon tool on a face with holes. If you want to further subdivide the region, apply Polygons → Triangulate first, as shown at the bottom left, and then clean up the object by deleting edges and/or vertices.

Converting NURBS to Polygons

Maya has an efficient NURBS-to-polygon conversion capability. The default is set to triangles and the tessellation method, with a standard fit, but you will often change the settings to suit your needs.

Choose Modify → Convert → NURBS to Polygons ❒ to open the option window. Quadrangles (quads) usually convert more cleanly than the triangles, and they make editing easier. The Count option lets you control the total number of faces of the converted surface. The Control Points option creates vertices that match the position of the NURBS CVs; you always end up with quadrangles with this option. The General option lets you control how isoparms are turned into faces. As you will see later, the Control Points and General options often offer the best conversion method. Figure 6.12 illustrates various conversion options. After the conversion, you can also edit the conversion settings in the Attribute Editor or the Channel Box.

Figure 6.11

Creating faces with holes

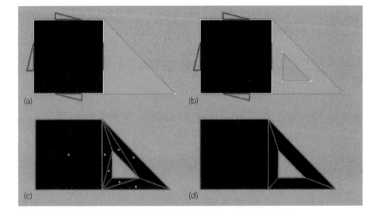

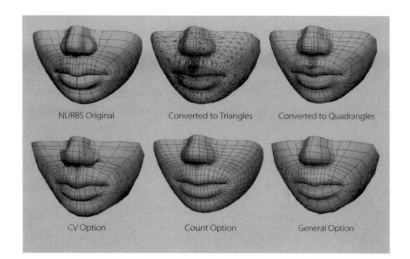

Figure 6.12

**A NURBS face con-
verted into polygons**

Editing Polygons

This section focuses on the tools for working with polygons. You have many options, ranging from moving polygon components to manually softening or hardening a polygon's edges. Maya also provides numerous ways to display polygons and select various components. As we do throughout the book, we will focus on the functions and the option settings that you are likely to use most often. Consult the Maya documentation if you need a complete list of the functions and their option settings.

Displaying Polygons

You can modify the display of polygons in several ways:

- From Display → Polygon Components, which is an easily accessible submenu

- From Display → Custom Polygon Display ❏, which provides more details and the ability to control the display of more than one polygon

- From Window → Settings/Preferences → Preferences (in the Display Polygons section), which also lets you control multiple polygons, similar to the Custom Polygon Display dialog box

- From the Attribute Editor's Shape tab (in the Mesh Component Display section), which focuses on the selected polygon

The following sections describe the display options for the polygon surfaces that are available through these dialog boxes.

Displaying Vertices

You can set vertices so that they are visible even when the polygon is not selected. Vertex normals can also be made visible. The Backface Culling option for vertices is turned on by default in the Custom Polygon Display Options dialog box (shown in Figure 6.13), but it has no effect if the Backface Culling option is set to Off.

Figure 6.13

The Custom Polygon Display Options dialog box

There are three degrees of backface culling, and they can be useful when you need to select only the front side of a surface. (The Attribute Editor and Custom Polygon Display Options dialog box have slightly different wording for these options.)

- Wire (or Keep Wire) mode blocks you from selecting vertices and faces of the back surface, while still enabling you to select edges. Wire mode displays the back faces.

- Hard (Keep Hard Edges) mode works like Wire mode, except that it doesn't display the back faces.

- Full (or On) mode does not display the back side at all, and you can't select anything at the back of the shape.

Figure 6.14 illustrates these three modes.

As mentioned in Chapter 4, "Modeling Basics," the Isolate Select tool is also a great aid in displaying only the parts of the polygon surface that you are working on.

Displaying Edges and Borders

The settings in the next area of the Custom Polygon Display Options window control how edges and borders are displayed. Edges can be displayed in three ways:

- The Standard setting displays all the edges.

- The Soft/Hard setting displays the soft edges as dotted lines.

- The Only Hard setting displays only hard edges.

Figure 6.14

The three modes of backface culling

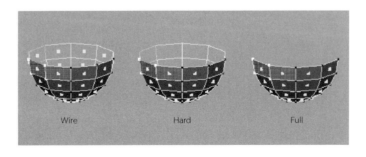

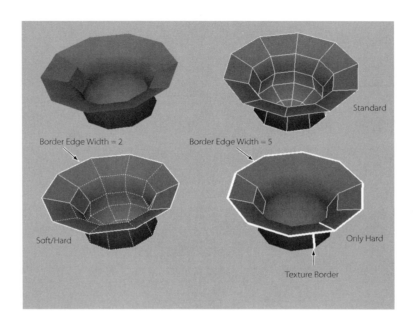

Figure 6.15

Different edge settings and border widths

Soft edges do not render as sharp edges, whereas hard edges do. For more discussion on these edges, see the "Reverse and Soften/Harden" section later in this chapter. The Border Edges setting is off by default. When you turn on this setting, you can see the border edges in thicker lines. The default width for border edges is 3, but you can increase the thickness. The dialog box also includes a Texture Borders option, which represents the starting point and end point for the texture UV placement. Figure 6.15 illustrates the effect of different display options for edges and borders.

Displaying Faces

In the Custom Polygon Display Options window, the choices for displaying faces are Centers, Normals, Triangles, and Non-planar. The Triangles option is available if the faces are not tri-

Figure 6.16

The effect of different display settings for faces

angular, and it displays the faces in triangles made up of dotted lines. (Note that the Triangles option for face display is different from the Triangulate function, which actually adds the edges to the faces. With the Triangles option, the surface itself does not change; it only *displays* triangles.) Non-planar detects any face that is non-planar. Figure 6.16 illustrates the effect of different settings for displaying faces.

You can also choose to display face normals, as well as vertex normals, and set different length lines to represent them.

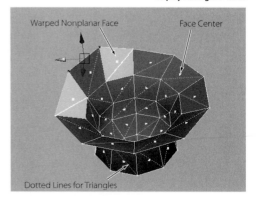

Displaying Numbers

You've seen that the order in which faces, edges, and other elements are created can affect the way Maya works with them. Using the Custom Polygon Display Options dialog box, you can display numbers representing the order of creation for vertices, edges, faces, and UVs of polygon surfaces. Figure 6.17 shows examples of item numbering for vertices, edges, and faces.

Coloring Vertices

You can color vertices in Shaded mode by checking the Color In Shaded Display option in the Custom Polygon Display Options dialog box. To apply color to vertices, select them and choose Edit Polygons → Colors → Apply Color ❐. In the option window, you can create the color you want for the vertices and then click the Apply Color button to see the result shown in Figure 6.18. (See the Color Gallery on the CD for the full effect.)

Displaying the Polygon Count

Another display function that is useful in working with polygons is Display → Heads Up Display → Poly Count. In many game productions, keeping a model's polygon count below a certain number is crucial in maintaining real-time interactivity of the game.

As illustrated in Figure 6.19, Poly Count shows the following statistics:

- The numbers in the first column show the total polygon count in vertices, edges, faces, and UVs for all the visible polygon surfaces inside the window.

- The numbers in the middle column show the numbers for visible selected polygonal objects.

- The numbers in the right column show the total polygon count for the selected components.

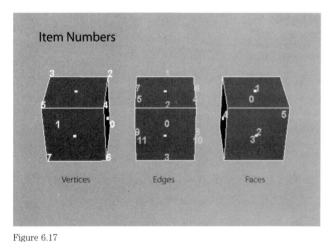

Figure 6.17

The effect of different number displays

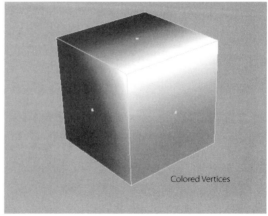

Figure 6.18

Colored vertices

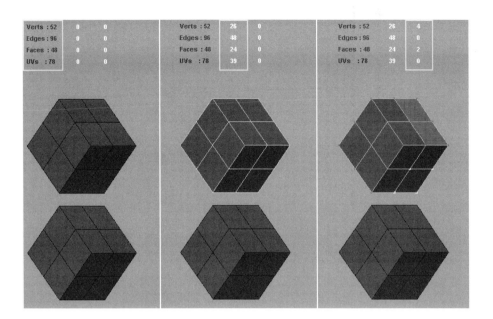

Figure 6.19

Displaying Poly Count statistics

Selecting Polygons

Before you can edit and manipulate your polygons, you need to select them. As usual, you can do so in several ways. You will most often select components using the selection mask, by RM choosing over the surface you're working on. Alternatively, you can use hotkeys and the tools on the Edit Polygons → Selection menu.

Selecting with Hotkeys

You can use the following hotkeys to select components of polygons:

F8	Toggles between object and component selection
F9	Selects vertices
F10	Selects edges
F11	Selects faces
F12	Selects UVs
Alt+F9	Selects vertices and faces

To select more than one component, select a component, pick-mask to another selection mode, and then Shift+select the other component. Figure 6.20 shows the marking menu list for the various polygon components.

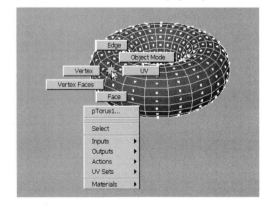

Figure 6.20

The marking menu for poly components

Using the Selection Tools

Maya also provides some tools to aid you in selecting components, as you can see in Figure 6.21. Choose Edit Polygons → Selection to display a submenu of selection tools. The Grow Selection Region function increases any selected component elements by one unit. Shrink Selection Region does the opposite. Select Selection Boundary leaves only the boundary of the selected component elements active and deselects the rest.

You can also convert any selected component element to another component type by using the Convert functions on the Selection submenu. As you can see in Figure 6.22, conversion is not cyclical—converting the selected vertices to UVs will give a larger region of UVs than the one you started with.

Constraining Selections

At the bottom of the Selection submenu is an advanced tool called Selection Constraints. Here are some examples of what you can do with this tool:

- You can constrain the selection to specific locations, such as border components or inside components.

- You can select only hard edges or only soft edges.

- You can select only triangular faces, only quads, or only faces with more than four sides.

- You can select components with a set amount of randomness.

- You can expand or shrink a selected region or select the selection's boundary.

Figure 6.21

The effect of the Grow, Shrink Region, and Select Boundary tools

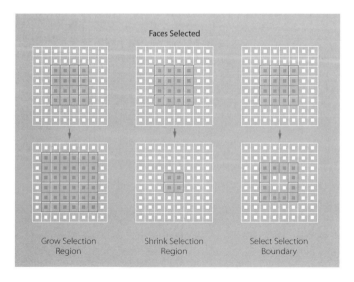

Figure 6.23 shows some examples of polygon selection constraints. You might notice that the n-sided faces look like they are quads or triangles. It's easy to confuse the two, but when you count the vertices or the edges, the selected n-sided faces have more than four. All the n-sided faces have smaller adjacent faces that divide their sides into two edges and three vertices. Another way to tell if a face is n-sided is to turn on the Triangles option in the Custom Polygon Display Options dialog box.

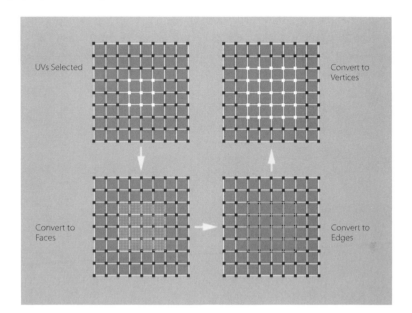

Figure 6.22

Convert Selection functions

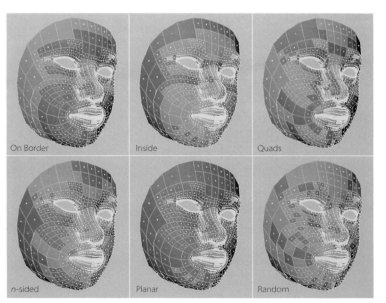

Figure 6.23

Polygon selection constraints

The contents of the Selection Constraint dialog box depend on the types of components being constrained. A good practice is to pick-mask the component you want to select and then open the dialog box. Another is to make sure to click the Constrain Nothing button before you close this dialog box.

Moving Polygon Components

You can move, rotate, and scale polygon components using the manipulator handles. Additionally, you can use the Move Component function under the Edit Polygons menu to translate, rotate, and scale the components.

The Move Component function has a local mode and global mode. You can switch between these modes by clicking the toggle handle, as shown in Figure 6.24. In local mode, the Z axis is always pointing in the direction of the surface normal.

Figure 6.24

The move manipulator in local and global modes

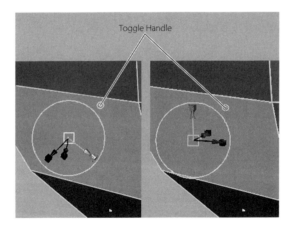

Extruding and Duplicating Faces

When working with faces, you can use the Duplicate Face and Extrude functions on the Edit Polygons menu. With both these functions, you can either keep the resulting faces together or keep them separate by toggling Polygons → Tool Options → Keep Faces Together. Figure 6.25 illustrates all four options. Notice that the duplicated faces are discontinuous from the original faces, and they become separate objects from the original polygon object. You can turn off the Separate Duplicated Faces setting in the option window, which will keep them as components of the original polygon object.

Figure 6.25

Extruding and duplicating with Keep Faces Together toggled on and off

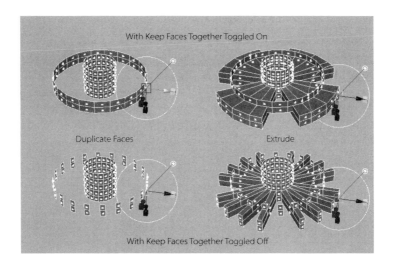

The Extrude Edge command, in the Edit Polygons menu, works the same way as Extrude Face, except that it works on edges. This command is especially useful for extending border edges, to give thickness to polygon shells. In Figure 6.26, the edge of the surface has been extruded twice and then converted to a subdivision surface.

Making and Filling Holes

You can use faces to create holes in other faces. The examples in Figure 6.27 were created by duplicating the face using Edit Polygons → Duplicate Face Options and clearing the Separate Duplicated Faces option. Then choose Edit Polygons → Make Hole Tool. Click the first face in which you want to make a hole, and then click the second face in which you want to make a hole. Next, either press Enter or click again to create the hole. Alternatively, you can produce holed surfaces by selecting Merge settings in the option window of the Make Hole tool. If you do not want to disturb the position of the original surface, set Merge to First.

Figure 6.26

Extruding an edge to give thickness to a polygon shell

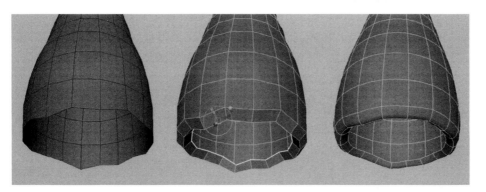

To get rid of unwanted holes in surfaces, select edges around the hole, and then choose Edit Polygons → Fill Hole. Figure 6.28 shows the result.

Performing Boolean Operations

You can perform simple Boolean operations—such as union, difference, and intersection, as illustrated in Figure 6.29—on polygons at the object level. These simple functions can aid you greatly in working with polygons. You'll find them on the Polygons → Booleans submenu. At times, two polygonal objects can intersect in a way that makes it impossible for Maya to carry out the necessary Boolean calculations. You might get an error message, or the two surfaces might disappear. In such a case, move one of the objects slightly and try again. At other times, you might need to clean up the objects first. For example, you might need to delete faces with zero area.

Figure 6.27

Different ways to make a hole

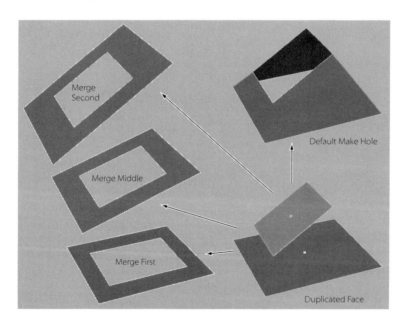

Figure 6.28

Filling the default hole created in Figure 6.27

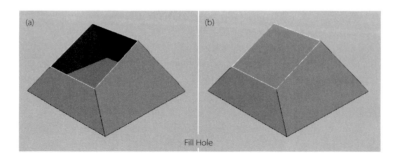

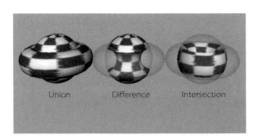

Figure 6.29

The result of three different Boolean operations

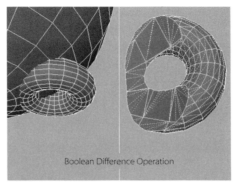

Figure 6.30

After a Boolean difference operation, this torus requires some cleanup.

After a Boolean operation, the vertices will often end up not matching well, requiring cleanup. For example, in the Difference operation, the first selected object remains, minus the intersecting part. In the operation shown in Figure 6.30, the torus ends up with a messy surface area at the intersection point, which will need to be cleaned up.

Combining, Extracting, and Separating Polygons

The Combine function on the Polygons menu is similar to the Boolean union operation, but there are differences. The Combine function takes any collection of polygonal surfaces and turns them into one object, as the Boolean union does, but as you can see in Figure 6.31, it does not trim away the unnecessary parts. You also can see that the union operation actually attaches the edges and vertices of the objects being joined together, whereas the Combine operation leaves them unshared, or extracted.

Figure 6.31

The Boolean union and the Combine operations

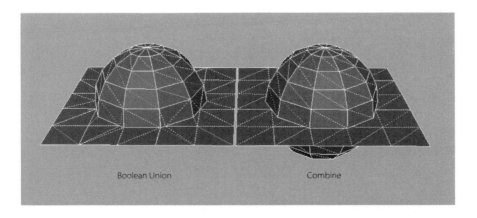

Combining polygon objects is simple, but dividing one polygon object into separate objects is a bit more involved. Before any faces of a polygon object can become separate objects, they must be extracted to become different shells.

> An object that was created through the Combine operation already has extracted pieces. Thus, you can simply apply the Edit Polygons → Separate operation to undo the Combine action; you don't need to use Extract.

The Extract function, also on the Edit Polygons menu, does exactly what it says: It extracts the selected faces from their neighbors so that the edges and vertices of the extracted faces are no longer shared. Figure 6.32 shows the result. The default setting separates any extracted faces automatically, so they become separate objects. If you want to extract faces but keep them as part of the original object, toggle off the Separate Extracted Faces setting in the Extract command option window.

In Maya 4.5, the Edit Polygons → Split Vertex option performs a function similar to the Extract command. It applies to vertices and splits each vertex into unshared vertices, also splitting adjoining edges into unshared edges, or border edges. It has as its opposite the Merge Vertices command, discussed in the next section.

Merging Vertices and Edges

Merging is the opposite of extracting. Whereas the Extract function separates vertices and edges so that they are no longer shared, the Merge function makes them shared by faces.

The Edit Polygons → Merge Vertices function merges vertices so that instead of there being several overlapping vertices at one point, only one vertex is shared by the edges, and the edges become shared edges. Often, you will not see any difference until you try moving the edges or faces, as shown in Figure 6.33. In order for Merge Vertices to have an effect, you must enter a Distance value greater than zero, even if the points you are attempting to merge are right on top of each another.

The Edit Polygons → Merge Edge Tool merges border edges. When you select the tool, the border edges become thicker. Click the first edge, and the second selectable edge turns purple. Next, click the second edge and both edges turn orange. When you click again, the two edges merge. There are three Merge mode options:

Middle The default mode, merges the first and the second edge at the halfway point

First Snaps the second edge to the first edge.

Second Snaps the first edge to the second edge

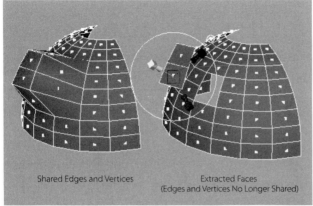

Figure 6.32

Extracting selected faces

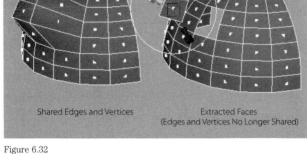

Figure 6.33

Merging vertices

After the merge, you are still in the Merge mode, and the tool asks you to select another first edge. You can keep merging this way, as in the two faces on the left in Figure 6.34, or if the edges to be merged are obvious, you can use the Merge Multiple Edges command. Select the edges near the area where the merging will occur, as in the top-right image, and then apply Edit Polygons → Merge Multiple Edges to merge all the border edges. As you can see in the face on the bottom right, this command sometimes leaves a few edges unmerged. You can merge those with the regular Merge Edge tool. If merging edges produces weird connections, undo the operation, and check the normals of the faces whose edges are being merged. If the normals are not consistent, you need to reverse some of them. (See the "Reverse and Soften/Harden" section later in this chapter.)

Figure 6.34

Merging two adjacent objects: (left) by merging individual pairs of edges and (right) by using Merge Multiple Edges

Deleting and Collapsing Polygon Components

Although deleting polygon components is straightforward, you need to keep a few in mind:

- You can delete only corner vertices, or vertices that are joined by only two edges (called *winged* vertices).

- You cannot delete border edges.

- You can always delete faces.

- When you delete edges, be sure to delete the winged vertices that often get created in the process. You will see them when you pick-mask Vertex over the surface.

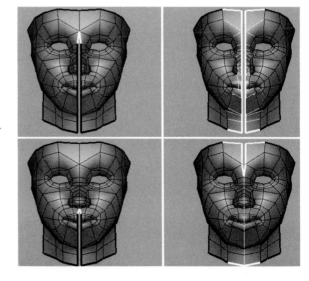

The Edit Polygons → Collapse function does not work like Delete. Instead, it let you collapse faces and edges so that the remaining vertices are shared, as illustrated in Figure 6.35.

Splitting Polygons

The Edit Polygons → Split Polygon Tool is probably one of the tools you'll use most frequently as you work with polygons. With this tool, you can divide faces into smaller pieces. (Do not confuse the Split Polygon tool with the Append To Polygon tool on the Polygons menu. The latter creates faces at the border edges of a surface, whereas the Split Polygon tool divides existing faces.)

Let's go through an extended example of modeling with a simple cube. Create a cube, and choose Edit Polygons → Split Polygon Tool. The mouse cursor changes into an arrow. Click one of the top edges, and a bright green dot appears, representing a vertex. Click the other edges as in Figure 6.36, and make the last click on the first green dot to complete a triangle of edges. Notice that you can move the last dot along the top edge. Press Enter to complete the action. Select the three corner edges in front and delete them, and you will end up with the corner of the cube chopped off.

Now what if you want to repeat the process on another corner of the cube, but this time make the split polygon put vertices exactly at one-third the length of each edge? Maya doesn't provide us with such an option (yet) with the Split Polygon tool, but it can subdivide the edges to help us.

Choosing Edit Polygons → Subdivide automatically and evenly divides an edge or a face into equal parts. The default setting is Subdivision 1, which divides an edge into two edges or divides a face into four quads or triangles. If you want to refine a rough polygon shape, subdividing provides a quick way to gain more control points. (Don't confuse Subdivide with Subdivision Surfaces, discussed later in this chapter.)

Figure 6.35

The difference between deleting and collapsing components

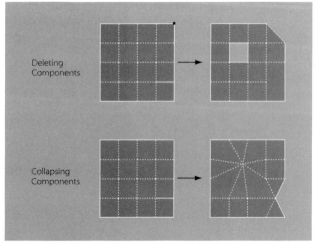

Deleting Components

Collapsing Components

To try the Subdivide option, select the three edges on a different corner of the cube, choose Edit Polygons → Subdivide, choose Subdivision Levels 2, and click Subdivide. Pick-mask Vertex, and you should see two extra vertices placed evenly apart on each of the three edges, as in the second image in Figure 6.37. Now you can proceed with Split Polygon, and then by deleting the corner edges, cut another corner of the cube. When you want to place a vertex at the end of an edge, don't click the endpoints of that edge. You may select the wrong edge that way. Instead, click the middle of the edge you want and drag to the endpoint.

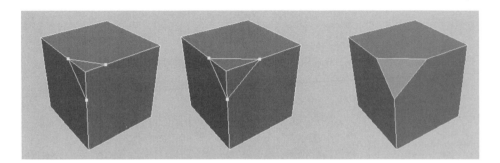

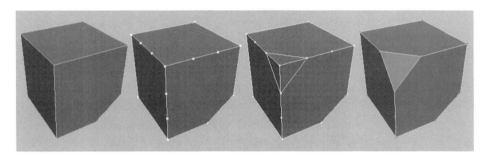

When we look at the cube now, we see that it has triangles, quadrangles, and n-sided faces. We can delete the winged vertices easily, and to make the cube "clean," we can split the triangles and n-sided faces further into quadrangles. First subdivide the triangle faces, as seen on the left in Figure 6.38, and then split polygons to turn all the faces of the cube into quadrangles, as shown on the right.

> To make sure different splitting polygon edges intersect each other correctly in the middle of a face, set to 2 the Subdivision setting in the Split Polygon tool option window for the first split polygon going across the face. This creates an extra vertex right in the middle.

Smoothing Polygons, Averaging Vertices, and Beveling Edges

Smoothing is a simple but indispensable function that you will use over and over again with polygons. The Smooth tool on the Polygons menu subdivides a surface or selected faces of a surface according to the Division setting in the option window (the default setting is 1) to create as smooth a surface as its Division setting will allow. Unlike the Subdivide command, the Smooth tool actually moves the vertices to make the faces appear smoother (see Figure 6.39). It always produces quads, and you should generally leave the Subdivision setting at the default. If

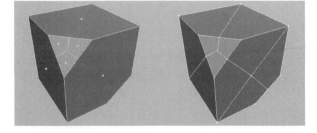

you are going to apply Smooth more than once, you will usually want to tweak the surface before applying it again. We will see Smooth in action in the hand tutorial later in this chapter.

Choosing Polygons → Average Vertices smoothes a surface without subdividing the faces into smaller pieces. It keeps the same surface topology and essentially produces the same result as the Sculpt polygon tool does in Artisan's smooth operation. It can be used with the Transfer command to produce clean UVs on complex models (see Chapter 17). In Figure 6.40, the middle face has Average Vertices applied once, and the right face has it applied five times.

Choosing Edit Polygons → Bevel lets you easily smooth sharp corners and edges. In Figure 6.41, a simple cube's corner edges were selected, and then Bevel was applied. The middle cube's bevel has its Segment option set to 4. This produces an n-sided face, which you can clean up into quadrangles, as in the third cube.

Figure 6.39

Using the Smooth tool

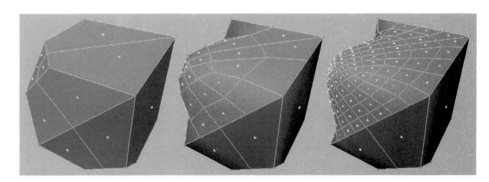

Figure 6.40

Using the Average Vertices option

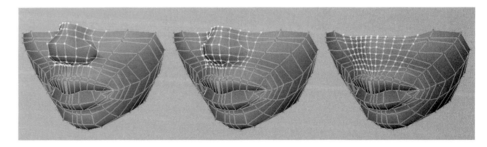

Figure 6.41

A cube, beveled and rounded

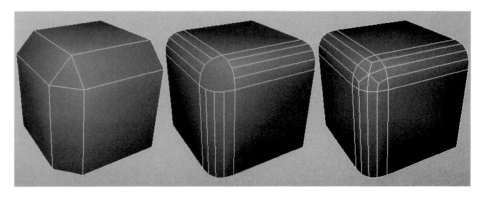

Mirroring Geometry

One more polygon modeling tool needs to be introduced: Polygons → Mirror Geometry. It's like copying the left half of the face in Figure 6.42, scaling it to –1, putting it on the other side, and then merging all the border edges, all in one step. But it's better than that, because mirroring also takes care of the normal flipping, keeping the copied side's normals the same as the original side. Mirroring makes it easy for you to concentrate on modeling just one side of a human face and then to see quickly how it will look as a whole face. (Looking carefully at the face on the right, you'll see a slight gap in the upper lip. Mirroring doesn't always do a perfect job.)

Reverse and Soften/Harden

Finally, normals play a significant role in editing polygons in Maya. A surface needs all its normals on the same side. When you're working with various polygonal objects, separating and attaching them, you may find that normals on some of the faces have become inconsistent. This can cause problems such as the border edges not merging properly or textures being mapped incorrectly. The Reverse function, found on the Edit Polygons → Normals submenu, reverses the front and back sides of the selected faces, reversing their normal direction as well. The Reverse And Propagate option not only reverses the normals of a selected face, it also "propagates" to other faces, reversing their normals as if they are facing the same side of the surface as the first selected face.

Soften/Harden, another function found on the Normals submenu, can manually determine if a polygon's edge is to be hard (edgy and sharp) or soft (smooth and rounded). Let's try out this tool:

1. Create a polygon sphere and set its subdivisions to 10.
2. Choose Display → Custom Polygon Display □. In the dialog box, turn on both Vertices Normals and Face Normals.

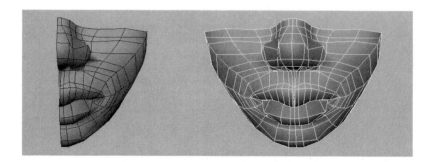

Figure 6.42

Mirroring to create a face

3. Zoom in to look closely at the vertices of the sphere in Shaded mode. You should see normals, as shown in Figure 6.43.

4. It may appear messy, but if you look carefully, you can see that each vertex has four normals coming out of it, with each normal parallel to its corresponding face normal. Pick-mask Edge and select the upper half of the sphere.

5. With the upper sphere's edges selected, choose Edit Polygons → Normals → Soften/Harden ☐.

6. Click the All Soft (180) button, and then click the Soft/Hard button. Each vertex on the upper half of the sphere now has only one normal coming out, which is not parallel to any of its face normals, as shown in Figure 6.44. The other vertex normals are not shown because the edges are now soft edges. Notice that the upper half of the sphere is rendered smoothly.

7. Open the Attribute Editor for the sphere and go to the polySoftEdge1 tab.

8. Open the Poly Soft Edge History. You'll see the Angle slider set at 180. Try moving the Angle slider down. From about 35 degrees and lower, you should see the deleted vertex normals popping back in and the edges becoming hard edges again.

Subdivision Surface Modeling

The Catmul-Clark's B-spline subdivision surface scheme was first introduced as a geometric modeling technique more than 20 years ago, but only recently has the technology for using subdivision surfaces been developed enough for use in commercial computer animation software such as Maya Unlimited.

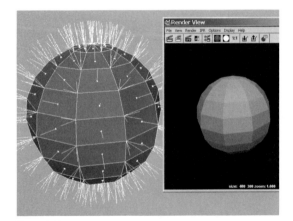

Figure 6.43

A hard-edged sphere and its rendered picture

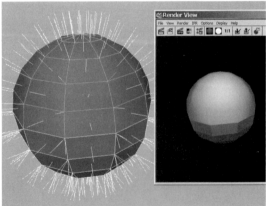

Figure 6.44

A soft-edged sphere and its rendered picture

You can use subdivision surfaces not only for modeling, but also for texturing, animation, and rendering, making it a real alternative to using NURBS or polygons. Subdivision surfaces are useful for the following reasons:

- They can exist on arbitrary topology, such as polygon surfaces, bypassing the difficulty of creating a form in four-sided patches.

- They are smooth and continuous, like NURBS surfaces. They do not have the problem of creating a faceted look, as polygons do.

- They allow a hierarchy of as many as 13 levels of detail, which allows isolated areas of highly detailed modeling and allows binding at the base levels.

Creating Subdivision Surfaces

Maya 4.5 Unlimited now has Subdivision Surface primitives, which are located in the Create → Subdiv Primitives submenu. However, to better understand them and their full potential, we will be creating them from polygon and NURBS surfaces. To convert a polygon surface to a subdivision surface, select the polygon object and choose Modify → Convert → Polygons To Subdiv. To convert a NURBS object to a subdivision surface, choose Modify → Convert → NURBS To Subdiv. When you convert NURBS to subdivision surfaces, the conversion doesn't recognize trimmed areas, and it treats chord-length surfaces as if they were uniform surfaces. Converting NURBS directly to subdivision surfaces produces the same result as first converting the NURBS surface to polygons using the NURBS To Polygon command with the Control Points tessellation method, and then converting to subdivision surfaces, as in Figure 6.45.

Conversion from polygon to subdivision surface requires that the polygon surface meet the following conditions:

- The surface cannot have nonmanifold topology, such as three or more faces sharing an edge, or faces sharing a vertex but no edge.

Figure 6.45

Two ways of creating subdivision surfaces

- There can't be any winged vertices.

- No adjacent faces can have opposite normals.

In addition to these requirements, the following guidelines that will help you produce good and efficient subdivision surfaces:

The polygon or NURBS surface should be light.
Using subdivision surfaces makes the most sense when the surface being converted is simple. The subdivision surface smoothness contrasts with the polygon edges. If the polygon is heavy, it may appear smooth already, so there is less reason for using subdivision surfaces. Because subdivision surfaces are

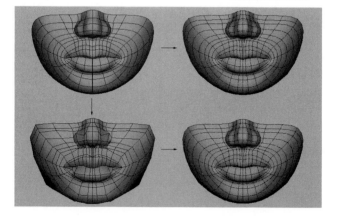

Figure 6.46

Converting a simple
polygonal object to
subdivision surfaces is
much more efficient
than converting a com-
plex object that already
appears smooth.

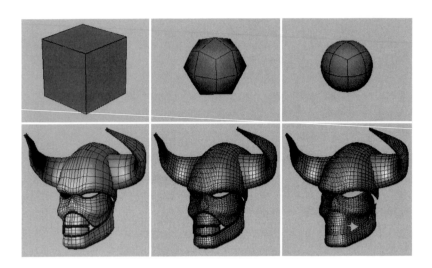

Figure 6.46

Converting a simple
polygonal object to
subdivision surfaces is
much more efficient
than converting a com-
plex object that already
appears smooth.

heavier to move and render than a smoothed polygon with the same topology, using them is preferred if the polygon looks smooth enough. In Figure 6.46, the smoothed cube (top center) still looks faceted, as opposed to the subdivision surface (top right), but the monster, when smoothed (bottom center), looks very smooth with no noticeable difference in the subdivision surface (bottom right). You might want to use the smoothed polygon in such a case, and not the subdivision surface.

Figure 6.47

Extraordinary points
resulting from triangle
and five-sided faces,
and the corrected
subdivision surface

The polygon should be quadrangles. With NURBS conversion, the resulting subdivision surfaces are clean, because NURBS are by definition four-sided. Converting nonquadrangular faces of polygons, however, creates what are called *extraordinary points*–points connected by less than or more than four edges, as seen in the pictures in Figure 6.47. Notice that the

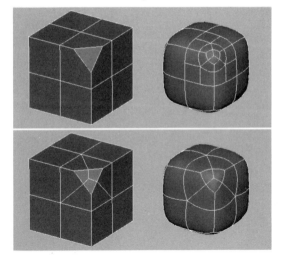

triangle and the five-sided faces on the cube produce subdivision surface points connected by either three or five points. These points make the subdivision surface unnecessarily heavy and could make the area appear bumpy. The cube at the bottom left in Figure 6.41 is heavier than the one at the top left because it has more edges, but the resulting subdivision surface is actually lighter, because the extra edges have changed the triangle and the five-sided faces into quadrangles.

As with NURBS and polygons, whether to use subdivision surfaces depends on the model you want to build. Subdivision surfaces are ideal for creating organic models. When dealing with sharp, rigid edges, polygons would still be more efficient, because they are lighter and come with edges already. If you want to create perfectly circular objects, such as mechanical parts, again, you might want to use NURBS. The sphere on the left in Figure 6.48 is a subdivision surface created from a cube, and a circle is surrounding it. The right sphere is a default NURBS sphere, also surrounded by a circle. If you look carefully, you will notice that the subdivision surface sphere is not perfectly circular.

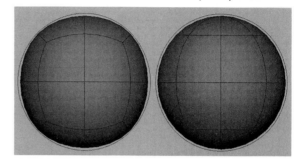

Figure 6.48

Unlike the NURBS sphere on the right, the subdivision surface sphere on the left is not perfectly circular.

Working with Subdivision Surfaces

You can refine and edit subdivision surfaces in many ways. You can work in Standard (hierarchical) mode or Polygon Proxy mode, transforming components of subdivision surfaces such as points, edges, and faces the same way you would with polygons. You can add detail in isolated areas or collapse levels of detail, create creases, mirror or attach surfaces, or convert them back to polygons.

Standard Mode

This is the default mode for subdivision surfaces. To try it, create a simple sphere out of a polygon cube (create a polygon cube and then convert it to a subdivision surface by choosing Modify → Convert → Polygons to Subdiv), and then RM click it to show the pick mask menu. As with polygons, the components displayed depend on what you select, as illustrated in Figure 6.49. You can travel the different levels of hierarchy with the Finer and the Coarser commands. A newly created subdivision surface has only two levels: level 0, called the base mesh, and level 1.

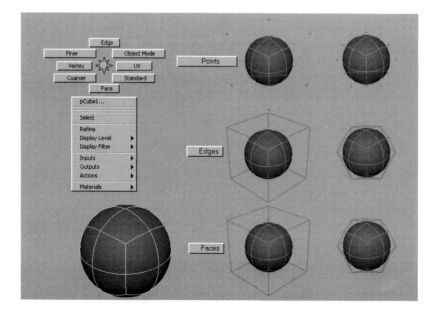

Figure 6.49

The pick mask menu for a subdivision surface sphere

Figure 6.50

Working with hierarchy levels

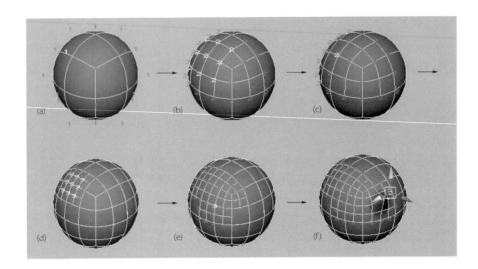

Pick-mask Point to display points, and then pick-mask Finer to travel to the level 1 display of points. Select a point as shown in Figure 6.50 step (a), and pick-mask Refine. That point becomes an area of nine points (b). Repeat the process again to show level 3 points. Select a point at the end, as in (d), and choose Subdiv Surfaces → Expand Selected Components. Notice that level 3 points expand to cover more areas (e). Select another level 3 point at the end and move it out, as in (f), and the same number expansion happens again.

Once the point is pulled out, the sphere retains this as level 3 edited point information. If you go into the Polygon Proxy mode and come back to Standard mode, you can pick-mask Point again and go back to level 3 to where you left off. You will only see level 3 points in the area affected by the edited point. You can toggle Show Edited/Show All to see more precisely which are the edited points. If no points were edited, when you go into Polygon Proxy mode and come back, the sphere will show only levels 0 and 1 again because no change in any of the levels was recorded.

> On rare occasions, switching to Polygon Proxy mode will delete the edited point information of levels 1 and higher. This should not happen; but if it does, undo, save the file, exit Maya, and start again. The edited points should now stay edited when you switch.

You can edit points up to 13 levels of hierarchy, but you usually don't want to go anywhere above level 2 or 3, because the hierarchical connection can significantly slow down the system. As you will see later in our tutorials, there is also an argument to be made for not tweaking anything—even in level 1.

One thing you cannot do in Standard mode is delete any points, edges, or faces or change the underlying topology of the surface. In level 1 or higher, if you select some edited points, edges, or faces and "delete" them, the edit information disappears, and they move back to their original unedited positions. If you move a point in the base level, however, that tweak is permanent and will only disappear with an undo. If you want to delete points or change the underlying structure of a subdivision surface, you need to switch to the Polygon Proxy mode.

> If you switch to Polygon Proxy mode when you are in a high level of hierarchy and no points have been edited, you might not be able to display any points, edges, or faces when you come back to Standard mode. In such a case, select the surface, go to the Shapes section of the Channel Box, and switch the Display Level to 0 or 1. This should make things display properly again.

Polygon Proxy Mode

Polygon Proxy mode allows you to edit a subdivision surface as if it were a polygon. To switch into Polygon Proxy mode, RM over a subdivision surface and pick-mask Polygon. This creates a polygon that matches the base-level control mesh of the subdivision surface, with its edges displayed surrounding the surface. The polygon is procedurally connected to the subdivision surface, so whatever changes you make to the polygon also occur on the subdivision surface. This lets you edit the surface just as if it were a polygon object by editing the polygon "proxy": deleting points, edges, faces and appending or splitting polygons. You can perform almost any polygon operation on the subdivision surface when you are in this mode.

You can switch back and forth between Polygon Proxy mode and Standard mode at any time by toggling the pick mask Standard and Polygon. Every time you switch from Polygon Proxy mode back into the Standard mode, you delete all the history that accumulates with polygon operations. Frequent switching back to Standard mode is actually recommended, because it "bakes" the polygon operations and makes the changes a permanent part of the subdivision surface.

For example, in the simple subdivision surface in the cube on the left in Figure 6.51, you cannot create a hole on one side in Standard mode. Switch to Polygon Proxy mode, extrude twice, and then delete the extruded face. The result is as you see in the third image. To make this topological change more stable and permanent, switch back to Standard mode, deleting the history of the polygon operations in so doing.

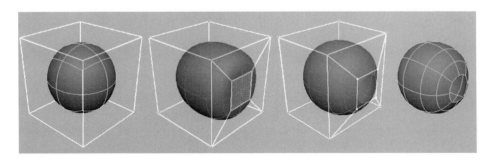

Figure 6.51

Working in Standard and Polygon Proxy modes

Because the Polygon Proxy mode can change the topology of the subdivision surface under it, edited points under or near a change may disappear or produce unpredictable changes. Try to make all the changes having to do with the topology of the surface before you start editing in the higher levels of the Standard mode.

If you are not changing the topology of the subdivision surface but only transforming the base points, edges, or faces, work in Standard mode rather than in Polygon Proxy mode. Standard mode is the more direct and efficient method.

Displaying Subdivision Surfaces

The Display menu has Subdiv Surface Components and Subdiv Surface Smoothness submenus for working with subdivision surfaces. The Components submenu lets you display subdivision points, edges, faces, and normals. When you are pulling points of a subdivision surface, you will find it helps a great deal if you can see the edges displayed.

The smoothness of the subdivision surface display can be changed in the same way as NURBS: 1 for Rough, 2 for Medium, and 3 for Fine display, as in Figure 6.52. When set to Fine, subdivision surfaces display extra faces, which are for display purposes only. The Smoothness submenu also contains the Hull setting, which displays subdivision surfaces like polygons. This can increase the interactivity quite a bit when working with heavy subdivision surface models.

You can also use the window panel's Show → Isolate Select → View Selected command with subdivision surface faces. When you are in the Polygon Proxy mode and you use View Selected, only the selected polygon faces stay visible, and the subdivision surface is not displayed.

Figure 6.52

Display smoothness settings

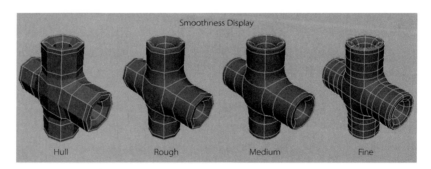

Extract Vertices and Tessellate

Rather than switching to Polygon Proxy mode, you might want to actually convert subdivision surfaces to polygons. To do so, choose Modify → Convert → Subdiv To Polygons ❑. Using the default Adaptive tessellation method converts each face of the subdivision surface to a polygon face, as in the left picture in Figure 6.53. The Vertices option, on the other hand, converts the surface's mesh points to the polygon vertices. The default setting converts the base level points to vertices, as in the picture on the right in Figure 6.53. The middle picture shows Extract Vertices with the level 1 option setting. Notice that although the resulting shape is similar to that of the tessellated polygon, the shape is a bit bigger.

The Vertices option with the default level 0 conversion setting is especially useful, because it converts a subdivision surface to polygons the same way as switching it to Polygon Proxy mode. This means that whatever editing you want to do in Polygon Proxy mode, you can also do with the converted polygon and then reconvert it back to the same subdivision surface again. The advantage of doing this is that the polygon surface is much lighter as a standalone than when it is in Polygon Proxy mode. This makes it more efficient to work with, particularly for doing texture work, as you will see in the later chapters. The limitation of such a process is that Extract Vertices destroys higher-level edit information. Any detail work done in level 1 and higher will be lost in the conversion.

> When a polygon has been extracted from a subdivision surface, it carries an invisible poly-SurfaceShape node, which can cause problems with commands such as Polygons → Mirror Geometry. If you need to issue such a command, select the polygon, go to Hypergraph and turn on Invisible Nodes display (or go into Up And Down Stream Connections mode), and then delete the invisible node.

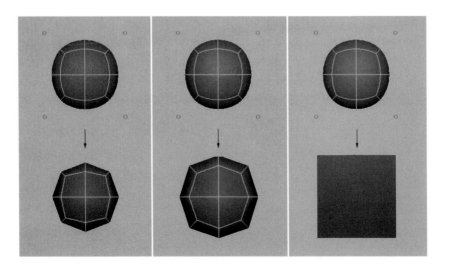

Figure 6.53

The effect of the Extract Vertices and Tessellate commands

Creasing Edges and Vertices

In Standard mode, you can create creases with edges or vertices, or you can uncrease existing creases. In Figure 6.54, we selected four edges, applied Partial Crease Edge/Vertex twice on the third shape, and applied Full Crease Edge/Vertex on the fourth shape. Partial creasing creates soft edges, whereas full creasing creates sharp edges. To uncrease the edges, select them and apply the Uncrease Edge/Vertex command. The crease information behaves similarly to higher-level edit points. The information is kept when the surface switches to the Polygon Proxy mode, but it is deleted when the surface is converted to polygon via Tessellation or Extract Vertices.

Mirror and Attach

A common technique for modeling is to build only one side of a model and then duplicate it and scale it to –1 on the necessary axis, thus creating a mirror image of the model. For subdivision surfaces, you use the Subdiv Surfaces → Mirror command instead. If you use the duplicate and negative scale technique, the results will disappoint you. You should be in Standard mode when using this command.

Once a subdivision surface has been mirrored as in Figure 6.55, you can choose Subdiv Surfaces → Attach to complete the process. Again, you need to stay in Standard mode in order to attach. Note that the crease and edit information carries over into the mirror and attach actions.

Figure 6.54

Partial and full creasing

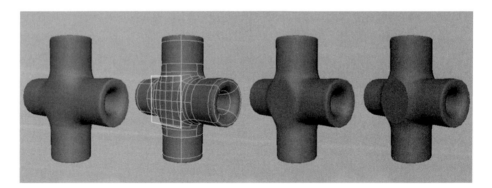

Figure 6.55

Mirroring and attaching

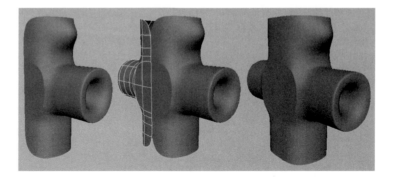

Remember that you can always switch to Polygon Proxy mode and edit subdivision surfaces like polygons. If attaching does not completely attach all the edges, you can use the Edit Polygons → Merge Edge tool in the Polygon Proxy mode to complete the attachment.

Hands On: Building a Hand

It's time to practice using the tools and actions we've covered in this chapter by building a polygon hand. Hands are usually built as polygons because it's difficult to build a NURBS hand that is not heavy and at the same time deforms well.

Building the Rough Hand

We begin by building the rough hand, starting with a poly cube.

1. Start a new scene. Create a poly cube. Select a face on the X axis and extrude it three times. Scale it until you see something like the image in Figure 6.56. Delete the faces at the back side.

2. Choose Polygons → Tool Options and turn off Keep Faces Together. Select the four front faces and extrude them three times, as shown in Figure 6.57. These will be the fingers. As you are extruding, scale the faces down a bit each time to taper them. At every point, tweak the vertices to try to form a rough hand shape. For example, try to roughly round the wrist area at the back.

Turn on the Backface Culling option's Keep Wire setting. This will help you avoid accidentally selecting vertices or faces at the back side of the hand.

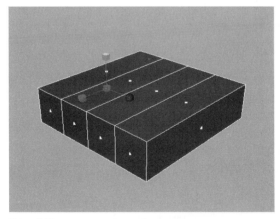

Figure 6.56

A poly cube, extruded and scaled

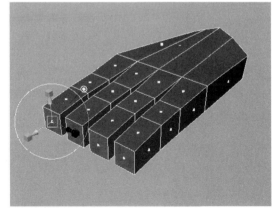

Figure 6.57

Fingers extruded and tapered

3. Push back the pinky finger, pulling it away from the ring finger to the side, and pull the middle finger out a bit. You can select faces to do this; however, in this situation, moving vertices seems to work best. Push up the two vertices where the knuckles should be.

Creating the Thumb

Building the thumb is one of the trickiest things you'll do in this tutorial. We'll use the Split Polygon tool to create the shape.

1. On the negative x side of the hand, draw two edges using the Edit Polygons → Split Polygon Tool. Next, at the bottom (the palm of the hand), draw four more edges. Pull out the vertex at the side and the one at the bottom beside it, and then pull them down. Select the face that sticks out with the vertices, and extrude it twice, turning and scaling it as you do. (See Figure 6.58 for guidance.) This is going to be the thumb. Save the file as hand_one.

2. Add two lines of edges going around the hand using the Split Polygon tool. Use the tool to place extra faces around where the thumb bends into the hand, and move the triangular face farther into the palm.

3. For the wrist, select the border edges, apply Edit Polygons → Fill Hole to create an n-sided face, select it, and then extrude the face at the back, as shown in Figure 6.59. After you extrude it, delete the face again.

Keep the faces you are creating limited to quads and triangles. They should also run smoothly along set lines and not be placed haphazardly.

Figure 6.58

Faces added, and thumb extruded

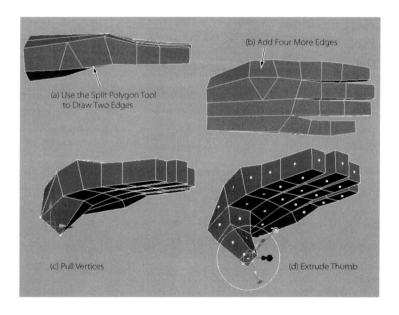

(a) Use the Split Polygon Tool to Draw Two Edges

(b) Add Four More Edges

(c) Pull Vertices

(d) Extrude Thumb

4. Scale out the hand to make it wider. Bend the thumb into the palm at an angle, as shown in Figure 6.60.

5. A lot of history has accumulated on the hand by now. Delete the history from the object and save the scene as hand_two.

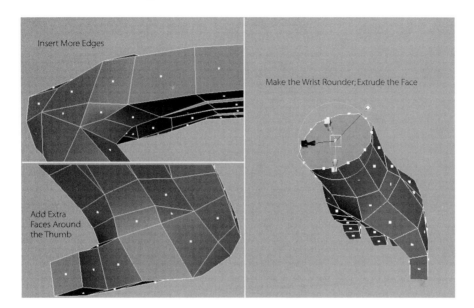

Figure 6.59

Extra faces for the thumb and wrist extrusion

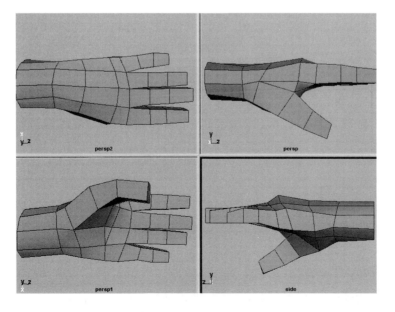

Figure 6.60

Views of the rough hand

Creating a Procedural Connection

The rough hand is now ready for smoothing. Once smoothing is applied, however, the hand becomes more difficult to shape because there are many more vertices to deal with. To make things easier, we'll use the rough hand as a lattice around the smoothed hand.

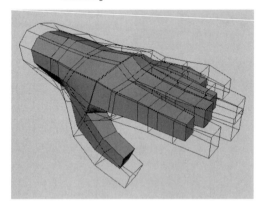

Figure 6.61

Preparing the hand for smoothing

1. Make a copy of the hand and scale it up a bit. We'll call this the rough hand and call the original one the smooth hand (it isn't yet, but it soon will be).

2. Using Hypershade, assign a material to the rough hand, and make it totally transparent. In the Shaded mode, the rough hand should still display as a wireframe, as in Figure 6.61.

3. Choose Window → General Editors → Connection Editor. Select the rough hand, press the Down arrow key to select its Shape node, and load it to the Outputs window by clicking the Reload Left button. Load the smooth hand's Shape node to the Inputs window the same way.

4. Scroll down in the left window until you find Out Mesh and select it. Scroll down in the right window until you find In Mesh and select it. Both attributes become italicized, and World Mesh becomes World Mesh[0], as shown in Figure 6.62. When you select the rough hand, the smooth hand turns pink to show that the hands are procedurally connected.

5. Select and move some vertices on the rough hand, and the smooth hand should deform along with the rough hand. Note that you can also move the smooth hand's vertices independently. Save the scene as hand_three.

Figure 6.62

Creating a procedural connection

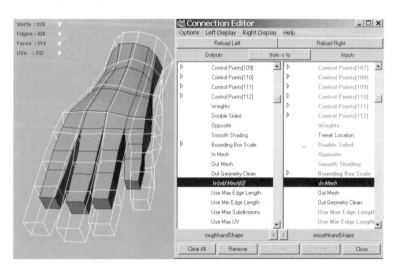

Smoothing, Layering, and Rough Tweaking

Now we need to smooth and tweak the hand. We will need to do this in two stages, beginning with applying Smooth and fixing some problems.

1. Select the smooth hand and apply Polygons → Smooth to it with the default setting. Some things immediately stand out as needing improvement, such as consistency in the width and the direction of the fingers. We need to fix these problems before we can apply Smooth again.

2. Before we start to tweak, let's put the smooth hand and the rough hand on different layers. Once the smooth hand is in a layer, select the Reference setting for the layer. The Template setting will only display the hand as a wireframe, but the Reference setting will display the hand in Shaded mode, while still disabling it from being selected.

3. Tweak the rough hand until you are comfortable with the shape it has created in the smooth hand. You can hide the rough hand for now and move back to the smooth hand by switching from Reference to Standard in the Layer menu.

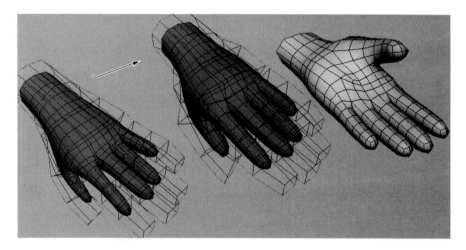

Fine Tweaking, Smoothing, and Applying Artisan

Now we will do some tweaking to prepare the hand for another smoothing. We will also use the Sculpt Polygons tool to get more surface definition and smooth out any unwanted creases.

1. Place vertices around the fingers and the thumb where the joints will bend. (One example is shown in Figure 6.63.) Think ahead to how another edge line will be placed between every line with the second Smooth. The area between the fingers needs a bit more space, and the knuckles should stick out more as well. (Don't worry too much about creating hard edges or creases at this point.)

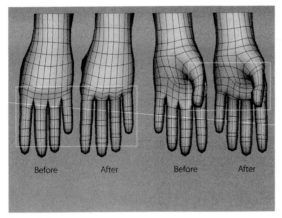

Figure 6.63

Fine-tuning the finger spans for deformation

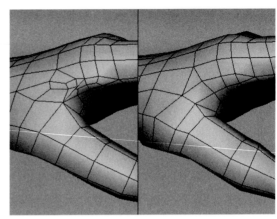

Figure 6.64

The thumb area

2. The thumb area needs special attention. Get rid of the extra edges, as shown in Figure 6.64. Make sure that there are no winged vertices left behind. If you need to make adjustments that require moving a whole area, use the rough hand. Save the scene as hand_four.

3. Apply Smooth one more time. At this point, the density of the surface calls out for the Sculpt Polygon tool. But such areas as the finger joints and fingernails should still be modified by selecting vertices. Notice the vertex placements around the finger joint areas and fingernails shown in Figure 6.65.

Figure 6.65

Tweaking the second smoothed hand

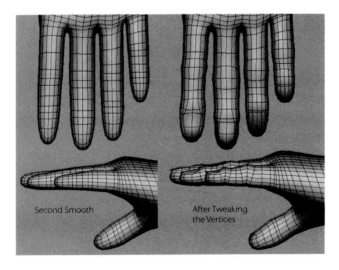

4. Using Edit Polygons → Sculpt Polygon Tool (see Chapter 7, "Working with Artisan," for more information), start pushing and pulling to get more definition for the hand, especially the palm, the knuckles, and the wrist area. Smooth out where the thumb joins the hand as well. If you want to build a more mature-looking hand, you can try making the bones protrude along the back of the hand and put more space between the fingers.

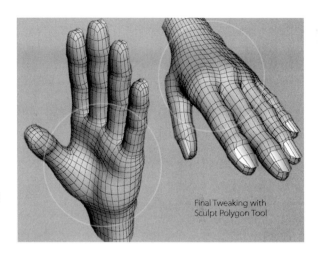

Final Tweaking with Sculpt Polygon Tool

Change the Radius setting according to the specific area you are sculpting, and always set the Opacity low. It may be frustrating to need to click many times, but retaining control of the tool you are using is important.

The hand model is just about finished at this point. We will come back to this hand in Chapter 8, "Organic Modeling," when we resume our character tutorial.

Hands On: Building a Character II (Advanced)

In the previous chapter, we built a NURBS head, an eye and patches surrounding it, and an ear. In this tutorial, we will continue from where we left off. We will finish building the head by converting its elements to polygons, editing them, and then refining them as subdivision surfaces.

1. Open the `Character_NURBS.mb` file from the Chapter 5 folder on the CD-ROM. This file incorporates all the work we did on the character in Chapter 5.

2. Duplicate the NURBS head, scale it to –1 in X, and then attach it using Blend. Apply Open/Close Surfaces to make the head periodic in V. You can edit the attached head until you're satisfied with the way it looks. If the number of isoparms going around the mouth is more than the isoparms of the head in Figure 6.66, get rid of the extra isoparms.

Figure 6.66

The head becomes a polygon surface.

3. Convert the head to a polygon surface using NURBS To Polygons, with the Tessellation Method set to Control Points. You should see a polygon head like the one in Figure 6.66. Don't mind the pointy chin.

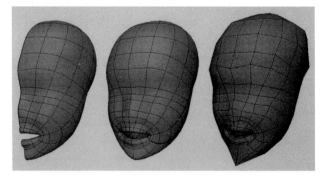

4. Delete the faces of the head on the right side and also the nine faces around the eye, as selected in Figure 6.67. The head_parts layer, which contains the various parts of the head, is set to Invisible, so click the left layer indicator to make it visible.

5. Convert the NURBS eye area patches (all eight patches) to polygon pieces, this time with the Tessellation Method set to General and the U and V Type set to Per Span # Of Iso Params. You should have polygon surfaces with three faces on each of the four sides. Check to make sure all the surfaces have the same normal direction, using Reverse to correct any wrong normals.

6. Combine and then attach the faces using the Merge Edge tool, making sure there are no border edges separating faces in the eye area.

The options Control Points and General with Per Span # Of Iso Params Tessellation Methods produce different results. The Control Points method produces extra faces at the open edges because of the extra CVs there, and you might need to clean them up, whereas the Per Span method does not. But on the other hand, polygons from the Control Points conversion become subdivision surfaces that more faithfully conform to the NURBS original. In this example, it was important to keep the shape of the head, so we used the Control Points method for that. By contrast, for the eye patches, it was more convenient to have the converted polygons' border edges match the number of edges surrounding them.

7. At the back of the head, delete four faces where the neck will join. Get a polygon cylinder with 12 faces in Axis and 3 faces in Height. Delete the top and the right half of the cylinder, and shape them roughly like the cylinder in Figure 6.68. Repeat the attaching procedure of step 2 to merge the neck to the head. If you set the Merge Edge tool's Merge mode to First, and click the head edge first and the neck edge second, the results will be more satisfactory. Remember to always keep an eye on the form as you work, moving points whenever necessary to keep shaping the head.

Figure 6.67

Attaching the eye area

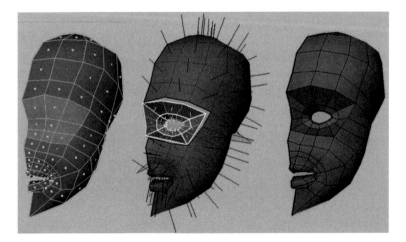

8. Repeat the same procedure with the ear. If the NURBS ear is not periodic in V for some reason, make it so. Convert the ear with the Control Points option because we want to keep the shape of the ear. Delete four faces where the ear should join as in Figure 6.69. Four faces produce eight border edges, and our converted polygon ear should have the same number. The vertices should move to make the ear area rounder, but don't do any careful tweaking for now, as that can be done on the subdivision surface.

9. Mirror the head and merge the edges. Create a subdivision surface to see what the head looks like. You will notice extraordinary points at the top of the head, because of the triangles at the pole area. Extract vertices to get the polygon surface again, and delete every other edge at the top, as in Figure 6.70. The result will be cleaner topology. You can go back and forth between polygon and subdivision surfaces and tweak the shape of the head.

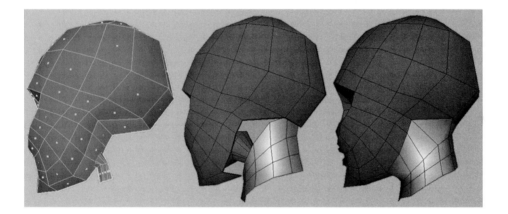

Figure 6.68

Joining the neck

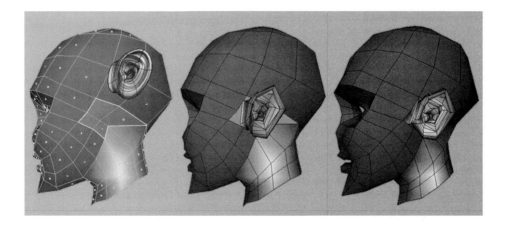

Figure 6.69

Joining the ear

Figure 6.70

Cleaning the topology

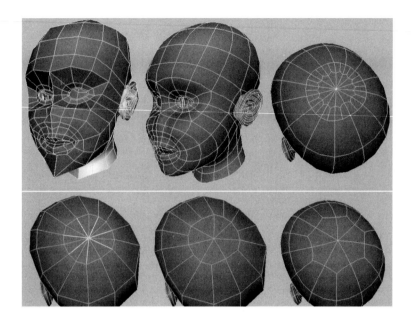

10. For the nose area, you could work either in polygons or in the Polygon Proxy mode of subdivision surfaces. Grab three faces where the nose would be, and apply Extrude Face. Translate in Z, and scale according to the shape you are aiming for. The second Extrude should include extra faces to create the shape for the nostril area. As you work, continue to tweak the nose shape, as in Figure 6.71. After the rough shape is created, do another Extrude for the nostril. You are really shaping just the left side of the nose, as the right side will be mirrored later, but extruding and tweaking the right side along with the left side is helpful in judging the overall shape of the nose.

> Build the mouth and the eye areas as lightly as possible, because they will be deforming for animation—fewer points make it that much easier for animation. The ear and the nose areas, however, can be heavier, because they take little or no part in animation.

11. The head is almost done. All that is left now is tweaking. Stay in the base level for all your tweaks, because this lets you go back and forth between subdivision surface and polygon heads. Place the eye in the proper place on the left side of the head, and tweak the eye area to fit the eye. Also tweak the left side of the head, around the ear, the nostril, the mouth, and other spots that need to be detailed. Delete the right side, mirror

the head, and merge any border edges that remain. Duplicate the eye for the right side, too, and the head modeling is done (see Figure 6.72). You can find the completed `character_head.mb` file in the Chapter 6 folder on the CD-ROM. We will create hair in Chapter 8, along with the body for the character.

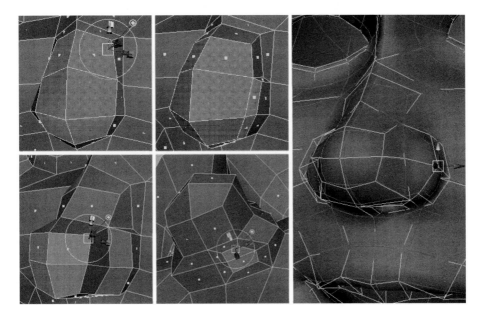

Figure 6.71

Creating the nose

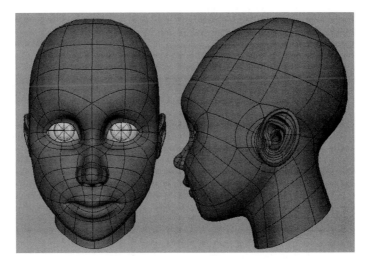

Figure 6.72

The finished head

Summary

In this chapter, you were introduced to polygons and subdivision surfaces. You learned what polygons are, how to create them, and how to work with them with the tools and actions in Maya. You then learned how (and when) to work with subdivision surfaces. The first major exercise used polygon techniques to build a hand, and the second used subdivision surfaces to continue our advanced level character modeling tutorial.

In Chapter 8, we will go back to a specific kind of NURBS modeling, called *patch modeling*. We will build a dog model in many separate NURBS patches, covering several relevant advanced modeling concepts as we go. We will then complete the final part of the character modeling tutorial.

CHAPTER 7

Painting with Artisan

Artisan is a set of 15 tools available in the standard Maya interface. (Paint Effects, another paint tool, is the subject of Chapter 19.) Artisan tools are implemented throughout the Maya workflow, the primary feature that links them being that they all act like virtual paintbrushes, "painting" on everything from shapes to goal weights. Similar to the paint or airbrush tools in a program such as Adobe Photoshop, the Artisan tools paint attribute values onto virtually any object or component you select—but Artisan does this in three dimensions. Taken together, the tools that make up Artisan provide one of the easiest and most intuitive ways to model, texture, weight, and generally edit attributes available in any graphics software today—and it's all built seamlessly into Maya!

In this chapter, you'll learn about the following:

- **The Artisan tools**
- **Sculpting polygons**
- **Sculpting (NURBS) surfaces: sculpting across seams**
- **Creating sets**
- **Painting selections and cluster weights**
- **The 3D Paint tool**
- **Painting soft body goal weights, skin weights, and jiggle weights**

The Artisan Tools: An Overview

Here is a quick run-down of the 15 tools in Maya Artisan, with a brief description of what each does and how to open it.

Sculpt Polygons Use this tool to sculpt polygonal shapes as if they were made of virtual clay. To open this tool, choose (from the Modeling menu set) Edit Polygons → Sculpt Polygons Tool.

Sculpt Surfaces Use this tool to sculpt NURBS surfaces as if they were virtual clay. To open this tool, choose (from the Modeling menu set) Edit NURBS → Sculpt Surfaces Tool.

Paint Set Membership Use this tool to paint on membership in sets, rather than having to select each point and assign it. To open this tool, choose (from the Animation menu set) Deform → Paint Set Membership Tool.

Paint Selection (newly redone in 4.5) Use this tool to select vertices on a NURBS, polygonal, or subdivision surface by painting on the surface rather than selecting points individually. To open this tool, choose Edit → Paint Selection Tool.

Script Paint Use this tool to paint the output of a MEL script onto an object using your mouse or graphics tablet, instead of manually running the script at each point. To open this tool, choose Modify → Script Paint Tool.

Paint Vertex Color Use this tool to paint colors directly onto individual polygons on a surface. To open this tool, choose (from the Modeling menu set) Edit Polygons → Colors → Paint Vertex Color Tool.

3D Paint (newly redone in 4.5) Use this tool to paint color, transparency, bump map, incandescence, and other attributes directly on NURBS or polygonal surfaces. To open this tool, choose (from the Render menu set) Texturing → 3D Paint Tool.

Attribute Paint (newly redone in 4.5) Use this tool to paint any (paintable) attribute onto your selected model. You can paint on colors, goal weights, or other attributes that you assign to be "paintable." To open this tool, choose Modify → Attribute Paint Tool.

Paint Cluster Weights (newly redone in 4.5) Use this tool to set the weights of clusters of vertices by simply painting on a surface. To open this tool, choose (from the Animation menu set) Deform → Paint Cluster Weights Tool.

 Paint Soft Body Weights (new in 4.5) Use this tool to interactively adjust the goal weights of the selected object. To open this tool, choose (from the Dynamics menu set) Soft/Rigid Bodies → Paint Soft Body Weights Tool.

 Paint Jiggle Weights (new in 4.5) Use this tool to paint on secondary motion—or jiggle—in areas of your model to allow for more lifelike animation follow-through. To open this tool, choose (from the Animation menu set) Deform → Paint Jiggle Weights Tool.

Paint Skin Weights (newly redone in 4.5) After smooth binding skin to bones, use this tool to modify the weights of the bound points to each joint in your bone chain, resulting in smoother, more natural skin motion. To open this tool, choose (from the Animation menu set) Skin → Edit Smooth Skin → Paint Skin Weights Tool.

Paint Fur Attributes (Maya Unlimited; newly redone in 4.5) Use this tool to paint particular fur attributes on specific areas of a fur description without affecting the entire node. To open this tool, choose (from the Rendering menu set) Fur → Paint Fur Attributes Tool.

Paint Cloth Properties (Maya Unlimited; newly redone in 4.5) Use this tool to paint cloth properties (such as wrinkling) on specific areas of cloth, even if that area spans more than one cloth "panel." To open this tool, choose (from the Cloth menu set) Simulation → Properties → Paint Cloth Properties Tool.

Paint Fluids (Maya Unlimited; new in 4.5) Use this tool to paint properties of fluids across the areas or volumes in which they operate. To open this tool, choose (from the Dynamics menu set) Fluid Effects → Add/Edit Contents → Paint Fluids Tool.

> Tools that are new or newly redone for Maya 4.5 have a different User Interface look than tools which retain their look from previous versions of Maya. The most apparent difference is that the Tool Settings window for the new tools has a single pane with twirl-down arrows revealing different sections of the options window (see Figure 7.20), whereas the "traditional" tools have a series of tabs at the top of the Tool Settings window (see Figure 7.2). The functionality of the two different Tool Settings layouts is the same, but the new layout is more efficient, as you can see all the elements you need at one time.

Because they work as paintbrushes, Artisan tools are most efficiently used with a graphics tablet. In this book, for the most part, we're assuming a "plain vanilla" configuration that doesn't include a tablet, so the instructions in this chapter show how to use Artisan with a mouse and keyboard as the only input devices. If you do have a tablet, it should be configured, for the most part, automatically when you launch Maya. In general, most attributes that are continuously adjustable (such as brush width and opacity) can be set to react to pressure from a stylus on a tablet, more closely matching the way one would actually paint or draw on a surface.

Because the Artisan paint tools all behave in much the same way, we'll describe how several of them work to accomplish tasks, rather than present a cursory description of each and every tool. If you need more information about the options for a tool not discussed here or about how to set up and use a graphics tablet with these tools, see the online documentation under Using Maya: Painting.

Sculpting Polygons: Deforming a Sphere

Let's begin our work with Artisan by modifying a polygonal object using the Sculpt Polygons tool. Open a new scene in Maya and create a polygon sphere (choose Create → Polygon Primitives → Sphere). Then follow these steps:

1. In the Channel Box, under Inputs: polySphere1, set the subdivisions X and Y to 40, as in Figure 7.1.

> When using Artisan sculpting tools, it is always important to work with a large number of points—either vertices (for NURBS surfaces) or facets (for polygon surfaces). If you don't provide enough points for Artisan to work with, it will not push and pull the objects' surfaces in ways you expect.

2. With the sphere selected, choose Edit Polygons → Sculpt Polygons Tool ❐ (from the Modeling menu set) to open the Tool Settings window shown in Figure 7.2, which is similar for all Artisan tools. (Because most settings are the same from one tool to another, we'll introduce them here and refer to them in later sections of this chapter.)

3. In this window (be sure you're in the Sculpt tab), change the Radius U and L to about 0.2, set the Operation mode to Push, and set the Maximum Displacement to about 0.5. When you move your mouse over the sphere now (don't click anything just yet), you'll see a red circle with an arrow pointing inward (toward the center of the sphere) and the label *Ps*. The circle shows your brush's radius of influence, the arrow indicates both the direction of the effect and the amount of influence it will have (longer arrows mean bigger pushes and pulls), and the *Ps* stands for "push," the current mode of the brush.

4. To see how this feedback works, try changing the radius of the brush to a smaller value in the Sculpt tab; the red circle will diminish to match. You can also change the direction of the effect, or reference vector; under Sculpt Variables, choose the X-axis radio button. As you now move the mouse around, you will see that the arrow always points down the X axis. You can try the other settings here as well—when you're done, set the reference vector back to Normal.

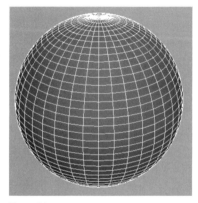

Figure 7.1

A polygon sphere with 40 divisions in X and Y

If you have a tablet, you can set the pen pressure to interactively change the radius of the brush. In the Stroke tab, click the Radius radio button. You can also use the stylus to adjust the opacity of the effect you are working on by clicking the Opacity radio button, or you can alter both elements at the same time by clicking the Both button.

5. Now that you have a feeling for some of Artisan's settings, try clicking and dragging the mouse over the surface. You should see the sphere dent inward as you drag your mouse across its surface, the dent always pointing inward toward the center of the sphere (because the brush option is set to Normal). If you make a few drags across the sphere, you will end up with something like Figure 7.3.

6. If you don't like what you have (or just to see how this works), you can erase your work. Click the Erase radio button (under Operation); then paint over the parts you don't like. If you want to reset the entire sphere, click the Flood button near the top right of the window. This will "flood" the entire sphere with the Erase command, thus resetting the sphere to its original shape.

You can use the Flood button with any operation, such as push and pull, to apply a certain value to an entire object. You can then fine-tune specific parts of your surface by painting on them as normal.

You might notice that, as you make several strokes on top of one another, the polygon facets tend to get jagged (as if the sphere were made up of crinkly paper instead of clay). You can smooth out your strokes in a couple of ways: by using the Smooth operation or by using the Auto Smooth option. Let's start with Smooth.

7. Once you have several strokes deforming your sphere (try pulling the points out this time), switch to the Smooth operation by selecting its radio button in the Sculpt tab. Now brush over the sphere, concentrating on the sharpest edges. You'll see these edges move back toward their original positions on the (undeformed) sphere, and the strokes you made will smooth out. The Smooth operation "relaxes" whatever you paint over, making it tend to return to its original position, and thus smoothing the shape back out.

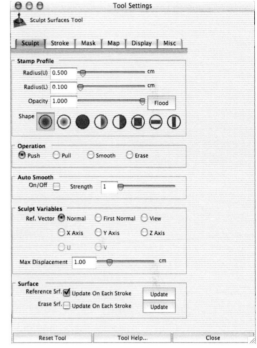

Figure 7.2

The Tool Settings window, open at the Sculpt tab

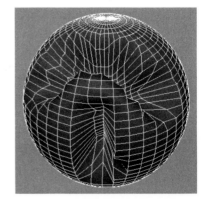

Figure 7.3

A dented polygon sphere

8. Now erase your sphere back to normal, check the Auto Smooth option, and set the Strength slider to about 5. As you paint strokes over the surface of the sphere (be sure you're in push or pull mode), you will notice that the polygons don't become as jagged as they did when the Auto Smooth option was off. To create smoothly organic shapes, use a combination of the Auto Smooth option and the Smooth operation mode.

Besides adjusting radius, modes, and other options, you can also change brush shapes, using the Shape row of buttons near the top of the Sculpt tab—the graphic on each button shows its stamp shape. *Stamping* is simply clicking and releasing your mouse button (without dragging). The brush creates a "stamp" of its shape right on your object's surface. When you drag over the surface, you lay down a series of stamps. You can see this effect if you drag quickly over your object's surface: if the mouse is moving quickly, each stamp will be noticeably separate from the others, rather than all running together.

9. Erase the sphere back to neutral, and then try stamping the sphere with each of the brush shapes to see how they compare. Because the Sculpt tool is set up by default to update its effects on each stroke, every time you make one stroke on top of another, the sphere will deform more and more (as if the effect were layering on top of itself—see Figure 7.4).

10. To set a maximum amount by which your strokes can deform the sphere, clear the Update On Each Stroke option. The same strokes will then produce something like Figure 7.5.

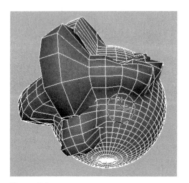

Figure 7.4

The polygon sphere, showing the layering effect of Update On Each Stroke

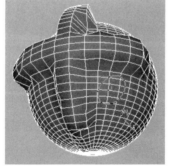

Figure 7.5

The deformed sphere, with Update On Each Stroke turned off

As you have probably noticed, you can also set the *opacity* of your brush. Opacity refers to the percentage of a tool's total effect that each painted stroke will have on your object. As an analogy, consider a real-world paintbrush: if the paint you're applying is highly opaque, one coat may be enough to cover your wall, whereas a semi-transparent paint would take several coats. In Artisan, if you set your brush to Push with a maximum displacement ("push in") set to 1, and your opacity is 0.5 (or 50%), clicking on the surface of your sphere will push it in only about 0.5 units, instead of 1. You can use the opacity setting to reduce the effect of your strokes, making each one subtler, thus allowing you to deform your objects in smaller increments than we have done thus far.

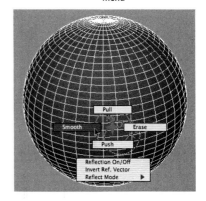

Figure 7.6

The Artisan marking menu

When an Artisan tool is active, you can open a marking menu that includes several Artisan options (see Figure 7.6) by simply holding down the U key and pressing the mouse button.

In addition to the settings available in the marking menu, hotkeys are defined for several of the most common tasks, and you can create your own hotkeys for most Artisan settings.

To modify the *upper* brush radius, hold down the B key while dragging your mouse left or right. Max displacement is mapped to M plus mouse-dragging right and left. To find out how to map other tool settings to hotkeys, see the Maya help files, or Chapters 3, "Techniques for Speeding up Your Workflow," and 20, "MEL."

If you have a graphics tablet, you can set the pressure of the stylus to map to brush radius, displacement amount, or both using the Stylus Pressure setting in the Stroke tab. See the Maya help files if you have problems with your stylus, which should work automatically with the Artisan brushes.

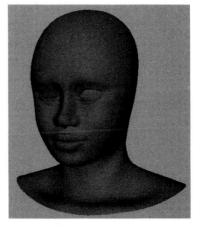

Figure 7.7

A basic NURBS head without ears or eyes

Once you are familiar with Artisan's marking menu and hotkeys, you need not keep the option window open for most operations. While you are starting out, however, it is a good idea to keep the window open. Throughout this chapter, we'll access all Artisan tool settings via the option window, though experienced users may find it more efficient to access them through the marking menu or hotkeys.

For a complete list of Artisan's hotkey functions (and those that are not yet mapped), choose Window → Settings/Preferences → Hotkeys, choose the menu set for your Artisan category (Brush Tools: ModifyUpperRadius, for example), and click the command in which you're interested. If you map any new hotkeys, be sure to save your preferences for future use (click the Save button at the bottom of the Hotkey Editor window).

Sculpting (NURBS) Surfaces: Sculpting across Seams

We're now going to look at Maya's Sculpt NURBS Surfaces tool and use a NURBS head model (**7head** on the CD) to see how Artisan works with complex issues such as surface seams.

1. First things first: we don't want to alter the shape of the person's ears or eyes, so hide them from view (select each, and then choose Display → Hide → Hide Selection). The resulting head is shown in Figure 7.7.

2. Drag-select the remains of the head, and then open the Sculpt Surfaces tool (choose Edit NURBS ➝ Sculpt Surfaces Tool ❐). The entire surface of the head will now be available for sculpting. (If you select only one portion of the head, it would be the only part available for sculpting.) You will see yellow bands where each surface is stitched to the others. If you see all the surfaces' isoparms, in the Display tab clear the Show Wireframe check box.

Because there are stitched seams in this model, sculpting this surface without pulling apart the seams will be a bit more challenging. Seams—which are described in Chapter 5— are a highly complex surface structure. Although Artisan does a great job of treating the object as a whole, you have to know how to adjust the Sculpt Surfaces tool settings to get it to work well. For the present, think of seams as stitched areas between different NURBS patches.)

Before you start deforming the face shape, it is a good idea to save a temporary version of the project file. As you play with the Sculpt Surfaces tool, it is likely your model will get permanently bent out of shape, and it's easier to go back to a fully prepared file than to go back to the original and hide the eyes and ears again.

3. In the Sculpt Surfaces Tool window, click the Seam tab and adjust the Seam Tolerance and Min Length (under Multi Surfaces) to 1. Setting these options a bit higher than their defaults allows Artisan to "see" the common edges more easily as you work with the tool. You can also set the Stitching Mode to Tangent in the Common Edge tab at the bottom of the window—sometimes this produces better effects than the default Position setting.

> One problem you will run into (if you let your brush stray too far) is that the upper head will not deform correctly—it has too few isoparms to deform well with Artisan. If we were planning to model the upper head next, we would need to insert more isoparms. But since we are not, we can just leave it alone for now. (You can even deselect it if you want to be safer.)

Let's create a heavier pair of eyebrows, using the Pull mode. We don't need to pull out each brow individually, because Artisan has a Reflect mode that lets us do both sides simultaneously.

4. Click the Stroke tab, click the Reflection check box, and set the reflection mode to V Dir (Horizontal). When you now pass your mouse over the head, you will see two brushes, mirrored around the center line of the head.

5. Now turn back to the Sculpt tab, set the Operation mode to Pull, adjust the radius of the brush(es) to something that looks appropriate for eyebrow size, turn the opacity down to about 0.5, and set Max Displacement to about 0.5 as well.

By holding down the B key and moving the mouse left and right, you can interactively adjust the brush size and see the changes in the brush right on the face. (The range of sizes the brush can take on is determined by the brush minimum and maximum settings in the Sculpt Surfaces option window.) This is a much faster way to adjust brush size to a desired radius.

6. Starting close to the center, pull a stroke along the top of the eyes (where the brows are), and pull out a heavier eyebrow, as shown in Figure 7.8. You'll notice that both sides pull out with just one stroke—a great time-saver! If you don't like your work, remember that you can return your model to its original state by using the Erase function.

7. Once you're pleased with the eyebrows, try creating an indentation below the cheeks that goes back toward the ears—specifically, across the seam boundary between the face and cheek patches of the face. Set your brush to push mode, and paint some strokes.

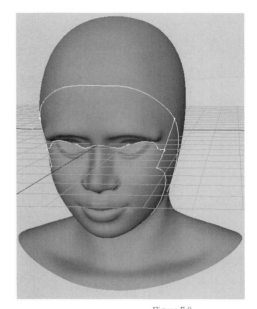

Figure 7.8

The head with heavier eyebrows

This is a well-modeled face: the stitches occur in places that would normally get no "tweaking" by tools such as Artisan (even though we're going to do that here). Placing seams in areas that won't move is good practice: even though Artisan works well with stitches, it is not perfect. Whenever possible, it is better if you don't have to tweak the boundaries of stitched surfaces in the first place.

You will probably get unsatisfactory results at this point (and you may have to reopen your saved temp file; even erasing sometimes fails to set the stitches back to normal). The two surfaces are obviously not working as one, each one deforming a different amount under the brush's pressure. The solution is to increase the number of surfaces the tool looks for as it works. (Be sure to start with a clean copy of your head!)

Figure 7.9

Head with sunken cheeks

8. Click the Miscellaneous tab, set the number of surfaces to two or more (or just click the Infinite radio button), and turn on the Use Common Edge Info option. With these new settings (and a bit of practice—try starting with the brush completely on one surface, then moving it to the other), you should get a nice "sunken cheek" look, as shown in Figure 7.9. Save this project for use later in this chapter.

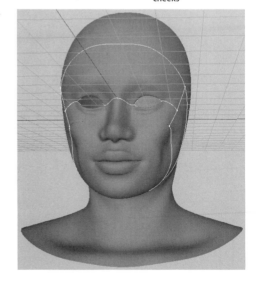

As you continue painting, you may find that areas around the seams bunch up or even start to crack. You can try resolving this issue by clicking the Stitch Now button (with either Position or

Tangent selected) in the Seam tab of the Sculpt Surfaces tool. If the effect is not strong enough, click the button several times.

Although this was a fast and simple introduction to real-world modeling using Artisan, it should give you an idea of just how powerful the tool can be for making subtle adjustments to your models. All it takes is a bit of practice and some knowledge of what the Sculpt Surfaces tool can do.

You can actually stitch surfaces using the Sculpt Surfaces tool. For more information on how to do this, see Maya's online help (NURBS Modeling: Editing NURBS Surfaces: Sculpting Surfaces).

Creating Sets

An Artisan tool that is sometimes useful is Paint Set Membership. With this tool, you can edit the set membership of points—for grouping with bones, for example—without having to select individual points. (And if you've ever had to do that, you know why this is a useful tool!)

Let's use our base head from the last section and create a few sets of points on it (or you can use 7head on the CD-ROM).

1. Drag-select the entire head, and then open the Paint Set Membership tool (choose Deform → Paint Set Membership Tool ❐) from the Animation menu set. With the tool open, the head should now be composed of several colors, each representing one of the sets that was created for the head.

   If you do not see a colored face, click the Display tab and be sure the Color Feedback and Display Active Vertices options are on. While here, you can also (if you prefer) turn off Active Display Vertices, which hides the isoparms and CVs on the head.

2. In the Set Membership tab, select set2 as the Set To Modify, and you should see the CVs in the lip area, as shown in Figure 7.10 (in color in the Color Gallery of the CD).

The Paint Set Membership tool works in three modes: Add, Transfer, and Remove. Add adds the painted points to the selected set; Remove deletes points from the selected set; and Transfer transfers points to the selected set. It is important to understand the difference between Add and Transfer. Add places the painted points into the selected set but does *not* remove them from membership in any other sets. Transfer both adds points to the selected set and removes them from membership in any other sets. The set you select in the Paint Set Membership Tool window is the set the points will transfer *to*. Points from any other set will be moved into your selected set.

There is no opacity setting; all points are either in a set or not—there is no in-between.

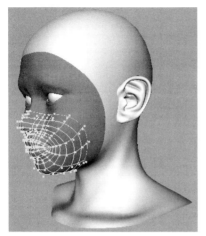

Figure 7.10

The head with set memberships colored

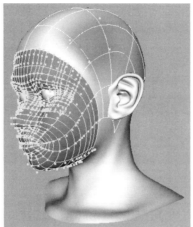

Figure 7.11

Painting new points into the shapeSet set

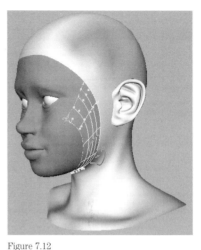

Figure 7.12

Points removed from the jaw set

3.　Let's add some points from the top of the head to the shapesSet that has all face points in it (in the Set Membership tab, select shapesSet under Select Set To Modify). With your brush mode set to Add (you can adjust the radius just as you did previously), paint some points on the top of the head into the shapesSet. The newly added points will change color as they are added to the set, as shown in Figure 7.11 (in color on the CD).

4.　Now let's remove some points from set3 (the set around the jaws). Set your Paint Set Membership tool to Remove and paint out some of the points. As the CVs are removed, they disappear from view, as shown in Figure 7.12 (in color on the CD).

Figure 7.13

Points transferred to the jaw set

5.　Finally, let's transfer some points from one set to another. With the Paint Set Membership tool set to Transfer, select set2 (the set of CVs around the mouth), and then paint over the area below the eyes. You will notice that the points change color as they are transferred from their old set to set2, as in Figure 7.13 (in color on the CD).

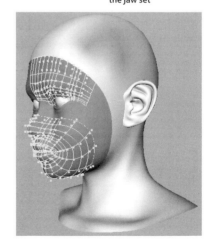

The Paint Set Membership tool can be useful if you have several objects (such as this head) and you want to form selection (or deform) sets across object boundaries for use in later deform processes or just for ease of selection. Instead of needing to carefully select points (and taking pains not to accidentally select points on the back side of the object), you can intuitively paint these points into your sets with a brush.

Painting Selections

Akin to the Paint Set Membership tool, the Paint Selection tool lets you select vertices (or polygon facets) that you can then manipulate in standard ways. To see this tool in action, follow these steps:

1. Open a new scene, create a NURBS plane, scale it out a bit, and set its U and V patches to about 50 each (to give Artisan enough points to work with).

2. Now open the Paint Selection tool (choose Edit → Paint Selection Tool ❑). The selection types are Select, Unselect, and Toggle (which selects unselected points and vice versa). There are also Select All, Unselect All, and Toggle All buttons.

3. To quickly see how Select works, select a brush shape and paint over part of the plane to select its points. You can now use the Move, Rotate, or Scale tools to alter just these points.

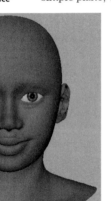

Figure 7.14

A smiling face

The advantage of being able to paint selections onto objects may not be obvious with a simple plane, where you could just as easily drag out selections with the Marquee tool. But on something more complex, such as our head model, the Paint Selection tool can be a great asset.

Once again, open your neutral head project (**7head** on the CD-ROM). Then, using the Paint Selection tool, select points around the mouth and make the face smile, using the Move tool and the Scale tool—you will probably have to move back and forth between the Paint Selection tool (changing the points selected) and the Move and Scale tools. A resulting smile is shown in Figure 7.14.

Remember that the Reflect mode lets you select points on both sides of the head simultaneously—cutting your selection time in half. Open the Reflection portion of the Paint Selection Tool settings window and click the Reflection: X checkbox.

Painting Cluster Weights

If selecting CVs via painting doesn't give you enough control over the points you're manipulating, you can use the Paint Cluster Weights tool to set the goal weight (the amount of effect a manipulation will have on a given vertex or facet) of each CV in an intuitive manner. (You can set CV weights in several other ways, but the Paint Weights tool is so easy to use, it's often not necessary to go beyond it.)

To see how this tool works, let's create an Aztec (stair-stepped) pyramid just by painting different weights on a simple NURBS plane.

1. Open a new scene, create a NURBS plane with about 50 U and V patches, and scale it out to about the size of the scene grid (for easier viewing).

2. There is one step before we can use the Paint Weights tool—we must first make the plane's CVs into a cluster so their weights can be manipulated. Select the plane, and then choose Deform → Create Cluster from the Animation menu set. If you forget this step (which is easy to do), you will be extremely confused by the tool's lack of responsiveness!

3. Now drag-select both the cluster and the plane it is mapped to, and open the Paint Weights tool (choose Deform → Paint Cluster Weights Tool ❑ in the Animation menu set).

You should see the plane turn white, indicating that its goal weights are all set to a value of 1. If this doesn't happen, be sure you created a cluster from the plane, and then check to see if color feedback is on (it's under the Display section of the tool settings window). It may be hard to see the color with the plane's isoparms showing, so turn off Show Active Lines as well.

Next, we need to flood the entire plane/cluster with a goal weight of 0, or no influence (CVs with a 0 weight won't react to any manipulation).

4. Set the operation mode to Replace (which replaces the old goal weight with your selection), set the Value (of the goal weight) to 0, and click the Flood button. The entire plane should turn black, indicating it now has a goal weight of 0. This is the base of our pyramid, which will not move.

5. Now we need to paint our "stairs." Choose the square brush option (the button that looks like a blue square) from the Brush section of the tool settings window, and change the value to 0.1 instead of 0. Also be sure the Rotate To Stroke check box is *off*. If this option is on, the square imprint from your brush will likely rotate each time you draw a new stroke. This next part is a neat trick: instead of having to increase the goal weight value manually each time, we can place the Paint Weights tool in Add mode (by clicking that radio button), and each brush stamp will increase the goal weight by 0.1. Thus, the more times you click a spot, the higher the goal weight goes, and the lighter the area's shade of gray will become.

This tool also has Smooth and Scale operation modes. The Smooth mode smooths transitions between areas of different goal weights. The Scale mode scales (or multiplies) the object's goal weight by the number in the Value box. With the new user interface of Maya 4.5, the brush tool can be made into the shape of any image file you choose. Simply click the Browse button at the right of all the shape icons and choose an image file on your computer; the brush will then be shaped like this image (a high-contrast or black-and-white image works best for the brush shape).

6. With the square brush chosen, set the radius of the brush larger than the edges of the plane, center the brush around the origin, and stamp a higher goal weight onto a large square area of the plane. (You will probably find this easier to do in the top orthographic view.) You should see a large square portion of the plane become a slightly lighter gray than before.

In general, you can set the orientation of any brush that's not round. In the Stroke tab, you can choose from Up Vector (default), U and V Tangent (horizontal and vertical aligned), and Path Direction (which changes the orientation depending on your stroke).

7. Make the brush radius a bit smaller and repeat the stamp—now a smaller portion of the plane should get just a bit lighter. Continue this process until you are at the center with a small radius. Your plane should look similar to Figure 7.15.

8. To make your pyramid, switch to the Move tool, select the cluster weight *only* (not the plane—you may need to do this in the Hypergraph or Outliner), and then move it straight up the Y axis. You should see something that looks like a stair-stepped pyramid, as Figure 7.16 shows.

As a further exercise, try making a hilly terrain by using a simple plane, a cluster, and painted goal weights.

Let's now return to our favorite head—either open your own file or use 7head from the companion CD—and examine how to weight the mouth clusters to allow for better manipulation of facial expressions when the character is eventually animated.

1. With the head showing, select only the lower face section (with the mouth) and create a cluster out of it.

2. Shift-select the cluster and mouth, and then open the Paint Cluster Weights tool (you should see the area turn white, indicating a goal weight of 1 for all points). As before, first flood the area with a goal weight of 0 (so the areas we don't want to move won't).

3. Using the Add (or Replace) and Smooth modes, paint the areas around the lips, giving the corners of the mouth, and the cheeks above them, the highest weighting.

Figure 7.15

A plane with stair-stepped goal weights

Figure 7.16

The completed pyramid

4. Try to imagine where the skin bends and stretches the most as you smile and frown (or look in the mirror), and then paint these creases onto the mouth. You may find it necessary to move the mouth and then repaint the goal weights to get the effect you want. Figure 7.17 shows the results of painting on these goal weights. Remember that turning on Reflection will cut your work in half.

5. When you are finished, try making the face smirk (as in Figure 7.18), purse its lips, and then frown. You should find that this method of creating facial animations can—after a bit of practice—become a powerful tool in your character animation bag. Chapter 24, "Dynamics of Soft Bodies," has a section describing how to use Artisan to paint goal weights for soft body hair.

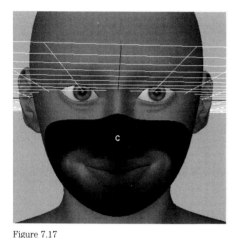

Figure 7.17

Painted weights in the mouth area

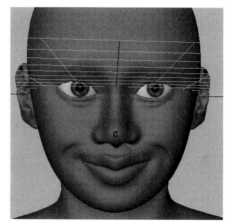

Figure 7.18

A smirking face

3D Paint: Painting Textures

Maya 4.5 has taken the useful Paint Textures tool, introduced in Maya 3, and made it even more useful. 3D Paint is a tool that lets you paint color, transparency, bump, incandescence, or other texture attributes directly on NURBS and (well-formed) polygon and subdivision surfaces. You can even paint on portions of file textures created in other programs such as Adobe Photoshop. This tool supplants and extends the Paint Vertex Color tool, relegating that tool to something of a legacy role.

When you create or modify a texture using the Paint Textures tool, Maya creates a new file texture (or renames one that already exists) for the selected material and paints on that file texture. Any scene objects that have this material applied to them will then be

updated when you save the brush strokes out. For a polygonal or subdivision surface to be "well formed," it must have non-overlapping UVs that fall within the 0–1 range in texture space
(a condition that is automatic for NURBS surfaces). To create proper polygonal or subdivision surfaces, use automatic mapping of UVs. For more on textures and rendering, see Chapter 16, "Rendering Basics."

Let's begin with a simple example: we'll paint some colors on a standard NURBS sphere.

1. In a new scene window, create a NURBS sphere (choose Create → NURBS primitives → Sphere), and change it to high resolution and texture shading (press the 3 and 6 keys on the main keyboard).

2. Now let's assign a material to this sphere: open the Hypershade (choose Window → Rendering Editors → Hypershade) and, in the materials section of the Create Bar panel, click the phongE material swatch .

Figure 7.19

Creating a new phongE material

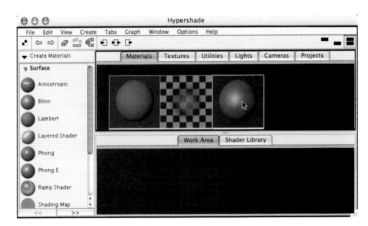

3. Now MM drag the texture onto the sphere in your scene window as shown in Figure 7.19.

4. If you want to check to be sure the material is applied, open the Attribute Editor (double-click the phongE1 material in the Hypershade) and alter the color under the Common Material Attributes section. You should see your sphere update with the same color. If not, go back and MM drag the material onto your sphere, or select the sphere and then, with the mouse over the phongE1 material, RM choose Assign Material To Selection.

5. We have a basic material applied to our sphere; now let's do some painting! First, save your scene if you haven't before (otherwise, the Paint Textures tool will remind you to

do so—it needs your scene name to name its textures); then select your sphere, and choose Texturing → 3D Paint Tool ❑ in the Rendering menu set. You will see an Artisan window similar to the other "new architecture" tools you have worked with in this chapter. This tool has a few different features, most notably the File Textures section, shown in Figure 7.20.

6. In the File Textures section, set the Attribute To Paint to Color (the default—you might want to look at—or try—the other attributes you can paint in the pop-up menu).

With version 4.5 of Maya, you can now safely choose the Update On Stroke and Save Texture On Stroke check boxes, because Maya will let you undo a saved texture—a welcome addition indeed! Under the Color section, you can adjust the color of your brush via the Color and Flood Color controls, and you can change the opacity of the brush. In the Paint Operations section of the window, you can choose to paint, erase, or clone (duplicate one area of a texture with another) with Artisan brushes, or paint, smear, or blur using a Paint Effects brush (see Chapter 19 for more on Paint Effects). You can also choose a blend mode for your brush strokes, similar to the way blending works in a program such as Photoshop (lighten, for example, lightens the underlying layers of paint or texture, rather than just painting over them as with the default brush).

7. Open the File Textures section of the window and click the Assign Textures button. Choose the default (256 × 256) file texture size and click OK. The new file texture will be saved in the 3DPaint-Textures directory of your project. Your file texture must always have a size ratio of a power of two (128 × 256, or 512 × 512, for example). If not, Maya will automatically convert the texture to such a ratio. This is important to remember if you create a texture in a paint package and intend to use it as a basic file texture to paint over later in Maya.

8. If you want to start with a single color on your surface, try clicking the Flood button (in the Paint tab). You should see the entire sphere's surface update to the color you chose in the Color Value section of the Paint tab.

9. Once you flood the sphere, change the color (either adjust the slider or click the color chip and choose a new color there) and paint several strokes on your sphere, as in Figure 7.21. You have just painted colors directly onto your sphere!

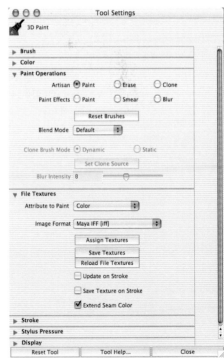

Figure 7.20

The Tool Settings window

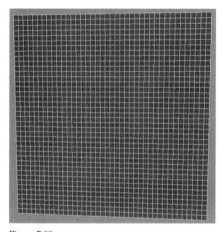

Figure 7.21

Painted texture strokes on a white sphere

If you want to paint on other attributes (such as transparency or bump map), be sure to choose that texture attribute, and then click the Assign Textures button—otherwise nothing will happen as you paint!

Now let's try a slightly more advanced example: let's paint the front of a polygon cube so it looks like a cartoon adobe house with a door and a window.

1. Create a new scene and save it; then choose Create → Polygon Primitives → Cube ❑. In the option window, set the subdivisions along width and height to about 40 (you can set the depth subdivisions too, but we won't be using them), and create the cube.

2. Rotate your view so you can see the front of the cube, as in Figure 7.22, and, with the cube selected, choose Texturing → 3D Paint Tool ❑. You might want to check the Show Wireframe check box (under the Display section), because we'll be using the faces of the polygons to mask our painting.

3. Under the Paint tab, choose Assign Texture, give it a resolution of 1024 × 1024, and click the Assign Texture button.

4. Under the Brush section, turn off Rotate To Stroke (the strokes are then painted on at a normal angle). Now change the Flood Color to whatever you want your "base coat" color for the house, and click the Flood All button. Your entire cube house should now be the base color (we chose an off-white).

5. Now let's paint on a door. First, we need to mask out the polygon faces we'll use as the door: go into Select mode (or press the Q key), and then RM choose Faces with the cursor over the cube. Shift-select a number of faces on the front of the cube that will become the door area, as in Figure 7.23.

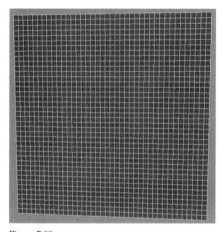

Figure 7.22

A polygon cube, set for painting

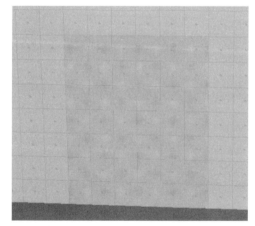

Figure 7.23

The door faces selected

6. Switch back to the Paint Textures tool (or press Y), choose a new color for your door, and paint over the door faces. If you want, you can reset the brush to a small size and paint a door-knob on as well. Figure 7.24 shows a close-up of the finished door. You can, if you want, set the Flood Color and then click the Flood Selected button to flood all selected faces with that color.

Now let's paint a window into the house. First, we'll paint a transparency map on the windowpanes, so they are semi-transparent; then we'll paint a color over the top where the crossbars of the window would be.

7. Select a group of faces on your cube that will be the window area—a good-sized picture window, as in Figure 7.25, will do nicely.

8. Under the File Textures section of the 3D Paint tool, select Transparency for the Attribute To Paint, and then click the Assign Textures button and assign a 1024 × 1024 texture to the transparency map. You will see the cube turn a light gray.

9. Set the Flood Color Value to black (completely opaque) and click the Flood button, making the entire cube opaque. Now raise the color to a light gray (color doesn't matter for transparency, only shades of gray), and paint into your window area with a large brush, or change the Flood Color to light gray and click the Flood Selected button. You might want to go back with a smaller brush and paint some streaks of "dirt" on the window, where it won't be as transparent—or you can wait and do this when you paint on your colors, next.

Figure 7.24

A close-up of the door and doorknob

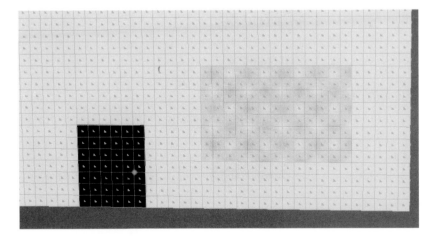

Figure 7.25

Faces selected for a picture window

Figure 7.26

Rendered house façade

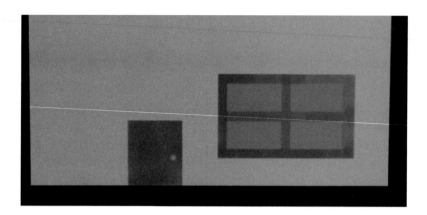

10. Now choose Color from the texture Attribute To Paint (your house will become mostly white again), choose a small brush, and paint in crossbar supports for your window. You might want to go back to the transparency image and paint on the dark crossbars there as well, so they don't render semi-transparent.

11. Finally, render out a test image to see what your cube house looks like. You should see something like Figure 7.26. If you don't like the look, just return to the Paint Textures tool and adjust to your heart's content.

Obviously, you can paint on many more features using this new tool—specularity maps are a good example. All the other texture attributes you can paint, however, behave like color and transparency, so you should now find using them rather intuitive.

Painting Weights

Let us now examine how Maya can be used to paint weights for various elements directly on objects. Whether for soft body goal, jiggle, or skin weighting, it is much more intuitive (not to mention faster) to paint weights on using an Artisan brush than it is to select and alter weights numerically on a per-vertex basis.

Painting Soft Body Goal Weights

The Paint Soft Body Goal Weights tool, which evolved from the Attribute Paint tool, is useful for modifying the uniform goal weights of a soft body. For our work, we're going to use this tool to paint on the particle goal weight of a simple cylinder, turning it into a bendable fishing rod. Soft bodies are collections of Maya particles that look like a solid object. They are useful for creating malleable objects such as the surface of water—or a flexible fishing pole. For information about creating and working with soft bodies, see Chapter 24. We could also use the Script Paint tool to do this; it has a predefined script, paintGoalPP, that will do the same thing. However, using this tool is more complex, and it is essentially a legacy tool from before the Paint Softbody Goal Weights tool was created, so normally there would be no reason to use this alternative tool.

1. Open the file **7rodSB** on your CD-ROM (or build a skinny cylinder, animate it, and make it a soft body). If you play back the animation, you will see that the entire "fishing rod" moves back and forth as one solid piece—we're going to change that by reducing the goal weights at the top of the rod.

2. Select the rod and open the Attribute Paint tool (in the Dynamics menu set, choose Soft/Rigid Bodies → Paint Soft Body Weights Tool ❑).

3. Under the Paint Attributes section, be sure the first button is set to copyOfnurbs-Cylinder1ParticleShape-goalPP and the second button is set to Filter: particle.

4. Be sure the Paint Operation is set to Replace, set the Value to 0 (goal weight of 0), and click the Flood button. The entire cylinder should become black, indicating that all soft body particles now have a goal weight of 0 (are not affected by motion of the original goal object). If you do not see the cylinder turn black, check under the Display section to be sure that Color Feedback is on. You can now play back the animation, which should show no motion because the soft body is no longer reacting to motion of its goal object.

5. Once you see how the Goal Weight attribute works, flood the entire rod with a value of 0.5, so there will be some connection between the rod and its animated parent. You will notice, on playing back the animation, that the cylinder moves a great deal more than does the original cylinder, because it tends to overshoot the motion of the goal object. Remember that you must rewind animations using soft bodies before playing them back. If you don't rewind, the animation will start giving you bizarre results.

6. Once you have the entire rod set to 0.5, set your Paint Operation to Add, and set your Value to 0.1—we're going to increase the goal weight as we go down the rod by simply painting on a lighter color. Set your brush radius fairly large, so it wraps around the whole cylinder—you can also change the brush shape to square if you prefer. To get a smooth transition from dark to light, you will probably need to use the Smooth mode as well as the Add mode. Run a couple of frames of the animation frequently to see how you are progressing. A good method for getting smooth transitions on an object like this is to start at the top and make a series of downward brush strokes, each one going down a bit farther. Figure 7.27 shows the rod in motion.

Although it can take a bit of practice to paint goal weights onto objects effectively, learning how to do so can really improve the control you have over soft body animations, allowing you to create much subtler variations of motion than would be feasible without such a paint method for applying goal weights.

Figure 7.27

The weighted rod in motion

Painting Jiggle Weights

Closely related to soft body goal weights are Maya's jiggle weights, which also can be painted on using the new Paint Jiggle Weights tool. One classic example of jiggle is the stomach of a rotund character such as Santa Claus. We will use a rudimentary stomach object (a deformed sphere) to demonstrate how jiggle can create a secondary animation when this "character" laughs.

1. Open the `belly.mb` file from the CD, or create your own rotund belly from a NURBS sphere. Feel free to practice using the Sculpt Surfaces tool discussed earlier in this chapter to give your belly some character. Figure 7.28 shows the model from the CD. If you create your own belly, be sure to keyframe in a rotating motion that looks like a laugh (see the CD file, which is animated already).

2. Before we can paint jiggle weights, we have to first create a jiggle set. In the Animation menu set, with the belly object selected, choose Deform → Create Jiggle Deformer. Now when you play back your animation, you will see the entire stomach sphere jiggling around out of control—obviously we need to control the weighting of the jiggle deformer so that only the front part of the belly jiggles!

3. Again in the Animation menu set, choose Deform → Paint Jiggle Weights ❐. The belly should turn all white, indicating that the entire object has a jiggle weight of 1, which is too high for most of it. (If the belly doesn't turn white, check under the Display section to be sure Color Feedback is on, or click Reset Tool to revert to the default settings.)

4. Under the Paint Attributes section, be sure jiggle1.weights is selected in the first button, Filter: jiggle is selected in the second, and that the Paint Operation is set to Replace. Next set the Value to 0 (no jiggle weight), and then click the Flood button. This will set your entire object to have a jiggle weight of 0, which means it will look like the original animation.

Figure 7.28

A simple rotund "belly" that will be made to jiggle

5. Now change the Paint Operation to Add, make the Value something like 0.5, set Opacity to about 0.5, and then use a large-sized brush to paint over the protruding stomach area (move out from around the belly button) until you are happy with the area and the amount of jiggle. Be sure to play back the animation frequently to check your progress. We found that the jiggle weights are sensitive to variations on the surface (what looks like splotches of brighter or darker color), so liberal use of the Smooth tool, plus a large brush size, is highly recommended. Also if the jiggle becomes too extreme, you can alter the Jiggle Weight (under Inputs: jiggle1 in the Channel Box) to something less than 1. We found 0.7 suited our needs much better. Figure 7.29 shows the jiggle weights painted onto our model.

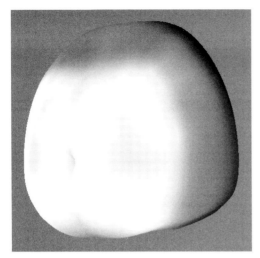

Figure 7.29

Jiggle weights painted onto the "belly"

Figure 7.30

The "belly" in motion, showing jiggle deformation of the lower stomach area

Once you complete your work, you should have a wonderful secondary jiggle to the front part of the stomach, as in Figure 7.30.

Painting Skin Weights

If you are working with smooth-skinned, jointed characters, the Paint Skin Weight tool is just what you need for precise control over how your character's skin bends in relation to joint movement. We'll use a simple "character" setup of a cylindrical arm and an elbow joint to explore use of this tool. You can either create this scene on your own or use the 7arm file on your CD-ROM.

Figure 7.31

Arm, showing joint1's influence

1. With your project open, try moving the joint up and down (drag-select the bottom IK handle, and then use the Move tool to move it—and the arm—up and down). You will notice that, while the bound skin moves with the joints, the elbow area doesn't respond correctly: the inner elbow area needs to crease a bit more.

2. Select the cylinder (not the skeleton) and open the Paint Skin Weights tool (in the Animation menu set, choose Skin → Edit Smooth Skin → Paint Skin Weights Tool ❑). You should see a grayscale image of the cylinder, and, under the Influence section, you will have a choice of three joints (joint1 at the shoulder, joint2 at the elbow, and joint3 at the wrist). If you select joint1, as in Figure 7.31, the color of the cylinder will show how heavily bound to the shoulder joint each point is. White represents a bind weight of 1, fully affected by any joint motion, and black is a bind weight of 0, not affected at all.

If your cylinder is not colored, be sure Color Feedback is on (under the Display section), and also be sure your scene is set to Shaded mode (press the 5 or 6 key on the keyboard). To get rid of the wireframe, clear the Show Wireframe check box in the Display section.

3. You can see by looking at the color feedback that the inside of the elbow is dark when either joint1 or joint2 is selected, indicating it is not being influenced by either joint very much. Let's paint slightly higher values into this area.

4. First, bend the arm some so you can see your results as you work (you might first want to note the translate information for the IK handle so you can easily return it to its rest position). Next, select joint1 in the Tool Settings window, set your Paint Weights mode to Add, set the value to about 0.1, and set your opacity fairly low (like 0.1 or 0.2). Set your brush to a fairly small radius, zoom in on the elbow area, and start painting higher goal weights on, switching between joints 1 and 2 and watching what happens. Your goal is to get a nicer crease between the upper and lower arm here, and setting higher goal weights at and just above (below for the elbow joint—joint2) the elbow will increase the joint's influence, making it pull the elbow area into more of a crease.

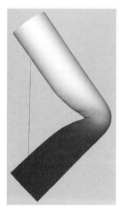

Figure 7.32

Arm with goal weights adjusted

If your strokes make the elbow area too lumpy, use the Smooth mode to smooth out the lumps—you might not want to smooth out all the lumps, however, because skin does wrinkle as it bends! Once you have worked a while, you should end up with something like Figure 7.32.

The effect here is subtle, but subtlety is what this tool is all about. The difference between Figures 7.31 and 7.32 is not great, but the second is far more appealing and "realistic" than the first—and getting this elbow bend without the Paint Skin Weights tool would be difficult and time-consuming. Once again, Artisan makes a difficult, painstaking task a lot easier.

Summary

This chapter has presented a selection of Artisan tools, and, although each tool does something different, they all behave in a similar fashion, so you should have a good feel for how Artisan works. You may be thinking at this point that virtual painting is something of an "art" to master (hence the name "Artisan"), but don't be intimidated. Consider this: how would you accomplish any of the tasks in this chapter without Artisan paint tools? Only when you imagine working without these tools is their power really evident. Artisan's tools take highly complex tasks that used to require custom programming and/or hours of dull, painstaking work and place all these jobs within easy reach. Artisan is also highly intuitive, especially if you use a stylus with it: after all, just about anyone understands how paintbrushes work. After reading this chapter, you might save yourself hours of time and frustration if, the next time a job seems too difficult, you try Artisan on the problem.

CHAPTER 8

Organic Modeling

The types of modeling covered in previous chapters—NURBS, polygons, and subdivision surfaces—are techniques based on specific Maya tools and their underlying math. Organic modeling, by contrast, is a process that embraces various techniques and is defined by its subject matter: organic forms, especially people and animals. These forms are typically more complex than mechanical forms (although their symmetry makes them good candidates for mirroring techniques). And they usually deform as they move, which makes this chapter a fitting preparation for the animation techniques that follow in Part III.

This chapter features the following topics:

- **Selecting and Inserting Isoparms**

- **Dividing the Surface into Patch Regions**

- **Rebuilding the Parameters**

- **Stitching tools**

- **Mirroring and Attaching the Model**

- **Globally Stitching the Model**

Laying the Groundwork for Modeling

One of the worst ways to start your modeling process is to plunge in without knowing how you want your model to look. Such an approach will make your work sloppy and waste valuable time. For our work, we'll use a sketch of a puppy (see Figure 8.1) as a background image.

Figure 8.1

A reference sketch for the modeling project

The next thing we need to know is what this dog will be doing. Let's say the dog will be walking or running, so we only need concern ourselves with the movements of the dog related to those specific actions (walking and running are fairly easy to set up). If the dog were also to move in more complicated ways, such as sitting or rolling over, we would need to build the dog accordingly to account for those movements as well.

In studio productions, models are not considered complete until they have gone through many extreme poses to test their suitability for animation. The designer may need to modify the model if it fails to hold its shape under certain extreme poses at the testing stage. In some cases, different versions of the model may be required for different animation situations.

MODELING GOOD WORK HABITS

This is a fun chapter. It demonstrates the various organic modeling procedures by working through two projects. First is a real-life project, in which we will build a NURBS dog from scratch to finish. Then, for the advanced Hands On tutorial, we will complete the third and final part of the character-modeling project. This more advanced tutorial uses a combination of subdivision surfaces, polygons, and NURBS techniques. Hands-on exercises are the best way to get down to the nitty-gritty details of organic modeling.

At the same time, this is a difficult chapter. The time required to build these models will depend on your skill level and familiarity with organic modeling, but you shouldn't build the whole dog, for example, in one session. Keep in mind that you are not producing a work of art at this point. Focus on learning the tools and techniques of organic modeling. (And you can always use the prepared model found on the accompanying CD instead of building it from scratch.)

As with any real-life project, things may get messy as you work your way through this chapter. It is important to practice good work habits. Save your work often, name things carefully, and take regular breaks to clear your head. Always consider *why* you are doing each step, instead of blindly working through them. You will learn much more that way.

Building the Head and Body

Let's start at the top, with the head and body. Building a good body piece with the minimum number of isoparms and proper isoparm distribution is important, because it influences the shape and the placement of the legs.

1. Create a new scene and go to side view. To bring in the image of the dog from the accompanying CD, in the window panel, choose View → Camera Attribute Editor, go to Environment, and click the Image Plane Create button. You can use the Image Name field to browse for the image `puppy_sketch.tif` on the CD. If you find the image plane too bright, you can darken the picture by lowering the Color Gain setting in the Image Plane Attributes section of the Attribute Editor.

2. Create a NURBS sphere, rotate it 90 degrees in the X axis, and scale it out. In the Channel box, open makeNurbSphere1, and set Sections to 10 and Spans to 20. Translate the sphere to about where the puppy's body is, as shown in Figure 8.2. Delete the history of the NURBS sphere by choosing Edit → Delete By Type → History.

3. Pick-mask the sphere's CVs or hulls and transform them using translate, rotate, and scale procedures to get the same profile form as the dog in the picture. Space the isoparms as shown in Figure 8.3. One of Maya's more elegant features is the ability to use the arrow keys to go up and down the UV parameters with the selection of CVs. This technique is especially useful when you are selecting hulls.

   The Face Two rows of CVs should do for the nose area, because we will place a sphere for the nose later. Also, since we are not including eyelids or a mouth, we can use a minimum number of isoparms for the face—three rows of CVs will do.

   The Body Use three rows of CVs for the back of the head and the neck, and three more for the chest area. Use one row for the stomach area, and three rows for the back leg area. The stomach shape is actually created by three rows of CVs; the row for the stomach area works together with the last row of the chest area and the beginning row of the back leg area.

   The Tail Two rows "tie" the tail to the back of the torso, and two more make the tail curve tightly toward the end. The last three rows shape the endpoint of the tail—they are one more than we need, so select the third row of CVs from the end of the tail and press the Delete key to remove it. Scale the last two rows out to fit the profile of the tail. It's important that the deformed NURBS sphere has no history when you delete its row of CVs. Otherwise, upon deletion of the CVs, the whole shape of the object will change.

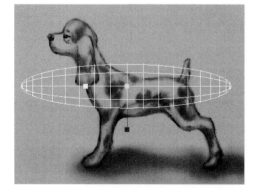

Figure 8.2

A picture of the image plane and sphere

**Transforming CVs and
hulls to get a profile
shape**

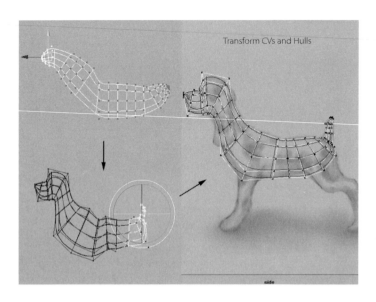

Figure 8.4

**Dog being shaped in
the perspective view**

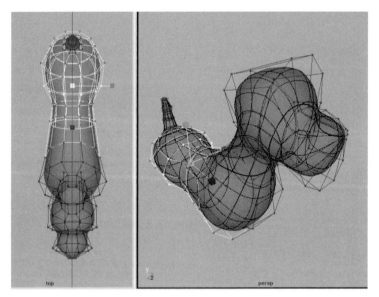

4. Switch to a two-view layout by choosing Window → View Arrangement → Two Panes Side
By Side. (You can also use the marking menu and choose Panels → Layouts → Two Panes
Side By Side.) Make one window perspective view and the other top view.

5. Select hulls again, and scale in the X axis to make the shape look more like a puppy. The
hulls can be scaled in the Y or Z axis as well, to fine-tune the profile shape. You should
end up with something like the shape shown in Figure 8.4.

HOW MANY CVS DO YOU NEED?

As you are building your model, always ask yourself how many CVs you need to get the shape you want. Remember, it takes only three CVs to curve a line. It follows that only three rows of CVs are needed to curve a surface. When you study models with this rule in mind, it's surprising to see how often unnecessary isoparms are placed for simple curvatures on surfaces.

You might want to add one more row to "tie" a curve, making it very tight and edgy. Another way to tighten a curve is to increase the CV weights, instead of adding more CVs. The drawback to this technique is that sometimes the weight information gets lost when models are transferred to other programs.

Be a minimalist when you are starting out. The fewer CVs you have, the easier it is to control the surface area. You can easily insert more isoparms to refine your model, but it is more difficult to get rid of them without disturbing what you've already built. Having fewer CVs also lets you concentrate on the big blocks of the model you are creating and ignore the details, which is a good drawing and sculpting principle to follow.

Cutting Up the Body

Now that we've defined the basic shape of the head and body, things are going to get a bit more complicated. To add legs, we need to make holes for them, which means we need to cut the body into pieces. But first, we need to put more isoparms in select places for smoother stitching later.

Selecting and Inserting Isoparms

To insert isoparms, you need to select existing isoparms and specify where you want to put the new ones.

1. In the perspective view, select the Select tool from the Tool Box. Pick-mask Isoparm and click the first vertical isoparm going around the nose area. The Help line (below the Command line) should read "U Isoparm 19.000." When you select the next isoparm, it should read "U Isoparm 18.000," and so on.

2. Click the horizontal isoparm around the eye level. You should see "V Isoparm 9.000" in the Help line. The isoparm around the mouth level should be "V Isoparm 1.000," and so on. If your isoparms show opposite numbers, such as 1.000 in place of 19.000, you can reverse the parameter values by choosing Edit NURBS → Reverse Surface Direction ❑, setting the Surface Direction to V, and then clicking the Reverse button with Keep Original unchecked.

When selecting isoparms, you have usually selected the proper isoparm if the number ends neatly, such as 1.000 or 1.25. If the number ends not so neatly, such as 9.01 or 15.476, usually you've missed the isoparm. One way to be sure is to select any U or V isoparm near the isoparm you want and then enter the exact value for the isoparm in the numeric input field in the far-right corner of the Status line. To do this, you need to switch from Selection mode to Numeric Input mode.

3. Shift+click U isoparms 13, 12, and 11. Then choose Edit NURBS → Insert Isoparms ▢, select Between Selections, and click Insert. You should see two U isoparms inserted: 12.5 and 11.5.

4. Repeat the procedure for V isoparms 7 and 8 to insert an isoparm 7.5.

5. Insert three isoparms between V isoparms 2 and 3 to get 2.25, 2.5, and 2.75. The inserted isoparms should be placed as shown in Figure 8.5.

Dividing the Surface into Patch Regions

Now we're going to cut the puppy in pieces. Yes, this seems cruel, but it will help us a great deal in reducing the amount of work we need to do.

1. Select the V isoparms 2.5 and 7.5, and then choose Edit NURBS → Detach Surfaces. Delete the right half. The image should look like the one shown in Figure 8.6.

2. Select the V isoparms that will be cut to create the holes for the legs shown in Figure 8.7. (The V isoparm values may be either 2.375 and 1.875 or 2.25 and 1.25, depending on the way you split the body into two pieces.) Choose Edit NURBS → Detach Surfaces again to detach those areas. Now there are three pieces. We need to divide these into 15 separate regions.

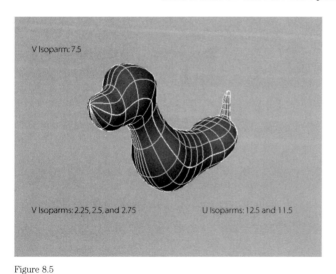

V Isoparm: 7.5

V Isoparms: 2.25, 2.5, and 2.75   U Isoparms: 12.5 and 11.5

Figure 8.5

The puppy with inserted isoparms

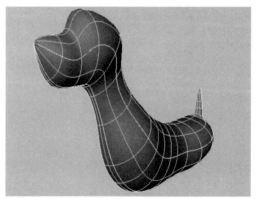

Figure 8.6

Half a puppy!

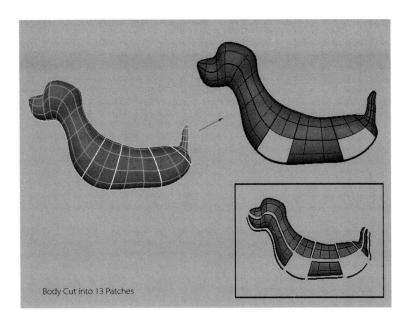

Figure 8.7

**Three regions cut into
15 smaller regions**

Body Cut into 13 Patches

3. Select the U isoparms 12.5, 11.5, 9, and 7 along the three pieces and detach them. You might want to do this in several steps. Get rid of the patches where the legs will be. We end up with 2 holes and 13 patches.

4. This is a good place to pause and clean up. Group the 13 pieces and name them if you wish. If you haven't saved the file yet, do so now. While you are in the middle of building a model, the object names and their groupings are simply for your convenience, and they don't need to be organized too carefully. The scene name, however, should describe what you've done, such as Dog_13pieces, or where you are in the modeling stage, such as Dog_model_1.

It is simplest to rename objects in the Outliner. Just double-click the node, type the name, and press Enter on the keyboard. When you are naming a series of nodes, such as obj1, obj2, obj3, and so on, you can also copy one name and paste it repeatedly—the numbers will be updated automatically.

After you cut up the surface, the smaller patches retain the parameter values they had before they were detached. They must be parameterized again using Rebuild Surfaces before you can apply stitching. If you don't do this, the results will be unpredictable. We will deal with this a little later in the chapter, in the "Rebuilding the Parameters" section.

Building the Legs

Because we are now dealing with only half the puppy's body, we need to come up with just one front leg and one back leg. Later, we'll duplicate these to add the other two legs.

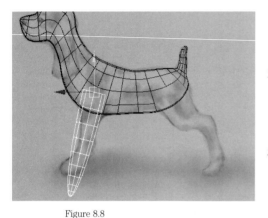

Figure 8.8

Transforming the half puppy

1. Create a layer, name it Dog Body, and assign the 13 patches to it. We can hide them or turn them into templated objects later when we are working with the legs.

2. Create a sphere and set its spans to 20. Detach it in the middle to get a half sphere with 10 spans. Delete its history and the top half. Use move, rotate, and scale procedures to transform the bottom half to the position shown in Figure 8.8.

3. Select hulls and build the leg in side view (in the same way that we built the profile of the dog's body). Notice the way that the rows of CVs are distributed in the side view shown in Figure 8.9. This will greatly simplify the setup process when we rig the puppy for animation in Chapter 12, "Binding." Next, scale the leg to the proper size in the X axis in the perspective view or the front view.

4. Move the leg to where it should be on the dog, a bit to the side, and tweak the CVs to place the top opening of the leg near where the hole is on the dog's body, as shown in Figure 8.10. Try to place the two spans of the leg geometry next to the two spans of the hole on each side, so they will stitch smoothly. How well the leg is being positioned for stitching with the body pieces involves some guesswork. After you gain some experience in stitching, your guesses will become more accurate.

> Typing numbers to position items is often not possible when you are building models. Organic modeling in particular is both fun and frustrating at the same time because you need to trust your artistic sense more and "guesstimate," as opposed to being precise. Do not think of guessing as being sloppy. "Guessing" here means doing things roughly now, knowing that you will be tweaking later.

5. Create a layer and name it Dog Legs. Assign the front leg to it, and turn off its visibility.

6. Build the back leg the same way you created the front leg. Ten spans of isoparms are enough. You now should have something similar to the illustration in Figure 8.11. Notice how the isoparms are placed around the joints as you are moving the hulls and the CVs. Also, the top end of the back leg is a bit higher and farther back than the hole on the body. This was done intentionally in preparation for stitching.

7. As a final step, we need to cut the legs into four pieces, as shown in Figure 8.12. Select V isoparms 1, 3, 5, and 7 and detach them. For both the front and the back legs, the isoparm values should be the same. Group them accordingly, name them, and assign them to the Dog_Legs layer.

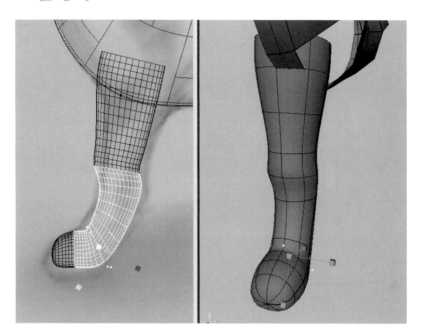

Figure 8.9

Leg CVs laid out for animation

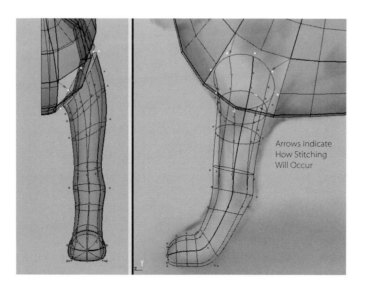

Figure 8.10

The front leg in its proper position

Figure 8.11

**Build the back leg
similar to the front.**

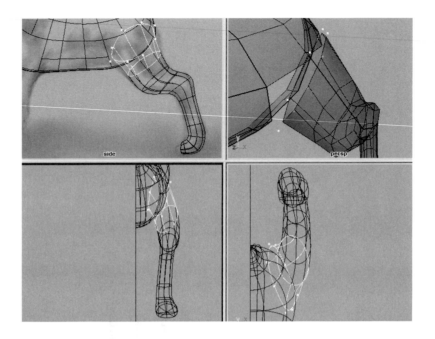

Rebuilding the Parameters

Now that we have the patches built, we are almost ready to stitch them together. However, first we need to rebuild the parameters. Currently, the smaller patches have the parameter values they had before they were detached. We need to reparameterize so that we can have the proper calculations between the patches for stitching.

1. Choose Edit NURBS → Rebuild Surfaces and make sure the settings are as in Figure 8.13. The Keep CVs box should be checked. Don't close this dialog box.

Figure 8.12

**Cutting the legs into
pieces**

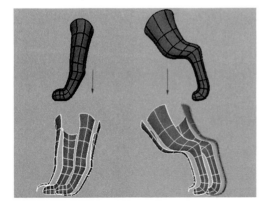

2. In the modeling window, press Ctrl+A to open the Attribute Editor. Select the top patch of the dog's head, and look at the NURBS Surface History of the geometry. In the Spans UV field, the values are 8 and 3, but the Min Max Range for U and V have different numbers. We need to reparameterize the patch to get the Max Range numbers to match the Span values.

3. Select all the geometry pieces in the modeling window and click Rebuild. You should see slight changes in the isoparm placements, as shown in Figure 8.14. Although the changes may seem insignificant, they are necessary for proper calculations between the patches. Select the dog's top head patch again. The Max numbers for UV should now match the corresponding Span values.

Stitching tools

The next stage of building our puppy model will be to stitch together the parts we've created. Stitching involves a set of Maya techniques and tools that we haven't used in earlier exercises, so before we continue, let's take a brief break from building the puppy and see how stitching works in Maya.

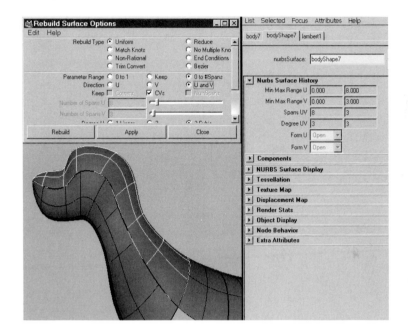

Figure 8.13

Settings in the Rebuild Surface Options dialog box

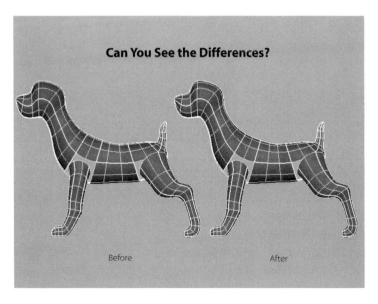

Figure 8.14

Reparameterized patches

Stitching Basics

In Maya, three types of stitching are available by choosing Edit NURBS → Stitch: Stitch Surface Points, Stitch Edges Tool, and Global Stitch. We will use the Stitch Edges tool to put together the parts of the dog and continue to shape its body, and then we'll use the Global Stitch function to keep the patches seamless.

Stitching Surface Points

Stitch Surface Points is a simple tool used to join CV points from different surfaces. To use this type of stitching, select one CV you want to stitch from each of the surfaces and apply Stitch Surface Points. The points should snap together, meeting each other halfway as shown on the left side of Figure 8.15.

Another way to use Stitch Surface Points is to open its option window and turn off the Assign Equal Weights setting. Then, when you select CVs and apply the stitching, the first point will stay where it is, and the other points will snap to the first point, as on the right side of Figure 8.15. The points in this setting are said to be in a *master-slave relationship*. The point that does not move is the master, and the point that moves is the slave.

Stitching Edges

You use the Stitch Edges tool to join two surface edges together. The default setting joins the edges in a master-slave relationship, as shown in the upper half of Figure 8.16. When you open the option window for this tool, you will see that Weighting Factor On Edge1 is set to 1 and Weighting Factor On Edge2 is set to 0. This means that the first edge isoparm you selected will not move, and the second edge isoparm you selected will snap to the first edge, as in the top right of Figure 8.16. If you want to apply equal weighting for both edges so that they will both move to meet in the middle, adjust the Weighting Factor settings to 0.5 for both edges, as shown at the bottom left. The edges will then meet halfway, as shown on the bottom right of Figure 8.16.

Figure 8.15

Two ways to stitch surface points

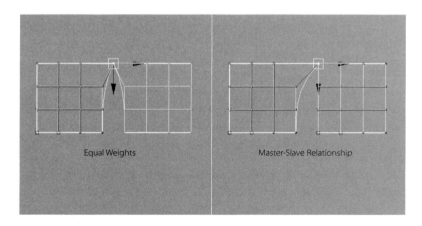

Equal Weights   Master-Slave Relationship

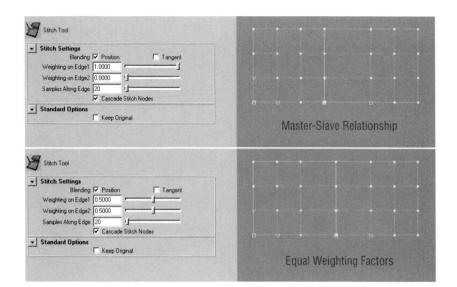

Figure 8.16

**Two ways to use the
Stitch Edges tool**

Global Stitching

Global Stitch can stitch all the edges of adjacent surfaces together. It automatically gives all
the surface edges being stitched equal weights and holds the pieces together like rubber. For
Global Stitch, the edges of the surfaces must be closer together than the Max Separation setting in the options, or it will not apply to the surfaces correctly.

> For both the Stitch Edges tool and the Global Stitch function, you can maintain C0 continuity
> or C1 continuity, also known as *tangent continuity*, between the stitched edges. See Chapter 5,
> "NURBS Modeling," for more information about the degrees of continuity.

Stitching between Two Edges

Now it's time to put the pieces of the dog together into a seamless whole. For the following
procedures, you might want to get into the wireframe or the x-ray viewing mode, because
either of these modes makes it easier to select isoparms. To switch to the x-ray viewing mode,
go to the modeling window and choose Shading → Shade Options → X-Ray.

First, we'll attach the legs to the dog's body by stitching the leg edges.

1. In perspective view, select the front leg and press the F key to center the geometry so
    that you can rotate around it. Choose Edit NURBS → Stitch → Stitch Edges Tool ❒ and
    click the Reset Tool button to make sure you're using the default settings. Then check
    the Tangent setting and close the option window.

2. Select the top-edge isoparm (it's also called a *surface boundary* isoparm) of the leg patch. Then select the patch edge located at the top side of the hole. The patch edge should snap to the leg patch, and the two patches should turn bright green, as shown in Figure 8.17. (You don't need to press Enter to complete the stitching process at this point.)

3. Go to the next boundary isoparm of the leg and repeat the stitching with the side edge of the hole.

4. Repeat the process with the next two edges. You should have a cross shape of green patches coming out from the body to the leg patches, as shown in Figure 8.18.

5. Press Enter to complete the action.

> In addition to pressing Enter to complete the stitching action, you can press any of the tool hotkeys, such as Q for the Selection mode. To repeat the stitch action, press Y.

6. Repeat the procedure with the back leg, as shown in Figure 8.19. Make sure to select the leg boundary isoparm first and the body boundary isoparm second, because the order of selection determines the master-slave relationship. The slave edge snaps to the master edge, and it is important that the leg patches function as master edges.

Stitching the Corners

So far, we've stitched seven body patches to the legs. Six corner patches still need to be stitched. Let's try stitching one of the head patches as an example.

1. To stitch the top patch of the dog's head to the adjacent (shoulder) patches, choose Edit NURBS → Stitch → Stitch Edges Tool (leave the default settings). Select the boundary edge of one of the adjacent patches, and then select the edge of the head patch, as

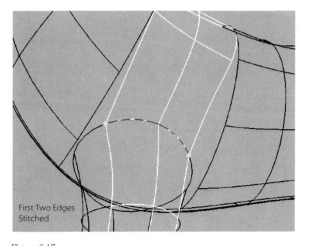

Figure 8.17

Stitching the first edge

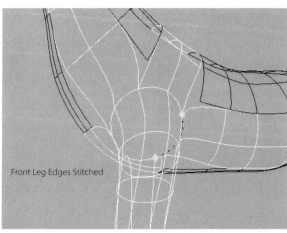

Figure 8.18

Stitching the four front leg edges

shown on the left in Figure 8.20. Complete the action by pressing Enter. Then repeat the procedure with the other adjoining patch as shown on the right in Figure 8.20. Even though the head patch may look as if it is lined up after the first stitching, you still need to stitch it to the second adjacent patch to make sure that the patches are lined up properly.

2. Repeat the procedure to stitch the corners on the other five patches. Figure 8.21 is an example of one of the patches that must be stitched three times. The patch represented as number 2 needs to be stitched to three other number 1 patches. Select the number 1 patch boundary isoparms first each time, and then select the boundary isoparm of the number 2 patch being stitched.

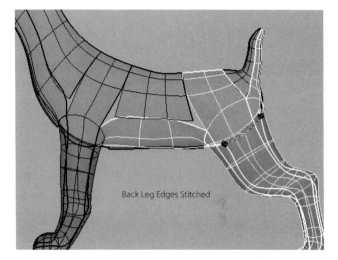

Figure 8.19

Stitching the back leg edges

Tweaking the Stitched Surfaces

When you look at the final stitched surface in Shaded mode, you will probably notice creases. The places where the creases occur and their severity will vary with how you've built your model. At this point, yours should look similar to the model shown in Figure 8.22. Unfortunately, there is no easy way to get rid of these creases.

Figure 8.20

Stitching the corner patch

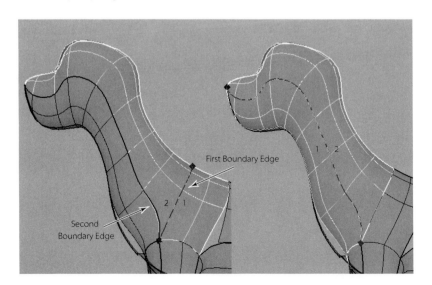

Figure 8.21

A patch being stitched

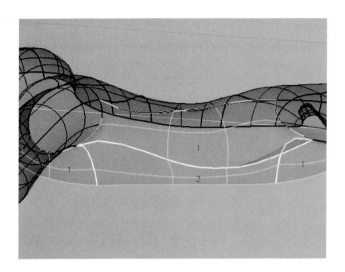

Figure 8.22

The puppy model with all the patches stitched

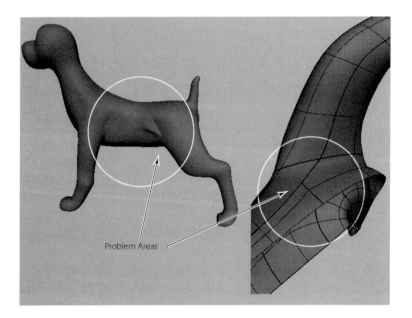

Problem Areas

Where the stomach meets the back leg, the isoparm has actually folded (as shown on the right in Figure 8.22). In such situations, you need to tweak the CVs of the master edges (the leg patches in our example) to get rid of the creases. Figure 8.23 shows some of the ways CVs have been pulled and rotated to correct the problems. Generally, you should move two CVs from the master edge to keep control of the surface tangency. Where the four patches are being joined at the corner as in the top-left picture in Figure 8.23, you might want to move the four CVs on each of the two master patches, eight CVs in all, together in order to maintain their tangency. When you move the CVs on the master edges, the slave edges will follow to keep the tangent continuity between the surfaces.

At this point, we have accumulated a lot of construction history. Choose Edit → Select All By Type → NURBS Surfaces, and then choose Edit → Delete By Type → History. We will lose our stitches on the body, which is fine—we no longer need them. Next, apply Freeze Transformations to ensure that your objects can be easily put back into place in case they are moved, accidentally or otherwise.

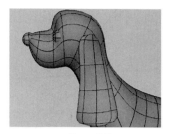

Figure 8.24

A basic dog's face

Building the Face

In contrast to the elaborate modeling that went into building the body, we'll keep the dog's face simple. Use spheres for the eyes, nose, and ears, as shown in Figure 8.24.

Place the eye and the nose in the appropriate positions, and pull in a couple of the CVs on the head to make room for the eye (but don't touch the two end CVs along the boundaries). You can create the ear by deforming the hulls of another sphere.

Figure 8.23

Manipulating CVs to eliminate creases

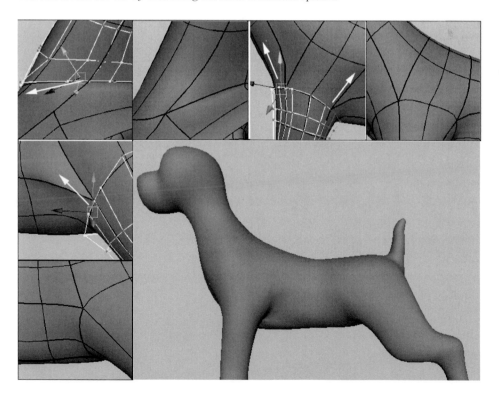

Mirroring and Attaching the Model

Mirroring is a common modeling technique. As its name implies, mirroring duplicates the selected items as a mirror image of the original items along a selected axis. Again, the symmetry of human and animal bodies means that we can take advantage of mirroring to greatly reduce the work of modeling such a body. We will use mirroring to duplicate the right half of the puppy.

1. Select all the objects in the modeling window except for the nose. Group them. This sets up the surfaces for mirroring because the pivot point for the group node is at the origin. Choose Edit → Duplicate ❐, set Scale X to –1, and click Duplicate. You should have a mirrored group of objects.

> As mentioned previously, the location of an object's pivot point is crucial to how it scales and rotates. In order for the model to scale properly, you might need to select all your patches, press Insert to enter Transform Pivot mode, and X+LM drag their pivot points to 0 on the X axis. When you are done, press Insert again to toggle out of Transform Pivot mode.

2. You now see the whole model of the dog. Before you attach the middle patches, make sure you like what you see. Are the body parts proportional? Are the legs too close or too far apart? If you want to modify any parts of the dog, undo the duplication and make the necessary changes before continuing.

3. When you are satisfied with the way everything looks, select the edge isoparms of all the patches that meet at the middle, or the Y axis, and attach them using the default settings. You should end up with 10 attached pieces making up the profile of the puppy, as in Figure 8.25.

Cleaning Up the Model

Now we can clean up our model by deleting the history and the transformation information. We can also group the model parts. In our particular project, the history and the transformation information of the patches are no longer needed, so we can delete them. In other situations, however, this information might be important. For example, you might want to animate a complex object procedurally, by controlling a simpler node that carries the history or the transformation information of the complex object. So, you'll need to decide whether to delete or retain this information on a case-by-case basis.

1. Select all the patches in the modeling window and choose Edit → Delete By Type → History.

2. Choose Modify → Freeze Transformations. Ignore the warning.

3. Group the legs and name them. Give the group nodes sensible names, such as Front_Legs or L_frontleg. You might not feel you need to name the leaf nodes. However, it is a good idea to rename everything, rather than leaving a node named something like leg33detachedSurface2detachedSurface2.

4. Group the body and the face, renaming them appropriately.

5. Put the face and body pieces into the Dog_Body layer. Put the leg pieces into the Dog_Legs layer.

Globally Stitching the Model

Finally, we should apply global stitching to the puppy. Unlike regular stitching, global stitching doesn't have a master-slave distinction; all the pieces are held together with equal weight. When we were building the model, we needed the control provided by the regular stitch; namely, the master-slave relationship of the edges being stitched. Now that the model is put together seamlessly with first-order continuity (C1) among the patches, we can easily stitch all the pieces together with one command.

Figure 8.25

The final mirrored and attached model

1. Select all the pieces except for the face objects, and then choose Edit NURBS → Stitch → Global Stitch ❒.

2. From the Global Stitch Options Box, choose Edit → Reset. Then click Global Stitch. Now if you move any of the patches, you will notice that they behave like rubber, stretching to keep themselves together.

3. The model is now ready to be set up for animation. Save the final scene as Dog_Final_Model. You can find this finished version in the Color Gallery on the CD.

> The puppy was built in NURBS to illustrate the patch-modeling techniques. It would be easy for us to take the NURBS puppy at this point and turn it into a subdivision surface puppy, using the same techniques that were used to build a character's head in the previous chapter.

Hands On: Building a Character III (Advanced)

In Chapter 5, "NURBS Modeling," we began the project of building a character, a young boy, using NURBS-modeling techniques to create the face. Then, in Chapter 6, "Polygons and Subdivision Surfaces," we continued the project using polygons and subdivision surfaces to finish building the head. In this tutorial, we will combine various techniques to create the character's body, hands, feet, and hair.

1. We are going to take advantage of subdivision surfaces again to build a seamless body, using basically the same techniques that were used for building the head. First build a rough outline of the body with a NURBS cylinder as in Figure 8.26, with 15 U spans and 12 V spans. Cut it in half, keep the left side, and add another V isoparm where the arm will attach. The selected surface patches on the right in Figure 8.26 will be where the arm will attach. The number of spans will be three for top and bottom and two for front and back, so the arm should have 10 spans to fit the body cleanly.

2. Convert the body to polygons using the Control Points setting (choose Modify → Convert → NURBS To Polygons ❏), and delete the six faces where the arm will attach. You might also want to delete unnecessary faces at the bottom or the top. Roughly tweak the vertices to make the hole round, as on the left in Figure 8.27. Build the arm from another cylinder, with 10 U spans and about 10 V spans for the length of the arm. Place the arm near the hole on the body as on the right in Figure 8.27, convert it to polygons, and then combine the two surfaces as shown in Figure 8.27.

Figure 8.26

A rough body shape

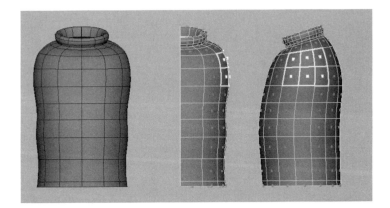

Figure 8.27

The arm attached to the body

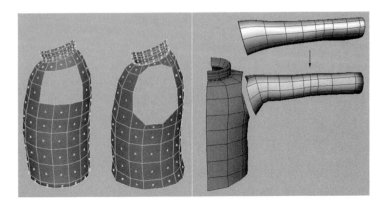

3. Once the two are combined, you can merge them using the Merge Edge tool. Once the arm has been attached, more tweaking is needed. For the hand, we can use the smoothed polygon hand we built in Chapter 6, but for the purposes of this tutorial, let's also make a subdivision surface hand. Either one will work well, although for close-up shots of the hand, the subdivision surface hand will render more smoothly. Take the polygon hand before smoothing, and edit the edges and vertices to turn all faces into quadrangles, as shown in Figure 8.28. You can put in extra edges where the fingernails will go and then use the Full Crease Edge/Vertex command to create sharp edges around the fingernails, as in the third hand in Figure 8.28.

4. The leg is a bit tricky. Start with a NURBS cylinder. Down the length of the leg could be about 14 or 15 U spans, and around the leg should be 10 V spans. Deform the CVs to make it look like half of the lower torso and the leg, as on the left in Figure 8.29. Turn the cylinder into polygons using the Control Points setting, delete the extra edges and vertices at the middle, and select the top four faces. See how the hole that would be created from deleting the four faces matches up with the body.

5. Because the body has three faces for the side but the leg only has two for its side, it needs one more edge to match the body. Split three of the faces as in the second image in Figure 8.30. Because one of the top faces now has five vertices, when the top four faces are deleted, the leg now has an open space with nine edges. Tweak the vertices to make it look more like the last leg in Figure 8.30. The leg should now match up cleanly edge for edge with the body.

Figure 8.28

The hand subdivided

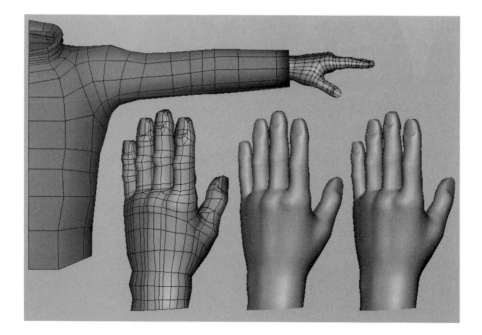

Figure 8.29

Deforming the CVs to
build the leg

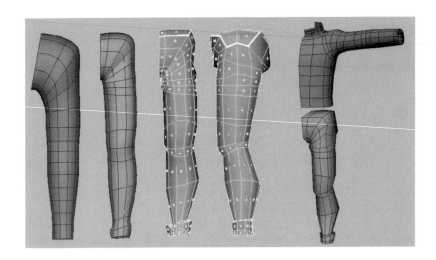

Figure 8.30

Adding an extra edge
for the leg

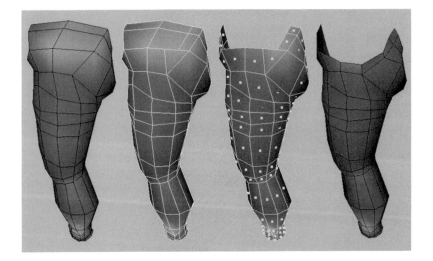

6. Combine the body and the leg; then merge them. You'll see the image on the left in
    Figure 8.31. Tweak the vertices, taking care to raise the waistline and push the circle
    of the shoulder line farther into the body, as in the middle image in Figure 8.31.
    Mirror the body and merge the edges, and tweak more until you are satisfied with the
    way the body looks. Convert the polygon into a subdivision surface (choose Modify →
    Convert → Polygons To Subdiv) to get something that looks like the right image in
    Figure 8.31.

If the Modify → Convert → Polygons To Subdiv command gives you an error message and does not convert the polygonal object, its polygon count may be too high. In that case, increase the value of Maximum Base Mesh Faces in the option box. Or it could mean that you forgot to delete winged vertices.

7. You can go back and forth at any time between polygons and subdivision surfaces, work with half a body for a while, and then mirror and merge again. You should also fit the head into the neck area by scaling the body and tweaking the vertices. To put the finishing touch to the body, select the top nine faces on the shoulder area, as shown on the left in Figure 8.32, and then extrude them twice. When converted to subdivision surfaces, the extrusion becomes a shoulder pad, as shown on the right in Figure 8.32.

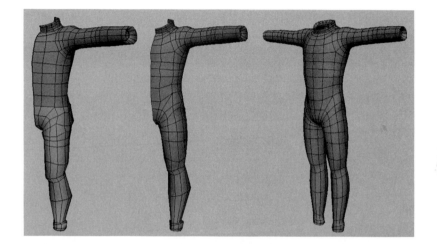

Figure 8.31

Tweaking and merging the body

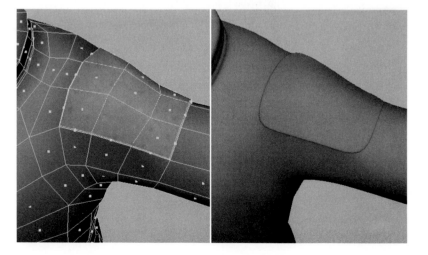

Figure 8.32

Extruding a shoulder pad

8. The shoes and hair are left to model. Start with a NURBS sphere and get a rough shape of the shoe. Convert it to polygons, and edit the tip of the shoe to get rid of the pole as in (a) in Figure 8.33. Extrude to create the bottom part, as in (b). Look carefully at how the edges have been edited to create quadrangles in (c). The areas where the edges are placed closely together are there to get sharp edges. Extrude the top two rows of faces twice to get more detail, as in (d). Convert to subdivision surfaces and tweak the top area to fit around the ankle, as in (e).

9. Finally, the hair on our character is composed of many simple NURBS strips. Try to place them as if they were tufts of hair, and layer them so you won't see any "bald" spots from any normal camera angle, as shown in Figure 8.34. We will texture them with transparency maps later to simulate hair strands.

The character model is now done. You can see a rendered image in the Color Gallery on the CD. The next step is to set up the character for animation and then bring him to life.

Figure 8.33

Modeling Subdivision surface shoes

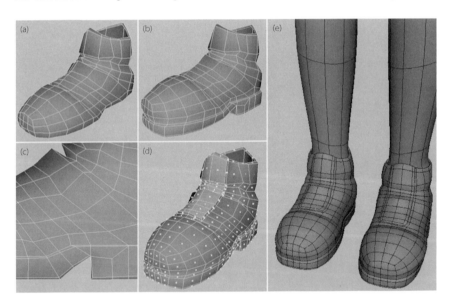

Figure 8.34

Placing NURBS strips for the hair

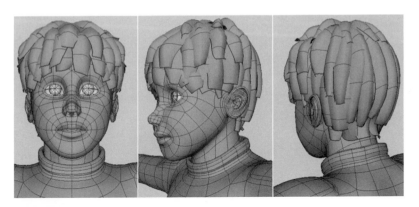

Summary

In this chapter, we stepped through building a complicated patch model of a dog, from start to finish. In addition to learning one specific method for building a dog in patches, we also covered the concepts and techniques for building complex models in general. These techniques included rebuilding surfaces, mirroring and attaching parts, and stitching to create seamlessness.

We also finished our character-modeling project, building a seamless body, arms and legs, with simple shoes, and what will hopefully be considered stylish hair. We will come back to our models for character setup tutorials in Chapter 13, "Character Animation Exercises."

PART III

Animation

In Part III, *you will learn all about animating in Maya. A computer animator makes things move and come alive inside the computer. In the following seven chapters, we'll cover the basics of keyframe animation, and you'll learn to animate with paths, skeletons, and deformers. You will also learn to bind surfaces using different methods, set up a character hierarchy for animation, and then practice different ways to make that character come alive by applying various principles of animation and by using the Trax Editor. You will also be introduced to ways to realistically simulate physical forces acting on objects using rigid bodies.*

CHAPTER 9

Animating in Maya

This chapter introduces you to animating in Maya. We will go over the fundamental concepts of keyframing in Maya, the various interface controls, and the tools for creating and editing keyframes. The tutorial in this chapter demonstrates how to use Maya's Set Driven Key tool. The techniques you'll learn in later chapters are quite challenging, so be sure to get a firm grasp of the basic tools in this chapter. This chapter features these topics:

- **Keyframe animation**

- **The Time Slider and Range Slider controls**

- **Techniques for creating keyframes**

- **Techniques for editing keyframes**

- **Hands On: Animating a finger**

Keyframe Animation

Animation, at its basic level, is *change over an interval of time*. In Maya, almost anything can be changed over time; in other words, almost anything you create in Maya can be animated.

You've learned how Maya has a node-based structure. Any attribute within the node that has a numeric value is *keyable*. Keying, or *keyframing*, in Maya is the act of assigning a numeric value to a node attribute at a specific time frame. As the frames change, so can the attribute value. For example, the basic attribute Visibility actually has a numeric value of either 1 (for on) or 0 (for off), so it can be keyframed and animated.

Keyframing is a concept taken from classic 2D animation. Senior animators draw important "key" poses of characters being animated at certain frame intervals, called *keyframes*. The junior animators then take over and draw all the frames between the keyframes, which are called *in-betweens*. The same thing happens when you are animating in Maya, as shown in Figure 9.1. You are the senior animator who establishes the key poses of whatever it is you are animating, and the computer is the whole department of junior animators drawing the in-betweens for you.

Other kinds of animation you may decide to explore on your own in Maya include rotoscoping, which is actually a kind of keyframe animation, and motion capture, a process of creating function curves from live actors' performances.

Figure 9.1

Key poses for a sphere with the in-betweens

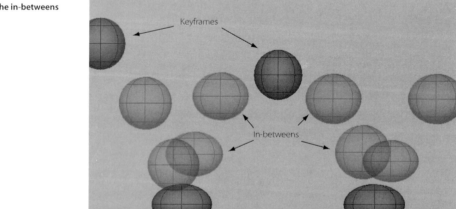

ARE YOU AN ANIMATOR?

There are levels of animating. At the basic level, you move things from A to B, which almost anyone can do. The next level involves learning and intelligently using certain animation principles, such as squash and stretch, anticipation, key posing, and so on. The 2D cell-animation schools are still the best places to learn these principles, although computer animation schools are beginning to offer classes in this area. If you want to be an animator, there is no way around it—you must learn them.

The ability to bring life to a character, however, requires more than just following animation principles. A successful animator also has a good sense of timing, which belongs to the realm of performance. Timing is a skill you are born with as much as something that is learned, and certain individuals are naturally better at animating than others, just as some people are naturally better dancers or singers than others. In fact, the ability to create authentic emotions and pathos in animated characters requires great acting skills.

A good way to discover whether you are an animator is to go through a whole animation project and ask yourself which parts of the project you enjoy spending time on the most. An animator's focus will generally be different from that of other 3D artists. Modeler and texture artists, for example, are usually interested in how things look; they want to create beautiful images, evoking certain feelings. Animators are usually most interested in telling a good story.

Animation Controls

Before we go further into keyframing, let's look at some animation control tools: the Time Slider and the Range Slider (see Figure 9.2). These and the other tools discussed in this chapter are in Maya's Animation module.

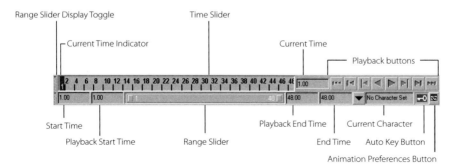

Figure 9.2

The Time Slider and the Range Slider

Playing Back and Updating Animations with the Time Slider

The Time Slider comes with playback buttons, which look like those on a video player control panel. You can also use the following hotkeys, shown to the right, to control the playback.

Alt+V	Toggles between play and stop
Esc	Stops the playback
. (period)	Moves to the next keyframe
, (comma)	Moves to the previous keyframe
Alt+. (period)	Moves to the next frame
Alt+, (comma)	Moves to the previous frame

You can click or drag in the Time Slider to do various things. When you click a frame number, that frame becomes the current time. If you drag the mouse, the animation updates interactively, which is called *scrubbing*. Scrubbing is great for viewing animation if the scene is light, because the object(s) being animated will update almost in real-time, but it loses its effectiveness as the scene becomes heavier.

When you MM click or drag, the current time indicator moves to where the mouse is without updating the animation. This is a valuable function when you want to quickly keyframe the values of one frame to other frames. MM dragging is also used for scrubbing only the audio, as opposed to scrubbing the whole scene.

The Time Slider can also become a virtual Time Slider inside the modeling window, the Graph Editor, or the Dope Sheet. To use it inside these windows , press the K key at the same time as you press the left mouse button. By K+dragging in any window, you can scrub the animation. By K+MM dragging, you can move the current time without updating the scene and scrub only the audio. This technique can be especially useful when you are editing function curves in the Graph Editor. The Graph Editor and Dope Sheet are discussed later in this chapter, when we get to the topic of editing keyframes.

RM choosing inside the Time Slider opens the Key Edit menu. This menu offers the standard key-editing functions, which we will discuss later in the chapter in the "Editing Keyframes" section. It also provides access to several useful submenus:

- With the Set Range To submenu, you can control the playback range in various ways. One option here is the Sound Length setting, which you can also use to discover the length of an audio file.

- With the Sound submenu, you can show, hide, or rename any of the audio files that have been imported.

- With the Playblast function, you can preview your animation as real-time movie clips (the Playblast function is discussed in Chapter 10, "Paths and Bones").

To play an audio file, you need to set the Playback Speed setting to Real-time in Animation Preferences. Click the Animation Preferences button (the last item on the Range Slider which is right below the Time Slider), and look for Playback Speed under the Playback section.

Controlling the Playback Range with the Range Slider

The Range Slider is a simple tool used to control the playback range of the Time Slider. You can set where the Time Slider starts and ends by sliding, shortening, or lengthening the Range Slider, and you can hide the Time Slider by toggling the Range Slider Display button at the left of the Time Slider.

The Auto Key button on the Range Slider (the next-to-last item on the slider) lets you set keys automatically as you transform the selected object in the modeling window. Using Auto Key for keyframing is explained in the "Creating Keyframes" section of this chapter.

The Animation Preferences button on the right end of the Range Slider lets you view the animation settings in the Preferences dialog box. The animation settings include options that let you adjust the Time Slider. For example, setting the Height to 2x or 4x, as shown here, can help you see the audio waves more clearly, which is helpful when you are scrubbing audio files.

2x   4x

You can also go to the Settings section of the Preferences dialog box and adjust the Time setting under Working Units. The default setting is Film 24 fps (frames per second).

Creating Keyframes

You can create keyframes in many ways in Maya. You can use the hotkeys, the Set Key or Set Breakdown function in the Animate menu, the Channel Box, the Graph Editor, or the Attribute Editor. All these methods are described in the following sections.

Using Hotkeys for Keyframing

Several hotkeys are useful for keyframing:

S	Keyframes a selected object at a specified frame (same as choosing Animate → Set Key, discussed in the next section)
Shift+W	Keys the translations
Shift+E	Keys the rotations
Shift+R	Keys the scales

Keyframing with Set Key

The standard way to keyframe a selected object at a specified frame is to choose Animate → Set Key. In the command's option window, the default setting is to Set Keys On: All Manipulator Handles And Keyable Attributes. With this setting, when you click the Set Key button in the Set Keys Options dialog box (or press the S hotkey), all the attributes displayed in the Channel Box are keyed. This setting may not be practical when you need to set keys only to a few attributes, such as the translation attributes, for example.

Set Key Settings

When you change the Set Keys setting to All Manipulator Handles, all the manipulator values are keyed. When the setting is Current Manipulator Handle, as shown in Figure 9.3, only the active manipulator handle is keyed. This is a useful setting if you want to restrict the keying to the attribute values you are changing, such as the Y-axis translation.

The Prompt setting lets you set keyframes at multiple frames. If you select Prompt, you are prompted for the frames to keyframe when you click the Set Key button (or press the S hotkey). Enter the frame numbers you want keyframed and click OK.

Keyable Attributes

All keyable attributes are displayed in the Channel Box. The default attributes are Translation, Rotation, Scale, and Visibility.

In Maya, each object can have its own keyable attribute settings. You can add or remove the keyable attributes of an object by using the Channel Control. Select an object, and then choose Window → General Editors → Channel Control to open the dialog box shown in Figure 9.4.

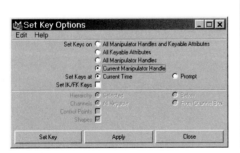

Figure 9.3

The Set Key Options window

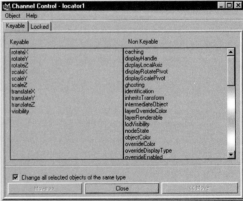

Figure 9.4

The Channel Control dialog box

The Channel Control dialog box displays a long list of nonkeyable attributes on the right and a list of ten default keyable attributes on the left. When you select an attribute in either list, the Move >> or the << Move button becomes active, and you can move the selected attribute to make it keyable or nonkeyable. Any changes you make in the Channel Control dialog box are reflected in the Channel Box. The Channel Control dialog box also has a Locked tab . When an attribute becomes locked, its value becomes static and nonkeyable. The fields for the attribute also become gray.

> Some people find using the Channel Box to lock attributes easier than using the Channel Control dialog box or the Attribute Editor.

Keyframing with Set Breakdown

Set Breakdown works the same way as Set Key, except that instead of setting keys, it sets *breakdowns*. What distinguishes breakdown frames from keyframes is that when regular keys are inserted into a breakdown curve, the breakdown frames become "bound" by the regular keys, and the breakdowns maintain a proportional time relationship to those keys.

To get a better idea of how breakdowns differ from keys, you can try the simple exercise in the "Working with Breakdowns" section later in this chapter. First, however, you need to become familiar with some further tools for controlling animation, particularly the Time Slider and the Graph Editor.

Keying Attributes in the Channel Box

You can key different attributes in the Channel Box. Select an object, open the Channel Box, select any attribute(s), and RM choose the attribute names. A long menu pops up (Figure 9.5), offering many key-editing functions.

The Key Selected command keyframes the attributes that are selected in the Channel Box. Key All keyframes all the keyable attributes for the selected object. The Breakdown Selected and Breakdown All commands work the same way for breakdowns. The Lock and Unlock commands work on selected attributes.

Keying Attributes in the Attribute Editor

You can also set keys in the Attribute Editor the way you do in the Channel Box. A difference is that when you RM choose the keyable attributes in the Attribute Editor as in Figure 9.6, you don't get as many functions in the menu that pops up.

You can lock attributes and set keys, but the keys are set for all X, Y, Z values of translation, rotation, or scale attributes. One advantage of using the Attribute Editor is that you can easily access nonkeyable attributes and make them keyable.

Figure 9.5

The Channel Box with pop-up menu

Keyframing with Auto Key

Auto Key is an efficient way to keyframe in many situations. When you click the Auto Key button on the right side of the Range Slider, the key icon turns white and the background turns red. Once this feature is turned on, any changes you make to the attributes of selected objects at any frame are automatically keyframed. The only precondition with Auto Key is that a keyframe must already exist for an attribute before that attribute can be auto keyed. The Auto Key button is a toggle; click it again to turn the function off.

As an example of using Auto Key, follow these steps:

1. Create a sphere and set keys for its translation attributes at frame 1.

2. Click the Auto Key button to turn on the function.

3. Move to frame 10, and translate the sphere to a different position. The change is automatically keyframed.

4. Move to frame 20 and try rotating the sphere. Nothing is keyed because there are no initial keyframes for the rotation attributes.

If you use Auto Key, make sure to toggle it off when you are finished, or you may unknowingly keyframe objects and end up with a lot of undesirable animation.

Custom Attributes and the Connection Editor

Figure 9.6

The Attribute Editor
with the pop-up menu
for a selected attribute

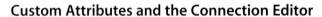

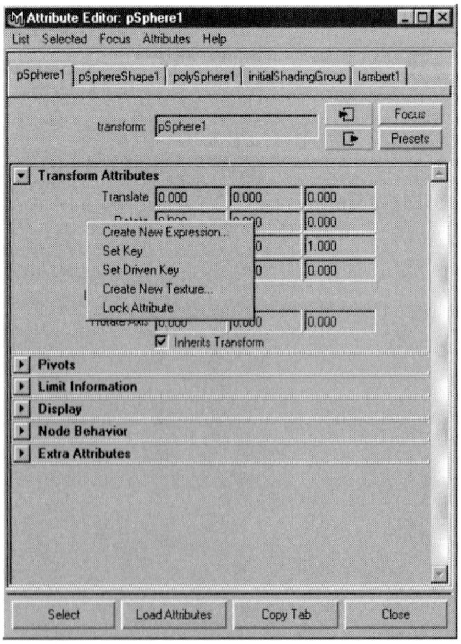

A lot of Maya's power comes from its ability to create custom attributes and connect them from one node to another. Before we begin, however, it is important to know about attribute types and how they are significant. Maya's Connection Editor offers a quick and easy way to automate animation tasks that would otherwise need to be done on an attribute-by-attribute basis. Connected attributes are advantageous because there is little calculation overhead. Additionally, direct, proportional relationships are established between attributes, resulting in mathematically precise animations. In this section, we will create a sphere and torus that behave similarly, despite being two different types of objects.

Working with the Connection Editor

Start a new scene, create a NURBS sphere and a NURBS torus, and choose Window → General Editors → Connection Editor. For this exercise, we are only interested in keyable attributes, so open the menu for Left Display at the top of the Connection Editor and clear the Show Non-Keyable check box. Do the same for the Right Display. Make sure the Channel Box is visible, and select the sphere. In the Channel Box, click the makeNurbsSphere1 input, and then click the Reload Left button at the top of the Connection Editor. All the sphere's keyable attributes should appear in the left column, along with its creation parameters. Next, select the torus, and click the makeNurbsTorus1 input in the Channel Box. Bring the torus and its creation parameters into the Connection Editor by clicking the Reload Right button at the top; the Connection Editor should look like Figure 9.7. Position the Connection Editor so that you can see the sphere, the torus, and the Channel Box.

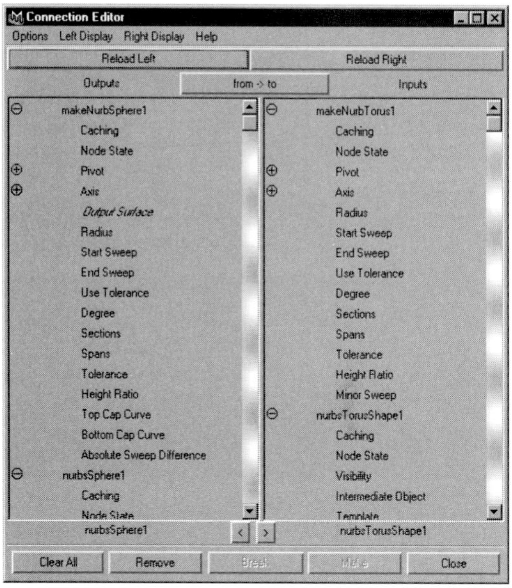

Attribute Types

Only attributes of the same type can be connected. In the Connection Editor, click the Translate entry for the sphere (in the left column). Most of the torus's creation parameters (in the right column), along with its visibility, will turn gray, indicating that they cannot be connected to the sphere's translation.

FLOAT ATTRIBUTES

You will most often work with float attributes, which contain values that are floating-point numbers, such as 3.14159. Translate X and Translate Y are common examples of float attributes. Connect the Start Sweep attribute of the sphere to the Start Sweep attribute of the torus. Then select the sphere and click the makeNurbsSphere1 input in the Channel Box. Select the Start Sweep attribute and MM drag to the right in the view port. Both the sphere and the torus open (as in Figure 9.8) and close. Now select the torus, and click the makeNurbsTorus1 entry in the Channel Box. Its Start Sweep attribute is orange (green on Irix), indicating that it is connected.

INTEGER ATTRIBUTES

Integer attributes contain whole numbers and require fewer calculations for the computer. In the Connection Editor, select the Sections attribute of the sphere and connect it to the Sections attribute of the torus. Select the sphere and click the makeNurbsSphere1 input in the Channel Box. As you change the Sections attribute for the sphere, the number of sections for the torus will update accordingly.

VECTOR ATTRIBUTES

Vector attributes are a collection of three floating-point numbers, used most often for operations on an object's X, Y and Z axes. In the Connection Editor, Translate, Rotate,

Figure 9.7

The Connection Editor with the sphere and torus attributes loaded into it.

Figure 9.8

Sphere and torus partially opened due to a connected Start Sweep attribute.

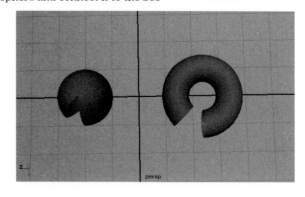

and Scale all have a plus sign (in a circle) to the left of their entries, indicating that they can be expanded. When you click the plus sign next to the sphere's Translate entry in the Connection Editor, the Translate X, Y, and Z entries display in the same manner they appear in the Channel Box. Do the same for the torus's translate entry. Click the sphere's Translate Y entry, and connect it to the sphere's Translate X entry. Because both values are floating-point numbers, Maya allows us to do this—what they are named does not matter. Now move the sphere up on its Y axis. The torus will move to the right. If you move the sphere down, the torus will move to the left. Set the sphere's Translate X attribute to 0 via the Channel Box, and disconnect the torus's Translate X attribute by clicking it in the Connection Editor. The X, Y, and Z components of a vector can be connected individually or collectively. In the Connection Editor, click the Sphere's Translate entry and connect it to the torus's Translate entry. Now if you move the sphere, the torus will follow. The advantage this has over simply parenting the two objects is that they can still rotate and scale independently.

BOOLEAN ATTRIBUTES

Boolean attributes have only two values—on and off—and can be entered as on or off, true or false, and 0 or 1. Visibility is a Boolean attribute. Connect the sphere's visibility to the torus's visibility.

ENUMERATED ATTRIBUTES

Enumerated attributes can have any number of values and are represented by items in a list. The Degree attribute of a NURBS curve or surface is an example of an enumerated attribute. Select the sphere, and click the makeNurbsSphere1 input in the Channel Box. Click the Degree attribute to display a drop-down list. You can change an enumerated attribute by either using its drop-down menu or specifying a number that indicates the position in the list where the value is located, starting with 0. For example, if your sphere has an enumerated attribute called Color with Red, Green, and Blue, respectively, as entries, you can set its value to Green by typing the number 1. You can also modify enumerated attributes by typing the entry as it appears in the list—just remember that they are case sensitive. Connect the sphere's Degree attribute to the torus's Degree attribute.

> It is possible to connect Boolean, integer, and float attributes to one another. Think through this action carefully before you take it. Connecting these attributes can result in unpredictable behavior that is difficult to track down.

Maya also lets you create custom attributes and rename or delete them. To try out this feature, create a sphere and choose Modify → Add Attribute to open the Add Attribute dialog box. You can also open the Add Attribute dialog box through the Attribute Editor; by opening the Attributes menu. In the Add Attribute dialog box, you use the options on the Control tab to create simple new attributes with values ranging from 0 to 1. You use the options on The New tab to control the new attribute's keyability, data type, and, in some cases, minimum, maximum, and default values, as shown in Figure 9.9.

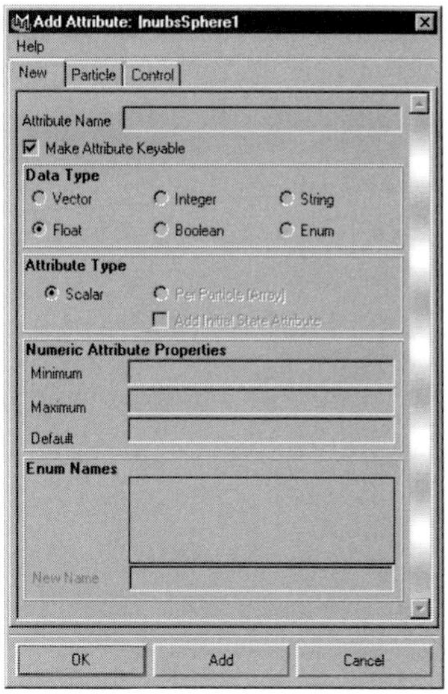

Make sure the sphere is selected and create an attribute called Junk with the default settings; you should see the additional attribute for the sphere in the Channel Box. The added custom attributes can be useful when setting up set-driven keys or expressions, as you'll see later in the Hands On tutorial.

You can rename custom attributes by choosing Modify → Edit Attribute. To delete custom attribute, in the Channel Box, RM-click next to the custom attribute, and select Delete Attributes. (You might need to deselect and select the object again to update the Channel Box.) You can rename or delete only the additional custom attributes you assign to nodes; you can't rename or delete the built-in attributes that are assigned to nodes by Maya.

Figure 9.9

The Add Attribute dialog box

> RM-clicking next to a custom attribute and selecting Delete Attributes does not work for all types of custom attributes. To ensure a custom attribute's removal, use the interface that displays when you choose Modify → Delete Attribute.

Editing Keyframes

After you create the keys or breakdowns, you can edit them by choosing Edit → Keys or by using the Channel Box, Graph Editor, Dope Sheet, or Time Slider. We'll cover the Graph Editor first, because it is the most important keyframe-editing tool, and you will want to use it most often.

Working with Animation Curves in the Graph Editor

When you create a series of keyframes in the Timeline, these keyframes can be represented as function curves or animation curves inside the Graph Editor (choose Window → Animation Editors → Graph Editor). The Graph Editor works like a regular orthographic window in that you can use hotkeys such as A and F for viewing the function curves, you can use Alt+MM drag to track, and you can use the Ctrl+Alt+LM or MM marquee for zooming. However, the settings for the Move and Scale tools change in important ways when the Graph Editor is the active window.

If you are not familiar with animation curves, the Graph Editor may look complicated. It is more complex than most other editors in Maya, but it is important that you learn to work with the Graph Editor and the animation curves. Experienced animators know how to "read" animation curves, visualizing how an object will move differently when the curves are edited a certain way. This alone can often separate the good animators from the bad ones.

To see how the Graph Editor works, let's create some animation curves:

1. Create a sphere. Key translation and rotation animation to it over 30 frames.

2. Using the marking menu hotbox, select Persp/Graph View. The top window should now show the perspective view, and the bottom should display the Graph Editor, as in Figure 9.10.

3. Press A to fit all the curves to the window. You should see six animation curves, one for each channel of the six attributes.

4. Marquee-select a few keyframes near the current time indicator. Notice that the graph outliner to the left shows which curve keys are selected. Move them, and you will see the sphere update interactively.

5. You can also work with only the curves you want by selecting those curves in the graph outliner. Select the translate curves to display only those curves.

Figure 9.10

The Graph Editor

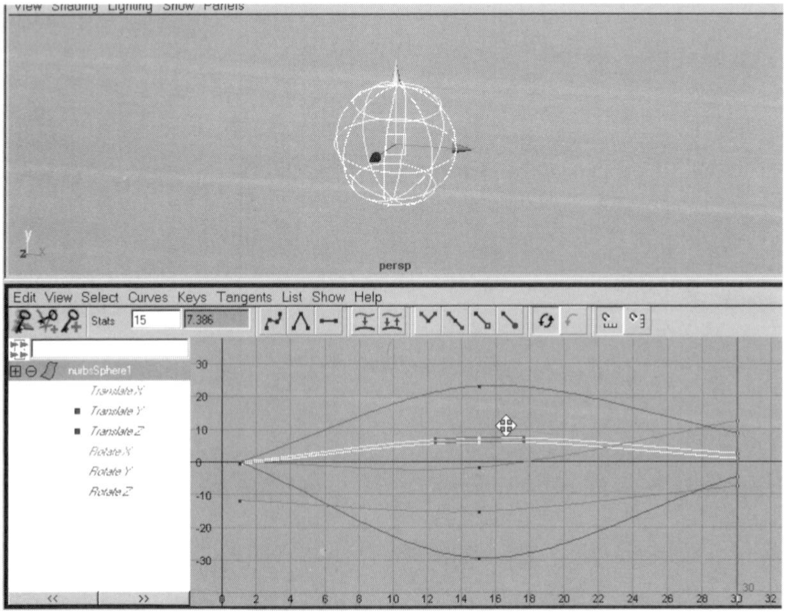

6. The options for the Move tool change when it's used inside the Graph Editor. Either double-click the Move tool icon or choose Modify → Transformation Tools → Move Tool ❐ to open the option window. Then click inside the Graph Editor to make it the active window, and you will see the options change. As shown in Figure 9.11, listed under Move Key Options are Move Only and Move Over. The default Move Over setting lets you move selected keyframes over other keyframes. The Move Only setting allows you to move the keyframes only between other keyframes.

Figure 9.11

The Move Graph Editor window

7. Open the Scale tool's option window. Again, you'll see settings that are different for the Graph Editor. The default Gestural setting sets the pivot point for scaling the selected keys to where you place the mouse. The Manipulator setting lets you create a box to move and scale, as shown in Figure 9.12. This may be the preferable setting for many situations.

Using the Graph Editor Tools

The Graph Editor provides many tools to help you edit curves, as shown in Figure 9.13.

THE TIME SNAP AND VALUE SNAP TOOLS

The Time Snap tool, which snaps the keyframes to frames, should always be turned on, because it makes editing keyframes so much easier. You will have fewer occasions to use the Value Snap tool, which snaps the keyframes to the nearest integer value of the attribute you are keying. Before moving on to the other tools, turn on Time Snap. Instead of working without the snap function and then needing to snap the keyframes later, it is much better to have the Time Snap tool on from the beginning.

> There are Time Snap functions in the Graph Editor, the Dope Sheet, and the Time Slider. You can also access Time Snap in the Preferences dialog box. Choose Window → Settings/Preferences → Preferences, and then choose Timeline in the Categories section. In options, Snapping is on by default.

Figure 9.12

The manipulator box

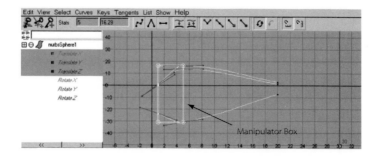

Figure 9.13

The Graph Editor tools

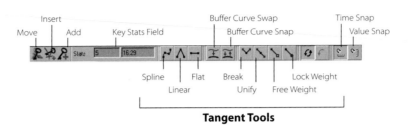

THE MOVE NEAREST PICKED KEY TOOL

The Move tool in the Graph Editor is actually the Move Nearest Picked Key tool, and it works differently from the standard Move tool. These two similar yet different tools can sometimes be frustrating if you confuse their functions. The Move tool moves all selected keyframes or their tangent handles; the Move Nearest Picked Key tool moves only one keyframe or tangent handle at a time–the one nearest the mouse pointer. It will not move curves. You can constrain the tool using the Shift key for horizontal or vertical movements, just as you can constrain the regular Move tool.

THE INSERT KEY AND ADD KEY TOOLS

The Insert Key and Add Key tools are similar. Insert Key inserts a key on the curve at the selected frame. Add Key adds a key to whatever value and frame you are clicking, changing the curve shape accordingly.

THE TANGENT TOOLS

The tangent tools let you change the shape of the curve around the keyframes. The Spline (the default shape), Linear, and Flat tools let you select those shapes. You can see other types on the Tangents menu. Select a few keyframes and play with the types to see how they behave.

If you want to break the tangent or increase the roundness of the curve at specific keyframes, you can use the Unify or Break tool (also available from the Keys menu), with the results shown in Figure 9.14.

Figure 9.14

A smooth tangent and a broken tangent

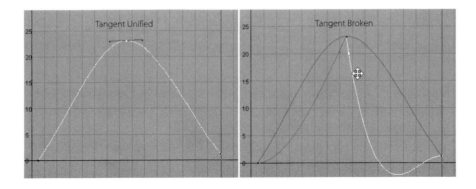

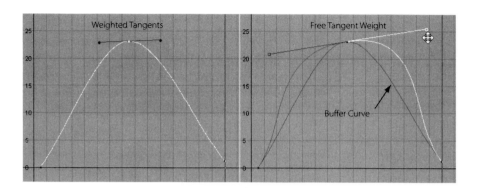

Figure 9.15

**A keyframe with
weighted tangents
(left) and with unlocked
weighted tangents**

Before you can free a keyframe's tangent weight and change it, the tangent of the keyframe must become weighted. Select the keyframe (you can also select the entire curve) and choose Curves → Weighted Tangents. The tangent handles change as shown on the left in Figure 9.15. You can then unlock the weights, using the Free Weight tool, and change the curve shape as shown on the right. After you finish adjusting the curve shape, you can use the Lock Weight tool to lock the tangent weights of the keyframes.

THE BUFFER CURVE SNAPSHOT AND SWAP BUFFER CURVE TOOLS

The Snapshot and Swap tools are similar in function to the Undo command. When you choose View → Show Buffer Curves and edit a curve, changing its shape, the original shape remains as a buffer (as shown in the Figure 9.15 example of the free tangent weight). The Swap Buffer Curve tool snaps the changed curve to the original buffer curve. The Buffer Curve Snapshot tool makes a new buffer curve from the changed curve.

THE KEY STATS FIELDS TOOL

The Key Stats Fields tool lets you enter precise values for keyframes. It is especially handy when you need to assign the same values for multiple keyframes. When the values of the selected keyframes are not the same, the field turns purple, but it turns white again when those keyframes are assigned the same value.

Using the Graph Editor Menus

The Graph Editor menus provide some of the same tools as the toolbar, as well as some other useful functions.

CUT, COPY, AND PASTE FUNCTIONS

Using Edit menu functions, you can cut, copy, and paste selected keyframes. Before you paste, however, make sure to set the proper options, or unexpected results could occur. Choose Edit → Paste ❒, for example, and look over the different settings.

The curves shown in Figure 9.16 were copied from the original curve (shown in white) and then pasted with different option settings back to the original curve. The first example shows a curve inserted into the current time with the Connect setting checked. Notice that the curve being pasted has moved up so that its starting point connects to the original curve at the current time indicator. If you turn off the Connect setting, you get the second example shown in Figure 9.16. The pasted curve is still inserted into the original curve, but it is not translated vertically to connect with the original curve. The Merge setting produces the third example, in which the curve being pasted merges with the original curve. Notice that the last keyframe of the resulting curve is the same as the pasted curve. The fourth example is pasted with the Time Range set to Start and the Time Offset set to 30. In this case, you get the same result if you set the Time Range to Clipboard and Time Offset to 29, because the copied curve on the Clipboard starts from frame 1.

> When using functions that have numerous optional settings, you can often produce the same result in different ways. Certain settings are optimal, depending on the situation. In order to know which settings are optimal for a particular purpose, you need a clear under-standing of what the settings do. It's frustrating to discover that a function that works in one situation will not work in another because different settings are required, and you don't know what those setting changes should be.

PRE- AND POST-INFINITY CYCLES AND EXTRAPOLATIONS

Choosing View → Infinity displays the curve values before and after the first and last keyframes, to infinity. In the Curves menu, you can select Pre and/or Post Infinity cycles or extrapolations. The pre- and post- infinity settings will radically modify the motion graph as shown in Figure 9.17.

The effects of the pre/post infinity settings are as follows:

- The default setting is Constant, which means the values for the first and last keyframes are maintained.

- The Linear setting takes the slope of the tangent.

- The Cycle setting repeats the curve segment, where the first keyframe of the next cycle occupies the same frame as the last keyframes of the current cycle. This can lead to jerky, skipping motion if the first and last keyframes don't have the same values.

- The Cycle With Offset setting takes the last keyframe value as the starting point for the next cycle.

- The Oscillate setting mirrors the cycle before it.

THE ADD AND REMOVE INBETWEEN FUNCTIONS

Two other nifty functions are Add Inbetween and Remove Inbetween, found on the Keys menu. These are simple functions that either add or remove a frame at the current time, moving all the keyframes after the current time one frame forward or backward.

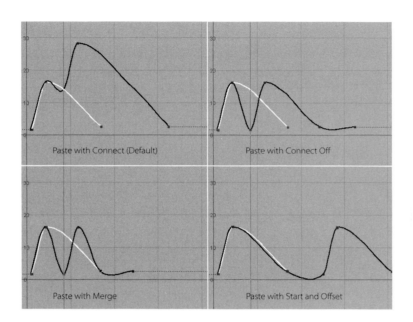

Figure 9.16

Curves pasted with different settings

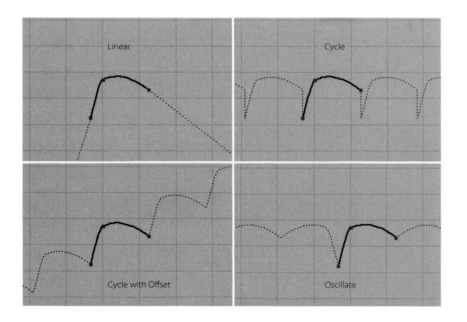

Figure 9.17

Various cycles and extrapolations

THE AUTO LOAD OPTION

In some situations, you might want to deselect one object and select another but still maintain the keyframes of the first object. In such a situation, you can turn off the Auto Load function on the List menu.

Editing Key Times with the Dope Sheet

The Dope Sheet has many of the same editing functions that are available in the Graph Editor. To open the Dope Sheet, choose Window → Animation Editors → Dope Sheet; you'll see the window in Figure 9.18. Because the Dope Sheet edits only key times, it is designed to allow you to move easily around keyframes, curves, and whole groups of curves.

Figure 9.18

The Dope Sheet is an alternative to the Graph Editor.

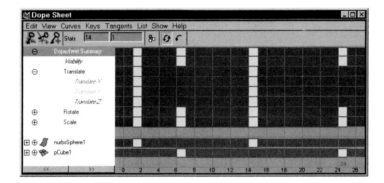

The Dope Sheet has a Dopesheet Summary line, which selects all the keyframes of the selected objects for editing. Alternatively, you can open the summary to select all the specific keyable attributes of the selected objects for editing. For example, you can select the Move tool, select all objects in the modeling window, select the Dopesheet Summary in the Dope Sheet, and move all the keyframes for the entire scene. You can also open the Dopesheet Summary, select Rotate, and then move only the rotation keyframes of all the selected objects in the scene.

Editing Keys in the Channel Box

Key editing in the Channel Box works the same as in the Graph Editor or the Dope Sheet, except that you don't have access to the option windows. The Cut, Copy, Paste, and Delete functions, when RM chosen in the Channel Box, are performed with the default settings.

> The difference between Delete and Cut is usually not significant, but it is worth knowing. Cut puts the keyframes into the Clipboard; Delete simply deletes them. If you have keyframes in the Clipboard that you want to keep, use Delete to remove animation from the selected attributes so that you don't replace the Clipboard items.

Using the Keys Submenu

You can access several key-editing functions from the main menu by choosing Edit → Keys. The functions on this submenu work differently from those with the same name in the Graph Editor, and it's important not to confuse them. The functions in the Keys submenu edit keyframe curves at the object level. You primarily use them to transfer animation curves between objects.

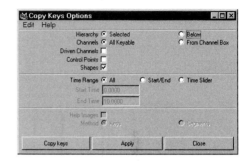

Figure 9.19

The Copy Keys Options dialog box

Cut Keys and Copy Keys have the same option settings. Choose Edit → Keys → Copy Keys ❐ to open the Copy Keys Options dialog box shown in Figure 9.19. The Hierarchy setting Selected copies only the animation curves of the selected object. The Below setting copies all the animation curves of the selected object plus all the objects on the hierarchy below it. You can also control the time range of the curves being copied by clicking Start/End and typing values in the Start Time and End Time boxes.

The Paste Keys options are the same as the Graph Editor's Paste options. If you copy animation curves from a hierarchy, you can paste them into the same hierarchy as well as into other similar hierarchies.

> You can cut or copy curves from multiple objects. The objects' selection order is important because the curves are copied in the same sequence. Also, when you are pasting to multiple objects, their selection order needs to be the same as the order in which the objects were selected for the Copy Keys function.

Working with the Time Slider

The Time Slider has several key-editing functions, which you can access by LM choosing an object that has keyframes. When you do this, the Time Slider displays key *ticks*—red vertical lines showing where keyframes are, as illustrated in Figure 9.20. (Breakdowns are displayed as green ticks.)

By Shift+clicking and dragging, you can select a frame or a range of frames. This range is displayed in a red block with arrows at the start, in the middle, and at the end of the block. You can then move the frame or frame range by dragging the arrows in the middle of the block, scale it by dragging the arrows at the side, or edit it by selecting functions with RM choose.

The Cut, Copy, Paste, and Delete functions are the same as those in the Graph Editor, without the options. The Paste function has Connect set to Off. The Paste Connect function works like the Graph Editor's Paste function with the default settings.

Working with Breakdowns

Now that you've worked with the Time Slider and Graph Editor, we can move on to the topic of breakdowns. This short exercise demonstrates how breakdowns work in Maya.

1. Create a sphere and keyframe it in the X axis at frame 1.

2. Translate it in the X axis to 5 at frame 20, and 0 again at frame 30, setting breakdowns. You can set breakdowns by RM choosing in the Channel Box or by choosing Animate → Set Breakdown (see Figure 9.21). Everything should be the same as if keyframes were used, except that the ticks in the Time Slider are red at frame 1 and green at frames 20 and 30.

Figure 9.20

The Time Slider

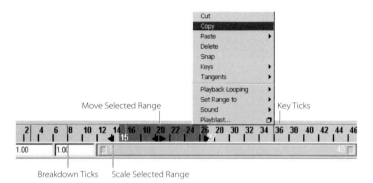

Figure 9.21

The Time Slider showing breakdowns

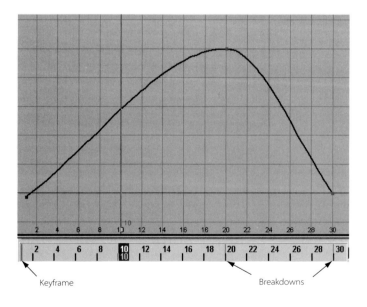

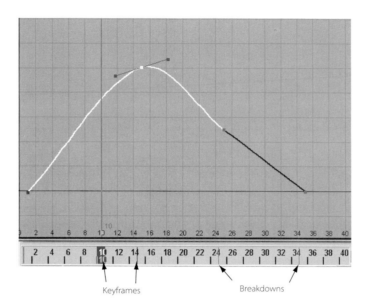

Figure 9.22

The breakdowns are bound to the keyframes.

Keyframes

Breakdowns

3. Set a keyframe at frame 10 with the X-axis translation value of 10.

4. Open the Graph Editor, select the keyframe at frame 10, and try moving it to frame 15. Notice that the breakdowns at frames 20 and 30 move as well, maintaining their curve shape with respect to the keyframe being moved as in Figure 9.22. This is what is meant by breakdowns being "bound" by keyframes.

Hands On: Animating a Finger

In some cases, when one object's attributes change, another object is affected accordingly. For example, consider the way that fingers fold: whenever the second joint of a finger folds, the third joint generally folds as well. Or whenever a button is pressed, a light may be turned on or a door open. It would be nice if you could make such processes automatic. The Set Driven Key tool lets you do this. You can open the tool from the Channel Box, Attribute Editor, or Animate menu (choose Animate → Set Driven Key → Set ❒). The function of the Set Driven Key tool is to link attributes in a master-slave relationship, similar to the Connection Editor. The attributes that influence the other attributes are called *driver* attributes; the attributes that are influenced are called *driven* attributes. Setting driven attributes has several advantages over connecting them, although setting them takes longer. You can easily establish nonproportional relationships, and you need not worry about data types. You can also set up animations that occur only when a value is within a specific range.

We will use the partial hand shown in Figure 9.23 for our tutorial. You'll find the file `finger_setup.mb` on the CD, but if you want to, you can create a simple joint hierarchy like the one we'll be using (for a full discussion on creating joints, see Chapter 10).

Using One Driver Attribute

We will start by using the Set Driven Key tool with a single driver attribute.

1. Open the file `finger_setup.mb` from the CD-ROM. It's a simple setup of a partial hand that has been smoothed, skinned, and weighted to a hierarchy of joints.

2. In the Outliner, select all the joints in the hierarchy, and choose Window → General Editors → Channel Control. In the Channel Control window, select all the attributes on the left side except the rotation attributes, and click the Move>> button. This leaves us with joints that can only be keyed in their rotation attributes, as in Figure 9.24.

Figure 9.23

Use this partial hand as the starting point for an exercise in setting driven keys.

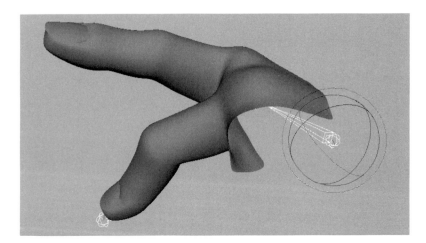

Figure 9.24

Limiting keyable attributes via the Channel Control box

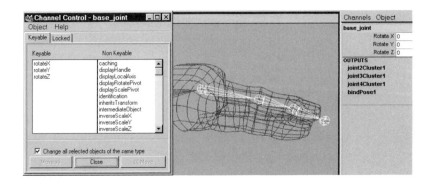

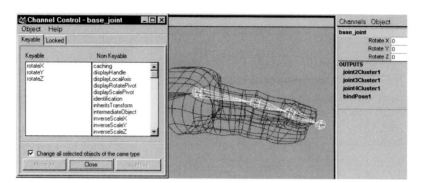

Figure 9.25

Using Set Driven Key to simplify animating

3. Select base_joint, mid_joint, and end_joint; then choose Animate → Set Driven Key → Set ❐. The three joints are listed as Driven, and the Driver list is empty. Click the Load Driver button to load the three joints as Driver items. Select base_joint from the Driver list, and select mid_joint from the Driven list. Their rotation attributes appear on the right side, as shown in Figure 9.25. Select rotateZ on both lists, and click the Key button. Select just mid_joint; in the Channel Box, you will see that the Rotate Z attribute field has turned orange (green on Irix). This indicates that the attribute has animation, but no red ticks are showing in the Time Slider, because there are no explicit keyframes. The mid_joint Rotate Z value is now driven by the base_joint Rotate Z value.

4. Select base_joint, and in the Channel Box change its Rotate Z value to 90; then select the mid_joint and change its Rotate Z value to 100. Click the Key button again in the Set Driven Key window. Now, whenever you rotate the base_joint to 90 degrees, the mid_joint will be driven to rotate 100 degrees. With mid_joint selected, open the Graph Editor. You will see a curve representing the way base_joint drives the mid_joint, as shown in Figure 9.26.

5. Because the values before the first key and after the last key are constant by default, if you rotate the base_joint to a negative value or a value greater than 90 degrees, the mid_joint will remain at 0 or at 100. If you want the mid_joint to be driven by the base_joint for all values, select the curve, open the Curves menu in the Graph Editor, and set the Pre Infinity and Post Infinity values to Linear, as shown in Figure 9.27. Now the mid_joint will be driven by the base_joint for all values. Repeat the same procedure with the end_joint as well, except perhaps make the end_joint rotate 80 degrees when the base_joint rotates 90 degrees, as the end joint tends to rotate a bit less than the middle joint.

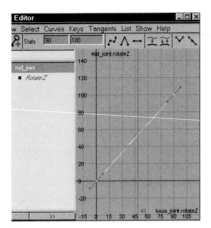

Figure 9.26

The Set Driven Key curve for mid_joint

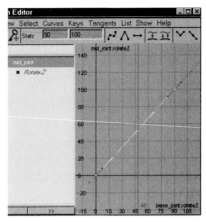

Figure 9.27

Tangents for mid_joint.rotateZ set to linear in case rotational bounds are exceeded.

As you can see from this example, using Maya's Set Driven Key feature is not difficult. One limitation, however, is that once the mid_joint and the end_joint become driven objects, they can't be keyframed. What if you want a finger bending as in Figure 9.23 earlier (as you would when snapping your fingers)? Because the end_joint is already constrained to the rotation value of the base_joint, trying to rotate the end_joint the other way doesn't seem possible. We can solve this problem by using multiple driver attributes.

Using Multiple Driver Attributes

While the end_joint cannot be keyframed, it can be driven by more than one driver. Although you can set up another driver to drive the end_joint in any node, logic dictates that you use the same base_joint node for the second driver.

1. Select the base_joint, and choose Modify → Add Attribute to open the Add Attribute dialog box. In the New tab's Attribute Name field, enter **reverse_rotation**, leave all the settings at their defaults, and click OK. In the Channel Box, you should see a new attribute with the same name. You can use this attribute to drive the end_joint.

2. Select the base joint and end_joint, open the Set Driven Key window if it was closed, and click the Load Driven button to load those objects as drivers as well. Select the base_joint, and click the Load Driver button. Select base_joint reverse_rotation as the driver attribute, select end_joint rotateZ as the driven attribute, as in Figure 9.28, and click the Key button to set your new keys.

Figure 9.28

Setting up a reverse_rotation driver for the end joint.

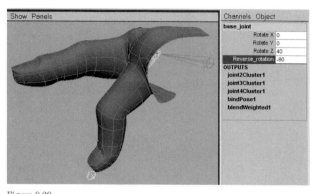

Figure 9.29

Snapping the fingers

3. In the Channel Box, make the reverse_rotation value 90, do the same for end_joint rotateZ, and click the Key button in the Set Driven Key window again. With the end_joint selected, open the Graph Editor and set the Pre and Post Infinity to Linear for the curve representing the new connection to the Reverse_rotation attribute. You can now use the base_joint's attributes, Rotate Z and Reverse_rotation, to animate the fingers more freely, as in Figure 9.29. The final Rotate Z value of the end_joint is roughly 40 minus 80, which is about –40 degrees.

Summary

In this chapter, we covered the basic concepts of keyframe animation and the tools Maya provides for creating and editing keyframes. Some of the interfaces are more challenging than others, especially the Graph Editor if you are not already familiar with function curves. It is the Graph Editor, however, that you will come to love using as you become more familiar with animating in Maya. The next few chapters are going to be challenging, so by all means, take a break!

CHAPTER 10

Paths and Bones

In this chapter, we will continue our examination of animation in Maya by exploring path animation and skeleton construction. Our examples include a chair drifting at sea with a camera following it, a dummy human being built with a skeleton and spheres, and a hierarchy of nodes to set up a character model for binding and animation.

This chapter features these topics:

- **Path animation**

- **Skeletons with bones and joints**

- **Forward and inverse kinematics**

- **Constraints**

- **Hands On: Setting up a character and hierarchy for animation**

Path Animation

Path animation is essentially animating objects along a designated path created with a curve. With the proper settings, the objects can move differently and even deform as they follow the path. This type of animation is ideal for animating things such as roller coasters, ships, and moving cameras.

Attaching an Object to a Path

For path animation, you attach an object to a path. To see how this works, let's create a simple path animation.

1. Create a curve and a cone in the front view port, as shown in Figure 10.1. Make sure that the Time Slider starts at frame 1 and ends at 48.

2. With the cone still selected, select the curve as well. Then choose Animate → Motion Paths → Attach To Motion Path ❏. Reset the options to make sure that you're using the default settings, and then click Attach. You should see the cone snap to the beginning of the curve. Try scrubbing through the frames (by dragging the mouse across frames in the Time Slider) and watch how the cone moves.

3. Under Inputs in the Channel box, you will see motionPath1. Click it to display the U value, which is 0 at frame 1 and 1 at frame 48.

4. Go to frame 15 and verify that the U value is 0.298. MM drag the current time indicator back to frame 1. The U value should still read 0.298. Click the U value, RM choose, and use Key Selected to keyframe that value at frame 1. Now the starting point has changed to U value 0.298, and the cone travels only about 70 percent of the curve from frame 1 to 48, as shown in Figure 10.2.

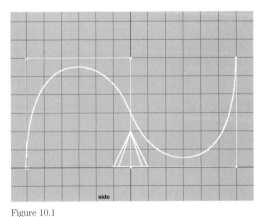

Figure 10.1

A curve and a cone

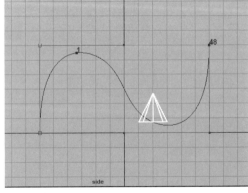

Figure 10.2

The cone doesn't travel the entire path.

5. Open the Attribute Editor, and click the motion-Path1 tab. Set Front Axis to X and Up Axis to Y. Scrub the Timeline on the Time Slider, and you will see how the cone moves differently. Click Inverse Up to flip the object vertically. Set Front Axis to Y and Up Axis to Z. Click Inverse Front to flip the object along the curve. Figure 10.3 shows the effects of setting different attributes for the motion path.

Now that you have an idea how path animation works, we'll try a more complex exercise.

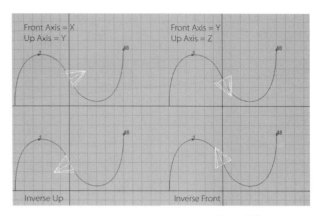

Figure 10.3

Different settings for a motion path in the Attribute Editor

Making an Object Float

In this section, we'll create a short animation of a chair floating at sea. In addition to exploring further how to use path animation, we'll introduce using cameras and previewing in Maya.

1. Open the living room scene you created in Chapter 4, "Modeling Basics." and select the chair group node. Rename it to Chair, and then choose File → Export Selection and save the file as `Chair.mb`. (You can also find this file on the accompanying CD, in the Chapter 10 folder.) You've just exported only the chair hierarchy into a new file.

> Maya's default Export function exports everything associated with the model(s) being exported, including its history, expressions, and animation. If you want to export only the model, turn the other settings off in the option box.

2. Start a new scene, create a NURBS plane, scale it to 100 uniformly, and increase the Patch UV spans to 30.

3. Switch to the Modeling module. Choose Edit NURBS → Sculpt Surfaces Tool ❏ and click Reset Tool. Switch to the Map tab and load the `Wave.tif` file from the CD. You will see the plane become wavy, but it's not wavy enough. Click the Reload button three times. Each time, you will see the waves become more pronounced (see Figure 10.4), as the displacement is compounded.

Figure 10.4

A wavy plane

4. Go to the top view and create a simple curve near the middle of the wavy plane. Select both objects, and create a curve on the surface by choosing Edit NURBS → Project Curve On Surface (see Figure 10.5).

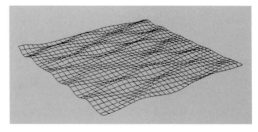

> If you want to create the Wave.tif file yourself, create a plane and open the Hypershade
> window. Assign a Blinn material with the water texture, and manipulate the variables until
> you see something like the Wave.tif file. In the Hypershade window, choose Edit → Convert
> To File Texture, and then convert the .iff file to .tif format using Fcheck. See the discussion
> of Hypershade in Chapter 17, "Shading and Texturing Surfaces," for details.

5. Hide the original curve (make it invisible). It's better not to delete anything until you are sure you no longer need it. In this case, you might want to use the original curve to adjust the curve on the surface later, when you animate the camera.

6. Import the Chair.mb file into the scene.

7. Set the Time Slider to start at frame 1 and end at frame 240. Select the top hierarchy of the chair, and then select the curve on the surface. Switch to the Animation module and choose Animate → Motion Paths → Attach To Motion Path, with the default settings.

8. Open the Attribute Editor and click the motionPath1 tab. Set World Up Type to Normal. Try different settings for Front Axis and Up Axis until the chair is sitting upright. (X for Front Axis and Y or Normal for Up Axis should work, but you might need to use different values.) Your scene should look something like Figure 10.6. When you're using curves on a surface as the path, using Normal for the World Up Type setting works well, because it makes the attached object's up direction the surface's normal. However, when you're using regular curves as the path, the Normal setting does not work as well, because a curve's normal will reverse if the curve's path goes from convex to concave. The attached object can end up flipping as it animates along the curve.

Moving the Chair

Figure 10.5

**Creating a motion path
on the water's surface**

The chair is a bit too low in the water, but if you try to move it, it will snap back when you scrub the Time Slider because it's attached to the path. You can move the node below the top hierarchy to move the chair up, which is actually the best solution, because the node below the top hierarchy isn't constrained to the path, However, for this exercise, we'll move the top node.

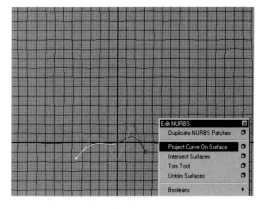

1. Select the top Chair node and press Insert to display the pivot manipulator. Drag the Y-axis handle down, as in Figure 10.7, and you will see the chair go up because the pivot is constrained to the path.

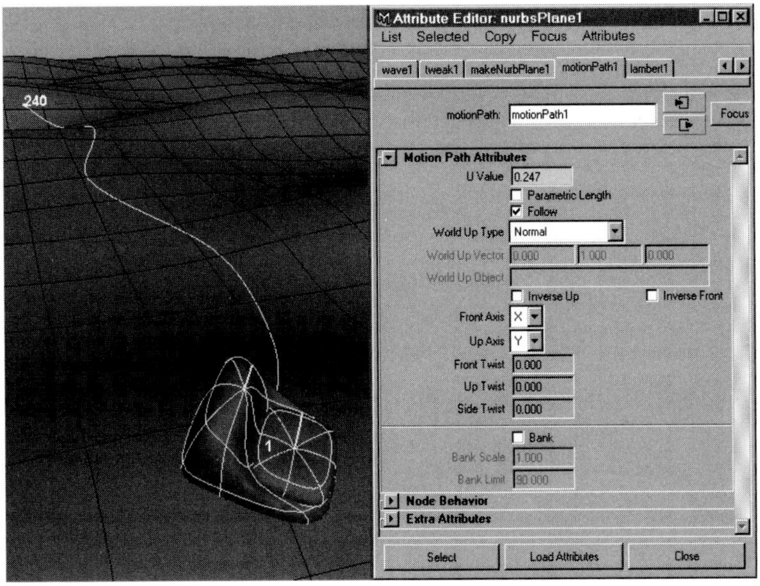

Figure 10.6
The chair attached to a curve on the surface

2. Press Insert again to turn off the pivot manipulator. Select the node that is one below the top Chair node and verify that its Y rotation value is 0 in the Channel box. Then use Key Selected at frame 1. Move to frame 240, enter **360** for Y rotation, and keyframe it.

3. Now as you scrub the animation, the chair should slowly rotate as it floats along the curve on the surface. View the animation to see how the chair moves.

Animating the Camera

The chair seems to be floating, but the water isn't moving. We can make it seem as if the water is moving by animating the camera.

1. In any modeling window, choose Panels → Perspective → New to create the Persp1 view. This will be our animated camera.

2. With the Persp1 camera still selected, zoom in to the curve on the surface and Shift+select it. Choose Animate → Motion Paths → Attach To Motion Path ❏. Choose Follow, X for Front Axis, Y for Up Axis, and Normal for World Up Type. Click Attach.

3. Switch to perspective view and press F to center in on the Persp1 camera. You should see the camera positioned as shown in Figure 10.8.

4. As you can see, the camera isn't aimed exactly where it should be. We need to adjust its direction and also position it a bit behind the chair. Click motionPath2 in the Channel Box, and you will see the Front Twist, Up Twist, and Side Twist input variables. Select them one at a time and try MM dragging in the modeling window to see the effect each has on the camera.

If the Twist attributes are grayed out, you probably attached the camera to the curve on the surface a bit differently. This isn't a problem. Just select the grayed-out areas, RM choose, and select Unlock Selected to unlock the attributes and make them keyable.

5. Return the Front Twist and Side Twist values to 0, and set the Up Twist value to –90. The camera should now be looking along the curve.

6. Select the curve on the surface. In the Channel Box, select motionPath1. This is the path animation for the chair. Go to frame 60, and then MM drag the current time indicator back to frame 1. Select the U value, which should be at 0.247, and keyframe it using RM in the Channel Box. If you scrub the Timeline now, the chair should start in front of the camera, as shown in the top picture in Figure 10.9.

7. Select motionPath2. This is the path animation for the Persp1 camera. Go to frame 200, and then MM drag to frame 240. Select the U value again, which should be at 0.8333, and keyframe it. Now the camera should finish behind the chair at the end of the animation, as shown in the bottom picture in Figure 10.9.

8. The only thing that remains is to adjust the height of the Persp1 camera. It's sitting too low on the surface plane. Go to Four Views layout, and make one window Persp1 camera view and another one the perspective view.

9. Select the Persp1 camera in the perspective view, select the Move tool, and press Insert to display the pivot manipulator. Grab the Y-axis handle and push it down to move the camera up. You should scrub the Timeline back and forth to come up with the ideal height for the camera. You might even want to move the chair farther from the camera.

10. When you are satisfied with the camera view, use Playblast, as described in the next section, to see how everything looks. Save the scene as `Wave.mb`. You might want to use it again later to try texturing the water and the sky.

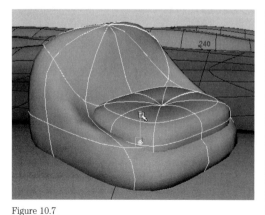

Figure 10.7

The chair resting higher on the water's surface after adjusting the pivot center

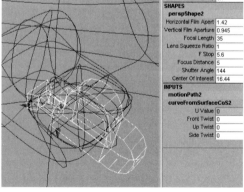

Figure 10.8

The camera attached to a curve

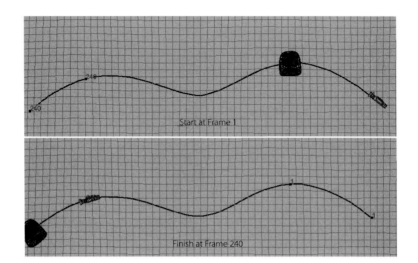

Figure 10.9

**Start and finish posi-
tions for the chair
and the camera**

You can find a finished version of the floating chair on the accompanying CD. It's named
`cam_anim.mov`.

Previewing and Playblasting

When you are previewing an animation, even with powerful machines, you often cannot get
real-time playback. Here are some suggestions (by no means exhaustive) to help you achieve
faster playback speed:

- Before you play the animation, make the active viewing window as small as you can
  without losing important details. Select the Four View window setting, and then drag
  the active window to a smaller size.

- If you can see the animation well in wireframe, by all means preview it in wireframe.

- In the shaded mode, make the NURBS display Rough (choose Display → NURBS Smoothness), or in the modeling window, choose Shading → Flat Shade All. Check if you can still
  preview the animation clearly. (Press Alt+V to play; press Alt+V again to stop.)

- For animation with joints, you can turn off the geometry display altogether, or use simple
  primitive proxy geometry to stand in for the more complicated geometry.

Playblast provides a quick way to view scenes as movie clips (or picture sequences,
although you will rarely use that option). Choose Window → Playblast ❐, click Reset Settings,
adjust your Time Slider range to about 30 frames for testing purposes, and then click Playblast. Maya quickly captures the active window view for the duration of the Timeline and creates an `.avi` movie clip in your computer's default temp directory. This movie clip will be
deleted automatically when you exit Maya.

Many of the Playblast options are self-explanatory, but a few are not so straightforward:

- The default compressor for the movie player is the standard Microsoft Video 1, which you can change to suit your computer's own capacity by clicking the Compression button.

- Instead of using the From Window setting for Display Size, specify a Custom setting of 320 × 240 or something similar in ratio, with Scale set to 1.0, to gain more control over the size of the movie clip you are making.

- Choosing Fcheck creates picture sequences instead of a movie clip. The Fcheck setting lets you acquire wireframe renders for your model turnarounds in minutes. You can save the .iff picture sequences into any directory by using the Save to File setting, or you can convert them to other image formats using Fcheck's Save Animation option.

Making the Camera Move

In this section, we will set up a moving camera attached to a path that can remain focused on an object. We will continue working with our floating chair.

Animating Waves

Open the scene you just created. The surface plane appears wavy, but it is not actually moving. Let's create some animated waves on it.

1. Select the plane and choose Deform → Create Nonlinear → Wave to apply Wave deformation. (See Chapter 11, "Deformers," for more information about Maya's deformers.)

2. Translate the waveHandle node to (−100, 0, 100) and scale it to 300 uniformly.

3. Select the wave1 in the Channel Box's Input section to open the wave attributes, and set the Amplitude to 0.005, the Wavelength to 0.1, and the Max Radius to 3. Leave the other properties at their default values.

4. Keyframe translate X at frame 1. Keyframe translate again at frame 240 with the X value at −60.

The waves look more realistic now. The surface still needs smaller ripples, but that's a texturing matter. (See Chapter 17 for details on texturing techniques.)

Adding a Three-Node Camera

We will use path animation with a three-node camera to get the effect we want. The default camera Maya creates is a single-node camera, which is what you see in perspective view or when you create a camera from the Panels menu. A two-node camera also has a camera_aim node, which determines the camera's center of interest. A three-node camera has an additional camera_up node.

1. Create another simple single-span curve above the surface to act as the camera path, as shown in Figure 10.10. Observe carefully where the CVs are placed in relation to the floating chair. The CVs have been positioned so that the camera can follow the chair from behind and gradually catch up from an angle.

2. Choose Create → Cameras → Camera, Aim And Up.

3. Select the camera_group node, and then select the curve. Use the Attach To Motion Path function with the Follow and World Up Type Vector or Scene Up settings selected.

4. Select the chair, Shift+select the camera_aim node, and then choose Constraint → Point. The camera_aim node should now be constrained to the chair. (Constraints are discussed in detail later in this chapter.)

5. Switch to the camera1 view and scrub through the animation. You may find some of the surface plane edges come into camera view for a few frames as the camera swoops down. You can try to fix this by accessing the motion path's properties and rotating the Front Twist setting or by moving the CVs of the motion path curve.

6. Use Playblast to see how the camera moves (see Figure 10.11). You may need to tweak the curve a few times to make the camera behave exactly the way you want it to.

Figure 10.10

Camera path above the surface

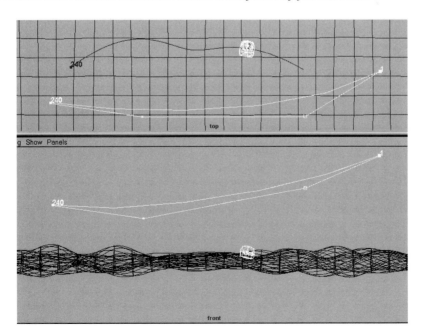

Figure 10.11

Camera view over the floating chair

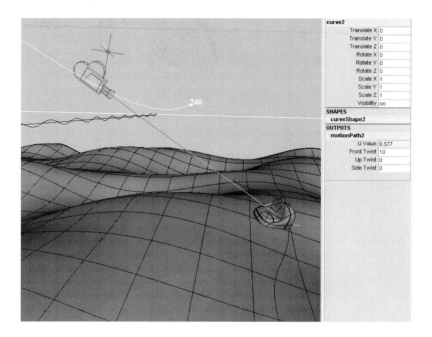

As you've seen in this example, path animation is relatively easy and can be useful when you want your animation to follow a particular route. Now we'll turn to the more complex techniques of animating characters using skeletons and kinematics.

Skeletons and Kinematics

"The knee bone is connected to the hip bone…." Bones are connected, and together they make up a skeleton. A skeleton is a protective structure that houses the vital organs of people and animals, maintains their shape, and enables them to move about.

There are no vital organs in a digital character to protect (not yet anyway), but Maya does provide joints, which let us animate characters efficiently and maintain or deform their shapes properly. Using skeletons at a basic level is easy in Maya, but it can also become quite complex.

Skeletons are built with bones and joints. You choose Skeleton → Joint Tool, and then click to place joints in the modeling window, much as you would edit points for a curve. Maya connects the joints by bones.

In building skeletons, it's good to know the kinds of joints you should be creating:

- A ball joint can rotate in all three axes, like the neck bone. This is the default Joint tool setting.

- A universal joint can rotate in two axes, like the wrist bone.

- A hinge joint can rotate in only one axis, like the knee bone.

Some people find it better to limit the joints they create according to their functions, such as a universal joint or a hinge joint, because it means more efficiency in animation and fewer calculations for Maya to perform. For example, you might use universal joints for wrists and ankles and hinge joints for knees.

Using Forward Kinematics

Forward kinematics works well for free rotational motions, such as a character's arms swinging when they walk or their spine rotating when they turn. Our main concern with forward kinematics is setting up the joints correctly for animation. Let's use the Joint tool to build a human skeleton.

Building a Leg

We will begin by building our skeleton's leg. We need to place leg, knee, and foot joints.

1. Choose Skeleton → Joint Tool ❐. Click Reset Tool to set all the options to their defaults, and then choose Auto Joint Limits.

2. Go to the Side View window and X+click the joints to snap them to the grid, as shown in Figure 10.12. When you've created all the joints, press Enter to complete the action.

> At any time during the creation of joints, you can MM drag to adjust the position of the last joint you created, or you can use the Up arrow key to go back to other joints. If you go back up a few joints and click with the left mouse button, you will add another bone branching from the joint.

3. Name the joints Lleg, Lknee, and Lfoot (*L* for left). You don't need to worry about the last joint in the chain, because that joint never takes part in the setup or animation of a character.

4. Go to the perspective view, select the knee or the foot joint, and try rotating it. You will see that you can rotate it only in the Z axis and that there is a limit to the Z rotation. The Auto Joint Limit setting creates a hinge joint, which will not rotate past its parent joint or bend away from it more than 180 degrees, as shown in Figure 10.13. It works well here with the knee.

If you want the foot to rotate in the X or Y axis as well, you can set this up through the Attribute Editor. In the Joint section, select X and Y for the Degrees Of Freedom setting. The joint limit for the Z axis will still apply, unless you turn off the Rot Limit Z setting in the Limit Information section.

In the leg you created, notice that the bones are placed *at an angle*, not in a straight line. This is because the angles between the bones are needed to determine which way the bones will bend. Also, the default joint orientation in Maya is determined by the joint's relationship to the child joint. This means that when a joint is created, its local X axis points into the bone—to the child joint. The Y axis points toward the bending direction, perpendicular to the X axis. The Z axis is perpendicular to the bending direction and the X axis. A hinge joint, therefore, will rotate around only the Z axis. You can display a joint's local rotational axes, as shown in Figure 10.14, by choosing Display → Component Display → Local Rotation Axes.

When joints are created with the default setting, the local Z-axis rotation will always bend the bones, and the local Y-axis rotation will rotate them from side to side. A corollary of this is that the window in which you decide to build the joints is important. Figure out how you want the bones to bend, and then build them accordingly in the proper window. For example, if your model is facing the front view, build its spine and legs in the side view. You will see examples of creating joints in different windows when we build the rest of the skeleton, which will be right after we mirror the joints in the next section.

Moving and Mirroring Joints

You can use the Move tool to move the joints you created. If you select a joint and move it using the Move tool, the joints below its hierarchy move with it. If you select the Move tool and then press Insert to display the pivot manipulator and move the pivot, only the selected joint moves. You can also use Maya's other tools on the Skeleton menu to edit the joints you created (or are in the process of creating)—by inserting, removing, connecting, and disconnecting joints—and even to reroot a skeleton.

Now we can use mirroring to create the other leg. Because joints behave differently from regular object nodes, we need to use the Mirror Joint command to duplicate the right leg symmetrically.

1. Move the leg hierarchy to (2, 0, 0). Then choose Skeleton → Mirror Joint ❐, select YZ as the setting, and click Mirror.

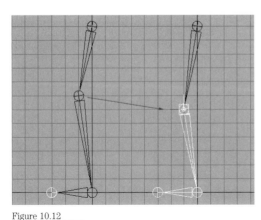

Figure 10.12

The leg being built

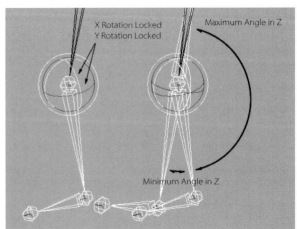

Figure 10.13

Leg being rotated in Z

2. Try rotating the left and right knee together. They should rotate as mirror images of each other, as shown in Figure 10.15.

3. Name the mirrored joints Rleg, Rknee, and Rfoot.

As you saw in this example, when you mirror joints, the rotational limit information should copy into the mirrored joint.

> If you find that the joints are not being mirrored properly, try grouping them under another joint, mirroring them, and then ungrouping them.

Building the Rest of the Skeleton

We will quickly go through the steps for adding the spine and shoulder hierarchy of joints.

1. Go to the side view and create the spine chain with the default Joint Tool option settings, as shown in Figure 10.16. The spine joints need to be ball joints. Once again, choose Skeleton → Joint Tool, reset its settings, and then close the window. From the top view, create the left shoulder chain, as shown in Figure 10.16. (Remember that we're creating a simple skeleton.)

2. Name the spine hierarchy waist, chest, neck, and head. Name the shoulder hierarchy Lshoulder, Larm, Lforearm, and Lhand.

3. In the front view, translate the shoulder chain up until it's a little below the neck bone.

4. In the Hypergraph window or the Outliner, group the legs under waist, and the Lshoulder chain under the chest. You should see something like the hierarchy and picture in Figure 10.17.

5. To put rotational limits on the shoulder joints, open the Attribute Editor and select the Lshoulder joint. The shoulder does not need to rotate in the X axis, so turn off X in the Degrees Of Freedom setting. We want the Larm joint to rotate like a ball joint, so don't change its settings. Lforearm is a universal joint that cannot rotate in the Y axis, so turn off Y. Lhand is also a universal joint that cannot rotate in the X axis, so turn off X.

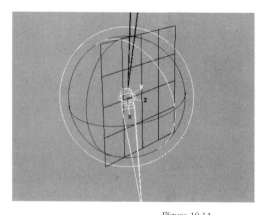

Figure 10.14

Viewing a joint's local rotational axes

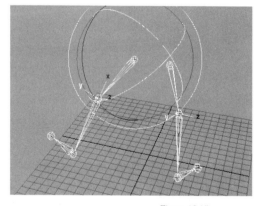

Figure 10.15

Legs mirrored

6. For these joints and others, you can also set specific minimum and maximum rotational limits. Let's do this for the Lforearm joint as an example. Select Lforearm. In the Attribute Editor, open the Limit Information, Rotate attribute. You will see three Rot Limit fields. Put checks in the four Rot Limit X and Z boxes to unlock the Min and Max fields.

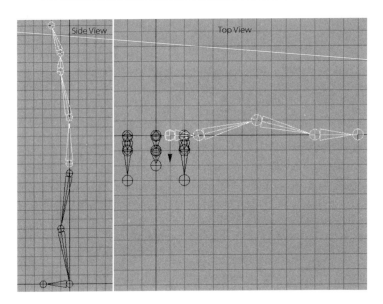

Figure 10.16

Side view and top view of the joints

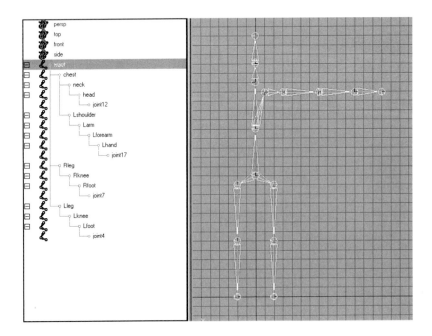

Figure 10.17

Front view of simple skeleton

7. In the top view, try rotating the Lforearm joint in the Z axis. When it's straight, the current degree reads about –28, so enter **–30** for the Min value. When it starts overlapping Larm, the degree is about 137, so enter **130** for the Max value.

8. For the X rotation, let's assume that the palm is facing straight down. In this case, Lforearm should be able to rotate about –90 degrees to make the palm face front, and about 45 degrees the other way. Enter those values for the Min and Max fields (see Figure 10.18).

> At times, you might want to use limits for Translate and Scale as well. Maya also has Rotation Limit Damping settings, which allow the joints to ease in and out of the rotational limits.

9. Select the Lshoulder joint and mirror it. You should now have a complete, albeit simple, human skeleton.

10. Create several NURBS spheres, one for every joint in the character, excluding the neck joint. Remember that the waist and chest are considered only one joint each, even though they appear to be three.

11. Scale, rotate, and translate the spheres to various positions and group them to their respective joints in the Outliner or Hypergraph window. It's not important exactly how the spheres are shaped or where they are placed, as long as they roughly represent the body parts being controlled by the individual joints. The final dummy human is shown in Figure 10.19.

12. Save this scene as `Dummy_human.mb`.

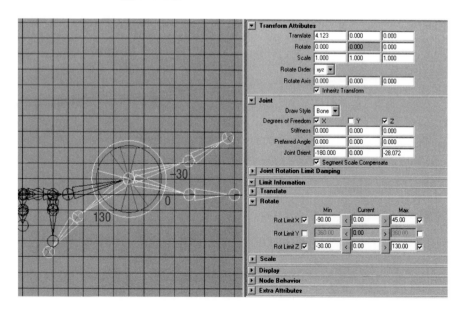

Figure 10.18

The Attribute Editor Rot Limit fields

Figure 10.19

The Outliner hierarchy and the sphere human

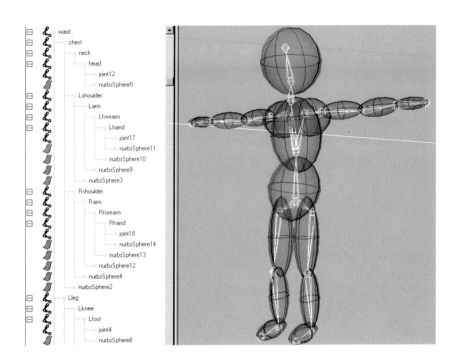

Figure 10.20

Various poses for the dummy

REORIENTING LOCAL AXES OF JOINTS

To gain precise control over how the joints rotate, you need to know how to reorient joints. In the skeleton you just created, let's say you've translated the shoulder joint down one unit using the pivot manipulator. If you display the local rotational axes, you will see that the X axis is no longer pointing directly into the bone's center. It's off about –24 degrees.

To reorient the X axis, select the Rotate tool and switch to the component mode. RM choose the question mark button (Miscellaneous), check Local Rotation Axes, and then select the shoulder joint. You can rotate the Y-axis handle in the front view until you see the X axis pointing directly into the shoulder joint. You can also enter precise rotational values by entering a MEL command in the Command Line field; for example, type **rotate -r -os 0 -24 0** to relatively rotate the local axes –24 degrees around the Y axis.

You can also use the `joint -e -oj xyz -zso` MEL command, which reorients the local axes of a joint automatically. But be careful how you use this command, because it destroys the mirror properties of symmetrical hierarchies.

Animating the Dummy

As mentioned earlier, using forward kinematics mainly involves setting up the joints the right way. Now that we've created and grouped the joints and applied the proper limits to them, all we need to do is transform the joints and keyframe them. Work on the top hierarchy first, and then move down to the lower joints until you achieve the poses you want. Figure 10.20 shows some sample poses.

Using Inverse Kinematics

For goal-oriented motions, such as having a character plant their feet on the ground or reach out their hands to open a door, working with forward kinematics can be difficult and tiresome. For these and other types of motions, you'll want to animate using inverse kinematics (IK).

Inverse kinematics uses *IK handles* and *IK solvers*. An IK handle runs through the joints being affected, which are called the *IK chain*, and a handle wire runs through them. A *handle vector* begins at the start joint and finishes at the end joint, where the IK handle's *end effector* is located. The parts of an IK handle are shown in Figure 10.21.

An IK solver looks at the position of the end effector of an IK chain and performs the necessary calculations to make the joints rotate

Figure 10.21

Components of an IK handle

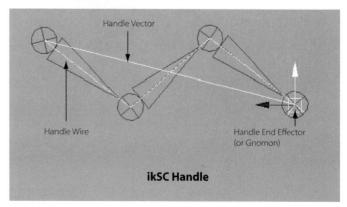

Handle Vector

Handle Wire

Handle End Effector (or Gnomon)

ikSC Handle

properly, from the start joint to the end joint of the IK chain, in such way that the end joint will be where the end effector is. When the end effector moves, the IK solver converts the translation values of the end effector to the rotational values for the joints, and the joints update accordingly. Usually, the IK chain will span only three joints, but it can handle more, as in the example in Figure 10.21.

Maya has three kinds of IK solvers: the ikRP (Rotate Plane) solver, the ikSC (Single Chain) solver, and the IK Spline solver. Each type of IK solver has its own type of IK handle.

Using the ikRP Handle

Since the ikRP solver is the default setting for the IK handle tool, let's see how that works first. As you work, refer to Figure 10.22, which shows the components of an ikRP handle.

1. In the side view, draw a simple joint chain by choosing Skeleton → Joint Tool (as in the inset on the upper-left corner of Figure 10.22).

2. Choose Skeleton → IK Handle Tool ❐, and reset the tool to its default settings.

3. Click the first joint, and then click the last joint. You should see that an IK handle has been created. The circle at the top looks complicated (as shown in Figure 10.22), but it's actually a fairly simple setup, once you've learned what its components are.

The ikRP solver calculates only the positional value of the end effector, which means it ignores the rotational values of the end effector. The joints are rotated by the ikRP solver in such a way that their Y axes are planar, their X axes are pointing to the center of the bones, and their Z axes are perpendicular to the bending direction. This is the default local orientation set up for joints. If you do not see the rotate disc, select the end effector and press the T key to display the Show Manipulator tool.

Figure 10.22

**ikRP handle
components**

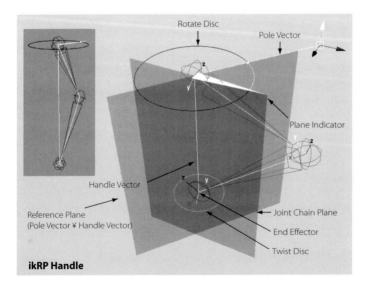

The plane along which the joints are bending is represented by the plane indicator. The plane itself is called the *joint chain plane*. You can rotate this plane about the handle vector using the twist disc, which rotates the IK chain. The Twist degree is measured relative to a reference plane created by the handle vector and the pole vector, which can be translated and keyframed.

At times, the way you want the arm to bend will cause the IK chain to flip with the default reference plane setting. To avoid this flipping, adjust or animate the pole vector.

In the Attribute Editor for the ikRP handle, you will see Snap, Stickiness, and Solver Enable settings. These are discussed in the "Switching between Inverse and Forward Kinematics" section, following the discussion of the ikSC handle.

The advantage of using the ikRP solver over the ikSC solver is that it offers more precise control over the rotation of the IK chain. The disadvantage is that it necessarily has more components to deal with.

Using the ikSC Handle

The ikSC handle is simpler than the ikRP handle. Let's experiment with it.

1. Go to the side view and draw another simple joint chain.

2. Choose Skeleton → IK Handle Tool ❏ as before, but this time, select the ikSC solver setting. Close the option box.

3. Click the first joint, and then click the last joint. You will see the ikSC handle.

4. Select Rotate and try rotating the IK handle. You will notice that only the local X and Y rotate handles seem to have any effect and that they snap back to certain angles after you release the handles.

Figure 10.23

An ikSC handle

If you press T to display the Show Manipulator tool, you will see nothing, because there are no extra manipulators for the ikSC handle—everything is controlled by the IK handle. The ikSC solver calculates the rotational values of the end effector and rotates the IK chain in such a way that all the joints in the chain will have the default local orientation for joints. The joint chain plane exists in the ikSC solver, although you do not see any representation of it in the handle. As with the ikRP handle, the plane cuts across the chain so that the X and Y axes are lying on the plane, as shown in Figure 10.23.

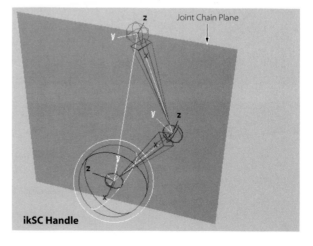

In the Attribute Editor for the ikSC handle, you will see Priority settings. The ikSC handles can have a Priority assignment when two or more chains are overlapping. The handle with the Priority 1 setting will rotate the joints in its chain first, then the handle with the Priority 2 setting will rotate its joints, and so on. The Po Weight setting determines the handle's position/orientation weight. If the weight is 1, the end effector will try to reach only the handle's position; if the weight is 0, the end effector will try to reach only the handle's orientation. You should leave this setting at the default value of 1. The Snap, Stickiness, and Solver Enable settings are discussed in the next section.

The advantage of using the ikSC handle is that you need to use only the IK handle to control the IK chain. If do not need a great amount of IK chain rotations, this is the more economical way to animate.

> When you are using the ikSC handle to rotate IK chains, use the Graph Editor to interactively adjust the rotational values. It produces the most predictable results. See Chapter 9, "Animating in Maya," for more information about the Graph Editor.

Switching between Inverse and Forward Kinematics

Maya lets you switch back and forth between using ikRP or ikSC handles and rotating joints (forward kinetics). It's easy to do, and you may find it useful. Let's go through the technique using the ikSC handle we created in the previous section.

1. Go to frame 1 and turn on Auto Key. Without this setting, the process becomes cumbersome.

2. Keyframe the IK handle, move to frame 10, and translate the IK handle. You should have another keyframe automatically set.

3. In the Attribute Editor, turn off Solver Enable to locally disable the ikSC solver for this IK handle.

4. Select the two joints in the IK chain and keyframe them. Go to frame 20 and rotate the joints. Go to frame 30 and repeat the action.

5. Select the ikSC handle again. In the Attribute Editor, turn on Solver Enable to enable the ikSC solver. You will find that the IK handle acquired the keyframes for frame 20 and 30 in the same positions where the joints were keyframed.

In order for this switch to be possible, you need the IK handle's Snap setting on and the Stickiness setting off in the Attribute Editor. If Snap is off or Stickiness is on, the IK handle will not snap to the end joint when the joints are rotated.

One more thing to be aware of in switching back and forth between inverse and forward kinetics is that the movements generated by the rotation of the joints and the corresponding keyframes of the end effector will not always match. They will be roughly the same, but you may need to tweak the end effector's animation.

If you build a chain in a straight line, ikSC or ikRP solvers will not be able to calculate and bend the chain. To fix this problem, first rotate the child joint(s) to angle the chain—even a fraction of a degree should do. Then choose Skeleton → Set Preferred Angle. Delete the existing IK chain and create a new one. Now the ikSC and ikRP solvers should be able to bend the chain.

Using the IK Spline Handle

The ikRP and ikSC handles are similar in their attributes, but the IK Spline handle is quite different in the way it functions. The IK Spline solver takes a NURBS curve as part of its handle and rotates the IK chain to follow the shape of the curve. The CVs of the NURBS curve, rather than the end effector of the handle, are animated. The IK Spline handle is ideal for animating curvy or twisty shapes, such as tails, spines, snakes, or tentacles. Let's try out this type of IK handle.

1. In the side view, build a joint chain, as shown in Figure 10.24. For IK Spline handles, the joints need not be built at an angle, but the bones should be short to ensure that the chain will move smoothly.

2. Choose Skeleton → IK Spline Handle Tool ❒, and select Number Of Spans 4. Leave the other options set to their defaults and close the option box.

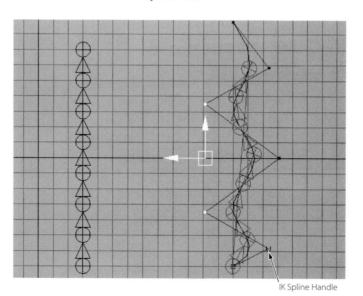

Figure 10.24

Joint chains and the Spline handle

IK Spline Handle

3. Click the top joint, and then click the last joint. You will see the IK Spline handle.

4. In the Outliner, select the joint chain or the IK handle and try moving the joints. The joints have become attached to the curve, and the IK handle doesn't show a manipulator.

5. Select the curve, display its CVs, and move them around, as shown in Figure 10.25.

You can also create your own NURBS curve and have the IK Spline handle use that curve. Turn off the Auto Create Curve setting in the IK Spline Handle option box. Click the root joint, the end joint, and then the curve to create the IK Spline handle.

6. Open the Attribute Editor for the IK handle. You will see the regular attributes and some specifically for the IK Spline handle. Try entering numbers for the Offset, Roll, and Twist settings in the IK Solver Attributes section.

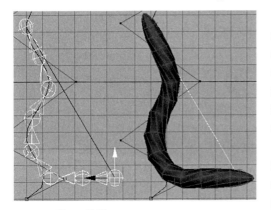

Figure 10.25

Joint chain dragged to side of curve

Offset translates the joint chain along the curve, with 0.0 as the start of the curve and 1.0 as its end. Roll rotates the whole joint chain. Twist gradually twists the chain from the second joint on. If the Root Twist Mode setting is turned on, the twist begins from the root joint. The Root On Curve setting constrains the root joint to the start of the curve. Turn it off, and you can move the root joint off the curve, but notice that it is still constrained to the curve.

As you have seen, skeletons can be moved and rotated with forward or inverse kinematics to animate various parts of a character. In addition to the IK tools, Maya provides the Constrain menu in the Animation module. The constraints on this menu are often used in conjunction with the IK tools to set up a character for animation.

Constraints

Objects in real life are "constrained" in many different ways. For example, if you are holding a baseball, the ball moves and rotates when your hand moves and rotates, because the ball is constrained by your hand movements. As another example, consider a tennis player whose eyes are always looking at the tennis ball. If you want to imitate these actions in Maya, it would be difficult and time-consuming to try to reproduce the motions of the baseball or the eyes by keyframing them. Instead, you can use constraints to automate such animation tasks.

Maya's Constrain menu provides Point, Aim, Orient, Scale, Geometry, Normal, Tangent, and Pole Vector constraints. All the constraints work in the same way. You select two or more objects, and then select the constraints that you want to apply. The first objects you select act as the targets that constrain, and the last object you select is the one being constrained. When you select more than one constraint target, the constrained object is shared between the targets according to the weights you set for the targets.

Using the Point Constraint

The Point constraint makes the center of the constrained object stick to the center of the target object. When you have more than one target, the Point constraint places the object being constrained at a point between the targets' pivot points, with the placement determined by the average value of the weights of the targets, as shown in Figure 10.26.

Because their weights can be animated, point constraints are excellent when you want an object to switch parents. Let's take a look at how this is applied.

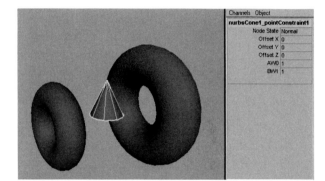

Figure 10.26

Using the Point constraint

1. Begin a new scene and set the first frame to 0 and the last frame to 20. Switch to the perspective view port, and make sure Auto Key is turned on.

2. Choose Create → NURBS Primitives → Torus, and rename it A. Create a second one, and rename it B. Then choose Create → NURBS Primitives → Cone.

3. Set A's X, Y, and Z scale to 3, and position it at -3 on the X-axis. Then set B's X, Y, and Z scale to 5, and position it at 10 on the X axis. Rotate A 90 degrees on its Z axis, and then rotate B -90 on its Z axis.

4. Select A, select the cone, and then choose Constrain → Point. Select B, select the cone, and choose Constrain → Point again. The cone should now be between the two tori, as in Figure 10.26.

5. Make sure the Channel Box is visible, and select the cone. Below the cone's transform attributes, there should be an entry that says something like nurbsCone1_pointConstraint1 that includes these three attributes underneath: Node State, AW0, and BW1. Set BW1 to 0. The cone should now be resting on top of the torus named A.

6. Now we will animate the weighting between the two tori. Go to frame 0, select AW0, RM choose, and use Key Selected to keyframe that value at frame 0. Do the same for BW1.

7. Go to frame 20, and set AW0 to 0 and BW1 to 1. Click Play to see the cone move from torus A to torus B over 20 frames. Notice also the offset attributes. By default, Maya's constraints move one object to another based on their pivot points. The offsets let you adjust a constrained object so it will not intersect with its target.

8. Now move torus A to -6 on the X axis, and click Play again. No matter where you move either of the tori, the cone will always start on torus A and end on torus B. Move torus A back to -3 on the X axis. Save your work as POS_Constrain.mb.

Maya also has a Point On Curve Locator constraint (choose Deform → Point On Curve Locator), which creates a locator at a selected point on a curve or an edit point. This constraint makes the locator position constrain the curve at that point, without breaking the curve's tangency.

Using the Aim, Orient, and Scale Constraints

The difference between the Aim and the Orient constraints can be a bit confusing. The Aim constraint creates an Aim vector (the default setting is the X axis of the object), which points the object being constrained to the *position* of the Aim target, as shown in Figure 10.27. In the example on the right in the figure, with two tori, notice the tilt toward the torus on the right. This is because that torus's weight input is 1, and the other torus's weight input is 0.7.

Figure 10.27

Using the Aim constraint

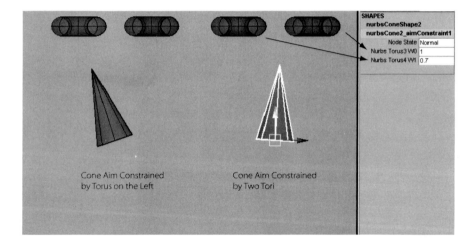

The Orient constraint causes the rotation values of the object being constrained to be the same as the *rotation* of the Orient target. In the example on the right in Figure 10.28, the cone has the average rotation value of the tori.

Like Point constraints, Orient constraints can be weighted and blended over time. Let's take a look at blending Orient constraints.

1. Load the POS_Constrain.mb scene you created in the previous exercise.

2. Select torus A and rotate it -45 degrees on its Z axis. Rotate torus B 45 degrees on its Y axis.

3. Select torus A, and then select the cone. Choose Constrain → Orient. Next, select torus B and the cone, respectively. Again, choose Constrain → Orient. The cone's rotation should now be the average of the two tori.

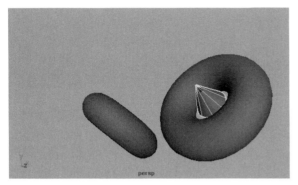

Figure 10.28

Using the Orient constraint

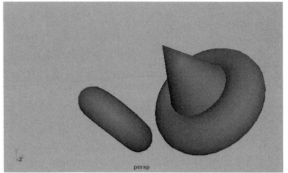

Figure 10.29

Using the Scale constraint

4. Select the cone. The weights for the Orient constraint should be visible. If not, click the nurbsCone1_orientConstraint1 entry. Go to frame 0, select AW0, RM choose, and use Key Selected to keyframe that value at frame 0. Do the same for BW1. Make sure BW1 is set to 0 at frame 0.

5. Go to frame 20, and set AW0 to 0 and BW1 to 1. Click Play to see the cone orient itself from torus A to torus B over 20 frames. Again, no matter how you orient the two tori, the cone will always find the proper rotation. Without the Point constraint we applied earlier, the cone only rotates in place. Orient Constraints also have offset attributes. Save your work.

The Scale constraint functions the same way as the Orient constraint. The object being Scale constrained has the same scale values as the target object, or the average scale values of the target objects, as shown in Figure 10.29.

To familiarize yourself with the Scale constraint try the following:

1. Load the POS_Constrain.mb scene you created in the previous exercise.

2. Select A, select the cone, and then choose Constrain → Scale. Select B, select the cone, and then choose Constrain → Scale again. The cone's scale should now be the average scale of the two tori.

3. Select the cone. The weights for the Scale constraint should be visible. If not, click the nurbsCone1_scaleConstraint1 entry. Go to frame 0, select AW0, RM choose, and use Key Selected to keyframe that value at frame 0. Do the same for BW1. Make sure BW1 is set to 0 at frame 0.

4. Go to frame 20, set AW0 to 0, and set BW1 to 1. Click Play to see the cone match its scale to torus A and then to torus B over 20 frames.

5. A nice feature of constraints is that they are hierarchy independent. Create a locator, and parent the cone to it. Move, rotate and scale the locator around. No matter what you do to the locator, the cone will still move properly between the two tori! Unlike Orient and Point constraints, Scale constraints do not have offset attributes.

6. Save your work.

Aim constraints are especially useful for quickly making a character look at or focus on different objects. Like the other constraints discussed thus far, the weight of their focus can be blended over time. Think of the aim constraint as a single-joint IK chain that can have any object as a goal.

1. Begin a new scene, set the first frame to 0, and set the last frame to 20. Switch to the perspective view port, and make sure Auto Key is turned on.

2. Choose Create → NURBS Primitives → Cone, and then choose Create → Locator. Rename the locator A. Create a second locator, and rename it B.

3. Move locator A to -5 on the X-axis and 5 on the Z axis. Set locator B's Z position to 5 on the X axis and 5 on the Z axis, and rotate the cone -90 degrees on its Z axis. With the cone still selected, choose Edit → Delete By Type → History, and then choose Modify → Freeze Transformations.

4. Select locator A and then the cone. Choose Constrain → Aim □. In the Aim Constraint options box, choose Edit → Reset Settings, and then click the Add/Remove button. Next, select locator B and then the cone, and choose Constrain → Aim.

5. Select the cone. The weights for the Aim constraint should be visible. If not, click the nurbsCone1_aimConstraint1 entry. Go to frame 0, select AW0, RM choose, and use Key Selected to keyframe that value at frame 0. Do the same for BW1. Make sure BW1 is set to 0 at frame 0.

6. Go to frame 20, set AW0 to 0 and BW0 to 1, and then click Play. The cone will now point from one locator to the other.

7. Stop the animation, and go back to frame 0. Move locator A around. Because the weighting is set to 1 for A and 0 for B at frame 0, the cone follows A exclusively.

8. Now go to frame 20 and move locator B around. Because we set the weighting to 0 for A and 1 for B at frame 20, the cone will point exclusively at B. Note the offset attributes. Save your work as `Aim_Constraint.mb`.

Using the Geometry and Normal Constraints

The Geometry constraint makes the center of the constrained object stay on the surface of the target object, as in the example on the left in Figure 10.30. It doesn't lock the attributes of the constrained object, allowing it to slide along the target surface. Unlike the other constraints we have discussed so far, the Geometry constraint will not blend an object's position smoothly between multiple objects. Instead, the constrained object will simply snap to the surface of the object with the greatest influence. The Normal constraint, however, can be blended smoothly between objects. Don't let the name fool you: Geometry constraints can be used on polygonal objects as well as on NURBS surfaces and curves. Another nice feature of the Geometry constraint is that the objects being constrained to one another do not need to be of the same type.

The Normal constraint works somewhat like the Aim constraint. The difference is that the aim vector of the object being constrained aligns itself with the normal vector of the surface that passes through the constrained object's center, as shown in the example on the right in Figure 10.30. Let's investigate the Geometry and Normal constraints.

1. Begin a new scene and create a NURBS sphere. Set its X-, Y-, and Z-scale to 3.

2. Create a polygon cube. Select the sphere, select the cube, and choose Constrain → Geometry.

3. Move the cube around. Notice that it is now constrained to the surface of the sphere. If you move the sphere, the cube will slide around on its surface.

4. Once again, select the sphere, and then select the cube. Choose Constrain → Normal, and move the cube around the sphere's surface. The cube will now align itself to the sphere's surface.

5. Select and move some of the CVs on the sphere's surface. No matter how you distort the sphere, the cube will remain on its surface and aligned to its normals. Save your work, if you like.

Figure 10.30

Using the Geometry and Normal constraints

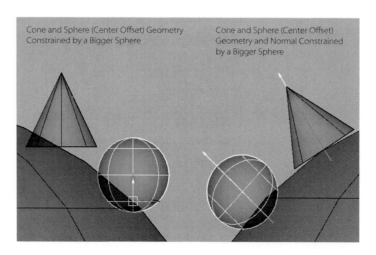

Using the Tangent Constraint

The Tangent constraint aligns an object's aim vector to the tangency of the target curve, as you can see in the example in Figure 10.31. It works in much the same way as the Aim and Normal constraints. Let's take a look.

1. Start a new scene and switch to the side view port. Create an Edit Point curve with four knots, and then create a NURBS cone.

2. Select the curve, and then select the cone. Choose Constrain → Geometry. If you move either the cone or the curve, the cone will slide predictably over the curve.

3. Once again, select the curve, and then select the cone. Choose Constrain → Tangent. The cone will now orient itself to the contours of the curve.

Using the Pole Vector Constraint

The Pole Vector constraint is a Point constraint specifically designed to constrain the pole vector of an ikRP handle. (We discussed ikRP handles earlier in this chapter.) This constraint is shown in the example in Figure 10.32. The ikRP solver by itself does a good job of figuring out a set of rotations for a hierarchy of joints. But if, for example, you need complete control of a character's knees and/or elbows, the Pole Vector constraint can be an invaluable asset. Pole Vector constraints let you decide exactly where a knee or an elbow will point. Like several of the other constraints, you can have multiple targets assigned to a Pole Vector constraint and

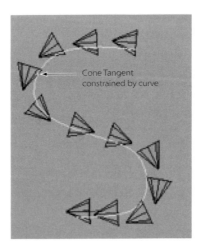

Figure 10.31

A cone oriented to a curve via the Tangent constraint

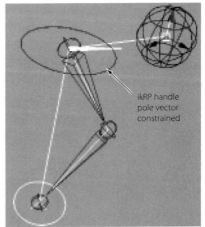

Figure 10.32

Using the Pole Vector constraint

weight them smoothly over time. To get a better idea of how the Pole Vector constraint works, try the following:

1. Begin a new scene, and switch to the side view port. Create three joints. Make sure there is a slight bend in them.

2. Choose Skeleton → IK Handle tool, and create an ikRP solver, with the first joint as the base and the third joint as the end.

3. Create a locator and move it to the side of the joint chain. In the Hypergraph or Outliner, select the locator, select the IK handle, and then choose Constrain → Pole Vector.

4. Switch to the perspective view port, and move the locator around. The bend in the joint chain should now always point to the locator.

Hands On: Setting Up a Character for Animation

Let's build the skeleton for the character that we finished modeling in Chapter 8, "Organic Modeling." We will also put IK handles and constraints on the character and organize all the nodes into a proper hierarchy to get ready for binding and animation.

Creating the Skeleton

To begin, choose Skeleton → Joint Tool to give our character bones and joints. The root joint will be used to move the entire upper body. Two spine joints and the chest joint will be used to deform the body. The neck and head joints will animate the head.

1. Load the `character_model.mb` file, from the Chapter 10 folder on the CD.

2. Convert the head, body, and the shoes to polygons using the Extract Vertices command (polygons will be lighter to deal with). Since the hands have creasing information, they shouldn't be converted; otherwise, the information will be lost.

3. From the side view, use the Joint tool with the default settings to draw the backbones and the leg as shown in Figure 10.33. Make sure that the knee joint is at the lower end of the knee area, and place the ankle joint down at the lower end of the ankle area. Once the leg chain is created, name the joints as shown in the figure.

4. Move the leg and the foot joint chains to the left side, and group the leg joint under the root joint, as shown in Figure 10.34.

5. We want the shoulder joint to primarily rotate up and down, so create it in the front view, as shown in Figure 10.35.

6. Create the arm chain in the top view, because we want the chain to bend forward, as shown in Figure 10.36. Notice the Lforearm joint's placement; it doesn't matter exactly where the joint is placed, as long as it lies in a fairly straight line between the Lelbow and the Lwrist joints. We will be using this extra joint later to deform the forearm.

7. Open the Lforearm joint's Attribute Editor, Joint section, and turn off its Y and Z Degrees Of Freedom, because we want it to rotate only in the X axis.

8. Group the Larm joint to the Lshoulder joint, and then group the Lshoulder joint to the chest joint.

9. Select the Lshoulder joint and all the joints below it, and choose Display → Component Display → Local Rotation Axes. Notice how the local axes for the shoulder joint and the other joints are different (see Figure 10.37). This is because they were created in different windows. We want the shoulder joint to rotate differently from the arm joints. That's why the shoulder joint is created in the front view, and the arm joints are created in the top view.

Figure 10.33

Backbones and leg

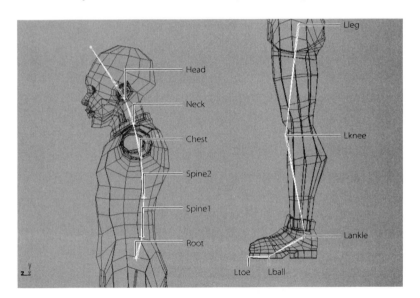

Figure 10.34

Leg and foot moved to the left leg

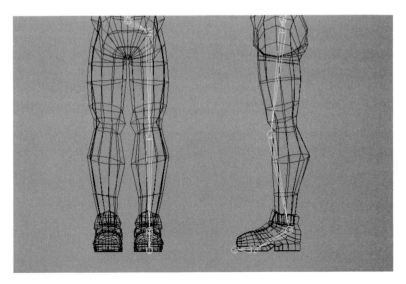

10. From the front view, create the first finger chain, as shown in Figure 10.38. You must create the finger joints carefully if you want clean Z-axis rotations. To better see the joint placements, you might want to reduce the joint size by using the Display menu.

11. Create the other finger chains. You can move the index and index1 joints, but you shouldn't move its child joints, because that will complicate the finger rotation. You can also scale the joints in the X axis to make sure that the joints are placed exactly where you want them, but don't scale them in Y or Z. It might actually be better to create the other finger joints individually, rather than copying the first index finger chain and trying to make that fit the other fingers. You should end up with finger joints placed somewhat like the picture on the right in Figure 10.39.

12. Select a finger joint and choose Display → Component Display → Local Rotation Axes. As with the shoulder joints, notice how the local rotation axes are displayed on the finger joints (see Figure 10.40). They should all be consistently pointing in the same direction.

Figure 10.35

Shoulder joint in front view

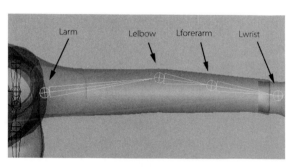

Figure 10.36

Arm joint in top view

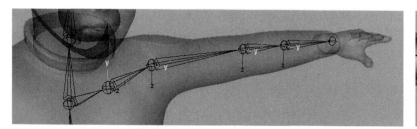

Figure 10.37

Shoulder and arm joints

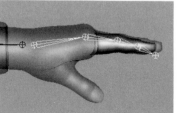

Figure 10.38

First finger chain

Figure 10.39

Creating the finger joints

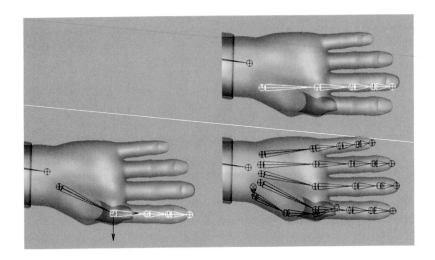

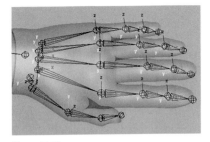

Figure 10.40

Local rotation axes

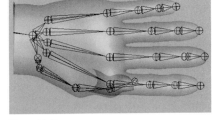

Figure 10.41

Grouping joints

13. When you're finished creating the joints, name them appropriately, such as Lindex, Lindex1, Lindex2, and so on, and group them to the wrist joint, as shown in Figure 10.41.

14. Select the Lshoulder joint, and then mirror it and its children by choosing Skeleton → Mirror Joint. In the option window, make sure Mirror Across is set to YZ and Mirror Function is set to Behavior. You should see a skeleton like the one in Figure 10.42. Do the same for Lleg.

15. Assign the same names for the mirrored joints, but use the letter *R* for right in the prefix (instead of an *L* for left).

This completes the creation of the joints that we will use to animate our character. The `character_skeleton.mb` file on the CD (in the Chapter 10 folder) contains the completed skeleton setup.

Adding IK Handles and Constraints

Now we're ready to put IK handles on the arms and the legs of our character. We will then create foot and hand controls. Finally, we will add constraints for the eyes. This section is long and involved, so save your work often and take a break occasionally.

Let's start with the arms. This setup will result in a forearm that rotates properly no matter how the wrist is bent. Furthermore, if the hand is grabbing on to something and the body moves, it will remain properly aligned.

1. The elbow is a hinge joint and therefore rotates on only one axis. Open the Attributes Editor for Lelbow, and limit its Degrees Of Freedom to Z only in the Joints section. Do the same for Relbow.

2. Choose Skeleton → IK Handle Tool. With the default setting, which gives us the ikRP solver, click from the Larm joint to the Lwrist joint. Create a second IK handle, this time going from the Lforearm joint to the Lwrist joint. Rename the IK handles Solver_LArm and Solver_Lforearm.

3. Create two locators. Name one Goal_Lwrist, and the other PV_Lelbow. Snap Goal_Lwrist to Lwrist, and PV_Lelbow to Lelbow. Move PV_Lelbow to -15 on the Z axis. PV_Lelbow will become the Pole Vector for the left elbow, and Goal_Lwrist will be used to move and rotate the left wrist.

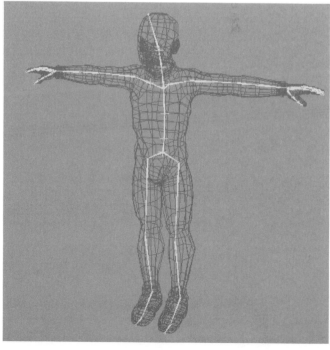

Figure 10.42

Complete skeleton

4. Next, we will create an Orient constraint for Lwrist. Before we do that, we need to be sure that Goal_Lwrist matches the Lwrist joint's rotation. Otherwise, we run the risk of accidentally rotating it out of place and spending a lot of time trying to solve the problem. Select Lwrist, and then select Goal_Lwrist. Choose Constrain → Orient. Goal_Lwrist will rotate itself in world space to match Lwrist's local rotation.

5. Open the Outliner window, and find Goal_Lwrist. Click the plus sign to the left of Goal_Lwrist, and delete the newly created Orient constraint that appears underneath it. Select Goal_Lwrist, select Lwrist, and once again choose Constrain → Orient. Lwrist will now be Orient constrained to Goal_Lwrist without having lost its original rotation.

6. Create a third locator, and snap its position to Goal_Lwrist's. Rename it PV_Lforearm, set its position on the Z axis to -2, and parent it to Goal_Lwrist.

7. Select Solver_Larm and Solver_Lforearm and parent them to Goal_Lwrist. Next, select PV_Lelbow, select Solver_Larm, and choose Constrain → Pole Vector. Then, select PV_Lforearm and Solver_Lforearm, respectively, and once again choose Constrain → Pole Vector.

8. Create a circle, rotate it 30 degrees in the Y axis, and set its X, Y, and Z scale to 3. Under Inputs in the Channel Box, set Degree to Linear and Sections to 1. This will result in a triangle shape. Snap its position to Goal_Lwrist, freeze transformation, and delete history. Parent Goal_Lwrist to Mover_Lwrist, and turn off Goal_Lwrist's visibility. We will use this triangle to position the hand. Because its transformations have been frozen, it is now easy to set it and the hand back to the starting position.

9. Again, create a circle, and rotate it 90 degrees in the Z axis and 180 degrees on X. Under Inputs in the Channel Box, set Degree to Linear and Sections to 1, once again resulting in a triangle. Snap its position to PV_Lelbow, and rename it Lelbow_Pole. Freeze its transformations and delete its history.

10. Finally, Parent PV_Lelbow to Lelbow_Pole, and set PV_Lelbow's visibility to 0. Select Lelbow, open the Attributes Editor, and in the Display section make sure Display Handle is checked. Repeat these steps for the right arm, but change the prefixes from L to R (PV_Relbow, GoalRwrist, and so on).

Applying Leg Constraints and Attributes

Now that we have the arms working to our satisfaction, let's set up the legs. In this exercise, we will create what is known as a "reverse foot," which will greatly simplify heel-toe motion. In addition, our hierarchy will remain intact, which will greatly simplify other animation tasks, such as jumping or swimming.

1. Create an ikRP solver that goes from Lleg to Lankle. Create a second one that goes from Lankle to Lball, and a third that goes from Lball to Ltoe. Name them Solver_Lleg, Solver_Lball, and Solver_Ltoe, respectively.

2. Create four locators, and rename them as follows: Ankle_L, Heel_L, Ball_L, and Toe_L. Snap them into their appropriate places by holding down the V key and LM-dragging. Because there is no heel joint to snap to, place the heel locator as shown in Figure 10.43.

3. Parent Ankle_L to Ball_L, and Ball_L to Heel_L. Also parent Toe_L to Heel_L. While we're at it, let's parent the IK handles as well. Parent Solver_Lleg to Ankle_L, Solver_Lball to Ball_L, and Solver_Toe to Toe_L.

4. Create a fifth locator and rename it PV_Lknee. Snap its position to Lknee, and set its Z position to 10. Select PV_Lknee, select Solver_Lleg, and then choose Constrain → Pole Vector.

5. Create a circle, and rotate it 180 degrees in the Y axis. Under Inputs in the Channel Box, set Degree to Linear and Sections to 1, once again resulting in a triangle. Set its X and Y scale to 3, and its Z scale to 5. Rename it Mover_Lfoot, and snap it to Heel_L's position. Delete its history, freeze its transformations, and group Heel_L under it. Let's not hide Heel_L just yet.

6. Create another circle, and rotate it 90 degrees on its Z axis. Under Inputs in the Channel Box, set Degree to Linear and Sections to 1, resulting in yet another triangle. Snap its position to PV_Lknee, delete its history, and freeze its transformations. Group PV_Lknee under it, and hide PV_Lknee. Rename it Lknee_pole. Open the Attributes Editor, and in the Display section make sure Display Handle is checked.

7. Select Mover_Lfoot, and choose Modify Add → Attribute. Name it Heel_Toe, and give it a minimum value of -1, a maximum value of 1, and a default value of 0. Click OK.

8. Next, choose Animate → Set Driven Key → Set ❏. With Mover_Lfoot still selected, click Load Driver, and in the right column of the driver section, select the newly added Heel_Toe attribute. Next, select Heel_L and then click Load Driven. In the right column of the Driven section, choose rotateX as the Driven attribute, and then click Key.

9. With the Set Driven Key option box still open, select Mover_Lfoot again, and set Heel_Toe to -1. Then select Heel_L, set its X rotation to -30, and set a second driven key.

10. Select Mover_Lfoot again, and set Heel_Toe back to 0. Heel_L should rotate back into its original position. Select Ball_L and load it as the driven object. In the right column, select rotate X as the Driven attribute, and set a key.

11. Select Mover_Lfoot again, and set the Heel_Toe attribute to 1. Select Ball_L and set its X rotation to 40 degrees. In the Set Driven Key options box, set another key.

12. Close the Set Driven Key options box, and hide Heel_L. Select Mover_Lfoot, and MM drag its Heel_Toe attribute back and forth. The left foot should now rock back and forth from heel to toe, which will greatly ease the process of creating our walk/run cycles. Repeat these steps for the right leg, but change the prefixes from L to R (Solver_Rleg, Heel_R, and so on).

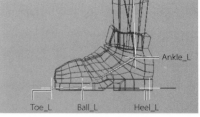

Figure 10.43

Placement of foot locators in side view

Setting Up the Eye Constraint

The last constraint we need to set up is for the character's eyes.

1. Create two more triangle nodes, similar to the knee nodes, and rename them Leye_c and Reye_c.

2. Group Leye_c and Reye_c under a locator, as shown in Figure 10.44. Rename the locator Lookat.

3. Apply the Aim constraint to the triangles, and template the triangles.

4. By scaling the Lookat locator, as well as moving it, you can have total control over how the eyes animate, as shown in Figure 10.45.

Setting up the Hierarchy

Finally, we need to place the different nodes into an animation-friendly hierarchy.

1. Select the root joint and choose Edit → Group. Rename the top group node Maya_Boy. This node will be used to move the whole character in scene placements.

2. Under Maya_Boy is the root joint, which will control the upper-body movements. Place the Mover_Foot and the knee_Pole nodes under Maya_Boy.

3. Place the Lookat node under Maya Boy as well. You might think you should place the Lookat node under the head joint, so that the eyes will look where the head is turning, but eyes that move with the rotation of the body joints tend to look dead, like those of puppets. In real life, people's gazes tend to stay fixed on specific objects, even if their bodies are moving.

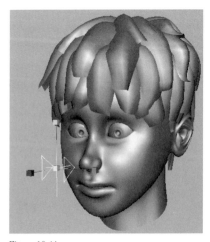

Figure 10.44

Grouped eye nodes

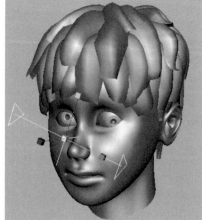

Figure 10.45

Scale the Lookat to control the eye focus

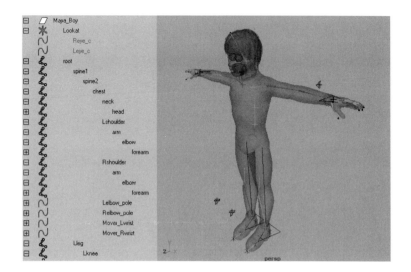

Figure 10.46

Outliner hierarchy

4. Depending on the kind of animation the character will be performing, you might want to place the knee_Pole nodes under the root joint instead.

5. Place the Mover_wrist and elbow_Pole nodes under the chest joint, because in most situations you want the arms moving with the chest. But you can place these nodes under the root joint or Maya_Boy node instead, depending on the kind of animation you want.

6. You should see something close to the hierarchy in Figure 10.46 when you are finished.

The character skeleton is now ready for animation. For your reference, a `character_setup_complete.mb` file is included in the Chapter 10 folder on the CD.

In your own work, there is no one right way to build skeletons or place constraints to set up a character for animation. In each case, you need to consider what the character will be doing, how the body should deform, and how the limbs should rotate. Different situations call for different solutions. A properly prepared character will move well under close scrutiny, will have the necessary range of movements, and will be easy to animate.

Summary

In this chapter, you learned how to animate objects and cameras along paths, build skeletons properly, and create different kinds of IK handles on joints. You were also introduced to using constraints. Finally, you built a hierarchy of nodes involving joints, IK handles, driven keys, and constraints to prepare the character modeled in the previous chapters for animation.

In the next chapter, we will cover how to use Maya deformers and prepare for facial animation.

CHAPTER 11

Deformers

If the only way to model and animate were by pushing and pulling points, life would be difficult for modelers and would be the bane of many animators' existence. Thankfully, Maya provides *deformers*, which let you bypass most of the menial work. With Maya's deformers, you can quickly build and animate deformed surfaces with a high level of control. Several deformers are indispensable for modeling and animating in Maya.

This chapter covers the following topics:

- **Creating deformers**
- **Editing deformations**
- **Advanced facial animation**

Creating Deformers

Maya provides many types of deformers, and they work in different ways. All deformers can deform anything with control points, including CVs on curves and surfaces, vertices on polygons, points on subdivision surfaces, and lattice points. Many deformers can also deform multiple surfaces, maintaining their tangency during the deformation process.

All deformers also work as sets, called *deformation sets*. You can edit the points being influenced by a deformation by changing their membership in the set using the Relationship Editor, the Edit Membership tool, or the Paint Set Membership tool (discussed later in the chapter, in the "Editing Deformations" section).

You'll find all the deformers and editing tools we cover in this chapter on the Deform menu in the Animation module.

Lattice Deformation

Lattice is one of the most frequently used deformers. When you apply Lattice to an object, Maya creates an influence lattice and a base lattice around the object. When you transform the influence lattice or its points, the object inside the lattice transforms with it or gets deformed by it according to the degree of difference between the influence lattice and the base lattice.

When using Lattice, you can control the deformation of complicated objects with fewer control points than you would need if you were deforming the objects directly. Creating the deformation is therefore easier, and the results are smoother.

Creating Lattices

You can apply Lattice deformation to a group of objects, to only some points of an object, or to points of a group of objects. You can even apply Lattice to points of a lattice, as shown in Figure 11.1, on the right. The lattice on the left in Figure 11.1 is made up of points from four objects. The shape in the middle is two tori, with the top torus latticed at the object level and the bottom torus latticed at its two top rows of CVs.

To apply Lattice, simply select the points or object(s) you want deformed and choose Deform → Create Lattice. You should see the influence lattice. The base lattice is also created, but it is not visible and appears as a wireframe cube only when selected in the Outliner or the Hypergraph.

If you are animating the object being deformed, you want the lattice to transform with the object. To make this possible, group the lattice and its base lattice under the deformed object. Grouping is available as an option setting when you create the lattice, or you can group after you create the lattice.

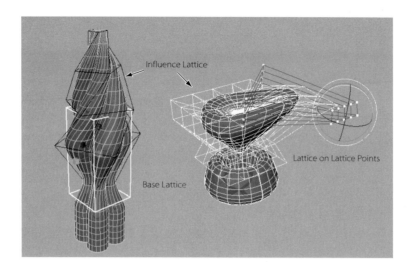

Figure 11.1

Examples of Lattice deformation

Lattice has its own local space, which parallels the XYZ coordinate system, called STU space. When you create or edit a lattice, you can adjust the STU divisions of the lattice, giving it more or fewer lattice points than the default setting.

> Skinning an object indirectly with Lattice can be a great way to animate because Maya's Lattice is so efficient, but sometimes you run into a situation in which an object is being transformed twice from the lattice and skinning. See the "Editing Deformations" section later in this chapter for an example of how to deal with double transformation problems.

Another way to adjust a lattice is through the Local Divisions setting, which is activated with the Local Mode setting. When Local Mode is turned on, each point exerts influence according to the Local Divisions setting, as shown in the left two examples in Figure 11.2. The default is 2, 2, 2, which means each point exerts influence up to two points away in STU space. When Local Mode is turned off, each point in the lattice exerts influence on the whole area. You usually want to leave Local Mode turned on.

The Freeze Geometry setting locks the object where it is being influenced. With this setting, when the object transforms, the deformed part of it stays fixed, as shown in the right two examples in Figure 11.2. You can activate Freeze Geometry in the Attribute Editor after you create a lattice. You can also move the deformed object partially first and then turn on Freeze Geometry to lock the object here it is.

Tweaking Lattices

To tweak a lattice, pick-mask Lattice Point over it, and you can manipulate its points in the same way as you manipulate regular control points.

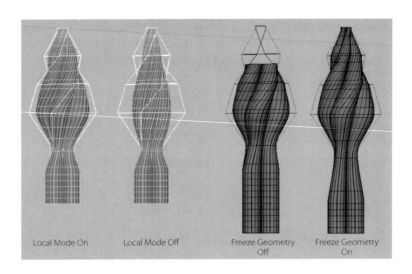

Local Mode On   Local Mode Off   Freeze Geometry   Freeze Geometry
                                                    Off   On

You can also manipulate the lattice to fit around an object better by transforming both the influence lattice and the base lattice. You can select the hidden base lattice in the Outliner. As long as the two lattices are being transformed together, no deformation occurs. When you are doing this, make sure that all the control points of the object being deformed remain inside the lattice, or they will not deform with the lattice.

> The lattice is created to fit an object's bounding box. If you find that some points are not deforming along with the lattice, try scaling up the lattice and the base lattice just a bit to make sure no points are straying outside the deformation.

If you've been tweaking the lattice points and you decide to start over from the original shape or to add more STU subdivisions, you can choose Deform → Edit Lattice → Remove Lattice Tweaks. If you want to undo the transformations you've applied to the lattice at the object level as well as the tweaks to the lattice points, choose Deform → Edit Lattice → Reset Lattice, which moves the lattice back to its original point of creation.

Cluster Deformation

Unlike the other deformers, Cluster produces a weighted deformation. Applying Cluster to an object creates weighted points in the cluster set. This is probably the most useful thing about using Cluster.

The default weight of the clustered points is 1.0, but you can adjust their weights by using the Component Editor or the Paint Weights tool (Artisan). Let's try a simple exercise to see how to create clusters and adjust their weights.

1. Create a NURBS plane. Set it to span 10 patches in U and V.

2. Drag to select 25 CVs at the center of the plane. Choose Deform → Create Cluster with the default settings.

3. A cluster handle appears as the small letter c. Select the Move tool and pull the c up. You should see something like the picture shown at the top-left in Figure 11.3.

4. Select the surface, and start the Paint Cluster Weights tool (from the Deform menu). Apply a bit of smoothing with low settings around the edges of the clustered points. You should be able to get a more rounded shape, as shown in the picture at the bottom-right in Figure 11.3.

5. Select the clustered points and choose Window → General Editors → Component Editor. Click the Weighted Deformers tab. Select the points being deformed, and they should appear in a column called cluster1, with various values created by the application of the Paint Weights tool. You can enter lower weight values to round the cluster edges or use the slider at the bottom to interactively adjust the point values.

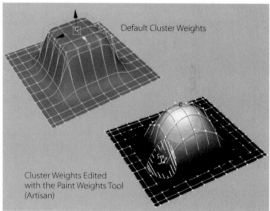

Figure 11.3

Adjusting Cluster defor-mation weights with the Paint Weights tool

Default Cluster Weights

Cluster Weights Edited with the Paint Weights Tool (Artisan)

In general, when you want precise control over the percentage of the weighted points and the points are easy to select in groups, the Component Editor is a good tool to use. When you want a more organic look or when the surface is dense, the Paint Weights tool (Artisan) is more efficient. (See Chapter 7, "Working with Artisan," for more information about using Artisan.) When you are working with clusters, the cluster handle c has a default Select Priority Level of 2, which means that it is selected along with the surface it's deforming. You can open the General Preferences dialog box and change the Select Priority Level for the cluster handle, or you can open the Attribute Editor and choose Display Handle in the Cluster Handle Display section. A handle with the highest Select Priority Level will appear, which lets you select the cluster over the surface.

When you move an object that is clustered, you would expect the cluster handle to move with the object, but it doesn't. If you want the cluster to stay on the surface as it moves, group it under the object. First, open the Attribute Editor, click the Cluster tab, and make sure the Relative setting is on for Cluster Attributes. Next, if the object is at the origin, you can simply group the cluster under the object in the Outliner or Hypergraph window. If not, group the cluster to itself once to move the center to the origin, and then group that node under the object. (Choosing Edit → Parent will produce the same result.)

Nonlinear Deformations

The six deformers in the Nonlinear submenu all deform in, yes, nonlinear fashion:

- Bend bends an object along a circular arc
- Flare flares out and tapers off an object
- Sine curves an object into sine waves
- Squash stretches and squashes an object
- Twist twists an object
- Wave creates circular ripples on an object

These are all simple functions, but they are remarkably effective in creating their intended effects, as illustrated in Figure 11.4.

Each of the nonlinear functions can deform only the selected points of objects, just like lattices or clusters. They can also deform multiple objects and maintain tangency between patches. The deformations start and finish along an axis line of your choice. The default setting is −1 and 1 of the local Y axis of the object being deformed, but it automatically transforms to fit the object. You can use the manipulator handles to interactively adjust the deformation attributes. Select the deformer in the Input section of the Channel Box, open the modeling window, and press T to display the Show Manipulator option.

You can combine any number of deformers. It's easy to create complex shapes by manipulating the attributes of the deformers. When you use multiple deformers, their order of creation is important. (See the "Changing the Deformation Order" section later in this chapter.) You can animate the deformers, and you can also animate the deformed objects.

Figure 11.4

The six nonlinear deformers

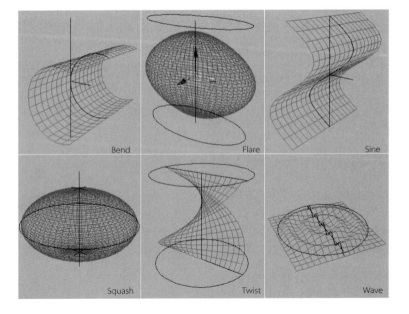

Let's try some examples with the nonlinear deformers. First, we'll use Bend and Sine to twist an object.

1. Create a NURBS plane. Set it to span 10 patches in U and V.

2. Apply Bend to it (choose Deform → Create Nonlinear → Bend), with Curvature set to 3. If the Bend deformer appears perpendicular to the plane, simply rotate it 90 degrees on its Z axis. Then rotate the plane about 15 degrees in the X axis. The plane twists, as shown in Figure 11.5.

3. Add Sine to it (choose Deform → Create Nonlinear → Sine), with Amplitude set to 0.5. Transform the plane back and forth in the X and Z axes. The twisting now seems more random, as shown in Figure 11.5.

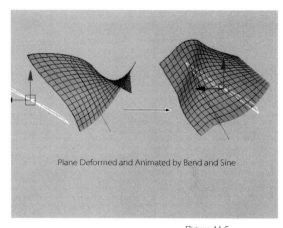

Plane Deformed and Animated by Bend and Sine

Figure 11.5

Twisting an object with the Bend and Sine deformers

4. Group the deformers and the plane. Now you can transform the deformers and the plane together as well.

You can quickly create the shape of a jet engine by applying Wave to a sphere, as shown in the left picture in Figure 11.6. You can start with any shape and play with the manipulator handles until you get the shape you want. Let's try creating an organic tree shape with the Flare, Sine, and Wave deformers.

1. Create a NURBS cylinder. Increase its sections and spans, and scale it up in the Y axis into a pillar shape.

Figure 11.6

Using nonlinear deformers to create shapes

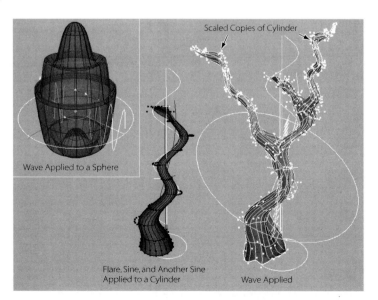

Scaled Copies of Cylinder

Wave Applied to a Sphere

Flare, Sine, and Another Sine Applied to a Cylinder

Wave Applied

2. Apply Flare to it (choose Deform → Create Nonlinear → Flare). Flare out the bottom and taper the top by adjusting the Flare parameters in the Channel Box.

3. Apply Sine to the object. Make the cylinder form about two waves by adjusting the wave length parameter.

4. Apply Sine again with a different wave length and rotate it to make the cylinder wave more randomly.

5. Apply Wave (choose Deform → Create Nonlinear → Wave), setting the Amplitude and Wave Length to about 0.1. Rotate the wave until the cylinder becomes gnarled like a tree, as shown in the middle picture in Figure 11.6.

6. Copy and scale the cylinder to make smaller branches, as shown in the picture on the right in Figure 11.6.

Sculpt Deformation

Sculpt deformation uses a sphere as a sculpting tool to make round or flat ring-shaped deformations. It can deform objects in three modes—Flip, Project, and Stretch—using the appropriate settings, as shown in Figure 11.7.

The Max Displacement and Dropoff Distance settings for Sculpt may seem similar, but they're not. The Max Displacement value determines the strength with which the sphere can push or pull a deforming point. The Dropoff Distance setting determines the area of points that can be influenced.

Figure 11.7

Sculpt deformation modes

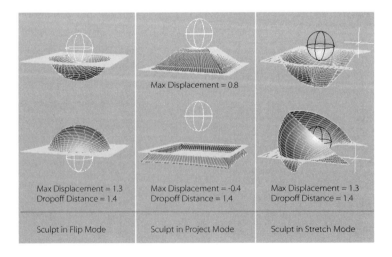

Using Sculpt in Flip Mode

When Sculpt is in Flip mode, the sphere acts as if it has a force field, pushing points away from its center in the direction of the sphere's normal vector. If the sphere's center crosses a point, there is a "flip," because the point being pushed is suddenly pushed in the opposite direction.

Using Sculpt in Project Mode

Sculpt's Project mode is the opposite of the Flip mode. In Project mode, the sphere acts as a magnet, causing the influenced points to snap to it. A Max Displacement value of 1 causes the points to snap to the sphere's surface; values between 0 and 1 cause the points to travel a percentage between their original position and the sphere's surface. Notice that the deformation shapes produced by Flip and Project are quite different in Figure 11.7.

Using Sculpt in Stretch Mode

In Stretch mode, the sphere calculates its position relative to a Sculpt stretch origin locator, which is created with the sphere and stretches the affected points away from the locator. With the Stretch mode, you can group the stretch origin locator and the sphere and animate them together, as in the example shown on the left in Figure 11.8. You can also change the Inside Mode setting to Ring or Even, as shown on the top-right in the figure.

You can use Sculpt in many creative ways. Just by sculpting a NURBS plane, you can easily fashion plant leaves, as shown on the bottom-right in Figure 11.8. Once you've stretched the plane, scale out the CVs at the top, tighten the CVs in the middle, and tweak the CVs a bit to make the leaves asymmetrical.

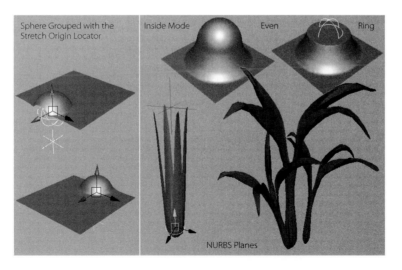

Figure 11.8

Examples of Sculpt in Stretch mode

Wire Deformation

Wire deformation works with an influence wire and a base wirelike Lattice deformation. The deformation occurs according to the relative distance between the two wires. Wire deformation is useful for creating facial expressions.

Applying Wire Deformation

Let's first try out Wire deformation on a simple shape.

1. Create a NURBS plane. Scale it out to 3, and make its patches U and V 16.

2. Place a circle on the plane, and draw a curve with one span inside, as shown in Figure 11.9 on the left.

3. Choose Deform → Wire Tool and accept the default settings. Maya asks you to select shape(s) to deform. Select the plane and press Enter. Maya then asks you to select wire curve(s). Select the curve inside the circle and press Enter. If the deformer has been created successfully, the plane should turn pink.

Figure 11.9

Wire deformation

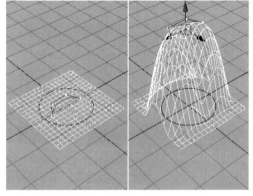

4. The curve is now called a *wire*. A hidden duplicate of the wire, called the base wire, has been created as well. Translate the wire up as shown in Figure 11.9 on the right. Then try moving up the base wire. As the distance between the two curves decreases, so does the intensity of the Wire deformation.

5. Return the wires to their original position, select the plane, and delete history. The Wire deformer node disappears, but the base wire remains, which you need to delete manually.

Using Holders

Let's repeat the process, but this time, we'll use the Holders option. Holders restricts Wire deformation by limiting the influence of the wires.

1. Choose Deform → Wire Tool □ and click Holders. As before, select the plane and press Enter. Then select the curve and press Enter.

2. Maya asks you to select a holder shape or clear the selection. Select the circle and press Enter. Maya now asks you to either select another wire (for more influence wires) or clear the selection. Clear the selection by deselecting all objects and press Enter to complete the wire creation. Notice that another invisible base wire is created.

3. Try moving the wire again and notice the difference. In the example on the left in Figure 11.10, the wire influence is overshooting the circle holder area.

4. In the Channel Box, select wire1 under Outputs and decrease the Dropoff Distance set-ting to 0.3. The wire influence is now restricted inside the circle holder, as shown in the middle picture in Figure 11.10.

5. Try moving the circle up to see the differ-ence between having a holder and not hav-ing one, as in the picture on the right in Figure 11.10.

6. Group all the wires—the influence wire, the base wire, and the holder wire—under the object being deformed so that they will move with the object.

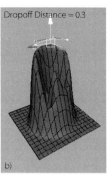

Figure 11.10

Wire deformation on a plane with the Holders option

Using Dropoff Locators

Wire deformers have an additional control tool called Dropoff Locators, which can give you subtle localized control over the Wire deformation. Let's continue with our plane example to see how this tool works.

1. Move the wire down nearer to the plane surface. RM choose over the wire and pick-mask Curve Point.

2. Select a point near the second CV, and then Shift+select another point near the third CV.

3. Choose Deform → Wire Dropoff Locator with the default settings, and you should see something like the top-left picture in Figure 11.11.

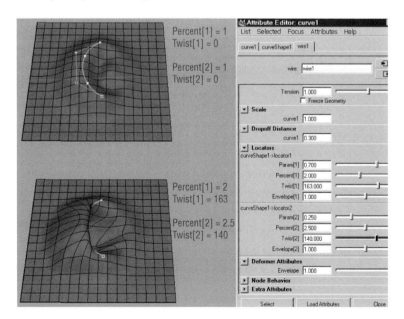

Figure 11.11

Wire deformation with Dropoff Locators and the Twist setting

4. Open the wire's Attribute Editor. There is now a Locators section, where you'll find sliders to control the locators' positions, their influence percentages, and their twist. The Twist setting simply twists the deformed points around the curve at the locator point.

5. Change the Locators settings as follows: Percent[0] to 2, Twist[0] to 163, Percent[1] to 2.5, and Twist[1] to 140. You should see something like the bottom-left picture in Figure 11.11.

Forming Facial Expressions

Now that we've experimented with a basic shape, let's look at how Wire deformation works on a face.

1. Open the Demo_Head.mb file from the Chapter 11 folder on the CD, or if you saved the one you created yourself in Chapters 6 and 7, open that file. Select the face and display the mesh edges and vertices by using the Display → Subdiv Surface Components submenu.

2. Create a NURBS circle with the number of sections that match the points going around the mouth, which should be 14 sections.

3. Choose Isolate Select to view just the mouth area and the circle, as shown in Figure 11.12. To do this, select the circle, select the subdivision faces around the mouth area, and then choose Show → Isolate Select → View Selected in the modeling window. Snap the CVs to the points around the mouth. This circle can be used as a wire to give subtle control to mouth shapes.

4. Create a curve that goes under the eye area and another one over the eyebrow area by snapping CVs to the points on those areas, as Figure 11.13 shows.

Figure 11.12

Molding a circle to the shape of the mouth for Wire deformation

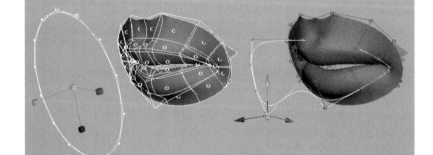

5. Use the Wire tool on the face (choose Deform → Wire Tool), using the three curves as wires. In the Outliner, you should see base wires created for each wire curve.

6. In the Channel Box, open wire1, and reduce the values of the three Dropoff Distance attributes for the three curves to about 0.5. You generally want to localize the influence of the wires to only about this much or less. But try moving the curves, pulling CVs, and see what you think is the best setting for each of the curves. Remember that you can also animate the strength of the influence.

7. Try moving the CVs to see what facial expressions you can create, as in the image on the left in Figure 11.14. You can also create Blend Shapes with the wire curves and animate them as well, as in the picture on the right; the wires are hidden, and the curves beside the face are blend targets.

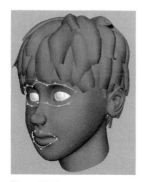

Figure 11.13

Building wires for the face

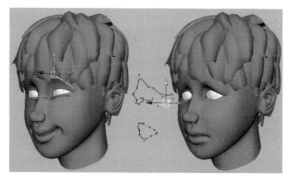

Figure 11.14

Creating facial expressions by (left) moving CVs and (right) creating Blend Shapes

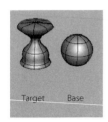

Figure 11.15

A sphere and the shape it will become

Figure 11.16

Default behavior of Blend Shapes

Figure 11.17

Blend-Shaping only two rows of CVs

Figure 11.18

Blend-Shaping with Origin set to World

Blend Shape Deformation

Blend Shape is different from the other deformers. It is specifically designed to perform morphing tasks, and it has a separate slider editor. You can also access Blend Shape sliders in the Attribute Editor or through the channels in the Channel Box.

Blend Shape is especially useful for facial animation. In this type of animation, a group of set shapes such as certain phonemes or facial expressions need to be readily accessible, editable, and, as the name suggests, blendable.

Applying Blend Shape Deformation

Blending works best when the *target object* and the *base object* have the same *topology*, meaning they have the same number of CVs in the same order. Although Maya lets you blend objects that have different topologies, you might not always get the results you want.

To see what we mean, let's go through some examples.

1. Create two spheres. Change the first sphere's shape by pulling points, as shown in Figure 11.15.

2. Select the first sphere, which will be the target, and then Shift+select the second, which will become the base. Choose Deform → Create Blend Shape and accept the default settings.

3. Choose Window → Animation Editors → Blend Shape. An editor opens with a target slider. A blendShape node is created, and the target slider is an attribute of that node. Maya has a Horizontal orientation option, which displays the sliders horizontally. The default setting is vertical. Slide the vertical slider to 1, and the second sphere should morph into an exact replica of the first sphere, as shown in Figure 11.16.

4. You can also Blend Shape points. Select the first two rows of the first sphere (target), select the same for the second (base), and then create another Blend Shape. You get something like the picture shown in Figure 11.17.

5. Notice that there is now another slider in the editor. Repeat step 4, but set the Origin setting to World in the Blend Shape option box. The blending calculates not only the relative translation of the target points, but their world space coordinates as well, as shown in Figure 11.18. The morphing points of the base object translate exactly to where the target points are, no matter how the base object is transformed.

6. Select the middle CVs of the second sphere and delete them, as in shown in Figure 11.19. The topology of the second sphere has changed; it now has eight fewer CVs than the first sphere.

7. Apply Blend Shape to the spheres again. Maya replies with the message, "Error: No deformable objects selected." This is because the default Blend Shape setting verifies that the topology of the target object matches that of the base object. Set Origin back to Local, and turn off the Check Topology setting in the option box. Maya proceeds to morph the base object the best it can. The result is as shown in Figure 11.20.

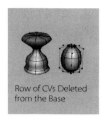

Row of CVs Deleted from the Base

Figure 11.19

Modifying topology after applying Blend Shape

Blend-Shaping Hierarchies and Editing Shapes

When you are morphing a group of objects, the hierarchy of the target objects must be the same as the base objects' hierarchy for the morphing to work properly.

In Figure 11.21, the face on the left is the base, and the one on the right is the target. The face is actually made up of four NURBS patches, as listed in the Outliner in Figure 11.21. Notice that the hierarchy of nodes under Face and Smile are in the same order. Selecting Smile, selecting Face, and then applying the default Blend Shape produces a Smile slider . You'll find an example NURBS_face.mb file with Blend Shapes in the Chapter 11 folder on the CD.

To add more target shapes to a surface that already has a Blend Shape, create more target shapes, select them, select the base object, and choose Deform → Edit Blend Shape → Add. If you see an error message saying you must specify a blendShape node, open the Add option box, choose Specify Node, and enter the name of the existing blendShape node.

Another way to add a shape is to open the Blend Shape Editor and click the Add button for that Blend Shape. This creates a copy of the base shape with the other Blend Shapes' influences on it. You can remove a target slider by selecting the same target shape you used to create that slider, selecting the base, and then choosing Deform → Edit Blend Shape → Remove. If you want to switch the order in which the target sliders are listed, you can do that two at a time by selecting two target shapes and then selecting Deform → Edit Blend Shape → Swap.

Blend Shape without Check Topology

Figure 11.20

Blend-Shaping objects with different topologies

Figure 11.21

Base and target objects for morphing

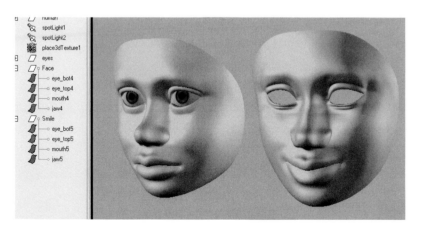

Figure 11.22

Examples of facial targets for Blend Shapes

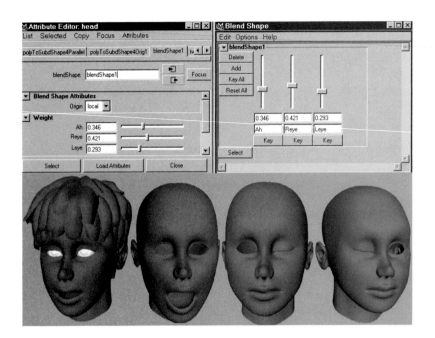

You also can edit the target values in the Channel Box or in the Attribute Editor, where the targets appear as sliders in the Weight section of the blendShape tab. Figure 11.22 shows some examples of target shapes, the blendShape1 tab of the Attribute Editor, and the Blend Shape Editor.

> Once you are satisfied with all the Blend Shape targets, you can delete the target objects to lighten the scene. This prevents you from further editing the target shapes, but because the blending information remains with the base object, you can always re-create a target geometry by copying it from the base object.

Editing Deformations

Deformations depend on the relationships among points and their groupings. The controls you can use for editing deformations include the Relationship Editor, the Edit Membership tool, the Paint Set Membership tool, and the Prune Membership function. You can also edit the deformation order.

Editing Deformation Sets

Whenever you create a deformer, Maya creates a deformer set of the same name. This set shows up in the Deformer Set Editing module of the Relationship Editor. You can use this editor to edit the membership of points in the deformer sets. The editor's Edit menu lets you select any point in a set, add points to a set, and remove points from a set. It also lets you select or delete deformers. Let's go through a simple example.

1. Start a new scene. Create a NURBS cylinder.

2. Select the top two rows of its CVs and apply Lattice deformation with the default settings to the points (choose Deform → Create Lattice).

3. Select both the cylinder and the lattice in the model-ing window, and apply Cluster deformation with the default settings (choose Deform → Create Cluster).

4. Try moving the cluster. You will see that you have a problem commonly known as *double transformation*, which is illustrated in Figure 11.23. The points inside the lattice are being moved twice—once by the lattice deformer, and again by the Cluster deformer. To solve this problem, the cluster should stop moving the points inside the lattice, because you want the lattice to still be able to affect the points on the cylinder.

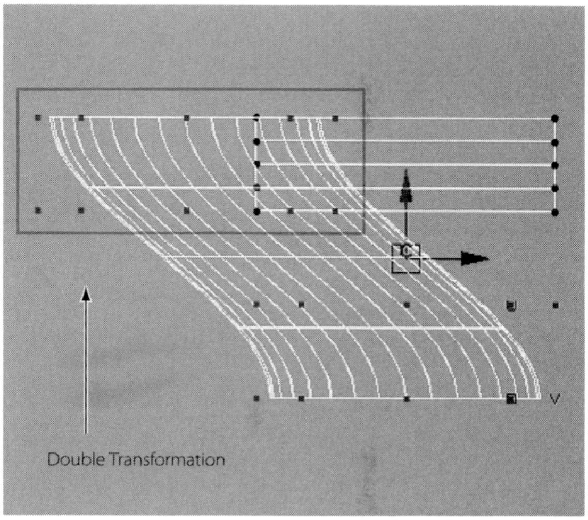

Figure 11.23

CVs transformed twice due to multiple deformers

Double Transformation

5. Choose Window → Relationship Editors → Deformer Sets. You should see the editor with two deformer sets on the left side: ffd1Set and cluster1Set. Click the plus signs to their left to display a list of all the points that are being deformed by the lattice and the cluster.

6. Highlight ffd1Set and choose Edit → Select Set Members. You also can highlight the points inside the set and choose Edit → Select Highlighted. In the modeling window, the points are selected.

7. Highlight cluster1Set, and either click the minus sign button at the top of the window or choose Edit → Remove Selected Items. Do not be alarmed if the points in the modeling win-dow remain highlighted—it is the feedback in the Relationship Editor that matters. The selected points are no longer part of the cluster set, and they are not transformed twice.

When you are in the Relationship Editor, you can unclutter the right window by RM choosing over it and clicking Show DAG Objects Only. (DAG stands for Directed Acyclic Graph.)

Using Tools to Edit Membership

Maya provides a quick way to do what we just did in the previous section without using the Relationship Editor. You can use the Edit Membership tools to solve the double transformation and other deformation problems. Let's try it.

1. Choose Undo to create the double transformation situation again (or repeat steps 1 through 3 in the previous section to re-create it).

2. Choose Deform → Edit Membership Tool. Maya asks you to select a set or a deformer. Our goal is to remove points from the cluster, so select it in the Outliner. All the points belonging to the cluster are selected.

3. Ctrl+click or marquee the points you want to remove. (If you want to add points to a deformer, you can Ctrl+Shift+click or marquee the points.)

The Paint Set Membership tool works in the same way as the Edit Membership tool. To use it in our example, select the cylinder, choose Deform → Paint Set Membership Tool □, select cluster1Set as the set to modify, choose the Remove operation, and brush over the cylinder, as shown in Figure 11.24. The advantage of using the Paint Set Membership tool is that it gives you color feedback, telling you which points belong to which deformer, which can be useful when you are editing rigid skinned objects. (See Chapter 13, "Character Animation Exercises." for more information about skinning techniques.)

Pruning Membership

With Lattice, Cluster, Sculpt, and Wire deformers, Maya provides a quick pruning function. The Deform → Prune Membership function removes all the points of a deformer set that, at the time of the pruning, have not been moved from their undeformed positions.

Figure 11.24

Using the Paint Set Membership tool

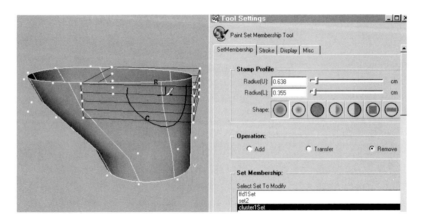

Although pruning can lighten a scene by reducing deformer calculations, you can remove points that seem unnecessary from sets and later find that they need to be deformed after all. In such cases, you can always add those points to the deformer set again, using the editing tools described in the previous sections.

Changing the Deformation Order

Deformation order, or the deformation chain, refers to how multiple deformers affect a surface in order. Their order is usually determined by their order of creation, but you can use the advanced option settings to change their placement in the chain. You can also use the Complete List window for a selected object to edit the order. The best way to understand how deformation order works is to go through another simple example.

1. Create a NURBS cylinder. Scale it up to 5 in Y, and increase its spans to 4.

2. Apply a flare deformer to the cylinder (choose Deform → Create Nonlinear → Flare), with Start Flare set to 2 for X and Z and End Flare set to 0 on X and Z. You should wind up with a cone shape, similar to that in Figure 11.25.

3. Apply a Bend deformer to the cylinder (choose Deform → Create Nonlinear → Bend). Set its Curvature to 1, and retain the other settings. You should wind up with something that looks like a bent cone, similar to the one in Figure 11.26.

4. RM click over the cylinder and choose Inputs → All Inputs to invoke the List Of Input Operations window.

5. In the List Of Input Operations window, notice that the history of the node chain starts from the bottom. MM drag the Non Linear(bend1) node down to the Non Linear(flare1) node until a box appears around it, and then release the mouse button. The nodes' placements have switched. The tip of the cone has opened up, and the cone itself has gone from being round to oval; this is demonstrated in Figure 11.27. Order of operations for deformers is crucial, especially if you intend to apply animation later.

Figure 11.25

A cylinder, tapered into a cone

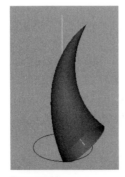

Figure 11.26

The same cylinder with a bend added

Figure 11.27

Different deformation orders

Figure 11.28

The same deformers with modified construction history

6. Undo the change of deformation order by pressing Z until the top end of the cone is closed once again. Select the cylinder, and click the makeNurbsCylinder1 input . Increase its number of sections to 16. Because the cylinder's construction happens before the deformations, and because we applied the deformation to the entire object (as opposed to some of its CVs), the deformations still work in a predictable manner, as illustrated in Figure 11.28. The List Of Input Operations window also works well on Blend Shapes, but you need to be careful not to delete any of your target shapes beforehand.

Advanced Facial Animation

A discussion of advanced facial animation techniques could quickly fill an entire book. Here, we will deal with only several basic points. At the simplest level, you can have a character talk with two shapes: open_mouth and close_mouth. Consider any muppet character, and you will see what we mean. For facial expressions at the simplest level, you need only close_eyes and open_eyes (and perhaps not even those). For a more realistic setup, however, the number of facial shapes, or targets, can quickly grow to dozens.

Creating the Teeth, Tongue, and Oral Cavity

Before you can work on facial shapes, you need to create the teeth and gums, as shown in (a) in Figure 11.29. The upper teeth do not move because they are fixed to the skull; the lower teeth should rotate with the jaw. Use Set Driven Key to have the lower teeth driven by open mouth shapes such as *ah* and *oh*. Make sure the rotation pivot for the lower teeth is similar to the jaw bone's, around the ear area. (See Chapter 9, "Animating in Maya," for details on the Set Driven Key feature.)

> If you are building a cartoony character, you might want to use a simple folded plane as teeth. It can actually look better on a character than more realistic teeth. The bugs in Pixar's *A Bug's Life*, for example, have such simple teeth.

You might also want a tongue, its tip clustered, to strike the back of the upper teeth for what the linguists, if not the dental experts, call the *alveolars* (s, z, t, d, n, l), or to strike the bottom of the upper teeth for the *th* sounds. An example is shown in (b) in Figure 11.29.

Figure 11.29

Teeth, tongue, and oral cavity for facial animation

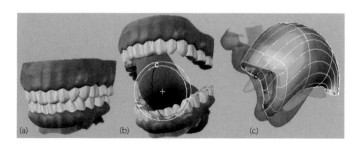

(a)   (b)   (c)

Another necessity is the oral cavity. A good way to proceed is to offset two or three curves from the boundary isoparms of the lips so you can maintain a procedural connection with the mouth shapes, create copies of those offset curves, translate them into the throat area, and loft. This is illustrated in (c) in Figure 11.29. You might want to wait until you finish building the face before creating the oral cavity. It should become a morphing part of all the mouth targets.

Creating the inner mouth parts can be tricky and time-consuming. If you are not going to have close-up shots of a character's mouth, it might not be worth the effort. As an alternative, you can create a textured plane, curve it, and position it inside the mouth.

Creating Mouth Shapes

There is no fixed list of facial shapes you should create, nor is there a standard guide for how to set them up for facial animation. Specific projects call for specialized solutions, and animators always experiment.

Setting up well-thought-out mouth targets might take longer, but it will save time in the long run, especially if you will be using the character repeatedly. Using Blend Shape for lip synching and Wire deformation for fine tweaking and facial expressions will probably give the best results. Figure 11.30 shows a sample list of Blend Shapes for lip synching.

The *ah* and *oo* shapes are absolute necessities—*ah* because it opens the mouth and lowers the jaw, and *oo* because it can also be the shape for sounds such as *ch*, *sh*, and *w*, not to mention kissing and whistling.

Figure 11.30

Mouth shapes for lip synching

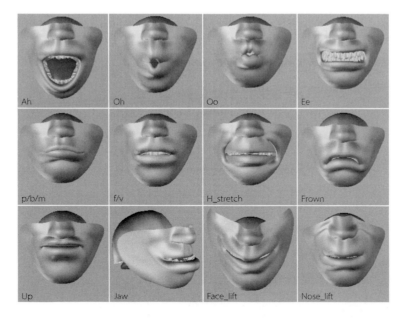

You can get by using one shape for *oo* and *oh*, but they are quite different shapes. The jaw drops for *oh*, creating a hollow space inside the mouth, whereas for *oo*, everything pushes up. The *ee* shape shown in Figure 11.30 is an extremely strong shape, which can double as an expression of anger or, combined with *ah*, screaming. For unaccented *ee* shapes, you might want to use the H(horizontal)_stretch instead.

For H_stretch, Frown, and Face_lift, you could separate them further into Left and Right targets. But be careful not to disturb the few middle CVs of the face, or you will get a double-transformation effect (described earlier in the "Editing Deformations" section).

For many of these shapes, if you build the targets carefully, you can also use their negatives. Figure 11.31 shows the negatives of some of the shapes.

The sounds discussed here are spelled like regular words; they are not accurately spelled phonetic sounds. For proper phonetic spelling, follow the IPA (International Phonetic Alphabet). Different dictionaries use slightly different spelling methods, but *ah* would generally be listed as [a:], *oo* as [u:], *ee* as [i:], and so on. The representation of letters such as *c* depends on how they are used. A soft *c* is [s]; a hard *c* is [k].

Setting Up Multiple Blend Shapes

One advantage of working with a face that's been built in patches, such as the one in Figure 11.32, is that when you are setting up your blending targets for the face, you can separate mouth shapes from facial expressions. This approach makes the setup more economical and efficient than throwing everything in together. You create two groups of Blend Shapes. The mouth and the jaw patches hold mouth shapes such as those described in the previous section. The eye patches hold facial expressions such as eyes closing and showing emotions—happy, sad, angry, and so on. Setting things up this way can be a bit more complex, however, and requires the use of the Set Driven Key feature.

Figure 11.31

Negative value mouth shapes

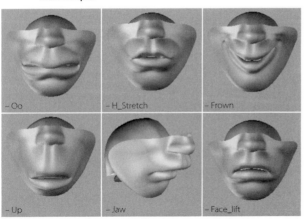

In the example in Figure 11.32, Blend Shape was applied not to the top Face node, but to the Eye_area and Mouth_area nodes. This creates two Blend Shape groups: one for the mouth area and another for the eye area. The two targets, Ah and Eyeclose, are applied to the base objects, Mouth_area and Eye_area. The two shapes are independent of each other so that when the eyes close, the mouth area is not affected, and vice versa. The third shape, Smile, however, is a combination of two target shapes: the Sm_eyes and Sm_mouth shapes. In the bottom-right picture in Figure 11.32, both shapes are at their maximum target value.

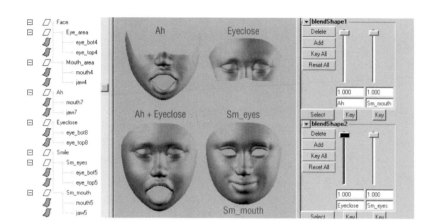

Figure 11.32

Blend Shapes for two areas of the face

The two shapes must move together, or you can run into problems with patches overlapping or separating. When only the Sm_mouth slider is moved, creasing occurs, as shown in Figure 11.33. This is because the Sm_eyes slider does not deform the eye area, so there is overlapping. We can prevent this problem by making the Sm_mouth slider a driver for the Sm_eyes slider.

RM choose over a numeric input field in the Blend Shape Editor to pop up a menu. Select Set Driven Key. You can select the blendShape node in the Blend Shape Editor by clicking the Select button. Specify Sm_mouth as the driver and Sm_eyes as the driven. Key them at 0 and 1. Sm_mouth should now drive Sm_eyes, as shown in Figure 11.34.

Discerning Spoken Sounds

When you are setting up lip synching, one of the worst mistakes you can make is to try to figure out the mouth shapes by going through the alphabet, spelling out what is spoken. It is better to reference a list of phonemes if you can, but better still to just follow the mouth shapes as the sounds are made. Here are a few rules that can help you get started:

Figure 11.33

Creasing caused by overlapping

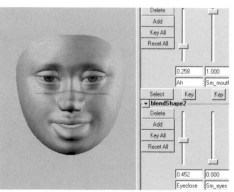

- Consonants are greatly affected by the sounds that surround them, which is a phonetic phenomenon called assimilation. For example, the consonant *d* in "how *do* you do?" and "how *did* you do?" forms two different mouth shapes, because the vowels that follow the *d* are different. A good rule to follow is to go through the vowels first, because they often dictate how the neighboring consonants will be shaped. Once you figure out the vowels, the consonants will naturally fall into place.

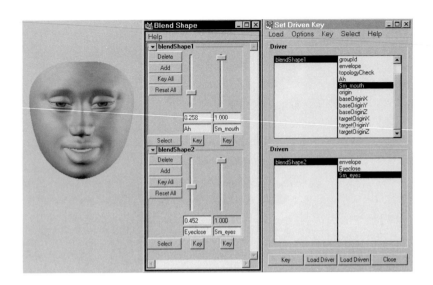

Figure 11.34

Making the Sm_mouth slider a driver for the Sm_eyes slider

- Vowel reduction or omission is a specific type of assimilation. For example, a phrase such as "how did you do?" is often spoken "how ju do?". In a case like this, it helps to "unlearn" your reading skills; instead of trying to find sounds from the words, just listen.

- English is an intonational language. It's rhythmic, with regular beats of accented and unaccented syllables and a few strong emphases punctuating different parts of sentences. Listen to these emphases and figure out where the beats are falling. You can then skim through the unaccented segments and concentrate on nailing the accented syllables.

- For animation, be concerned only with what will be seen. If a character's back is toward you, for goodness sake, don't animate its face! If that seems obvious, then in the same way, you don't need to animate what goes on inside the mouth. Consonants such as s, z, t, d, n, and j, among others, can often be shown as just a slight up and down movement of the mouth. Consonants such as k, g, ng, and h matter only in that they fill time between vowel shapes. The th sounds (as in "thing" and "they"), too, are indistinguishable in terms of shapes and should be treated as one sound.

For many animators, lip synch is not such an important part of facial animation. Far more important is creating proper facial expressions, especially in the eye area, and body poses that fit the action.

Keyframing and Tweaking Mouth Shapes

There are various methods of keyframing mouth shapes. You can use the Channel Box, the Attribute Editor, or the Blend Shape Editor. It is generally not a good idea to keyframe individual shapes, because the shapes that are not keyframed may end up "floating" between their keyframes. A much more efficient method is to keyframe all the shapes and then tweak them individually in the Graph Editor.

You can lock certain targets to exclude them from being keyframed if you know you won't be using them for a specific scene. For example, you might lock a smile target in a scene if you know the character isn't going to smile.

Keyframing with the Channel Box or the Attribute Editor

You can use the Channel Box and the Attribute Editor to keyframe facial animation much like you use the Blend Shape Editor, although the Blend Shape Editor offers more functions.

To use the Channel Box, you need to select the base object. The Attribute Editor has the Copy Tab button at the bottom, which creates a copy window that will still remain when the object is deselected. Another advantage of the Attribute Editor's torn-off copy is that it has sliders. The Channel Box's targets are restricted to a value range of 0 to 1 for the targets, but you can set the Attribute Editor sliders to a wider range of target values. Simply enter numbers such as –1 or 2 in the numeric input field, and the slider range will adjust accordingly.

You can use Key All in the Blend Shape Editor and in the Channel Box, but not in the Attribute Editor. One way to get around this is to use the hotkey for setting keys. You might need to adjust the Set Key options to All Keyable Attributes in order to keyframe blended shapes. Figure 11.35 shows the Attribute Editor sliders and the Channel Box being used to keyframe the Blend Shapes.

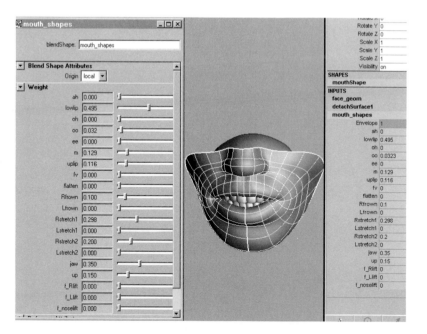

Figure 11.35

Using the Attribute Editor and the Channel Box to keyframe Blend Shapes

Tweaking with the Graph Editor

Once you've roughly animated the mouth shapes, you can use the Graph Editor to tweak the animation curves. You can also tweak using the Channel Box or the sliders (turning on the Auto Key function will help), but only the function curves can give you a clear picture of how the shapes are moving through time. Figure 11.36 shows an example of the curves for the *oo* shape's rising and falling values in the Graph Editor.

You usually want to select either one or only a few targets in the Graph Editor and focus on tweaking only those curves at one time, as shown in Figure 11.37. You might also want to turn off Curve in the Select menu if you are editing only keyframes.

Figure 11.36

Facial animation curves in the Graph Editor

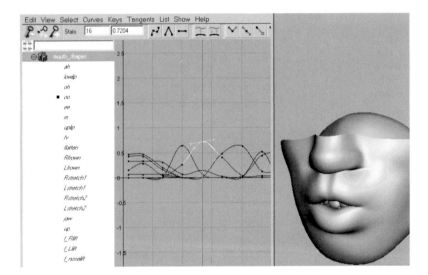

Figure 11.37

Tweaking a curve in the Graph Editor

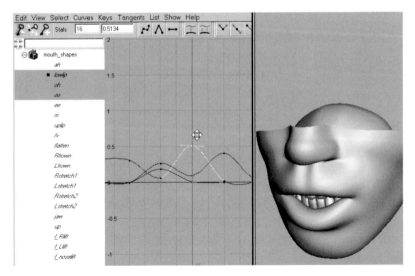

When you're lip-synching a character's mouth movements to an audio file, the best approach seems to be to hit the sounds to the mouth shapes exactly and then, at the end, move the keyframes about 2 to 4 frames backward on the Timeline. Lip synching looks most natural when the target mouth shape is hit a bit before the sound is actually heard. Just remember this principle: seeing comes before hearing.

Summary

In this chapter, you learned how to apply various kinds of deformers to objects or parts of objects. One of the wonderful things about deformers is that they can be combined in different orders to produce some remarkable effects. In particular, Wire and Blend Shape deformation lets you produce high-level facial animation. Lattice can also be a useful tool for both smooth and rigid skinning.

In the next chapter, we'll discuss how to bind and weight characters.

CHAPTER 12

Binding

In this chapter you will learn how to attach surfaces to skeletons and make them deform properly for animation. The attaching process is called *binding*, the bound geometry becomes the skeleton's *skin*, and the skin's deformation is affected by a process known as *weighting*. All this terminology will soon become familiar as you go through the examples and exercises that follow. We will first bind the character model, and then we'll spend the rest of this chapter setting up and binding the puppy.

This chapter features:

- ■ **Skinning**

- ■ **Binding and subdivision surfaces**

- ■ **Hands On: Binding a character**

- ■ **Hands On: Binding a puppy**

Skinning

We've already talked about how skeletons can bind objects and deform them properly as they move. The process by which skeletons do this is called *skinning*, and the objects that become bound to skeletons this way are called *skins* or *skin objects*.

Like other deformers, skeletons can skin anything that has control points, such as CVs, NURBS curves, surfaces, polygonal vertices and objects, subdivision surfaces, and lattices. Although you will most often skin whole objects, it is worthwhile knowing that you can bind only a selection of points as well.

There are two kinds of skinning: *rigid* and *smooth*. Rigid skinning creates a joint cluster for every joint binding the objects. These clusters can contain points of multiple objects, and you can use flexors or weighting to smooth the bends. Smooth skinning creates a skin cluster for every object being bound; this cluster is shared by a set number of joints with different influence percentages. You can use influence objects to manipulate the deformation of smooth skins. For both kinds of skinning, you can use the Artisan tools to edit set member-ship and weights of the skinned points. When you are working with dense organic models, the difference between using Artisan and using the regular tools can be quite noticeable.

Rigid Skinning

Rigid skinning is called "rigid" because only one joint can influence a CV. There is no sharing of CVs as in smooth skinning, and the joint clusters that are created have a default influence value of 100 percent, which results in a rather rigid deformation when joints are bent. You can edit rigid skins by using flexors (a special type of deformer) or other deformers or by changing skin point weights. All the tools we'll be using, unless stated otherwise, are avail-able in the Skin menu in the Animation module.

Creating Rigid Skin

Let's start with a simple example.

1. Create a NURBS cylinder and increase its sections to 10, its spans to 6, and its Height Ratio to 10.

2. In the side view, create a skeleton chain (choose Skeleton → Joint Tool) as shown in Figure 12.1 (a).

3. Select the cylinder and the skeleton—the order of selection here doesn't matter—and choose Skin → Bind Skin → Rigid Bind with the default settings. The cylinder turns pink to show that is bound, or skinned, by the skeleton chain. Try rotating the second joint in Z by 90 degrees; you'll see that all the points bound by it rotate fully, or "rigidly," as in Figure 12.1 (b).

You can skin selected joints in the same way that you skin complete skeletons. In the option windows for Bind Skin commands, change the setting to Bind To Selected Joints. You can then bind different geometries differently, such as rigid binding the hand and smooth binding the body, for example. Using the Selected Joints method gives you more control over the binding process. If you want to skin one object separately to two or more joints in a hierarchy, bind the control points, because Maya will not allow you to bind at the object level twice. You can, however, bind an object to separate joint chains as different partitions.

Rigid Skin Editors

Choose Window → Relationship Editors → Deformer Sets to display two jointSets, one for each joint. The two sets contain all the points of the cylinder, and if you remove any of the points from the sets, those points will no longer be bound by the skeleton. Choose Window → General Editors → Component Editor, and click the Rigid Skins tab. There are now two columns for the jointClusters. Select all the CVs of the cylinder, and click Load Components in the Component Editor. You will see the points weighted under the joints to which they belong. If you want, you can manipulate the weights here to smooth the bending. In most situations, however, you can smooth the blending in more elegant ways.

If you have trouble selecting CVs with a pick mask because the skeleton gets selected over the CVs, switch to Component mode and select them. Skeletons are not selected in Component mode. You can also disable the Joints object type in the Status line.

Figure 12.1

A cylinder with rigid skin

Flexors

The easiest way to make joints bend smoothly is to use a *flexor*, a special type of deformer that works with rigid skinned joints. There are three types of flexors: lattice, sculpt, and cluster. You will usually want to use the lattice.

THE JOINT LATTICE FLEXOR

To see how this tool works, select the skeleton and choose Skin → Go To Bind Pose. The cylinder is no longer deformed. Select the second joint and, from the Skin menu, choose Edit Rigid Skin → Create Flexor. Leave everything at the default setting and click Create. A joint lattice (or flexor) is created with its orientation the

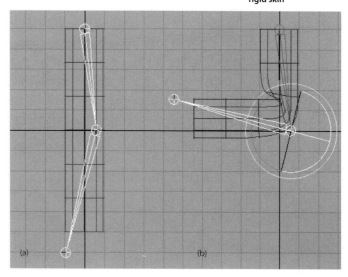

same as the joint's local axes. Rotate the joint 90 degrees again, and you'll see that the bending is smoother—the flexor deforms the cylinder around the joint. You can further change the way the flexor is deforming by selecting it and editing its attributes in the Channel Box. In Figure 12.2, notice how each attribute changes the way the flexor deforms the cylinder.

THE BONE LATTICE FLEXOR

You can also apply flexors to bones, but bone flexors are applied a bit differently. Their deformation is affected by the rotation of their child joint. Think of biceps and triceps bulging when you rotate your elbow. To try a bone flexor, select the first joint and apply Create Flexor. In the Create Flexor option window, turn off At Selected Joints and check At Selected Bones. Click Create to create a lattice around the first bone. Rotate the second joint 90 degrees, select the flexor, and, in the Channel box, change the values for the boneFlexor attributes. Notice that, instead of Creasing and Rounding, boneFlexor has Bicep and Tricep as the first two variables. You can easily get something like (a) in Figure 12.3.

You can move, rotate, and scale the flexors to adjust the way they are affecting the skin. In the Outliner, select the lattice group, which selects both the flexor and its latticeBase, and transform it. You can see the way the skin deformation changes while you are transforming the lattice group: Figure 12.3 (b) is the result of the lattice group being moved and rotated.

Figure 12.2

Joint flexor attributes

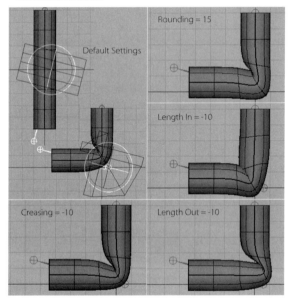

GO TO BIND POSE

Do not confuse the Skin → Go To Bind Pose command with the Skeleton → Assume Preferred Angle command. The latter rotates the joints back to their creation positions, which can be changed with the Set Preferred Angle command. Bind Pose instead keeps track of not just the rotation but all the transformation values of the joints when the object was skinned.

If you decide to detach and reattach skinned objects, reposition the skeletons to their Bind Pose. In order for Go To Bind Pose to work properly, the joints must not be locked. Often, however, some of the joints will become locked, because of constraints, expressions, or keyed IK handles. In such case, you can temporarily disable these nodes by choosing Modify → Evaluate Nodes and selecting the nodes that are causing the blockage.

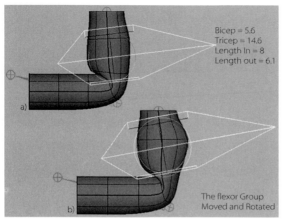

Bicep = 5.6
Tricep = 14.6
Length In = 8
Length out = 6.1

a)

The flexor Group
Moved and Rotated

b)

Figure 12.3

The bone flexor in different positions

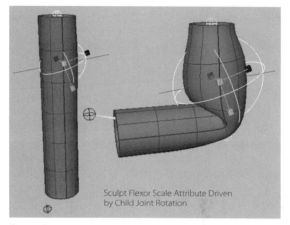

Sculpt Flexor Scale Attribute Driven
by Child Joint Rotation

Figure 12.4

The upper arm bulging

THE SCULPT FLEXOR

You can also use a sculpt sphere as a flexor. It works just like a regular Sculpt deformer, and there are no automated attribute controls as with lattice flexors. To have those controls, you need to use Set Driven Key. You can use the sculpt flexor as a bulging upper arm if you want, as shown in Figure 12.4, or as other parts of the body that regularly stretch with joint rotations, such as chest muscles. The Sculpt Flexor can be applied as a joint flexor as well, although it is generally used as a bone flexor.

THE CLUSTER FLEXOR

Cluster flexors have no options attached to them, and they exist only within joints. You can manipulate the smoothness of the joint's deformation, as well as the distribution of the parent and child joints' deforming influences. Create a cluster flexor, select the joint with the cluster flexor, and press T to activate the manipulator handle. The handle shows two rings: one for the child joint, and another for the parent joint. The center of the rings slide up and down the bones, changing the joints' Upper or Lower Bound values, and the radius of the rings changes the Upper or Lower Value values. Figure 12.5 shows some of the ways you can change the bending with a cluster flexor.

Figure 12.5

A cluster flexor

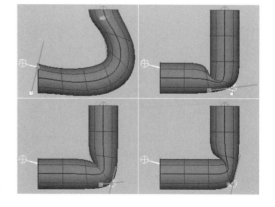

THE COPY FLEXOR

The Copy Flexor function allows you to copy flexors to other joints. This is useful for creating flexors on mirrored joints or finger joints. Simply first select the flexor you want to copy, select the joint you want it copied to, and choose Edit Rigid Skin → Copy

Flexor. If you have many copies of the same flexors deforming something like finger joints, and you are comfortable using the Hypergraph, you can try setting up the connections so that one flexor node can drive all the lattice nodes. This is especially helpful if you need to animate the attributes for all the flexors.

Edit Membership and the Artisan Tools

You've already been introduced to the Edit Membership, Paint Weights, and Paint Set Membership tools under the Deform menu. Rigid skin works with all these tools.

> Smooth skin does not work with these tools, because it has only one cluster set. It uses Paint Skin Weights (choose Skin → Edit Smooth Skin → Paint Skin Weights Tool) instead for weighting points.

We are back with the cylinder and the two joints. Delete all the flexors, choose Skin → Go To Bind Pose (with the skeleton selected), select the cylinder. and choose Skin → Detach Skin. Select the skeleton and the cylinder, choose Skin → Bind Skin → Rigid Bind ❑, turn on Color Joints, and click Bind Skin. Notice that the joints are now colored. Rotate the second joint 90 degrees as before. Choose Deform → Edit Membership Tool to change the shape of the mouse arrow. Select the first joint to highlight all the points belonging to it, as in Figure 12.6 (a). Ctrl+Shift+click the points at the bend to include them to the first joint, until you see something like Figure 12.6 (b). Remember that you should generally edit membership before editing the weights of the control points.

Select the cylinder, and choose Deform → Paint Set Membership Tool ❑. This tool performs the same function that Edit Membership provides. In the shaded mode, the cylinder shows two colors, representing the points that belong to the two joints. Because the joints themselves are colored, you can easily identify which joint is binding which part of the surface. Select the second joint in the Set Membership section, and you can add points to it with the paintbrush as shown in Figure 12.7.

With the cylinder still active, choose Deform → Paint Cluster Weights Tool ❑. Set the Operation setting to Smooth, select the second joint for the Clusters setting by clicking the first button in the Paint Attributes section, and then choose Cluster → joint2cluster1-weights. Now the cylinder's color has changed again. The

Figure 12.6

Using the Edit Membership tool to add CVs to the root joint

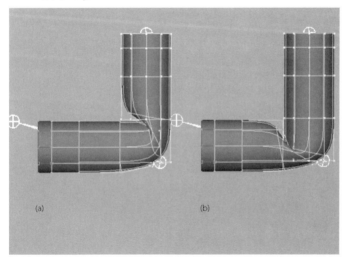

(a)   (b)

cylinder is black, except for the section bound by the second joint. The smoothing operation actually re-weights the points in the second joint, as shown in Figure 12.8. Always keep the brush at low settings. It may take some practice, but once you get used to smoothing the weights, you can efficiently smooth out the bend. Using these Artisan tools (introduced in Chapter 7, "Working with Artisan") is definitely faster than using the Component Editor when dealing with dense models.

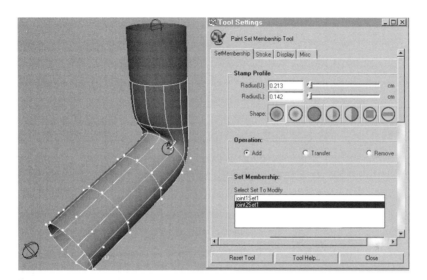

Figure 12.7

The Paint Set Membership tool

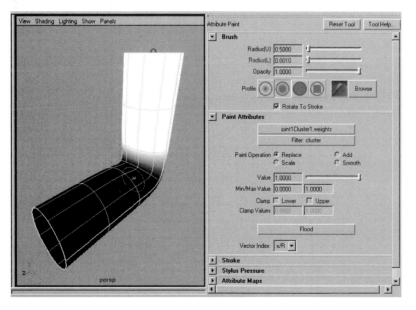
Figure 12.8

The Paint Cluster Weights tool

For fine control over deformations such as bending and bulging, use flexors and other deformers, but for simple smoothing tasks or creating organic weighting around a surface, use Artisan tools. They create a lighter scene, without the extra deformer nodes.

Do not confuse the Artisan tools Paint Set Membership and Paint Weights. The first tool determines which cluster the points will belong to, and the second determines how much the points will be influenced by that cluster.

Smooth Skinning

For each object being skinned, smooth skinning creates one cluster set of points, which can be influenced by more than one joint. The main advantage of smooth skinning is that more than one joint can exert influence on the control point. This can also mean a bit more involved weighting process, but as you will see in the "Hands On: Binding the Puppy" section, certain binding situations require smooth skinning to work. You can set the number of joints that can actually influence the points in the Smooth Bind option window, but all the joints in the skeleton can potentially influence the smooth skin.

You do not need flexors or the Edit Membership tool to edit points in the smooth skin cluster set. If you need that kind of deliberate control over the bends, you can always use deformers or influence objects, which are deformers specifically set up to work with smooth skinning. Artisan's Paint Skin Weights tool (see Chapter 7 for details on Artisan) is especially useful with smooth skin.

Creating Smooth Skin

Figure 12.9

Smooth skin deformation

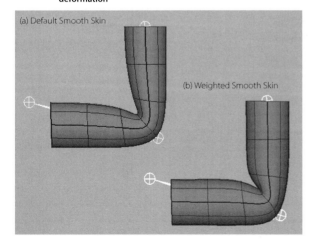

(a) Default Smooth Skin

(b) Weighted Smooth Skin

Let's get back to our cylinder. First, select the skeleton and choose Skin → Go To Bind Pose. Then, with the cylinder selected, choose Skin → Detach Skin. Again, select the cylinder and the joint chain, choose Skin → Bind Skin → Smooth Bind ❐, choose Edit → Reset Settings, and then slide Max Influences down to 2. The default Max Influences is 5, but you'd rarely need anything higher than 2 or 3. The default Bind Method is Closest Joint, meaning that joint influence priority is based on joint hierarchy. If you choose Closest Distance, joint hierarchy is ignored, and whatever joint is closest to the skin point will have the greatest influence. Unless you specifically want the binding to be created this way, this is not how a hierarchically structured character deforms, and you should generally leave this setting at default. Click Bind Skin, and the cylinder is smooth-skinned. Rotate the second joint 90 degrees, and notice the difference in the way it bends as in Figure 12.9 (a): the skin deforms a lot more smoothly. Too smoothly, in fact. We want a bit more rigidity around the bending area than the default setting, something like the second cylinder in Figure 12.9 (b).

Weighting Skin Points

Before we address the lack of rigidity, however, let's see the differences between the smooth-skinned cylinder and the rigid-skinned one. In the Relationship Editor, choose the Deformer Set Editor, and notice that there is only one set. In the Component Editor, in the Skin Clusters tab, you will notice three columns of joints, including the end one, and they all share in influencing the skin points. All the numbers in a row always add up to 1, meaning 100 percent influence. Select the cylinder, and choose Skin → Edit Smooth Skin → Paint Skin Weights Tool. Set the brush values low, set Operation to Add, and select the second joint to work on. The cylinder is black except for the area that is being influenced by the second joint. You can easily make the bend more rigid on the second joint, as in Figure 12.10. Repeat the process for the first joint. If you make a mistake, you can always undo it, and if you want to restart from the beginning, just select the object and choose Edit Smooth Skin → Reset Weights To Default.

> When you are in the Paint Skin Weights mode, you can also select different joints for weight-ing, by RM choosing Paint Weights over the joint you want.

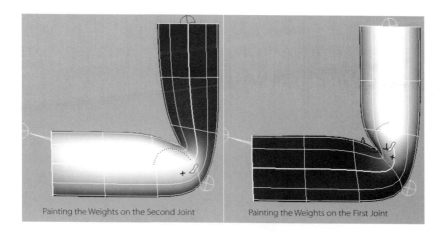

Painting the Weights on the Second Joint   Painting the Weights on the First Joint

Figure 12.10

The Paint Skin Weights tool

Influence Objects

Let's say we want the biceps and triceps to bulge. We can use an influence object to accomplish this. Create a NURBS sphere and scale it to fit inside the upper arm. Select the cylinder skin, select the sphere, and choose Skin → Edit Smooth Skin → Add Influence with the default settings. The sphere becomes an influence object, like a lattice deformer, with a hidden sphereBase object also created. You will generally leave the Base object alone, although you can optionally pull points of the Base object to change the deformation effect of the sphere. You can use Set Driven Key to automate the bulging by scaling up the sphere when the second joint rotates, as in Figure 12.11. The influence sphere and the sphereBase should be grouped under the first joint.

Do not delete an influence object the regular way, as it will mess up the smooth skin weighting. Select the skin, and select the Influence object, and then choose Edit Smooth Skin → Remove Influences.

We used a sphere, but we could have used any object with control points. The biceps and the triceps in Figure 12.11 look shapeless. Let's try the Influence object again, this time deforming a torus to get more definition for the biceps and triceps. Set up a torus as an Influence object with Minor Sweep at –180 and everything else at the default setting, as in Figure 12.12. Select the skin, and, in the Channel box, open the skinCluster and set Use Components to On. An easy way to do this is to enter **1** in the field. When this is turned on, component-level deformation of the Influence object will influence the skin as well. Sculpt the torus until the upper arm takes on the shapes for biceps and triceps as in Figure 12.12.

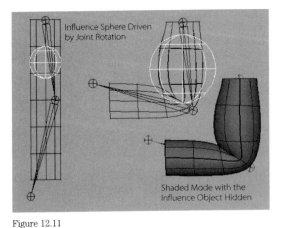

Figure 12.11

The sphere as an influence object

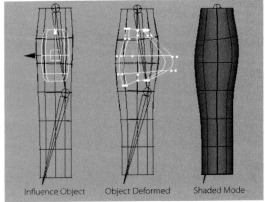

Figure 12.12

The influence object being sculpted

Keyframe the CVs, and move to a different frame. Rotate the second joint, and sculpt the torus again until you see bulging biceps and triceps as shown in Figure 12.13. Copy the bulging torus.

Move back to the frame where the torus CVs were keyframed. You can now delete the keyframe. Apply Blend Shape to the torus, making the copied torus its target. In the Channel Box, open the blendShape channels, highlight the nurbsTorus target, and RM choose Set Driven Key. Make the blend shape driven by the joint rotation, as shown in Figure 12.14.

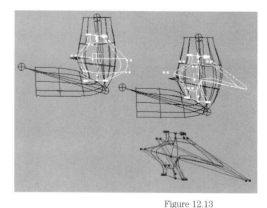

Figure 12.13

Bulging torus when the joint is rotated

Binding and Subdivision Surfaces

Before moving on to this chapter's exercises, we need to briefly discuss binding subdivision surfaces. The process of binding is exactly the same for NURBS, polygons, and subdivision surfaces. In each situation, we are binding the control points that will be weighted to move and deform the surface appropriately. As you will see later with the NURBS puppy, it is not easy to bind multiple-patch NURBS surfaces, and we will use the lattice deformers to bypass the problem. The great thing about polygons and subdivision surfaces is that we do not have to worry about seams appearing at the edges, as they are usually single continuous surfaces. Unlike NURBS modeling, however, with polygons we cannot use the arrow keys to travel across the points in U or V, nor can we select entire rows or columns. Weighting can become frustratingly tedious when you have to adjust weights on thousands of control points on a dense polygon model.

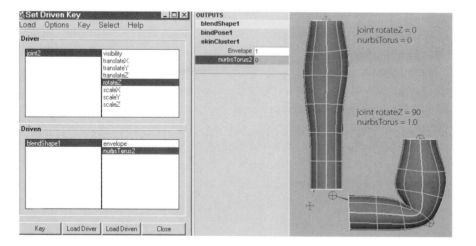

Figure 12.14

Set Driven Key causing the upper arm to bulge

Binding subdivision surfaces is advantageous in that we do not have to worry about seams as we do with multipatched NURBS surfaces, and because of its smoothing property, we usually end up binding a much smaller number of control points than we would with a comparable polygon surface. Again, as with modeling, we get the best of both worlds when we bind subdivision surfaces, as you can see in the bound cylinders in Figure 12.15. Cylinder (a) consists of four patches of NURBS surfaces, cylinder (b) is a comparable polygon surface with many more points, and cylinder (c) is a subdivision surface.

Figure 12.15

Different surfaces bound

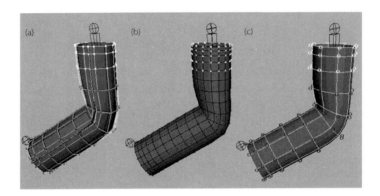

Hands On: Binding a Character

In Chapter 10, "Paths and Bones," we set up our character with a skeleton hierarchy. We will now proceed to bind the character to the skeleton. The binding procedure usually takes multiple steps, and different characters require different methods. For our situation, we will use rigid binding for the hands, body, and the head. For the shoes, we will use smooth binding.

Poly Proxy Binding

The straight approach to binding a subdivision surface is to bind the hierarchical surface at level 0. For our character, however, we will use an alternative "poly proxy binding" method: as the name suggests, the poly proxy mesh is bound to the joints, and it deforms the hierarchical subdivision surface. This approach has a couple of advantages compared with binding the subdivision surface directly. Because the poly proxy mesh is much lighter than the subdivision surface it is connected to, you can weight it faster, especially if you are dealing with a heavy model. Also, the proxy mesh can be used as a rough proxy model to animate with once the binding is done. When we hide the hierarchical surface and leave the proxy mesh visible, the model can be more quickly animated.

1. Open the `character_ik_setup.mb` file from the Chapter 12 folder on the CD-ROM. It already has everything set up except for the binding. Open the Hypergraph window

and turn on the Shape Nodes display option. You should see the subdivision shape nodes below their transformation nodes, as in the left side of Figure 12.16. RM over the surfaces in the perspective view, including the body, the hands, the head, and the shoes, to go to Polygon mode. In the Hypergraph window, you should see extra poly proxy mesh shape nodes with names such as subD_body-HistPoly below the subdivision shape nodes, as in the right side of Figure 12.16. We will be binding these poly proxy mesh nodes.

2. Select the subdivision shape nodes and hide them. The poly proxy meshes do not have any shading assigned to them yet, so connect them to a Lambert or Blinn material.

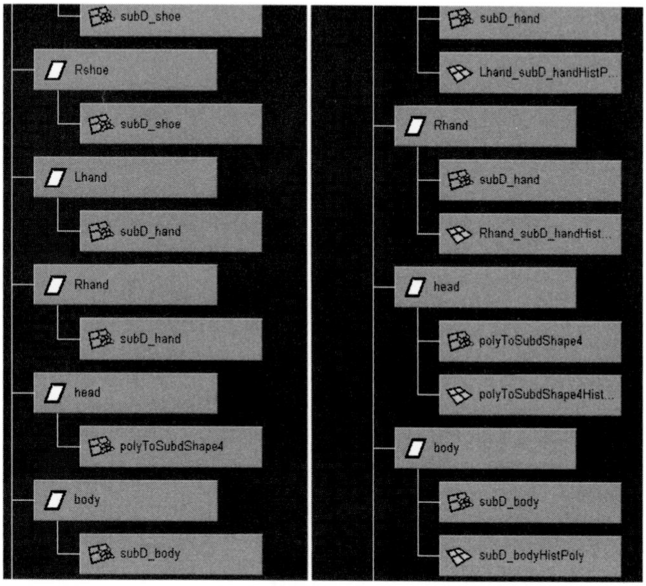

Figure 12.16

Shape nodes in the Hypergraph: (left) in Standard mode, only subdivision surfaces are created; (right) in Polygon mode, the display adds poly proxy mesh nodes.

Although for the sake of simplicity this example uses the subdivision surfaces' poly proxy meshes for binding, in production settings, you might want to create another set of poly meshes from the subdivision surfaces' poly proxy meshes and bind those duplicated meshes. You can then connect them to drive the deformation of the poly proxy meshes, which in turn will drive the deformation of the subdivision surfaces. This extra step will increase the complexity of the character setup, but it will also bring more flexibility and stability to it. Also, it's a good idea to group the subdivision shape nodes and the proxy polygon nodes to separate layers or sets, so that you can easily hide or show those shape nodes. If you create a set using the Set Editing Relationship Editor, the set will also appear at the bottom of the Outliner.

Binding Body Parts

Let's first bind the body.

1. Select the following joints in the skeleton hierarchy: root, spines, chest, neck, shoulders, arms, elbows, forearms, legs, and knees. In other words, leave out the wrists and the joints below them and the joints below the knee. With the appropriate joints selected, add the body poly proxy node to the selection, and choose Skin → Bind Skin → Rigid Bind ❑. Make sure you select the body poly proxy node, the subD_bodyHistPoly node, and not the DAG node above it, as this will also select the hidden subdivision surface as well.

2. Set the Bind To setting to Selected Joints and click Apply. Make sure the clusters have been created by testing to see if the body deforms with the joints.

Now we should edit the membership of the vertices. We can't go through all the sections of the body, so we will use the Lelbow joint as an example.

3. In the Animation module, choose Deform → Edit Membership Tool; then, in the modeling window, click the Lelbow joint. All the points that belong to the Lelbow joint are highlighted, as shown in Figure 12.17 (a). You want to transfer the membership of the points so that the rows of points above the elbow area also become part of the elbow joint's

Figure 12.17

Membership before and after the weighting

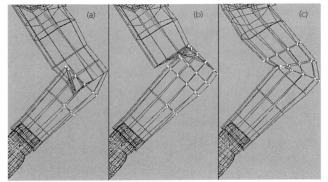

cluster set. This "over-reaching" may seem improper when those points deform the way they do in Figure 12.17 (b), but such rearrangement of point membership is necessary if you want parts of the upper arm area to deform when the elbow joint rotates. Once the weighting is properly assigned, the deformation will appear more agreeable, as in Figure 12.17 (c), in which some of the points on the forearm have also been transferred to the forearm joint.

When you complete all the membership assignments for a joint, it's a good idea to create a set for those points using the Relationship Editor for Sets. When you move on to weighting, this can help you greatly in selecting the relevant points.

4. Use the approach just described to assign memberships for different joints. In particular, the membership for the knee joints should also include the lower thigh area above the knee, as we did with the elbow and for the same reason. Keep in mind how the points will deform after you've lowered the weights. The shoulder area is tricky to weight properly, and carefully assigning the most appropriate points to the shoulder joints will go a long way in enabling the shoulder area to deform well. You might also have to reassign some points as you go through the weighting process. Figure 12.18 shows the membership assignments for different sections of the body. For a closer examination of how the points are assigned, look at the `character_bound.mb` file in the Chapter 12 folder on the CD-ROM.

5. Select the head and the neck joints, add the head proxy mesh (not the DAG node above it) to the selection, and apply Rigid Bind. Figure 12.19 shows the membership assignment for the head and neck joints.

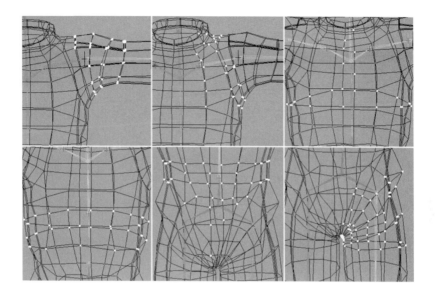

Figure 12.18

Point membership for sections of the body

6. The head is the easiest part to bind and assign weights. The hand, by contrast, is probably the hardest part to work on. Select the Lwrist joint and the joints below it, add the
Lhand proxy mesh node to the selection, and apply rigid binding. You will most likely
want to adjust membership assignments as you are weighting the points for the fingers.
The first finger joints also deform the palm area, so they need extra attention and deliberation. Reassign the last two rows of the hand to the Lforearm joint. Again, Figure 12.20
shows the membership assignments for certain areas of the hand, but for a closer examination, refer to the `character_bound.mb` file in the CD-ROM.

The shoes need to be bound differently. Since we created an inverse foot setup for the
feet, the joint chain for the foot is separate from the leg joints. If we rigidly bind the shoes,
we have a weighting problem that cannot be solved—the knee joint and the foot joint will
deform the ankle area from two separate pivot points, and choosing membership for one will
exclude the other influence. What we need is for the ankle area to be influenced by both. We
can make this area deform correctly by smooth-binding the shoes, which will enable the
points to be shared by the knee and the foot joints.

7. Select the Lknee, Lfoot, and Lball joints, add the Lshoe poly mesh node to the selection,
and apply Smooth Bind, making sure to set the Bind To setting to Selected Joints. Since
the shoe has smooth bind, there is no need to assign membership to its control points.

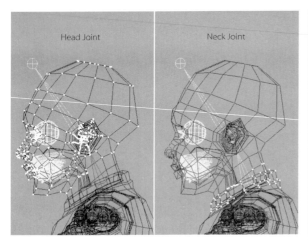

Figure 12.19

Membership assignment for the head and neck joints

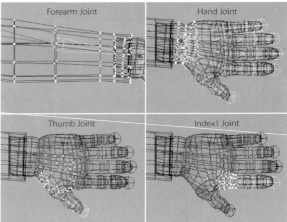

Figure 12.20

Membership assignments for Lforearm, Lhand and finger joints

8. Before we move on to the weighting process, make sure the other parts of the head, such as eyes, eyelashes, hair, and teeth, are grouped under the head joint. Since these body parts need not deform with the joint rotation, they needn't be bound. You could bind them, if you wanted to, but it would only make the model heavier, without improving the setup.

Editing Skin Weights

This is the fun part of binding a character—you get to punch a lot of decimal figures into a spreadsheetlike Component Editor. Using the Artisan tool is an alternative to entering numbers, but even with that, for final weighting refinements, you do have to use the Component Editor. Once you become used to it, however, this tool really can become an interesting part of character setup. Let's do the knee area for a simple example.

1. First, keyframe the Lfoot_c control node to make the left knee bend over a span of frames. You can then drag along the Timeline to see how the knee will bend as you are assigning the weights to the Lknee joint. The default weights clearly do not do a good job of deforming the knee, as shown in Figure 12.21.

2. Display the hierarchical subdivision body shape node you had hidden, to see how the weighting affects the deformation. Select the points on the body mesh that belong to the knee joint, and choose Window → General Editors → Component Editor. On the Rigid Skins tab, scroll across until you come to a cluster column with the numbers showing.

As you can see, the default numbers are all 1, meaning 100 percent influence. Edit the weights as follows: assign the points around the shin area a value of 1, the next row, 0.9, and then 0.6, 0.3, 0.1, and 0.01. As you assign the values, notice how the deformation of the knee area changes, as Figure 12.22 shows.

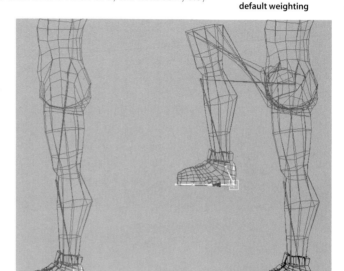

Figure 12.21

Knee bending with default weighting

3. Surface areas such as the fingers and the neck are much like the knee area and are fairly easy to weight. The head is the easiest—the whole head should remain fully weighted at 1 to the head joint, deforming starting from the neck area. But certain parts are much harder to deform properly, such as the thumb and palm area, the shoulders, and the legs. The legs, for example, can be weighted to move correctly to the front and back, but that will not necessarily improve their side up and down movements or twisting from side to side. You should, therefore, keep your goal weights for the character's movements and try to reach for those specific movements as you are weighting the different sections of the character. As you weight the different areas to test various character poses, keyframe as many different movements as you can. What seems to be deforming well in one pose may not hold up well in another, or it may deform incorrectly while changing to another pose. Figure 12.23 shows some example poses.

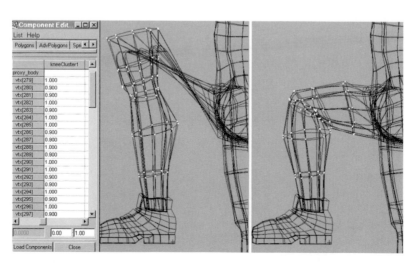

Figure 12.22

Knee area weighting

Figure 12.23

**Various areas
where weighting
needs editing**

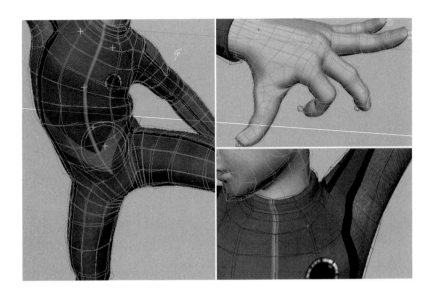

Figure 12.23

**Various areas
where weighting
needs editing**

There is obviously a limit to the control you can achieve with point weighting. To aid you in getting exactly the shapes you want, you can also use deformers such as flexors, Influence objects, or Blend Shapes. You will usually use Set Driven Key or expressions to connect the deformers to the joint rotations.

4. With the shoe, the weighting is a bit more involved. Select some points on the shoe, and open the Component Editor (see Figure 12.24). For smooth-skinned surfaces, the cluster values show up under the SkinClusters tab. As you can see in Figure 12.24, three joints can potentially exert influence on each point, so you need to input more values per point.

Figure 12.24

**Cluster values in the
Component Editor**

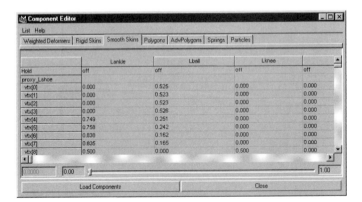

5. A good way to proceed weighting skin cluster points is to give one joint 100 percent influence and then subtract a certain value from it by adding it to another joint. For example, let's say we want to make the weighting at the top of the shoe 95 percent influenced by the knee joint and 5 percent influenced by the foot joint. We can initially assign a value of 1 for those points under the knee joint column. The other two joints' influences drop to zero. So enter a value of **0.05** under the foot joint. Now the values at the knee joint drop to 0.95, and the ball joint values remain at 0.0. The area below the ankle should generally be 100 percent influenced by the foot joint, as the shoe is a rather rigid object. Since the knee should not influence the ball of the foot area at all, begin weighting the relevant points by assigning a value of 1 to either the foot or the ball joint. The shoe should deform as shown in Figure 12.25.

Cleaning Up

The character is now ready for animation. Hide the subdivision surfaces and display only the poly proxy mesh surfaces. Some animators like using the Hypergraph window to select the control nodes; others, the Outliner window. Still others prefer to keep only the modeling window open and select the handles inside the camera view. Use layers to convert the poly meshes into reference objects now that you don't need to select them. You can hide the geometry if you'd like and work only with the skeleton for even faster interaction. Display selection handles for the root joint and other control nodes if you want to select them in the window. Some animators, however, prefer not to display anything but the geometry. You might also want to rename nodes to make them easier to identify, such as renaming subD_bodyHistPoly node to something like proxy_body. Delete anything that you no longer need, whether it's geometry, curves, history, or empty nodes, and save it as `character_bound.mb`. We will use the completed character in the next chapter to demonstrate various animation tasks.

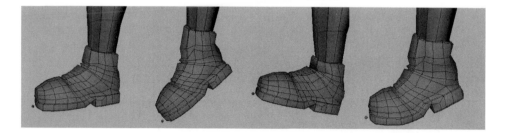

Figure 12.25

Shoe deformations

Hands On: Binding a Puppy

Our final exercise in this chapter will be to set up and bind the multipatched NURBS puppy we built in Chapter 8, "Organic Modeling." We will briefly go through the skeleton setup, put on IK handles and constraints, and organize the hierarchy to get it ready for animation. Then we will apply smooth binding to the puppy to make it deform with the skeleton.

Creating the Skeleton

We'll begin by using the Skeleton → Joint Tool to give the puppy bones and joints.

1. Bring in the file `dog_model.mb`, the final global-stitched model of the dog, from the Chapter 8 folder on the CD.

2. In the side view, draw the backbone as shown in Figure 12.26, starting from the hip area and finishing at the nose. Draw the tail. Draw the front leg and the back leg with Auto Joint Limits turned on. Notice where the wrist is—that is where the IK end effector will be placed.

3. To make the back leg the proper shape, increase the grid division and use X+click. This is important because we will be using IK with the three joints of the leg. If the bones are not built as a *Z* shape as in Figure 12.27, they may not bend the way we want them to.

4. Name the joints. The backbone chain should be hip, back, chest, neck, and head. The tail-bone chain should be tail1 and tail2. The front leg chain should be named Larm, Lelbow, Lwrist, and Lpaw. Finally, the back leg chain should be Lleg, Lknee, Lhock, and Lpad.

Figure 12.26

Side view of the dog and its joints

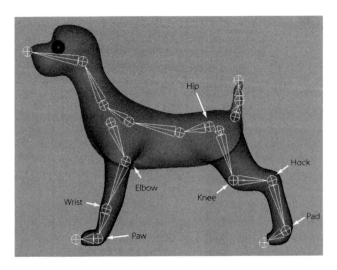

Adding IK Handles and Pole Constraints

Now we're ready to apply inverse kinematics to the puppy, using the Skeleton → IK Handle Tool.

Figure 12.27

Applying an IK chain to the back leg

1. In the perspective view, move the leg joints to the left side so that they are placed properly as shown in Figure 12.28. Put ikRP handles on them to test how they bend. For the back leg, try to keep the three bones that will use IK coplanar. Think also of how the skin is going to stretch with the skeleton as the joints are moving.

2. Mirror the front and back legs on the Y-Z axis. The ikRP handles should copy as well. Check to make sure the joint limits are working. If the ikRP's plane indicator for the mirrored leg does not mirror properly, try mirroring with the option set to Orientation instead of Behavior.

3. Group the front legs to the chest. Group the back legs and the tail to the hip joints. Name the joints properly, such as Rarm and Relbow. Name the IK handles Lfront, Rfront, Lbackleg, and Rbackleg.

4. Create four locators and place them as pole vector constraints for the legs. Two should go directly behind the front legs, and two should go directly in front of the back legs. Your drawing should look something like Figure 12.29.

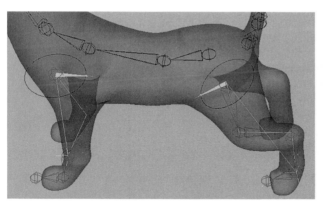

Figure 12.28

Legs moved to side and set up for IK

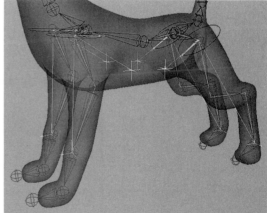

Figure 12.29

Bones set up for IK and grouped

Constraining the Legs

We have a problem with the puppy's legs. We would like the paws planted on the ground when the dog walks, but because the IK chain is to the wrist, the rotation center is the wrist, not the paw. To a lesser degree, we have the same problem with the pads rotating when the body moves. We'll solve this problem by using locators and the Orient constraint.

1. Create four locators. Snap them to the paw and pad joints. Name them Lfront_c, Rfront_c, Lback_c, and Rback_c (the *c* stands for "control").

2. Select Lwrist (make sure you select this joint and not the Lpaw joint), select Lfront_c locator, and choose Constrain → Orient. The locator should rotate to match the rotation values of Lwrist.

3. Repeat step 2 for the right side of the leg. Also orient-constrain the two back_c locators to the back pad joints. You should see them rotated and positioned as in Figure 12.30.

4. Open the Attribute Editor for the Lwrist joint. Click the X and Y Degrees of Freedom settings. They need to be activated before the joint can be constrained. Repeat this process for Rwrist and the two back pad joints.

5. In the Outliner, delete the constraint nodes under the four control locators. In the modeling window, select the Lfront_c locator, select Lwrist (not the Lpaw joint), and then choose Constrain → Orient. Do the same for Rfront_c and Rwrist. The rotation attributes of the wrist joints are now constrained to the control locators. Repeat the process for the back locators and the pad joints.

Figure 12.30

Locators placed at the paws

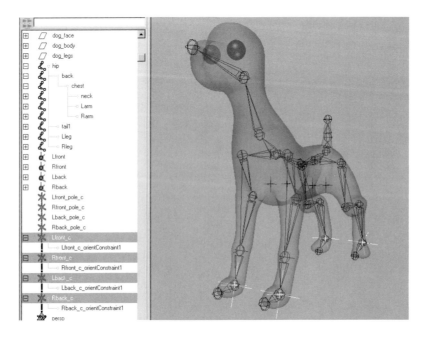

6. In the Outliner, group the Lfront ikRP handle with the Lfront_c locator by MM dragging it to the locator node. Do the same for the Rfront ikRP handle and the Rfront_c locator. Now if you try moving or rotating the Lfront_c and Rfront_c locators, the legs should follow, pivoting around the paws. Place the IK handles for the back legs under the back_c locators as well.

> When you group the IK handle under the control locator, the handle may flip to a weird angle. This is not a problem; the IK handle just hasn't updated. After you group all the IK handles, select the pole vector constraint locators, move them, and press Z to undo the move. The IK handles should snap back to their original angles.

7. Select the hip joint and group it to itself by choosing Edit → Group with the default setting. This produces a parent node. Name the node Puppy, and group the pole vector constraints and the control locators under it. The Puppy node is the top node and will move the whole dog. Create an extra attribute channel in the front_c locator to rotate the paw joint via Set Driven Key. Hide the channels that will not be animated, such as the Translate attributes for the joints, using the Channel Control. In the Outliner, you should see a hierarchy like the one shown in Figure 12.31.

In your own work, it's important to remember that there is no one proper way to build skeletons or place constraints to set up a character for animation. In each case, you need to consider what the character will be doing, how the body should deform, how the limbs should rotate, and so on. Different situations call for different solutions. A properly prepared character will move well, will have the necessary range of movements, and will be easy to animate.

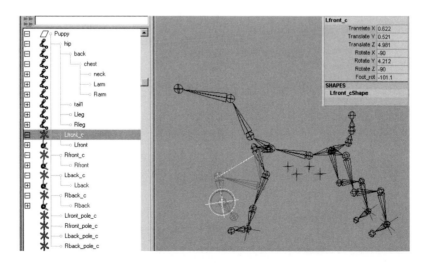

Figure 12.31

The Puppy hierarchy

Binding the Puppy

To deal with the NURBS puppy's multiple patches, we are first going to create two lattices: one for the puppy's head, another for the body. We'll then bind the two lattices plus the tail and the legs to the skeleton as smooth skin. The skeleton will deform the lattices, which will then deform the puppy's head and body. This method of indirectly moving the puppy using lattices is easier to weight, and it produces smoother deformation.

1. Create a skeleton layer to control the visibility of the skeleton, IKs, and constraints. Hide the layer for now. Select the head patches, eyes, ears, and nose; then in Component mode, select all the CVs, except the last two rows of the neck area, as shown in Figure 12.32. Create a default lattice and increase its STU divisions to (4, 5, 5).

> We didn't have to include the eyes and the nose with the lattice deformer. We could simply group them to the head joint instead. If they are bound to the lattice, however, you can deform them along with the rest of the head. For cartoon effects, you might want to weight the head lattice to something less than 100 percent.

2. Creating the body lattice is a bit more involved. You have to select rows of CVs from different patches, and it will help to create a set in the Relationship Editor to contain all the points for selection purposes. Figure 12.33 shows the stages of selection. First select all the CVs of the body patches (a). Select the two rows of CVs from the neck area (b). Select the top three rows of the front leg patches (c). Select the top two rows of the back leg patches(d). Finally, select the bottom three rows of CVs of the tail patches (e). The resulting lattice should look like (f).

Figure 12.32

CVs and the head lattice

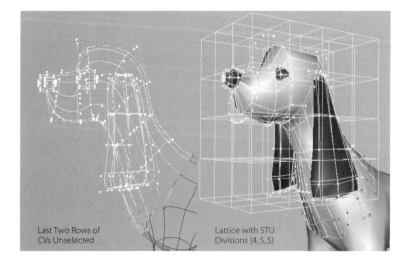

Last Two Rows of CVs Unselected

Lattice with STU Divisions (4, 5, 5)

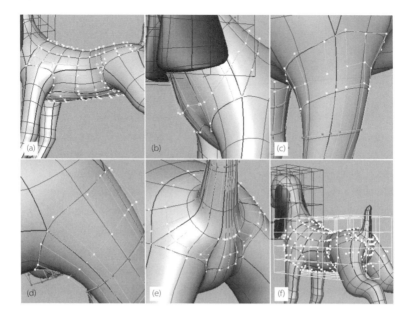

Figure 12.33

Selecting CVs for body lattice

3. Try moving the lattices to see that none of the points that should be included have been left out. Select the lattices, the leg patches, and the tail patches. Unhide the skeleton, and include it in the selection as well. Choose Skin → Bind Skin → Smooth Bind ❑, choose Edit → Reset Settings, reduce Max Influences to 2, and click Bind Skin. Maya starts to create a skin cluster for each of the patches and the lattices. Open the Relationship Editor and go to the Deformer Set Editing module. You should see 24 sets altogether. There are two lattice sets and 22 skin cluster sets: 16 for the leg patches, 4 for the tail patches, and 2 for the lattices. Remember, the lattices are now also smooth-skinned objects.

4. We have a double-transformation problem with the lattices (discussed in Chapter 11, "Deformers"). Try moving the top skeleton joint node —some of the leg CVs and the tail CVs are translating farther than they should because they are getting translated twice. There is a simple way to fix this problem. In the Relationship Editor window, highlight the body lattice set, choose Edit → Select Set Members, and you should see the CVs for the body lattice get selected as shown in Figure 12.34.

Figure 12.34

CVs for the body lattice selected

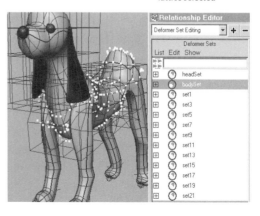

5. Highlight all the skin cluster sets (not the lattice sets) and click the minus button at the top, or choose Edit → Remove to get rid of the selected items. The offending CVs are removed from the skin cluster sets, and the dog should look normal again.

Editing Skin Weights

We'll start weighting from the head. You have to use the Component Editor to weight the lattice points.

1. Rotate the head joints and see how the integrity of the head shape holds up. The head area should mostly be fine with the default setting. For places where the deformation is occurring too much, such as the back of the head shown in Figure 12.35, enter a higher value for the head joint in the Component Editor.

2. Create a cluster on the ears. Select the CVs as in Figure 12.36, and apply Create Cluster with Relative mode on. Weight the points so that the bottom of each ear gets deformed the most. Group and parent it to the head joint. The ears should deform well enough within the lattice, but in cases where they are going through the head geometry, or for secondary animation, you can use the cluster to adjust the ears.

3. As you are weighting the different parts of the body and rotating the joints, you can always use Go To Bind Pose. But if you move the IK handles or the constraints, the Bind Pose will not work. One way to handle this is to keyframe those nodes. After you test them, you can return them to their original positions, after which the Bind Pose should work again.

4. Let's go through a simple example of lattice tweaking at the chest area. The four points in Figure 12.37 are being influenced by Rarm, Relbow, Larm, and Lelbow. The elbows, however, shouldn't be influencing the chest area, so enter 0 in the elbow columns. The arms are each assigned the value of 1 for two points. But the chest bone should be influencing the chest as well, so assign 0.5 in the chest joint. The value for the arm joints drops to 0.5 accordingly. As you can see, a lot of weighting actually consists of getting rid of unnecessary influences and thinking about which joints should be influencing the points. You might find it makes the process more efficient if you weight the point at 1 for one joint at the beginning and then start adding influence values to the other joints.

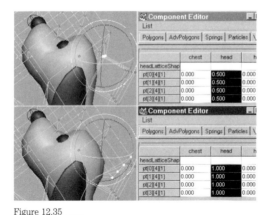

Figure 12.35

Weighting with the Component Editor

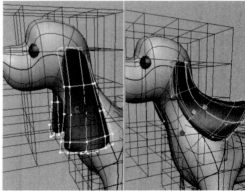

Figure 12.36

Ears clustered

5. You can use the Paint Skin Weights tool for the legs and the tail if you want, but apply them only if you see the need. In our case, the default skinning has done a decent job of weighting. Once you are done with weight tweaking, save the file as `puppy_bound.mb`. In Chapter 13, we'll try a four-legged walk cycle with it.

Summary

In this chapter we covered rigid skinning and smooth skinning, using the subdivision surface boy character as an example of the former and the NURBS puppy as an example of the latter. You learned how to edit point set membership and weight the points using the Component Editor. And that's it. No more tweaking CVs, applying IKs, or constraining. We are now ready to animate, and that is what we will do starting in the next chapter.

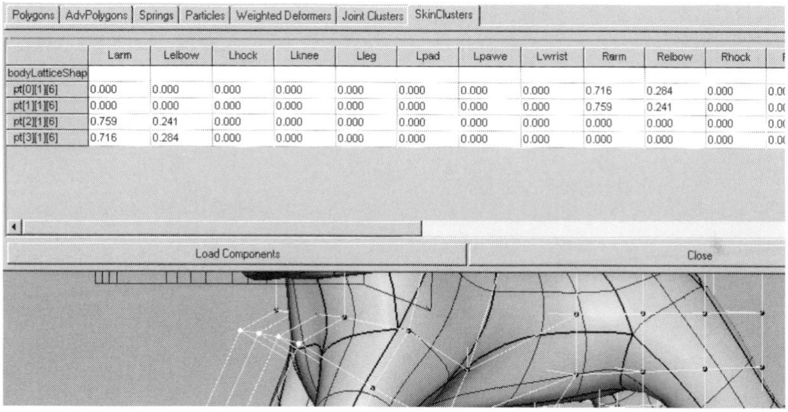

Figure 12.37

Weighting the chest area lattice points

| Polygons | AdvPolygons | Springs | Particles | Weighted Deformers | Joint Clusters | SkinClusters |

	Larm	Lelbow	Lhock	Lknee	Lleg	Lpad	Lpawe	Lwrist	Rarm	Relbow	Rhock	
bodyLatticeShap												
pt[0][1][6]	0.000	0.000	0.000	0.000	0.000	0.000	0.000	0.000	0.716	0.284	0.000	0.00
pt[1][1][6]	0.000	0.000	0.000	0.000	0.000	0.000	0.000	0.000	0.759	0.241	0.000	0.00
pt[2][1][6]	0.759	0.241	0.000	0.000	0.000	0.000	0.000	0.000	0.000	0.000	0.000	0.00
pt[3][1][6]	0.716	0.284	0.000	0.000	0.000	0.000	0.000	0.000	0.000	0.000	0.000	0.00

Load Components   Close

CHAPTER 13

Character Animation Exercises

It's been long time coming, but here we are, with a fully built model ready to be animated. In this chapter, we'll use the character and the puppy we built to produce simple walk cycles. We'll then go through some more animation exercises, such as running and throwing a ball. Along the way, we'll selectively present a few of the more important classical animation principles.

In this chapter, you will find the following animation exercises:

- **A step-by-step walk cycle**
- **A dog walk**
- **A run cycle**
- **Tossing a ball**
- **A Maya character**

Step-by-Step Walk Cycle

Walk cycles are often used as animation lessons because nothing is probably more familiar than walking—just about anyone can go through the motions (or watch others walk). At the same time, a walk cycle requires you to be aware of and properly apply many fundamental animation principles. If you already have an animation background, this section may help you get some needed sleep, but if you are just starting out, it may be quite educational. Take time to read through the explanations and understand them fully.

> For a fuller treatment of classical animation and its mysterious ways, try perusing *The Illusion of Life: Disney Animation* by Frank Thomas and Ollie Johnston, which, 21 years after its first publication, is still the most enlightening, entertaining, and inspiring reference book for animators. For studies of how people and animals actually move in real life, Eadward Muybridge's photo books are a great reference source for many artists.

When creating a walk cycle, you can choose between two types. The simplest type is a stationary walk, in which the ground seems to be moving under the character. The other type is a more realistic walk in which the character actually moves forward. This second type is a bit more complex than a stationary walk but involves the same principles. We'll animate the simpler stationary walk, so that we can take more time dealing with the animation principles behind the movements. (You can see sample walk cycles in the Chapter 13 folder on the accompanying CD-ROM.)

Setting Up for the Walk Cycle

Animation is an iterative procedure. You can try to animate everything at once, right from the beginning, and some people prefer to work like this. But, usually, you end up working at a much slower pace, and you can easily lose sight of the forest for the trees; that is, you can lose your perspective on how the character is animating over all because you are bogged down on translating and rotating so many control nodes.

It's much better to key in rough poses one or two nodes at a time, working on different parts of the character in stages, much like painting or sculpting. For the walk cycle, this will be our workflow:

- Animate the hip (root joint) and the left leg.
- Transfer and offset the animation to the right leg.
- Animate the spine joints.
- Animate the head.
- Animate the arms.

Once the rough animation is done, you can tweak and refine the function curves and change subtle details of the walk to give it more personality. At every stage, you'll want to do simple playblasts to see how the keyframes make the character move in real time.

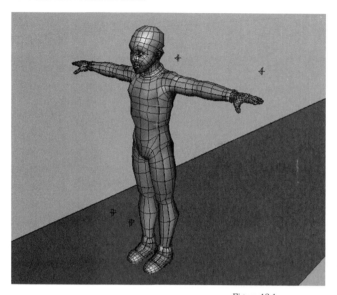

Figure 13.1

The character on the plane

1. Choose File → Open Scene and bring in the `character_setup_complete.mb` file from the Chapter 10 folder on the CD.

2. Create a plane and stretch it out. This will serve as the ground.

3. Translate the Maya_Boy node up or the ground plane down until you see the boy's feet just on the ground, as shown in Figure 13.1.

4. Make sure the subdivision surfaces are hidden and only the poly proxy meshes are showing, because you want to concentrate on quickly creating rough poses. You can work with only the skeleton if you wish (as some animators do).

Animating the Hip and the Legs

Hip movement is probably the first joint you want to animate, because it is the most basic movement from which much of the other joints' movements spring.

An important decision is how many frames the walk cycle should be. Bigger and heavier characters tend to walk slower, and lighter characters walk faster, but you can infer more than just that. Different walks can reveal much about a character. For instance, a slow walk done well can convey seriousness, dignity, and grace in a character, such as a king or a queen at a coronation. A fast, bouncy walk can convey the lightheartedness of a clown or the intense energy of a soldier. Long steps can imply confidence, energy, or urgency. Small steps can imply shyness, weakness, or leisure.

We'll do a brisk walk and make it cycle in 18 frames. Generally speaking, it's better to make a character move faster, not slower, than what you would consider normal speed. Producing quick movements does not necessarily produce better animation, but it does discourage "floating" in your animation.

When animation is being examined, people often comment about there not being enough weight or enough snap to a character's movements, and comments such as "You know, this character just floats" usually sound the death knell for the animator.

The pelvic area moves in many different ways in a walk cycle. You need to translate the root joint up and down, but it also must rotate in the X and Y axis. (For the root joint created in the side view, the X axis mainly spins the body, Z rotation bends forward and back, and Y rotation moves sideways.) You can translate the root joint in the X axis as well, for side-to-side movement, if you want. A female walk usually has greater X translation, making her hips sway; a male walk generally doesn't have any noticeable sway.

How much the feet are apart can change the look of the walk quite a bit. No one really walks with their feet straight below their shoulders, as in the left picture of Figure 13.2, although this is a common mistake with beginning animators. You might, however, intentionally want a character's feet placed like this, to animate a Frankenstein walk, for example. Our character's feet will be placed together closely enough to be almost brushing against each other when they cross, as in the center picture. This is probably the most natural distance for a regular walk. The feet can also come closer together, even cross each other in a walk, as in the right picture. Such overlapping produces a more feminine walk, such as the way fashion models walk down a runway.

Before you begin, check to make sure that the animation speed is 24 frames per second by choosing Window → Setting/Preferences → Preferences, and confirm that the working unit for Time is Film (24 fps) in the Settings section.

1. Rotate the root joint in the direction of the front leg. Since we want the left leg forward at frame 1, in the top view, rotate the body clockwise for about 15 to 20 degrees, and press Shift+E to create a keyframe for the rotation attributes.

2. Repeat the keyframe at frame 19. At frame 10, it should be rotated about the same amount in the opposite direction.

Figure 13.2

Different spreads between feet produce different walks.

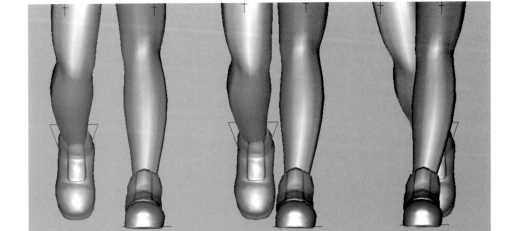

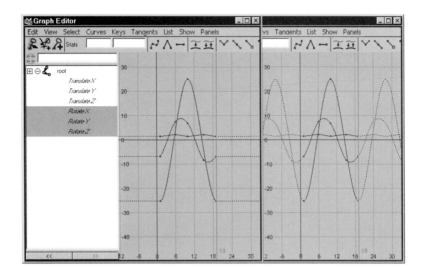

Figure 13.3

Graph Editor function curves for the root joint

3. You should see waves in the Graph Editor that look like the left picture in Figure 13.3. Choose Curves → Pre Infinity → Cycle And Curves → Post Infinity → Cycle to make the waves repeat as in the right picture in Figure 13.3. If you don't see the waves repeating choose View → Infinity from the Graph Editor.

When you are cycling function curves, use the tangent handles to get rid of sharp breaks that may occur.

Moving the Left Leg

We will set up the left leg first and then copy its nodes for the right leg.

1. In frame 1, translate the Mover_Lfoot node in the X axis to about 1. Move it forward in the Z axis, and set the Heel_Toe attribute to –0.6, as in the picture on the left in Figure 13.4, where the legs are widest apart. The heel is just touching the ground, and the toes are curled. You might need to move the root node down on the Y axis to achieve the desired pose. Keyframe Mover_Lfoot's position, and set a keyframe for Heel_Toe by RM choosing Key Selected over its input field.

2. Copy the keyframe at frame 19 by MM dragging the current time indicator and setting keyframes again.

3. Go to frame 10, which is the halfway point in the cycle, and translate and rotate the control node and the toes to the back, as in the picture on the left in Figure 13.4. Set Heel_Toe to 1. The toes at this frame are just about to leave the ground.

4. Keyframe the in-between frames for the left foot, and adjust the root joint's values accordingly as shown in Figure 13.5. At frame 3, the left foot is planted solidly on the ground, and the body is at its lowest. At frame 6, the left foot passes under the body, and the body is at its highest. Around frame 8, the left foot actually pushes the body forward. Notice how the root joint's Y translation values increase and decrease at different frames, as shown in Figure 13.5. At frame 10, set Heel_Toe to 0 and rotate Mover_Lfoot 22 degrees on the X axis and move it up on the Y-axis so the boy's left toe is slightly higher than the sole of his shoe. Move Mover_Lfoot on the Z axis so the toe of his left foot is at about the mid-point of his right foot .

At frame 1, the front foot's heel touches the ground, but the weight of the body still makes it sink before it can spring back up. This is why the body is lowest around frame 3. Then, around frame 5 or 6, the body reaches its highest position. The heavier the body, the longer the recoiling will take. So if the recoiling process takes longer, the steps become a heavy, serious walk. If the body hangs around its highest position a bit longer, meaning the recoiling happens faster, the steps become a light, bouncy walk.

Figure 13.4

The left-leg walk cycle

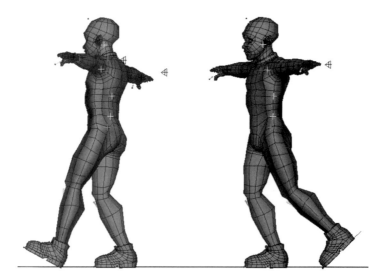

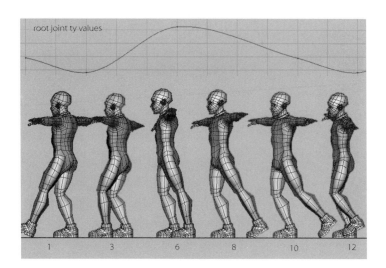

Figure 13.5

The left leg in between keyframes

The Graph Editor in Figure 13.6 shows the root joint's Translate Y curves for different walks of another character. Just by looking at these curves, you should be able to tell that the first one is a fairly bouncy walk, the second is an extremely bouncy walk, and the third is a heavy walk.

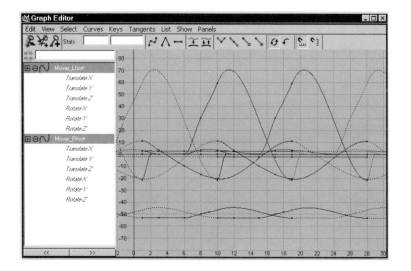

Figure 13.6

Animation curves for different types of walks

Moving the Right Leg

Now we can work on the animation for the right leg, but first we need to refine the root joint's rotations a bit.

1. Rotate the root joint a bit from the side view to make the body lean forward, as in the left picture in Figure 13.7. Also, at the extreme positions at frames 1 and 10, the hip is horizontal, but at frames 6 and 15, when the foot is passing the body (or rather, in reality, the body is going over the foot), the hip on the side of that foot should be lifted up by rotating the root joint in the front view, as shown in the middle and right pictures in Figure 13.7.

> Walking is often referred to as a continuous falling. When you walk, your body is pushed by the leg in the back position, and then the body leans and falls forward. If it weren't for the back leg speeding ahead of the body to break the fall, your body would actually fall to the ground.

2. Now we need to copy the animation from the left leg to the right. Select the Mover_Lfoot node and, in the Graph Editor, choose Edit → Copy, with the default settings. Select the Mover_Rfoot node and choose Edit → Paste, again with the default settings. The right foot should snap to the left foot.

3. Select both control nodes, open the Graph Editor, and choose View → Infinity, choose Curves → Pre Infinity → Cycle, and then choose Curves → Post Infinity → Cycle. The two nodes should have identical function curves.

Figure 13.7
Root joint's rotations

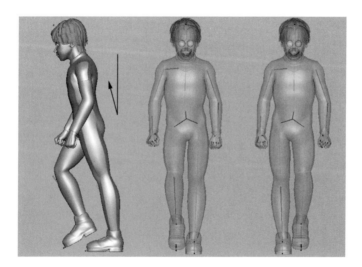

4. Now we need to change the Translate X curve values for the Mover_Rfoot node from positive to negative. In the Graph Editor, select the Translate X curve, choose Edit → Scale ⬚, change the Value Scale/Pivot setting to −1, and click the Scale Keys button. The curve should now be a negative mirror of the original.

5. Turn on Time Snap, and select all the Mover_Rfoot curves and move them 9 frames forward, so that the first keyframes are positioned at frame 10.

Now the legs should step and cycle indefinitely, with the right leg's animation trailing the left leg's by nine frames.

SQUASH AND STRETCH, RIGIDITY, AND VOLUME

One of the corollaries of a character (or anything) having weight is a principle called *squash and stretch*. In classical animation, this is considered one of the cardinal principles. In our preceding example of the body sinking to its lowest recoil position in frame 3, the character is being "squashed" by the force of gravity and the resistance of the ground. When it bounces up, the body "stretches" to its highest point. What is a subtle movement in real life often becomes greatly exaggerated in animation. Especially in cartoony animation, squash and stretch in characters can become extreme.

To use the squash-and-stretch principle properly, you need to always apply it as a consequence of weight. Weight is force times mass (remember high school physics?), so something that has more mass will squash more; it will also squash more if more force is applied. This principle, however, needs to be balanced with another factor called *rigidity*.

In real life, rigid bodies such as tables or chairs do not squash or stretch at all, or so little as to not be noticeable. In animation, especially in cartoony animation, this physical reality is often overlooked, and you will see objects such as an anvil or a boulder being squashed and stretched as if they were made of rubber. But the fact is that the more rigid a thing is supposed to be, the less it should squash and stretch. Carelessly applying squash and stretch to what is supposed to be a rigid object (or character) can undermine its believability. A steel hammer, for example, even if it walks and talks, should stay mostly rigid if we are to believe that it is made up of steel—that it is a hard object. If it squashes and stretches like some soft, rubbery substance, its characteristics as a hammer are undermined.

When applying squash and stretch, another factor to keep in mind is consistency of *volume*. When a water-filled balloon is put on a hard surface, for instance, gravity causes the mass of the water to exert pressure on the rubber, causing the balloon to squash. But as it flattens, it also stretches out sideways because the volume of the water hasn't changed. Even cartoon characters need to have a sense of volume, and once a character's form becomes easily recognizable, that sense of volume must be maintained.

Animating the Upper Body

The upper-body movements in a walk cycle are mostly a matter of counter-rotating and counter-counter-rotating to balance the root joint's animation. In a natural walk, when the pelvis is rotating one way, the shoulders rotate in the opposite direction, moving to counter-balance the upper body against hip rotation.

Upper Spine and Chest Rotation

Much of the counter-rotation happens in the lower back area. The upper spine and chest joints' rotations are added to this to produce an "over-rotation." Because the face should always be looking straight ahead, the neck joint needs to be counter-rotated to correct the over-rotation, as shown in Figure 13.8.

Notice that the shoulder rotation in Figure 13.8 isn't as apparent as the hip rotation. However, the rotation is a rather exaggerated movement in that you would rarely see this much shoulder rotation in real-life normal walks. You must also be careful to make the head as stationary as possible. If the spine and chest counter-rotations are not properly done, the head may noticeably move from side to side, which could make for a good cartoony animation, but generally is not found in normal walks.

Figure 13.8

Upper body rotations

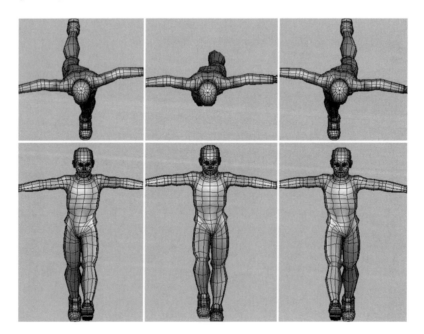

Arm Movement

Arm movement follows the shoulder—specifically the shoulder rotation—transferring the motion like a wave starting from the shoulder and moving down to the fingers. First, you need to lower the shoulder joints about –15 to –20 degrees in the Z axis. Because the shoulder-bind position is for outstretched arms, when they come down, so should the shoulders. Move and roughly rotate theMover_Lwrist node, as shown in Figure 13.9. The poses are captured at frames 1, 5, 9, 14, and 18.

If you look at Figure 13.9 carefully, you will see that the arm is still in the process of swinging back at frame 1. The Mover_Lwrist node follows the shoulder rotation about three frames behind; it reaches its extreme position at frame 4. This is called *follow-through* or *overlapping action* in classical animation. Loose limbs such as the arms do not stop when the object they are attached to stops moving, but rather continue to move for a few more frames, perhaps dangling a bit, before coming to a full stop. So when the shoulder rotation changes direction, the arms follow through and change their directions a few frames later. This is also called overlapping action because the change in the direction of the shoulders overlaps with the change in direction of the arms. The curves in Figure 13.9, the spine rotate.x curve, and the Mover_Lwrist translate.y that follows illustrate this animation principle.

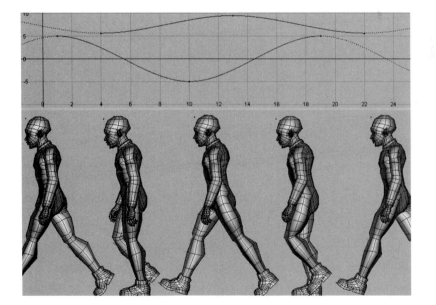

Figure 13.9

The arm movements

Hand Movement

Once you are satisfied with the way that the arms are moving back and forth, rotate the hand to make it follow through the arm movement about two frames behind. It may help to get rid of the rough rotations you had keyframed and start over from frame 6. The hand rotation in real life is usually nonexistent or very subtle. But again, as with the shoulder rotations, you might want to exaggerate the rotation to make it more noticeable. Examine the poses and the overlapping curves shown in Figure 13.10.

Copy the animation from the left hand to the right hand control node, offsetting and adjusting the values as you did with the feet. Check to make sure that the curves are cycling properly, so that there are no broken tangents or values skipping at the start or the end of a cycle. Sometimes, an extra keyframe can lengthen a curve segment, causing it to not cycle correctly. One way to find out is to playblast the animation over a few hundred frames. You can see a movie clip of the final walk in the Chapter 13 folder on the CD.

EXAGGERATION AND FOLLOW-THROUGH

There is a fine line between keeping movements true to real life and exaggerating to achieve certain effects. In our exercise, we noted that shoulder rotations are hardly noticeable in normal real life walks, yet we made the shoulders rotate more. We did this because when we try to imitate reality completely, we often end up with terrible animation. Exaggerating certain movements greatly improves the animation. This concept is clearer if you consider actors acting out a scene. Actors often exaggerate their movements to make their acting more "real" to the audience. Exaggeration, when properly executed, can communicate the meaning of the action to the viewers better than unexaggerated movements.

In animation, you can exaggerate in more varied ways, such as squashing and stretching characters and making them move in ways that are not physically possible. However, you do need to make sure that your exaggerations are serving to make the actions more "real" to the viewers, not less. Think of it as creating a caricature. If you draw a person, exaggerating that person's distinguishing features, the resulting caricature makes us see who the person is more clearly. If you just exaggerate without a good reason, you end up with a bad drawing.

Another animation principle that often works together with exaggeration is follow-through, or overlapping action. Again, you have already seen an example of this with the arm movements of the walk cycle. Because the arm is dangling from the shoulder, the arm still moves in the same direction for a few more frames when the spine and chest joints change their direction of rotation. It is following through, or overlapping with, the rotation action of the body. Follow-throughs and overlapping actions occur all the time in real life. Any situation in which things are dangling or flapping, such as appendages or soft body parts, require them. Follow-throughs are also the conclusion of any good, graceful motion. Anyone learning golf will be reminded of the importance of a good "follow-through" to their swing. In the same way, the follow-through motion of a character that occurs after the "hit," whatever that is, is just as important as the "hit" motion itself.

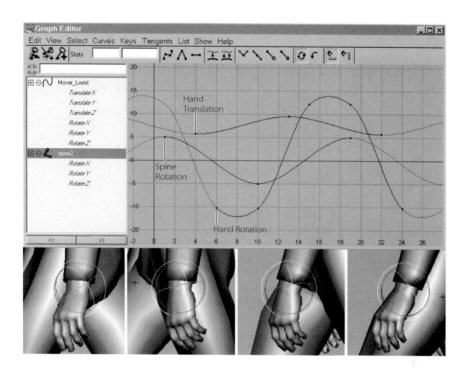

Figure 13.10

Hand rotation and function curves

Creating More Interesting Walks

Our current walk has all the characteristics of walking, but it's rather boring. And boring in animation is synonymous with *dead*. But you can easily tweak the curves, now that you have them to play with, to create more interesting walk cycles.

For an example, let's edit our walk cycle to a happy walk. The walk we created is already fast, so just increase the bounce to be a bit snappier, a bit higher, which is more characteristic of a happy walk. Here are the modifications you can make:

- Raise the front knee a bit more when the body is passing its highest point. Rotate the root joint forward, and then rotate the spine joints back so the spine will arch back.

- Rotate the neck as well so the character's chin will be pointing up.

- Animate the shoulders to lift a bit when the arm is forward. Bend the arms and lift them up more when they are forward, and by translating the arm Pole Vector constraints, make the elbows come out to the side.

- You might also want to rotate the body more noticeably.

Figure 13.11

A happy walk

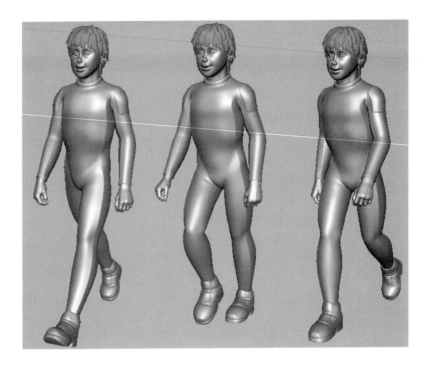

Of course, putting a smile on his face isn't a bad idea either, as shown in Figure 13.11. You can see a movie clip of the happy walk in the Chapter 13 folder on the CD.

As you can see, once a walk has been established, it's easy to edit the keyframes to create different walks. If you want a sad walk, slow the pace down, make the legs cover less ground, and rotate the back to be more hunched down. The head should be looking down as well, and the body should rotate less. Think of other kinds of walks you could create: a stiff, proud walk; a loose, drunken walk; an urgent walk; a leisurely walk; or a sexy, cat walk. Isolating and exaggerating the characteristics that define such walks can be a useful exercise in character animation.

A Dog Walk

Now that we have gone through a step-by-step walk cycle, we can tackle a more difficult four-legged walk cycle. We'll also make the puppy move forward, to make the exercise more realistic.

A four-legged walk is basically two sets of two-legged walks that are offset by a frame or two. You will also find that the puppy is just good enough in terms of its weighting for a walk, but not much more, so you want to keep an eye on how the dog's form holds up as you move it around.

To use the puppy for more extreme deformation situations, such as running or sitting, you would need to build the model itself more carefully. It would need more control points and better weighting. You would also want to use blend shapes and expressions to accommodate specific poses the puppy would assume.

Animating the Body

The first thing we want to do is to make the upper body move, and then we want to make the legs follow. The first several keyframes are necessarily rough guesses, the values of which will probably change as you animate and refine the other control nodes of the puppy. We'll make the walk cycle in 16 frames.

1. Open the `Puppy_final.mb` file from the Chapter 12 folder on the CD.

2. Keyframe the hip joint at frames 1, 5, 9, 13, and 17.

3. In the Graph Editor, select the translate Z curve and delete the keyframes on it except for 1 and 17.

4. Move up the keyframe at 17 until you think the puppy has covered enough distance for two steps, or a cycle. When you work on the steps, it will become apparent whether you need to increase or decrease this value.

5. Take the translate Y keyframes at 1, 9, and 17 and lower the body a bit. This is when the puppy's steps are at their extreme positions.

6. Do the opposite of step 5 with keyframes 5 and 13, when the legs are crossing each other and the body position is at its highest.

7. Cycle the translate Y curve. For the translate Z curve, apply Cycle with Offset or Linear. Your function curves should look like those in Figure 13.12.

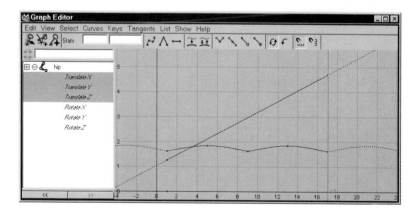

Figure 13.12

Root joint translation curves

Animating the Legs

Now we will make the legs move. To pull off this task of coordinating the legs and the body as the dog walks forward, we will need to work in the Graph Editor. Trying to keyframe in the modeling window or the Timeline for this type of work would be inefficient and frustrating.

1. Move the left legs, front and back (Lfront_c and Lback_c nodes), as follows and shown in Figure 13.13:

    - From frames 1 to 9, the front leg stays stationary, while the back leg moves up with the body, as shown in the left picture in Figure 13.13, with an extra keyframe at frame 5 to lift the leg.

    - From frames 9 to 17, the front leg moves up with the body, with another keyframe at frame 13 to lift the leg, while the back leg stays stationary, as shown in the right picture in Figure 13.13 (the right legs are hidden for now). Their translation values are also shown in Figure 13.13.

    - You should also rotate the legs appropriately. Note that the front leg's paw is controlled by the Foot_rot attribute.

2. Cycle all the curves, but with the translate Z curves, apply Cycle with Offset.

3. With the left leg control nodes still selected, also select the hip joint.

4. In the Graph Editor, select only the translate Z curves to view them. Zoom out until you can see how the curves behave over a few hundred frames. You will probably see something that looks like the top picture in Figure 13.14, where the curves diverge over the Timeline.

Figure 13.13

The left legs move up

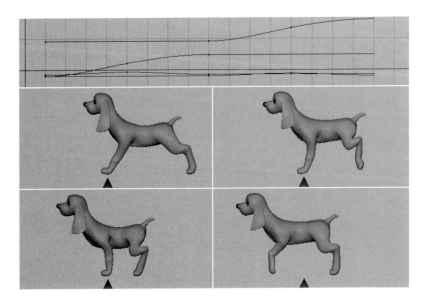

5. Move the keyframes of the legs and/or the hip joint at frame 17 to adjust the values so that the curves will stay parallel over at least a couple of hundred frames, as in the bottom picture in Figure 13.14. It's important that the relative distances between the leg control nodes and the hip joint are not only maintained, but that the legs stay right under the body, so that it will look like they are supporting the body as the puppy walks.

6. Once the legs are cycling properly, we can copy the animation to their right leg counterparts. Copy Lfront_c's animation to the Rfront_c node, and then move the curves back 8 frames, so that their first keyframes will be at frame –7. The most telling curve is the translate Z curve, and when you compare the values for the two front legs, you should see the translate Z curves crisscrossing, as shown in the top picture in Figure 13.15.

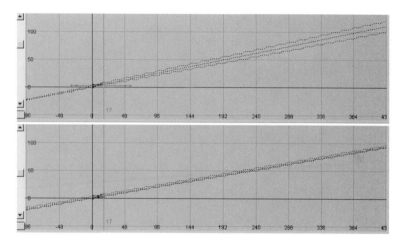

Figure 13.14

Translate Z values of legs and hip joints

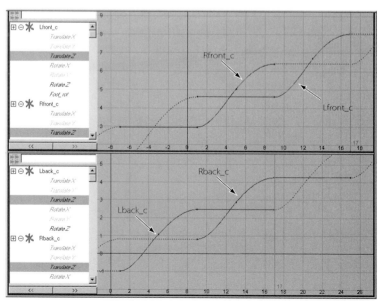

Figure 13.15

Translate Z values for left and right legs

7. Repeat step 6 with the back leg control nodes, except that this time, push the copied curves forward 8 frames, not back. Again, see how the translate Z curves for the back legs crisscross in the bottom picture in Figure 13.15.

Refining the Walk

The legs are moving fairly well now, but something still doesn't quite seem right. There should be a couple of frames of delay between when the back leg comes up and the front leg moves forward. The back leg has to first push the puppy forward, which then makes it possible for the front leg to push off the ground as well. Select the front_c nodes, and then in the Graph Editor, push all the curves forward two frames. These two frames of overlapping action make the movements of the four legs more natural.

The body moves in arcs, as you can see in the lines drawn above the pictures in Figure 13.16. The side-to-side rotation cycles once in 16 frames, with the body arching in toward the side where the back leg is coming up. The up-and-down rotation cycles once every 8 frames, with every step, with the body arching down when the body is up. In exactly the same way as with the human walk, the back joint of the puppy counter-rotates to compensate for its hip-joint rotation. The chest joint rotates the body in the opposite direction, which the neck joint counter-rotates again to keep the puppy's head looking straight ahead, as shown in Figure 13.16.

Finally, you might want to create and animate a camera so that it will keep up with the puppy as it moves forward. An easy way to do this is to copy the translate Z curve of the puppy's hip joint to the camera and then move the entire curve up and down to adjust the camera view. You can see a movie clip of the final dog walk in the Chapter 13 folder on the CD.

A Run Cycle

From two to four legs, and now back to two legs again—after the previous exercises, doing another two-legged cycle should be easy.

Figure 13.16

Body rotations

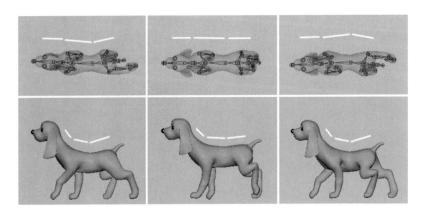

Running differs from walking in that when the body is at its highest position, both feet are actually off the ground. A slow jog is almost exactly the same as a bouncy walk, except for this one fact: A runner is constantly leaping or bouncing forward. As the run becomes faster, the body leans forward more.

Setting the Distance

We'll cycle the run in 16 frames. As you saw with the puppy walk cycle, the most important thing to establish at the beginning is the distance covered.

1. Start out by keyframing the Mover_foot nodes and the root joint in an extreme pose, as shown in Figure 13.17. Keyframe the knee_Poles as well, because they will also need to move forward with the character.

2. Go to frame 17, move the root joint, the knee_Pole nodes, and the Mover_foot nodes in the Z axis up to a position that would cover the distance for two leaping steps, as shown in Figure 13.17. Cycle with Offset the translate Z curves. This distance will likely need to be refined later.

3. Keyframe the root joint at frames 5, 9, and 13. Get rid of the keyframes for the translate X and Z curves. Move the keyframes as follows to create the curve shapes shown in Figure 13.18:

    *   Rotate X should rotate from about 20 to –20 degrees.

    *   Rotate Y should rotate between –10 to 10 degrees.

    *   Rotate Z should cycle every 9 frames, rotating a few degrees.

    *   The tangents for translate Y should be broken at the bottom to make the bounce quick and snappy. Note that the keyframes for the body at its lowest have been moved to frame 4.

Figure 13.17

Extreme running poses

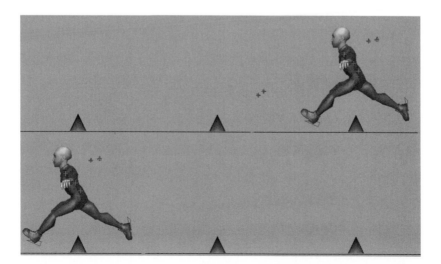

Figure 13.18

**Function curves for
the root joint**

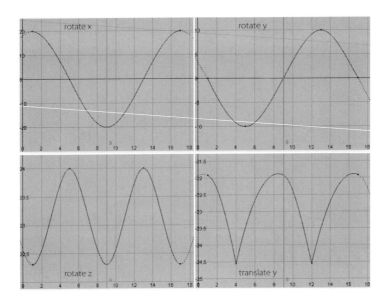

Animating the Run

We'll concentrate on keyframing the Mover_Rfoot control node through the cycle and then copy the keys to the Mover_Lfoot node.

At frame 1 (and frame 17), adjust Mover_Rfoot 's keyframes to accommodate the root joint's rotations. The root joint's translate Y value, on the other hand, should adjust to the leg. If the body is too low, the leg will be bent all the time; if the body is too high, the leg will stretch too much. Each time you edit a keyframe at frame 1, make sure to move its counterpart at frame 17. Also, the right foot should be just touching the left foot, which means a translate X value of about –2.2.

Keyframe the Mover_Rfoot as shown in Figure 13.19:

- At frame 1, the toes should be curling up.
- At frame 3, the foot should be planted on the ground.
- At frame 5, the body is passing over, and the foot should be starting to spring back.
- At frame 7, the foot is kicking off from the ground.
- At frame 9, move the foot so that it doesn't stretch or lag behind the body too much.
- At frame 12, the foot is passing the body, moving just above the ground.
- At frame 14, the knee is coming up, and the foot is rotating in preparation to hit the ground again.
- Frame 17 should show the same leg position as frame 1.

Copy the keys from Mover_Rfoot to Mover_Lfoot. The Mover_Lfoot node needs to be edited a bit:

- The translate X value should be the opposite of the right foot's, which is 2.2.

- Select all the curves, and then push them forward 8 frames.

- The first keyframes should start at frame 9.

- The translate Z curve needs to be pushed up, until it is crisscrossing with the Mover_Rfoot node's translate Z curve, as shown in Figure 13.20. Do not, at this point, try to adjust individual keyframes of the translate Z curve, or the symmetry between the right leg's movement and the left leg's will be broken. Move the entire curve instead.

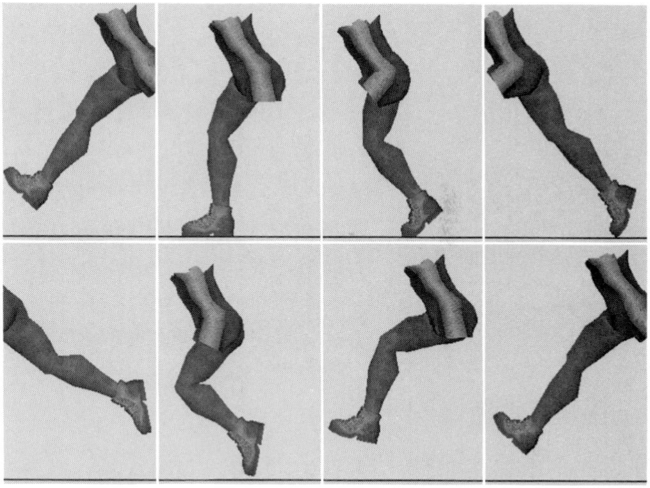

Notice that there aren't any flat curve segments in translate Z curves for the legs. The flat segments occur when the foot is firmly planted on the ground for a while, which happens with walking. This doesn't happen with running.

Figure 13.19

Right leg poses

Animating the Runner's Upper Body

By now, counter-rotating the spine and the neck joints to compensate for the hip movements should be a familiar task. In a run, the shoulders move, the body rotates more noticeably, and, of course, the arms swing much more dramatically. But for our character, let's try a bit of drama and have him keep his arms stretched out, perhaps trying to stop someone in front of him.

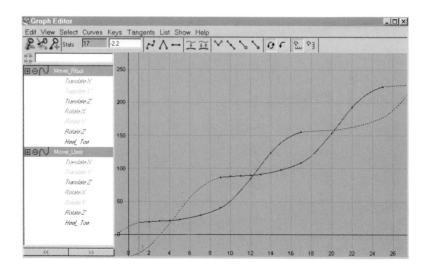

Figure 13.20

Translate Z curves for the legs

ARCS AND STAGING

Arcing is another important classical animation principle. To imitate life, you need to show motion as arcs, or waves. Nothing in this world moves in a totally straight line. Nature is composed of arcs and waves, including all motion that occurs within it, as Tai Chi practitioners like to point out. We are told that even something as apparently straight as a ray of light is not perfectly straight. A run cycle, such as the one we just created, is all wave motions, as you can readily see in the Graph Editor.

But it's one thing to create wavy function curves and quite another to show them as wavy motions. Consider the often-used example of head-turning. Although the motion itself is an arc, depending on the angle from which you are looking at the head, the head-turning can appear as a straight-line motion. To show it as an arc movement, you need to either change the view or dip the head as it turns and then bring it back up.

When you have roughly animated your character, get into the habit of going to the camera view and checking the lines the character's motions are creating. If you see a lot of straight lines even though the motions themselves are arcs, perhaps the camera view needs to be changed.

This brings up yet another important animation principle called *staging*. No matter how great the action is in a scene, it must be seen clearly to be appreciated. Staging a character involves making sure that the character's actions are being accurately transmitted to the viewers. The run cycle exercise, for instance, was shown in the side view because it best staged the motions of the body. If the same steps were captured in the front view, you would have a much harder time grasping what was going on. Classical animators often only look at the silhouette of a character to determine whether the character's actions are being staged properly.

Staging also involves making sure that only one principal action is being presented at a time. If you want to show a character get up from a chair and also flash a smile, it would be poor staging to have her do both at the same time. It would be much better to have her stand up first and then flash a smile or vice versa.

Rotate the shoulder joints down a bit and forward, and keyframe his arms stretched out. The rotations of the spine joints should be toned down to keep the chest looking straight forward, to keep the arms from swinging wildly from side to side. Aim for something like the poses shown in Figure 13.21 through the cycle.

If you want the arm movements to not repeat every 16 frames, try lengthening the cycle for the arms to something like 32 frames. This approach can make the movements seem more random. You can see a movie clip of the final run cycle in the Chapter 13 folder on the CD.

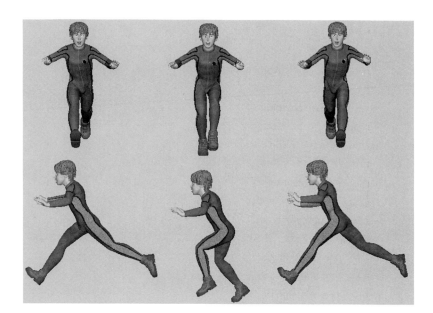

Figure 13.21

Rotations of the runner's body

Ball Tossing

Animating a character interacting with things or other characters is always more challenging than working with a solitary character. Fortunately, it is more rewarding as well, because you can develop a character much more fully when it is acting and reacting in a more complex setting. But what may be an easy task in real life, such as two people shaking hands, can cause severe headaches for the person trying to animate such a scene.

Consider the perils of animating something like a battle between two sword fighters. How do you make them grasp their swords with both hands, clash blades, briefly stick the swords together, and then merrily continue in their deadly ways? Sorry, it's not for this book to figure out such things for you—you can tackle that one at a later date.

Here, we will go through a simple task of grabbing and throwing a ball by animating constraints, which will, hopefully, help you solve more complex problems such as sword-play. You can see movie clips of this animation in the Chapter 13 folder on the accompanying CD.

Grabbing the Ball

We'll start by setting up the hand holding the ball.

1. Create a ball (sphere) scaled to 1.5 uniformly, and group it with itself, creating a parent node.

Figure 13.22

The hand grabbing the ball from the surface of the table

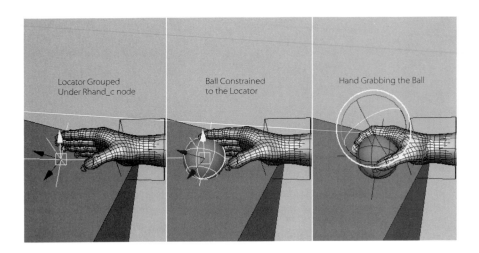

2. Choose Modify → Center Pivot to make sure the parent node's pivot point coincides with the ball's.

3. Place the character's hand on a table (a simple cube will do), as demonstrated in Figure 13.22.

4. Create a locator, scaled to 3 uniformly, group it under the Mover_Rwrist node, and place it somewhere near the hand. Refer to the left picture in Figure 13.22.

5. Point and Orient constrain the ball's parent node to the locator, and the ball should snap to the locator positionally and orientationally, as in the middle picture in Figure 13.22.

6. Move the locator closer to the hand, and rotate the fingers to make it look as if the hand were holding the ball.

7. Keyframe the finger joints and the Mover_Rwrist node at frame 15, as in the right picture in Figure 13.22. This is how the hand will be seen as grabbing the ball.

8. Select the ball's parent node, and you will see pointConstraint and orientConstraint attributes in the Channel Box.

9. Select Node State, where it should say Normal for each attribute, and keyframe NodeState at frame 15. In the Graph Editor, you can see that a value of 0 is created.

10. Go to frame 14. In the Channel Box, click the Node State field to open the submenu, and choose Block. Keyframe that for both attributes. You should then see a value of 2 created in the Graph Editor. (Note that the curve created is a stepped curve.)

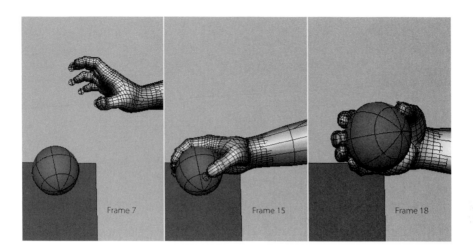

Figure 13.23

The hand grabbing the ball

Frame 7   Frame 15   Frame 18

11. Try moving the hand, and you will see at frame 14 that the ball is not constrained to the locator. Keyframe the ball where it is (at frame 15) just to make sure that the ball will be at that spot when the hand grabs it.

12. Now you can animate the Mover_Rwrist node and the finger joints, starting from a distance at frame 1 and then swooping in to scoop the ball at frame 15, as shown in Figure 13.23.

Throwing the Ball

Animating throwing a ball is essentially the same thing as animating grabbing a ball, except that you are working backward.

1. Start at frame 25 with the ball constrained to the hand. Swing the character's arm as if he were throwing the ball, and reach the point of release at frame 30. This means he should be flicking his wrist between frames 30 and 32. Finish the throw at frame 35.

2. Once you are satisfied with the throwing motion, go back to frame 30 and keyframe the ball where it is.

3. Go to frame 31, select the ball's parent node, and, in the Channel Box, change the Node State setting to Block for the Position and Orient constraints.

4. At frame 35, translate the ball to the direction where the ball has been thrown, and keyframe.

Now, when you move the Time Slider, the ball seems to be thrown from the hand at frame 31 and then shoots out from there, as shown in Figure 13.24.

Figure 13.24

**The hand throwing
the ball**

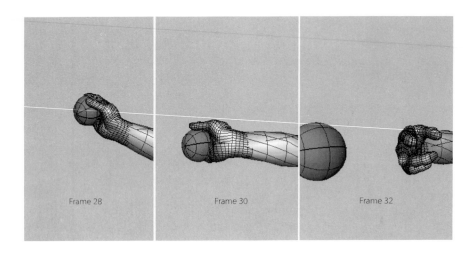

Frame 28   Frame 30   Frame 32

Maya Character Creation and Animation

The Trax Editor (covered in the next chapter) has made Maya's character node a useful aid in enabling animators to animate more intuitively. A *character*, as defined and used in Maya, is essentially a node under which you can collect all the attributes you want to use to animate as a single entity. This usually will be the control nodes of a character you've created and want to animate. However, it could also be a collection of things that you want to animate together as a group, such as the lights and doors of a haunted house or two characters interacting closely.

Creating a Character

First, let's go through the steps for creating a character.

1. Bring in the `character_bound.mb` file from the Chapter 12 folder on the CD.

2. Select all the major control nodes for animating the character: the root, spine1, spine2, neck, head, shoulders, hand controls, foot controls, and pole-vector controls for arms and legs. These should add up to a total of 15 control nodes.

3. Choose Character → Create Character Set ❏. The option window's default settings, as shown in Figure 13.25, include only the translation and rotation attributes for the selected nodes to the character node. You would rarely want to include the other attributes, which are selected for exclusion.

4. Click Create Character to display a node with a human icon named character1 in the Outliner. You can rename it if you want.

5. Open the node, and you will see all the X, Y, and Z translation and rotation channels for the nodes you selected, as shown in Figure 13.25.

Editing a Character

Consider all the attributes in the character1 node we just created. Perhaps certain attributes are not needed for the animation of the character, and maybe some extra attributes should be added. The Character menu in Maya provides the functions to perform this type of character node editing. For this example, we don't want the rotation attributes of the Lookat node to be part of the character1 node; instead, we want to add its scale X attribute. First, the character1 node must be set as the current character, or the functions won't work.

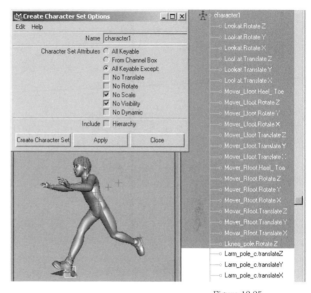

Figure 13.25

The Create Character Options box and character node

1. Either choose Character Set → Current Character Set → character1 or click the inverted triangle at the bottom right of the Maya window, beside the Auto Keyframe button. This opens the character pop-up menu. Choose character1 from the menu.

2. Select the Lookat node, select all its attributes in the Channel Box, and choose Character → Remove From Character Set to remove the attributes from the list.

3. Select the translate attributes, scale the X attribute of the Lookat node, and then choose Character → Add To Character Set.

The translation and the scale X attributes are part of the character node now. Why did we remove the translation attributes and then add them again? This was done to make the Lookat node's attributes stay together in the character node's list of attributes.

To quickly select all the nodes included in the character1 node, you can choose Character → Select Character Set Node → character1. To delete a character node, just delete the node using the Outliner or the Relationship Editor as you would remove any set. The attributes listed under it are not deleted.

Creating and Editing a Subcharacter

Maya also has the ability to create a hierarchical structure within the character node, by creating a subcharacter node. You create and edit a subcharacter node in the same way as you create and edit a regular character node. Let's try grouping the upper-body joints and control nodes together.

First, set the character1 node as the current character (as described in the previous section). Then simply select the nodes you want to group and choose Character → Create Subcharacter Set, with the default settings. A subCharacter1 node is created inside the character1 node. You should see a hierarchical structure that looks something like the one shown in Figure 13.26.

Figure 13.26

A subcharacter node in the Outliner

A subcharacter node is essentially another a character node. If you want to add or remove attributes from it, you must set it as the current character. If you open the Set Current Character submenu now, you should see that character1 has an arrow beside it. It has itself become a submenu, containing the subcharacter1 node. When attributes are removed from a subcharacter, or the subcharacter node is deleted, they don't return to the parent character node. You need to put them back in manually.

Animating a Character

When using the character or the subcharacter in Maya, it's important to set the current character properly. Let's say that we want to keyframe Mover_Lwrist node, and only that node, at frame 1.

1. Set Current Character to None. At the bottom right of the Maya window, the field should read "No Character Set."

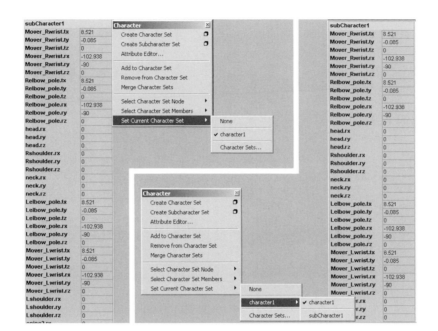

Figure 13.27

The current character settings

2. Keyframe Mover_Lwrist, and then select subCharacter1 in the Outliner. In the Channel Box, you should see that only that node's translate and rotate attributes have been keyframed, as shown in the left side in Figure 13.27.

3. Undo the keyframe, set the current character to subCharacter1, and keyframe Mover_Lwrist again. This time you should see that all the attributes in the subCharacter1 node were keyframed, as shown in the right side in Figure 13.27.

4. If you keyframe Mover_Lwrist with the current character set to character1, all the attributes under the character1 node, including the attributes in subCharacter1 node, will be keyframed.

You can choose to keyframe only the attributes of a character or a subcharacter that you want by selecting them in the Channel Box and RM clicking Key Selected, but this defeats the purpose of using the character node. It's much better to use the regular Set Key command and keyframe all the attributes each time.

As we said at the beginning of this section, a character node collects all the disparate elements from a character's setup into a single entity, eliminating the need to deal with a large number of controls—15 control nodes in our example. The real advantage is that the character node frees the animator to concentrate on animating the character. Keyframing all the attributes in the character node freezes the character into a pose and thus encourages a "pose-to-pose" approach to animation, as shown in Figure 13.28. Once you are in the character mode, you can forget about nodes and just animate!

Summary

In this chapter, we went through a simple walk cycle step by step, and then we examined more complicated animations such as a four-legged walk cycle, running, and grabbing and throwing a ball. We also covered the concept of character and subcharacter nodes in Maya and how they can aid animation.

In the next chapter, you will learn about the Trax Editor, a nonlinear animation-editing tool introduced back in Maya 3.

Figure 13.28

**Animating
pose-to-pose**

CHAPTER 14

Animation Using the Trax Editor

One of the most-used features of recent versions of Maya is the Trax Editor, a nonlinear animation editor that simplifies many of an animator's jobs and is especially useful for game developers. In essence, nonlinear animation helps resolve two problems common to keyframed animation: reusing keyframed motion and stacking keyframed motion.

Although reuse of animation segments grew out of game development needs (in which short animations need to be reused and blended), Trax, as this chapter will show, has advantages that go way beyond the gaming world. This chapter covers the following topics:

- Creating characters and subcharacters

- Creating poses

- Creating, modifying, blending, and sharing clips

- Hands On: Creating a walk cycle

- Hands On: Using Trax to lip-synch

Characters

Before you can work with Trax in Maya, you must first create a character. A character can be anything from a single geometric primitive to a complex, fully functional virtual human, complete with skeleton and blend shapes. What ties a character's disparate objects together is that, once they are properly joined as a character, they are all grouped under a single node, and you can animate the appropriate channels on all the objects in the character from one convenient place. Basically, when you create a character, you key multiple attributes from different objects as one.

A character is not equivalent to a grouped set of objects for an important reason: character nodes are set nodes, not geometry or transform nodes. Because characters are sets, you can place other nodes in the set, or more importantly, you can place *only certain channels* of other nodes in the set. Thus, only channels that are relevant to animating a character are added to that character, eliminating much of the hunting through excess channels and extra keyframes that can occur when animating without using character sets.

Creating Characters

You create a character by selecting objects and choosing Character → Create Character Set ❐ from the Animation menu set. In the options window, shown in Figure 14.1, you can give your character a name (character1 is chosen by default), and you can set three options that specify which object attributes to include in your character:

- The All Keyable option places all the attributes that appear in the Channel Box into the character (often, this is too many).

- The From Channel Box option lets you select specific channels to include by highlighting them in the Channel Box before opening the options window. This option allows you to include the exact attributes in the set for which you plan to set keys. It is a good idea to include only the keys you need in the character.

Figure 14.1

The Create Character Set Options window

- The All Keyable Except option (the most generally useful, and selected by default) lets you select which attribute groups to include in your character. For example, if you select No Scale, the Scale attributes from your objects are not included in the character.

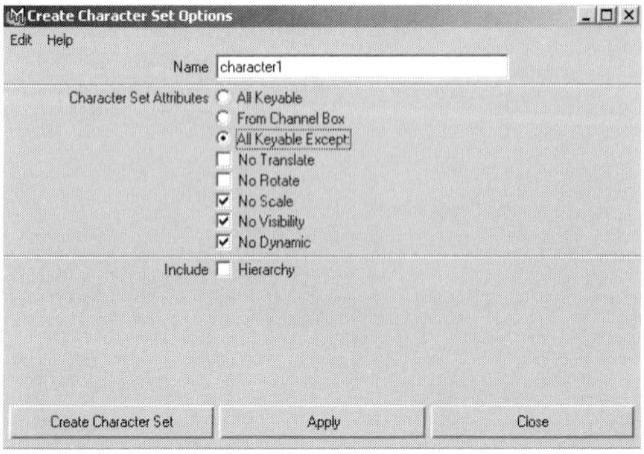

Additionally, the Include Hierarchy option, when checked, allows you to include the objects you have selected and every object or part of the hierarchy under the object you are including in the character set. The Object Hierarchy comprises all the connected nodes that make up the object. The attributes of the included hierarchy are the same as the attributes you set

Figure 14.1

**The Create Character
Set Options window**

for the selected objects. If the Include Hierarchy box is not checked (this is the default), only the selected objects are included in the character set.

Let's create a simple character and take a look at how character sets are actually structured in Maya and the differences in selecting or not selecting the Include Hierarchy option. Follow these steps:

1. In a new scene window, create a NURBS sphere and cone, and rename them ball1 and cone1, respectively. You can move the scene elements around, but you don't need to for this example.

2. Drag-select both objects, and then choose Character → Create Character Set ❐ from the Animation module. Choose Edit → Reset Settings, and click the Create Character Set button to create your character. Your character, named character1, will be created, and the character name will appear to the right of the Range Slider at the bottom right of your screen (as shown to the right).

3. Create two NURBS spheres and two cones, and name them respectively ball2, ball3, cone2, and cone3.

4. In the Outliner, select ball2, and then Ctrl+select cone2. Press the P key to parent the two objects. Select the cone, and choose Character → Create Character Set ❐. Change the name to character2, and check the Include Hierarchy option. Create your character.

5. Parent ball3 and cone3. Select the cone, and choose Character → Create Character Set ❐. Change the name to character3, and clear the Include Hierarchy option. Create your character.

Selecting and Examining Characters

By selecting the character and using the Channel Box, you can quickly locate and animate the relevant attributes of all your objects in one place—which is the primary advantage of creating a character.

Now let's select the character. Follow these steps:

1. In the Outliner, click character1 to highlight it. (Although you can see a character node in the Hypergraph when in Input/Output mode, it is much easier to deal with characters in the Outliner.)

2. Click the plus sign to the left of the character to see all the nodes that are currently in the character1 set (see Figure 14.2). These nodes appear in the Channel Box when you select the character. Because we allowed only translation and rotation keyframes, those (for both the ball and cone) are all that appear in the set. Compare character2, which uses Include Hierarchy, and character3, which does not use Include Hierarchy. Notice that attributes for both parent and child nodes are included when Include Hierarchy is checked. Including the hierarchy allows you to quickly add relevant members to the character set. However, be careful not to include unnecessary attributes.

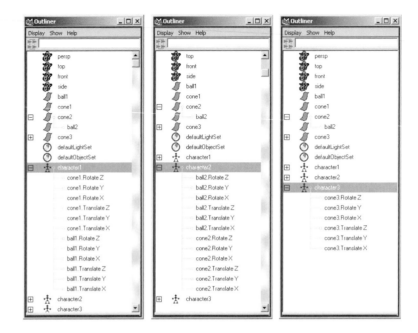

3. To see more clearly how the character is constructed (as well as how to add or remove attributes), open the character set's Relationship Editor by choosing Window → Relationship Editors → Character Sets. On the left side of the window, you see the character sets, just as in the Outliner. On the right side are all the objects in the scene.

4. Highlight character1 on the left, and all scene objects that are part of this set will be highlighted on the right (as in Figure 14.3).

5. Click the leftmost plus sign by character1 on the right side to display all the object attributes assigned to this set. This is the same as clicking the character1 plus sign on the left side. (Notice that all the attributes are highlighted on the right.) Furthermore, both the ball and the cone scene objects are highlighted, indicating that their nodes are (at least partially) in the character1 set.

6. Click the rightmost plus sign next to the cone to display all the cone's attributes. Scroll down, and you will see that the translate and rotate attributes are highlighted, indicating that they are part of the character1 set.

Removing and Adding Character Attributes

Removing an attribute from a character is simple in the Relationship Editor. Find the attribute you want to remove (the cone's translateX attribute, for example), and click it on the right side, removing the highlight from the translateX attribute. You will immediately see the translateX channel disappear from the character1 set, and from the Channel Box (assuming character1 is still selected).

To add an attribute, highlight it on the right side while character1 is selected on the left. Even if you have already begun animating your character, you can still add or remove attributes from the character set. Be aware, however, that if you remove a keyed attribute from a character, you lose any keyframes from that attribute.

You can also remove and add attributes via the Channel Box and the Character menu. Select a channel name (such as `cone.tx`) and choose Character → Remove From Character Set. To add an attribute this way, select the object, highlight the attribute you want to add, and then choose Character → Add To Character Set.

Figure 14.3

The Relationship Editor, showing objects connected with the character1 set

Setting a Working Character

To set a character as the working character, you can choose the character from the pop-up menu at the right of the Range Slider, or you can choose Character → Set Current Character Set → *<character name>*. Setting a current character means that setting keyframes will affect only keyable attributes of that character (those listed in the Channel Box).

Let's see how this works.

1. Create another character out of a simple cylinder and rename it character4.

2. Check in the character pop-up menu to be sure that character4 is set as the working character. Then choose *both* the cone1 from character1 and the cylinder from character4, and set a key by pressing **s** (do not press the Shift key) on the keyboard.

3. Move the Timeline to, say, 10 frames, and move the objects in both character1 and character4 some distance from their original positions. Press **s** again to set new keys.

4. Rewind your animation. You should see the cylinder move between the two positions you keyed over 10 frames, but the cone will stay where you last put it.

If your cone moves also, it is likely because you have auto keyframing on (the key icon at the bottom right of the window is red). When auto keyframing is on, anything that moves is automatically keyframed, even non-character objects. While this seems somewhat counter-intuitive, Alias|Wavefront has decided that this is the proper way for auto keyframing to operate. To avoid accidentally setting non-character keyframes when animating characters, be sure to disable auto keyframing (by clicking the key icon) before you begin animating with characters.

Why didn't the cone move? Because when you set keys, you set them on *only* the current character. Because the cone is part of character1, not character4, no keys are set as you move the objects around. If you try to set keyframes on the cylinder's Y scale, you will not be able to do so, because you did not define scale as keyable in character4. Although it may take a bit of time to get used to, the fact that Maya does not set keyframes on objects or attributes outside a character is a great way to avoid the numerous extraneous keyframes that always seem to crop up when doing animation work.

> If you want to keyframe the cylinder's scale, but don't want to add those attributes to your character, you can choose to disengage all character animation by setting the character pop-up menu (or choose Character → Set Current Character) to None. Setting keyframes will then work for all scene objects and attributes. When you choose a character once again, you will see that character's keyframes listed again and available for editing.

Creating Subcharacters

Finally, you can create subcharacters that are part of your main character but can be animated and keyed separately. If, for example, you want to animate a character's left arm separately from the entire body, you can create a leftArm subcharacter, which will be hierarchically a child of the main character.

To create a subcharacter for a left arm, first create a character for the whole body; then with the body set as your character in the pop-up menu, select the elements of the left arm and choose Character → Create Subcharacter Set ❐. Adjust the settings of the subcharacter to your liking, name it leftArm, and click the Create Subcharacter Set button. In the character pop-up menu, leftArm will appear as a submenu of the body character, indicating that it is linked below the main body character.

You can also create sub-subcharacters. Set the subcharacter as your current character (leftArm in this case), select the objects you want to be the subcharacter of the arm (left-Hand, for example), and choose Character → Create Subcharacter Set. In this manner, you can link multiple subcharacters in a hierarchy.

Now that you have a good idea of what characters are and how they are constructed, let's create a couple of simple poses and use them in the Trax Editor.

Poses

By storing and applying poses to characters during the animation process, you can quickly return to any number of default configurations for your character. Poses can save you time if the character commonly returns to certain positions during an animation.

Creating Poses

Let's first create a pose for character1. If you still have your simple scene from the last section handy, use it for this example. If not, create one character called character1 and another called character2 (characters made of simple geometric primitives are fine for our present purposes).

1. Once your characters are defined, set character1 as the working character using the Character pop-up menu (or choose Character → Set Current Character Set).

2. Open the Trax Editor by choosing Window → Animation Editors → Trax Editor. You will notice that, as shown in Figure 14.4, character1 and character2 are listed on the left side of the window, and the right side includes tracks for each character (empty at this point) and a Time Slider at the bottom.

You can navigate inside the Trax Editor the same way you navigate a Maya scene. To zoom in or out, increasing the number of frames you can see at one time, use Alt+LM, and MM. To scroll (track) through the frames, use Alt+MM.

3. Select character1 in the Trax Editor so that it appears in the Channel Box. (This is equivalent to selecting the character in the Outliner.)

4. In the Trax menu (or by RM choosing within the Trax window), choose Create → Pose ❑.

5. Name the pose startingPoint and click the Create Pose button. You will not see any difference in the scene when you create this pose, but Maya has saved the position and rotation data of character1 in a clip in the Visor.

6. Open the Visor (choose Window → General Editors → Visor).

7. Click the Character Poses tab. You will see a clip called startingPoint in this tab, which is the pose you just saved (as shown in Figure 14.5).

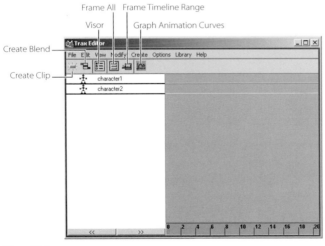

Figure 14.4

The Trax Editor, with character1 and character2

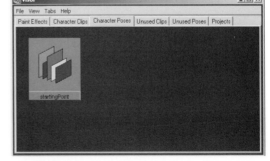

Figure 14.5

The Visor, showing a stored clip

8. A pose works as you would expect. Try moving your character (or parts of it) to a different position, so it is not at the origin anymore.

9. With the cursor over the pose in the Visor, RM choose Apply Pose. You should see your character return to its initial settings. (This menu also allows you to copy, instance, duplicate, or rename your clip or open the Attribute Editor.)

If you adjust, say, the scale of one of your character parts, it will *not* return to its original scale when you apply the pose. Scale data is not included in the character and thus is not recorded in the pose.

Placing Poses on the Timeline

You can also place poses in the Timeline of the Trax editor. Doing so can be beneficial in at least two ways. When working alone, you can place poses in the Timeline and move them around (by simply dragging them from place to place in the track) to get a quick "pose-to-pose" animation for your character, which you can refine later. In a multiperson production team, the lead animator can set poses for the most important frames in an animation (and adjust where those moments occur by moving the poses), and then the animation team can create the in-between animation necessary to fill out the scene.

When you place a pose or a clip into a track in the Trax Editor, you are actually creating an instance of the source clip stored in the Visor. When you drag the startingPoint1 clip, for example, into a track, it is called startingPoint1 (or 2 or so on), not just startingPoint. Because of this instance relationship, you can make any changes you want to an individual pose or clip in a track without affecting the source clip's values. On the other hand, if you adjust the source clip's settings (via the Attribute Editor), all instances of the clip in the tracks will be updated to reflect those changes. If you are familiar with a program such as Director, you might recognize that the relationship between a source clip and a track clip in Maya is similar to that between a cast member and a sprite in Director.

Let's try a simple pose-to-pose animation.

Figure 14.6

Dragging a pose into a character track

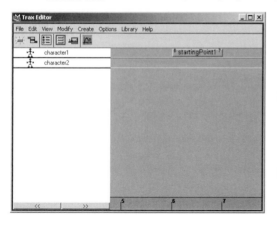

1. With the Visor and Trax Editor open, MM drag the pose from the Visor into the track for character1, pasting the pose into the track at a given frame, as shown in Figure 14.6.

2. Move your character objects to a different place in the scene (and rotate them if you want), and then create a pose with a different name (choose Create ' Pose r in the Trax Editor).

3. MM drag this new pose into the Timeline, as shown in Figure 14.7.

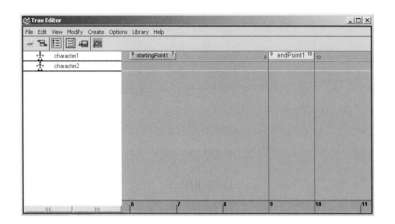

Figure 14.7

Inserting a second pose in a character track

When you play back the animation, your character will "pop" from one pose to another, giving you a rough idea of the timing involved in the animation you later create.

Clips

By allowing "clips" of animations to be stored in a sort of bin (akin to bins used in nonlinear video editors), Maya lets you reuse animations as easily as pasting them into your scene. Also, since animation is stored in clips, several clips can be stacked on top of each other, or blended together, allowing you straightforward, nondestructive control over large- and small-scale animation of an entire character, without needing to find and adjust specific keyframes in several character parts. Clips are useful when animating repetitive motions such as blinking, walking, or even talking. You can scale the clips up or down to increase or decrease the speed or exaggeration of the action. You can also cycle the clips to repeat the motion again and again.

Creating Clips

Creating a clip is much the same as creating a pose, except that instead of storing a single frame of position and rotation (and other) data, you store several keyframes of data. This allows you to create chunks (or clips) of an animation that you can later use in various places in a given track.

A clip can actually be composed of just one keyframe; however, a single keyframe clip can be difficult to use later, because it has no length to adjust or blend with other clips. You can alleviate this problem by selecting the source clip in the Visor, opening the Attribute Editor, and increasing the Duration of the source clip. However, it's easier to create a multi-keyframed clip in the first place.

Once you have some sort of animation in your Timeline, you can create a clip in the Trax Editor by RM choosing Create → Clip ❐. The Create Clip Options window, shown in Figure 14.8, allows you to choose how you want to create and use your clip.

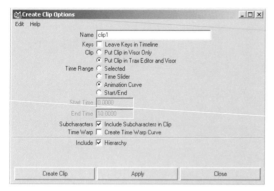

Figure 14.8

The Create Clip Options window

The Name field lets you name your clip (clip1 is the default name). You will find it helpful to rename the clips to form a description of what the clip does. For example, if you are creating clips of words for lip-synching, name each clip the word you are animating. The Leave Keys In Timeline check box lets you maintain the keyframes you use to create a clip in your Timeline. This can be useful if you want to create several similar clips and don't want to reproduce all the keyframes for each clip. In general, however, it is best to remove Timeline keyframes as you create a clip, so you don't get unexpected animation later.

The Clip radio buttons allow you to place the clip in the Visor only (if you don't plan to use it right away) or place the clip in the Visor and in a character track in the Trax Editor. The Time Range section provides four choices: use a selected time range (Shift+dragging in the Timeline), use the start and end values of the Range Slider, use the range of animation curves (from the first keyframe to the last for your character, which is the default method), or use a manually specified start and end frame. Finally, you can choose to include subcharacter keyframes when you create a clip.

Let's create a clip.

1. In your scene window, move the object that comprises character1 to a new position, set a keyframe by pressing the **s** key (be sure character1 is still selected, or you won't be able set keyframes on it). Change the time, then move the character somewhere else, and set another keyframe. (You can continue this process with as many keyframes as you like.)

Remember that you can apply your predefined poses to help you set keyframes on the character.

2. In the Trax Editor window (or under Animate in the Animation menu set, choose Create → Clip ❑. In the option window, name the clip anything you want, set the clip to go in the Trax Editor and Visor, choose Use Animation Curve Range to set the length of the clip, and click Create Clip. As shown in Figure 14.9, a new clip is inserted in the Trax Editor, ready for your use. In addition, in the Visor (in the Clips tab now, not the Poses tab) is a new source clip.

Figure 14.9

The Trax Editor with a new clip for character1

3. Click Play in the scene window, and you will see the time marker move across the Trax Editor Timeline as well. As it crosses the clip, your animation will play back, as it did when the keyframes were stored in the scene Timeline.

Once a clip is in a track, you can interactively change its position, length (or scale), and cycling options, as explained in the next section.

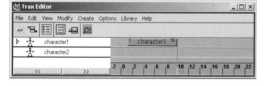

Modifying Clips

You can control the placement, length, cycling, and weight of a clip, as follows:

- To change the position (start and stop points) of the clip, just drag the clip (by its middle) to a new point in the Timeline.

- To change the length (or scale) of the clip, drag on the top-right corner of the clip, as shown in Figure 14.10. You should see an arrow pointing right and a bar. Alternatively, you can change the Scale value for the clip in the Attribute Editor or Channel Box. When you change the length of a clip, the animation will take a longer or shorter time.

- To change the number of times a clip repeats (its cycle settings), drag on the bottom-right corner of the clip (you will see a curled arrow with a bar), as shown in Figure 14.11. Alternatively, you can set the Cycle number in the Attribute Editor or Channel Box. When there are multiple cycles of the original clip in your track, Maya places a black tick mark in the clip at each point where the original clip repeats. You can choose to off-set the cycle for a clip in two ways. If you choose Absolute, the attribute values are reset to the original value on each repetition of the cycle. If you select Relative, the attribute value is added to the original value. For example, a Relative offset is useful when creating a walk cycle.

- To set the weight of a track, open the Attribute Editor and go to the Anim Clip Attribute section. Each keyframe in a clip is multiplied by the weight setting, so setting the weight of a clip to be greater than 1 exaggerates each keyframe. Reducing the weight means a corresponding reduction in the level of each keyframe.

By controlling the placement, length, cycling, and weight of a clip, you can fine-tune your animation to an exacting degree using the Trax Editor. If you want even more control over the shape of the underlying curves that make up a clip, you can graph the curves and adjust them as you would any animation curves in the Graph Editor. In the Trax Editor, choose View → Graph Anim Curves (or click the Graph Animation Curves button in the toolbar, labeled in Figure 14.4). The Graph Editor will appear with all the curves of your clip loaded in the window (you may need to press the A key to center the curves), as shown in Figure 14.12. You can then adjust the curves as you would any other animation curves, tweaking the motion until you are satisfied with it.

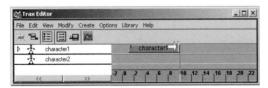

Figure 14.10

Interactively changing the length of a clip

Figure 14.11

Interactively changing the number of cycles of a clip

Figure 14.12

A clip in the
Graph Editor

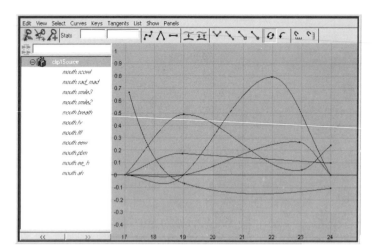

The animation curves of a clip loaded into the Graph Editor will *not* reflect any cycle, weighting, timing, or scale changes you made to the clip. You will always see the curves from the original, unchanged clip in the Graph Editor. (For more information about using the Graph Editor, see Chapter 9, "Animating in Maya.")

MOTION WARPING: ADDING KEYFRAMES ON TOP OF CLIPS

With Trax, you can also add keyframes over a track, tweaking the motion of a particular track while maintaining the integrity of the clip. This feature, called *motion warping*, allows a great deal of individual variation of a clip that might be used on several characters without affecting the underlying clip itself.

To create a motion warp, first set keyframes for the first and last frame on which the warp will occur (set these keys without changing the keyed values) to set the range of the warp. In the Trax Editor Timeline, the range of frames that set off the motion warp will be highlighted in blue, letting you know that a motion warp is in effect.

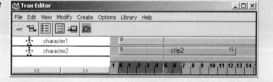

After you set a range, you can (within that range of keys) set any keyframes you want on the character. As you make adjustments, Maya will *add* the keyframes you set to the clip animation, modifying the clip with the new keyframes. Since the effect of any keyframes you set is additive, it is best to set keys that have more subtle effects.

By using motion warping, you can alter one iteration of a clip cycle, make subtle adjustments to a particular motion on your character, or modify several characters that share the same clip animations, allowing each to behave in a slightly different way. (See the "Sharing Clips" section later in this chapter for details on sharing clip animations.)

Blending Clips

If adjusting one clip at a time in the Trax Editor is not enough for your animation purposes, never fear—you can blend animations between different clips or even between a clip and itself. For example, you might blend between a walking and standing clip or between a walking and running clip, reducing the need to keyframe complex transitional states in an animation.

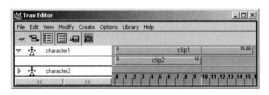

Figure 14.13

Two tracks, stacked on top of each other

To see how blending works, either use your simple character from the previous sections or create a character out of two primitives (such as a sphere and a cone), and then create two clips: one clip with the sphere and cone moving up and down in the Y axis in opposite directions, and the other with them moving in the X or Z axis in opposite directions. You may find it easier to create the second clip if you disable the first one. To disable a clip, select the clip in the Trax Editor, and then RM choose Enable/Disable Clip. A disabled clip's name is slightly grayed out, indicating that it no longer affects the character's motion. Enabling and disabling clips can be a useful way to test individual motion on a character with multiple tracks of animation.

When you finish, the Trax Editor should have two tracks for character1 (as in Figure 14.13), with both clips stacked on top of each other. Notice that Maya created a new track for character1 below the original one to accommodate the new clip.

If you now play back the animation, the motions from both clips combine, so the sphere and cone travel diagonally opposite each other. To allow each clip to operate on its own, simply move one clip down the Timeline until it is no longer overlapping the other.

> You can manually create new tracks in the Trax Editor by selecting the character and choosing Modify → Add Track in the Trax Editor. To remove an unused track, select the character and choose Modify → Remove Track (the bottommost unused track is removed).

Clips are blended based on which clip is first in the Timeline. In other words, if clip1 starts on frame 20 and clip2 starts on frame 30, clip1 will hold the initial values (at 100%) for the blend, while clip2 will hold the final values (100%) of the blend. This system breaks down if both clips start at the same time on the Timeline, so avoid blending two clips that start at the same time.

Adding a Blend to Overlapping Clips

Partially overlapping clips create additive animation during the frames when the two clips overlap. The trouble with the overlapped section is that the animation will "pop" when the new clip is introduced, because the values of the animated channels suddenly change.

To resolve the popping problem, you can add a blend to the clips, creating a smoother alteration from the values of one clip to the other. To create a blend, Shift+select the two clips and, with the cursor over one of the clips, RM choose Blend Clips. A curve will appear between the clips, as shown in Figure 14.14, indicating that the animations of the two clips are now blended across the frames the two clips overlap.

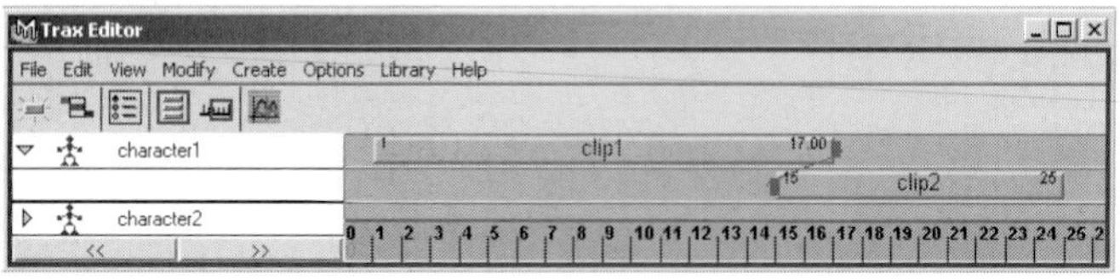

Figure 14.14

Two animation tracks blended

Blending works using the common attributes of the two clips. Blending will not be effective if the clips you are trying to blend do not share common attributes. Also, blending will create a smoother transition if a similar motion is maintained between the two clips.

Select Create → Blend □. Look at the options in the Initial Weight Curve and Rotation Blend. Under the Initial Weight Curve there are four choices that allow you control over the tangents used to create the blend. Linear, the first option creates an evenly weighted transition between the clips. Ease In assigns less weight at the beginning of the transition and increases the weight given to the next clip as frames in the blend progress. This makes the beginning of the transition less noticeable. Ease Out is the opposite of Ease In. More weight is placed on the beginning keys, and the effect of the first clip is more prominent than the second clip for a longer amount of time. The Ease In and Ease Out option is a combination of the two options above. You will discover that you achieve very different results with each option.

The items under Rotation Blend control how the rotation attributes from the first clip are combined with the second clip. Quaternion Shortest uses the least amount of distance between the rotations and the Quaternion Longest uses the greatest distance between the rotations. Basically, if you don't want the object to spin in the opposite direction as one clip blends into another, choose Quaternion Shortest. The Linear option merges the rotation values at a constant rate during the Blend. Experiment with the different options to see just how big a difference each choice will make. Once you are familiar with the way the blend works you will more easily achieve a successful transition between the clips.

Modifying Clip Blends

To change the length of the blend (the number of frames over which the blend takes place), slide one track relative to the other, changing the overlap. You can also blend tracks that are not on top of each other—the blend will occur between the last values of the first clip and the initial values of the second clip. Figure 14.15 shows a third clip (clip3) blended with clip2 in this manner.

To delete a blend that you no longer want, highlight the curve that represents the blend in the Trax Editor, and then press the Delete key.

Figure 14.15

A third clip, blended without overlapping with clip2

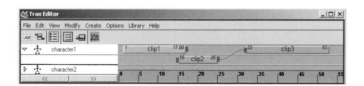

For more control over blending clips, you can graph the blend. To do so, highlight the blend and choose View → Graph Anim Curves from the Trax menu set (or click the Graph Animation Curves button in the Trax Editor's toolbar). The Graph Editor will open, showing the blend curve. As you can see in Figure 14.16, the default blend curve, Quaternion Shortest, is just a straight line on a scale of 0 to 1 in both the horizontal and vertical axes. When the curve is at 0,0, the blend is completely weighted toward the first clip in the blend (that is, character channel values are 100% those of the first clip). When the curve is at 1,1, at the end of the blend, the blend is completely weighted to the second clip in the blend.

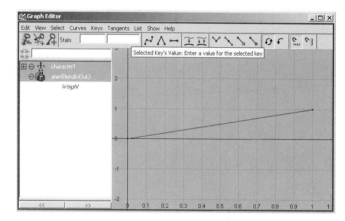

Figure 14.16

The Graph Editor showing a default blend curve

To create a different shaped curve (for instance, to ease the blend in and out), simply adjust the tangent handles of the two blend keyframes, or add other keyframes into the blend shape. Editing the shape of the blend is simple enough, yet if you seek ease in, ease out, or ease in and out effects, you might save time by deleting the blend and creating a new blend by selecting the appropriate options from the Create Blend menu. One possible curve shape is shown in Figure 14.17. (For details on using the Graph Editor, see Chapter 9.)

Figure 14.17

An altered blend curve displayed in the Graph Editor

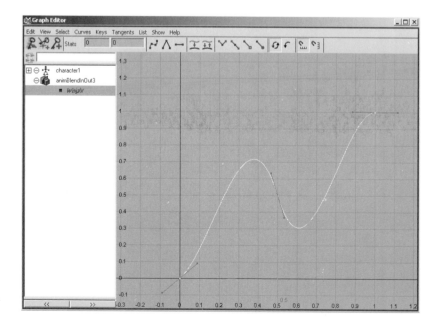

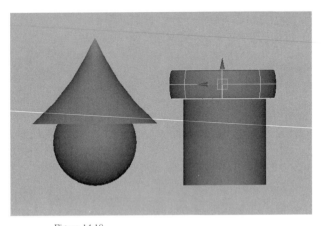

Figure 14.18

**Two primitive
characters**

Because the shape of the blend curve is independent of the length of the blend, you can adjust the shape of the blend and then increase or decrease the length of the blend in the Trax Editor (or vice versa), thus lengthening or shortening a blend without changing its shape. This separation of curve shape from length is one of the workflow benefits of using Trax as opposed to traditional keyframe techniques.

Blending clips allows for quick and easy transitions between different character animation states. Although these transitions aren't always perfect, they are generally good, and you can adjust them using the Graph Editor, by changing the blend lengths or even by adding keyframes on top of the blend (using motion warping, as discussed earlier). Another advantage of using Trax is that it provides the ability to share clips and poses among characters in a single animation or even in multiple, separate scenes. If you invest time planning your characters, you can save time when you are animating.

Sharing Clips

Maya's ability to share animation clips and poses among characters provides for massive time savings in a complex, multicharacter project or in several projects that can use each others' motion data. To see how sharing clips works, we'll first share clips within a single scene, then use a referenced scene to share clips, and finally use the import/export feature to share clips between scenes.

Sharing Clips in a Scene

You can share clips between characters within a single scene by copying and pasting clips from one character to another. If you have the simple project from the previous sections, you can continue to use it. If not, create a simple character with two geometric primitives (like those in Figure 14.18), and create two or three animation clips for it. When one character is animated with clips, create a second, similar character (for example, with two geometric primitives) and move it away from the first character in your scene, as shown in Figure 14.18.

You can share clips between characters that are quite different from each other, but much of the animation of each clip might be lost in the transfer. Thus, it is generally better to share clips between similar characters.

You can copy a clip from one character to another in two ways. The simplest method (if the clip is already being used by the other character) is to copy and paste it from the first character's track into the second character's track. To do so, RM choose Copy Clip with the cursor over the clip you want to copy. Then, in the second character's track, choose Edit → Paste, and the new clip will appear in the track for the second character.

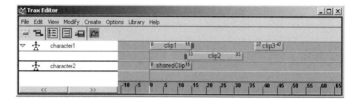

Figure 14.19

A clip copied from character1 to character2

The second way to copy and paste is to use the Visor. With character1 (*not* character2) set in the character pop-up menu, open the Visor and RM choose Copy, with the cursor over the clip you want to copy. Then, in the Trax Editor, place the cursor in a track for the second character and RM choose Paste, placing the clip into the track. The result is shown in Figure 14.19.

Copying and pasting from the Trax Editor and from the Visor are not identical operations. When you copy a clip from the Trax Editor itself, any changes (to scaling, weighting, or cycling) are transferred to the clip for the new character. When copying and pasting from the Visor, the original source clip is copied, with no modifications. Depending on your animation goals, one or the other method may prove more useful.

If you open the option box when pasting a clip, you can paste by attribute name, by attribute order, by node name, or by character map, as shown in Figure 14.20.

Generally, you want to use attribute name or attribute order to paste, because this places the animation curves on attributes in the new character that are either of the same name or in the same order as in the originating character. The By Node Name option will not work properly when the two characters are in the same scene (because two nodes cannot be named the same in a single scene). However, you can use this option when importing or copying clips into a new scene in which all the nodes have names identical to those in the original scene. The By Character Map option creates a user-modifiable MEL script that maps the curves from one character to another. This method can be powerful

Figure 14.20

The Paste Clip Options window

for pasting a clip from one character onto a very different character, but it is a fairly complex and specialized process and not generally useful for the average Trax user. For information about how to create and use a character map, see Animation → Nonlinear Animation → Using the Trax Editor → Working with Clips in the online documentation that comes with Maya.

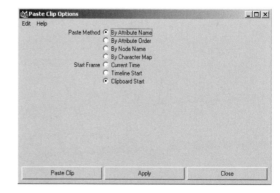

You will likely find that your new character will move to *exactly* the same place as the first character (so the two overlap). If this behavior is acceptable, you are finished with the pasting. If not, you can correct the problem in two ways:

- Activate the clip (bring its keys into the Timeline for editing by highlighting the clip, and then RM choose Activate/Deactivate keys) and move the character to the proper position at each keyframe.

- Graph the animation curves (choose View → Graph Anim Curves) and adjust the curves to move your character.

Graphing the animation curves generally tends to work more intuitively, because you can move the curve as a whole. Working with the individual keyframes in Activate mode can lead to forgotten or misplaced keyframes, and thus to unwanted behavior.

Using a Reference Scene to Share Clips

To copy clips from one scene file to another, you can reference a source scene into a new one. Save your current scene (with clips intact), and then open a new scene and create another simple character. Now choose File → Create Reference and select the source scene you just saved. You should see the geometry from your old scene appear in the new one, and if you look in the Character pop-up menu, you will see characters 1 and 2 (preceded by the scene filename) in the menu, in addition to the new character you just created.

In the Trax Editor, the two characters from your source scene will appear below your current scene character, as shown in Figure 14.21. You can then copy and paste clips as you want, using the techniques described in the previous section.

When you are finished copying clips, remove the reference from your new scene. To do this, choose File → Reference Editor. In the Reference Editor window, twirl down the arrow next to .\untitled, select the scene file you referenced, and choose Edit → Remove Reference. With the reference removed, all the geometry and extra clips from the source scene are removed, and you are left with just the copied clips you want to use in your new scene.

Exporting and Importing Clips

The third way to share clips is to export the clips themselves and then import them into a new scene. The exported scene will contain *only* animation clips (and poses), not geometry.

Reopen your old scene file (with the two characters) and open the Trax Editor or Visor. Select all the clips that you want to export (only selected clips will be exported), and choose File → Export Clip in the menu. A dialog box will appear, allowing you to save the exported clips into a new scene file (stored, by default, in the Clips directory of your project). Choose a name and export the file.

Figure 14.21

Referenced clips in the Trax Editor

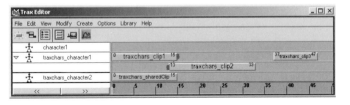

In a new scene file, create yet another simple character. In the Trax Editor, choose File → Import and import the clips you previously exported. When the file is imported, the clips from the other file are stored in the Visor of the new scene, under the Unused Clips tab. You can then use the Visor method of copying and pasting clips onto your new character, thus sharing the clips between files in this manner.

By exporting clips from scene files, you can create libraries of clips to use later. For example, if you create walk, run, jump, sit, and stand clips for a character, you can save just the clip data to a scene file (or multiple files if you prefer) and then import this animation data into any other character file you create in the future, saving you the time of rekeying all this motion data.

Using Trax to "create once, use many times" can drastically reduce the need to redo work, either in a single scene file or across dozens of scenes in ongoing projects. This, combined with the nonlinear, additive nature of Trax, makes it extremely useful for real-life animation work in which characters need to perform similar tasks many times or in which a number of characters need to share similar behaviors.

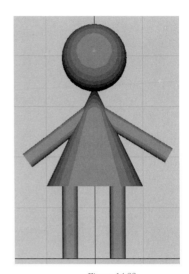

Figure 14.22

A simple girl character

To finish this chapter, we'll take a look at two more complex examples of using Trax to create useful animation. First, we'll create a walk cycle for a simple character. Then we'll use Trax with blend shapes to provide for rapid lip-synching in multiple characters.

Hands On: Creating a Walk Cycle

In this first hands-on example, we're going to create a "Scooby-Doo" type walk cycle, in which our character will glide across the ground rather than plant its feet as it walks. (Just check out any budget cartoon from the 1960s or early 1970s to see this effect.) Although the character and walk cycle generated here are simpler than that for a realistic human, shown in the previous chapter, a gliding walk style is perfectly acceptable for many cartoonish characters. Additionally, most of the techniques used for this simple style of walking transfer well to more complex walk types. (We'll cover a few differences at the end of this section.)In fact, if you have your completed human character from the last chapter, you can substitute him here and work on a more realistic walk cycle.

Creating the Character

We'll begin by creating a character and then creating subcharacters for arms and legs.

1. Open a new scene and create the "girl" character shown in Figure 14.22, using a sphere, a cone, and four cylinders. Be sure to move the pivot points of the arm and leg cylinders to where the shoulder and hip sockets would be (using the Insert key on the keyboard).

2. After you create the geometry, group all the parts into one group (select all, and then press Ctrl+G), and name the group girlBody.

3. Drag-select all the body and choose Character → Create Character Set ☐. In the option window, choose Edit → Reset Settings. Name the character girl (she will have only translate and rotate elements keyable by default). Click the Create Character Set button to create the girl character.

4. With the girl character set selected (the name should appear in the Character pop-up menu), select only the leg cylinders and choose Character → Create Subcharacter Set ☐. In the option window, set the name of the subcharacter to legs, be sure the Attribute radio button is set to All Keyable Except, and choose the No Translate option (because the legs will only rotate, we don't need or want the translate channels in this subcharacter). Click the Create Subcharacter button to make the legs subcharacter.

5. In the character pop-up menu, set the character back to girl (not legs, which will be selected now).

6. Select the arm cylinders and repeat step 4 to create a subcharacter called arms (again with no translate channels). When you're finished, you should have a character (girl) with two subcharacters connected to it (arms and legs).

7. To create a pose of the girl, set the character to girl, and then in the Trax Editor, choose Create → Pose. We'll use this pose to reset the girl to a standing position later.

Animating the Character

To animate the girl, we'll first animate the legs rotating for the walking motion, then animate the body moving forward through space, and finally animate the arms moving back and forth in countermotion to the legs. We'll create a 24-frame walk cycle, so each step will take 12 frames.

1. To animate the legs, set the active character to be the legs subcharacter (using the Character pop-up menu). You can then select the legs subcharacter (using either the Outliner or the Trax Editor) or just manually select each leg as you need it.

2. At frame 1, rotate the right leg forward about 40 to 50 degrees, and rotate the left leg back 10 to 15 degrees, as in Figure 14.23.

3. At frame 6, set the rotation of the right leg to about 15 to 20 degrees, and set the rotation of the left leg to about –20 to –25 degrees (see Figure 14.24).

4. At frame 12, key the left leg forward about 40 to 50 degrees, and rotate the right leg back about 15 degrees (see Figure 14.25). (This is halfway through the walk cycle, so the legs are essentially in opposite positions from frame 1.)

5. At frame 18, rotate the left leg to about 15 to 20 degrees, and rotate the right leg to about –20 to –25 (see Figure 14.26).

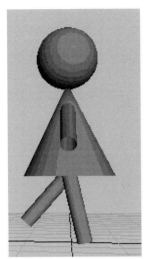

Figure 14.23

The first keyframe of the walk cycle

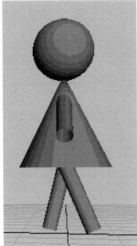

Figure 14.24

The second keyframe of the walk cycle

Figure 14.25

The third keyframe of the walk cycle

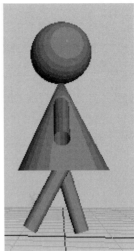

Figure 14.26

The fourth keyframe of the walk cycle

6. At frame 24, set the rotation of the two legs back to what they were at frame 1. (You might find it easier just to copy and paste the keys from frame 1 to frame 24.) At this point, you can either make a clip out of the leg animation you created or add body motion first and then create clips for legs and body simultaneously. We found it easier to create the body motion while the legs were still keyframed, so we opted for the latter approach.

7. To create the body motion, set the character back to girl (not legs).

8. At frames 1, 6, 12, 18, and 24, set the body position so that the girl's body moves forward as the legs rotate. (Don't worry if the motion isn't quite right yet; you can adjust it once the motion is turned into clips.)

Creating the Clips

Now that we have body and leg motion, we can create the clips.

1. With the girl character still selected, choose Create → Clip ❑ from the Trax Editor. Name the clip if you want, choose to put the clip in the Visor and the Trax Editor, use the animation curve range, and select the Include Subcharacters In Clip option so the leg clip is saved as well. Click the Create Clip button to create the animation clips.

2. In the Trax Editor, you will now have three clips: one for the girl character, one for the legs, and one for the arms (even though no keys have been set for the arms). Because we will create a separate clip for the arms, select the current arms clip and press the Delete key to get rid of it. You should then have animation tracks similar to those shown in Figure 14.27.

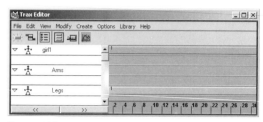

Figure 14.27

Leg and body walk cycle clips in the Trax Editor

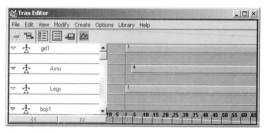

Figure 14.28

The arms clip moved back so it lags behind the leg and body motion

3. Now we need to create our arm animation. To make life easier (so the character doesn't walk away while you're animating the arms), disable the girl character clip by selecting the clip and, with the cursor over the clip, choosing Enable/Disable Clip.

4. Set the character to the arms subcharacter in the pop-up window, and then rotate the arms at frames 1, 12, and 24—24 being the same as frame 1—so that the arms move opposite to the legs (for example, when the right leg is forward, the right arm is back). We don't need to set keys at frames 6 or 18, because the motion of the arms is less complex than that of the legs.

5. In the Trax Editor, choose Create → Clip ❐, name and create the clip using the settings described in step 1, except for the Include Subcharacters In Clip option (arms has no subcharacter).

6. With the three clips now in the Trax Editor, reenable the girl clip (so she moves forward), and play the clips together. The first thing you will likely notice is that the arm swing is locked to the leg swing, making her walk look very mechanical. The arms should drag a bit behind the legs as the girl walks.

7. To correct the locked arm and leg swing problem, drag the arm clip back 3 to 4 frames behind the leg and body clips, as shown in Figure 14.28—a simple solution indeed!

8. If you now want to tweak the leg, body, and arm motions, you can graph the animation curves in the Graph Editor (in the Trax Editor, choose View → Graph Anim Curves) and adjust them so the feet stick to the ground as nearly as possible, as shown in Figure 14.29.

Creating the Walk Cycle

We now have one good step. To create a walk cycle, we need to repeat this motion. Fortunately, the Trax Editor makes this easy.

1. Double-click the girl clip in the Trax Editor to focus the Channel Box (or Attribute Editor) on this clip.

2. Set the Cycle channel to a number such as 3 instead of 1. Also, change the Offset setting to Relative instead of Absolute. (Otherwise, the girl will pop back to 0 between each step.)

3. For the legs and arms clips, set the cycle to be the same, but be sure the Offset is Absolute so that her feet and arms return to the same positions between steps.

The clips in the Trax Editor will update to show the cycle, and when you play back the animation, the girl will walk forward three complete steps.

You might notice that the girl's body gets ahead of (or behind) the leg motion as she walks or that the legs or arms don't return to exactly where they were. This is because of minor errors in how the character has been keyframed. Although these errors are too small to show up in one step cycle, they will appear as the cycles are added on top of each other.

To solve the problem of the body moving too far (or too little) for the legs, you can adjust the Weight setting of the body motion clip. By setting the weight a little greater (or less) than 1, you can adjust how far the body travels on each step, bringing the body back in line with the leg rotations.

To adjust problems with the legs and arms not returning to their rest positions, either change the Offset to Absolute (so the curves are forced to return to their exact starting values at the beginning of each cycle) or adjust the start and end keyframes for the rotations so they are exactly the same. Even small differences between start and end keyframes will add up over several cycles.

Blending the Clips

Once we have a walk we like, we can blend it with a standing clip to create a transition from walking to standing. First we need to create the standing clip.

1. Disable all the clips in the Trax Editor by RM choosing Enable/Disable Clip.

2. Open the Visor, find the standing pose you created earlier, and RM choose Apply Pose to the character.

Figure 14.29

Tweaked curves for the walk cycle

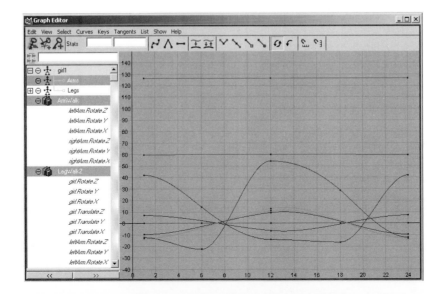

Figure 14.30

The Trax Editor showing a blend between walking and standing

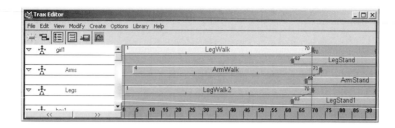

3. Key the values of the pose (be sure your character is set to girl), and then move forward some frames, apply the pose again, and key the values.

4. In the Trax Editor, choose Create → Clip ❑, give the clip a name (such as Standing), be sure that Include Subcharacters In Clip is selected, and create the new clip. Remember that clips of 0 duration (only one keyframe) are difficult to deal with. Even though both keyframes for the standing pose are the same, it is better to create two frames for the clip than just one.

5. Blend the walking and standing clips by Shift+selecting them and RM choosing Blend Clips to produce a transition between the walking and standing states for the girl, as shown in Figure 14.30 (see the "Blending Clips" section earlier in this chapter).

Sharing the Clips

As a last step, try creating a "boy" character, as shown in Figure 14.31. Then apply the walk cycle from the girl to the boy by using one of the methods described in the "Sharing Clips" section earlier in this chapter.

Figure 14.31

Creating a boy character

To make things a bit more challenging, make the boy taller than the girl, so that you need to reweight the body motion to get the body to travel correctly with the motion of the legs. (Since longer legs travel farther when they rotate the same amount, the body must move more on each step.)

A quick render of both characters' walk cycles is available on the CD-ROM as `14simpleWalk .mov`, and the project file is also available (`14simpleWalk`).

Making a More Complex Walk Cycle

To move from the simple walk cycle we created here to a more complex type is actually fairly simple (at least, once you have a nonslip foot setup working!). The only real adjustments that need to be made are as follows:

- The IK handles are manipulated for the legs (and often the arms as well). The legs sub-character should consist of the IK handles rather than the leg bones.

- Since IK handles are translated through space rather than rotated, set the legs (and arms) subcharacter so that it has only translate channels (not rotation ones, as in the hands-on example).

- Because the IK handles actually move though space rather than rotating, set the Offset for the legs (and arms) subcharacter to Relative, not Absolute. Otherwise, the charac-ter's legs will pop back to the origin at the start of every step.

Other than these adjustments, the method used in the hands-on exercise works quite well for realistic human walk cycles using nonslip foot techniques.

Hands On: Using Trax to Lip-Synch

One of the most complex and tedious tasks facing a character animator is the task of lip-synching. The repetitive nature of continually re-creating words for long-format animation is not a task for the faint of heart. Fortunately, Trax can greatly reduce the difficulty and tedium of creating lip-synching, while providing for a high degree of accuracy and flexibility. For our example, we will work with a cartoon character, but you can easily apply the same principles to the most realistic of 3D creatures.

We will not go through the steps to create eye clips and animation in this tutorial. However, the process for the other animation is the same as for lip-synching, and creating the animation with the included blend shapes is fairly straightforward.

At first, lip-synching will require lots of patience. You will find that it is really easy to over-work a word, causing the character's mouth to look as if it is moving out of control. Look in a mirror and say Tina's lines. (You'll find Tina's lines in a Tip later in this section.) Notice how little or how much your mouth moves as you speak. Do not set keys for every letter. Instead only set keyframes for the major sounds in a word. With these tips in mind, have fun lip-synching one of Tina's lines.

1. Open the 14Tina project on the CD-ROM (you can also follow along with a character of your own if you want). You will see a simple character (Tina) with an interesting hairdo, shown in Figure 14.32.

2. In your scene, import the 14TinaSound file from the CD into your project (choose File → Import). You might want to copy the sound file into your *<scene name>*/Sound folder first, which will significantly increase responsiveness.

3. To see the sound file in your scene, place your cursor over the Timeline and RM choose Sound → 14TinaSound. You will then see the sound's waveform in the Timeline.

4. To see the waveform of the sound better, you can increase the size of the Timeline. Choose Window → Settings/Preferences → Preferences, and then choose the Timeline category. You can set the Timeline to be default size (1x), twice normal size (2x), or four times normal size (4x).

5. To hear the sound file while in your Maya scene, scrub through the Timeline while holding down the middle mouse button. The faster you drag, the more quickly the sound plays back.

The actual line that "Tina" says is: "What I'm gonna do? I'm gonna rock your world's what I'm gonna do. I got some singing and some dancing and a little bit of hoochy koochy thrown in too—oooh!" This line is part of a longer animation created by a group of University of North Carolina at Asheville students. (Individual credits are given at the end of the 14Tina.mov file on the CD-ROM.)

Creating Tina

First, we need to create a character (Tina) and three subcharacters (left and right eyes and mouth). Then we will add the scene's previously created blend shapes to the subcharacters for eyes and mouth.

1. Select the Tina_Control node (select a body part and press the Up arrow key until you reach this node) and choose Character → Create Character Set ❒. Name the character Tina, allow scaling for the character (plus translate and rotate), and create the character.

2. With Tina set as the character, select nothing (you don't need to select any body parts here) and create subcharacters called REye_Tina, LEye_Tina, and Mouth_Tina.

3. To add blend shape elements for the mouth, set the mouth to be the active character using the Character pop-up menu, and then open the Blend Shape Editor by choosing Window → Animation Editors → Blend Shape. (For more information about blend shapes, see Chapter 11, "Deformers.")

4. In the Blend Shape Editor, find the Mouth_Tn blend shape node and click the Select button, as shown in Figure 14.33.

5. In the Channel Box, select all the Mouth_Tn attributes (starting with Envelope and ending with Tina_Closed), and then choose Character → Add To Character Set to add these attributes to the mouth subcharacter.

6. Repeat steps 3 through 5 for the left and right eyes. (Be sure to set LEye_Tina and REye_Tina to be the active character first.)

Creating the Word Clips

With the characters set up properly, it's time to start creating clips. Since Chapter 11 goes into detail about creating blend shapes, we'll cover just the process of converting them into clips here.

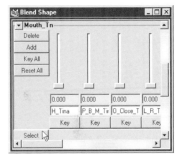

Figure 14.32

The Tina character

Figure 14.33

Selecting the Mouth blend shape node

1. Be sure that Mouth_Tina is the active character, and then create a series of about four keyframes that create the word *what*. We found that the O_Close, E, Ah, Smile, and Closed blend shapes created a decent *what* in four frames, but you may find using other shapes works better.

You don't need to worry about the length of a particular word, as long as each mouth shape is held for the correct relative length. (A long vowel sound might be several frames; most consonants are about one frame.) Since you can adjust the length and weight of the animation clip later, you don't need to match the words to actual sounds yet.

2. Once you have a word you like, open the Trax Editor and choose Create → Clip ❐. In the option box, reset the settings (choose Edit → Reset Settings), name the clip what, and create the clip. You will now have the clip for *what* in a track for the mouth subcharacter, as shown in Figure 14.34.

Figure 14.34

The clip for the word *what* in the Trax Editor

3. Move the word to about the start of the *what* sound in the Timeline (about frame 6 or 7), and scrub the animation (use the left mouse button in the Timeline, or hold down the K key and LM drag in the Trax Editor's Timeline). The scrub will play back fairly slowly, but you will be able to see the mouth update with the sounds as you scrub. You may find that you need to start the word earlier or shorten it some to fit the sound track, because the word is very short as spoken here.

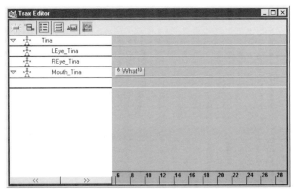

You can also use Playblast so you can hear and see the words as they are spoken. You may find, however, that the sound is not properly synchronized to the video track. (We're not sure why this problem exists, and it happens only on some computers.) If you do have this problem, the easiest way to view a quick render with sound is to hardware render the scene and then, in a compositing package (such as Shake, Fusion, AfterEffects, or even Quicktime Player Pro), add the sound file to the rendered image sequence. This method takes a few extra steps, but it guarantees proper alignment of sound and video, which is important here. See Chapter 16, "Rendering Basics," and Chapter 22, "Particle Rendering," for more information about hardware rendering.

4. When you are satisfied with your *what* animation, create clips for *I'm*, *gonna*, and *do*. Then scale and move them into proper position as well.

5. At this point—a space of about 10 frames without words—you might want to create a neutral mouth clip for the character—a state in which Tina's mouth rests when she's not speaking. We chose to create a mouth shape with lips slightly open and a medium-sized mouth width. (A completely closed mouth for such short pauses seemed to make the character's mouth work too hard.)

Remember to blend your clips (choose two clips, and then RM select Blend Clips with the cursor over one of the clips). This will create a natural motion from one word to the next. Also remember that you can adjust the curve of the blend by graphing the blend in the Graph Editor, as explained earlier in this chapter.

6. Now you can start to save time by using clips. Tina's next two words are *I'm gonna*, so you can just recycle those two word clips from before, placing them in the correct positions for the next words. You can copy and paste using any of the methods described earlier in this chapter, but the easiest way is to put the cursor over the clip, RM choose Copy, click in an empty area of the track, and RM choose Paste to paste the clip back in. You will likely find that you need to shorten the *gonna* word, because it's quicker the second time around (just click the top-right corner of the clip to interactively scale it, or use the Attribute Editor).

7. Continue creating and reusing word clips until you reach the end of the sound file.

Although it might take you a while to get really proficient, you should already see how rapidly you can create lip-synching using Trax. If you animate several minutes of dialogue, the time savings would become even greater. This is because the character would repeat many words, allowing you to store and reuse a library of word clips instead of needing to re-keyframe each word as it comes up. Additionally, because you can add keyframes on top of the basic mouth motion, you can layer expressions (smiles, frowns, and so on) layered on top of the speech. As you can see, using Trax is a rapid and flexible way to animate character speech!

If you want, you can look at a completed scene (with just mouth movement) by opening `14TinaAnimated` on the CD. You can also take a look at a completed render (including eye and body motion) by opening `14Tina.mov` on the CD.

One final step you can take when creating lip-synching is to transfer words from one character to another. You can create the blend shapes in the same order for another character; in other words, if Tina's mouth shapes are ordered as H, P_B_M, O_Close, and so on, you can create Joe's blends in the same order. Then you can reference the Tina file (or export the clips, as explained earlier in this chapter), copy source clips from the Visor, and paste them into the new character's mouth subcharacter using the Paste By Attribute Order option. Thus, you can share libraries of words from one character to another, with obviously huge time savings. Additionally, if each characters' blend shapes are slightly different looking (the smile blend, for example, being a sneer for an evil character), the words will look different for each character, because the Trax clips alter only the weights of the blend shapes, not what they look like.

Summary

Nonlinear animation has been an increasingly popular area of 3D animation over the past several years, and Maya's Trax Editor is one of the best, most robust NLAs (nonlinear animators) on the market. Using the Trax Editor, you can quickly produce animation from simple characters moving in simple ways to complex characters walking and talking. If you find yourself spending a great deal of time doing a repetitive animating task, ask yourself, "How can I use the Trax Editor get this done?" You will be surprised at how the Trax Editor can save you hours of time!

By creating and reusing poses and clips, you can save a great deal of time in animating repetitive tasks. By blending clips, different animation states can fuse into one another, reducing the need for complex transition keyframes. With motion warping, keyframes can be added on top of existing clips for final tweaks or to create individual motion for part of a character's animation. Finally, by sharing clips and poses between characters and scenes, you can leverage all the work done for one character or one scene for use in other scenes and projects. Maya's nonlinear animation is so powerful that once you begin using it, it's difficult to imagine complex character animation without Trax!

In the next chapter, we'll explore how to work with rigid body dynamics to produce simulated animation.

GALLERY

Maya 4.5 Color Gallery

This full-color section showcases some of the end results of projects in the book, as well as some spectacular uses of Maya in projects outside of this book. In these next few pages, you will find creations to inspire you to tackle your own worlds in Maya.

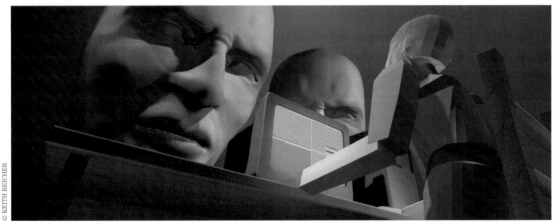

ABOVE: These mushrooms are in the process of auditioning for parts in a fictional TV show. The characters are both made with NURBS surfaces, and their movements are controlled by expressions and set-driven keys. The most difficult part of creating these characters was developing a way to attach the eyes to the body in such a way that body deformations did not deform the eyes. With high-level controls on the characters, and using the Trax Editor, the animation process is greatly simplified. **BELOW:** This is a scene from the CG animated short "Benjamin Task," created in Maya by Keith Reicher. The two heads in the animation were created using NURBS patches and the Stitch tool. For the facial animation, sixteen separate heads were modeled, each with a different facial expression, then combined using blendshaping. The lip synch was accomplished the same way by shaping several mouth phonemes for speech.

MODEL BY PETER LEE AND HAE YOUNG MOON, TRACKING BY KYOUNG SOO KIM. © STORYDALE INC.

The CG elements of Alexandria Kim—a historical figure at the turn of the century in provincial Russia, and subject of an hour-long Korean Broadcasting System documentary—were tracked and composited into footages recorded on a digital camcorder. The realistic face was sculpted using Maya's subdivision surfaces. For the shot inside the train, a whole CG body was created and composited into the scene, and Maya fur was essential in creating believable fur on the coat and the hat.

REBECCA JOHNSON, DEBORAH WRIGHT, AND UMA HAVALIGI

Bright Idea tells the story of the creative yet futile attempts of Blinky the lighting bug, trying to escape. He is trapped in a jar in a child's room, but he must also overcome bigger obstacles. The use of ray-tracing was advantageous to the reflections and refractions of the glass jar. Many of Maya's capabilities were used, including particles, dynamics, cloth simulation, and kinematics.

UMA HAVALIGI, REBECCA JOHNSON, DEBORAH WRIGHT

This scene of a kid's room, for an animation titled "SOS," was modeled mainly with NURBS surfaces; by deforming vertices, revolving curves and trimming. Maya's cloth was used to make the realistic looking bedspread. The use of ray-tracing was advantageous to the reflections and refractions of the glass jar. Glass shader, wood texture, and a lot of file textures helped create this happy cozy starry kid's room.

PS2 game cinematic work done for Joycast, Korea. The explosions include live footage and particles generated in Maya. Small debris was animated using dynamics.

PS2 game cinematic work done for Joycast, Korea. The character setup includes a combination of simple parenting to the bones and skinning polygon meshes, which in turn drive their smoother counterpart subdivision surfaces.

PETER LEE

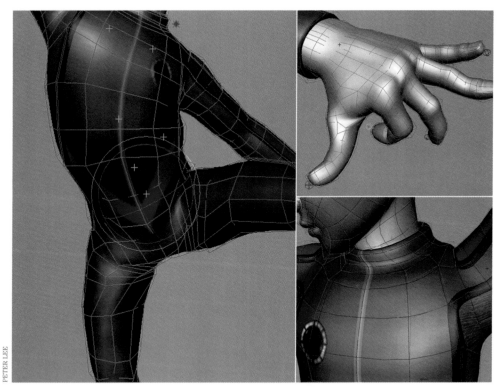

PETER LEE

ABOVE: A character node collects all of the disparate elements from a character's setup, eliminates the need to deal with a large number of controls, and frees the animator to forget about nodes and just animate. When you keyframe all of the attributes in the character node, it freezes the character into a pose, and thus encourages a "pose-to-pose" approach to animation, as shown here. **BELOW:** Surface areas such as the fingers, neck, knee, and head are fairly easy to weight. But certain parts are much harder to deform properly, such as the thumb and palm area, the shoulders, and the legs. Keep your goal weights for the character's movements, and try to reach for those specific movements as you are weighting the different sections of the character. Keyframe as many different movements as you can.

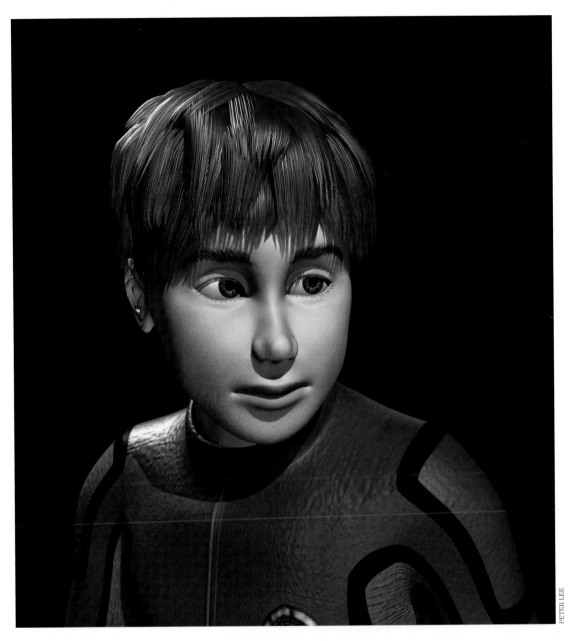

The finished character begun in Chapter 5 and completed in Chapter 17. He was raytraced to create the proper shadows for hair. File images used for color, bump, and specular maps were created using Deep Paint 3D. Texture maps for the body were created by Hae Young Moon at Storydale. The textured, constrained, and weighted model is also included in the Chapter 17 folder on the CD-ROM.

ABOVE: A still frame from the rocket model and animation project in Chapter 2, this shot shows how effective even a simple project can be. By building simple model parts, using some keyframed and some rigid body animation, and the addition of lights, textures, and glowing particles, we've made the cartoon-style rocket appear to leap off the pad for parts unknown. **BELOW:** The finished version of the dog begun in Chapter 8 and completed in Chapter 17. This simple puppy was built from NURBS patches, which were assembled using the Stitch tools and bound with Smooth Bind. The textured, constrained, and weighted model is also included in the Chapter 17 folder on the CD-ROM.

The shadows were positioned to create the impression of a sunset. The brick texture was retouched in Photoshop to make the bricks look more random.

Icewalker Penguin Extraordinaire is a super-hot penguin who catches all of the lady penguins' attention. Yet his narcissistic nature leads to his downfall and provokes the struggle for the Icewalker title. Will the new Icewalker succumb to the same mistake? Icewalker is a deceptively simple character created using NURBS. The stylized sunglasses, bright colors used for the body, and crazy hair are the secret to the character's appeal.

The scene was created using a combination of scripts, which enhance Maya's Paint Effects, in order to cover three dimensional objects with paint strokes to create an impressionistic animation.

Tury is one of the characters for a TV series concept called "Hello Asia," an educational show about Asian history and culture. NURBS surfaces' unique properties were used to create eyelashes, which were procedurally connected to the eyelids, and the eye groups were created separately from the face for easy cartoony scaling. An anisotropic shader was used to create the silky look of the hair.

DANIEL WILLIAMS

For the last six years, Daniel Williams has been a modeler at Blue Sky Studios in New York. To branch out and broaden his skill set to include character setup, animation, lighting, and texture work, he created a couple of "test" characters and began to try to learn as much as he could about those subjects. Eventually, he created Junker, using Maya and Adobe Photoshop (for the texture maps). These images were rendered using Maya's default renderer and Mark Davies' wonderful Ray Diffuse plug-in. Williams hopes to continue to utilize Junker as a learning tool and as a stepping stone toward his next animated creation.

"The Phantom Weapon" will hopefully be one of those fun little projects that make people laugh and send on the URL (blueyonderpictures.com) to their friends. With apologies and thanks to George Lucas, of course. The project started as an original idea by Marc Elmer, who plays the Jedi. The story surrounds the efforts of a Jedi weapons specialist to build and test the very first light saber, with comedically horrific results. The light saber is a simple cylinder model in Maya, attached to an IK chain on a NURBS soft body controller. A goal object was used to keep the elasticity of the saber in check, and the whole rig was tracked in Maya to the background plate of the Jedi. A simple shader glow was added to make the saber seem like a light beam, particles where added to create sparks and the whole kit and kaboodle was composited, re-tracked, and color tweaked in Adobe After Effects with some patience and a bit of sweat.

CHAPTER 15

Working with Rigid Body Dynamics

In this chapter, you will learn what rigid bodies are, when they can be useful, and how to apply rigid bodies in several situations in which keyframing would either take too long or would not look realistic enough. Topics include:

- What are rigid body dynamics?

- Creating a simple rigid body

- Converting a body from passive to active mode

- Using fields to add effects to rigid bodies

- Using the Rigid Body Solver

- Working with fields

- Using impulse and a Newton field to simulate orbital dynamics

- Converting (baking) a rigid body animation into keyframes

- Working with the Dynamics Simulator

- Adding constraints to a rigid body

What Are Rigid Body Dynamics?

If you've done any animation (either computer or traditional), you're familiar with the concept of keyframes, introduced in Chapter 9, "Animating in Maya." Rigid body animation, on the other hand, is essentially a physics simulator built into Maya that tries to mimic (or exaggerate, if you want) what happens to real-world objects as they move under the influence of forces (such as gravity or wind) and collide with other objects. If you've ever tried to keyframe even the simple motion of a ball bouncing on the ground, you know how difficult it is to make a keyframed animation work in this type of situation. If you try something more difficult, such as bouncing a cube off a wall, it can get really frustrating trying to make the collisions look realistic.

Fortunately, Maya has the answer for you: *rigid body dynamics* (often simply called *rigid bodies*). Using rigid bodies is straightforward: you create one or more rigid bodies; create one or more fields that influence them (if you wish); give the rigid bodies an initial position, velocity, and impulse (if you wish); and play back the animation. Maya's *dynamics engine* does all the calculations to make the body behave realistically, based on your initial information; you don't need a degree in physics, just a bit of practice with the settings.

Maya also uses its dynamics engine to create particle effects. See Chapters 21 through 24 to find out how Maya works with particle dynamics.

Rigid bodies come in two flavors: passive and active. Passive rigid bodies are *not* affected by fields and cannot be moved by collisions, though they can take part in collisions. Passive rigid bodies can be keyframed (so you can move them around). Active rigid bodies *are* affected by fields and will be moved by collisions. They cannot be keyframed (so you can't move them around on your own).

Generally, a passive rigid body is a floor, a wall, or some other object that is fixed to the world; an active rigid body is any kind of falling, moving, or colliding object (a basketball or a coin, for example). Although it would seem a great disadvantage that active rigid bodies cannot be keyframed, you can convert rigid bodies from passive to active at any time in an animation, allowing a rigid body to be passive for a time and then to become active. (We'll try an example of this shortly.)

Let's begin with a simple example to see how rigid bodies work.

Creating a Simple Rigid Body

In this example you'll create a simple rigid body—a bouncing ball—and experiment with a few settings that will affect the motion of the ball.

Start by creating a new scene in Maya. Create a NURBS plane and scale it out to about the size of the Maya grid. Now make a NURBS sphere with a radius of 1 and move it above the plane. Your scene should look like Figure 15.1.

Now select the plane and choose Soft/Rigid Bodies → Create Passive Rigid Body from the Dynamics menu set. The plane is now a passive rigid body.

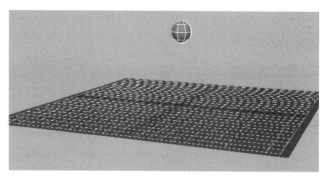

Figure 15.1

A sphere placed above a plane

Next, select the sphere and choose Soft/ Rigid Bodies → Create Active Rigid Body from the Dynamics menu set. The sphere is now an active rigid body.

To allow dynamics simulations to play back properly, the playback rate has to be set to Play Every Frame so that the physics engine can calculate what it needs before going on to the next frame. Either choose Window → Settings/Preferences → Preferences and choose Settings/Timeline or click the Animation Preferences button at the lower right of the screen to display the same window.

In the Animation Preferences window, choose Playback Speed: Play Every Frame from the Playback area.

Close the window, rewind the animation, and play it back.

Nothing interesting happened, right? Even though you have made two rigid bodies, you have not created any animation yet, because you have not added any fields (forces) or initial motion. For a dynamics simulation to work properly, you need to have either fields affecting one of the rigid bodies (a.k.a. rigids) or an initial motion set on one or more of them to give the object(s) movement. Let's create a gravity field to make things a bit more interesting.

THE IMPORTANCE OF REWINDING

You must rewind any animation that contains dynamics—otherwise, the animation will not play back properly. You also cannot "scrub" through an animation by sliding the time marker back and forth. All dynamics data is calculated frame by frame, so if any frame is skipped, the calculations break down and the animation goes berserk. If this happens, just rewind the animation and start over—all will be well again. To rewind, click the Back button on the playback controller (located in the lower-right corner of the screen, it looks like a VCR control). To play the animation, click the Play Forwards button on the playback controller. You will not be able to play back the simulation in reverse.

From the Dynamics menu, choose Fields → Gravity. Now open the Dynamic Relationships window shown in Figure 15.2 (choose Window → Relationship Editors → Dynamic Relationships), choose the nurbSphere1 name in the Outliner on the left side of the window, and

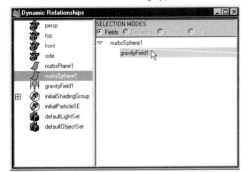

make sure gravityField1 is highlighted in the selection window on the right. If it's not, be sure to click gravityField1 to highlight it.

If you select the sphere and then click to create the gravity field, the two will automatically be connected. (If there are other active rigid bodies that you haven't selected, they will be unaffected by this force.) In addition, you can create an active rigid body by selecting the geometry you want to make into an active rigid and just create a field object. This converts the selected object to an active rigid and automatically attaches it to the field.

Figure 15.2

Highlight gravity for nurbSphere

Now rewind and play back the animation. You should see the ball fall toward the plane and bounce off it. If the animation is cut off too quickly to see this, increase the number of frames in the animation to 200 or more (type **200** in the text field to the right of the Time Slider).

Now let's examine the rigid body settings for our objects. In the Channel Box, you'll see rigidBody1 (or 2, or whatever) listed under the shape node for the object you select. For now, select the plane and then click the rigidBody1 text to expand the Channel Box attributes for the rigid body. You might want to expand the viewable area of the Channel Box by turning off the Layer Editor with the Show Channel Box icon seen in Figure 15.3.

Several text fields will pop up, giving you more control over the rigid body than you probably want. For now, just look down to these items: mass, bounciness, damping, static friction, and dynamic friction. Change the bounciness to 0.9 and replay the animation (remember to rewind first!). On the first bounce, the ball should bounce nearly as high as the height from which it was dropped, and it should take longer to settle to rest as the animation plays. Now try setting the bounciness to 2. What happens? The ball bounces farther up each time, soon disappearing from view—talk about a superball! In our virtual world, not only do we get to simulate reality, we get to break the rules if we want.

Figure 15.3

The Show Channel Box icon hides the Layer Editor and shows only the Channel Box to increase its viewable area.

The mass, bounciness, damping, static friction, and dynamic friction channels all contribute to how the ball reacts when it collides with the ground plane. Try playing with some of these settings, such as friction and damping—for both the ball and the plane to see how the bouncing of the ball changes. However, keep in mind that mass is a relative attribute—relative to other objects in the simulation. Since a passive rigid body essentially has an infinite mass, the mass setting won't matter for the plane or the ball colliding with it. Also, changing the mass of the ball won't make much difference because gravity is a universal force and it affects all active objects in the same way. Later, you'll see where mass can be used more effectively.

An idea to remember in dynamics work is that playing with the numbers is a great way to learn how rigid bodies work. Don't be afraid to try different settings for each of the channels of each rigid body—try to guess what your changes will do before playing back the animation and then take a few notes on how the behavior of the simulation changes with each change when you do play it back.

Catapult! Converting a Body from Passive to Active Mode

Now let's create a catapult and see how easy it is to turn the active key on and off for a rigid body. Again, start with a new scene. Create a NURBS plane scaled to about the grid size. Now create a cylinder, rotate it so it lies along the X axis, and squash it nearly flat. Position it to the edge of the grid, and zero the cylinder's attributes by choosing Modify→ Freeze Trans-formations. Freezing the transformations is generally a good idea when dealing with dynam-ics, because it zeros out the transform attributes of your rigid bodies, making them "cleaner" for Maya to deal with.

> "Zeroing" the transforms of an object resets all the values of that object's transformation attributes (move, rotate, and scale) without moving the object. This will effectually reset the object to seem as if it were created at its current position as opposed to the origin (or other point). Some Maya functions, particularly when dealing with history, respond much better when the object to be affected is first "zeroed."

Your scene should look like Figure 15.4. With the cylinder selected, press Ctrl+G to group the cylinder to itself. If you don't take this step, you may end up with strange behavior later. You'll eventually group a ball under this newly created parent node as well and use the par-ent node to animate the rotation of the cylinder and ball together, but hold on for now— we're getting there.

Now move the insert point of the new group from the origin all the way to the right end of the cylinder. To move the insert point, select the Move tool, press the Insert key on your keyboard (which will change the Move tool's handle from one with arrows to one without), and move the new handle around. Don't forget to press the Insert key again when you're done, or you'll stay in insert mode!

Once you have this set up correctly, add a sphere of radius 1 and place it on top of the left end of the cylinder, as in Figure 15.5.

In the Hypergraph or Outliner, MM drag the sphere onto the cylinder's parent group (probably called group1). This will make the sphere a "child" of the catapult's parent group, making it a sibling of the cylinder itself. This will make the ball rotate together with the cylinder.

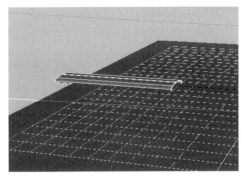

Figure 15.4

A plane with a squashed cylinder

Figure 15.5

A sphere added to the flattened cylinder

Now set a keyframe at your first frame on the parent node's rotation channels (select the rotation channels and RM choose Key Selected, or press Shift+E), move the Time Slider to about 15 frames, rotate the top node of the cylinder so it is close to upright, as in Figure 15.6, and keyframe this new setting. Make sure the parent node is selected and not just the cylinder when you keyframe the rotation so that the sphere will rotate with it. Also, remember that setting the Auto Keyframe button to On will make Maya automatically set a new keyframe whenever some channel changes—after you first manually set the first keyframe for that channel. This may save you some time in setting keyframes every time you make a change.

Next, go back to frame 1, select just the sphere, and make it into a passive rigid body by choosing Soft/Rigid Bodies → Create Passive Rigid Body.

Be careful here. Creating the rigid bodies *before* you group the sphere under the catapult might cause undesirable results. Rigid bodies can act strangely when they are grouped into hierarchies. Furthermore, it is highly inadvisable to group more than one rigid body into the same group. As a general rule of thumb, make sure that only the top node of an object is a rigid body, active or passive.

Figure 15.6

The cylinder moved into an upright position

Play back the animation. You should see the cylinder (and its attendant ball) rotate up in a few frames and then stay still.

Now let's shove this ball up and let it fly! Select the ball object. Go to frame 12 or so and set a passive key for the ball by choosing Soft/Rigid Bodies → Set Passive Key. This sets a keyframe of "off" for the Active attribute of the ball's rigidBody node, keeping it as a passive rigid body. Go forward a frame and set an active key for the ball by choosing Soft/Rigid Bodies → Set Active Key. This keyframe sets the Active attribute of the ball to "on," switching the ball from a passive rigid body to an active rigid body at that frame. This allows the ball to fly off the cylinder and become dynamic.

You can manually turn the Active attribute on and off through the Active attribute itself. Select the rigid body object, and in the Channel Box, toward the bottom of the rigidBody channels, is the Active channel. To change the body to an active rigid, type **on** or the number **1** to turn the object from a passive rigid body to an active rigid body and keyframe it. To toggle it back to passive, type **off** or the number **0** in the Active channel and set a keyframe. Although this method can work at times, A|W advises us to use the Set Active Key and Set Passive Key commands found in the Soft/Rigid Bodies menu instead.

What you have done here is to force the sphere to become an active rigid body *just as the sphere is being pitched up in the air by the cylinder*. This timing allows us to take advantage of some clever programming by the Maya developers: the sphere will "inherit" speed and rotation from the movement of the cylinder, and so it will fly away from the cylinder the moment it becomes an active rigid body.

To test this, rewind and play back the animation. The sphere should go flying off to infinity. Of course, to finish this simulation correctly, we need to add gravity. Select the sphere and then choose Fields → Gravity (the gravity will automatically connect to the sphere). Now play back the animation. The ball should (depending on how fast your cylinder rotates) either shoot or "plop" off the cylinder. If the ball flies off the catapult too slowly, try rotating the cylinder farther at its last keyframe, or shorten the number of frames over which it rotates up. If the ball flies off too quickly, rotate the cylinder less at the last keyframe, or increase the number of frames over which it rotates up.

We've already played with the numbers on the rigid bodies themselves in the last example. This time, let's play with the gravity field's attributes. In the Outliner or Hypergraph, select the gravity node you just created. In the Channel Box, you'll see several settings for gravity, including Direction and Magnitude. Direction defaults to –1 in Y, or down. Since gravity in the real world pulls down, it becomes a negative value in the vertical axis. Magnitude defaults to 9.8 (that's 9.8 meters—or 32 feet—per second squared, the force of earth's gravity). Let's make things a bit heavier. Try setting gravity to, say, 200 or so. Now, when the ball comes off the cylinder, it should drop like a *very* heavy stone. Or try a value of 2—now we're on the moon and it flies off the screen!

As you can see in this simple scene, rigid body dynamics is a balancing act of setting numerous attribute values. Adjusting certain settings on one rigid body, such as the ball in this scene, might get you similar results as adjusting attributes of a field, such as gravity. This balancing act of attribute settings can become a convoluted process at times, but with patience and some careful note taking, the process becomes easier to handle. Playing with the numbers over and over again is a great way to familiarize yourself with how dynamics works; you'll begin to see the forest through the trees.

Now, even though the geometry in this scene is simple, the results are not: this same trick can be used as a character throws a ball at a can or bottle, creating a nice mix of keyframed character animation and realistic physics.

Using Fields to Add Effects to Rigid Bodies

After you play with the gravity settings for a while, find a value for gravity that will give the ball a good long flight time—75 or so—because now we're going to add another field to affect the ball's flight.

Let's add some turbulence. Select the sphere and choose Fields → Turbulence. Play back the animation. With the default magnitude of 5, the effects on the motion of the sphere will be very subtle. If you set the turbulence field's magnitude to 50, or even 500 or more, and turn the Attenuation down to about 0.1 or 0, you will see the sphere move about in random ways as the turbulence field affects its motion. Try different numbers for the channels of the turbulence field and see what results. With rigid bodies, fields, and particle dynamics, it is a good idea to take a simple animation and experiment with what each channel does by changing the numbers and watching the results in the animation. It is only by this kind of experimentation that you can see how Maya's physics engine really works.

You've seen how different fields can change a rather humdrum animation into something more interesting. Now let's make the simulation engine work a bit harder by creating more complex shapes.

Using the Rigid Body Solver

When you work with more complex shapes, you may find that Maya's default settings don't provide the speed or accuracy that you are looking for in your rigid body simulation. For such occasions, Maya allows you to adjust how it calculates rigid body simulations by using the Solvers → Rigid Body Solvers pane. With the *Rigid Body Solver* you can adjust how Maya calculates the simulation, giving you the ability to fine-tune your simulation for speed or accuracy.

Figure 15.7

An angular shape, which will behave differently than a perfect sphere

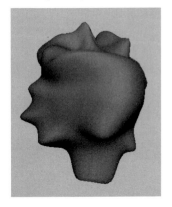

Let's look at the solver in action. Create another empty scene, add a plane and a sphere (at some height above the plane), and make the plane a passive rigid body. Select the sphere, and choose Fields → Gravity to automatically create an active rigid body out of the sphere and attach it to the gravity.

Now let's make the shape a bit more complex. First, increase the U and V isoparms to 16 or more each (on the makeNurbSphere1 node). Then take the sphere and mold it into some bizarre, angular shape, something like Figure 15.7.

You can create this shape quite easily using Maya's Artisan utility (choose Edit Nurbs → Sculpt Surfaces Tool ❒), as discussed in Chapter 7, "Working with Artisan." Or you can just pull individual CVs out of the sphere.

When you play back the animation this time, Maya will probably go just a bit slower—this time, it has to keep track of a lot more surfaces! If you play back the frames one at a time (and look under the plane), you'll probably also be able to see a few points where some of the sphere's surfaces poke through the plane.

At full-speed playback, you probably won't notice these errors, but at times you might want to correct problems like this—or perhaps speed up playback for a particularly complex simulation. In these situations, you can use the Rigid Body Solver menu to adjust how Maya calculates its rigid body simulations. Essentially, the Rigid Body Solver gives you some control over the way Maya's dynamics engine handles the mathematics involved in the movement and interaction of rigid bodies. As you've just seen, complex shapes interact in complex ways, and adjusting calculation options via the solver is useful when the result of using Maya's default settings isn't accurate enough or fast enough to look realistic.

You can get access to the Rigid Body Solver in one of two ways: either choose Solvers → Rigid Body Solvers, or select a rigid body, open the Attribute Editor (Ctrl+A), and select the Rigid Solver tab. Either way, you'll see the window shown in Figure 15.8, which allows you to adjust the solver to meet your needs.

Notice the Rigid Solver States and the Rigid Solver Display Options sections of the window. Here you can turn most major functions on and off. As an example, turn on the Display Velocity check box and play back the animation. You will see an arrow that points in the direction of the sphere's velocity; its length represents the speed of the sphere. If you clear the State check box, the animation will do nothing, because clearing this check box turns off the solver. (This is a good way to quickly eliminate dynamics so that you can concentrate on other elements of an animation.) If you clear the Contact Motion check box, the sphere will fall, but it will no longer bounce, because dynamic interactions no longer work. Try clearing each of the check boxes in turn and see what effect this has on playback. When you're finished, reset the check boxes to their default state.

The Rigid Solver Methods section of the window offers three choices, though normally you will use the default method, Runge Kutta Adaptive. If you have a complex simulation, however, and either want to view it more quickly in interactive playback or don't care about the accuracy of the simulation for your final rendering, you

Figure 15.8

The Rigid Body Solver window

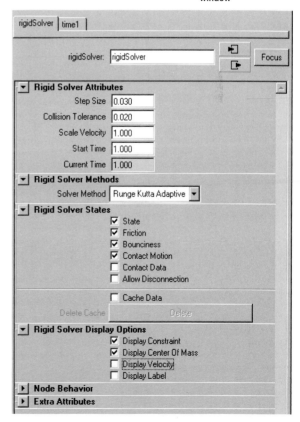

can (temporarily) set the method to either Runge Kutta or to Midpoint. Midpoint is the least accurate but fastest. Runge Kutta is a compromise between the two extremes. For your dented ball, you probably won't see much difference between the three methods.

> The Runge Kutta and Runge Kutta Adaptive options are named for the Runge Kutta solution, a mathematical method for solving an interlocking system of differential equations using first-order derivatives. In Maya, time is broken into discrete steps (referenced through the Step Size field), and the integral of the equations is approximated at each step. Though the technique is mathematically complex, it is fast and accurate enough for most applications.

The top—and most useful—section is labeled Rigid Solver Attributes. Using the Step Size, Collision Tolerance, Scale Velocity, and Start Time fields, you can alter the way in which the solver simulates rigid body dynamics. Let's look at each option:

Start Time Using the **Start Time** box, you can alter when the Rigid Body Solver begins to function (for example, if you set the Start Time to 50, the Rigid Body Solver will not start working until frame 50).

Scale Velocity is useful only if you have checked the Display Velocity check box in the Rigid Solver Display Options section—the Scale Velocity slider lets you scale the arrow that sticks out from the rigid body, making it fit within your window.

Step Size defines the "chunk" of time (measured in fractions of a second) into which the solver divides the Timeline. A smaller step size means more calculations per second of animation, but it can also mean a more accurate simulation. If you have trouble with rigid body *interpenetration errors* (meaning that two bodies have "pierced" each other, as in our example), reducing the step size is a good place to start.

Collision Tolerance tells Maya how carefully to evaluate frames where collisions take place. A large collision tolerance will speed up playback but can become very inaccurate.

Try making the collision tolerance 0.8 and playing back your animation. You will notice that the sphere doesn't bounce correctly on the plane. Now set the tolerance to 0.001 (the smallest possible value). If you saw points at which the sphere's points stuck through the plane before, they should no longer appear (or at worst should poke through only a little bit).

Experiment with different step sizes and collision tolerances, and see how the changes affect the simulation. Often you can get away with making either the step size or the collision tolerance very large, as long as you keep the other element small. Finding a compromise between speed and accuracy for a complex simulation is often the key to using rigid body dynamics effectively.

Speeding Up Calculations with Additional Solvers

Each additional object a rigid solver has to keep track of can geometrically increase the calculation time. To compensate for this, you can speed up calculations by isolating different
parts of a simulation from one another and assigning additional solvers to each part.

Let's see how this works, by making some changes in the deformed sphere scene you created in the previous example. (If you no longer have that scene, just create a ball and a
plane, make the ball an active rigid body and the plane a passive rigid body, and then create
gravity. Play back the animation to be sure the ball bounces off the plane.)

Now we're going to create a second Rigid Body Solver and assign the ball to it. Choose
Solvers → Create Rigid Body Solver to create a new solver, which will be called rigidSolver1
(or 2 or 3, depending on how many others you have created).

Now set the new solver as the default (so that all new objects will be assigned to this
solver): choose Solvers → Current Rigid Solver → Solver*X*, where Solver*X* is the solver you
want to establish as the default. Since we have already created both of our rigid bodies using
the same solver, we need to assign one of the two bodies (the ball) to the new solver—rigid-
Solver1. Unfortunately, there is no button to do this, but you can do it with a quick bit of
MEL (Maya Embedded Language) scripting.

In the scene window, select the sphere and then, in the Command line (accessed by
pressing the apostrophe key while you're in a scene window), type the following:

```
rigidBody -edit -solver rigidSolver1;
```

This command tells Maya to edit the rigid solver for whatever objects are selected in the scene.

For more on MEL scripting, see Chapter 20, "MEL."

Now play back the animation again. This time, the ball should pass right through the
plane. Although the plane and ball are both still affected by gravity, they no longer interact
with each other, because they "live" in different solver states.

If you want to edit the settings of your new rigid solver, be sure it is selected (choose
Solvers → Current Rigid Solver), and then choose Solvers → Rigid Body Solver. This opens the
Attribute Editor with the rigidSolver1 selected.

Finally, with rigidSolver1 selected, you can create a new plane (or other object), make it a
passive rigid body, and play back the animation. Because both the ball and the new plane
share the same solver, they will collide properly.

Speeding Up Calculations by Controlling Collisions

Keeping separate rigid body objects on different solvers can be an important workflow efficiency. Particularly in scenes with multiple dynamic rigid bodies that need to behave differently from one another, multiple solvers affords you better interactivity in the scene.

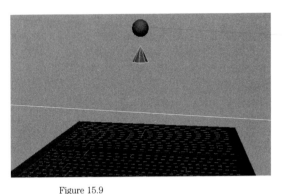

Figure 15.9

The cone below the ball

Furthermore, you can manage the collisions on rigid bodies on an individual object basis as well, for an even finer degree of control. By toggling the collision attribute (found toward the bottom of the Channel Box for the rigidBody node of the object) on or off for a rigid body, you can control whether that object collides with all other rigid body objects in the scene. This attribute controls only *all* the collisions of that object.

For more detailed control, Maya allows you to toggle the collisions between only two or more objects, as opposed to turning on or off all the object's collisions.

In a new scene, create a ball and ground plane, make the ball an active rigid body and the plane a passive rigid body, and then create gravity to attach to the ball to make it bounce off the plane. Check the playback to make sure the ball bounces off the plane properly.

Now add a NURBS cone to the scene and place it above the ground plane and one or two units directly under the ball. To make this cone an active rigid body and attach it to the existing gravity, all you need to do is pop open the Dynamic Relationships window by choosing Window → Relationship Editors → Dynamic Relationships, and connect the cone to the existing gravity. Maya will automatically create an active rigid body out of the cone and attach it to the gravity. Your scene should look like Figure 15.9.

Play back the simulation, and you'll see both the ball and cone fall to the plane. The ball will hit the cone, bounce off its tip, and push it to the side on its way back down. Now let's try to get rid of the collisions between the ball and the cone. But if we were to turn off collisions on the cone through its Collisions attribute, the cone would not collide with the ball, but it would also not collide with the ground and fly right through the plane. If you turned off collisions on the cone through the Collisions attribute, turn them back on.

Instead, select both the cone and the ball, and choose Solvers → Set Rigid Body Interpenetration. Play back the simulation, and you'll see that the ball and cone will both bounce off the plane, but not off each other. To turn the collisions between the ball and cone back on, select them both, and choose Solvers → Set Rigid Body Collision.

These commands will not toggle the individual Collisions attributes of the ball or cone.

In addition to the collision controls under the Solver menu, each rigid body object has an attribute called Collision Layer. This attribute separates object collisions in a scene so that not all objects in the scene have to collide. You can assign different layers of object collisions to speed up calculations, simplify animation, achieve particular effects, and so on.

Let's create an example in which only objects of the same color collide inside a box. Start a new scene, create a NURBS cube, and scale it to the size of the grid. Then scale it down in height and delete the top face of the cube to form a short open-top box.

Next, create 4 NURBS spheres and 4 polygonal cubes (polygonal cubes are easier to select than NURBS cubes and will be easier to work with here). Scale the cubes up to match the size of the spheres. Using simple Lambert shaders in the Hypershade or Multilister, color one of each of the spheres and cubes red, green, blue, and black, and place them inside the box, a quarter unit or so above the bottom of the box as shown in Figure 15.10.

Grab the planes that make up your box and press Ctrl+G to group them together. With that parent node of the box selected, turn the box into a passive rigid body. Make sure you make the parent node the rigid body and not the individual planes that make up the box. Next, grab all the cubes and balls and choose Fields → Gravity. This will make active rigid bodies out of the selected objects and attach them to the gravity field. Play back the simulation. You should see the objects bounce into the box.

Here's the fun part. Select all the cubes and balls again, and create a radial field. Set the magnitude of the radial field to –1.0. A radial field forces objects away from itself in a radial pattern. With a negative magnitude, it will pull objects toward itself. Play back the simulation, and you'll see the objects all head into the center of the box and bounce off one another.

Now, to make only similar colored objects collide, let's set Collision Layers. Grab both red objects, and on their Collision Layer channel—about three-quarters of the way down the Channel Box—set the number 1. Set a number 2 for the blue, number 3 for green, and number 4 for the black objects. When you play back the simulation, all the objects will fly into the center of the box, but will pass through it entirely. We need collisions with the inside of the box as well.

The objects pass right through the box because we have the box still set to its default Collision Layer of 0. Select the box, and set its Collision Layer channel to –1. This will make the box collide with everything, regardless of their Collision Layers.

Play back the animation, and you should see the balls bouncing off the bottom of the box as they head toward the center. The same color objects will now collide only with each other and pass right through the other objects.

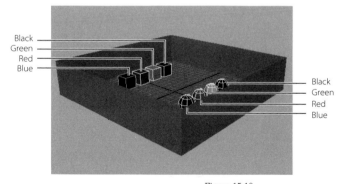

Figure 15.10

Place the colored objects inside the box.

Working with Fields

Once you create an active rigid body, you can control its movement in a few ways. One direct method is to set values for its impulse and initial velocity and spin attributes. You can also control it secondarily through collisions with other active or passive rigid bodies. Fields are another secondary way of affecting the movement of active rigid bodies, and they work by exerting a specific force on the active rigid.

For example, if a shot calls for particles of dust to blow around in a scene, you can use an air force to create a dynamic simulation to blow Maya particles around the scene. Fields are useful over the other methods of particle control in that they closely resemble forces in nature that affect the movement of objects in real life. To that end, they become more intuitive to use with particles.

All fields have the same primary attributes used to control them: Magnitude, Attenuation, Use Max Distance, Max Distance, and Volume Shape. The Magnitude attribute governs the strength of force applied from the field to the object(s), and Attenuation is the amount the strength of the field diminishes as the distance between the field and object increases.

Magnitude and Attenuation essentially govern how much the field affects the active rigid body object. The Use Max Distance, Max Distance, and Volume Shape attributes, however, directly affect the maximum area of influence the field has. These attributes allow dynamic changes in specific regions of the 3D space.

With Use Max Distance turned on, the Max Distance attribute dictates how close the object needs to be to the field for the field to have any influence. Objects beyond the Max Distance value from the field's location will not be affected at all.

An easier way to govern the region of influence on a field is to use Volume Shape to define a specific volume for the field. Dynamic objects in that volume are affected by the field's force. Volume Shape gives you a visual representation of the region of influence and is transformable as any object in Maya. Actually seeing the volume of influence of a field is much more interactive than using only the Max Distance to define its extents. With Volume Shape, you can see the particles and their proximity to the field and the extent of its influence, and you can animate the physical shape of the volume, as opposed to the Max Distance value, to create your desired effect.

In a new scene, create a passive rigid ground plane that is scaled to fit the grid and then create eight spheres. Place the spheres in two rows of four facing each other as in Figure 15.11, with one row closer to the origin than the other row.

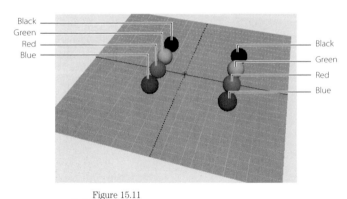

Figure 15.11

Eight spheres lined up to face each other

Select the spheres and create a gravity field. Then select the spheres again and create a radial field. Change its Magnitude to –1, and change its Volume Shape to Sphere. Set a keyframe for its scale to be 1,1,1 at the first frame. Go to frame 80 and scale the field's sphere volume up until it's about the size of the ground plane.

When you play back the simulation, you should see the radial field affect the spheres in the middle of the row closer to the origin first. As the volume of the field increases, it affects the other spheres as well. Try changing the Volume Shape to a cylinder or a cube and replaying the simulation. Also try changing the Magnitude of the radial field to try to get some of the spheres to escape the field's volume once they bounce around inside a bit.

Using Impulse and a Newton Field to Simulate Orbital Dynamics

Let's now see how to use rigid bodies to create a realistic simulation of a rocket ship going into orbit. We'll use a small cone for the ship and a big sphere for the planet, but you can model just about anything you want and substitute those objects in their places.

First, create a sphere with a radius of 25 units and name it planet. Scale your view out so you can see it clearly. Now, create a cone (named rocket) and scale it so it looks about the size of the sphere that you see in Figure 15.12.

It really doesn't matter how big the cone is, as long as it looks good to you (we just left it at its default settings). Just be sure to place the cone a little above the surface of the sphere, or you'll get rigid body interpenetration errors, like those we saw earlier.

Now make the sphere a passive rigid body (choose Soft/Rigid Bodies → Create Passive Rigid Body) and make the cone an active rigid body (choose Soft/Rigid Bodies → Create Active Rigid Body).

We could add a simple gravity field to these objects, but gravity pulls everything in the same direction. What we need here is a field that's centered on our planet; we'll use the Newton field (named after Sir Isaac). The Newton field creates a gravitational "well" in the planet that will attract all other active rigid bodies to it, its force depending on how far from the planet the object is.

Choose Fields → Newton; then Shift+select the sphere and choose Fields → Use Selected As Source Of Field. In your Outliner or Hypergraph, you will now see a Newton field parented to the planet. Choose the cone and open the Dynamic Relationships window (choose Windows → Relationship Editors → Dynamic Relationships). In this window, click the Newton field to highlight it—this connects the cone to the Newton field.

Figure 15.12

Scale your cone to this relative size.

By attaching a field to an object by selecting the field, Shift+selecting the object, and then choosing Fields → Use Selected As Source Of Field, you are using the object as a source of the field's force. The field will travel with its parent object and can be used to create a wake or turbulence as the parent object passes rigid bodies or particles.

Set the frame length to 1000 or more and play back the animation. The rocket should fall and land on the surface of the planet, bounce a bit, and stay there, or perhaps roll around a bit on the surface of the sphere. If not, try turning the magnitude of the Newton field to 6 or 7 and see if that helps.

Now we're simulating planetary gravity; but what we're missing is the thrust (or impulse) that every rocket uses to escape gravity. With the rocket selected, click the rigidBody2 text in the Channel Box and set the rocket's impulseY to about 0.5. The rocket should lift off the surface and fly out of the frame. Most likely, however, the rocket will go flipping around out of control as it rises, just like those early V-2 rocket tests. The reason is that the impulse (or thrust) is coming from the bottom of the cone, so any slight error in thrust spins the rocket. In reality, this is a serious and difficult aspect of rocket science. But in our virtual world, we have a quick fix: set the ImpulsePositionY to about 1 or 2, making the thrust come from atop the cone, and thus making it much more stable in flight. You might also want to change the Damping value on the rocket to a number such as 0.1; this reduces the chance that the rocket will spin as it is thrust upward, while still allowing orbital motion without much drag. When you now play back the animation, the rocket (if it has enough thrust) will smoothly rise and disappear from the screen.

At present, our rocket has infinite fuel, so it just keeps going. The attribute Impulse will continually apply a thrust to the rocket until it is keyframed to 0. To make a more realistic flight, we'll need to create a ballistic trajectory, allowing the rocket to rise for a time and then fall back to the planet as its thrust gives out.

To do this, keyframe the thrust (impulse) on and off. Select the Y impulse, set the Time Slider to the first frame, and set a value of 5 for the impulseY with the RM selecting Key Selected. Now go out to about frame 15 and set the value of impulseY to 0 (the impulse will fall off from 5 to 0 over those 15 frames). When you play back the animation, the rocket should launch, rise, and then fall back to the planet. It may take more than 1000 frames though, so adjust your time.

Instead of keyframing the Impulse channel to give the rocket a short thrust, you can also set its Initial Velocity attributes. The Initial attributes (Initial Velocity in XYZ as well as Initial Spin in XYZ) give the rigid body only a starting thrust of motion, but do not continue to provide thrust as Impulse does. Therefore, Initial Velocity is better to use for rigid bodies that should have a burst of motion only at the beginning of the simulation, and the Impulse attributes are better for acceleration at any time during the simulation. Notice that you'll need a much higher Initial Velocity Y setting than impulseY for the rocket to take off.

Getting this sequence to work right will take a bit of tweaking the numbers. It is easy to get the rocket stuck on the ground or flying off at an amazing speed. If you are completely stuck, try opening the `150rbit.ma` project on the CD that accompanies this book.

We've now gone suborbital; it's time to get into orbit! To do that, we need to add an in-flight correction to make the rocket move sideways as well as up and down. Move the time indicator to frame 10, and key the impulseX (at 0) on this frame. Now move to frame 11 and key the impulseX to 5. Move the time to 20 and key impulseX back to 0 (again, you may need to change these numbers to get good results). If all worked well, you will see the rocket orbit the planet (in a *very* scary looking, squashed orbit, but an orbit nonetheless) when you play back the animation. If you haven't given the rocket enough thrust, it will crash back into the planet in a rather spectacular manner.

To get our orbit a bit cleaner, we need to add yet another in-flight correction. At about frame 90, set another key on impulseY (at 0). At about frame 95, set a key on impulseY to –2 (so it pushes down on the rocket). At about frame 115, set another key on impulseY, this time back to 0 again. If these numbers work for you, you should see the rocket following a much cleaner orbital path. If not, try adding a negative thrust to the X impulse about frame 150.

As an exercise, see how close you can get the orbit to circular. Can you keep the rocket from spinning around as it orbits the planet? With all the tweaking involved, you can see why they're called "rocket scientists"!

Converting (Baking) a Rigid Body Animation into Keyframes

Once you've got an orbital motion you like, you can "bake" the rigid body animation into keyframes, which you can then change into other sorts of motions. *Baking* is the term Maya uses for creating a set of keyframes that mimic the dynamic motion of a rigid body simulation. As you will see shortly, baking an animation allows you to adjust motion paths and keyframes for what was once a dynamic simulation (and thus did not allow this kind of adjustment).

> If you might eventually want to return to your rigid body simulation, save a *different* copy of your project before you bake the simulation. You can't go back once the simulation is baked!

Select the rocket and choose Edit → Keys → Bake Simulation. The simulation will run, and when it's finished, you will have a baked animation (and a mess of keyframes in the time line).

Let's put this baked animation to good use, getting rid of that nasty rotation around the Z axis that the rocket developed. With the rocket still selected, open the Graph Editor (choose Window → Animation Editors → Graph Editor). On the left side, highlight the rotateZ channel, and then press F (to frame the selection). As in Figure 15.13, you'll see a curve with hundreds of keyframes on it—a few more than we need for our animation!

To get rid of the cone's Z rotation problems, we could first attempt to simplify the curve. Choose Curves → Simplify Curve from the Graph Editor's menu (or by RM selecting). Maya will remove many keyframes it considers unimportant to the curve. Unfortunately, even if you run the Simplify Curve command several times, the curve is still heavy—and we don't want any of that motion anyway! Let's just kill the whole curve. Be sure you're at your first frame before you delete the curve to ensure that the cone is at its initial Z rotation.

Drag-select the entire curve, press the Delete key, and away it goes. Now when you play back the animation, the Z rotation is gone—all of it. To get some form of rotation, you'll need to first delete the rigid body from the rocket (so it doesn't interfere with your setting keyframes). In the Outliner or Hypergraph, choose Options → Display → Shape Nodes to reveal the rigid body nodes. Select the rigid body associated with the rocket and delete it. Now set a 0 keyframe on the Z rotation of the rocket at about frame 15 (just where it begins to tip over). Go to the end of the animation and set a keyframe of about –1080 for the Z rotation. (This is three full revolutions, which matches the number of times the rocket goes around in the 1500-frame example animation.) To get the rotateZ curve to look right, you'll have to adjust its shape in the Graph Editor. (See Chapter 9, "Animating in Maya," for more information about the Graph Editor.)

For a finished project, see `15orbitBaked.ma` on the CD-ROM that accompanies this book.

Figure 15.13

The rocket's rotateZ curve in the Graph Editor

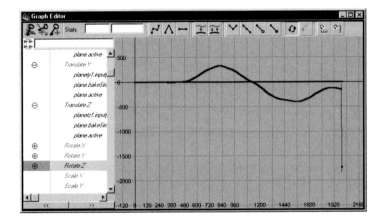

Throwing Dice: Working with the Dynamics Simulator

On a quick trip to Vegas, you might play craps, a game in which you throw two dice into a horseshoe-shaped pit and watch them bounce around (hoping for lucky 7). As you might guess, this is another great event to simulate in Maya using rigid bodies. Here, in a simplified version of the craps table, we'll see how Maya's dynamics simulator handles a more complex, multiple-body collision.

First, build a NURBS plane and stretch it to the size of the grid. Now build a second plane and place it near the end of the first, at a right angle to it. Figure 15.14 shows the initial scene.

Now add a cube of about default size or a little smaller, and name it something like die1.

> A NURBS cube is actually six pieces, or faces, and it is easy to choose only one of these faces by accident. A way to avoid choosing only a face is to be sure to name the cube itself (the parent level) something that you can easily recognize (like die1, in this case). The simpler option is to create a Polygon cube, which is one body.

Add a second cube and name it die2. You can add a checker 2D texture to the dice to make them stand out better if you want. (See Chapter 17, "Shading and Texturing Surfaces," for information about basic texturing and other rendering techniques.) When the dice are textured and placed at the front of the "table," the scene should look something like Figure 15.15.

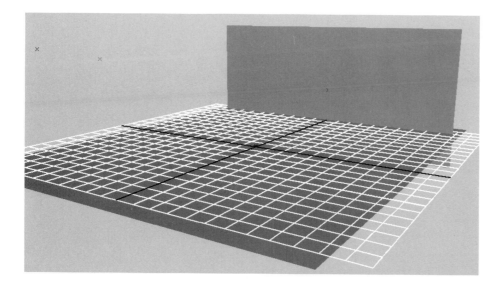

Figure 15.14

Two planes at right angles

Figure 15.15

Dice and a craps table

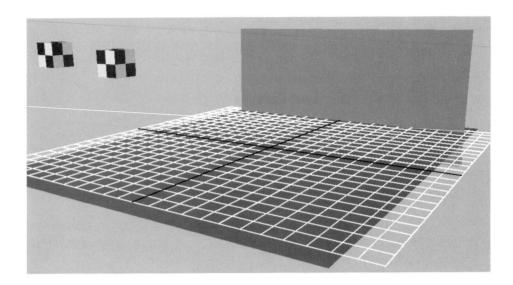

Select both of the planes and choose Soft/Rigid Bodies ➔ Create Passive Rigid Body. If you created NURBS cubes, use the Outliner or Hypergraph to choose the top level of each die. (Remember, it must be the top level, or you will get strange results!) For polygons, you can just select each cube. Now choose Soft/Rigid Bodies ➔ Create Active Rigid Body. Be sure both dice are still selected (or select them again), and choose Fields ➔ Gravity.

When you play back the animation, you should see both dice fall and bounce off the table. If the dice break apart, you have created the rigid bodies on the sub-faces of your NURBS cubes, not on their top levels, so you'll need to go back and try again. If you get stuck, try opening the file 15dice.ma on the CD.

To make life a bit more interesting, we need to give the dice some initial motion. Select one of the dice, click rigidBody1 in the Channel Box, and set the initial velocity to –15 or so in Z. Depending on your scene, you might have to set the Initial Velocity to as high as –100 or so. Repeat with the other die, but give this one a slightly different velocity. When you play back the animation, both dice should travel down the table and bounce off the far wall (if they don't, increase their velocities). You will notice, however, that they stay perfectly upright (that is, they don't rotate), which looks a bit odd. Give them an initial spin in X, Y, and Z or anything you like, and tweak the numbers until you get a nice-looking simulation. If the dice now bounce off the table, you can either scale the plane bigger or increase the plane's dynamic friction, which will make the dice "stick" to it more.

Finally, add a positive X velocity (maybe 5) to the left die, and add a negative X velocity to the right die, making them collide in mid-air before hitting the table. You will probably need to adjust their velocities in both X and Z to get them to collide. Because of the complexity of the collisions between the spinning dice, you will notice a slowdown when the two collide, making it a bit difficult to determine if the motion looks good. To get a better idea of how the scene really looks, you can playblast it and watch it play back in real time (to playblast a scene, choose Window → Playblast). The Playblast tool will record the animation one frame at a time, and when it is finished, you will get a window with the completed animation in it.

A fully rendered version of the dice throw is available as a QuickTime movie (15diceFinished.mov) on the CD that accompanies this book.

Building a Chain: Adding Constraints to a Rigid Body

As a final example of rigid bodies, let's build something a bit more complex: a link of chains like a child's swing would have. Along the way, you'll learn how to add constraints and how to adjust the rigid solver to speed up some difficult calculations.

Create a new scene, add a cylinder (named Bar), rotate it 90 degrees in X, and then scale it large on the Z axis so that it looks like Figure 15.16.

Now create a torus (named EmbeddedLink) and stretch it into the shape of your basic chain link. Rotate the torus into position below the bar, as in Figure 15.17.

Once the first link is in place, duplicate it, rename it Link1, rotate it 90 degrees around the X axis, and move it into place. Do this three more times, until you get a link of chains that looks like Figure 15.18.

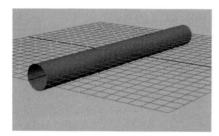

Figure 15.16

This cylinder will be the bar at the top of our swing.

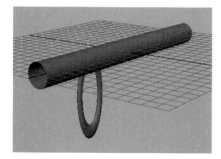

Figure 15.17

A link added to the bar

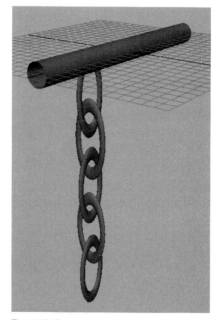

Figure 15.18

The bar with five links

Be sure there is a separation between each link (so they do not touch each other). Otherwise, when you create the rigid bodies, you will get an interpenetration error, and the simulation will break down. After you create your first duplicate and then move and rotate it, you can use the Smart Transform option in the Duplicate options window to do the rest. Each duplicate will be rotated and moved into position automatically.

Now select the bar and the first link, and choose Soft/Rigid Bodies → Create Passive Rigid Body. Next, choose all the other links and choose Soft/Rigid Bodies → Create Active Rigid Body. With all the links still selected, add gravity to the scene (choose Fields → Gravity). When you play back the animation, you should see all the links fall and then bounce off one another, finally coming to rest after about 200 frames (depending on how your bounciness settings are defined).

This is a good first step toward our chain link, but there are a couple of problems. First, the chains aren't in a "resting" position at the start of the animation, and second, they bounce all over the place when playback starts. Let's deal with problem two first (we'll deal with the first problem in a bit).

Our chains really don't need to bounce much; in fact, bounciness just slows down the simulation. So we could either turn all the Bounciness attributes down to 0 or take care of the whole thing in one fell swoop by turning off the Bounce state attribute. Choose Solvers → Rigid Body Solver, and in the attribute window, clear the Bounciness check box. This globally turns off all bounciness calculations and makes the remaining calculations run more quickly and smoothly. With the Bounciness calculations off, the links should just drop nicely into position when you play back the animation, coming to rest by frame 20 or so.

To finish our swing, we're going to add a weight to the bottom of the chain links. Create a sphere with a radius of about 3 (named weightBall), and position it just below the bottom link in the chain. (Remember not to allow the sphere to touch the link!) Looks a bit medieval, huh? First select the bottom link, and then Shift+select the sphere. Now choose Soft/Rigid Bodies → Create Constraint ❑. This opens a window that allows you to create a constraint between the two selected objects. Choose the Pin type of constraint, and leave the other settings at their default values. When you click the Create button, the sphere will be made into a rigid body, and a pin-type constraint will be added between it and the last link in the chain (as if the two were pinned together).

With the sphere selected, choose Window → Relationship Editors → Dynamic Relationships, and highlight gravityField1 (connecting it to the sphere). When you play back the animation, all the links plus the sphere should drop down (as before).

Now let's deal with the first problem: getting our links and ball into a resting position at the start of the animation so they will not fall into place to start every animation. Play the animation forward until the chain comes to a complete rest. Stop the playback, but don't rewind the animation. Choose Solvers → Initial State → Set For All Dynamic. This programs the current state of all dynamic objects into Maya as the initial state. When you rewind the animation now, it should remain in its current, rest position.

Great! We now have a completely lifeless simulation that does absolutely nothing! Let's make things a bit livelier. First, try adding an initial X velocity of about –10 to the weight. When you play back the animation, the ball (and the chain, following it) should swing out to the left and then pendulum back to the right, slowly settling back to stillness. You can try adding velocity in other directions to the ball, and even a rotation. When you have experimented a bit, reset all the initial velocities back to 0.

Instead of an initial velocity, let's now add an impulse of –4 or –5 in the X direction. When you play the animation back, the ball and chain will appear to be blowing in a wind from the right of the screen. (You could actually achieve the same effect by connecting an air field to the ball.) To allow the ball and chain to fall again, keyframe the impulseX back to 0 after 30 or 40 frames.

You might notice that the ball and chain get kinked up near the bar, and this slows down the animation considerably. To compensate, you might try adjusting the rigid solver settings. (Try a step size of 0.1 and set the solver to Runge Kutta—not Adaptive.) You might also get interpenetration errors, in which case you can reduce the step size a bit.

Finally, you might notice that the ball doesn't look very weighty in the way it is thrashed around by the chain. Try increasing the ball's mass to 50 or 100 (and set the impulse higher to compensate), and see how it looks now.

A rendered movie of a chain and ball is available on the CD (`15ballAndChain.mov`).

All in all, the only real drawback to adding mass to objects is that it drastically increases calculation times.

Summary

In this chapter, we saw how easy it is (relatively speaking) to get Maya to do the work for us when simulating real-world events such as falling and colliding objects. We also found that rigid bodies can be changed from passive (keyframeable and not affected by fields) to active (not keyframeable but affected by fields) and that, when a passive rigid body is made active, it inherits the motion it had before. This allows rigid bodies to work within a keyframed animation and with keyframed characters. Finally, we created more complex interactions, and we adjusted the rigid solver to give us realistic, but faster, simulations. In Chapter 20, we'll take the last example we worked on (the ball and chain) and automate the process of building it by creating a MEL script we can run from a single command.

Rendering

Part IV *of this book introduces the world of rendering in Maya. Rendering is an umbrella term for the many processes that actually create the images we see, such as setting up cameras to capture images, shading and texturing, lighting and shadowing the surfaces, and actually creating the image files. Rendering experts boast that 90 percent of all that we see in the final CGI output happens in rendering. The claim is justifiable. You can take poorly built models and still render out beautiful images with quality texturing, lighting, and camera work, but even the best models will end up looking terrible with poor rendering techniques. You will first learn the basics of rendering in Maya, and then learn to use the Hypershade to color and texture surfaces through numerous examples and hands-on tutorials. The last chapter is devoted to creating proper lighting, shadows, and special light effects.*

CHAPTER 16

Rendering Basics

Rendering is many-faceted process. First, you need a proper camera through which objects can be seen and captured into 2D images. You also need to decide on the quality and resolution of the image output. You can then select how you want to light the surfaces—your choices include four different lights or incandescence. Next, you need to create materials and textures for the surfaces. You might also want to create an appropriate background, such as a stage set, an image plane with live footage, or an environmental texture. Alternatively, you can render the surfaces in layers with alpha channels and put them together with compositing software.

In October 2002, Alias|Wavefront began offering a free version of "mental ray for Maya," a rendering plug-in from "mental images," to those who purchase version 4.5 of Maya Complete and Maya Unlimited. The companies announced that they are going to develop and integrate mental ray for Maya as a standard rendering feature in future versions of Maya. For those seeking more programmability, this is good news. For now, however, we will stick with Maya's built-in renderer, as that is what is included with version 4.5.

This chapter deals mainly with cameras and render settings and how to use Maya's IPR (Interactive Photorealistic Rendering) tool. We'll cover shading and lighting thoroughly in the following chapters. Topics include:

- **Camera and resolution setup**

- **The Render Globals dialog box**

- **The Render View window**

- **Interactive Photorealistic Rendering**

- **Image planes**

- **Batch rendering**

- **Rendering techniques**

Rendering an Object

As we've done in previous chapters, we will explore the rendering process by working through an example from beginning to end. To demonstrate rendering, we'll use a beveled text letter. We will light it, texture it, and animate it appearing and disappearing against a textured background. Then we will render the animation as a video-quality picture sequence.

Setting the Camera and the Resolution

First, you need to set the camera. As you learned in earlier chapters, cameras are windows through which you look at objects in Maya's world space. The four default views that you see when you start a new scene are actually four cameras that cannot be deleted: one camera with a perspective view and three cameras with orthographic views, which you know as the front, side, and top views. Generally, you use the orthographic views for modeling, texturing, and animation purposes, and rendering is done only through the perspective views.

To set the camera and the resolution, follow these steps:

1. Create a beveled text letter *M* (choose Surfaces ➝ Bevel), as we did in Chapter 5, "NURBS Modeling."

2. Create another perspective view by choosing Panels ➝ Perspective ➝ New. Persp1 camera is created.

3. In the Outliner, rename the view to Camera. Open its Attribute Editor, shown in Figure 16.1, and in the Film Back section, set Overscan to 1.1. In the Display Options section, check Display Resolution. (You can also turn on Display Resolution by choosing View ➝ Camera Settings ➝ Resolution Gate.) In the camera view, you will see a box that shows the exact area that will be rendered. The Overscan setting of 1.1 also shows a bit of the area just outside the box. In the Display Options section, also check the Display Film Gate setting. This displays another box, representing the Film Gate, the camera setting for the medium in which you want to display the images. The default resolution size in Maya is 320×240 pixels, which gives a width × height (*aspect*) ratio of 1.33333. If you see the Film Gate box overlapping the resolution box imperfectly, there is an imperfect match between the aspect ratio of the pictures being rendered and the ratio used in the final display medium.

You might want to render at a smaller size as a test render, but still maintain the correct (larger) aspect ratio, similar to the lock-aspect ratio feature available in Photoshop and other graphics software. Maya provides a setting for this in the Render Globals dialog box, discussed in the next section.

4. In the Film Back section, select different media in the Film Gate drop-down list, such as 70mm projection, to see how the aspect ratio changes. Change the preset to 35mm TV Projection, as shown in Figure 16.1. This setting has the 1.33333 ratio for television. The Film Gate and Resolution boxes should now match perfectly. (See the "Broadcast Standards" sidebar later in this section for more information on resolutions and ratios.)

5. The default resolution setting is at 320×240, which you can see at the top of the resolution gate in the camera view, but you will probably want to render the pictures at a higher resolution. Choose Window → Rendering Editors → Render Globals (or click the Render Globals button in the Status line) and open the Resolution section. For our example, set the Render Resolution to 640×480.

6. Adjust the camera view, dragging and rotating the camera until you have the proper composition for the letter M. Then keyframe the Camera attributes. (First, make sure you are at frame 1 on the Time Slider. Then, with the camera selected, RM click any of the attributes in the Channel Box and select Key All.) Now you can switch back to the regular perspective window and test-render the camera view as you make changes to the lighting and textures.

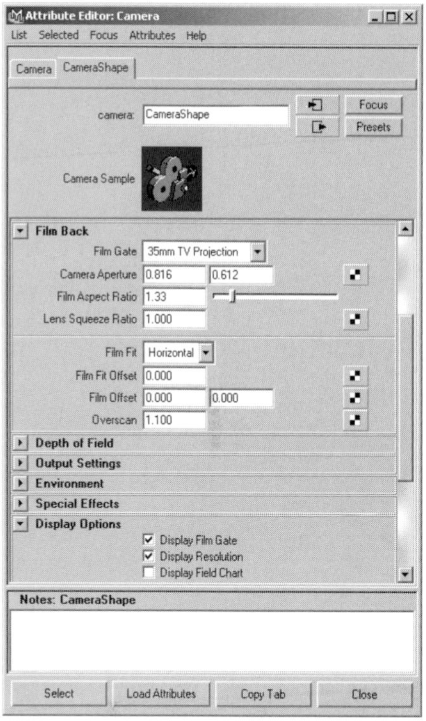

Figure 16.1

The Camera Attribute Editor

As you saw in step 5, Maya provides many Render Resolution presets. For television and video productions, the most common resolution setting is CCIR 601, which is 720×486, Device Aspect Ratio 1.33333, and Pixel Aspect Ratio 0.9. With this setting, the image is 720 pixels wide and 486 pixels high, but it is shown with a 4:3 width × height ratio because the pixel aspect ratio is not square. The 640×480 resolution that we are using has Device Aspect Ratio 1.33333 and Pixel Aspect Ratio 1, and it is considered the minimum broadcast-quality resolution.

Render Globals Settings

We need to set a few other objects in the Render Globals dialog box. As shown in Figure 16.2, this dialog box includes many settings, but for now, we will set the quality, the output filename and format, and some frame-rendering details.

1. Click the Render Globals dialog box in the Status line and open the Anti-aliasing Quality section. Set the Presets option to Intermediate Quality. You can change this setting to Production Quality when you are ready to render, but for test renders, the Preview or Intermediate Quality settings are usually good enough.

BROADCAST STANDARDS

Different broadcast standards are used in different parts of the world. The PAL (Phase Alternating Line) and SECAM (Sequential Color And Memory) systems are used in Britain and in Europe. The NTSC (National Television System Committee) system is used in North and South America and many Asian countries.

Unfortunately, these systems are incompatible in a number of ways. NTSC broadcasts 525 horizontal lines in a picture; PAL and SECAM broadcast 625 lines. NTSC transmits 30 fps (frames per second); the others transmit 25 fps. Systems also have different broadcast channel widths and types of signals. However, all these standards broadcast pictures at a 4:3 image aspect ratio.

Images are rendered at 640 × 480 resolution with square pixels, or 720×486 resolution with a pixel ratio of 0.9, to make them fit the 4:3 aspect ratio. A Device Aspect Ratio setting of 1.33333 is another way of stating that images are being displayed at a 4:3 width × height ratio.

With the coming of HDTV (high-definition TV), these standards are changing. Although there still isn't a universal standard for DTV (digital TV), the accepted image ratio for HDTV is 16:9, which is the same ratio as the wide-screen format used for films. This ratio translates to 1.777 Device Aspect Ratio. The minimum resolution for HDTV is 1280 × 720. For film, 1.85 framing and 2.35 (anamorphic; also known as Cinemascope) are currently the most commonly used aspect ratios.

Figure 16.2

The Render Globals dialog box

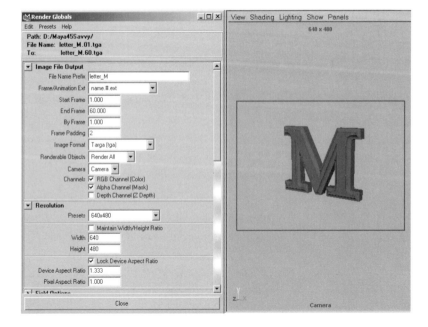

For production- or higher-quality anti-aliasing presets, Maya automatically turns on the Multi-pixel Filtering setting. Multipixel Filtering is good for situations in which you see thin surface edges. If there are no thin edges to anti-alias, it's best to turn off this option, because it can slow down the rendering process significantly.

2. Open the Image File Output section and type a name for the picture sequence you will be rendering in the File Name Prefix field. If you don't enter a name, the rendered pictures will automatically be assigned the scene filename.

3. Set Frame/Animation Ext to name.#.ext. The animation settings become activated. If you leave the setting at name or name.ext, only the current time frame will be rendered, unless otherwise commanded in a batch render.

4. Set End Frame to 60, because we will be rendering two seconds of animation.

5. Set Frame Padding to 2. This determines the number of digits that will be used for the frame number extension. Since we chose to render to frame 60, a double digit number, we are forcing frames 1 through 9 to have double-digit extensions as well (name.01.ext, name.02.ext, name.03.ext, and so forth). This keeps the files in numeric order in the output folder.

6. The default Image Format is Maya IFF (`.iff`) picture format. Change it to something more widely used, such as the Targa (`.tga`) format.

7. Set the Camera to Camera to make it the renderable camera. Before closing the Render Globals dialog box, check to make sure you have the settings shown in Figure 16.2.

Here's a quick explanation of the Image File Output settings we've just made:

Image Format: Targa Formats such as JPEG or GIF are usually not used as image formats, because they do not carry alpha channel (mask) information, and alpha channel information is often needed for compositing purposes. Regular color pictures have 24 bits of color information for each pixel, stored in three RGB (red, green, blue) channels. A picture with an alpha channel has an extra 8-bit channel, which contains the masking information for each pixel of the picture. The information is stored in the form of a grayscale picture, which often turns out to be the outline of the objects being rendered. The final renders should also, as a general rule, not be output as a compressed file format, such as JPEG or GIF.

Channels By default, Maya renders the RGB channels and the alpha channel. You can also render the depth channel (Z-depth) by checking the Channels box. Z-depth is similar to the alpha channel in that it is represented as an 8-bit grayscale picture. As its name indicates, it stores the depth information of pixels to be rendered. Like the alpha channel, it is mainly used for compositing purposes. If the image format is the default `.iff`, the Z-depth information is stored inside the image file being rendered, like other alpha channel information. If you are rendering in a format such as `.tga`, Maya creates a separate Z-depth file for every image it renders.

Renderable Objects This option is set to Render All by default, but you can switch it to Render Active if you want to render only what you've selected. Using the Render Active option is also useful if you are rendering in layers.

Camera In the Render Globals dialog box, you see Camera as the only view that will be rendered. If you want to render multiple views, open the other view's Attribute Editor, go to the Output Settings section, and turn on Renderable. Now if you go to the Render Globals dialog box's Image File Output section and look at the Camera menu, you will see that the other view is also identified as Renderable.

Working in the Render View

Now we will set up some spotlights and take a look at our letter in the Render View window. Follow these steps:

1. Create a default spotlight. Choose Panels → Look Through Selected, and move the spot-Light1 view to something like spotLight1 which is on the left in Figure 16.3.

2. Create another spotlight, and repeat the procedure to look something like spotLight2 which is on the right in Figure 16.3. This is a convenient and intuitive way to set lights. You do not need to fine-tune anything at this point—we will be doing that with the IPR tool soon.

3. Choose Window → Rendering Editors → Render View.

You can open and save many different images in the Render View window just as you would in any other graphics software. Here are some of the other things you can do in the Render View window:

- Keep multiple images by choosing File → Keep Image or by clicking the Keep Image button for each picture you want to keep.

- Turn off shadows and glow pass by choosing Options → Ignore Shadows and Options → Ignore Glows.

- Take wireframe snapshots of different cameras available for rendering or select a region to render only that area.

- Zoom in and out and drag the image by using hotkeys and mouse buttons, just as you do in a modeling view.

- Use the options on the View menu to change the view. Frame Image shows an entire image, Frame Region focuses on just the selected region, and Real Size shows an image without any zooming. The Display menu list also allows you to see a rendered image as separate color planes, to see its luminance, or to see its alpha channel (Mask Plane).

The toolbar in the Render View window includes buttons for the most-often-used functions. You can display their functions by placing the mouse arrow over the icons.

Using Interactive Photorealistic Rendering (IPR)

You use the Interactive Photorealistic Rendering (IPR) tool to edit colors, materials, textures, lights, and shadows interactively. When you invoke IPR, Maya creates an image file that stores both the shading and the visibility information of surfaces. An IPR file is considerably larger than a regular image file of the same resolution because it stores the extra visibility information. When you select a tuning region, Maya loads all the IPR information for the pixels in the region into memory. You can change the tuning region at any time, and the IPR will continue to load the pixel information for the new region.

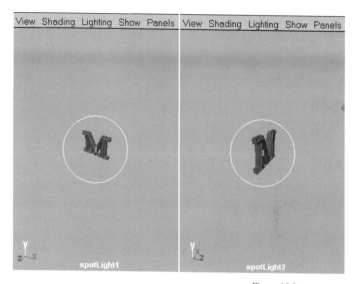

Figure 16.3

Looking through the Spotlight view

We will use IPR to render our letter *M*, but first let's get a snapshot. It's always a good idea to take snapshots before you do any rendering so that you can quickly see what you are about to render. Taking a snapshot also sets the camera you've chosen as the active camera, and you can later use the Redo Previous Render and Redo Previous IPR Render icons to render the same camera view.

1. In the Options menu in Render View window, turn off Auto Resize and turn on Auto Render Region.

2. Choose Render → Snapshot → Camera. You can also RM click to access the menu in the Render View window.

3. Click the IPR button to start the IPR process. When the letter *M* is rendered, select a region to start IPR tuning, as shown in Figure 16.4.

If the image is real size, the marquee box stays green. As soon as the image is zoomed in or out, the box turns red. The IPR icon in the top-right corner becomes activated as well; clicking it ends the IPR mode. The indicator to the left of the icon shows the size of the IPR file. Any changes you now make to the lighting or texture information relating to the letter *M* are updated within the tuning region automatically. You can also pause the updating of the IPR by clicking the Pause IPR Tuning button next to the IPR file size indicator. This allows you to adjust your scene without waiting for the IPR to finish.

Figure 16.4

An IPR rendering of the letter *M*

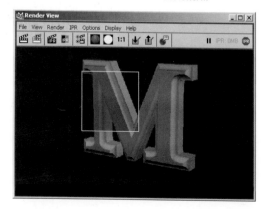

You can do some neat things within the selected IPR tuning region. You can Shift+click over any pixels within the region to find out which shades and lights are affecting them, and you can select those nodes. You also can drag materials and textures onto the objects within the region, and they will update accordingly. Any modification in the shading information is updated in the region with speeds comparable to that of a Hypershade swatch update, because the visibility calculations have already been made. (We will use the Hypershade window in the next section and examine it in detail in Chapter 17, "Shading and Texturing Surfaces.")

Having the visibility information already stored in the IPR file means that once the file exists, you can change the camera view and make changes in the surfaces without disturbing the IPR tuning region. Those changes are not recalculated until you start another IPR. Although this allows you to get more mileage out of a single IPR file as you are editing lighting and shading, keep in mind that if the changes in the surfaces' visibility are significant, the IPR updates can go out of sync with how the surfaces actually look. If this happens, create another IPR file.

Shading the Object

Next, we'll use the Hypershade window to shade the letter *M*. As in the Render View window, you can zoom in and out and move around using the hotkeys and the mouse buttons. We will go through the steps to shade a texture in our current example, without much explanation of the settings. You will learn more about the Hypershade in the next chapter.

1. Keep the Render View window open, and adjust the spotlights until you are fairly satisfied with the way the letter *M* is being lit in the tuning region. After you've shaded the letter properly, you can come back to this view and fine-tune the lighting.

2. Choose Window → Rendering Editors → Hypershade. On the left you will see the Create Bar panel. On the right will be a split panel display with different tabs in each panel. The top panel contains tabs with all the nodes that make up the scene (material nodes, texture nodes, utility nodes, and so on). The bottom panel shows Work Area and Shader Library tabs. You can choose to display these panels as the split panel display (the default) or in separate panels by clicking the buttons (Show Top Tabs Only, Show Bottom Tabs Only, or Show Top And Bottom Tabs) in the upper-right of the Hypershade. For now, click Show Bottom Tabs Only, the middle button.

3. To create a new material, click the button at the top of the Create Bar panel and choose Create Materials. (If you don't see any of this, click the checkered icon in the upper-left corner to display the Create Bar panel). Click the Blinn material swatch to create a new one in the Work Area on the right, as shown in Figure 16.5.

4. Click the Create Textures button at the top of the Create Bar panel. Scroll down to 3D Textures and MM drag the Brownian texture over the Blinn material you created. A list of possible input connections pops up. Connect to Color, and you will see the Brownian

texture appear on the Blinn material swatch. (You can easily move the swatches around in the Work Area by LM clicking and dragging them.)

5. MM drag the same Brownian texture (from the Work Area) over the Blinn material to see the list pop up again. This time, connect to Bump Map, as shown in Figure 16.6. You'll see the bump effect of the Brownian texture on the Blinn material, along with the creation of a Bump node.

6. In the Work Area of the Hypershade window, RM choose Graph → Rearrange Graph to sort the nodes. Press A on the keyboard to "frame all" the contents of the window.

7. Bring the Hypershade and the Render View windows close to each other, and drag the Blinn material onto the letter *M* inside the tuning region of the IPR window. Since our letter *M* has two surfaces, you'll need to apply the material twice. The material, along with the Brownian color and bump, should update on the letter almost immediately, as shown in Figure 16.7.

You can apply the Blinn material to the letter *M* in many other ways. One way is to MM drag the swatch onto the object inside the modeling window. Another way is to select the object, move the mouse over the Blinn swatch, and RM choose Assign Material To Selection.

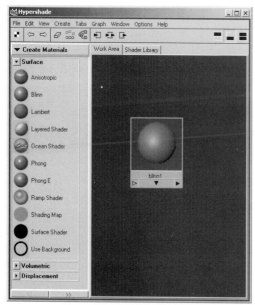

Figure 16.5

The newly created Blinn swatch in the Hypershade work area

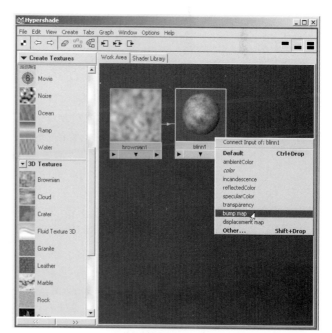

Figure 16.6

Connecting the Brownian texture to the Bump node of the Blinn material

Figure 16.7

The Blinn material, applied to the letter *M*, updates in the Render View window

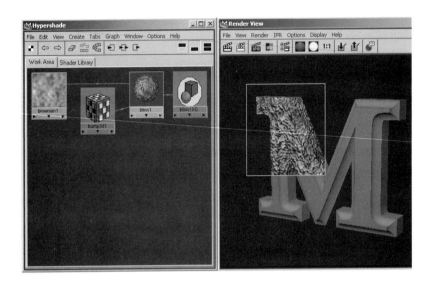

8. The default bump value is too high for our purposes. RM choose over the Brownian texture or double-click it to open its Attribute Editor, open Color Balance, and move the Alpha Gain slider down. You should see the bump on the letter *M* start to lessen in the IPR tuning region. Adjust the Alpha Gain value until you like what you see. To adjust the bumpiness in a different way, you can also try playing with the increment value slider in the Brownian Attributes section.

9. Work in the same way with Brownian's Color Gain and Color Offset values to adjust the color of the texture.

10. Go to the Blinn material and adjust Specular Shading by moving the Eccentricity, Specular Roll Off, and Specular Color sliders. (Specular Shading has to do with how the light is reflected from an object.)

11. Return to the spotlights and fine-tune the lighting, this time adjusting not only the angles, but also the Color, Intensity, and Dropoff values. You might also want to change the tuning region to different areas to make sure there are no hidden surprises. The updates we've made appear as shown in Figure 16.8. (You can also see this image in the Color Gallery in the CD.)

If you have been experimenting with the other sliders and fields, you've seen that some do not affect the letter *M* at all and that others should be left alone. It's easy to play with the texture, material, and light attributes and get immediate feedback from the IPR tuning region. One of the best things about IPR is that it frees you to experiment with the attributes and think of other possibilities—there is less reason for number crunching and more room for artistic expression.

If a single image is the goal, once you are satisfied with the way everything looks you can increase the Anti-aliasing setting to Production Quality and then click the top-left corner icon, Redo Previous Render, to render a final image. You can then save the image by choosing File → Save Image. But our example is for a sequence of images, which requires a bit more work.

Making an Object Disappear

We would like the letter *M* to appear and disappear against a textured background. Before working on the background, we will make the letter appear and disappear. We can accomplish this by using the Transparency, Specular Color, and Set Key attributes.

1. In the Blinn material's Attribute Editor, slide the Transparency value all the way up to white. In the IPR region, the letter's surface disappears, but the specular highlights still remain. Notice that the alpha channel for the letter also becomes black, which you can check by clicking the Display Alpha Channel button.

2. To make the letter *M* completely invisible, you need to turn down the Specular Color slider all the way to black. At frame 5, RM click over the Transparency attribute to display the pop-up menu, and choose Set Key to keyframe the value. Repeat for Specular Color.

Figure 16.8

IPR updates for shading and lighting

Figure 16.9

**The Blinn material's
keyframed attributes in
the Graph Editor**

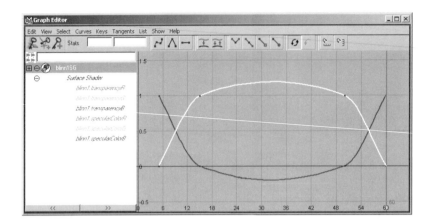

3. Go to frame 15, turn down the Transparency value to black, raise the Specular Color value to white, and Set Key those attributes. The letter *M* now fades in over a ten-frame time interval.

4. Repeat the process in the opposite direction between frames 50 and 60 to make the letter disappear. Notice that as you move the current time indicator in the Time Slider, the IPR tuning region updates the changing transparency and the specularity.

5. In the Graph Editor (choose Window → Animation Editors → Graphic Editor), you can see the Blinn material's keyframed attributes, as shown in Figure 16.9. Select all the curves and choose Tangents → Flat to make sure the Transparency and Specular Color attributes stay constant between frames 15 and 50. The gradual slope of the keyframe curves also ensures the smooth appearance and disappearance of the letter *M*.

Adding a Textured Background

Our work on the letter *M* is done. Now let's add a background for the letter. The Create button in the Environment section of the camera's Attribute Editor lets you create an image plane. You can set the display to show the image only through the camera view or to display it in all views. When you are modeling, you will want to be able to see the image in different views. You can hide the image temporarily by setting the Display Mode to None. You can also load any image to use as the background by clicking the browser button beside Image Name and placing the image anywhere in the modeling window using the Placement and Placement Extras attributes. For our example, we will create a texture to use as the background.

1. Select Camera and open its Attribute Editor. Open the Environment section and click the Create button to create an image plane.

2. In Image Plane Attributes, change Type to Texture. Click the Create button beside the Texture field to open Create Render Node and select a solid fractal texture.

3. Because background textures do not show up in the IPR, you need to render the region to test how the solid fractal matches up with the letter *M*. Adjust its Color Gain, Offset, and Placement attributes to get it to look the way you want—something like the image shown in Figure 16.10.

> You can select the image plane in several ways. One way is to first select the camera and then click the arrow beside the Image Plane Create button. Another way is to go into Component mode and click the question-mark icon, which enables image plane selection. A third option is to choose View → Image Plane → Image Plane Attributes. And then there's the Outliner, in which you can RM choose to toggle off Show DAG Objects Only and then scroll down to select the Image Plane node.

Batch Rendering

We are now ready to render. Before you save the scene, however, let's see where the rendered pictures will be placed.

1. Choose File → Project → Edit Current. The Edit Project dialog box (see Figure 16.11) tells you the location of the current project. Go to the Project Data Locations section and look at the field beside Images. If this field's entry is Images, there is a default subdirectory in the current project called Images, and the rendered pictures will be placed in that directory by default. If the field is empty, the rendered images will be placed in the current project directory.

2. Save the scene, entering the name **letter_M**. You can now either render from within Maya or from a Command Prompt window (the command line). To render from within Maya, from the Rendering menu set, choose Render → Batch Render.

3. Batch rendering from the command line allows you to render outside of Maya. This means you can close the Maya program, which will give you more memory to render with. This is useful for scenes with motion blur, highly complicated scenes, or for computers with low memory. In an ideal situation, you would be batch rendering from a computer dedicated to rendering so that you can continue to work in Maya on another computer. To render from the command line, save your scene, and exit Maya. Open an MS-DOS Command Prompt window. (If you are using SGI, open a Unix shell window.) In the directory where you saved your letter *M*, you will see the file listed as `letter_M.mb`.

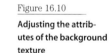

Figure 16.10

Adjusting the attributes of the background texture

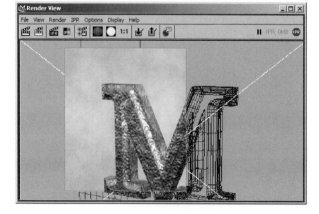

4. Type **Render –help** and press Enter to display all the options that you can use with the Render command.

5. For our example, enter a command such as the following (substituting your own project directory path):

```
Render –s 1 –e 60 –b 1 –rd D:\Maya45Savvy\Chapter16\Renders\ –n 2
    letter_M.mb
```

> You can reduce the time it takes to render your scenes by using some optimizing techniques. See Chapter 18, "Lighting," for some render optimization tips.

The Maya Rendering program will take the file `letter_M.mb`, render frames 1 to 60 using two available processors, and place the rendered pictures in the directory listed in the path.

In this example, we used the most common Render command options: `-s` for start frame, `-e` for end frame, `-b` for by frame or step, `-rd` for the directory path in which to store rendered images, and `–n` for number of processors to use. If your machine has two CPUs, for example, be sure to use the `–n 2` option, which will make the render go twice as fast. You can also omit the `–rd` option, render the pictures into the default render directory, and move the pictures out of that directory later.

Other options, such as `–mb` for motion blur and `–sa` for shutter angle, can also be handy in certain situations. For example, let's say you've rendered a run cycle, and while checking the rendered pictures, you notice that frame 12 is looking weird because of the motion blur. Rather than opening the file and fixing this, you can either render just that frame without the motion blur (`-mb off`) or reduce the motion blur by using a lower shutter angle value (`-sa 70`, for example).

Figure 16.11

The Edit Project dialog box

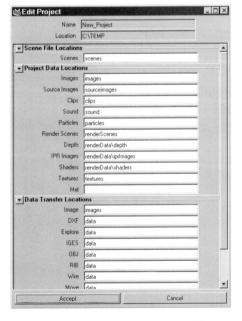

Once the rendering is done, you can view the rendered pictures using the Fcheck utility. Fcheck allows you to view a single image or a sequence of images, check their alpha channels, view the different color planes, and see the Z-depth information. You can also save the images into many different picture formats. (If you are working with SGI machines, you can use the `imgcvt` command to convert images into different formats.)

Using Other Rendering Techniques

So far, we've gone through the process of lighting, shading, and rendering a sequence of images for a simple beveled letter *M*. We've tried to keep the options, but rendering, by nature, is a rather complex endeavor. In the rest of this chapter, we'll cover some other rendering techniques that you may find useful in your projects.

Layer Rendering, Compositing, and Editing

What we've done with the letter *M* rendering is actually rather … dumb. Because the letter wasn't moving, the 60 frames of rendering were not necessary; only the first 10 frames need to be rendered. In studio environments, where meeting deadlines and work efficiency are always paramount, this kind of rendering redundancy would have been frowned upon.

With any editing software or with some renaming and renumbering script commands, you can extend frame 1 forward to frame 5, reverse the animation from frames 5 to 15 to make them frames 50 to 60, and hold frame 15 until frame 49.

Alternatively, we could have rendered the letter *M* separately from the fractal textured background. Since the background remains constant, only a single frame is necessary. Using compositing software, we could have composited the letter *M* onto the background.

In a production, the rendering pipeline is often set up to layer-render anything that can be layered. Figure 16.12 is a partial example of how the letter *M* can be rendered as multiple-layered render passes. The floor has been added to illustrate the shadow passes. (You can also see this image in the Color Gallery on the CD.)

Although it's not included in the sample pictures, there can also be a separate render for the floor, with the accompanying alpha channel. To create just the shadows on the floor, select the letter *M* surfaces, go to the Attribute Editor's Render Stats section, and turn off Primary Visibility. To create the shadow mask, color everything white, make the lights black,

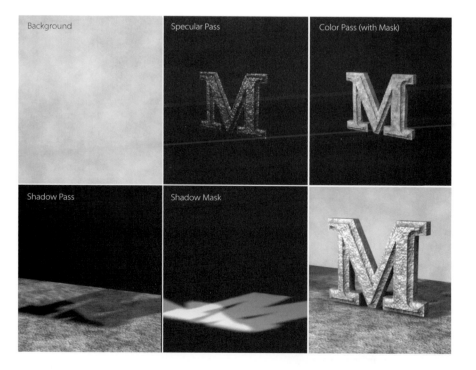

Figure 16.12

Render passes for different layers

and turn their shadow colors to white. Even if there are many lights, you will usually want two or three lights at most to create shadows. Separating these elements may seem like extra work, but it allows you much more control at the compositing stage, and it can ultimately save you time in terms of making changes or corrections in complex scenes.

You can increase or decrease only the specularity or change the colors on the letter *M*. You can darken or lighten just the shadows, sharpen them, or blur them. If you have the proper compositing software, such as Maya Fusion or Adobe After Effects, you can even transform and animate the different layer elements. If the rendering was done in one pass, you will need to re-render the whole scene each time you want to make changes. However, if you render these items as separate elements, you need to re-render only the elements you want to change. Ultimately, however, whether these refinements are worth the extra effort depends on your specific production situation.

Adding Depth of Field

Maya cameras can also imitate the depth-of-field functionality of real-world cameras. To use this capacity in any practical way, however, requires some setup.

Open the `letter_M` file, select Camera, and open its Attribute Editor. Go to the Depth Of Field section and check Depth Of Field. Its attributes become active. The Focus Distance attribute does what it says—it sets the distance for the camera focus.

It would be useful to have a way of interactively controlling that distance in the modeling window, instead of punching in numbers. An easy way to do this is to open the Connection Editor with the Camera Shape loaded on both windows and connect the Center Of Interest output to the Focus Distance input. This constrains the focus distance to the camera's center of interest, which shows up as part of the Show Manipulator handle.

In Figure 16.13, the F Stop value might be a bit too low. Also, the blurring, a post-effect, is expensive (meaning it takes longer to render). However, because it is a 3D blur, it adds much more realism to the rendered image than any post-effect 2D blur can. If you want more control, or just need the camera's center of interest and the focus distance to be separate entities, you can connect the focus distance to a locator instead.

Figure 16.13

Depth Of Field activated

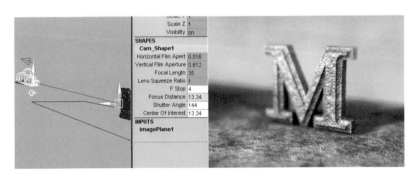

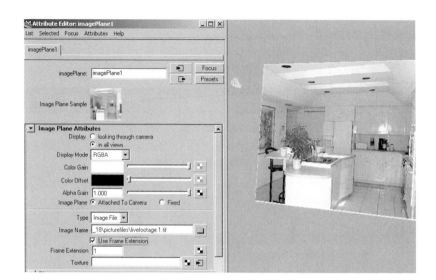

Figure 16.14

The first frame of live footage loaded into the image plane

Importing Live Footage

When you want to match an animation with live footage, you need to animate the image plane. Let's assume we have ten frames of footage properly numbered and with proper extensions. To bring in the sequence of images, in the image plane's Attribute Editor, turn on Use Frame Extension in the Image Plane Attributes section. Click the browse button (the folder icon) beside the Image Name field to load the first frame of the footage. The result should look something like Figure 16.14.

Go to frame 1, enter **1** in the Frame Extension field, and RM choose Set Key to keyframe it. At frame 10, enter **10** in the field and keyframe that. Now when you move the Time Slider, the frames update. If you open the Graph Editor for the image plane, you can see a linear curve for the Frame Extension, as shown in Figure 16.15.

Maya has a file texture node specifically for movie files. It works the same way as a regular file, or the image plane, in that you have to keyframe the sequences, but instead of reading in separate pictures, it reads in the frames of an `.avi` movie file. Shown in Figure 16.16 is a movie file applied as a texture to a polygon face. The movie file is designed to play back live footage more efficiently than the regular image files, and it can be a great tool for quickly referencing an action sequence for animators.

Loading in picture sequences or movie files is easy. Camera tracking the live footage, however, is a tedious and time-consuming affair—usually frame-by-frame matching work. Once the tracking is done, matching up lighting and shading to the live footage is yet another grim task. But as you will see in the next chapter, using IPR can make the editing of lighting and shading an enjoyable process.

Figure 16.15

The Frame Extension in the Graph Editor

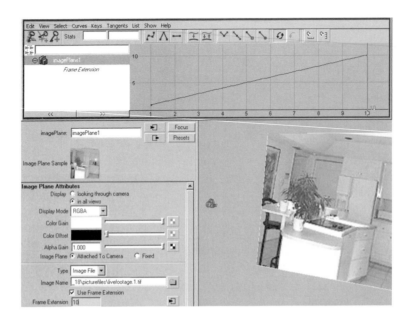

Figure 16.16

A movie file texture

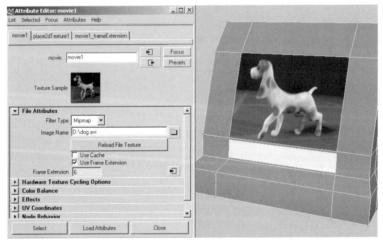

Summary

This chapter introduced you to the many varied parts of rendering. You learned how to create and set up a camera and how to set the resolution and the format of the output in the Render Globals dialog box.

We also covered the Render View window and the IPR tool. Then we took a brief look at other topics, such as working with image planes and batch rendering. The Hypershade window and lighting were also introduced. These topics are covered in depth in the next two chapters.

CHAPTER 17

Shading and Texturing Surfaces

Objects look different because they are made up of different materials. One way we can distinguish materials is by the way they reflect light. A metal object, for example, shines more than a wooden object. The brightest spot where the light is reflecting from an object is called the object's *specular highlight*. In Maya, materials are generally classified according to the way that specular light is calculated to represent them.

We also identify objects by their color and texture. Maya has many default textures, such as wood, rock, leather, and so on. These allow you to quickly create easily identifiable, every-day objects.

In this chapter, you will learn how to use these default materials and textures to create great-looking objects. We will use the dog, objects from the living room, and the human model from the previous chapters as examples. But first, you need to learn how to use the Hypershade. Topics include:

- **Hypershade operations**
- **Surface coloring**
- **Shininess and bumpiness control**
- **Transparency, incandescence, and glow**
- **Texturing techniques**
- **Working with polygons and subdivision surfaces**
- **Hands On: Texturing a character**

Using the Hypershade

Just as you can view and edit nodes and node network connections using dependency graphs in the Hypergraph, you can work with them the same way in the Hypershade for rendering. The Hypershade differs from the Hypergraph in that it uses swatches, which give a level of visual feedback that the Hypergraph lacks. For viewing and editing render nodes such as textures and materials, the Hypershade is indispensable.

Working in the Hypershade Window

When you choose Window → Rendering Editors → Hypershade, you see the Create Bar panel on the left side of the window. As you learned in Chapter 16, "Rendering Basics," you can click a node swatch to create nodes, or you can MM drag them onto the layout area on the right side of the window. The top-left button (the checkered icon) opens and closes the Create Bar panel; you can also open and close this panel by choosing Options → Create Bar → Show Create Bar. You can also customize the Create Bar panel by using the Options menu and selecting Display Icons And Text (the default) or Display Icons Only, which takes up less screen space.

Let's briefly go over some of the menu functions available in the Hypershade window, which is shown in Figure 17.1. We will then see how the nodes and networks work in the Hypershade.

Figure 17.1

The Hypershade window

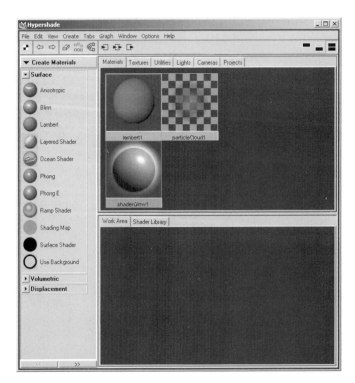

The Edit Menu

On the Edit menu, the Delete Unused Nodes function deletes all the nodes that are not assigned to geometry or particles in the scene. This is basically a cleanup command that you will want to invoke at the end of your session.

The Duplicate command has three options. The Blinn1 material with the checkered texture and its placement node in Figure 17.2 form a simple network of render nodes we can use to demonstrate these options.

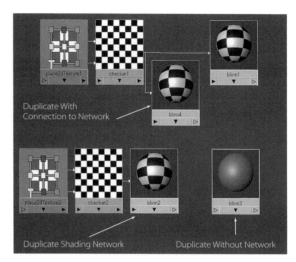

- Choose Duplicate → Shading Network to produce the Blinn2 node network, an exact duplicate of the first.

- Choose Duplicate → Without Network to produce just the Blinn3 node, which copies all the properties of the Blinn1 material, but not the network.

Figure 17.2

Duplicating the Blinn1 node

- Choose Duplicate → With Connections To Network to produce Blinn4, which inherits the same upstream node network connections as the original Blinn1 node. The network connections are not duplicated, as they are when you choose Duplicate → Shading Network, but shared.

The Convert To File Texture function converts a material or texture into an image file. You can adjust the image size and turn on Anti-aliasing in the command's option window. The image will be placed in your current project directory. You can select material nodes, 2D or 3D textures, or projections for the conversion. If you select the Shading Group node, the light information is baked into the image as well.

The Create Menu and Create Bar Panel

Within the Create Bar panel, at the top, is the Create Render Node button. When you choose the type of node you want to create, you will see subsections for each.

- The Create Materials section contains surface, volumetric, and displacement materials. When you click or MM drag one of these materials into the layout area, a Shading Group is automatically created and linked to it.

- The Create Textures section consists of 2D and 3D textures, Environment textures, and Other textures.

- The Create Lights section consists of ambient, area, directional, point, spot, and volume lights. (You'll learn about lighting in Chapter 18.)

- The Create Utilities section contains the General utilities, Color utilities, Switch utilities, Particle utilities, and Image planes. You can also find Glow here, which is an optical FX, useful for creating light effects such as glow, halo, and lens flare.

- The Create All Nodes section just lists all of the sections in one.

On the Create menu, the Create New Node command opens a window with tabs. This is just an alternative to the Create Bar panel. If you want to apply a texture as a projection or a stencil, you can use either the Create Render Node window or the Create Bar panel to change the setting from Normal to As Projection or As Stencil.

Hypershade Tabs and the Tabs Menu

Within the Hypershade window are several tabs, each displaying an area containing the nodes that make up the current scene. You can click each tab to view the specific nodes. The top Hypershade panel has six tabs by default: Materials, Textures, Utilities, Lights, Cameras, and Projects. The bottom Hypershade panel contains two tabs by default: Work Area and Shader Library. You can also create your own tabs.

You can view this layout area in three ways: Show Top Tabs Only, Show Bottom Tabs Only, and Show Top And Bottom Tabs. These buttons are in the upper-right of the Hypershade, or you can choose them from the Tabs menu. You use the Work Area (the bottom tab) to build shaders by dragging, dropping, and connecting different nodes to your material. To create your own tab, choose Tabs → Create New Tab. Type a name in the New Tab Name section, choose an initial placement, and select which nodes to show. Creating your own tabs is especially useful when you need to organize a scene with many rendering elements.

The Graph Menu

The Graph menu has several useful functions. The Graph Materials On Selected Objects command let you work with a select group of render nodes according to the surfaces you select. After you select an object in your scene, this command displays the render nodes for that object in the Work Area of the Hypershade. The Graph Materials On Selected Objects command is also available as a Hypershade window button.

The Clear Graph command clears the Work Area, and it is also available as a button.

The Up And Downstream Connection command performs the same function as it does in the Hypergraph, listing the nodes connected to the selected nodes in the Work Area. The Upstream Connection and Downstream Connection commands can also be useful when you know which stream you want to view and edit, because they reduce the clutter in the Work Area when you are working with a complex scene.

The Rearrange Graph command cleans up the Work Area and reorganizes the nodes for better viewing. This command is also available as a button placed next to the Clear Graph button. To see which button executes which command, point to the button to display a label, as shown in Figure 17.3.

Other Menus

The Window menu gives you access to the Attribute Editor, Attribute Spread Sheet, and Connection Editor.

The Options menu's Keep Swatches At Current Resolution command keeps the swatch resolution at a fixed size so that when you zoom in, the resolution doesn't update. This makes the swatches less accurate when closely zoomed in but increases their interactive speed.

Figure 17.3

Button label

Working with Nodes and Networks

To see how you can work with nodes, click a Blinn node in the Materials folder or MM drag it into the Work Area of the Hypershade. Then try the following:

- Either MM click or MM drag and drop a texture over the Blinn material. You see a list of the attributes that can be connected with incoming information, as shown in, Figure 17.4 (a).

- Roll over the right-bottom corner until the mouse pointer looks like a box with an arrow pointing to the right. LM click to display a list of the attributes that can go out to the other nodes, as in Figure 17.4 (b).

- RM choose over the material node. A box pops up with a list of operations you can perform on the material node, as in Figure 17.4 (c). Graph Network lists nodes that are connected to the material node. Assign Material To Selection assigns the material node to selected surfaces. Select Objects With Material selects all the surfaces that have the material node assigned to them. Frame Objects With Material selects and frames the surfaces with the material in the modeling window. You can also open the Attribute Editor for the material node or rename it.

Figure 17.5 is an example of a fairly simple network, which includes different swatches with which you will soon become familiar. (If you have a hard time seeing the lines of the diagram, it's also in the Color Gallery on the CD.) Working backward (upstream) from the right, the Blinn1SG (Shading Group) is getting its shading information from the Blinn1 material swatch and nurbsSphere node. The Blinn1 node is getting its color information from the checker1 node, which is also outputting its alpha channel information to a reverse node (reverse1). The reverse1 node, true to its name, reverses the information it's receiving and passes it on to the 2D bump node (bump2d1), which connects to the Blinn's bump channel input. The leather1 and brownian1 textures connect to the checker1 texture's color attributes, and there are placement nodes

Figure 17.4

Input/output connections, Node Operations

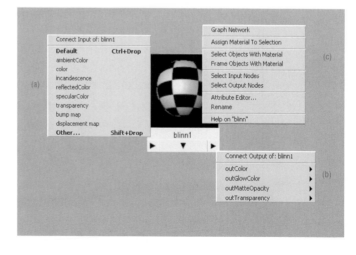

for each of the textures: a 2D placement node (place2dTexture1) for the checker1 texture and 3D placement nodes (place3dTexture1 and place3dTexture2) for the brownian1 and leather1 textures, respectively.

> You can assign different shading groups to different faces of a polygon object. For NURBS surfaces, different shading groups can also be assigned to different faces. However, with NURBS, the shaded surface patches will only be visible in the shaded view and hardware renders (in the modeling window) and cannot be software rendered by using the rendering command.

Figure 17.5

A network of swatches in the Hypershade (top) and Hypergraph (bottom) windows

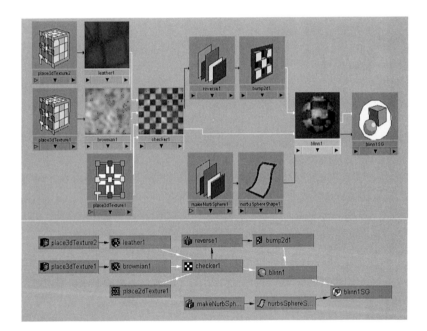

Everything is arranged exactly the same way as in the Hypergraph node network. Like the Hypergraph, the Hypershade lets you move the mouse over the lines connecting the nodes to find out exactly what attributes are being connected:

- The green lines are triple attributes, such as the RGB color information or the world space (XYZ) coordinates.

- The light-blue lines are double attributes, such as the UV coordinates of a geometry surface.

- The dark-blue lines are single attributes, such as the 8-bit grayscale masking values of the alpha information.

To check or change these and other color designations, choose Window → Settings/ Preferences → Colors and go to the Hypergraph/Hypershade section.

MM dragging a node over another node opens the appropriate connection list. Ctrl+MM dragging a node over another node lets Maya choose the default connection automatically. If you want to use the Connection Editor to connect the two nodes, Shift+MM drag the node. You can also drag a node into another node's Attribute Editor.

You can also import and export nodes and networks. To bring in a scene, choose File → Import. You can save specific nodes or node networks by selecting them and choosing File → Export Selected Network. The nodes will be saved as a Maya scene.

Using Shading and Texturing Attributes

Shading in Maya can be divided into categories of color, shininess, bumpiness, transparency, and self-illumination. We will go through these "global" material properties first and then proceed to cover some general texture properties.

Coloring Surfaces

When you create a material and open its Attribute Editor, you can find its default Color attribute in the Common Material Attributes section. The default is set as a gray color with zero saturation and 0.5 value in HSV or 0.5 RGB. You can adjust the color of the material in Maya in many ways:

- Use the Color Chooser. To access the Color Chooser, click the Color box beside the Color attribute.

- Connect textures or image files to the Color attribute, typically by dragging them to the Color attribute in the Attribute Editor. The Diffuse attribute acts as a scale factor for the color values, with 0.0 being black and 1.0 being the original color values. The default Diffuse setting is 0.8. The image files can be single pictures, sequences of pictures, or a movie file (as you saw in the previous chapter).

- Map 2D textures or image files to a surface as normal UV textures or as one of many types of projections: planar, spherical, cylindrical, ball, cubic, triplanar, concentric, or perspective.

- Apply 2D textures as stencils.

- Map 3D textures as if they were solid objects occupying space in and around the surface.

- Use a Surface Shader for coloring a material node. Although it is stored in the Materials section, a Surface Shader has the information for only the color, transparency, glow, and matte opacity of a material. When you want to use the same color for many materials or textures, Surface Shader enables you to have one node control the color information of many nodes.

- Use the Shading Map tool to color a surface. Shading Map is typically used for non-photorealistic, or cartoonish, shading effects. It takes the colors sampled by a regular shader and replaces those colors with a simpler color scheme using the brightness and hue of the original colors.

- Use the environmental shaders such as the Env Textures (Env Ball, Env Chrome, Env Cube, Env Sky, and Env Sphere) with an accompanying image file to simulate a surrounding environment, either as background image or reflections on surfaces.

Figure 17.6 illustrates some of the many ways you can create colors and textures on a simple sphere in the Hypershade.

You can also assign textures directly to surfaces. Make sure your object is selected first. RM click over the texture to display the Assign Texture's Material To Selection command. When the texture is assigned this way, Maya creates a default Lambert material prefixed with the texture name.

Controlling Shininess

Different materials reflect light differently on their surfaces. Lambert material does not have any specular highlight. Blinn, Phong, and PhongE materials have different variables for calculating specular highlight.

Blinn has the softest specular highlights among the three, as shown in Figure 17.7, and is usually the material recommended for surfaces with bumps or displacements, because it tends to rope or flicker less than the Phong materials. Blinn and Phong are called *isotropic* materials, which means that they reflect specular light identically in all directions.

Figure 17.6

Various ways to color a sphere

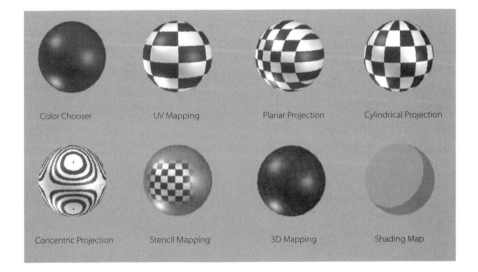

Anisotropic material reflects specular light differently in different directions according to its Specular Shading settings. It more faithfully adheres to the way materials such as hair, satin cloth, feathers, or CDs reflect light unevenly.

Shading Map also calculates specular highlight, but in a non-photorealistic way, as mentioned in the previous section. The Use Background Material's Specular and Reflectivity variables only work with raytracing. The Layered Shader does not have specular variables, because it creates layered materials. See the "Applying Textures" section later in this chapter for more information about layered shaders.

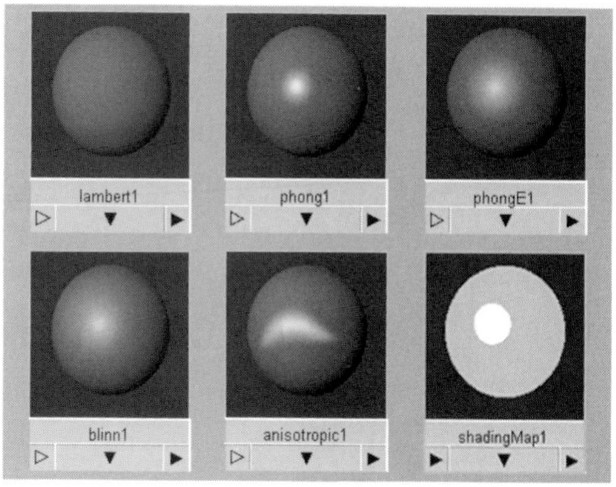

Figure 17.7

Specular highlight properties of materials

All the materials with specular highlight have Specular Color, Reflectivity, and Reflected Color attributes. You can use the Color Chooser to tint the specular color or map textures or image files in the same way that you can with material color. In Figure 17.8 (a), the Specular Color attribute in the sphere with the anisotropic shader has been tinted to match the color of the material. In (b), the sphere has a checkered texture mapped to Specular Color. You can also do the same thing with Reflected Color and fake reflection in this way, although true reflection only occurs with raytracing. In (c), the sphere has an Env Sky shader with the floor texture mapped to its Reflected Color, making it appear as though the sphere is reflecting a sky environment. The sphere in (d) is raytraced; notice the reflections on the floor and in the sphere.

Figure 17.8

Specular color and reflection

(a) (b) (c) (d)

RAYTRACING

Raytracing lets you create refractions and shadows through transparent objects. Although raytracing may be desirable and necessary when you want to create photorealistic images, it is also more expensive than the regular rendering. When the settings are high, the render time can increase dramatically.

To raytrace, you need to turn on Raytracing under Raytracing Quality in the Render Globals window. For refractions, you also need to open the material Attribute Editor of the selected surface and turn on the Refractions setting in Raytrace Options. To raytrace shadows, you also need to open the shadow casting light's Attribute Editor and check the Use Ray Trace Shadows setting in the Raytrace Shadow Attributes section. We'll discuss raytraced shadows in Chapter 18, "Lighting." You also can control whether a surface is visible in reflections on other surfaces, by using its Attribute Editor to turn on or off its Render Stats → Visible In Reflections setting.

Creating Bumpiness

You can create bumpiness on a surface in two ways:

- Apply a bump map to a surface, which fools the camera into believing that there are bumps on a smooth surface.

- Apply a displacement map, which actually moves the geometry to create the bumps.

Advantages and disadvantages are associated with both methods. Bump mapping is much more efficient to render, but it fails at the edges of a surface and cannot create the appearance of extreme bumpiness, as seen in Figure 17.9 (a). Displacement mapping does a better job of creating bumpiness because it actually displaces the geometry of the surface, but it takes longer to render. Also, often the geometry's UV spans or its tessellation count must increase before you see proper displacement, as shown in Figure 17.9 (b) and (c).

With displacement mapping, the surface is displaced efficiently, tessellating only the areas that need the bumping, reducing processing time and making this method more practical. Also, displacement mapping doesn't create an additional bump node, which makes it much easier to place separate bump maps on the surface being deformed.

Figure 17.9

Bump mapping and displacement mapping

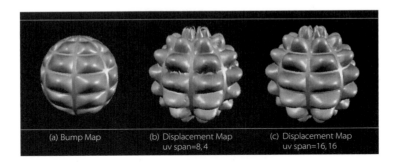

(a) Bump Map   (b) Displacement Map uv span=8,4   (c) Displacement Map uv span=16,16

When you drag a texture over a material node and connect to its bump map, or drag to its Bump Mapping field in the Attribute Editor, a bump map node is created. If the texture is 2D, a bump2D node is created. If the texture is 3D, a bump3D node is created. Projection bumps also create a bump3D node. The texture's alpha value, which is a single-channel attribute, connects to the bump node's Bump Value attribute. The bump node then outputs a triple-channel outNormal to the material's normalCamera attribute, which creates the appearance of bumpiness on the material surface.

When you connect a texture to a material's Displacement attribute, a displacement node is created. It connects not to the material, but directly to the material's Shader Group node. You can also bump a displacement map, to add more detail to a bump-mapped or displacement-mapped surface. In the example in Figure 17.10, we applied a ramp texture to a Blinn material as a displacement map, which we assigned to a plane, as seen in (a). We then connected a bulge texture to the middle color input of the ramp, adding detail to the displacement of the plane, as seen in (b). Another ramp texture with water texture as color input was then applied to the Blinn material as a bump map. The result appears in (c). The lower part of Figure 17.10 shows the whole sequence of connections in Hypershade.

Adding Transparency

Transparency is a triple-channel RGB color attribute, with black making the material opaque and white making it transparent. As with color and specular attributes, you can map textures or image files for transparency, as shown in Figure 17.11. Once a material becomes transparent, you can also turn on refraction for raytracing. The Refractive Index in the Raytrace Options section of the material's Attribute Editor controls how much the light bends as it

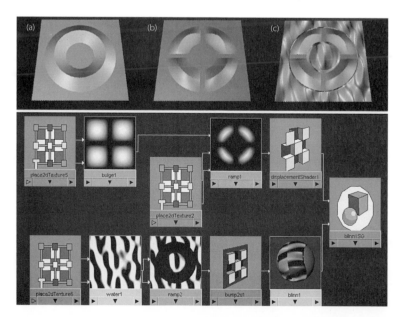

Figure 17.10

Adding a bump map to a displacement-mapped surface

Figure 17.11

Transparency and refraction effects

passes through the transparent material. For the refraction to have any effect, there must be more than one layer of surface that the camera can see through. You can set up a simple example with a sphere and a textured floor to test how these objects will raytrace with different Refractive Index settings, as shown in Figure 17.11 (and in the Color Gallery on the CD).

The Refraction Limit setting is in the Raytrace Options section of the material's Attribute Editor, and it's also listed simply as Refractions in the Raytracing Quality section of the Render Globals dialog box. Both settings need to be adjusted; the lower of the two values will act as the maximum refraction limit for the material.

You can also use transparency to layer different materials and textures on top of another with a layered shader. For more information about using layered shaders, see the section later in this chapter dealing with texturing the eyes.

A related material attribute that needs a brief mention here is Translucence. A translucent object isn't completely transparent, but it does transmit light through its surface. Objects such as sheets of paper, leaves, clouds, ice, and hair are examples of translucent materials, as shown in Figure 17.12. (This image is also in the Color Gallery on the CD.)

Adding Self-Illumination

You can add self-illumination attributes to materials through Incandescence, Glow Intensity, and Ambient Color settings.

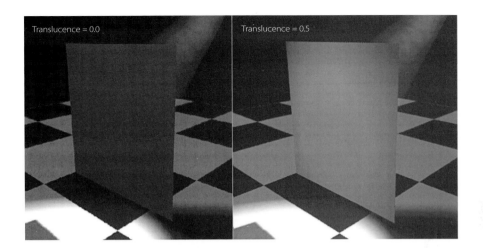

Figure 17.12

Examples of translucence

Incandescence

Most materials have Incandescence under their Common Material Attributes. This attribute makes the surface appear to give off light on its own. Red-hot metal and neon signs are good examples of noticeable incandescence.

You can also use incandescence more subtly in many other surfaces. With an almost unnoticeable amount of incandescence, a person's eyes seem much brighter, and flower petals and tree leaves look much more like living things. You can also map textures or image files to Incandescence, and you can combine this attribute with Glow (discussed next) as shown in Figure 17.13. (A color version appears in the Color Gallery on the CD.)

Glow Intensity

Materials can glow as well. Incandescence usually works better when it is combined with a bit of glow. Many materials have a Glow Intensity attribute under the Special Effects section in their Attribute Editor. When Glow Intensity is at zero, no glow is calculated; when the value is something other than zero, materials start to glow, as shown in Figure 17.14 (also in the Color Gallery on the CD). The Hide Source setting in the same section allows you to hide the surface with the material and show just the glow. Glow can be effective in creating certain atmospheric effects with surfaces, such as a hazy moon, a warm sunset, or candlelight, as shown in Figure 17.14. You can edit the Shader Glow Attribute Editor to control the way the surfaces (when its material's Glow Intensity is set to a number greater than zero) will glow in a scene. The Shader Glow swatch (shaderGlow1) is located by default in the Materials tab of the Hypershade. Halo Intensity, found in the Halo Attributes section of the Shader Glow Attribute Editor, works much like Glow Intensity, affecting the scene globally.

Figure 17.13

**Examples of
Incandescence
and Glow Intensity**

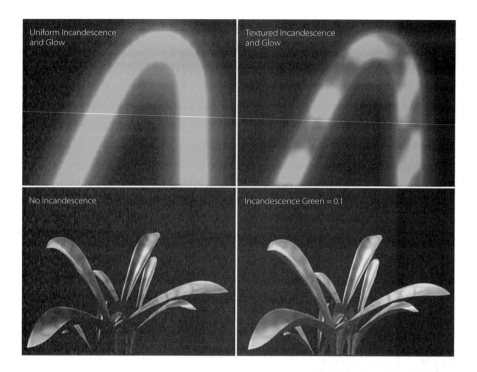

Figure 17.14

**Examples of Glow
Intensity**

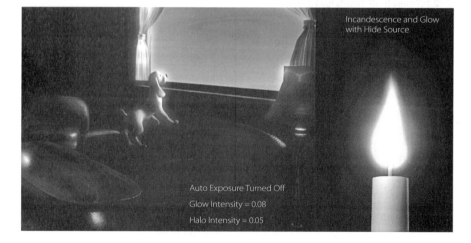

You need to be careful when using glow effects, because they can get tricky. Unlike the Incandescence attribute, glow is a post-process. It bases its calculations on the amount of light the surface is receiving from the light sources, including other objects that are glowing. In some circumstances, an object's glow intensity will visibly change when other glowing objects enter the scene, resulting in annoying flicker. In such a situation, you need to open the Shader

Glow Attribute Editor and turn off its Auto Exposure. This prevents Maya from automatically calculating glow intensity in a scene. But you will have to readjust the Glow Intensity and the Halo Intensity in the Attribute Editor to get the proper glow look for the surfaces in the scene.

Another thing to watch out for with glow effects is that their intensity can change with changes in the render resolution. When you test render with glow effects, test with the same resolution as the final output.

Ambient Color

Materials also have Ambient Color. This attribute is similar to Incandescence in the way it lights the surface, but Incandescence illuminates the material, and Ambient Color illuminates the material's color or texture. Ambient Color is also different from Diffuse, which brightens the material color in areas where the light is hitting the surface; Ambient Color lights the whole surface. You could render a surface only with Ambient Color if you wanted to do so.

Applying Textures

Maya's Create Bar panel provides 32 textures: thirteen 2D textures, thirteen 3D textures, five environment textures, and a Layered texture. With the exception of Layered, all the textures get a placement node when they are created. Most textures also have a Color Balance section and an Effects section in their list of attributes.

Texture Placement

3D textures or 2D projections are placed much like real objects, as opposed to 2D textures, which occupy the UV space on the surface. You can transform them in the world space, and you can shear them as well. Be aware that rendering them generally takes longer than rendering 2D textures. You can convert 3D textures or projections to 2D image files by choosing Edit → Convert To File Texture in the Hypershade window, but you may lose some quality in the process.

Because of the nature of 3D texture placements, when a surface with a 3D texture deforms, the surface will seem to swim through the texture, as you can see comparing Figure 17.15 (a) and (b). To solve this problem, you can use Reference Object, which enables the 3D textures or 2D projections to deform with the surface. After you assign a 3D texture to a surface, select the surface and choose Texturing → Create Texture Reference Object in the Rendering module. Maya creates a reference object over the surface. Notice that the texture in Figure 17.15 (c) is squashed and stretched with the surface.

You must create a reference object before applying any deformation or animation to the original surface. A texture's placement is determined by its relationship to the reference object, not to the original surface being deformed.

By default, a place2dTexture node completely covers whatever surface it is assigned to. The Coverage attribute of the place2dTexture node lets you control the percentage of the surface area the texture covers, and Translate Frame and Rotate Frame transform the texture over the surface in UV. Don't confuse these attributes with the UV Repeat, Offset, and Rotate attributes, which determine the way the texture is mapped within the coverage area. The examples in Figure 17.16 show how the various attributes affect the texture placement.

Color Balance and Effects

Typically, you use a texture's Color Gain and Color Offset attributes to control its color and brightness. The Default Color attribute is the color of the surface area that is not covered by the texture. Usually, you won't need to change this setting. However, if you are using the texture as a mask and the texture coverage is partial, you might at times need to turn the Default Color attribute to black or white.

Figure 17.15

Reference Object enables a texture to deform.

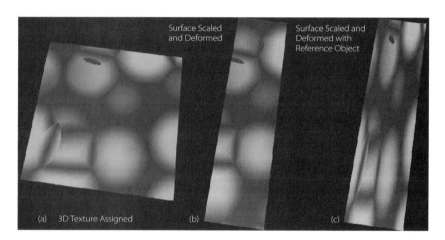

Figure 17.16

place2dTexture placement variables

The Alpha Gain attribute scales the alpha channel and is used for bump or displacement effects. The default value is 1.0, which usually produces a bit too much bumpiness for most situations. Figure 17.17 is an example of the fractal texture, first with the default settings of gray for Default Color and 1.0 for Alpha Gain, and then with Default Color turned to white and Alpha Gain turned down to 0.3 to tone down the extreme bumping. The fractal texture's Threshold value was also pushed up to 0.7.

> To use the texture image as a bump map, turn on Alpha Is Luminance. When the image is calculated for bumping, the values are determined by a grayscale version of the image, with white bumping up, and black bumping down.

In the Effects section, many textures have Filter, Filter Offset, and Invert attributes. The Invert setting inverts the texture's colors and hue, changing white to black and vice versa. It also inverts the alpha channel, changing bumps into dents and vice versa.

The Filter and Filter Offset attributes blur textures, and they are useful when the textures are too sharp or are aliasing. When a texture is too sharp, you may have shimmer or noise problems with the surface when the textured surface or the camera is animated. By blurring or smoothing the texture, you can usually make those problems disappear. Filter's default value is 1.0, but you can lower it to something close to zero. Filter Offset basically adds a constant value to the Filter attribute, and usually a tiny fractional value is sufficient to correct any excessive sharpness.

Figure 17.18 shows the same fractal texture as in Figure 17.17, but with Invert turned on, Default Color set to neutral gray, and Alpha Gain moved back to the default value of 1.0. The first half sphere has Filter set to 0.01, and it is a bit too sharp and may shimmer with a moving camera. The second half sphere has Filter Offset set to 0.005, and the bumps have been noticeably blurred, perhaps even a bit too much. But that much blurring has made the second surface safe from any problematic shimmering.

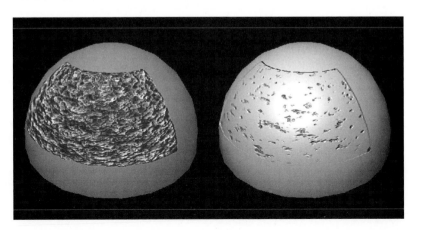

Figure 17.17

The fractal texture with different Default Color and Alpha Gain settings

Figure 17.18

**The fractal texture with
Filter and Filter Offset**

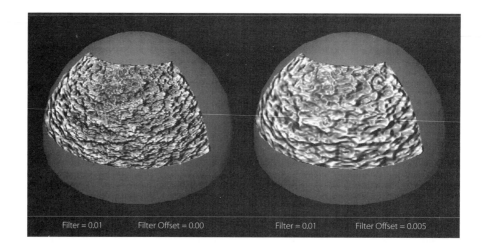

Filter = 0.01   Filter Offset = 0.00   Filter = 0.01   Filter Offset = 0.005

Figure 17.19

**Wrap, Local, and Blend
effects**

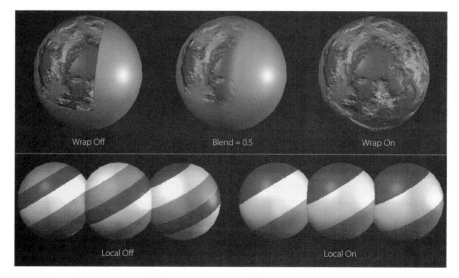

Wrap Off   Blend = 0.5   Wrap On

Local Off   Local On

For 3D textures, the Effects section has three extra attributes: Wrap, Local, and Blend, shown in Figure 17.19 (and in the Color Gallery on the CD). Because a 3D texture is placed as a solid cube around an object, if the object is partially moved outside the cube, that area is colored by the Default Color attribute, as shown in Figure 17.19. Wrap, which is on by default, enables the texture to extend to cover the whole surface. The Blend attribute mixes the Default Color to the texture color. It only works when Wrap is turned off. 3D textures are also by default applied globally, meaning that when a texture is assigned to three surfaces, those surfaces get different parts of the texture. When Local is turned on, the textures are applied locally, so that the three surfaces get the same texture placement.

Fix Texture Warp

For NURBS objects only, there's a Fix Texture Warp setting in the Attribute Editor, under the Texture Map section. Because of the parameterization of the UVs, NURBS surfaces sometimes warp the UV textures applied to them. Recall from Chapter 5, "NURBS Modeling," that chord-length parameterization of surfaces does a better job of mapping a UV texture to a surface than the Uniform method but is more difficult to model with. Fix Texture Warp calculates the NURBS surface in a way that decreases the warping, as shown by the bottles in Figure 17.20. The true advantage of the Fix Texture Warp function can be seen when the surface is being animated.

Layered Texture

Our presentation of textures would not be complete without briefly mentioning the Layered Texture node. It works like the Layered shader node, except that it works directly with textures, not materials, and it has more options to composite the layers in different ways. Plane (a) in Figure 17.21 has a Blinn material with a Layered texture connected to the material's color. There is a single layer of Checker texture assigned to the Layered texture. When a Leather texture is added to the Layered texture (connected to input color[1]), it is mapped under the first checker texture, as seen in the Attribute Editor window. Different values of Alpha and Blend Mode in the Checker texture layer will bring out or hide the leather texture layer. The settings seen in the window produce plane (b). An Alpha of 0.5 with Difference Blend Mode results in plane (c). Plane (d) is created by applying a circular Ramp to the Alpha channel of the top layer, causing the Leather texture to show only through the middle circle. You can add as many layers as you want into the Layered texture.

Figure 17.20

Three bottles with textures

Uniform
Parameterization

Chord-Length
Parameterization

Fix Texture Warp

Figure 17.21

Layered textures

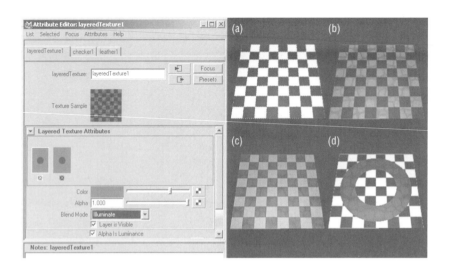

Using Shading and Texturing Techniques

Now we're ready to apply some of the shading and texturing techniques discussed in this chapter. We will work with the various models that we developed in previous chapters as examples.

Texturing the Puppy

In Chapter 8, "Organic Modeling," we constructed a dog model using many NURBS patches. Texturing each piece would be a complicated and tedious task. One way to get around this is to apply a 3D texture and create a reference object for the dog. Here are the general steps:

1. Select all the patches of the dog, except for the eyes and the nose, and assign a Blinn shader. (You could also assign a Lambert or an anisotropic shader, depending on the way you want the dog's fur to shine or not shine.) Adjust the specular settings until you are satisfied with the way the material looks.

2. Assign a leather texture as the color. You need to use a 3D texture, such as leather, for this example because a 2D texture will map differently to the different patches. Adjust the settings and the placement node until your dog looks something like the one shown in Figure 17.22 (and in the Color Gallery on the CD). Connect a solid fractal to Blinn's Bump attribute, and make it bump very subtly, as also shown in Figure 17.22. The Attribute Editor values on the left are only a rough guide. You will want to use the IPR tool to fine-tune the texturing.

3. When you are satisfied with the colors and the placements of the spots and their sizes, group all the patch surfaces under a group node, select the group node and choose Texturing → Create Texture Reference Object. The reference duplicate of the dog is created over the original dog.

Leather is a remarkably useful texture. It can serve as the basis for a great variety of surfaces, such as spots on dog fur, human skin, grunge, plant leaves, or a field of stars, just to name a few.

When you're finished, test the dog's legs or head to make sure the spots move and deform with the surface.

Adding Textures to the Living Room

We created the living room model in Chapter 5 and added a lamp to it in Chapter 6, "Polygons and Subdivision Surfaces." Now we will add some textures to make the floor and wall appear old, and then we'll refine the lamp with some texture and glow attributes.

The Floor and Wall Textures

Let's create a worn-out floor. It takes only a few more steps to go from a clean floor with a single texture to a more complicated dirty floor, but often the results (improvements?) can be startling.

1. Start with a Blinn material for the floor, and assign a marble texture to it as its color. Turn down the specular quite a bit.

2. Create a 2D fractal texture and a brownian texture. Connect them to the Vein Color and Filler Color of the marble texture, respectively, as shown in Figure 17.23 (and in the Color Gallery on the CD). You can adjust the texture settings as you see fit. You may want to also connect the same fractal texture to marble as a bump map, and turn down the Alpha Gain setting to a very subtle level.

3. For an old wall, first we need an acceptable wall pattern. Start with a Blinn material and apply a checkered texture as color. The placement node for the first picture shown in Figure 17.24 has a Repeat UV of 32 and 1. Connect a cloth texture to Color1 of the Checker attribute, and make its Repeat UV, 64 and 32. You should see something like the top-right picture of Figure 17.24, and we have our wall pattern.

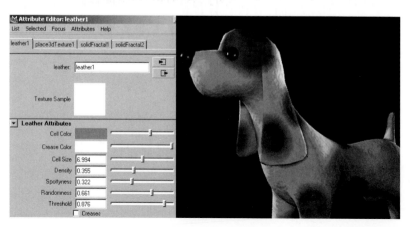

Figure 17.22

Leather values and the dog

Figure 17.23

Creating a dirty floor

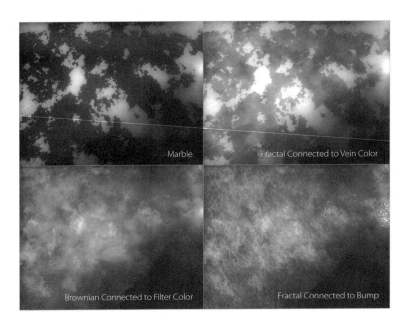

4. To create a worn-out look, you can use a handy technique called *smearing*. Take a brownian texture and connect its alpha channel to the Offset U and Offset V attributes of the placement node for the checkered texture, as in the bottom-right picture in Figure 17.24 (and in the Color Gallery on the CD). Reduce the Alpha Gain value to keep the smear effect from being too drastic. The bottom-left picture is the result of a subtle smear.

At this point, the colors themselves are still rather clean, but you can make the colors dirtier in many ways. You can map the Ambient Color attribute of the Blinn material or Color2 of the Checker attribute, tint the lights shining on the wall, or map their Color attributes. If you want complete control over the dirtiness of sections of the wall, you can reassign a layered texture to the wall, Blinn, and then add as many layers of dirt as needed.

The Lamp Textures

Let's try texturing the floor lamp we created in Chapter 5. The lamp stand, lamp shade, and lightbulb need shading and texturing. We will use a ramp texture for the lamp stand, but first we need to briefly go over what a ramp texture is.

A ramp basically consists of layers of colors, and it is one of the most useful textures. By default, the ramp texture has three layers of RGB colors, which are called color entries. You can create additional color entries by LM clicking in the ramp. The circles that appear at the left side of the ramp allow you to drag the color entries, or you can type a precise position value in the Selected Position field. The square boxes at the right side delete the color entries.

As you can see in the examples in Figure 17.25 (and in the Color Gallery on the CD), you can apply the ramp along the V isoparms, U isoparms, diagonally, radially, circularly, and so on. The color entries mix according to a set Interpolation type; if you set Interpolation to None, the color entries will not mix. You can also distort the ramp with waves and noise, and you can map other textures into any of the color entries.

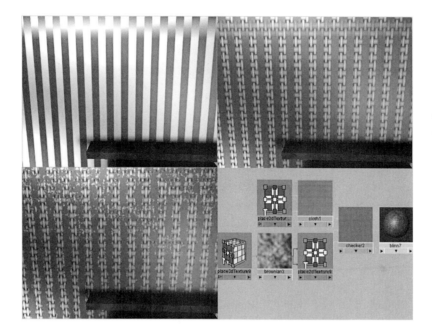

Figure 17.24

Creating the wall texture and the smear

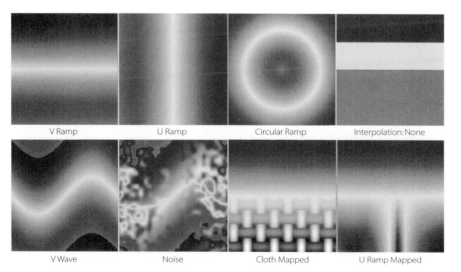

| V Ramp | U Ramp | Circular Ramp | Interpolation: None |
| V Wave | Noise | Cloth Mapped | U Ramp Mapped |

Figure 17.25

Examples of ramps

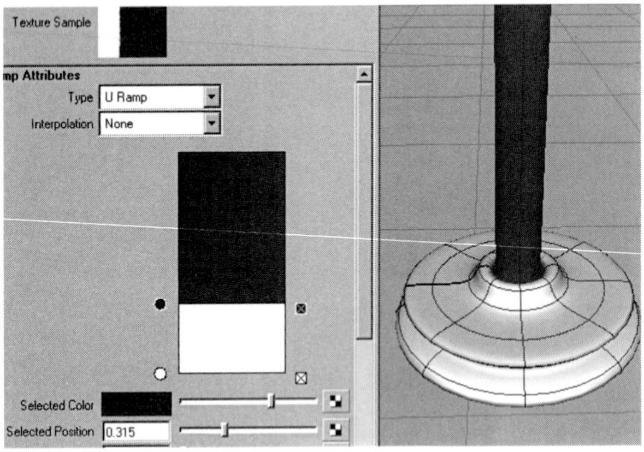

Now let's add textures to the lamp.

1. Assign a Blinn material to the lamp stand. Add a ramp to its color. Delete one of the color entries in the ramp texture, and set Interpolation to None. Make the first color entry white and the second entry blue. Adjust the position of the blue entry until you see in the model window that the white is covering only the lamp base and the blue is covering the lamp pole, as shown in Figure 17.26.

2. Apply a fractal texture to the ramp's white color entry, and apply a wood texture to the blue color entry. You could, for added effect, apply a subtle fractal bump on the Blinn material. You can use the same fractal texture for the bump mapping as you can control its Alpha Gain value without affecting its color values. Adjust the settings until you see something like the lamp stand in (a) of Figure 17.27. (This image is also in the Color Gallery on the CD.) A little glow was also added to the Blinn material.

3. We want the lamp cover to be thin and a bit transparent. Assign a Blinn material, and then assign a checkered texture as Color. The checkered texture for this example has a Repeat UV of 16 and 32. In the Blinn material's Attribute Editor, increase the Transparency setting a bit, as well as the Ambient Color attribute; add a tiny bit of Translucence. Glow Intensity should be fairly strong, but not so strong as to wash out the texture. Play with the values in IPR until you see something like the lamp cover in (b) of Figure 17.27.

Figure 17.26

The ramp texture applied to the lamp stand

Figure 17.27

The lamp stand, cover, and lightbulb

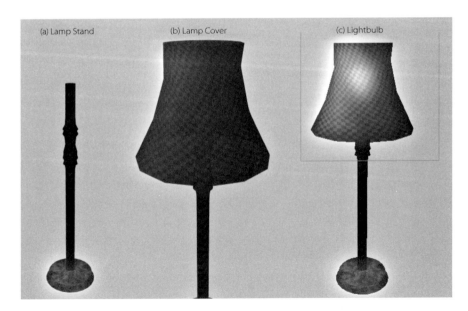

4. For the lightbulb, assign a Blinn to the bulb, make the color dark orange, and choose a darker orange for the Incandescence setting. Raise the Glow Intensity setting and turn on Hide Source. Start an IPR process and adjust the settings until you see something like the lamp shown in (c) of Figure 17.27.

> The glow on the materials will change slightly each time you introduce a new element into the scene, so don't spend too much time fine-tuning the glow until you have all the elements you want and know the resolution of the picture in the final render.

Shading and Texturing Polygons and Subdivision Surfaces

So far, we've worked only with NURBS surfaces. Shading works a bit differently with polygons, and unless you are firmly grounded in the basics, texturing polygonal surfaces can become confusing and frustrating. This is especially true of UV mapping in polygons. Texturing subdivision surfaces is essentially the same as texturing polygons, as you will see at the end of this section.

UVs in Polygons

As with NURBS, textures are mapped to polygon surfaces parametrically, with UV values. But UVs are not an intrinsic part of a polygonal surface. By definition, a NURBS surface has four sides and neatly arranged rows and columns of UV parameters. But because polygons have arbitrary topology, their UV information exists separately from the geometry and must be mapped to the geometry. The default polygon primitives in Maya come with UVs already mapped neatly to the geometry, but they can be lost or replaced with new sets of UV mapping. Figure 17.28 shows examples of primitives and their default UV mappings above them. The pictures below the primitives show how the primitives can take on different UV maps. A polygonal surface can acquire UV values through various types of projections, normalization, or unitization. The best way to understand these concepts and the other tools you need to use for texturing polygons is to try some examples.

Working in the UV Texture Editor

The UV Texture Editor window allows you to work on UVs that are already mapped to a polygonal surface. In the modeling window, you can RM click over polygons to select UVs, which occupy the same position as vertices. When vertices are selected, they turn bright yellow, but when UVs are selected, they turn bright green. You can also select polygon components the same way in this window, but the shapes shown are flat 2D representations of UVs being mapped to polygon faces. You can work on UVs only in the UV Texture Editor: you can transform them, copy and paste them, and access the texture-editing functions to edit them. Navigation in the UV Texture Editor is the same as in the modeling window. To dolly in and out, press Alt + the middle and left mouse buttons. To track, press Alt + the left mouse button.

First, let's create a polygon to work with in the Texture View window.

1. Start a new scene and choose Window → UV Texture Editor.

2. In the Modeling menu set, choose Polygons → Create Polygon Tool ❑. Make sure that the Texture option is set to Normalize.

3. Go to top view and create a triangle, as shown in Figure 17.29. Be sure you draw the triangle in the same order we did, with the first point at the top, the second point to the left, and the third point at the origin (0,0). Press Enter to complete the action, and you will see the triangle appear in the Texture View window.

4. Create a Blinn shader in Hypershade, assign a Diagonal ramp to it, and assign the shader to the triangle.

5. Press 6 to get into Textured Display mode, and select the triangle again. Your display should look something like the one shown in Figure 17.30. The triangle fits the texture horizontally in Texture View, which represents U parameterization from 0 to 1. Normalized UVs map the texture to the polygon surface in this manner.

It's a good idea to keep the UV Texture Editor window open when you are working with polygon textures. You can access most of the Texture submenu options from this window, and we will use it throughout this section.

Figure 17.28

Polygon primitives and UV mappings

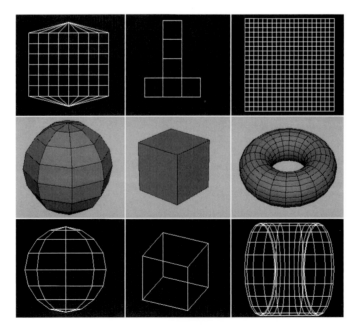

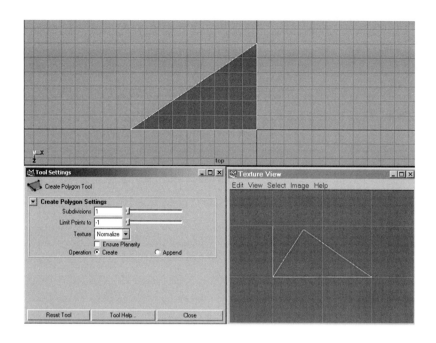

Figure 17.29

Create Polygon, UV Texture Editor, and a face.

In the UV Texture Editor window, select the Image Range options window (choose Image → Image Range ❑) to change how much of the texture displays. You can change the size of the image yourself by setting the Minimum U/V and Maximum U/V range, or you can use one of the presets. Grid Size allows the texture to fill the grid (as defined in the Grid Options window). Unit Size fills the 0 to 1 (or unit) texture space.

Transforming UVs

You can transform UVs in the UV Texture Editor window in the same way that you transform regular vertices. If the selected faces have a projection mapping, you can edit the Mapping manipulator as well.

Figure 17.30

Ramp assigned to triangle

1. In the UV Texture Editor window, RM click and choose UV to switch into component selection mode. Then, select all the UVs, and select the Move tool. A 2D Move manipulator appears. Move the manipulator, and you will see the texture in the triangular face update in the modeling window.

2. Select the Rotate tool, and a 2D Rotate manipulator appears. Rotate the UVs, and again, the texture inside the triangle updates accordingly, as shown in Figure 17.31.

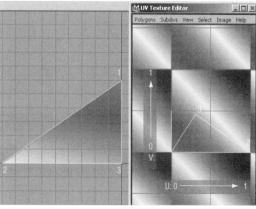

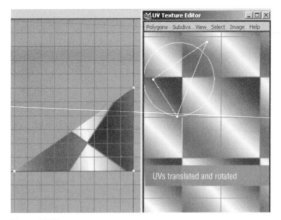

Figure 17.31

UVs moved and rotated

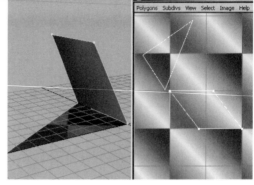

Figure 17.32

Diagonal face added

3. Append a quad face to the triangle. Open the Append To Polygon Tool window, turn off Ensure Planarity, and set Texture to Normalize. Select the right edge, switch to side view, and click the vertices up so that you end up with a diagonal face, as shown in Figure 17.32.

When it becomes part of the surface, the ramp texture is automatically assigned to the new quad face. As the UVs of the new face are normalized, the ramp texture is mapped to the diagonal face horizontally, from 0 to 1, as shown in Figure 17.32.

Sewing Textures

In our example, although the faces are attached to each other with shared edges and vertices, the UVs are mapped separately. This creates a problem if we want a texture that will go across the two faces. To have the two faces share the texture mapping, you can *sew* the textures.

1. First, let's position the textures properly. In the modeling window, select the UVs on the edge that joins the faces.

2. In the UV Texture Editor window, take note of which two UVs of the triangle and the diagonal faces are selected. Select all the UVs of the diagonal face, and then rotate and translate them so that the two UVs of the triangle and the diagonal face are next to each other, as shown in Figure 17.33.

3. Select the common edge of the two faces, and then, in the UV Texture Editor window, choose Polygons → Sew UVs. The UVs of the triangle and the diagonal face snap to each other and become shared UVs. The Polygons → Cut UVs command performs the opposite function. It takes shared UVs and separates them, creating two new UVs per vertex.

Unitizing UVs

Now let's see what happens when we unitize our polygonal surface, which makes the UVs of the selected faces fit into a texture UV unit.

1. Open the Append To Polygon Tool window. Set Texture to Unitize, and turn on Ensure Planarity.

2. In perspective view, select the longest edge of the triangle. When you see pink arrows, click the nearest edge of the diagonal face.

3. In front view, click a vertex straight up to the diagonal face's height. The new face is planar, and it should look something like the image in Figure 17.34. The Unitized setting stretches the UVs for the new face to fit the texture UV unit.

4. Repeat the sewing procedure: rotate and translate the unitized UVs to line up to the triangle and sew it. You should see something like the image in Figure 17.35 in the next section. Notice that now there is a smooth texture transition from the triangle to the unitized face.

Assigning UVs

From time to time, you will encounter models imported from other programs that carry no UV information with them. Or you might choose to delete the UVs of polygons you are working on. You will then need to assign UV values to those polygons before you can render them, following a procedure like the one outlined here.

1. Open the Append To Polygon Tool window again if you've closed it. Set Texture to None.

2. Select the top edge of the unitized face. When you see the arrows, select the top edge of the diagonal face. Press Enter to create a triangle, as shown in Figure 17.35. Although it is part of the polygonal surface, this new triangle has no UV information, and therefore no texture is displayed. Notice that nothing new appears in the Texture View window.

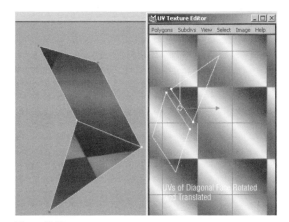

Figure 17.33

Diagonal face rotated and translated

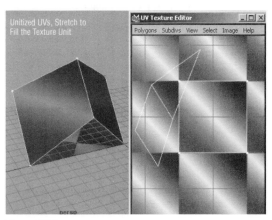

Figure 17.34

New face with unitized UVs

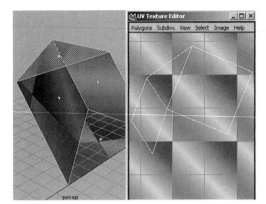

Figure 17.35

Triangle with no UV values assigned

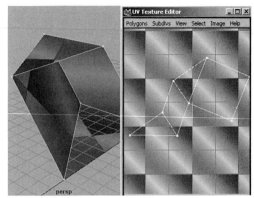

Figure 17.36

New face UV assigned and sewn

3. Select the face of the new triangle. Open the Normalize UVs option window by choosing Edit Polygons → Texture or by using the Polygons menu in the UV Texture Editor window. The default setting will make the triangle stretch from 0 to 1 in both U and V, which is not what we want for this example.

4. Select Preserve Aspect Ratio to normalize only one of the two values, in this case, U. Click the Apply and Close button, and the texture should appear on the new triangle in the modeling window. Accordingly, the triangle, in its normalized UV points, should appear in the UV Texture Editor window.

5. Sew the new UVs to the diagonal face by rotating and translating the new triangle and then sewing the triangle and the existing rectangle edges, as shown in Figure 17.36.

Projection Mapping

Maya has four types of projection mapping functions, which project textures on to the UV coordinates of the selected polygon surfaces, all available from the Texture submenu: Planar, Cylindrical, Spherical Mapping, and Automatic Mapping. There is also a Create UVs Based On Camera function, which creates UV values of a planar mapping projected from the camera view. Let's try out the planar mapping.

1. Start a new scene and create a polygonal cube. With the cube still selected, open the UV Texture Editor window. You should see the cube UVs laid out as shown in Figure 17.37. The default setting for the cube normalizes UVs, which means that each face will receive a whole texture, and the UVs are all connected for the whole object.

2. Rotate the cube on the Z axis 45 degrees. RM click the cube and choose Face to switch into component selection mode. Now, select the cube's front face. Make sure that the Assign Shader To Each Projection function on the Edit Polygons → Texture submenu is

checked, and apply Planar Mapping (choose Edit Poly-gons → Texture → Planar Mapping) with the default set-tings. The Assign Shader To Each Projection setting automatically creates a default polygon shader with a checkered texture and assigns it to the selected polygon. The default planar projection fits the texture to the bounding box of the selected object or face and projects the map along the Z axis.

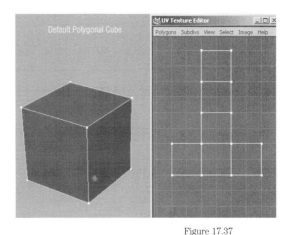

Figure 17.37

Default cube with UVs

3. The black-and-white checkered colors are too intense for viewing in the UV Texture Editor window. In Hyper-shade, select the checkered texture and assign dull blue to one color and green to the other. Notice how the UV points are mapped as a square rotated 45 degrees in the UV Texture Editor window.

4. Select the cube. If you don't see the texture in the UV Texture Editor window, as shown in Figure 17.38, choose Image → Selected Images → texturedFacets | pCube1.

Do not confuse UV projection mappings for polygons with the texture projections for NURBS objects; they are completely different processes. When creating textures for poly-gons in the Hypershade, use the Normal setting, which creates UV textures. If you need to create a texture as a projection, click the Interactive Placement button only for NURBS objects, not polygons.

Mapping would be a bit harder if, for example, we selected the face at the top and rotated it in the Y and X axes to make it nearly perpendicular and diagonal, as shown in Figure 17.39. If we apply the default planar (Z-axis) mapping, we get stretched UVs (as in the top-left image). Notice how the UVs are stretched in the UV Texture Editor window as well. If we set the option to Y-axis projection, again the result is not what we want (as in the top-right image). We could grab the manipulator handle and rotate and scale until the texture fits the surface straight, but that takes effort. Instead, we can set the option to Fit To Best Plane. The projection will extend in the direction of the surface normal, and as a result, we get a perfect fit (as in the bottom-left image). Another option is to apply planar mapping with camera direction (as in the bottom-right image). For the last example, we tried selecting the whole cube as an object, so all the UVs would map exactly as the UVs you see through the camera in the modeling window.

Figure 17.38

Planar mapped face and Texture view

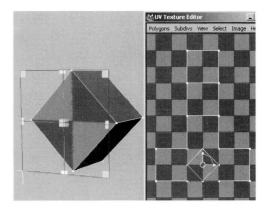

Figure 17.39

Projections and corresponding Texture views

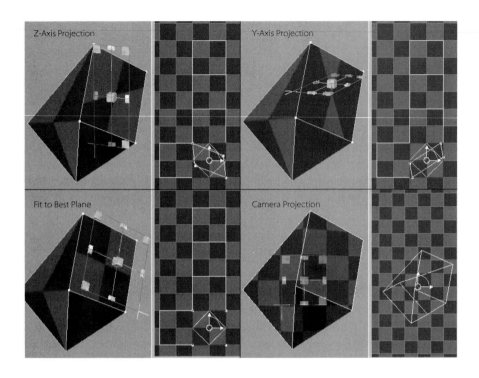

The Cylindrical and Spherical Mapping options are similar in principle to planar mapping, and you apply them in the same way. Often, the shape of the polygonal object will dictate which type of mapping is best suited for it.

One of the big difficulties with polygon UV mapping is that on complex models it is hard to get evenly spread out UVs. As the two examples in Figure 17.40 demonstrate, it's one thing to make a texture map evenly on a simple surface such as a plane, quite another thing to map it evenly on more complicated surfaces.

Figure 17.40

Mapping a ramp texture to a simple and a complex surface

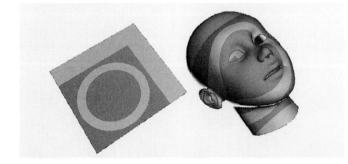

Let's look at the head more closely. Figure 17.41 shows the UV mapping that was applied to the head, which was a planar projection. When texturing the front part of the face, as shown in the middle picture, the UVs are evenly spreading the ramp texture. But when we try to map the ramp texture to the side of the head, we get stretching, as seen in the last picture. Getting rid of such texture stretching (or other problems, such as squashing or seams between faces) is often the more difficult part of working with polygons.

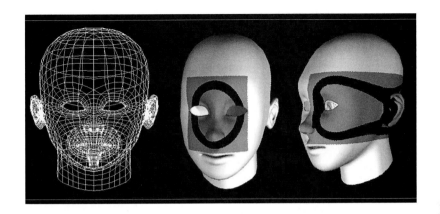

Figure 17.41

UV mapping of a human head

Creating Clean UVs

To avoid or reduce the stretching and overlapping of textures on polygon surfaces, we need to create clean UV coordinates. This usually means creating UVs that are neither overlapping nor stretched or squashed in relation to the actual surface areas of the corresponding polygon surfaces. Maya provides a variety of tools to help you to accomplish such a task.

Automatic Mapping

Automatic mapping can give us a starting point for creating a good UV map. The six projections of the head in Figure 17.42 illustrate this process. The first two UVs, (a) and (b), were created with Cylindrical Mapping and Spherical Mapping, and they are not at all practical for the head. As you can easily see, they will create overlapping textures that will stretch and squash. They will also create seams between some faces. UV map (c) was created using Automatic Mapping. Although this mapping creates many separate pieces of UVs, those pieces also reflect accurately the proportional sizes of the surface's faces. Although picture (c) is not in itself a good UV map, it does give us a basis from which to start building one. In (d), two pieces of UVs, representing the front part of the face and the left side of the head, have been dragged closely together. Using the Sew UVs or the Move And Sew UVs command, we can sew the two pieces together. Picture (e) shows the sewing process. As the UVs are being sewn, some distortion of the UVs is inevitable. The final UV map that resulted from this process is shown in Figure 17.42 (f).

Figure 17.42

Automatic Mapping produces the most accurate UVs, but the pieces must be sewn together.

Figure 17.43

**Using the Move And
Sew UVs command**

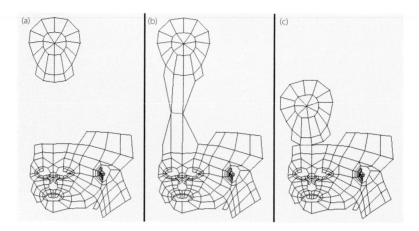

Automatic Mapping produces a UV map that lies within 0 to 1 texture space. This is important for texturing, especially if the texture will be created in a 3D paint program, because that space is where the texture will fit into exactly once. If any of the UVs go outside the 0 to 1 boundary, Automatic Mapping will map a repeating texture.

The Move And Sew UVs Command

We've just seen that another tool, Move And Sew UVs, is useful in working with UVs, especially if you create them with Automatic Mapping. In Figure 17.43, we have two separate UV patches, as shown in (a). If we apply the regular Sew UVs, we get stretching between the two pieces as their common edges are sewn, as seen in (b). But when we apply Move And Sew UVs, the smaller patch of UVs snaps to the larger piece, as shown in (c). This command can quickly sew together many separate patches of UVs while maintaining their proportional size and form.

Maya provides some other editing tools that we simply do not have space to get into, such as Relax UVs, Layout UVs (although we will cover this later in "Texturing Subdivision Surfaces"), and Flip UVs. If you will be working with polygons frequently, explore the other commands in the Texture submenu on your own. One related command that we do need to cover, though, is Polygons → Transfer.

Transferring UVs

The Transfer command copies vertex, UV, or Vertex Color information from the first selected polygon to the second selected polygon. As long as both polygons have the same topology, the command works. This enables us to create a clean UV map more easily on a smoothed-out version of a complex polygon surface and then copy that UV map to the original complex surface. You can create the smoothed version by using the Artisan smoothing brush or the

Average Vertices command. For example, face (a) in Figure 17.44 has a map in which the UVs around the nose and mouth areas are overlapping. Face (b) is a copy of the first, with the nose and mouth areas smoothed with Average Vertices. It may look ugly, but a planar mapping on this face creates a cleaner UV map, which then can be transferred to the first face, as shown in (c).

Texturing Subdivision Surfaces

Subdivision surfaces inherit the UV mapping from the polygon or NURBS surfaces they are created from. You can edit subdivision UVs just as you would edit any regular polygon surface. However, subdivision surfaces have their own mapping and editing operations, separate from the polygon operations.

UV Mapping for Subdivision Surfaces

There are two UV mapping methods for subdivision surfaces, Planar Mapping and Automatic Mapping, located under the Subdiv Surfaces → Texture menu. These mapping techniques are equivalent to the Planar and Automatic Mapping of polygons except that only one UV set is used for subdivision surfaces whereas polygons can have multiple UV sets.

Planar Mapping for Subdivision Surfaces

Planar mapping assigns UVs to a subdivision surface in a single direction onto a single plane. Although this method keeps the UV pieces low, it tends to cause the pieces to overlap since the projected UVs are striking both sides of the surface. To fix this, you will need to use Layout UVs to separate the overlapping pieces.

Figure 17.44

Transferring smoothed UVs to a complex surface

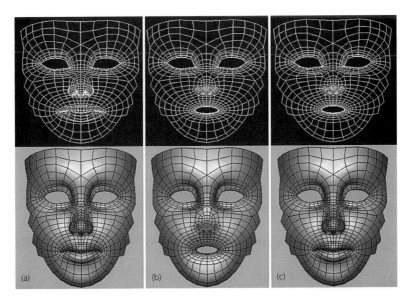

Automatic Mapping

Automatic mapping avoids overlapping UV pieces because UVs are projected onto subdivision surfaces inwardly from multiple planes. This will result in a greater number of smaller UV pieces, which may increase the difficulty of creating textures for the model. It would be a good idea to combine smaller UV pieces into larger pieces using the Move And Sew UVs operation.

UV Editing

In the UV Texture Editor, there is a separate menu for editing UVs for subdivision surfaces. It has the same operations as the polygon UV editing menu except for Layout UVs. Layout UVs separate overlapping UV pieces that typically result from planar mapping when more than one face is projected on the same area of the map.

Hands On: Texturing a Character

Let's now turn to texturing the human character we've been working with throughout this book. We will first deal with the hair and the eyes, which are NURBS surfaces, and then proceed to the subdivision surfaces—the head, body, hands, and feet.

Many image files were used to texture the character, and you can find them in the Chapter 17 folder on the CD-ROM. The image files are all squares such as 256×256 or 512×512. Maya works better with square image files whose dimensions are powers of 2, such as 128, 256, 512, or 1024. It's also a good idea to start out with a bigger size than you think you need and then shrink the image later, instead of starting out with a size that may pixelate when rendered.

Texturing the Hair and the Eyes

Texturing the NURBS parts of the human character is fairly straightforward. Although the following steps may not be the way to create the most photorealistic eyes and hair, they will give you good examples of how to work creatively with different render nodes.

1. Open the `character_bound.mb` file from the Chapter 12 folder on the CD-ROM. Make the subD_surfaces layer visible to see the hair. Assign an Anisotropic material to the hair strands and set SpreadX to 1.2, SpreadY to 1, Roughness to 0.1, and Fresnel Index to 3. You will probably change these settings as you refine the specularity of the hair later, but they will do for now. Apply a fractal to the Color attribute and set the Repeat UV to something like 5 and 0.2. You should see the fractal stretch as in Figure 17.45 (a). Connect a Ramp to the Color Gain attribute of the fractal to get color variation to the hair, as shown in (b). Create an image file to connect to the Transparency attribute of the Anisotropic material, and bring in the `hair_transparency.jpg` image from the CD-ROM. The hair should now look something like Figure 17.45 (c).

2. A few more steps need to be taken. Let's have a bit of bumping on the hair. Connect the fractal node to the Anisotropic material's Bump Mapping attribute. The initial bump value is too high, so bring down the Alpha Gain value of the fractal to something like 0.6. The hair geometry is transparent at the bottom end, but the specular still shines on what's supposed to be empty space. We want only the hair strands to shine. Create a Reverse node from the Create Utilities → General Utilities section. Connect the `hair_transparency` image file to the input of the Reverse node. Make a copy without a network of the fractal node, and connect the Reverse node to the Color Gain attribute of that copied fractal node. Then connect the copied fractal to the Specular Color attribute of the Anisotropic material. The specular now only shines where the hair is, as shown in Figure 17.46. The hair shading network is also shown for your reference.

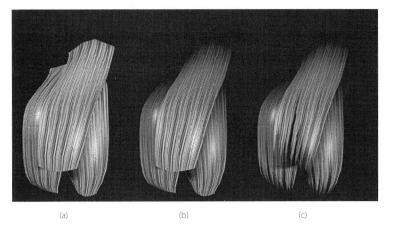

(a)　　　　　(b)　　　　　(c)

Figure 17.45

Hair transparency

Figure 17.46

Hair bumping and specularity

3. You can create good-looking eyes made of simple spheres and textures. In our example, however, the eyes are made of two spheres: an inner sphere for the pupil and the iris textures and a transparent outer sphere just for specularity. Start with a Layered shader, create a Blinn layer, and assign it to the inner sphere.

4. Start an IPR process to see how the values change as you work. Put a Ramp into the Color attribute of the Blinn material to create the pupil. Make the Ramp black and white and position the black color to start from the pupil area. Decrease the Blinn material's Eccentricity to 0.05, and increase Specular Roll Off to 1. Then push up the Specular Color's HSV value to 2.0. This will make the pupil shine with a tight and bright highlight, as shown in the first eyeball in Figure 17.47.

5. Create another Blinn material over the pupil layer to texture the iris area, and map a fractal to its color and bump. Make the fractal's Repeat UV 0.02 and 3. Put a ramp into the layer's Transparency attribute, and position the color entries so the ramp won't cover the pupil or too much of the eyeball area. It should look something like the second eyeball in Figure 17.47.

6. Create yet another Blinn layer over the third layer. This time, map a fractal just to its color, and make the fractal a bit darker. Put a ramp into its Transparency attribute so it will show up only at the edge of the iris, blending with the first fractal texture. You should see something like the third eyeball in Figure 17.47.

7. Assign a Blinn to the outer sphere and make it totally transparent. Decrease Eccentricity to 0.1, increase Specular Roll Off to 2, and push the Specular Color to totally white, or a value of 1. The outer sphere serves to make the eyes brighter with softer specularity, as you can see in the last eyeball in Figure 17.47, and it shows the convex shape of the eye lens.

Figure 17.47

The eye-texturing process

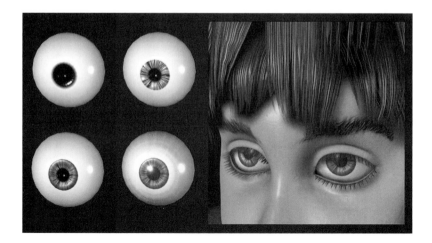

Instead of using Layered Shader, we could use Layered texture. That would make the network much more efficient, but we wouldn't be able to enter different values for specular shading in different layers.

Texturing the Head and the Body

Since we are using image files to texture the character, almost all the difficulty in texturing its subdivision surface parts lies in creating the appropriate UV maps. The UV map created for the head, for example, is not perfect; it stretches in certain areas and squashes and overlaps around the ears. The artist who worked on creating the texture, however, dealt with the UV map well enough. Often, the artist has to make compromises to try to balance the quality of what they are doing with the realistic demands of the situation. This is especially true in painting good organic textures. Figure 17.48 shows the UV map for the head, along with the color image and the Texture view of the two together.

1. Assign a Blinn material to the head, set its Eccentricity and Specular Roll Off to 0.3 and 0.5, and name it Skin. You can also give the material a tiny amount of Incandescence and a bit of Translucence to imitate the feel of living skin more closely. Connect an image file to Skin's Color attribute, and bring in `face_C.jpg` from the Chapter 17 folder on the CD-ROM. Then connect another image file to Skin's Bump Mapping attribute, and bring in `face_B.jpg`. As shown in Figure 17.49 (a), the default value for the bump map is too much. In the image file for the bump mapping, turn down the Alpha gain to about 0.2, and the bumping should seem more reasonable, as seen in (b). Also connect an image file to Skin's Specular Color attribute and bring in `face_S.jpg` from the CD-ROM. In this image file, bring up the Color Offset value to about 0.5, or gray color, and connect the bump map image file to its Color Gain attribute. This makes the specular shine only on the bumps. You should see something like in Figure 17.49 (c).

2. The body's UVs were collected into groups, as seen in Figure 17.50 (a). Then the artist mapped the appropriate textures on them: the `body_C.jpg` color file shown in (b), the `body_B.jpg` bump file in (c), and the `body_S.jpg` specular file in (d). Assign another Blinn material to the body, and connect the appropriate image files to the material. The specular intensity and the bump value should be fairly low.

The images for the head and the body are 1024 × 1024, which you may consider too large, but remember that it is always better to start big and then resize. For most purposes, these images could probably be resized to 512 × 512 without losing any quality.

Figure 17.48

UV map and image
for the head

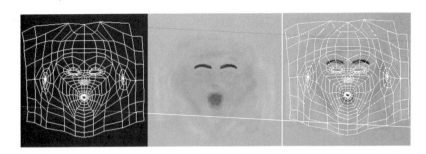

Figure 17.49

Bump and specular
mapping

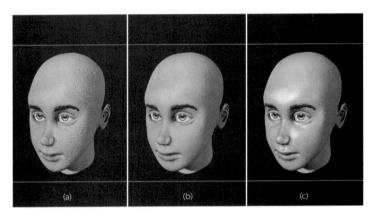

Figure 17.50

Image files for the
body

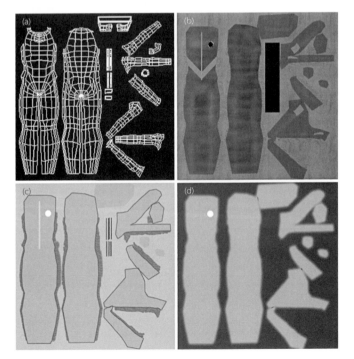

3. Repeat the same procedure for the hands and the shoes. They each have three image files in the Chapter 17 folder on the CD-ROM—one for color, one for bump, and one for specular. The artist has chosen to create separate files for the material's attributes, but you could easily use a bump map, adjusting its Color Gain and Color Offset, as a specular map as well.

4. The remaining image to be mapped is `eyelashes.jpg`, which should be applied in essentially the same manner as the `hair_transparency` image was used. Assign a Lambert material to the eyelashes, and then use the image file for both Color and Transparency attributes. You can see the finished images in the color section in this book or in the Color Gallery on the CD-ROM.

Summary

In this chapter, you learned how to use the Hypershade and work with various render nodes. We covered materials and textures, their various properties and attributes, and how to work with them in shading a dog, parts of the living room scene, and a human character.

Shading and texturing, as you have seen working with our examples, can make the simplest objects look good. But in creating the textures in this chapter, one essential part has been intentionally omitted from our discussion: lighting. In the next chapter, we will learn all about this other half of the equation in creating great-looking pictures.

CHAPTER 18

Lighting

Although in this book we discuss lighting after discussing modeling, animation, and shading, lighting is really a circular process, and it's difficult to confine it to any one stage in the production cycle. Before you can test-render anything, whether it's a model you are building or the textures of a model you've already built, you need to set up proper lights to view the scene properly. At the same time, if you want to control precisely how the lights shine on the objects, you should not fine-tune your lights until all the animation is finished. We'll discuss proper lighting techniques later in this chapter and conclude with some tips on optimizing the renderer once lighting is set up. But first, let's go over the six Maya lights and their attributes. This chapter's topics include:

- **Types of lights and their properties**
- **Shadows**
- **Light effects**
- **Lighting techniques**

Types of Lights

You can light surfaces using Ambient light, Directional light, Point light, Spot light, Area light, or Volume Light. Usually you'll combine different lights to get the effects you want. You can create any type of light from the Create menu (choose Create→ Lights) or by choosing it from the Create Lights section in the Create Bar panel of the Hypershade. Figure 18.1 shows the icons for the lights in the Hypershade and in the modeling window.

Ambient Light

Ambient light can shine, as its name suggests, everywhere uniformly—bathing all the objects in the scene from all directions. You can get similar effects from a material shader by controlling its ambient color. But Ambient light can also behave as a simple Point light, which shines from a specific point and in a specific direction. You can combine omnidirectional and directional Ambient light using the Ambient Shade setting in the Attribute Editor. When the Ambient Shade is set to 1, the Ambient light behaves exactly like a Point light; it lights a surface from a specific position. Ambient light can also cast shadows like Point light, but only when raytraced.

In Figure 18.2 (which also appears in the Color Gallery on the CD), you can see examples of different Ambient Shade values. The third picture is raytraced with Use Ray Trace Shadows turned on.

Figure 18.1

Maya's six types of light in the modeling window (top) and Hypershade (bottom)

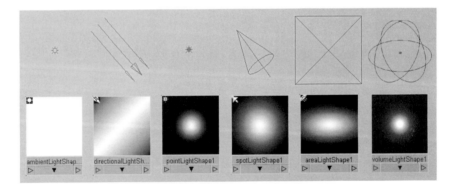

Figure 18.2

Various Ambient Shade values

Directional, Point, and Spot Lights

Directional light shines in the direction of its icon arrows. It imitates light coming from a distant source, such as the sun. Point light, by contrast, shines from a specific point to all directions evenly; it is ideal for imitating a light bulb or a candle. Spot light behaves exactly like a real-world spotlight, its direction defined by a beam of light that gradually widens. Spot lights are also good for imitating headlights or lamps. Figure 18.3 shows examples of these lights. Notice how the Point and Spot light shadows are a bit bigger than the Directional light's shadows. This is because the rays scatter for the Point and Spot lights, but not for Directional light. One significant difference between Point light and Spot light exists in the way they cast shadows. When Depth Map Shadow is turned on (see the "Shadows" section later in this chapter), Point light creates multiple shadow maps by default, whereas Spot light creates only one.

Ambient and Directional lights do not have Decay Rate attributes, whereas Point and Spot lights do. Spot light also has Cone Angle, Penumbra Angle, and Dropoff attributes. We'll look at these and other light properties in the following sections.

> You can change a light from one type to another in the Attribute Editor. When you do that, however, only the attributes common to both types are retained. Other attribute settings are lost.

Area Light

Area light behaves much like Point light, except that it shines from a flat rectangular area, which can be scaled like a regular plane. When you make the area larger, the light intensity increases proportionally. With Area lights you can create more realistic specular highlights, mimic radiosity better, and (when raytracing) create dissipating shadows.

Figure 18.4 (a) shows a shoe lit by a Spot light. Notice how the specular highlight is reflecting from the shoe. Picture (b) shows the same shoe lit by an Area light. The specular on the shoe is much more realistic. In (c), another Area light with low intensity was placed just behind the wall to imitate light reflecting off the wall and lighting the shoe. Again, the light seems to be bouncing off the entire wall, not just from a point.

Figure 18.3

Directional, Point, and Spot lights

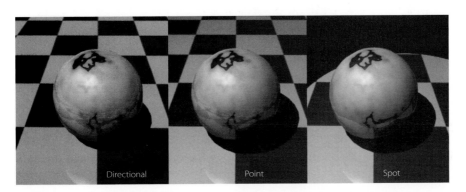

Directional   Point   Spot

Volume Light

Volume light illuminates within the boundaries of the light. You can choose its shape from either box, sphere, cylinder, or cone. As with Area light, you can control how much of your scene will be lit by adjusting the scale of the volume light. You can change the direction of the light as well, for different lighting effects: Outward simulates a Point light, Downward behaves like a Directional light, and Inward gives you inward illumination. Figure 18.5 (left) shows how the scene is lit by the Volume light, which is centered on the candle. The wireframe image (right) shows where in the scene the Volume light has been placed. As you can see, the light grows weaker as it moves away from the center. You can adjust this via the color range in the Volume light's Attribute Editor. More on this later in the chapter.

Light Properties

For all types of light, you can control the basic properties of color and intensity. For Point, Area, and Spot lights, you can vary the intensity over distance by controlling the decay rate, whereas the Volume light uses a color ramp (or gradient) to control its decay rate. Additionally, you can control the linkage between lights and the objects in a scene. Finally, Spot lights have some unique properties and attributes you can control. You can access all these controls in the light's Attribute Editor.

Color and Intensity

As with shading, you can use the Color Chooser to tint a light (usually subtly) or map textures that will be projected onto the surface. When textures mask or filter certain areas of light as in Figure 18.6 (a) and (b), the light is called a *gobo* light. You can also change the intensity or brightness of a light. Negative intensity values will actually take away light, which can be useful for creating shadowy areas such as dark corners in a room, as shown in exaggerated form in (c). You can also make the light color black and the shadow color white to create shadow masks, as illustrated in (d). To create the mask, you also need to change the floor to plain white color and turn off the primary visibility of the shoe.

Figure 18.4

Area light lighting a shoe

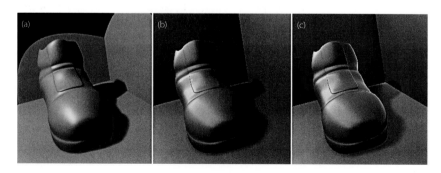

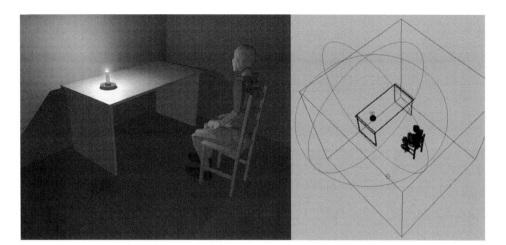

Figure 18.5

Volume light illuminating a scene

Figure 18.6

The gobo, negative light, and shadow mask effects

A *shadow mask* is used in compositing to put shadows into a scene when objects in the scene are rendered separately. It is especially useful when computer graphic elements are being added to live footage. The shadow mask allows the compositor to blur the shadows, if necessary, and to adjust the HSV (hue, saturation, and value) settings of the shadow to match the shadows in the live footage.

Figure 18.7

**A grid texture
mapped to the
Intensity attribute**

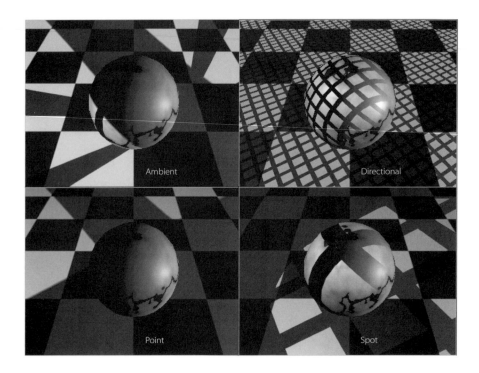

You can also control the intensity value of any light by mapping textures to it, which produces results similar to mapping texture to color. Figure 18.7 shows examples of a default grid texture mapped to the Intensity attribute of different lights with default settings. Notice how the grids are translated to intensity values differently for each of these four lights.

For Spot light only, you can also create Intensity and Color curves to control their values with respect to distance from the light source. To create the curves, click the Create buttons under the Light Effects section of the Attribute Editor. You can then edit the curves in the Graph Editor.

Decay Rate

You can decay the intensity of Point, Area, and Spot lights over a distance by turning on Decay Rate. You can choose from three decay rates: Linear, which decreases intensity proportionally to the distance; Quadratic, which decreases intensity proportionally to the square of the distance (distance × distance) and is how light intensity decays in the real world; and Cubic, which decreases intensity proportionally to the cube of distance (distance × distance × distance). In Figure 18.8 (and in the Color Gallery on the CD), you can see examples of each decay rate. Notice how the intensity value shoots up accordingly to light the sphere. You can hardly tell the differences in the sphere itself, but the differences are noticeable on the floor. Also, the Decay Rate setting begins to affect a light's intensity only at distances greater than one unit from the light source. Inside the one-unit radius, no decay of light intensity is possible.

To decay Volume lights, you use the color ramp in the Color Range section of the Attribute Editor. This gradient ramp affects the color of the Volume light from its center to the edge. You can change the way the light decays by changing the values on the ramp. The right side of the ramp represents the color at the light's center, and the left side is the color at the light's outer edge. The Interpolation settings determine how the colors on the ramp are blended.

Linking Lights and Objects

When a light shines on a surface, the two are said to be *linked*. All the lights have a setting called Illuminates By Default, which is turned on by default and shines the light on all objects; that is, the light is linked to all the objects in the scene. If the setting is off, the light will not shine on any object unless you manually link it to that object. You can also do the opposite and cut the link between individual objects and a light so that the light will not shine on those objects. If you are working on simple scenes, you usually retain the default settings and let all lights shine on all objects. As soon as the scene gets fairly complex, however, it's a good idea to start linking lights only to the objects they need to light, because linking affects rendering time significantly.

You can link lights and objects or sever the links from the Lighting/Shading menu in the Rendering module. Select the object(s) and light(s). Select Make Light Links to link them or Break Light Links to sever them. You can also control light linking in the Relationship Editor (choose Light/Shading → Light Linking). You can either open the Relationship Editor in what Maya calls a *light-centric* mode and link objects to a light, or open it in an object-centric mode and link lights to an object. Figure 18.9 shows examples of using a light-centric Relationship Editor to link objects to lights. On the left, the second and third spheres have been severed from pointLight1. On the right, the second sphere has been severed also from pointLight2 and, as a result, is totally black.

The Lighting/Shading menu also includes the Select Objects Illuminated By Light and Select Lights Illuminating Object commands. When you select a light and apply the Select Objects Illuminated By Light command, all objects linked to that light are selected. When you select an object and apply the Select Lights Illuminating Object command, all lights linked to that object are selected.

Figure 18.8

Linear, Quadratic, and Cubic decay rates

Linear
Intensity = 6.5

Quadratic
Intensity = 40

Cubic
Intensity = 220

Figure 18.9

Light-centric linking of objects

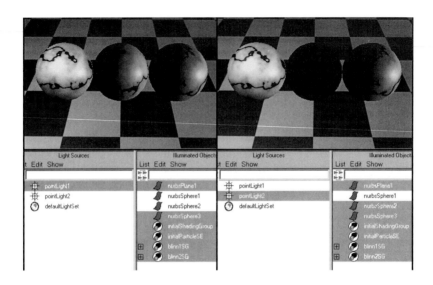

Spot Light Properties

Unique to Spot light are the Cone Angle, Penumbra Angle, and Dropoff attributes. Cone Angle controls the spread of the beam. It is usually sufficient to leave it at the default 40 degrees. Penumbra Angle, when given a positive value, blurs the area outside the cone to soften the edge. With a negative value, it blurs the area inside the edge to soften it. Figure 18.10 shows examples of different Cone Angle and Penumbra Angle settings.

> Be careful not to spread the Cone Angle too much, as it will create problems with shadows.

Dropoff is similar to Linear Decay Rate, but instead of decaying over a distance from the light source, it makes the intensity drop off from the center of the cone to its edge, much like the decay of Volume lights. Its results are often similar to the Penumbra Angle with a negative value. Figure 18.11 shows examples of different Dropoff values and their effects on the Spot light.

Spot Light Effects

In the Light Effects section of the Attribute Editor, two more attributes of Spot light are worth mentioning: Barn Doors and Decay Regions. They are both turned off by default. Barn Doors act just like masks, or shutters, to cover the edges of the cone from four corners. You input values to set the angles between the Spot light's center and the barn doors. The Decay Regions option lets you create regions within the Spot light beam where the light does not illuminate, as well as regions where it does illuminate. The example of Decay Regions in Figure 18.12 has light fog applied to it. (The effect is similar to a smoky nightclub. You'll learn more about fog effects later in this chapter.)

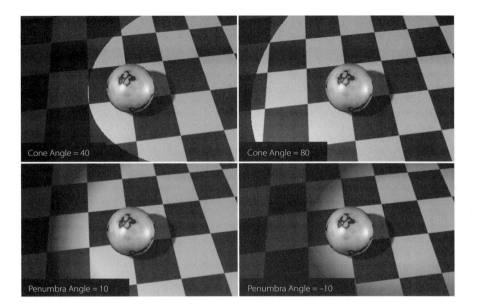

Figure 18.10

Examples of Cone Angle and Penumbra Angle settings

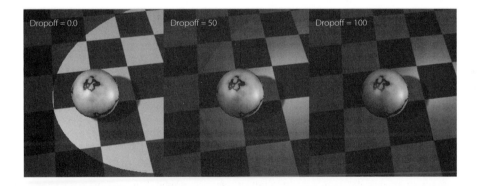

Figure 18.11

Examples of different Dropoff values

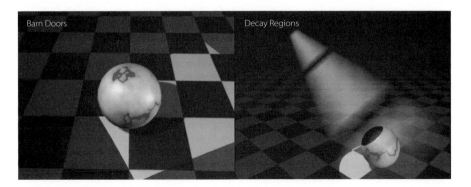

Figure 18.12

Barn Doors and Decay Regions

Shadows

The default light setting in Maya produces no shadows. This is because shadows can be computationally expensive and, in general, you want only one or two main lights to be casting shadows. You can set all lights to produce either Depth Map Shadows or Ray Trace Shadows, with the exception of Ambient light, which can only produce Ray Trace shadows. To activate shadows, open the Shadows section of a light's Attribute Editor, and check Use Depth Map Shadows in the Depth Map Shadow Attributes section, or check Use Ray Trace Shadows in the Raytrace Shadow Attributes section.

Depth-Map Shadows

Most of the time you will want to use depth-map shadows, because they are much more efficient than raytraced shadows. When a depth-map shadow is turned on, during rendering Maya creates a *depth map*, which stores the distance from the shadow casting light to the surfaces that the light is illuminating and uses this information to calculate shadows. The depth map, as you can see in Figure 18.13, is a Z-depth (see Chapter 16, "Rendering Basics") image file created from the light's point of view, and it enables Maya to calculate whether one surface is behind another surface with respect to the light. In this case, areas of the floor are found to be behind the sphere and the cone, and are thus rendered as shadows. A small area of the cone is also found to be behind the sphere and becomes a shadow as well.

Color

The default Shadow Color setting is black, but you might want to lighten it or tint it with other colors or even map textures to it, depending on the look you want. Mapping into color can also be a good way to fake transparency. Depth-map shadows do not recognize transparent objects; only raytraced shadows do. But for simple situations, you can often get away with clever use of Shadow Color, as in the examples in Figure 18.14 (also in the Color Gallery on the CD). On the left, a darkened version of the marble texture was connected to the Shadow Color; on the right, a ramp was used to create the more transparent upper area of the shadow.

Figure 18.13

A depth map and the resulting shadows

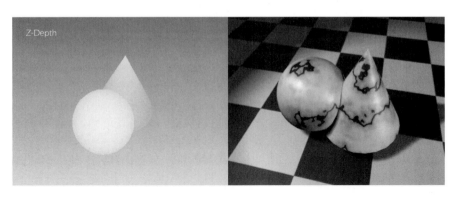

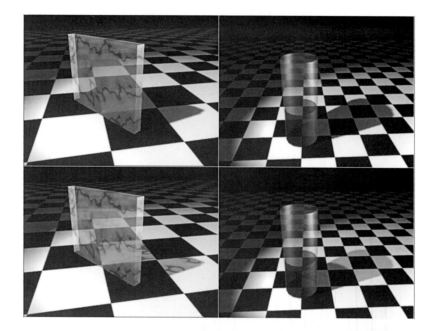

Figure 18.14

Examples of faking transparency

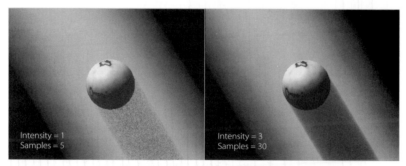

Figure 18.15

Fog Shadow Intensity and Fog Shadow Samples

Intensity = 1
Samples = 5

Intensity = 3
Samples = 30

Fog Shadow Intensity and Fog Shadow Samples

When the Light Fog attribute (discussed shortly) is applied to a light, you can control the intensity and the graininess of the fog shadow as well. The darkness of the shadow is controlled by the Fog Shadow Intensity setting, and the graininess is controlled by Fog Shadow Samples, as seen in Figure 18.15. Increasing the value in the latter increases the rendering time, so keep its values as low as is acceptable.

Dmap Resolution, Filter Size, and Bias

Dmap Resolution sets the size of the depth map that Maya creates. The default value is 512, which creates a square depth-map file 512 pixels in width and height. If you need sharper shadows, you might need to increase the resolution, but for softer shadows, you can get good results with resolutions as low as 128 or even 64. The Dmap Filter Size blurs, or softens, the shadow edges. As with any filter, the higher the number, the more expensive it gets, so keep the filter size as low as is acceptable. In Figure 18.16 are examples of various resolution and filter size settings and their effects.

Dmap Bias controls how much the shadow is offset from its source. It should generally be left at its default value, except to correct situations in which the shadow placement seems off, as in the left image in Figure 18.17.

Disk Based Dmaps

The Disk Based Dmaps feature can make rendering go much faster when used properly. The default setting is Off, which means that every time Maya renders, it creates depth maps for shadow calculations. But since a depth map stores information about the distance between a light and the surfaces it illuminates, you can reuse the depth map as long as the relative distance between the light and its linked surfaces in a scene does not change. Even if the camera and any other element in the scene are being animated, you can still reuse the depth map.

Figure 18.16

Examples of Dmap settings

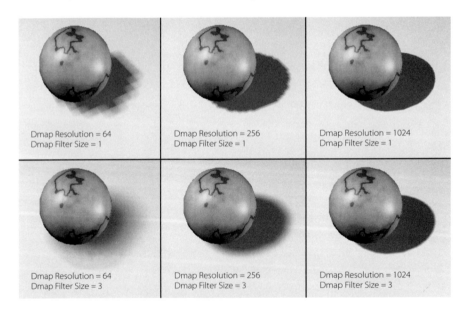

Figure 18.17

Examples of Dmap Bias

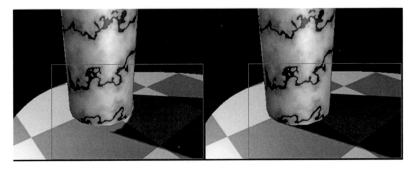

Switch the setting to Reuse Existing Dmap(s) to activate other settings. The default Dmap Name is `depthmap`, and Dmap Light Name is checked, which means that when the depth map is saved to disk, it will be assigned the name `depthmap` plus the name of the light generating the depth map. For example, for a Spot light named Spot, a depth-map file named `depthmap_SpotShape1.SM.iff` is created. The first time around, Maya looks for a depth map in the current project directories; and when it doesn't find one, it creates the depth map and places it in the current project directory, in the `\depth` subdirectory. The next time Maya renders, it uses this depth map to shadow the surfaces, thus reducing rendering time.

If the distances between the light and its linked surfaces do change over time and you will be rendering the sequence more than once (as often happens with animation test-renders), you can still create a sequence of depth maps and reuse them by checking Dmap Frame Ext.

The other Disk Based Dmaps setting, Overwrite Existing Dmap(s), overwrites any existing depth maps. If you make positional changes to a light or any of its linked surfaces, you should overwrite existing depth maps. Once you've rendered and created new depth maps, change the setting to Reuse Existing Dmap(s) again.

By default, Use Only Single Dmap is turned on. This means Maya will generate a single depth map for the spotlight. Most of the time this is sufficient, but if the cone angle is large (90 degrees or more), additional depth maps may be needed to avoid jagged-edged shadows. For higher-quality shadows, clear the Use Only Single Dmap check box. Maya will then generate as many as five depth maps for the spotlight in six possible directions: positive or negative X, positive or negative Y, and positive or negative Z. By default, all directions are turned on, but you usually need only a few directions for the light to cast shadows in. Turning off depth maps in certain directions will also reduce rendering times.

Raytraced Shadows

Raytracing gives you better renders than depth-map shadows; the images have a clean, crisp feeling that regular rendering cannot completely match. For example, when you are creating shadows for transparent objects that have reflections and refractions, and you need photorealistic accuracy, raytraced shadows are the only way to go. The cost, however, is rendering time. For many situations, you can get almost exactly the same quality with depth-map shadows, with much more efficient render times.

To use raytraced shadows, you need to turn on Use Ray Trace Shadows in the individual light's Attribute Editor and also turn on Raytracing in the Render Globals.

When Use Ray Trace Shadows is turned on, Shadow Radius becomes active for Ambient light, Light Angle for Directional light, and Light Radius for Point, Spot, and Volume lights. (This option is not available with Area light.) These different attributes all affect the softness of the shadow edges. Zero, which is the default setting, gives you sharp, hard shadow edges, and as the values increase, the edges become softer. The value range is different for different lights.

As the shadow becomes softer, the edges at the default setting become grainier, as in Figure 18.18 (a). The Shadow Rays setting blurs the graininess of the edges. Shadow Rays is render-intensive, so it is best to keep the values as low as you can.

Soft edge shadows can be much more efficiently created with depth-map shadows. Ray-traced shadows are more useful for creating sharp, crisp shadows.

Ray Depth Limit sets the maximum number of times, minus one, that a ray of light can be reflected or refracted and still create a shadow. If the value of the Shadows attribute in the Raytracing Quality section of the Render Globals is lower than the Ray Depth Limit value, that lower value becomes the maximum limit. In Figure 18.18 (c) and (d) (and in the Color Gallery on the CD), a Ray Depth Limit of 1 isn't showing the shadow behind the transparent sphere. By contrast, a Ray Depth Limit of 3 shows it.

Raytracing with Area light can also give you dissipating shadows. The depth-map shadows on the left in Figure 18.19 are quite soft, but we still have a solid area of shadow. The ray-traced shadow with Area light, in contrast, dissipates as it goes away from the object, as shown on the right.

Figure 18.18

Examples of Shadow Rays and Ray Depth Limit

Figure 18.19
Raytracing can produce a dissipating shadow with Area light.

Light Effects

In addition to the properties we've looked at so far, Maya offers various special effects you can apply to lights. These include fog and various optical effects such as glow, halo, and lens flare. You can access these effects from the Light Effects section of a light's Attribute Editor.

Light Fog

The Light Fog attribute can be applied to Point, Spot, and Volume lights. Point light fog is spherical, whereas the Spot light fog is cone shaped. Volume light fog takes the shape of the light, whether it be box, sphere, cylinder, or cone shaped. When light fog is applied, a separate fog icon appears along with the light icon, which you can transform to create the size and shape of the fog you want. Figure 18.20 shows examples of Point light fog and Spot light fog with different scales.

The Fog Type and Fog Radius attributes are available only for Point light fog. Under Fog Type, the Normal setting lets the fog intensity remain constant regardless of the distance from the light source. The Linear setting decreases the fog intensity as the distance from the light source increases, and the Exponential setting decreases the fog intensity as the distance increases exponentially. Fog Radius determines the spherical volume of the fog. Figure 18.21 shows examples of Point light's Fog Type and Fog Radius settings.

Fog Spread is an attribute available only for Spot light fog. It functions much like Spot light's Dropoff attribute. It determines the decrease in fog intensity as distance from the center of the cone increases, as in the examples in Figure 18.22. The decrease in intensity as the distance increases from the light source is determined by the Spot light's Decay Rate setting.

You can go to the lightFog node and adjust the Color and Density attributes of the light fog, or you can combine light fog with light glow (discussed next) to produce a combination effect. When using light fog, you will often also want to map textures into the light's Color attribute to imitate smoke or bigger dust particles. The example in Figure 18.23 (also in the Color Gallery on the CD) has a solid fractal texture mapped to the Color attribute of Spot light and Point light.

Figure 18.20

**Point light fog and
Spot light fog**

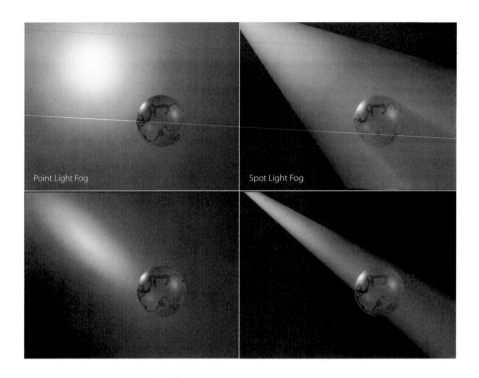

Figure 18.21

**Examples of Fog Type
and Fog Radius**

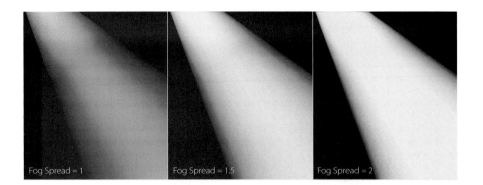

Figure 18.22

Examples of fog spread

Fog Spread = 1   Fog Spread = 1.5   Fog Spread = 2

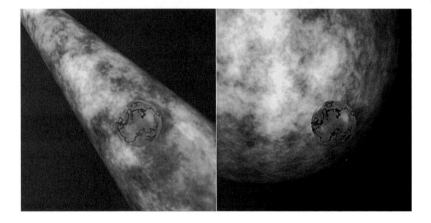

Figure 18.23

Solid fractal mapped to light color

OptiF/X

Maya has an optical light effects node (called OptiF/X) that can produce glow, halo, and/or lens flare effects for Point, Area, Spot, and Volume lights. The light effects are useful in imitating different camera filters, as well as stars, candles, flames, or explosions. The light sources have to be inside the camera view for the light effects to show, and the effects are all post-processes, applied after all the regular rendering is done. In the Light Effects section of the light's Attribute Editor, click the Light Glow box to create an opticalFX node. OptiF/X turns on when the Active box is checked and Glow Type and Halo Type are set to something other than None. For Lens Flare, you also need to check the Lens Flare box separately. Figure 18.24 shows examples of these three light effects.

Glow and Halo

Both Glow and Halo have the same list of types: Linear, Exponential, Ball, Lens Flare (which shouldn't be confused with the OpticalF/X Lens Flare effect), and Rim Halo. Figure 18.25

(also in the Color Gallery on the CD) shows examples of the various types for Glow and Halo. For the glow examples, Halo Type was set to None, and vice versa, but you would usually combine their effects.

Glow and Halo have same color and intensity attributes as regular lights, and you can change their sizes through the Spread attribute. Halo attributes are limited to those illustrated in Figure 18.25. Glow, however, has the additional stars and noise attributes.

Working with glow effects can be confusing because these additional attributes are scattered in different sections of the Attribute Editor, with three of them in the Optical FX Attributes section, and some of the others in the Noise Attributes section. The pictures in Figure 18.26 (also shown in the Color Gallery on the CD) have glow beam effects with various settings. Starting from the top left, the Star Points setting determines how many regular beams will come out of the light source. Their sharpness, or width, is determined by the Glow Star Level setting, and randomness in the beams is introduced by Glow Radial Noise. Once you have a nonzero Radial Noise setting, you can adjust both the frequency of the random beams and their width by using the Radial Frequency attribute. The beams can be rotated with the Rotation attribute. The two last pictures show more combinations of different possible glow settings.

Noise attributes produce a fractalized look you can use to imitate a variety of effects such as fog or explosions, as you can see in Figure 18.27 (and in the Color Gallery on the CD). Glow Noise produces the fractalized glow, which should always be adjusted together with Glow Intensity and Glow Spread (among other settings) to achieve the desired look. The Noise section enables you to adjust the Noise Threshold, along with its vertical and horizontal Scale and Placement.

Figure 18.24

Glow, halo, and lens flare effects

Glow   Halo   Lens Flare

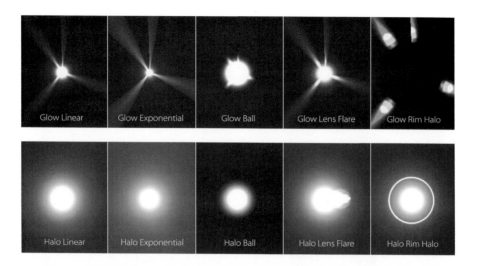

Figure 18.25

Examples of glow and halo

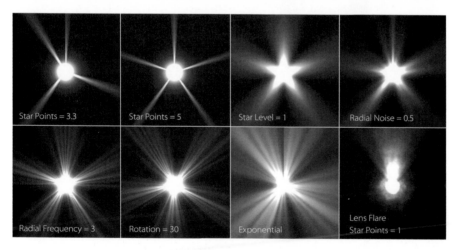

Figure 18.26

Glow settings

Lens Flare

Lens Flare re-creates the effect of physical imperfections in an optical lens, which become particularly apparent as the lens is trained toward a light source. Flare Color in the Lens Flare Attributes works a bit differently from the regular Color attribute in that Lens Flare color is a spectrum of colors, the range of which is determined by the Flare Col Spread attribute. Flare Num Circles determines how many circles (hexagons if Hexagon Flare is turned on) will show in the lens flare beam, and Flare Length determines the length of that beam. The Flare Min and Max Size attributes limit the sizes of the smallest and largest circles, and Flare Focus can blur or sharpen the flare circles, as seen in Figure 18.28 (also in the Color Gallery on the CD). Lens Flare beam doesn't rotate but is placed in different positions with Flare Vertical and Horizontal controls.

Figure 18.27

Examples of noise

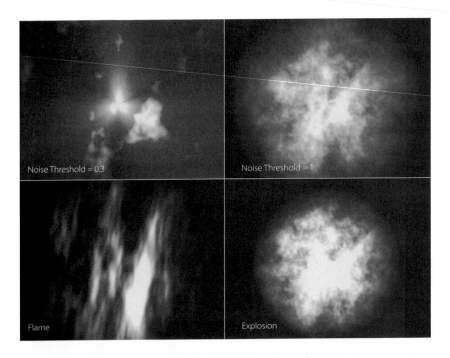

Figure 18.28

Examples of Lens Flare with different attributes

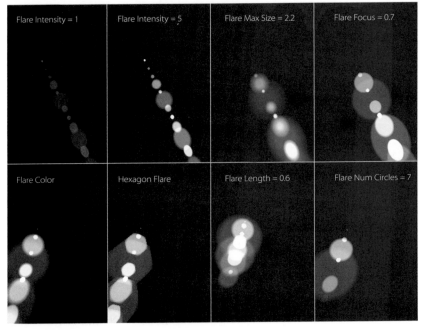

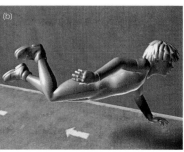

Figure 18.29

An example of bounce light

As you've seen, lights in Maya can have many different properties and effects to manage, and a complex scene can have numerous lights. Chapter 20, "MEL," shows how to build a MEL script that creates a graphical interface window for controlling all the lights in a scene.

Lighting Techniques

The art of lighting is a whole world unto itself, and studies in painting or photography will certainly be of great help. We will be able to cover only the basics in the remainder of this chapter.

The Basic Rules

One of the first things to realize about digital lighting is that there must always be a proper mixture of the real and artificial. First, lighting has to be believable. If a character is in a room, for example, you need to think about what and where the light sources are. Is there a window? Sunlight or moonlight? Are there lightbulbs or fluorescent lights? You also need to create additional lights to imitate bounce lights, or reflected light. In Figure 18.29 (a similar effect is also shown in the Color Gallery on the CD), the light in (a) has problems because the character's face in the shadows is totally dark, even though the corridor is lit. Picture (b) is better, as it accounts for the bounce lights in similar brightness level as the rest of the corridor.

> When you are dealing specifically with lights, you might find it better to get rid of textures for a while, as we did with the character in our examples. The absence of textures will help you think only about lights and shadows.

On the other hand, lighting is always an artificial endeavor. Stages and movie sets use many artificial lights to create the best possible lighting environment, setting the proper atmosphere and making sure the characters will be lit well. This often involves cheating reality, such as flooding characters with bright blue light for a night scene when in reality the light would be much darker, or creating a strong rim light (see the picture in the next section) on a character for a close-up, when the setting doesn't have any such strong light source coming from the character's backside. Good lighting often means that the dramatic needs of storytelling override reality. But computer lighting also has the additional burden of making the overall result look as if real lights had been placed in the same spots. You need to make sure the shadows look proper, bounce lights exist, and colors don't get washed out. You also have to worry about issues such as render time, transparent objects casting shadows, linking lights only to specific objects that need the lights, and so on.

Three-Point Lighting

When it comes to lighting a person, there are no hard and fast rules—different light setups can serve different purposes, and experimentation is often the only sure rule. Generally speaking, however, *Rembrandt* lighting is considered a good starting point. This means light hitting a subject from an angle so as to bring out its contours, as in Figure 18.30 (a) (a similar effect is also shown in the Color Gallery on the CD). It creates a triangle of lit area on the dark side, as can be seen in many of Rembrandt's paintings. This light is usually called a *key light*. In our example, Spot lights and Area lights are being used; but Point lights will work just as well.

Another light is then placed to shine on the dark side of the subject, as in (b), usually from the side and lower in intensity. This light is called *fill light*, because it fills the dark shadowy parts of the surface with light. The general rule is that if the key light color is warm, the fill light color should be cool, and vice versa. The third light is usually placed at the back and shining down on the subject, creating an outline of the head and shoulders, as in (c). Its intensity can vary from soft to very intense, the latter creating a glow. This light is called *back light*, and it's good for separating the foreground character from the background. Some people use the term *rim light* to describe this light as well.

Figure 18.30

Three-point lighting

These three lights make up what is known as *three-point lighting*, a standard lighting setup in photography. Because Maya does not automatically generate the bounce lights from these three lights, you might want a fourth light to act as a low-intensity second fill light shining from the front or the bottom to soften the dark areas between the key light and the first fill light, as also illustrated in (c). Then, as in picture (d), all the lights are combined to produce the final lighting.

A good technique for placing lights is to select the light and then, in the modeling window, choose Panels → Look Through Selected. This lets you view the scene from the light's point of view. Then, as you move and rotate in the modeling window, the light position adjusts accordingly. It's also a good idea to work on one light at a time, as in Figure 18.30.

Although three-point lighting will always give you a fairly satisfactory setup to work with, don't fall into the trap of making it the rule for all situations. Especially with lighting, the best examples are the ones that break the rules. (Of course, the same can be said of the worst examples.) Figure 18.31 shows some examples of extreme lighting setups. As a general rule, you do not want the key light to be shining directly from the front, because it makes the subject look flat, but it can produce a good live video camera effect if the intensity fall-off is carefully handled, as in (a). Hard light shining down as key light or having two back lights as key lights can also produce good dramatic effects, as in (b) and (c). And there's always the "I-am-the-spawn-of-hell" lighting, the key light shining almost vertically up from under the subject, as in (d).

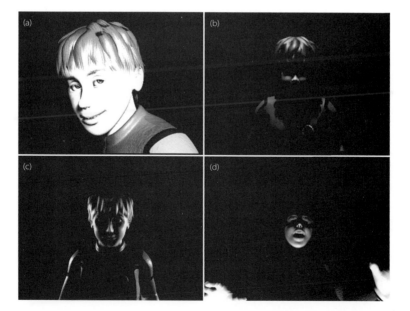

Figure 18.31

More lighting examples

RENDER OPTIMIZATION TIPS

You've read through the rendering information in this book, and you've set up your scene carefully. You've put in only the lights you really need, and you've set shadow casting for most of the lights. But your render times per frame are still through the roof! What's going on?

Most likely, the problem is that the render has not been optimized. You can optimize in many ways, and modelers have their own ideas about where to compromise quality and to what extent. However, it's possible to optimize rendering without reducing the quality of your work. Here, we present some production-tested ideas to help make your scenes renderable in your lifetime.

First, and most important, link lights to the surfaces they will be illuminating, as discussed earlier. Linking lights causes the renderer to calculate only the rays necessary to illuminate the linked object and any shadows that are being cast by that linked object. The other objects in the scene are ignored.

For example, this technique might be helpful when you have a Directional light illuminating your objects. If this light is also raytraced, the light will cast shadows from *everything*, which could take a while (to say the least). An alternative is to create a duplicate of the Directional light, exclusively link it to the objects that will not be casting shadows (don't link it to the floor either), and make this copied light non-shadow casting. Now link the original raytraced light only to the objects that will be casting shadows (plus the floor). The result will be a faster render, with raytraced shadows for only those objects that need it.

Another way to optimize this scene is to eliminate shadow casting for the floor itself, since we will never see the shadows it casts (which fall below the floor itself). Also, lowering the tessellation of distant objects will help conserve memory. Remember that a floor (unless curved) does not need to be highly tessellated!

Maya has the ability to selectively raytrace objects and surfaces (parts of objects), which you should use.

One of the best ways to reduce render times and give yourself more flexibility is to render in layers with alpha and depth channels. Then, if you need to make adjustments later, you only need to rerender the particular objects on a specific layer, not everything else too. The real power comes later, during compositing, because you can tweak colors, lighting (to an extent), contrast balance, layer order, and so on. These things would take far too long to adjust and test in a full-scene render, but that isn't the case with a few intelligently rendered layers. You can render separate passes for the shadow, highlights, ambient color, reflection, and so on. Then later, in the composite, you can interactively tune these parameters to your specific needs. This takes some time to set up and initially results in longer render times. However, huge time savings can be earned when you are tuning a scene in real time, changing the amount of reflection, highlight size, shadow color, and opacity—all in a compositor, not in the renderer. An excellent example of this can be found at Jeremy Birn's website, `http://www.3drender.com/jbirn/ea/Ant.html`. (Although this rendering was done in a program other than Maya, the principle applies to any 3D application.)

Here are some other render-optimization tips:

- Reduce bump maps, especially on objects far enough from the camera to not be noticed. An intelligently created color map, added to the base color map of your object's texture, can suffice to simulate the bump map from a distance, and it will greatly reduce render times.

- Only model what viewers will see. This is especially important if you are going to be raytracing— too much geometry to raytrace (in reflections and shadows on floors) will grind your render to a halt. The other reason to do this is to reduce the time you spend modeling, so that you can have more time for rendering! Don't spend time doing amazing things backstage where the audience can't see them.

- Limit your shadow map light's field of view to encompass only the objects casting shadows. This reduces the computations Maya must perform and allows that savings to be applied to a larger shadow map.

- Check that only surfaces that are supposed to be reflecting are set to have some amount of reflectivity. If the shading group was created as a Phong, PhongE, Blinn, or anisotropic shader, these surfaces might be set to the default of 50 percent reflectivity.

- Selectively tune the render attributes of each object. Turn off Shadow Casting if you won't be seeing the object's shadow. Turn off Visible for reflections or refractions if that visibility isn't needed for the object. Turn off Motion Blur if the object doesn't move too fast (and if the camera doesn't fly past it too fast). Turn off Double Sided for enclosed objects that have no transparency.

- Test your render with the render diagnostics script. In the Render View window, choose File → Render Diagnostics. This will alert you to any problems immediately, and it's always better to know about problems sooner rather than later.

- Use environment reflection maps whenever possible. They should be a size that is divisible by 2, such as 256 × 256. These maps also don't need to be high resolution, if the pixels that are reflecting don't take up much screen space. You can create animated environment maps if those are needed, since the render times wouldn't be long for each frame at the small resolution. You can also simulate blurred reflections, by running the frames through a blur filter in a compositing program first.

- Use texture maps whenever possible, because they aren't as render-intensive as procedural maps. Procedurals don't take up as much memory as image files, but this shouldn't make a huge difference if you keep a close eye on your texture map file sizes. Don't apply texture maps bigger than you need. This is especially true for output to television, because the color space and ultimate resolution are limited to begin with.

- Render frames with motion blur and not fields whenever possible. The hit you take with motion blur will rarely exceed the hit you take with rendering another whole field (or frame if you are going to interlace them later in a compositor).

- Use 2D motion blur whenever you can. It is smoother than 3D motion blur, it is almost as accurate (as far as the human eye can tell), and the render times are a fraction of those of 3D motion blur at the same quality level.

- Last but not least, read the release notes. They can warn you of problems or slow areas of the renderer before you start pulling out your hair!

Summary

In this chapter we went through the six types of light available in Maya, their properties, the two ways of creating shadows, and the fog, glow, halo, and lens flare effects available for Point, Spot, and Volume lights. We also discussed how to light characters in a scene using the standard three-point lighting setup.

This chapter completes the coverage of all the basic stages of producing character animation in Maya. We started with the interface in Part I and continued through the discussions of modeling techniques (Part II), animation (Part III), and rendering (Part IV), of which this is the last chapter. In Part V, we will move on to advanced effects in Maya, including Paint Effects, MEL, particles, dynamics, and the new Fluid Effects feature.

Advanced Tools and Techniques

If you have *worked through the book thus far, you are well on your way to high-level modeling, animation, scripting, texturing, and lighting skills. There is, however, another exciting facet of Maya that deals with large groups of objects. The effects available with both Paint Effects and particles require some practice, but once you understand the basics of working with large groups of objects, you can create stunning scenes with fire, water, clouds, flowers, and other elements. What's more, you can control both particles and Paint Effects strokes to create specific effects.*

And Chapter 25 introduces you to the newest advance in Maya—fluid effects.

CHAPTER 19

Paint Effects

The dream of rendering a fully 3D natural environment or other organic object (such as hair, plants, or food) has traditionally been an onerous task involving proprietary software and loads of difficult modeling and animation. It's little wonder that, until recently, most CG work has involved lots of space ships and desert planets! The complexity of the problem facing the computer artist in re-creating nature's many wondrous sights has been daunting, to say the least; not only are there thousands of details to re-create, they must all look natural (for example, include no straight lines or simple repetitive textures), and, ultimately, they all need to move about in a realistic fashion. This bewildering array of technical and artistic problems has kept all but the bravest CG pioneers firmly in the land of artificial objects or simple backdrops.

With Maya's Paint Effects (released with version 2.5), the rules changed. Paint Effects is a brush-based paint program that lets you create both 2D and 3D objects—many of which can be animated as well! You can paint hair, trees, grass, corn stalks, pasta, or many other default Paint Effects brushes into your scene, or you can get really creative and start making your own brushes, either using the included brushes as a template or designing them from scratch. As you proceed through this chapter, play with Paint Effects as much as you can; you will discover that a bit of guided interaction with a particular brush is your best instructor. This chapter features these topics:

- **Paint Effects theory**
- **Strokes and brushes**
- **Painting on a 2D canvas**
- **Modifying and saving brushes**
- **Painting a 2D texture on a 3D object**
- **Painting in a 3D scene**
- **Rendering**

Paint Effects Theory

Paint Effects creates its look with strokes that you paint into the scene using preset or custom-made brushes. These strokes emit dynamic tubes that, when rendered, reproduce the selected effect, be it human hair or a bush of flowers. The tubes render with a high-quality look without using geometry, so the render is much faster than a similar geometry-based scene.

Because the brushes are tubes (actually just curves) that can be rendered into three dimensions, you can work interactively with the brushes (especially in wireframe mode) while producing astoundingly realistic effects. Also, because final rendering is done on the fly, you can freely move a camera (or the Paint Effects objects) in the scene, and the brushes will render properly from any angle. The combination of interactive "modeling" (though painting is closer to one's actual interaction with Paint Effects), fully 3D renders, and high-quality texturing and shadowing make Paint Effects an eminently usable feature, right out of the box! Also, being able to add forces such as turbulence, wind, and gravity to any Paint Effects brush means that you can animate your scene in a quick, intuitive manner that looks great.

However, the forces you apply to Paint Effects brushes are not actually calculated by Maya's dynamics engine, but are in fact expressions applied to the brush tubes. Maya's main engine then runs these expressions, so there is no need to access the dynamics engine for the entire scene's dynamics attributes. Consequently, there is no need for Maya to run up a dynamics scene to calculate positions and attributes for every object to create its calculations for a single stroke. Thus, you can animate several trees or the hair on someone's head with little penalty in interactivity or rendering.

Paint Effects takes advantage of the depth buffer to do its rendering magic. The Paint Effects renderer uses the depth (or Z) buffer, in addition to six other buffers, to figure out where to place paint strokes in the 3D scene, and then it splats the objects there, fully anti-aliased and rendered. The Paint Effects renderer is not a scan line–based rendering pass; it is actually a post process, meaning that all geometry is rendered first, and then the Paint Effects elements are added into the render. Although Paint Effects is a post process, it allows effects such as transparency (which is traditionally *not* possible in depth buffer effects), out-of-order draw, glowing paint strokes, depth of field, and motion blur (both 2D and 3D). The strokes are tubes that can be fully drawn along their length and separated by gaps, and nearly all Paint Effects elements (or attributes) can be keyframed or animated—or both.

If Paint Effects sounds fantastic, just wait until you see how easy it is to use. After reading the pages that follow, you should be up and running with this feature, which is worth the price of Maya Complete in and of itself. But enough superlatives—let's get painting!

Strokes and Brushes

Artists always begin by selecting their tools. To use Paint Effects, you must first decide which line and effect you're going to produce—or, in this case, what your stroke and your brush should look like. Once you have a clear vision of the look you're after, you can create or modify the tools (strokes and brushes) to match what you want. Working with Paint Effects is a great deal like choosing a traditional paint brush and paint (the brush) and then setting down the appropriate line (or stroke) for the effect you're after.

Strokes

Strokes are the basic elements that underlie all that Paint Effects does. They are, in essence, curves drawn in real time by your mouse or graphics tablet, and they can take the form of curves on a canvas, on a 3D surface, between surfaces, or even on the Maya grid plane.

Wherever they are placed (or "painted on"), strokes are the curves that either define the shape of a brush directly (as in a stroke of air-brushed paint) or "emit" brush tubes from them (as in grass blades, hair, or entire trees). Brush strokes are not particles, but if they are set to emit tubes from their base curve, they can "grow" these tubes as you paint—the blades of grass, hairs, or branches of a tree sprouting up from the stroke curve. In the case of trees, for instance, the strokes can emit a base branch, sprout further branches and subbranches, and then sprout leaves, buds, or flowers. Alternatively, if you have already created a curve, you can convert it into a Paint Effects stroke, and your selected brush will be applied to the curve. If the stroke uses only the base curve you draw, paint is applied to the curve itself. If the stroke emits tubes, the original curve renders invisible, and the paint is applied to the tubes emitted from the curve.

Because these tubes can be emitted from a Paint Effects brush, you can animate their growth, as well as many other features. Thus, you can create a field of flowers that grow up from the ground or lengthen a model's hair while the animation plays.

Brushes

Brushes are a group of growth and render options (or attributes) you set for a given curve; more simply, they are the "paint" with which you choose to paint. Thus, although strokes define the shape of the curve you paint (as in a painter's brush strokes), brushes define the look of the paint.

There are more than 400 built-in brushes, including tube-shaped animals (snakes), animal elements (flesh, hair), natural phenomena (clouds, lightning, stars), traditional brushes (oil, felt pens, airbrushes), metals and glass, plants of all varieties, and even food (pastas, hamburger, corn). As you would expect from Maya, you can infinitely adjust and animate all these preset brushes, modifying the built-in brushes to your fancy and saving these new brushes for later use.

There are also at least two Paint Effects brush exchanges online, at www.highend3d.com/maya/paintfx and www.aliaswavefront.com/en/Community. At both sites, you can look for new brushes, and at the highend3d site, you can also submit your creations for others to use.

Brushes are stored in the /Maya4.5/brushes folder (in Windows, the path would likely be C:\Program Files\AliasWavefront\Maya4.5\brushes) and are accessible in Maya in the Visor window (choose Window → General Editors → Visor). On opening the Visor, scroll down to the bottom of the window and click the plus sign next to the C:\Program Files\AliasWavefront\ Maya4.5\brushes text. This allows you quick access to Paint Effects' 30 folders of brush presets, as shown in Figure 19.1.

Figure 19.1

Contents of the Paint Effects brushes folder in the Visor

Open any folder to display brushes on the right side of the Visor. To select a brush, simply click its icon. Point to an icon to display its name. Navigating the right side panel of the Visor is just like moving about in a work window; you can pan or zoom into the icons for a better look. When you select a brush (say, Delphinium from the Flowers folder), your mode is set to the Paint Effects tool in the Tool Box, as shown in Figure 19.2, and your cursor changes to a pencil icon with a red circle under it (similar to the Artisan cursor).

Click inside your scene window and paint a stroke or two. You will see the outline of several flowers, as in Figure 19.3. As soon as you release the mouse button, the flowers reduce to a rudimentary outline, and you will see the base curve (the actual curve you drew) highlighted on the scene grid. To keep the scene responsive to your input, Maya automatically reduces the complexity of the curves and tubes it draws with the Paint Effects tool. You can adjust this reduction to your liking (see "Animating Brush Strokes" later in this chapter).

Figure 19.2

Paint Effects Brush tool

You might also notice that the flowers are painted on the Maya scene grid; this is because the Paint Effects tool defaults to painting on the scene grid (or the X–Z plane) if no other objects are selected and set to be paintable.

You might wonder why your brush strokes, while interesting, look nothing like a fully rendered flower. To see what your brush strokes will look like when rendered, you must either do test renders as you go or paint in a special Paint Effects window, rather than in the default scene windows. You can define this window either to be a 2D canvas or to mimic the perspective (or other) camera in your scene. We will begin with painting on a 2D canvas in the next section and then move on to painting in a 3D environment later in this chapter.

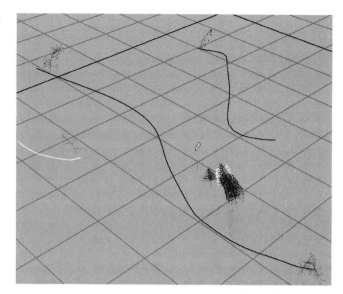

Figure 19.3

Painting flowers in the scene window

Painting on a 2D Canvas

At its simplest level, using Paint Effects on a 2D canvas works a lot like a traditional paint program (Corel's Painter, for example). You simply paint on colors—or alter colors already present—and create a painterly image in two dimensions.

Start with a new scene window (or erase the strokes you painted previously—choose Edit → Delete All By Type → Strokes), and then choose Window → Paint Effects to open a floating Paint Effects window. In this new window, you will probably see what appears to be your perspective view with a new set of icons at the top of the window. This is, in fact, the 3D environment for painting in Paint Effects. For now, we want to paint on a canvas, so choose (from the window's menu bar, or RM choose) Paint → Paint Canvas. You will now see a large white canvas on which to paint, with icons at the top of the window (see Figure 19.4) similar to the preceding set.

To switch your main scene view window to the Paint Effects window and back, press the 8 key on your keyboard (not on the numeric keypad). Because you will likely switch back and forth from the Paint Effects window to the scene window(s) many times in a project, it is a good idea to memorize this shortcut. When you are in the Paint Effects window, you can momentarily access the scene window (to select an object, say) by holding down the Ctrl key and clicking in the window.

First, try painting on a few brush strokes. If you've been painting and have a brush still selected, you will see that brush painted on the canvas. If you have just opened a new session of Maya, you will see a black brush stroke (the default brush) painted on the window.

Figure 19.4

Icons in the Paint Effects window

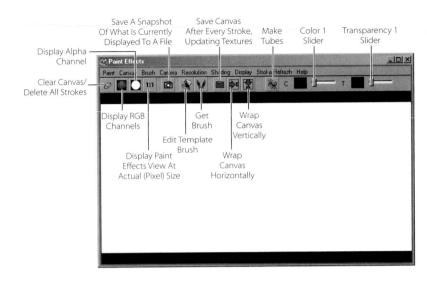

In the 2D view, you have only one level of Undo, and you can access it only via the panel menu (choose Canvas → Canvas Undo)—not by the usual Z key. You can assign this function to a hotkey (such as Ctrl+Z) via the Hotkey Editor. (See Chapter 3, "Techniques for Speeding Up Workflow," for more on assigning hotkeys.) There is, however, an Erase Scene icon, so you can clear the entire canvas at once.

After you paint a few brush strokes, you might want to clear the canvas so that you can paint on new strokes. To do so, choose Canvas → Clear or click the eraser icon in the toolbar to reset the canvas to its initial color (probably white). To change the background color of the canvas, choose Canvas → Clear ❏, and choose a new color from the Clear Color color chip or slider.

Clear your canvas, choose a new brush from the Visor, and paint something interesting! You might find that on a traditional canvas such as this, the more traditional brush types (oil paint, pens, airbrushes, and such) look better than the organic brushes, but it's your canvas, so you get to decide. If you have a graphics tablet, you will find that many brushes have a built-in dependence on pressure, changing everything from color to size as you press harder with your stylus. You will also notice that as you move your cursor faster, many brushes will segment, not following your strokes in a continuous manner; this is because the brush strokes are merely a collection of "stamps" that the program places as you drag your mouse or stylus over the canvas. Thus, if you paint fast enough, you can "outrun" the spacing of the stamps and produce blank spaces in between. Sometimes this effect might be useful and sometimes not, so remember that Paint Effects is actually responding to the speed at which you draw your curves.

After you experiment a bit, clear your canvas once again (choose Canvas → Clear or click the eraser icon) and turn on horizontal and vertical wrap. From the rendering menu set, you can choose Paint Effects → Paint Effects Globals → Canvas and toggle on Wrap H and Wrap V, but it's simpler just to click the Wrap icons in the Paint Effects window toolbar.

Now that you have wrap on, try painting a brush stroke that goes beyond the edge of the canvas. You should see the stroke continue on the other side of the canvas, as if the canvas were wrapped into a ball where all sides meet, like the canvas shown in Figure 19.5. This effect is, of course, extremely valuable for creating seamless tiles you can use as repeating textures in your Maya scene.

Figure 19.5

Brush strokes wrapped in the horizontal and vertical directions

If you want to see how the edges of your canvas look for this or any set of brush strokes, you can roll the canvas in any direction by choosing the Canvas → Roll → *<item>* commands. You can, for example, roll the canvas halfway horizontally (by choosing Canvas → Roll → 50% Horizontal) to see the vertical seam in the middle of the canvas. Another roll of 50% Horizontal, and your image is back to where you started.

If you have a texture that is not currently seamless (or just for other effects), you can change the brush mode from Paint to Erase, Smear, or Blur, and you can alter the paint that is currently on the canvas. Choose Paint Effects → Template Brush Settings (from the Rendering menu set), or click the paintbrush icon in the toolbar to open the Paint Effects Brush Settings window, which allows you access to all the brush's settings. For now, just change the Brush Type pop-up at the top of the window to Erase (or whatever you prefer) and paint over your image. You will see that the brush stamp is now painting on an erase (or smear or blur) effect, which can make for very intricate effects, as shown in Figure 19.6.

Figure 19.6

**Brush strokes,
partially erased**

To save your image (if you wanted to use the image as a texture file, for example), you can either click the Camera (Save Snapshot) icon or choose Paint → Save Snapshot and name the file. You can further modify the image in another program (such as Adobe Photoshop) or use the file as a file texture on a scene object. (See Chapter 17, "Shading and Texturing Surfaces," for more information on using file textures.)

Modifying and Saving Brushes

In addition to simply using the Paint Effects presets, you can alter just about every parameter for a brush and then save this modified brush setting for later use. You can modify the look of a brush in several ways; we'll go from the simplest method to the one that offers the most control.

Using the Toolbar Sliders

To make basic adjustments to color and transparency, you can simply change the color chips or sliders that reside on the top-right side of the Paint Effects toolbar, as shown in Figure 19.7.

Figure 19.7

Color sliders and chips

Clear your canvas, and then choose the puttypaint brush from the Oils folder. Draw a few strokes onto the canvas to see what the default brush looks like.

You might want to scale your brush up to see the strokes better. To do so, use the same hotkey as the outer brush radius for Artisan: the B key. By holding down the B key and dragging your mouse left and right, the brush stamp size will interactively change on the canvas, allowing you to see how large your brush will be.

For the puttypaint brush, you will see only two color chips and sliders in the toolbar (one pinkish, which sets color, the other a dull gray, which sets transparency). Change the pinkish color to something else by clicking the color chip; then paint a few strokes to see your new brush in action. Next, increase the transparency (the gray color) by moving the slider to the right, and paint some more. Your new strokes should look less solid (or more transparent) than before.

You might have noticed that changing a brush setting does *not* affect your old brush strokes. Paint Effects strokes are each stored on a separate node (or, in the case of 2D work, they are just painted pixels) and thus will not automatically update when the brush profile is altered. In 3D scene painting, you can select and change old strokes.

If you like the brush you have created and want to use it again in future work, you'll want to save the profile so you don't have to make the same changes again. You can save the brush either to a shelf or in the Visor. To save the template, choose Paint Effects ➜ Save Brush Preset to open the Save Brush Preset dialog box, which is shown in Figure 19.8. In the Label field, name your brush (**Blueputty**, perhaps); in the Overlay Label field, type any letters you would like printed on the icon overlay (this will only be visible if the brush is saved to a shelf). Choose either To Shelf or To Visor, and, if you want to save the brush to the Visor, type the path to the directory where the brush will be saved. Finally, you can capture an image of the brush as an icon by clicking the Grab Icon button and then drawing a marquee around some strokes your brush made.

Many users seem to prefer saving brush presets to a new shelf tab created just for brush presets, rather than to the Visor. This way, you have ready access to different brushes in a convenient shelf. Of course, the choice of where to save brushes is completely up to you! For more information on creating shelves, see Chapter 2, "Your First Maya Animation."

Blending Brushes

For broader brush control than is available through the color and transparency sliders, you can easily combine two or more brushes into a third brush that shares the qualities of both parents. Reload your basic puttypaint brush by selecting it again in the Visor. Now let's combine this brush with something natural, such as the fernOrnament brush in the Plants folder. Be sure the puttypaint brush is already selected, open the plants folder, point your mouse on the fernOrnament brush icon, and RM choose Blend Brush 50%. (You will see several other blend

Figure 19.8

The Save Brush Preset dialog box

modes that you can play with as well.) Now when you paint strokes onto the canvas, you will see that your brush has become a sort of hybrid between the putty and fern brushes. If you continue to RM choose Blend Brush 50% from the fern brush, you will continue blending the brush toward the fern look, and your strokes will look more and more like the basic fern preset. An in-between state of the brush is shown in Figure 19.9.

Figure 19.9

A brush blended from the putty and fern brushes

For even more control over the blending of shape and shading between two brushes, choose Paint Effects → Preset Blending to open the Brush Preset Blend dialog box, and adjust the two sliders, as shown in Figure 19.10. If you choose another brush preset, it will be blended in with the other brushes according to the percentages you set. This way, in just a few minutes of experimentation, you can create completely new, unique, and fun brushes for your own use. Try some blend of ferns, grass, and hair, and see what you come up with! To remove the blending effect, simply close the Brush Preset Blend dialog box, and the next brush you select will be loaded at 100%.

Using Brush Settings

Figure 19.10

The Brush Preset Blend dialog box

The final way to adjust brushes is to use the Paint Effects Brush Settings window (choose Paint Effects → Template Brush Settings, or click the Edit Template Brush icon in the Paint Effects toolbar), shown in Figure 19.11.

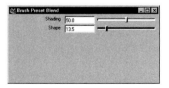

Here you have access to the "guts" of any Paint Effects brush, with control over everything from brush profile to lighting and shadowing effects to animation and forces. You can adjust literally hundreds of settings here (try twirling down some of the arrows to see how many nested menus there are!), so we can't cover all of them here. If you need information about a specific setting, look in Maya's online documentation under *Paint Effects Tool-settings*. You may also find that simply altering a setting and examining the resulting look of the brush will give you enough feedback about the setting's purpose that you need look no further.

For the purpose of becoming familiar with brush settings, let's take a look at a few settings, and you can experiment with others as you go. Getting to know the Template Brush Settings window is paramount to becoming a skilled Paint Effects user. This window is where all the action is, and you need to understand enough to make intelligent changes to the settings in this window to control how your brushes will look.

Let's start with a simple brush. Choose the markerRed brush (in the Markers folder). Paint a few strokes to see what the marker looks like in its default setting, and then clear the canvas. Open the Template Brush Settings window (choose Paint Effects → Template Brush Settings) and twirl down the Brush Profile settings. From this group of controls, you can set, for example, the Brush Width, Softness, and Stamp Density of the brush (how frequently the brush creates a new stamp of its image as you drag your mouse). Try setting the Brush Width bigger, the Softness very small, and the Stamp Density to a large number (such as 10). You should end up with a series of large, distinct circles, maybe something like the brush in Figure 19.12—a very different-looking brush from the default marker! The Stamp Density placed the circles close together, the Brush Width (obviously) increased the size of the stamp, and reducing Softness created sharply defined circles instead of a blurred stroke.

Under Shading, you can adjust the color, incandescence, and transparency of the marker brush. Illumination allows you to "light" the strokes (when Illumination On is checked), choose the light's direction (the Real Lights setting will not function properly in Canvas mode), and add effects such as specular highlights to the brush. By setting Fake Shadow to On under Shadow Effects, you can add either a 2D offset shadow (a drop shadow) or a 3D cast shadow (the 3D cast works best in scene painting mode). Under the Glow section, you can set several Glow attributes. You can set gaps in your brush so that it appears more like a dotted line than a continuous curve, via the Gaps submenu. Finally, under Flow Animation, you can actually animate your brush

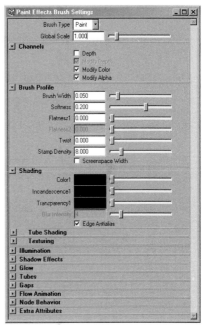

Figure 19.11

The Paint Effects Brush Settings Window

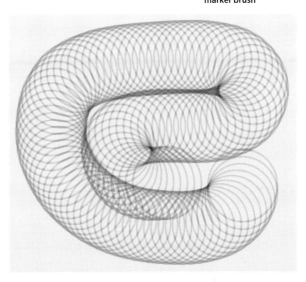

Figure 19.12

An altered marker brush

strokes (more on this in the "Painting in a 3D Scene" section, later in this chapter). Experiment with any or all settings and see what your brush ends up looking like. Figure 19.13 shows a sample of a further modified marker brush.

> If you have a graphics tablet and want to map brush properties to stylus pressure, open the Paint Effects Tool Settings window (choose Paint Effects → Paint Effects Tool ❑). In this window, you have control over any three attributes you want to map to pressure. Simply pull down the mapping pop-up, choose an attribute to map, and set the min/max values.

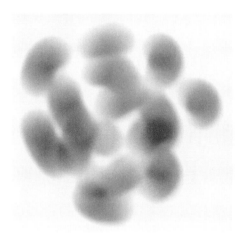

Now let's try a growing tube-based brush, to see how we can actually alter the attributes of the tubes that grow from a brush like this. From the Plants folder, select the fernOrnament brush, draw a few test strokes, and then open the Template Brush Settings window. You can, of course, alter any of the color, lighting, shadow, and other settings we discussed earlier, but here let's look at the Tubes attributes. Twirl down the Tubes settings, and then twirl down the Creation submenu. If you set the Tubes Per Step very high (like 7 or 8), you will no longer get individual fern fronds, but a mass of fern-looking things, as in Figure 19.14.

While interesting, this density is calculation-intensive, so reset the Tubes Per Step to a low value (such as 0.2). The Creation section includes, among many others, controls for making your ferns very long by adjusting the Length Max setting, changing the tube start and end widths by adjusting the Tube Width1 and 2 settings, altering the number of segments for each tube (more segments means more of a flowing curve), and, of course, randomizing the Tube or Width settings so that each fern doesn't look identical to its neighbor.

Creation is just the start, however; under the Growth settings, you can turn any of the following on or off and adjust settings for them as well: Branches, Twigs, Leaves, Flowers, and Buds. The default fern only has leaves and buds turned on, so try turning on branches, twigs,

Figure 19.13

A new look for the marker brush

Figure 19.14

A bunched fern brush

Figure 19.15

Fern with flowers

and flowers, and see what happens. Without even changing the default settings, just turning on these options creates a rather interesting shrublike brush, shown in Figure 19.15.

Inside each of these Growth sections, you have control over how many items will be created, at what angles they split off from their parent tubes, whether all tubes will have children (the Dropout rate), whether the new tubes will twist (and how much), and how large they will be compared to their parent tubes. In addition, there are several specialized settings for each element. As an experiment, let's create something that looks like a flowering wild rose tree. Our leaves and flowers are obviously too large for a tree, so we'll have to modify our Growth settings. The settings we chose for different aspects of the brush were done mostly by trial and error; we made adjustments and painted strokes until we were happy with the look of the tree. Table 19.1 lists a collection of settings that produces the rose you see in Figure 19.16.

Be sure to experiment with all these settings as you go, and draw on the canvas to see how your changed settings are affecting the brush.

Figure 19.16

**The fern brush turned
into a rose tree brush**

Of course, there are a multitude of possibilities here; although we can't cover the effects of all these options, here are a few highlights. Twig Start specifies where the twigs will begin appearing. Leaf Start determines how high up on the tree its trunk and branches are bare. For the buds, choose a color that stands out from the branch color. You can also change the two base leaf colors and how the two colors are randomized—try setting the randomization values very high and see what happens. When you are finished, you should have a shrublike tree with large reddish flowers on it. The color version of Figure 19.16 can be found in the Color Gallery on the CD.

Because tubes are drawn using recursive, fractal algorithms, where each layer of tubes depends on the settings for the previous layer, all tube sizes, lengths, and such are relative, not absolute measures.

ASPECT	SETTING	VALUE	
Branches	Num Branches	4	Table 19.1
	Branch Dropout	0.15	**Settings for a Wild**
	Middle Branch	on	**Rose Tree**
Twigs	Twigs In Cluster	4	
	Num Twig Clusters	2	
	Twig Dropout	0.3	
	Twig Length	0.25	
	Twig Base Width	0.9	
	Twig Tip Width	0.7	
	Twig Start	0.4	
	Twig Angle 1	107	
	Twig Angle 2	45	
	Twig Twist	0.3	
Leaves	Leaves In Cluster	4	
	Num Leaf Clusters	4	
	Leaf Dropout	0.25	
	Leaf Length	0.1	
	Leaf Base Width	0.05	
	Leaf Tip Width	0.001	
	Leaf Start	0.7	
	Leaf Angle 1	105	
	Leaf Twist	0.5	
	Leaf Flatness	1	
	Leaf Size Decay	0.48	
Flowers	Petals In Flower	10	
	Num Flowers	5	
	Petal Dropout	0.14	
	Petal Length	0.03	
	Petal Base Width	0.03	
	Petal Tip Width	0.01	
	Flower Twist	0.1	
Buds	Bud Size	0.02	
	Bud Color	a muted red	

In addition to color, you can actually map texture files onto flowers, leaves, and the main object tube itself. To map the main tube, go to the Brush's attributes in the Attribute Editor, choose Shading → Texturing, click the Map Color check box, set Texture Type to File, and choose an image to map in the Image Name text field. (To browse textures, click the folder icon to the right of the Image Name field near the bottom of the Texturing section.) To texture Leaves and Flowers, twirl down the Leaves (or Flowers) section under Tubes and then Growth, clear the Leaf (or Flower) Use Branch Tex(ture) check box, and then choose an image in the Image Name field (or browse textures by clicking the folder icon). See the birchBlowingLight texture in the Trees collection for a demonstration of texture-mapping colors on a brush.

Painting a 2D Texture onto a 3D Object

Creating a texture map for a scene object using Paint Effects is a straightforward process. First, create a side-by-side layout (choose Panels → Layouts → Two Panes Side By Side), and make the right side the Perspective view and the left side the Paint Effects window (still set to Paint On Canvas mode). In the scene window, create an object you'd like to paint a texture on—for the example shown in Figure 19.17, a simple sphere will suffice.

Figure 19.17

A split view with a sphere object

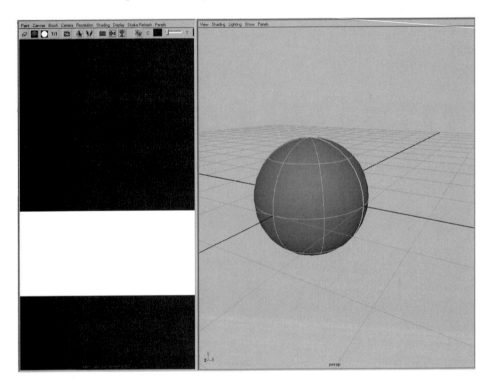

For information on creating, modifying, and saving layouts, see Chapter 3 and Chapter 20, "MEL."

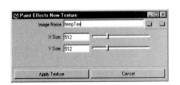

Figure 19.18

The Paint Effects New Texture dialog box

Next, open a Hypershade window, create a new material, and assign a file texture to its color channel. (For more on how to create textures, see Chapter 17.) From the Hypershade window, first MM drag the material onto your scene object (to assign the material to it), and then MM drag the file texture onto the Paint Effects canvas to open Paint Effects New Texture dialog box, which is shown in Figure 19.18. You use this dialog box to assign the name and size (in pixels) of your texture. Click Apply Texture, choose Yes to save the file, and save it in your /sourceImages directory. Before painting on the canvas, choose Canvas → Auto Save to turn on Save After Each Stroke. When you release the mouse button each time, you will see your texture updated on the scene object(s) to which the material is being applied. Try painting with several brushes onto the canvas and see how your texture map updates. Remember, you might want to turn on Wrap Horizontal And Vertical to allow your map to be seamless as it wraps around the objects in your scene. Figure 19.19 shows how wrapping appears on your canvas and can be found in the Color Gallery on the CD. If the textures are not updating in your window, click the Shading menu in your current panel, and turn on Hardware Texturing.

Painting in a 3D Scene

Now that you understand strokes and brushes and how to use them in 2D, let's get on to the really interesting aspect of Paint Effects: painting in three dimensions. Because all Paint Effects brushes are 3D curves that can (optionally) create tubes, you can paint in a scene as easily as on the canvas. If you open a new scene, choose a Paint Effects brush, and start painting, you will automatically paint on the scene grid (as we mentioned at the start of this chapter). This can work well if you want to paint trees, grass, or other elements on the "ground." If you want to paint on an actual scene object (or multiple objects), however, you need to select that object and then tell Paint Effects that the object can be painted.

Figure 19.19

File texture applied to a sphere

In a new scene, create a NURBS Cylinder (be sure to cap the cylinder). In the scene window, select the object and choose Paint Effects ➝ Make Paintable. (Remember, holding down the Ctrl key in the Paint Effects window momentarily enables the scene window so you can select objects in the Paint Effects window as well as in the main scene window.) If you're not in the Paint Effects window, press the 8 key on your keyboard to choose that mode. If you are still in Canvas mode in the Paint Effects window, choose Paint ➝ Paint Scene to toggle on display of your scene.

We could choose to paint some hair on this object, but we'll wait on this until the hands-on project later in this chapter. Instead, let's paint some other brushes on, such as one of the grasses, an oil paint, and a waterfall (under the Liquid folder). Remember that you can alter the scale of the brush by pressing B and dragging the mouse. Also, because painting on an object simply creates curves on the object's surface, you can select, move, modify (alter individual CVs), or offset these curves from the surface, giving you a great deal of control over the look of each curve.

> Many of the Paint Effects brushes require real lighting to appear, so you might need to add one or more lights to your scene to see your brushes in all their splendor.

If you tumble the Paint Effects window, you will notice that the brushes revert to an outline of their fully rendered selves in order to speed up redraw, so you don't have to wait for the full effect of the brushes to render each time. To change how Paint Effects simplifies the *display* of your strokes (not the actual strokes themselves), open the Template Brush Editor, open the Tubes section, open the Creation section, and then alter the Simplify Method. If you choose Tubes Per Step, the redraw removes many of the initial tubes from display. (This is good for elements such as hair, which have many tubes.) Choosing Segments removes portions of each tube object, but retains the initial tube for each one. (This is good for trees, flowers, and the like.) Choosing Tubes And Segments will (of course) reduce display of both. You can also force Paint Effects to redraw the entire window each time you move in the scene (choose Stroke Refresh ➝ Rendered in the Paint Effects window), but this will slow your interaction with Paint Effects a great deal.

After some painting, your cylinder will probably look a great deal more interesting than it did in the first place; an example of what you might create is shown in Figure 19.20.

Although painting in the Paint Effects canvas window is great for getting the look of brushes down, it is often far more interactive to paint in the scene view for large-scale jobs. When you switch over to the scene window, you will be limited to painting in wireframe, but the painting will go much faster. One workflow example might be to create an interesting look for a tree brush or two in the Paint Effects window, save these (in the Visor or on a shelf), and then switch to the Scene window and paint a forest of these trees. When you create the forest, you already know what the trees look like—you just want to paint them into the scene quickly and interactively, and the scene window is better suited to this than the Paint Effects canvas window.

Additionally, if you want to delete the last stroke you made in 3D paint mode, the normal Undo feature works fine. To delete selected strokes, simply select them (in the scene or Hypergraph window) and press the Backspace or Delete key. To delete all strokes in one fell swoop, simply choose Edit → Delete All By Type → Strokes.

Take some time now to play with different brushes (altering them as you want or just using different defaults) and get a feel for how various brushes act in a 3D scene as opposed to a 2D canvas.

Instead of drawing the Paint Effects curve using the Paint Effects tool, you can create a curve first and then attach a brush to the curve. Select the curve in your scene window and then choose Paint Effects → Curve Utilities → Attach Brush To Curve. In this manner, you can "multipurpose" curves for brushes and other functions within your scene or even use existing curves to which to attach a new Paint Effects brush.

Editing Previous Brush Strokes

As you experiment with brushes, you may find yourself wishing you could go back and alter strokes you've already laid down. (Remember that each new stroke is a new node, so changing a brush will normally not affect older strokes.) Because Paint Effects strokes are just curve nodes in a 3D scene, you can choose these curves and alter any attributes via the Attribute Editor or Channel Box.

As an example, let's choose one of the strokes you created on your scene object and modify it. You can try to select a curve via the Select tool, but you will likely choose many curves at the same time; using the Hypergraph is a better way to choose an individual curve (you can also zoom in very close to a stroke and select it that way). When you open the Hypergraph, you will see dozens of nodes named *stroke<item><number>*, in which *<item>* is the name of the brush and *<number>* is the number of that brush's stroke. Figure 19.21 shows some sample strokes in the Hypergraph window.

Figure 19.20

A cylinder with multiple brush strokes applied to it

Figure 19.21

The Hypergraph showing Paint Effects stroke nodes

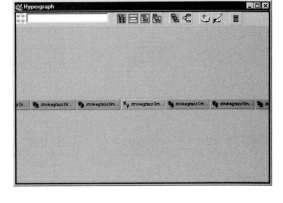

Figure 19.22

Altered grass brush strokes

Choose one of the Grass strokes (for example), and then open the Attribute Editor (press Ctrl+A). Under the grass<*type*><*number*> tab (the second tab from the right), you will have access to all the settings that were available via the Template Brush Settings window, only this time the changes will be made to the existing stroke. Try adding some flowers to the grass (under /Tubes/Growth), and change the color of the grass to something other than green (/Shading/Tube Shading). As exemplified in Figure 19.22, you have complete control over your brushes, even after you create them!

If you have several strokes that you want to vary all at once, you can elect to "group" them so that they share one brush setting. This way, as you adjust one brush, all the strokes update simultaneously—a real time-saver. To accomplish this, select all the strokes that you want to share one brush. These strokes can have any brush attached to them, but be sure to select *last* the stroke with the brush shape you want to assign to all of them, because the last stroke selected supplies the shared brush. Next, choose Paint Effects → Share One Brush to make them all share the same brush settings. If you now open the Attribute Editor and change the attributes of the current brush, all the strokes you selected will update together.

If you chose, for example, to share the vineLeafy2 brush (in the Plants collection), you can change the default brush settings to include twigs, and all your strokes would look something like Figure 19.23. To remove sharing between strokes, simply select the strokes, and then choose Paint Effects → Remove Brush Sharing.

You can also select all the brushes you want to alter and change the Paint Effects attributes through the Channel Box. Any attribute you change affects that attribute on all the selected strokes in the scene.

Adding Forces to Paint Effects Brushes

If creating still lifes isn't enough for you, don't worry: you can add dynamics to your Paint Effects brushes (at least the tube ones) and animate the brushes over time.

Paint Effects brushes actually don't use dynamics (as do particles and rigid bodies) but use recursive expressions on the tubes nodes. Although expressions aren't quite as wide-ranging as Maya's dynamics engine, using them was a clever trade-off between speed and natural motion. Using Maya's built-in dynamics engine, even a single tree could take minutes per frame to update, whereas the expression solution allows for fast updates and even allows you to scrub the animation back and forth, which dynamics simulations cannot handle.

Figure 19.23

An altered vine look on the cylinder

To see how to add dynamics, let's create some grass that blows in the wind. In the Visor, select the grassClump brush (in the Grasses folder), and, using the Paint Effects Template Brush Settings window, change the grass's Length Max (under /Tubes/Creation) to about 4 so that there's a lot of grass to blow around. (There are, of course, preset grasses that include wind, but by starting with a grass that has no forces applied to it, you can build your own.) Paint a single stroke on the ground plane. If you play back the animation now, you will see that the grass stays perfectly still as the animation plays. Although you can adjust your brush settings in the Brush Settings window, and then paint a new stroke each time, it is easier to simply select the stroke, open the Attribute Editor, and make changes. Your selected stroke then updates as you make changes, allowing you to see the effects of what you are doing.

You will find it far more interactive to switch to the scene window (by pressing the 8 key) rather than trying to watch animation play back in the Paint Effects window or by just working in the scene itself.

With the stroke selected, click the grassClump1 tab in the Attribute Editor, and open the /Tubes/Behavior subsection, in which there are several menus: Displacement, Forces, Turbulence, Spiral, and Twist. (Paint Effects is a deep program with lots of controls!) Feel free to play with any of these behavior modifiers, but we will concentrate on just a couple as examples.

First, twirl down Forces and adjust the Gravity setting. You will notice that the blades of grass bend over as if they're growing heavier and heavier as you adjust this setting higher. Due to the relatively few segments on the grass blade, the grass will bend at sharp angles when gravity is applied (of course, you can change this by setting /Tubes/Creation/Segments to a higher number, such as 20). You can also make the grass stretch under gravity by setting the Length Flex to a number greater than 0. Although a heavy, stretchy look might be great for some items, it's not particularly appropriate for grass, so set the Length Flex back to 0. Still, we can make the grass a bit heavier by setting gravity to about 0.12. Because all Paint Effects brush behaviors are based on expressions, you can either type a value for most attributes or create an expression or a Set Driven Key to control that attribute. To create an expression or to set keys, RM choose Create New Expression (or Set Key) for an attribute; in the case of an expression, you then write an equation that alters the value of said attribute. Try this simple equation to make the grass do "the wave." With your cursor over the Gravity setting, RM choose Create New Expression, and then, in the expression window, type the following:

```
gravity = sin (time);
```

When you play back the animation, your grass should wave up and down as the expression gives the gravity alternating values between 0 and 1 based on a sine wave running over time.

> You can also enter an expression rather easily through the Attribute Editor. Simply erase the current value for the given attribute, and then type an equal symbol (=) and the rest of the expression. Maya creates a new expression based on that attribute for you. Now, if it would just make coffee.

Now let's add some wind to our grass. First, delete the gravity expression from the Expression Editor, or RM choose Break Connections over the word *Gravity* in the Channel Box. Twirl down Turbulence, and choose Grass Wind from the Turbulence Type pop-up menu. Leave the Turbulence Interpolation set to Smooth Over Time And Space (or feel free to experiment with the other settings), and try adjusting the Turbulence, Frequency, and Speed settings while your animation plays back. At their default settings, the grass will wave back and forth a bit, fairly quickly. To make it wave more slowly, set the Turbulence Speed to a small number. To make the grass blow stronger, change the Turbulence slider to a large number. Turbulence Frequency controls how much space the turbulence field varies across the stroke. In other words, setting the Turbulence Frequency to 0 makes every blade of grass blow just the same; setting Turbulence Frequency to 1 makes all blades blow independently.

If you now go back and adjust the /Forces/Length Flex to 1, you'll get grass that stretches as it blows—an interesting, if unrealistic, effect.

If your playback speed is set to Free, you might find that your animation runs too quickly, giving the illusion that your objects are moving around much faster than they will in the final render. To compensate for this, you might try setting the playback rate to Normal (choose Window → Settings/Preferences → Preferences, and then choose the Settings/Timelines section); or if your scene is complex (slowing down playback) or depends on Free playback for dynamics, just playblast the animation (choose Window → Playblast) to get a better idea of its output speed.

Finally, once you get just the brush you are looking for, you will probably want to save it for later use. With your brush stroke still selected, choose Paint Effects → Get Settings From Selected Stroke, and then save the brush to your shelf or the Visor.

> The Color Gallery on the CD contains a still and an animation of a water fountain that we will create in the next several chapters; this fountain includes Paint Effects trees, grasses, moss, and such (see 22fountain.mov for the finished animation). This animation shows off just a small portion of the possibilities Paint Effects opens to your modeling and animation endeavors.

Animating Brush Strokes

In addition to animating the tubes on your brush strokes, you can animate the appearance of your strokes over time, enabling you to "grow" hair on a head or flowers in a field. Let's do the latter, using the brush flowerTallRed (in the Flowers folder). First, make a nice long stroke in your Paint Effects or scene window, as Figure 19.24 shows, so that you have a nice bunch of flowers to work with.

Figure 19.24

A curve of flowers painted in the scene window

First, we need to change the simplification mode of the flowers (so we can see them better as we animate their growth). With the stroke selected, click the flowerTallRed1 tab in the Attribute Editor, and, under Tubes/Creation, set the Simplify method to Segments. Now twirl down Flow Animation to get at the settings for animating brush growth. Set the Flow Speed to a number greater than 0 (drag the slider, or, if you want, you can set a value greater than 1 by typing in the number field). Next, check the Time Clip box, set the start time to 0 and the end time to a larger number (the default is 1000), and play back the animation. You should see all your flowers rise out of the ground at the same time, growing to full height over 100 or so frames. Figure 19.25 shows a still from this animation process.

Figure 19.25

Flowers half grown all together

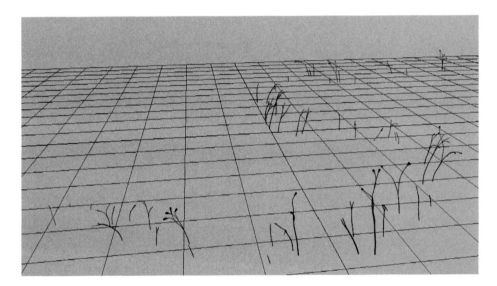

Setting the start time to a number greater (or less) than 0 allows the objects to begin growing after (or before) the animation starts. Setting the end time to a small number (such as 1 or 2 seconds) will make the objects "decay" after that much time: they will disappear, starting at the roots. Although this effect isn't quite right for flowers, you can use it in other instances (as in water drying up at its source or streaks from fireworks) to good effect.

Having all the flowers appear at once may not be what you're after. If, instead, you want the growth pattern to follow your brush stroke, simply click the Stroke Time check box to enable the brush to remember the direction of your strokes. With both Time Clip and Stroke Time enabled for various brush strokes, you can create a field of grass and trees or grow hair on a model's head just as easily as drawing the curves! The flowers shown in Figure 19.26 are growing at different rates.

Figure 19.26

Flowers growing at different rates

Instancing Brush Strokes

You can instance brush strokes as particles, allowing you to, for example, rapidly create a field of flowers (by instancing flower strokes to a grid of particles) or—as we'll do here— make a showering fountain of feathers. Obviously, some uses of instancing are more realistic than others! (Particles are covered in depth starting with Chapter 21, "Particle Basics." For the purposes of this chapter, we'll just work with basic particle emitter and field settings.)

In a new scene window, open the Particle Emitter Options window (choose Particles → Create Emitter ❑ from the Dynamics menu set). Set the Emitter Type to Directional, the Rate to 50, the DirectionY to 1 (set X and Z to 0), the Spread to 0.4, and the Speed to 20 (you will have to twirl down the first three subsections of the window to find these settings). When the proper options are set, click the Create button. Play back the animation; you should see little purple dots shooting up into the air. Select these dots (not the emitter) so that they turn green, and then choose Fields → Gravity ❑, choose Edit → Reset Settings in the Gravity Options menu, and click the Create button. Now when you play back the animation, you should see the particles shoot up, and then fall down again as they succumb to gravity's influence—you might need to zoom your view out to see the particles better.

If you don't see the particles falling back down, however, select the particles again and open the Dynamic Relationship window (choose Window → Relationship Editors → Dynamic Relationships). Click the gravityField1 text to the right (highlighting it pale orange), and your particles should be connected.

Figure 19.27

A fountain of feathers

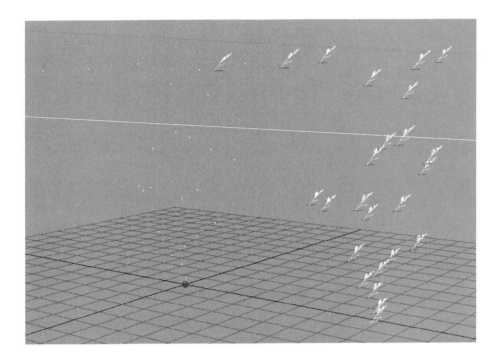

Now that we have a fountain, let's instance a Paint Effects feather to it. In the Visor, choose a feather brush (down3, for example), and, anywhere in the scene window, paint a short stroke until you see a single feather. With the feather still selected, Shift+select the particles (not the emitter) and choose Particles → Instancer (Replacement). Now, when you play back the animation, you should see the basic fountain *and* a fountain of feathers, offset from the emitter, as in Figure 19.27. You can then hide the original fountain and move the first feather wherever you want the fountain to go. You have a great deal of control over how the instanced geometry interacts with the particles by clicking the instancer1 tab in the Attribute Editor— however, you might find it easier to adjust settings by using the Instancer Options window when you first create your particles.

Rendering

Although Paint Effects is a deep program with a great many controls, rendering is a relatively transparent process. To render a scene with Paint Effects brushes in it, all you need do is batch render (or test render into the Render View window) as you would normally. When a render including Paint Effects brushes is launched, Maya first renders all the geometry in the scene and then, in a post-render process, adds the brushes, fully rendered. Although Paint Effects rendering is a post-render process (after all geometry), the renderer is intelligent enough to place Paint Effects brushes properly in 3D space. In other words, a brush that is partially behind some geometry (such as a cube, for instance) will render with that portion hidden from view. This way, though Paint Effects rendering is done after normal rendering, you don't generally have to deal with the difficulties of masking and compositing the two elements together; Maya does this for you. The hands-on tutorial that follows covers the issue of partially occluded Paint Effects brushes in more detail.

There is an exception to the rule that Maya precomposites Paint Effects brushes with geometry renders: refractions (for semitransparent objects) and reflections. If you render a raytraced scene with refractions or reflections, you will not see the Paint Effects brushes in the objects that are refracting or reflecting. To circumvent this problem, you must render out your geometry and the Paint Effects brushes in separate passes and composite them together in a compositing package (such as Maya Composer, Maya Fusion, or AfterEffects). The final fountain on the CD (`24fountain.mov`) uses compositing to get the appropriate reflections and refractions in the water.

Although most of the controls in a Paint Effects brush that have to do with rendering are fairly self-explanatory (color, textures, illumination, and so forth), two items are worth noting here. First, there is a Translucence setting (under Illumination in the Paint Effects Template Brush Settings window, or Attribute Editor for existing strokes) for brushes (high translucence allows diffuse light to pass through an object), which can be useful for plants, tree leaves, and hair. Second, you have two choices for shadowing (under Shadow Effects): a 2D offset shadow (the drop shadow we discussed earlier in the chapter) and a 3D cast shadow. The 3D cast shadow is a "fake" shadow and thus might need some adjustment to have proper size and density in your scene. The following hands-on section discusses this issue further.

> You can quickly enable or disable Paint Effects strokes in your renders (or choose to render *only* Paint Effects strokes). In the Render Globals window is a section for Paint Effects with Enable Stroke Rendering and Only Render Strokes check boxes. With Enable Stroke Rendering on, Paint Effects brushes are rendered. When off, only the geometry of the scene is rendered. If Only Render Strokes is on, geometry in the scene is hidden, and only Paint Effects brushes are rendered. In such a case, you need to previously render out your geometry and include a depth map image with your render—you then choose this depth map (under Read This Depth Map) to inform the Paint Effects brush strokes where to render. Using these render features can be valuable when you want to use a compositing program to adjust and assemble render passes.

A few exceptions notwithstanding, rendering Paint Effects brushes is a painless (and quick!) experience. With your basic understanding of the principles of rendering in Maya, you will find yourself producing great-looking images right from the start.

Hands On Maya: Painting Hair on a Head

Up until now, the boy we created earlier in the book has been stuck with somewhat plastic-looking hair. (For a different way to animate the boy's hair, see Chapter 24, "Dynamics of Soft Bodies.") Although you could explain his hairdo away as an overzealous use of hairspray, a better option is to give him some "real" hair, which is where Paint Effects comes in.

Start by opening one of your head models or the scene file 19hair.mb on the CD. The included project defaults to a close-up of the boy's bald head.

Open the Side window full-screen. You should be in shaded, textured mode. The hair is not graphics-intensive, so we will be able to run at a fairly high window-display setting. This is good, because we will need the fine details to decide how and where to paint the hair. Select the head object and press the 3 key to increase the display quality.

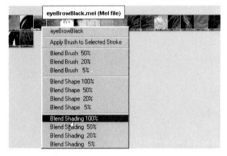

Figure 19.28

Creating a brush blend for dark hair

In the Visor, go to the brushes directory under the folder where you've installed Maya (by default it's C:\Program Files\AliasWavefront\Maya4.5\brushes) and open the Hair folder. Select the hairBlondeNoShape brush. Now, since the boy actually has black hair, we will blend the shading of the eyeBrowBlack brush at 100%. With your mouse over the eyeBrowBlack icon, RM choose Blend Shading 100%, as shown in Figure 19.28.

Because you cannot apply Paint Effects brushes to polygon or subdivision surfaces, we first need to make a skull cap of NURBS curves on which we will paint. (This cap will then be hidden after the hair is applied.) With the head selected, choose Display → Subdiv Surface Components → Vertices to display the vertices of the head. Using point snap (press and hold V or click Point Snap in the Status Line), trace NURBS curves vertically along the head to make a skull cap that more or less conforms to the Subdiv head. Draw the curves from the forehead hairline to the top of the head where the vertices all meet, and work your way clockwise around the head. You may need to tweak the positions of your CVs to better match the head, as tracing the subdiv vertices will not exactly match the head outline. When all your curves are drawn, select them (in order from left to right) and choose Surfaces → Loft to loft a skull shape, as shown in Figure 19.29. Next, select the lofted surface and choose Edit → Delete By Type → History, and then delete all the curves you used. Finally, delete the polygon head (not the original subdivision surfaces head!) and redisplay the original head, if you want.

> The skull cap has been completed for you in the 19hair.mb file on the CD. If you want to create the curves on the head using this file, simply erase the lofted surface and make them yourself.

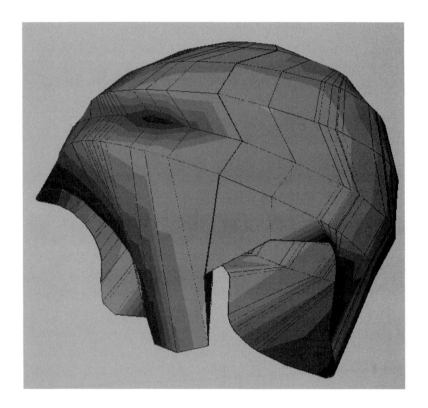

Figure 19.29

A NURBS skull cap on which to use the Paint Effects hair brush

With the skull selected, choose Paint Effects → MakePaintable. Now let's try a few strokes; click and hold down the mouse while drawing a line on the head (remember, only the skull-cap portion can be painted). You will instantly see hair sprouting from the head, although it will probably not be long enough to give the impression that this child has much of a hair-style. We need to change the brush size.

Interactively resize the brush with the B key (as shown previously in this chapter). You might have to experiment to get a size that works for you. Try painting different brush sizes, and once you get the hair size you want, delete all the strokes to start fresh (choose Edit → Delete All By Type → Strokes). You now have a clean head and a properly sized hair brush.

The next step is to decide how the hair will be added to the child's head. You can accomplish this in quite a few ways. For this exercise, we explored many options for getting hair on the head. It turns out that the most obvious, in this case, seemed to work the best for us: just paint the hair following the topology of the head model from front to back.

With that in mind, let's start giving this poor boy something to comb. We will start on the left side of the boy's head. Start your first stroke from the sideburn area and paint up and around the ear, to where the hair would naturally stop growing, as shown in Figure 19.30.

The reason for starting here is that the more hair we add, the harder it will become to see the strokes as we make them. The area around the ear is the most critical (because it has to match the boy's sideburn and ear line), so we begin here.

If you are painting a huge model or one with very intricate curves, you can select your brush and, before you paint, choose Paint Effects → Paint Effects Tool, and change the Display Quality to 0. You will still see the hairs as you paint them, but when you lift your finger from the mouse button to get another stroke ready, they will disappear. You will be left only with the curves on the surface visible, showing you where you painted without slowing down your work. Remember, this setting affects only the display, not the rendering of the strokes.

If you have a tablet, now is the time to use it. You will find that painting the boy's hair will be much easier with a tablet than a mouse!

We are now going to set things up so that from this point on the hair will be shaped to the head as we paint. (The brush actually isn't shaping itself to the head as much as following the direction of the curve that we are painting.)

With the hair brushstroke still selected, open the eyeBrowBlack1 tab for this brush in the Attribute Editor, twirl down the /Tubes/Behavior/Forces triangles, and find Path Follow. Path Follow defaults to 0 for this brush because hairBlondeNoShape is controlling our hair's shape, while eyeBrowBlack is in control of the shading, but we need something a little different, so change the value to 0.7.

Figure 19.30

Hair painted around the ear area

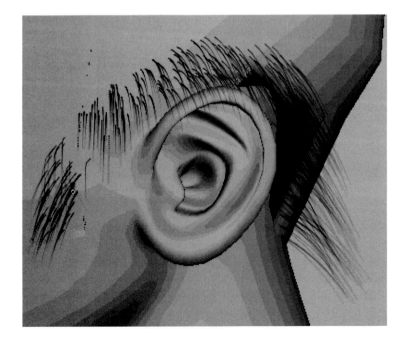

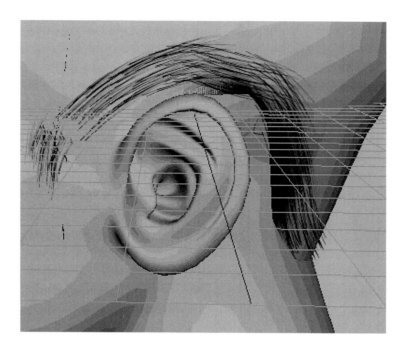

Figure 19.31

Hair following the curve of the head

Now you will notice that the hairs that are already on the model's head have nicely aligned themselves to the shape of the head (actually the curve we painted), as in Figure 19.31. Feel free to play with values in this field to get different results.

After you have a shape you like for your hair stroke, choose Paint Effects → Get Settings From Selected Stroke. This will ensure that as you paint each new stroke, the settings you changed on the stroke you already painted will be used for each subsequent stroke. Give it a try. It makes painting the hair and designing the shape of the hair style much more intuitive.

If you also change the value of Path Attract to a non-zero number, the hairs will tend to "lean" toward the curve as well as follow its direction. This can be particularly useful when you paint braided hair and you want the hairs to be more compressed to the head in evident rows. You can also enter a negative number to repel the hair and get an "Einstein" look.

Now start working your way up the head, drawing slow, even strokes from the front of the head toward the back. You will notice that the hair sticks straight up and has no real defined shape. This is by design, since we picked the hairBlondeNoShape brush. The reason we did this is to allow us to shape the hair after we paint it, to give us more eventual control over the hair, and faster feedback while drawing, without all the added dynamics that are built into some of the other hair presets. You should end up with somewhere between 10 and 15 brush strokes, which can be seen as curves on the surface and show up in the Hypergraph window as stroke-eyeBrowBlackShape1, strokeeyeBrowBlackShape2, and so on. Figure 19.32 shows the results.

Figure 19.32

Hair strokes on one side of the boy's head

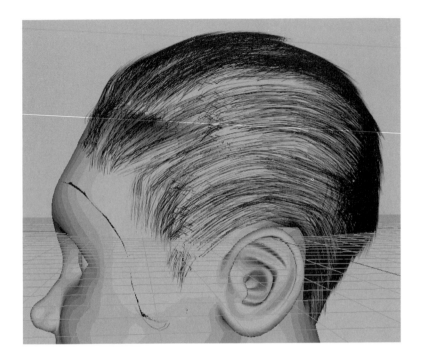

Now rotate your view and repeat the process for this side of the head. As Figure 19.33 indicates, our boy now looks as though he has a premature case of male pattern baldness, because we haven't yet painted the top of his head.

Switch to the Top camera (or rotate your perspective view again) and start at the forehead, painting toward the back of the head. Finally, rotate your view to the back and finish the job. You might want to swirl the boy's hair around the crown of the head, imitating the way hair grows there. Figure 19.34 shows a completed head of hair.

Now, add a light or two and do a test render. Notice anything wrong? More than likely, the specular highlights on the hair strands are blown out. You can control this for the entire head by choosing Edit → Select All By Type → Strokes. With all the strokes selected, open the Channel Box and open the Inputs for the brushes. Change the following settings to affect the specularity: Specular to 0.085 (this sets the brightness of the specular highlight, based on the specular color settings) and specular Power to 10 (this is the size of the specular highlight, where a larger number means a tighter highlight).

Do another test render. Much better! However, the hair is looking a little gray, so change the Color 1 and Color 2 settings to the following: color1 R, G, and B to 0.01 each; color2 R, G, and B to 0.02 each.

Figure 19.33

Missing hair on top of the boy

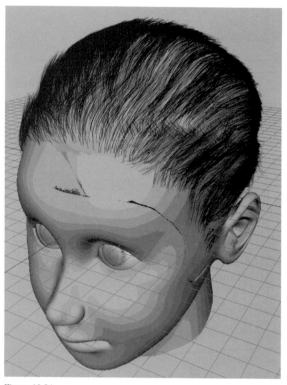

Figure 19.34

A head full of hair

Now with another test render, you should notice more natural-looking hair color and specularity. You will find that different lighting conditions may warrant changing these settings, so feel free to experiment with them.

Something still seems to be missing here, though; the boy is looking like a fairly cheap hair-transplant recipient. This is because the default settings for density on the original brush weren't high enough.

To change this, select all the strokes, and, in the Channel box under Shapes, change the Sample Density value to a larger number, such as 5. This will give you a thicker head of hair, as shown in Figure 19.35, because the brush stroke is more densely populated by hairs along its path. Now make everything visible on the boy model and do a test render.

For even more control of the hair shape, change the number of segments for the tube (under Inputs for the stroke) to a higher number. This will cause the hair shape to not only look more realistic, but act more predictably as you paint.

Figure 19.35

Same boy, but the hair has a higher density

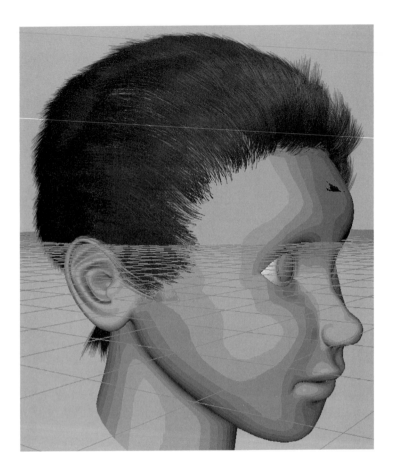

If you look closely at the render, you will notice that the hair is also casting nice fine shadows onto the boy's head. These are fake shadows, caused by Maya placing additional black strokes on the surface of the head to simulate shadows. It guesses where the surface is in 3D space and draws a shadow paint stroke where it thinks the surface lies. This method isn't perfect, but it allows nice fine shadow details when it works. To prevent the hair from casting shadows onto other objects, or to give yourself another type of shadow option when the fake shadows aren't working, set Fake Shadow to None in the Attribute Editor (remember to select all your strokes first!).

Alternatively, you can change the shadow setting to 2D offset, but this is for creating a drop-shadow effect. Although it works well for ferns that are painted on the side of a brick building, it isn't good for hair on a curvy surface such as a head.

(a)

(b)

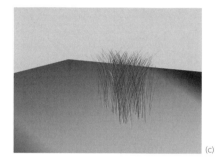

(c)

Figure 19.36

**Three shadow types.
(a) Shadow mapped
shadows (with Cast
Shadows on);
(b) 3D cast shadows;
(c) No shadows**

With Fake Shadow set to None, scroll up to the top of the Inputs section and set Cast Shadows to On. Make sure your light is set to cast Depth Map Shadows. The Cast Shadows setting only works with Depth Map Shadows, because none of the Paint Effects elements can be raytraced. Compare the various shadow types shown in Figure 19.36.

Although they cannot be raytraced, all Paint Effects brushes can be motion-blurred, both in 2D and 3D. Most people will opt to use 2D motion blur, because it's usually faster and smoother than 3D. Also note that there will probably be some visibly chunky lines near where a brush stroke (hair or otherwise) is occluded by the geometry. This is because the hair is rendered into place using the Depth Buffer, and therefore there can be no anti-aliasing of the edge where they meet; depth is either true or false for a given depth. As Duncan Brinsmead (co-creator of Paint Effects) stated, "We don't have the notion of an anti-alias for the depth. It's sort of an on or off thing. It's either at that depth, or it's at a different depth for that whole pixel in the Depth Map." You must therefore take steps to compensate for this problem if it is apparent in your renders.

To alleviate this edge, we suggest you render your geometry first without the Paint Effects elements and then render the Paint Effects elements without the geometry (remember what we said previously about rendering in passes). Using various compositing tricks, such as blurring and shrinking the elements slightly, you should be able to eliminate these chunky lines. They are really only a problem in very close shots or when there is little to no motion. Another quick way around aliasing problems is to use 2D motion blur, which we found almost totally hid these areas.

Now that you have given your model a full head of hair with shadows, take away some of his dignity and have some fun with your brush. Select all the strokes and, in the Visor, with your cursor over the Hyacinth brush (in the Flowers folder), RM choose Apply Brush To Selected Stroke. Do a test render, as in Figure 19.37, and enjoy the boy's fancy new 'do. Have fun with these experiments, and try applying several different brushes to your strokes to see what they look like.

Figure 19.37

A head of flowers!

Summary

Although there is no way to fully explore the depths of Paint Effects in just one chapter (that could be the subject of another book!), this introduction should enable you to grasp the underlying elements of the Paint Effects tool set, and you should now be comfortable enough with this feature of Maya that you can experiment intelligently, using the built-in presets or creating your own unique brushes. You have learned how to paint in both two dimensions (on a canvas) and three (in a scene), how to interactively create texture maps, how to animate your strokes, and what many of the Paint Effects options do. Furthermore, you went through a "real-world" example of using Paint Effects to create hair on a head—a process you might repeat often in a production environment. By now, you should have an appreciation of both the depth of Paint Effects and how it can help you accomplish tasks that were heretofore too difficult or time-consuming to attempt.

Paint Effects is a great deal like Artisan: you will likely need to experiment with it creatively for a while before you will feel comfortable. However, you should now have enough knowledge to use simple Paint Effects elements in your scenes right away and to understand how to experiment with the package to create more complex and interesting effects in the future. With Paint Effects—and Maya as a whole—you should have fun re-creating reality or creating anything you can imagine.

In the next several chapters, we turn to another area of advanced effects work: particles. Using particles (introduced briefly in this chapter), you'll be able to create a number of effects—from dust clouds to jiggly, "fleshy" bodies—that would be very difficult to create in any other manner.

CHAPTER 20

MEL

This chapter introduces Maya's embedded scripting language, MEL. You will learn how Maya uses MEL, and you'll see how you can increase your productivity by automating repetitive tasks and getting Maya to do exactly what you want it to do.

Although MEL does require a bit of programming savvy, you really don't need to know a great deal about computer programming to use it—at least not at the basic level. If you have some programming background, MEL's basic syntax will seem straightforward. If you know the C or C++ programming language, MEL's syntax will seem like second nature.

If you have never looked at a computer program before, MEL will at first seem baffling, but don't worry. Even if you never intend to do any real programming with MEL, you will find that this chapter contains many nuggets of information that will allow you to use MEL to control Maya in powerful, high-level ways, often without the need for doing any programming yourself.

Before reading this chapter, you should be familiar with basic Maya concepts, such as interface conventions, how to create and animate objects, and how to move around Maya's windows and menus (see Chapters 1 and 3). If you have some knowledge of computer programming, that will also prove helpful, but it is not necessary. This chapter features:

- **Fundamentals of MEL and scripting**

- **The Script Editor**

- **Getting Maya's help with MEL**

- **Variables, loops, and branching**

- **Debugging MEL scripts**

- **Creating a GUI**

- **Using procedures and scripts**

- **Placing objects using a marking menu**

- **Using expressions with MEL**

MEL Is Fundamental

Maya Embedded Language (MEL) is the ground from which you interact with Maya. When you open Maya, the program first runs several MEL scripts that actually build all the windows you see—that's right: Maya itself has no interface whatsoever. You can even run Maya from your operating system command prompt by typing **Maya -prompt**! Behind nearly everything you see in Maya is a MEL script.

What does this mean to the average Maya user? Simple: whatever the original programmers did, you also can do. You can write windows that have sliders, tabs, text fields, and buttons in them; you can create attributes in the Channel Box; you can even add menu items to the main menu bar. The fact that Maya is built on MEL is one of the program's most powerful features.

> Because Maya's syntax is similar to that of the C and C++ programming languages, a good primer on one of these languages is your best preparation for MEL. The publisher of this book offers numerous titles on C and C++, including *Visual C++ 6 In Record Time* by Steven Holzner (Sybex, 1998) and *Mastering Visual C++ 6* by Michael J. Young (Sybex, 1998).

What Is a Scripting Language?

MEL is a scripting language, not a complete programming language (like Java or C++). A program written in a programming language is compiled and becomes an independent program (like the core program, Maya, which just runs off your computer's operating system). A scripting language, on the other hand, resides on top of another program (in this case, Maya) and is interpreted at every line rather than compiled. Because scripting languages are interpreted by the "mother" program, they are a bit slower than compiled programs—however, they require much less programming overhead than do compiled programs.

If you are a real "propeller head" and like to get into the guts of a program, you can create plug-ins for the program itself using the C or C++ programming languages. Maya has its own API (application programming interface)—appropriately enough named Maya API. MEL does just fine for 95 percent of the things most people want to do, however, and it isn't too difficult to learn.

> Although the API is outside the scope of this book, you can contact Alias|Wavefront about using the Maya SDK to develop plug-ins for Maya.

The Script Editor

One of the best ways to get to know MEL is to use the Script Editor. MEL is a huge language (with more than 600 commands and about 75 functions), but the Script Editor will clue you in on how commands are used and allow you to "cut and paste" whole scripts together without the need to program a thing yourself. You don't even need to use the command line to enter the MEL commands. Operations you perform in the Maya interface are recorded as MEL commands in the Script Editor. With no knowledge of programming, you can actually copy-paste together a fairly complex script.

> The command line, which we discussed in Chapter 1, "The Maya Interface," is just one input
> line in the Script Editor. When you type a command in the command line, it appears in the
> Script Editor's history window.

You can open the Script Editor in two ways: either choose Window → General Editors → Script Editor, or click the button ⊞ , in the lower-right corner of the screen, that looks like a square with lines in it. When opened, the Script Editor will look like Figure 20.1.

Notice that there are two panes in the editor. The top pane is called the history pane; the bottom, the input pane. With the Script Editor open, create a polygon cube (from the Modeling menu set, choose Create → Polygon Primitives → Cube). Now look at the history pane. The last lines of that pane should read something like:

```
polyCube -w 1 -h 1 -d 1 -sx 1 -sy 1 -sz 1 -ax 0 1 0 -tx 1 -ch 1;
// Result: pCube1 polyCube1 //
```

What you see in the top pane is the command you told Maya to perform when you made your menu selection. The `polyCube` command creates a polygon cube; all the characters preceded by dashes (`-w`, `-h`, `-ax`, and so on) are "flags" that tell `polyCube` how to build the cube. For example, `-w` stands for width, which is the width of the cube, and `-ax` tells Maya which axis is the "up" axis for the cube (in this case, the Y axis). Finally, the semicolon at the end of the line tells Maya the command is finished. (Nearly every line of MEL code needs a semicolon at the end.)

Sometimes, more characters will fit into the input pane than we can squeeze into the printed page, so the semicolon is also your guide to where one command actually ends and the next begins. As you enter commands from this book into the Script Editor, you generally need only press the Enter key after semicolons.

Change some of the attributes of the cube (scale, rotation, translation, and so on), and look at what appears in the history pane of the Script Editor. You can see that every command you perform in the interface is relayed to Maya's core program via MEL commands. For

Figure 20.1

The Script Editor

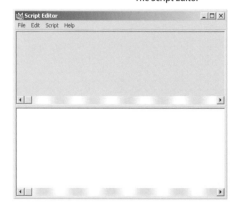

ease of reading, you can clear the top pane at any time. Choose Edit → Clear History to clear the top pane of all commands.

Now try opening one of Maya's windows (for example, the Hypergraph window: Window → Hypergraph). What do you see in the history pane? Probably nothing at all. To keep from cluttering the history pane, Maya's programmers created a filter that blocks from view in the history pane many of the MEL commands that programmers don't commonly need to see. Sometimes, however, it is useful to see what's really going on in Maya. Close the Hypergraph window, choose Edit → Echo All Commands in the Script Editor, and reopen the Hypergraph window. Now you should see something like this:

```
editMenuUpdate MayaWindow|mainEditMenu;
HypergraphWindow;
tearOffPanel "Hypergraph" "hyperGraphPanel" true;
addHyperGraphPanel hyperGraphPanel1;
HyperGraphEdMenu hyperGraphPanel1HyperGraphEd;
createModelPanelMenu modelPanel1;
createModelPanelMenu modelPanel2;
createModelPanelMenu modelPanel3;
createModelPanelMenu modelPanel4;
buildPanelPopupMenu hyperGraphPanel1;
// Result: hyperGraphPanel1Window //
showWindow $gCommandWindow;
```

All these strange lines represent the steps by which Maya builds the Hypergraph window for you. (Actually, nearly all the words, such as `buildPanelPopupMenu`, are calls to other MEL scripts in the `\Maya4.5\Scripts\Others` directory. You can look through them to see how the window is actually constructed.) So you see, even the windows in Maya are created through MEL.

The next-to-last line

```
// Result: hyperGraphPanel1Window //
```

is called the *result line*. The two slashes at the beginning of the line are a comment marker that tells MEL to ignore the rest of that line. (You'll see these comment lines in all well-written MEL scripts, and we'll discuss them later in this chapter.) MEL then displays the result of the operation (in this case, that it created the window as you asked). If a problem occurs while making the Hypergraph window, the result line contains an error message instead of a result message.

Now let's take a look at the input pane (the pane on the bottom half of the Script Editor window). First empty the scene of all objects, and clear the history pane; place your cursor in the bottom pane, and type the following:

```
polyCube -name myCube;
```

Press the Enter key on your numeric keypad (not the one on your main keyboard) or, alternatively, press Ctrl+Enter on your main keyboard. You should see the text disappear from the input pane and appear in the history pane. (You will also see another result line, telling you that the command was successfully completed.) At the same time, you should see a cube appear at the origin of your scene, named myCube. Congratulations, you have just executed your first MEL command!

> If you're wondering why you have to use the numeric keypad's Enter key or Ctrl+Enter, it's because the alpha Enter key is reserved for inline returns. In other words, pressing the alpha Enter key just creates a new line in the editor window. To force the contents of the editor window to be evaluated (executed), you must use one of the two other options.

Now try this: delete the cube from your scene, and then triple-click the line in the history pane that you typed earlier (`polyCube -name myCube`). Once you have the entire line highlighted, copy that line into the input pane (simply MM drag into the input pane). Now press Enter. You should see the exact same cube (called myCube) created at the origin of your scene, meaning that you have copied a command from the history pane and made a mini-script (called a macro) out of it. This is a simple example, but consider the power this little cut-and-paste trick gives you: you can "record" anything you like from the history pane and turn it into a MEL macro (or even a full-blown script). By storing this little script, you can return to it any time and, by cutting and pasting text or even at the click of a button, make all those actions happen.

As noted in Chapter 3, "Techniques for Speeding Up Workflow," you can create buttons for MEL commands simply by highlighting those commands and then MM dragging the command lines up to a shelf.

What Is an Attribute?

As you likely understand from reading earlier chapters, an attribute (MEL uses the term `Attr` to refer to attributes) is any item that lives on a Maya node. (A Maya node is anything you can see in the Hypergraph, or the tabs at the top of the Attribute Editor.) This sounds a bit obscure, but it's really fairly straightforward: anything in the Channel Box, such as `rotateX`, `transformY`, or `scaleZ,` is an attribute of an object (more specifically, an object's transform node).

When you build, alter, or animate an object, you're changing one or more attributes on one or more nodes in the object—and, of course, all of these changes are just MEL commands, so you can make Maya do the work for you. In this section, we'll take a quick look at how MEL works with attributes; in a later section, we'll get into more detail about how to build complex scripts using attributes.

You might have noticed when you adjusted certain attributes of myCube in the previous section that the Script Editor was filled with statements that started with setAttr. The setAttr statement tells MEL to set a certain attribute to a certain value. Likewise, the getAttr statement gets (reads) the value of an attribute on a certain object, so you can use that value in another MEL statement. The addAttr statement tells MEL to add a custom attribute to a certain item. Essentially, using the setAttr statement is the same as opening the Attribute Editor window and changing a value in one of its fields. (Try changing a value in the Attribute Editor, and you'll notice that the Script Editor history pane shows that a setAttr statement has been executed.)

The syntax (the rules of what goes where) for an Attr statement is as follows:

```
setAttr [flags] objectName value;
```

Flags, as you've seen, are any special requests for MEL to complete; the object name is the name of the item's attribute to set (such as myCube.translateX); and the value is the value to set the attribute to. The getAttr and addAttr commands have similar syntax. For example, we can move a cube called "box" to 10 on the X axis by typing the following in the Script Editor:

```
setAttr box.translateX 10;
```

Once you execute this command, your box moves from where it is to 10 on the X axis. (Of course, if you have no object called "box," you will get an error message.)

The way MEL (and Maya) references an attribute is similar to the way C++ and other object-oriented programs work. You reference the node, then a period, then the attribute: Object.Attribute. If you don't specify the node on which the attribute is located , you'll get an error message. For example, typing setAttr translateX 10; generates an error message, because Maya doesn't know what to translate.

Setting the translateX attribute is much like giving the move command: move 10 0 0. Unlike giving the move command, however, setting the attribute of translateX does not affect the other two attributes (the Y and Z translate attributes). Also, the setAttr statement is far more flexible than the move command, which can translate only an object.

As a quick example of how setAttr can work, let's make a box and manually set several of its attributes. Type the following in the Script Editor's input pane:

```
polyCube -n box;
setAttr polyCube1.sw 3;
setAttr polyCube1.w 5;
setAttr box.rotateY 45;
setAttr box.translateX -2.5;
setAttr box.translateY .25;
setAttr box.scaleY 0.5;
```

Can you figure out what each command does on your own? Try highlighting each line and pressing the numeric Enter key to execute it. Highlighting one line at a time is a useful way to figure out what's happening in a script—and to see where things go wrong!

To change the way your cube is constructed, you reference the shape node (`polyCube1`), not the transform node, which you have renamed `box`.

The first line builds a cube. The rest of the lines change some of the attributes, either on the shape node of the cube (the `pPolyCube1` node) or on the transform node (the `box` node). After the `polyCube` command, the next two `setAttr` statements change the subdivisions along the width and then the width of the cube (now a rectangle) itself. The last four lines change the rotation, position, and scale of the cube's transform node (named `box`). The finished product should look like that in Figure 20.2.

If, for some unknown reason, you need to create a flattened box over and over again in different scenes, you can simply MM drag these commands to your shelf and make the object at the click of a button—quite a time-saver!

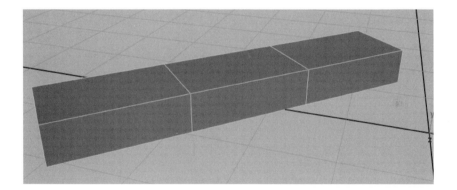

Figure 20.2

The box, squashed

How to Get Help with MEL

Before we delve any further into the world of MEL, let's examine the powerful Maya help tools—and how easy they are to use.

First, you have Maya's internal Help function. Because there are so many MEL commands and functions (about 700), the Help function is a quick and useful feature. (You can even type **help help** to get a look at how the `Help` command works.)

Here's an example of the type of information available in Help. Open the Script Editor and type the name of the command you want help with into the input pane (or just type it in the command line below the main window). For example, to get help with the `setAttr` command, type:

```
help setAttr;
```

Execute the command (press Enter on the numeric keypad, or press Ctrl+Enter on the keyboard), and in the Script Editor's history pane, you'll see the following result lines:

```
// Result:
Synopsis: setAttr [flags] Name[...]
Flags:
   -e -edit
   -q -query
  -av -alteredValue
   -k -keyable        on|off
   -l -lock           on|off
   -s -size           Index
 -typ -type           String
  //
```

These result lines give you a quick look at the `setAttr` command: a synopsis of its syntax (or how to use it) and a list of flags that you can use with the command.

If you're an experienced programmer, this information might be all you need to use the command. If you're just starting out, however, you'll probably want more guidance. In that case, try typing the following in the input pane:

```
help -doc setAttr;
```

When you execute this command, Maya automatically opens your browser of choice (usually Netscape Communicator or Microsoft Internet Explorer) and finds the correct HTML page in your online documents (contained on your hard drive) that contains the command you want help with. In the case of the `setAttr` statement, the following is displayed (this is merely an excerpt—the actual page contains much more information):

Name
```
    setAttr
```
Synopsis
```
    SetAttr
        [flags] object.attribute value [value..]
```
ReturnValue
```
    None.
```
Description
```
    Sets the value of a dependency node attribute. No value for the
    attribute is needed when the -l/-k/-s flags are used. The -type flag
    is only required when setting a non-numeric attribute.
The following chart outlines the syntax of setAttr for non-numeric
    data types:
{TYPE} below means any number of values of type TYPE, separated by a space
[TYPE] means that the value of type TYPE is optional
A|B means that either of A or B may appear
```

Examples

```
sphere -n sphere;
// Set a simple numeric value
setAttr sphere.translateX 5;
// Lock an attribute to prevent further modification
setAttr -lock on sphere.translateX;
// Make an attribute unkeyable
setAttr -keyable off sphere.translateZ;
// Set an entire list of multi-attribute values in one command
setAttr -size 7 "sphereShape.weights[0:6]" 1 1 2 1 1 1 2
// Set an attribute with a compound numeric type
setAttr "sphere.rotate" -type "double3" 0 45 90;
// Set a multi-attribute with a compound numeric type
setAttr "sphereShape.controlPoints[0:2]" -type "double3"
    0 0 0 1 1 2 2 2;
```

As you can see, a few examples can do a lot to clarify how a command is used.

You can also access an entire MEL manual online, for a more in-depth look at the structure of the scripting language itself. In Maya, choose Help → Library to open the main reference page in your web browser. Choose the Using Maya/MEL link to display a menu of introductory material, frequently asked questions, and other resources for learning MEL. Between the internal Help files and the online help on your hard drive, you can access excellent reference material rapidly.

Examining other users' scripts as guides for what you want to do is another great way to learn more about MEL—you can even copy and paste portions of scripts for your own use (just be sure that you have the author's permission). For some example scripts you can study, see the accompanying CD-ROM or the new Maya Gems section of the online help.

A Comment on Commenting

Comments are a way for you, as a programmer, to document your code. Comments can be useful when you revisit old code, when you're writing code that may be confusing, or when others are reading your code.

Comments are identified by two forward slashes (//). When the script executes, the interpreter ignores anything that follows the two slashes. Here are some examples of legal comments:

```
//Script written by: John Doe
polyCube -n myCube;      //create a cube named myCube
```

As you can see, a comment can be on a line by itself or at the end of a line of code.

Always include comments at the top of a script about what the script does, which arguments (inputs) it needs (you'll learn about arguments later in the section on procedures), who wrote (and modified) it, and when it was last modified. It's also not a bad idea to put in a "use at your own risk" line to indicate that some unforeseen problem could arise while using the script and that the author is not responsible for any mishaps because of the script's usage (ah, the joys of a litigious society!).

You might think that these comments are of use only to others and not to yourself, and you'd rather not bother with them if you don't plan to distribute the script. But remember that two months after you create the script, you might need to modify it, and if you can't figure out what you did or why, you'll waste a great deal of time hunting through the script instead of getting right to your modifications.

Always comment your scripts well (even the simplest ones). It's a habit (and for once, a good one), so get into it! Commenting well doesn't necessarily mean commenting everything though. In this chapter, the scripts are a little over-commented for instructional purposes, but in most cases, if you have more comments than code, you have overdone it. Good code is self-documenting with comments included where you or someone else might need a little extra information about what is happening. Here is an example of poor, or overdone, commenting technique:

```
// z equals x plus y
$z = $x + $y;
```

Hands On: Building a Room Automatically

Let's put all this information to some use now. We're going to record several actions we perform to create a default room setup, copy those actions into a macro, and place that macro on a shelf. Once we've done that, we can automatically set up a room for any scene we want, at the click of a mouse.

1. Open Maya or begin a new scene.

2. Open the Script Editor and clear the history pane.

3. Build a room with three walls, a floor, and a ceiling (polygon cubes or planes). Leave one side of the room open to see inside. Place a cube and a sphere inside the room. Create a point light and place it in the center of the room, and shine a spotlight into the room. Then create a camera to see inside the room.

4. Once you're happy with the room, simply select everything in the history pane and MM drag the highlighted text up to the shelf of your choosing. If you're not happy with your room, you can use a sample room script, `room.mel`, on the accompanying CD-ROM. Simply load it into the input pane of the Script Editor by choosing File → Open Script. Once the script is loaded, highlight it and then MM drag it up to a shelf. A new button appears `mel` .

5. Let's see if it worked. Select everything in your scene and press Delete. (Or you can type **select -all; delete;** in the Script Editor to do the same thing.)

6. Once your scene is empty, go up to the shelf and click your newly made button. After a couple of seconds, you should see your room magically appear in the scene, just as you had it set up.

Not bad for a couple minutes of work and no programming! If you like, you can make several more room configurations.

One problem you might notice right away is that the default MEL shelf buttons all look alike. Fortunately, Maya can handle this problem quite easily.

1. From the main menu, choose Window → Settings/Preferences → Shelves to open the Shelves window, which is shown in Figure 20.3. (Or, alternatively, choose Shelf Editor from the Shelf menu, the black triangle at the left of the shelf icons.)

   Figure 20.3

   The Shelves window

2. Click the Shelves tab. The main pane lists all current shelves, along with buttons to add, delete, or move shelves up and down in the order they appear on screen. Click the New Shelf button to display a new shelf titled **shelfLayout1**. You can either rename this to create a shelf for you (such as **myShelf**) or click the Delete Shelf button to remove the new shelf.

3. Now select Shelf1 from the list and click the Shelf Contents tab. The main pane lists all the buttons on the selected shelf (see Figure 20.4). Click the first item in the list (probably CV Curve Tool), and look at the area below the main pane. Here, you'll see the Move Up, Move Down, and Delete Item buttons, as well as other buttons and fields:

   Figure 20.4

   The Shelf Contents tab

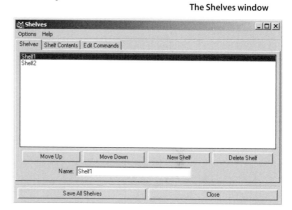

   - The Label & Tooltips text field contains the text you see in the pane above this section (the internal label for the button; see Figure 20.4).

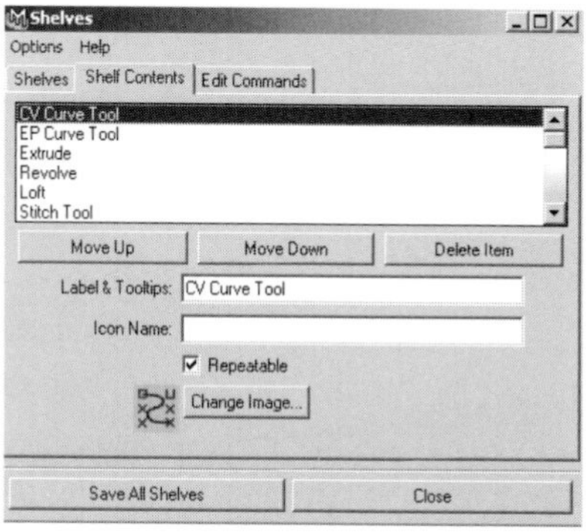

   - The Icon Name text field contains the text you see under the button when the icon is displayed in the shelf itself. For the CV Curve Tool button, highlighted in Figure 20.4, this is blank, so there is no text on the shelf icon. Try adding text and see what happens!

   - The Change Image button allows you to find or create the bitmapped image that appears on the shelf—in the case of the CV Curve Tool button ![icon], it's stored in the \Maya4.5\Bitmaps folder.

You can also navigate to the `\Maya4.5\extras\icons` directory and browse through many prebuilt icons for your use in creating shelf buttons.

> You can also create your own icons. In Windows, Mac OS X, and Linux, the icons can be in BMP, JPG, or XPM formats. (BMP and JPG are supported by nearly all graphics-editing packages.) In IRIX, you must save the image in XPM format (using XPaint or another program). The icons are 32 × 32 pixels, and you should make your images that size. If you want to place text at the bottom of the image, leave a blank space for it, because both the text and the image must fit within the 32 × 32 area.

4. Now go back to the Shelves tab and select the shelf that contains your new room button.

5. Return to the Shelf Contents tab. Add an icon name and a label to your button. Now change the image of the button to one of the images in `\Maya4.5\extras\icons`. (If you want text on your button, a good choice of icons is the `UserMenuIcon` group in this directory. The buttons in this group have room for text at the bottom of the button.)

The Edit Commands tab is for more advanced users. This window actually allows you to rewrite the scripts for the menu buttons right inside the Shelves window. The script for whatever item you select in the Shelf Contents tab appears in the main window. You can then change any commands you want or add comments to the script.

To make these changes "stick," however, you *must* press the Enter key on your numeric keypad (not on your keyboard); otherwise, when you select another tab, all your changes will be lost! For practice, try adding a comment line such as the following to your room macro:

```
//This is my macro to make a simple room.
```

Click another shelf button and then return to the Edit Commands tab. Did your changes hold? If not, try again, this time remembering to press the Enter key.

Before leaving the Shelves window, it is always a good idea to click the Save All Shelves button at the bottom of any of the tabs (assuming you want your changes to stick!). This button writes all the changes you just made to your `\Winnt\Profiles\<user name>\maya\4.5\prefs\shelves` directory (for Windows), so that the next time you start Maya, your shelves will look just as they do now.

In this example, you learned to record your actions, save them as a macro, place them in your shelves, and finally change the text and image of the button to customize its look.

Variables, Loops, and Branching

If you've done any programming at all, you've probably been waiting for this point: the main reasons to program are (1) to create flexibility and (2) to take care of repetitive tasks. Flexibility comes through variables and branching; repetition is made possible through looping.

Variables

It's actually much easier to see what a variable is than to talk about it. Type the following in the Script Editor:

```
string $myVariable;
$myVariable = "hi there";
print $myVariable;
```

When you execute these commands, you'll see that "hi there" is displayed in the last line of the history pane, indicating that when you told Maya to print $myVariable, it displayed "hi there." The first line of this script is called a declaration of the variable: string is the variable's type (a string is just text contained in quotes), and *$myVariable* is its name. The second line of the script assigns the string "hi there" to the variable *$myVariable*, and the third line tells the print command to output the contents of the variable *$myVariable*, which as you can see is "hi there".

> Every MEL variable must start with the $ symbol so that MEL knows it's a variable. (This is easy to forget, and it causes strange errors—so remember your $ symbol!)

In the previous example, we could have typed the following after the print statement

```
$myVariable = "goodbye";
print $myVariable;
```

which would change the data in the variable *$myVariable* to the string "goodbye" and display it on the screen just after "hi there". As you see, variables can be useful, because they can store different data at different times as a program runs.

MEL has a convenience feature built into it for variables: you can declare and assign a variable in the same line. In other words, you can write the previous script as follows:

```
string $myVariable = "hi there";
print $myVariable;
```

There is no real difference between the two scripts, except for less typing and better readability—you can use whichever method appeals to you (though most seasoned programmers opt to save keystrokes!). You can also save keystrokes when declaring and assigning values to variables in other ways. Following are some examples of ways to declare variables:

- Integer

```
int $months = 11;   //standard declaration & assignment
int $days = 11, $year = 1977; //2 assignments, comma separation
int $dollars = $pounds = $pesos = -14; //multiple assignments
```

- Float

```
float $distance = -7.1;  //standard
float $height, $weight = 87.8; //declare 2, assign 2nd
    $length = 3.4; // implicit declaration
```

- String

```
string $greeting = "Hello World!"; //standard
string $empty = "",      //comma separator
    $hello = "HI!";  //2nd line ends declaration
```

- Array

```
int $bits[5] = {0, 1, 0, 1, 0}; //standard
float $lengths[10]; //10 element float array with no values
    $lengths[0] = 4.6; //assignment of 1st element
string $class[5] = {"Jim", "Davy", "Dave", "Deborah", "Wil"};
```

TYPES OF MEL VARIABLES

You use the following types of variables in MEL:

int An integer number—used to represent a whole number, such as 3 or –45.

float A decimal number—used to represent a "real" number, such as –35.4725.

string A set of characters surrounded by quotes—used to store text, such as "hello world".

vector Three decimal numbers that make a vector number—used to represent a point on a three-dimensional grid, such as (26, 31.67, 5.724). A vector number is useful for three-dimensional information such as position (X, Y, Z coordinates) or color (red, green, blue colors).

array A list of numbers—used to store lists of integers, floats, strings, or vectors. Arrays are useful for storing data about many similar items, such as the color of each of a group of particles.

matrix A two-dimensional array of floats, or an array of float arrays. If it sounds a bit confusing, you can think of it as a graph of rows and columns of floating point data.

We'll examine vectors, arrays, and matrix variable types more closely when they are needed in this chapter.

It is always easier to read code that has appropriately named variables. Like well-written comments, well-named variables make life much easier when you revisit old code or deal with complicated scripts. For example, a variable named `$whisker_length` is much more meaningful than `$wl`.

Looping

Next, let's examine looping. Say you want to create five cubes in your scene using MEL commands. You can either type **polyCube -n box** five times or have MEL do it for you using the `for` loop. To build our five cubes, type the following:

```
int $i;
for ($i = 1; $i<= 5; $i++){
    polyCube -n box;
    }
```

Voilà, five cubes named `box1` through `box5`. (However, you'll need to move them away from each other to see them as separate objects. We'll do that in a moment.)

MEL supports implicit variable declaration, so the `int $i` line is not strictly necessary. However, in most cases, it is preferable to declare all variables explicitly to avoid possible complications in the script.

Notice that there is no semicolon after the `for` statement: MEL expects one or more commands (contained within the { } brackets) after the `for` statement, so a semicolon is unnecessary. Additionally, the closing bracket (}) functions as a semicolon, so a semicolon is also unnecessary on the last line. The syntax for the `for` loop is as follows:

```
for (initial value; test value; increment)
```

The *initial value* is what the counting variable is set to at the beginning. The *test value* is a Boolean statement (yes or no, 1 or 0, off or on, true or false) that determines whether to continue with another iteration of the loop (see Maya's documentation on Boolean operators). The *increment* is how quickly the counter increases in value (`$i++` is a simple way of saying "increase the value of `$i` by 1 each loop"). The `for` loop in the previous example can be read as follows: for i starting at 1, while i is less than or equal to 5, increment i by 1 every time the statements inside the brackets are executed.

To make this loop do a bit more for us, let's have it move the cubes on top of one another on the Y axis as it creates them:

```
for ($i = 1; $i<= 5; $i++){
    polyCube -n box;
    move -r 0 (2 * $i) 0;
    }
```

Now as the spheres are created, each one is moved up by twice the value of $i, placing them just atop one another.

There are several other types of loops in MEL. The following sections provide the syntax and an example of each.

for – in

Syntax:

```
for (element in array){
    statements;
}
```

Example:

```
string $student;
string $class[3] = {"Brian", "Nathan", "Josh"};
for ($student in $class){
print ($student + "\n");   // \n = go to the next line
}
```

while

Syntax:

```
while (test condition){
    statements;
}
```

Example:

```
int $i = 0;
while ($i < 5){
   print $i;
   $i++;   //increment i by 1
}
```

do – while

Syntax:

```
do{
    statements;
}while(test condition);
```

Example:

```
int $i = 5;
do{
    print $i;
    $i-;    //decrement i by 1
}while($i > 0);
```

Branching

The last basic program structure we'll look at is branching. Branching provides a way to ask a question and decide whether to take some further action given the answer. (The for statement actually contains a branch in its *test value* statement.) Let's use the same script as previously, only this time let's put a conditional statement inside it:

```
for ($i = 1; $i<= 5; $i++){
    polyCube -n box;
    if ($i<=3){
        move -r 0 (2 * $i) 0;
        }
    else{
        move -r (2 * $i) 0 0;
        }
    }
```

What happens when you execute these commands? The first three cubes are stacked up on the Y axis (when $i is less than or equal to 3), and the last two are stacked along the X axis (when $i is 4 and 5, and therefore greater than 3). In abstract, the syntax for the if statement is as follows:

```
if (test){
    commands;
    }
else if (test){
    commands;
    }
else{
    commands;
    }
```

The else if and else statements do *not* have to exist for the if statement to work. The else if statement, listed here, allows you to make as many tests as you like (your conditional statement can have as many else if statements as you wish), allowing you to test for multiple possibilities within one large conditional statement. The else statement must always be last in such examples, and it is the "default" answer if no other conditions are met. All the commands for an if, else if, or else statement must be enclosed in brackets ({ }). If we want, we can increase the complexity of our create-and-move-box code with an else if statement:

```
for ($i = 1; $i<= 10; $i++){
    polyCube -n box;
    if ($i<=3){
        move -r 0 (2 * $i) 0;
        }
```

```
        else if ($i>3 && $i<=6){
            move -r 0 0 (2 * $i);
        }
        else{
            move -r (2 * $i) 0 0;
        }
    }
```

Here, the cubes will stack along the Y axis if $i is less than or equal to 3, along the Z axis if $i is between 4 and 6, and along the X axis if $i is greater than 6.

If there is only one line of commands after the if statement, you do not need the brackets. However, it's a good idea for readability to always include them anyway. Always be consistent with the placement and alignment of your brackets. It becomes easy to forget a bracket with multiple if else statements, which can lead to unnecessary debugging.

Another way of branching is to use the switch statement. A switch statement branches based on a control. The control can be of type int, float, string, or vector. If the value of the control is equal to the value of one of the specified case values (which must be of the same type as the control), the statements following that case value execute. Following is the basic syntax of the switch statement.

```
    switch (control)
    {
        case value1:
            statement1;
            break;
        case value2:
            statement2;
            break;
        case value3:
            statement3;
            break;
        ...
        default:
            statement4;
            break;
    }
```

The break statement is used to exit out of the switch statement and prevent execution of subsequent case statements. The default statement executes if none of the other case statements are a match for the control. The default statement can be omitted.

Here is an example of the `switch` statement with our box example:

```
for( $i = 0; $i < 3; $i++){
    polyCube -n box;
switch($i){
case 0:
    move -r (2 * $i) 0 0;
break;
case 1:
    move -r 0 (2 * $i) 0;
break;
case 2 :
    move -r 0 0 (2 * $i);
break;
default:
break;
}

}
```

Here we create three cubes and move them each along a different axis. When i is equal to 0 we move it along the X axis, 1 along the Y axis, and 2 along the Z axis. When i is 3, we arrive at the default condition, which does nothing, so no new box is created.

Debugging MEL Scripts

If you were careful typing in the previous sections, you might have gotten away without seeing a MEL error message; in the work ahead, however (and certainly as you begin building MEL scripts of your own), you will encounter error messages, the most common of which is the syntax error. Every command has a particular structure or form that must be followed to execute successfully. Otherwise, the script interpreter won't know what to do with your command and will most often return a syntax error.

Although debugging a script is a bit of an art form, you can help yourself in a couple of ways. First, check the history pane when you execute a script: if the last line of your script is the last line in the history pane, the commands executed without an error. If, however, you get a comment line such as the following:

```
setAttr box 5;
//Error:  line 1:  No attribute was specified. //
```

you know that there has been at least one error in parsing the script.

Parsing is the programming term for the search that the script interpreter makes through the script to ensure that all the commands are correct.

The Feedback line (at the bottom-right of the screen) turns orange-red to indicate that the MEL interpreter has discovered an error in your code. One way to quickly identify where these errors might lie is to turn on the Show Line Numbers option in the Script Editor. Generally, it's a good idea to keep this option on at all times. It does not slow Maya down in any significant way, and it provides useful information about where errors are occurring.

As you begin scripting, one error that will probably creep in is forgetting the final semicolon at the end of a line. This can be difficult to spot if you're not aware of the problem. If you are getting errors in your script that don't make sense, try looking at lines above where the error occurred to be sure they end with a semicolon.

Finally, since MEL is an interpreted scripting language, you can execute a script one line at a time, rather than as a whole. This can be a useful way to figure out where a problem is occurring in your program. A brief exercise will illustrate:

1. Type the following, but don't execute it yet:
```
print "hello, world!";
print hello, world;
```

2. Now highlight the first line and execute it (by pressing the Enter key on your numeric keypad or Ctrl+Enter on your keyboard). You should see `hello, world!` displayed in the history pane.

3. Now highlight and execute the second line. You should see something like the following:
```
// Error: print hello, world; //
// Error: Line 1.12: Syntax error //
```

The first line executed properly, but the second had an error in it—the `print` command needs a string to work with, and you need to include quotation marks to identify the string. In a two-line script, spotting the error is simple; in a longer script, this method of going through the script one line at a time can be a great way to uncover problem spots.

Great. You know how to get help and debug a script—now let's get down to business!

Hands On: Making a Mountain

By now you should have a good understanding of some of the basic concepts of writing MEL scripts. You know about variables, loops, and branching. You also know how to create an object. Now we'll put these concepts to work in a MEL script that creates a mountain.

First, let's create a simple polygon plane that will eventually become our mountain. Type the following in the Script Editor:
```
int   $subDivW = 20, $subDivH = 20,
      $scaleW  = 20, $scaleH  = 20;
polyPlane -name mountain -w $scaleW -h $scaleH -sx $subDivW
                    -sy $subDivH -ch 0;
```

As you can see, we've named our plane `mountain`, which it will soon become! We've also declared four variables that determine the scale and the number of subdivisions of our plane. We've used variables in our creation of the plane so that we can go back and change these attributes later if we want to do so. The –`ch` flag, when set to 0, turns off the construction history of the plane, which will be useful when we want to deform it to make the mountain.

Using variables inside scripts rather than "raw" numbers is good practice. Not only is *$scaleW* easier to understand than 20, if you used the *$scaleW* variable multiple times while writing a script, you could just return to the top of the program and alter the definition of the variable to change its value in all instances in the script. Using a variable here saves you the time (and potential errors) of hunting down all the instances where you used this value in the script.

Our algorithm for making the mountain is to raise each of the vertices of the plane a certain amount based on its distance from the mountain's peak. To do this, we need a `for` loop to make our way through each of the plane's vertices. For simplification, the peak of our mountain will be in the center of the plane. Now edit what we had before to look like this:

```
int    $i,
       $subDivW = 20, $subDivH = 20,
       $scaleW  = 20, $scaleH  = 20,
       $num_vertices = ($subDivW + 1) * ($subDivH + 1);

polyPlane -name mountain -w $scaleW -h $scaleH -sx $subDivW
                         -sy $subDivH -ch 0;

for($i=0; $i < $num_vertices; $i++){
    select -r mountain.vtx[$i];
}
```

We added another integer variable *$i* to be our vertex index in the `for` loop that we also added. You can see that it's easy to select a vertex on the plane with the `select` command. In our `for` loop, our test case is based on whether *$i* is less than *$num_vertices*, a variable we created based on the subdivisions along the width and the height of the plane.

To make the mountain take shape, we'll need to add a few useful commands. Edit the code again as follows:

```
int    $i,
       $subDivW = 20, $subDivH = 20,
       $scaleW  = 20, $scaleH  = 20,
       $num_vertices = ($subDivW + 1) * ($subDivH + 1);

float $peak = 15, $height,
      $dist, $max_dist,
      $position[3],
      $roughness = 1.5;
```

```
$max_dist = sqrt ($scaleW * $scaleW + $scaleH * $scaleH) / 2;
polyPlane -name mountain -w $scaleW -h $scaleH -sx $subDivW
                         -sy $subDivH -ch 0;

for($i=0; $i < $num_vertices; $i++){
    $position = `xform -worldSpace -query
                       -translation mountain.vtx[$i]`;

    $dist = `mag(<<$position[0], $position[1], $position[2]>>)`;
    $height = $peak * (1 - ($dist / $max_dist) ) +
                           rand(-1 * $roughness, $roughness);

    select -r mountain.vtx[$i];
    move -r 0 $height 0;
}
select -r mountain;
```

The first thing we added were six **float** variables. The *$peak* variable is the height of the mountain, *$height* is how high to move the vertex, *$dist* is how far the current vertex is from the center, *$max_dist* is the farthest vertex from the center, *$position[3]* is an array to hold three floats that represent the x, y, and z of a vertex, and *$roughness* is the roughness of the mountain's surface.

To calculate the maximum distance from a point on the plane to the center of the plane, we used some high-school geometry. We use the **sqrt** function to calculate one-half the length of the diagonal of the plane (using the Pythagorean theorem). This should be the distance of the farthest point on the plane to the center. The **xform** command queries the world coordinates of the current vertex. The **mag** function calculates the length of a vector. Since we want to find the distance of a vertex to the center (<<0, 0, 0>>) of the plane, we can use the vertex's world position as the vector argument in the **mag** function. We then calculate the height of our point based on the peak and a ratio of the distance of the current point to the maximum distance of a point. We then add a random amount to the height with the **rand** function, which gives us a number between the first argument and the second argument—in this case –1.5 to 1.5 since the value of *$roughness* is 1. And, finally, we move the point up on the Y axis with the **move** command. (For more information on these commands, see the Maya documentation.)

When you execute the code, you should see a mountain appear after a second or two of calculations. Convert it to a subdivision surface (Modify → Convert → Polygons To Subdiv) to smooth it out some. Your mountain should look something like Figure 20.5. (It will look slightly different due to the randomness of the points.)

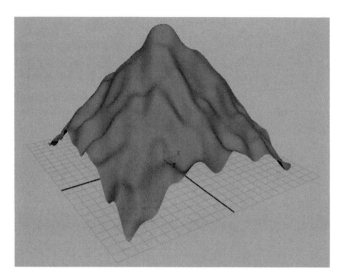

Figure 20.5

A MEL mountain

Now we can modify our script and change the size, subdivision, roughness, and height of our mountain by changing only a few variables at the top. Let's not stop here though. Let's make a few more simple additions and modifications to really make our script dynamic. Edit the code once more:

```
int $i,
    $subDivW = 20, $subDivH = 20,
    $scaleW  = 20, $scaleH  = 20;

float $peak = 15, $height,
    $dist, $max_dist,
    $position[3],
    $roughness = 1.5,
    $jitterX, $jitterZ, $overhang = 1.0,
    $crater_radius = 5.0, $crater_depth = 10.0,
    $crater_roughness = 1.0;

$max_dist = sqrt ($scaleW * $scaleW + $scaleH * $scaleH) / 2;
polyPlane -name mountain -w $scaleW -h $scaleH -sx $subDivW
        -sy $subDivH -ch 0;

for($i=0; $i < ($subDivH +1) * ($subDivW + 1); $i++){
    $position = `xform -worldSpace -query
                -translation mountain.vtx[$i]`;
    $dist = `mag(<<$position[0], $position[1], $position[2]>>)`;
```

```
    if($dist > $crater_radius)
        $height = $peak * (1 - ($dist / $max_dist) )
                            + rand(-1 * $roughness, $roughness);
    else
      $height = $peak - ($crater_depth +
                  rand(-1 * $crater_roughness, $crater_roughness));

        $jitterX = rand(0, ($scaleW / (float)$subDivW) * $overhang);
        $jitterZ = rand(0, ($scaleW / (float)$subDivW) * $overhang);
        select -r mountain.vtx[$i] ;
        move -r $jitterX $height $jitterZ;
    }
select -r mountain;
```

Now we have several new features in our mountain script. First, we added variables to jitter the vertices along the X axis and Z axis as they are raised. You can see that this is also a random value and is controlled by a variable called *$overhang*. If $overhang is greater than 1.0, the vertices may overlap.

We also added the capability to turn our mountain into a volcano. You can see the variables *$crater_radius*, *$crater_depth*, and *$crater_roughness*. Since we are basing the height of our vertices on where they are in relation to the center, we can create a radius around that center, in which the heights are dropped rather than raised. The *$crater_depth* tells us where the bottom of the crater is in relation to where the peak would be, and the *$crater_roughness* is how rough the surface is inside the crater. You can see the if-else statement that determines what to do with a vertex based on its distance from the center. Figure 20.6 shows some examples of the mountains you can create by just changing a few variables:

Figure 20.6

Several MEL mountains

Creating a GUI

Although typing commands into the command line or input pane of the Script Editor is useful for simple tasks, it is often much more elegant (not to mention user-friendly) to create a graphical user interface window in your script to give users access to all the script's commands in a comfortable point-and-click environment. Although creating these windows can be somewhat challenging, nearly all high-quality scripts use them, so it is good to learn at least the basics of GUI creation using MEL.

Windows in Maya can be complex (just look at the Attribute Editor window for an example), but the basic way to create a window is fairly simple. At a minimum, you need three commands to make a window:

```
window -title "title" -wh 400 200 myWindow;
some kind of layout;
showWindow;
```

Executing the `window` command creates a window with a name that appears at its top (the `-title` flag), optionally a predefined width and height (the `-widthHeight` or `-wh` flag), and an optional name (the last item in the `window` command). The title of a window and its name are *not* the same. Maya refers to the `myWindow` name, while a user sees the window's `title`.

The `showWindow` command displays the window on the screen. (It will never appear if you forget this line.) This command usually resides at the end of a "make window" series of commands.

The layout commands specify the layout of the window. Some common types are `column-Layout`, `scrollLayout`, `rowColumnLayout`, and `formLayout`. The column layout creates a column, the scroll layout makes the window a scrollable window, the row-and-column layout makes a grid of rows and columns (like a table), and the form layout creates a flexible space that can be laid out in many ways. These layouts can also contain other layouts nested within them, creating the ability to make complex windows relatively easily. (The form layout is often the parent layout, with many other layouts inside it.)

Let's create a simple window that contains one button and one slider. Type the following in the Script Editor:

```
window -t "The Big Window!" -wh 400 200 myWindow;
columnLayout -cw 200;
button -l "Click this button" myButton;
text " ";
attrFieldSliderGrp -l "Slide this around" -min 0 -max 10 theSliderGroup;
showWindow myWindow;
```

Figure 20.7

The Big Window!

These commands create a window (which Maya knows as `myWindow` but, as you see in Figure 20.7, is titled The Big Window!) with a width of 400 and a height of 200 pixels. A column layout is then set with a width of 200

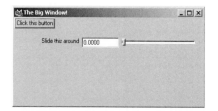

pixels. Next, a button (labeled Click This Button and known to Maya as `myButton`) is created; then a field-and-slider group is created (labeled Slide This Around and known as `theSlider-Group`) with a minimum value of 0 and a maximum value of 10. The `text` command just puts a space between the button and the slider group. Finally, we display the window via the `showWindow` command. Obviously it's not too difficult to create windows with buttons, sliders, or other objects in them.

If you make some errors typing the MEL script and then go back and try to run the script again, when you try to re-create the window, you might run into the following error message: `Error: Object's name is not unique: myWindow`. If you get this message, you need to delete the window `myWindow`: even though it doesn't appear on the screen, MEL has created a UI object named `myWindow` (the `showWindow` command is last, so an object can be created and not shown). Thus, while `myWindow` doesn't appear, it can exist in your scene, and it needs to be deleted. To do this, type **deleteUI myWindow** in the command line or Script Editor and execute it. This command is useful as you create GUI windows, so commit it to memory.

Now let's make our buttons do something. Clear all objects in your scene and create a sphere called "ball." Edit your script to include the −`command` and −`attribute` flags, as follows:

```
window -t "The Big Window!" -wh 400 200 myWindow;
columnLayout -cw 200;
button -l "Click this button" -c "setAttr ball.ty  5" myButton;
text " ";
attrFieldSliderGrp -l "Slide this around" -min 0 -max 10 -at ("ball.tx")
    theSliderGroup;
showWindow myWindow;
```

The −c flag for `button` tells Maya to perform the quoted instruction each time the button is clicked. Thus, when this button is clicked, Maya sets the ball's Y position to 5 units. The −`at` flag in the slider group tells Maya to connect the slider and text field to the quoted attribute (in this case, the X position of the ball). When you click the button, the ball jumps up to 5 on the Y axis. When you slide the slider (or enter numbers in the text field), the ball moves back and forth between 0 and 10 on the X axis.

You can set the slider and text field at different minimum and maximum values. The −`fmn` and −`fmx` flags give the field's min and max values. The −`smn` and −`smx` flags give the slider's min and max values. This allows the user to enter numbers outside the slider's bounds, which can be useful.

You can also create radio buttons and check boxes that perform functions when selected. (See the MEL documentation for more information on these.)

As an exercise, what command could you place on the button to move the ball up 5 units *every* time the button is clicked? Hint: it's relative motion instead of absolute.

Now that you've seen how quickly you can create a basic window as an interface to your scripts, let's make a script that automatically creates a useful window. Make a new scene, and then create several lights and aim them at an object in the scene. Now enter the following in your Script Editor window:

```
string $sel[] = `ls -lights`;
string $current;
string $winName = "lightWindow";
if (`window -exists $winName`)
    {
    deleteUI $winName;
    }
window -title "Lights" -wh 600 300 $winName;
scrollLayout;
rowColumnLayout -nc 2 -cw 1 150 -cw 2 400;
for ($current in $sel)
    {
    text -l $current;
    attrFieldSliderGrp -min (-1) -max 10 -at ($current + ".intensity");
    }
showWindow $winName;
```

When you execute this script, Maya automatically creates a "light board" for you, allowing you to control the intensity of all lights in the scene from one floating window.

The most interesting portion of this script is the first line:

```
string $sel[] = `ls -lights`;
```

This line assigns to the variable string array *$sel[]* the name of every light in the scene. The `ls` command tells Maya to list the items that come after (in this case, `-lights` means "list all lights in the scene"); then the reverse apostrophes tell Maya to evaluate this command (which returns the name of each light) and read the result into the array *$sel[]*.

Next, other variables are declared to store the "current item" (*$current*) and the window name (*$winName*), and the script checks to see whether the window already exists—if it does, the script kills the old window (using the `deleteUI` command) so it can write a new one. This little piece of code is good to include in all your GUI scripts, to ensure that you don't accidentally generate any errors if a window by that name already exists. Then a window is created with a scroll layout (so the window can scroll if it's too small) and a row/column layout (a table). Next the script performs a variation of the `for` loop, called the `for...in` loop. The `for...in` loop looks through an array (in this case, *$sel[]*) and does one loop for each item it finds, placing the value of $sel[number] in the variable *$current*. The type of *$current* must therefore match the type of *$sel[]* (in this case, they're both strings).

> If you want only the lights you previously selected in the scene to be in the window, you can add the flag `-selected` to the `-ls` command on the first line.

As you can see in Figure 20.8, the loop then displays the name of the light (in column 1) and makes a field slider group that's attached to the light's intensity setting (in column 2).

This little script should indicate how powerful a workflow enhancer MEL can be: in just a few lines of script, you have created a way to control potentially dozens of lights in a complex scene in a completely simple, intuitive manner. If you needed to create just the right light levels on 20 lights in a scene, it could take hours navigating to each light and adjusting it individually. This script could make the job a 10-minute effort instead!

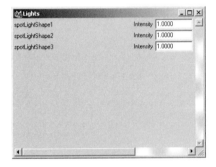

Figure 20.8

A GUI window showing light controls

As an exercise, try creating sliders that let you adjust the light's colors as well as its intensity. (Hint: three attributes, `colorR`, `colorG`, and `colorB`, control the red, green, and blue intensities.) If you really want to get crazy, try placing each group of controls for each light in its own sub-window (so `intensity`, `colorR`, `colorG`, and `colorB` are all inside a window). You'll need to know about the `setParent` command, as well as how to make a frame layout with the flag `-cll` (collapsible) set to true (to make each window close by clicking its triangle). You could also add check boxes to turn off each light's visibility, so that you can see the effects of each light separately. You can find help for these commands in Maya's online reference documents, and if you get stuck, check out `lightBoard.mel`, a finished MEL script included on the CD.

Using Procedures and Scripts

In the past few sections, we've touched on most of the basic elements of MEL. However, all the pieces we've created so far won't work well if we try to give them to someone else or save them to our scripts directory. We haven't done anything to save the commands we've written in a format that Maya can read as a whole. Now, we need to turn these bits of code into full-fledged (standalone) scripts that you can port from one place to another and trade with others.

In this section, we'll look at procedures and scripts. A *procedure* is the basic building block of a MEL script. At its fundamental level, it's simply another declaration line that tells Maya that all the contained lines form one named function. A *script* is just a collection of one or more procedures.

Procedures

In abstract, a procedure looks like this:

```
proc myProcedure ()
{
commands
}
```

Maya executes all the commands in the curly braces every time you type **myProcedure** in the command line or the Script Editor's input pane. MyProcedure is the name of the procedure, and the parentheses can contain any number of declared variables that can either be called from another procedure or entered by the user when executing the procedure. As a simple example, let's write a procedure that creates a user-defined number of spheres.

```
global proc makeBall (int $num){
int $num;
for ($i=1; $i<=$num; $i++){
        sphere -r 1 -name ("ball" + $i);
    }
}
```

Enter this text in the Script Editor, and then execute it. You will notice that nothing happens in Maya. This is because the script as a whole has been "sourced" into Maya's memory. Because the script now resides in memory, whenever you type **makeBall** in the command line or input pane, followed by an integer number, you'll get that many spheres (called ball1, ball2, and so on) in your scene. Typing **makeBall 5**, for example, makes five spheres named ball1 through ball5 in your scene. We've made this procedure "global" so that Maya can reference the procedure from within your \Winnt\Profiles\<user name>\maya\scripts (for Windows) directory (more on this in a moment).

You know that a procedure is just a bunch of MEL commands contained in braces and given a name; so how would you turn our series of light board commands into a procedure? If you didn't guess, it would look something like this:

```
///////////////////////////////////

global proc lightBoard (){
string $sel[] = `ls -lights`;
string $current;
string $winName = "lightWindow";
if (`window -exists $winName`){
    deleteUI $winName;
  }
window -title "Lights" -wh 400 300 $winName;
scrollLayout;
rowColumnLayout -nc 2 -cw 1 150 -cw 2 400;
for ($current in $sel){
    text -l $current;
    attrFieldSliderGrp -min (-1) -max 10 -at
 ($current + ".intensity");
  }
showWindow $winName;
}
///////////////////////////////////
```

Once you source (enter) this procedure, each time you type **lightBoard** in the command line, the procedure runs, and you get a light board for all your lights.

It is a good idea to comment the beginning and end of every procedure (so it's easy to see where they start and stop).

Scripts

What is the difference between a procedure and a script? A script is just a collection of one or more procedures. Thus, the lightBoard procedure we just wrote is actually a script as well. A true script is also saved as an external text file and given a name, which must end in .mel, and the name of the script *must* be the same as the name of the last (global) procedure in the script (plus the .mel extension). For our light-board example, we save the script as lightBoard.mel and store it in our \Profiles\<user name>\maya\scripts directory (for Windows NT; for other operating systems, the location is similar). (When you choose Save Selected in the Script Editor, this is the default directory, so just save it there).

Now let's make a simple script that contains two procedures, to see how that's done.

```
//Source this script, and then type "makeBall <number>" in
//the Command line or Script Editor.  The procedure will make
//the number of spheres you specify and call them "ball1,"
//"ball2," etc.
//Created by:  John Kundert-Gibbs.
//Last Modified:  October 24, 2000.
//Use at your own risk.

//makeIt creates the spheres and gives them names.
//This procedure is passed the number of balls you specify
//from the main procedure.
proc makeIt (int $theNum)
{
//$theNum must be redeclared internal to the procedure.
int $theNum;
for ($i=1; $i<=$theNum; $i++)
    {
    sphere -r 1 -name ("ball" + $i);
    }
}
//end, makeIt.

//makeBall is the main procedure you call.
//It just calls the procedure makeIt and passes it the number
//of spheres you specify.
global proc makeBall (int $num)
```

```
{
int $num;
makeIt ($num);
} //end, makeBall.
```

All we've done with this script is to create a subprocedure that actually creates the spheres. The main (or global) procedure merely calls the subprocedure. (This is often the case with complex scripts—just look at the end of a script, and you'll often find a small procedure that simply calls all the other procedures in the script.) The *last* procedure is the one that you call by typing **makeBall 5** in the command line. This is (and should be) the only global procedure in the script—the `makeIt` procedure being a local procedure (and therefore not visible to Maya outside the script).

> There are times when Maya, for some reason, does not see a local procedure even when it is correctly placed within a script. When you get a "Procedure Not Found" error, try redefining your local procedures to global and see if that removes the error.

Hands On: Creating, Moving, and Naming an Object—with One Keystroke

Let's say you often make a NURBS sphere, rename it to **ball**, and move it some distance from the origin. (You can modify this exercise to use a light, a plane, or whatever; but for now, we'll just do it with a sphere.) Even though Maya has an efficient workflow, it's a waste of your time to do the same things over and over, so let's make Maya do it for you at the press of a key.

1. Choose Window → Settings/Preferences → Hotkeys to open the Hotkey Editor, a rather scary-looking window, which is shown in Figure 20.9.

2. Before we create a command, let's query a key to see if it's free for us to use. In the Assign New Hotkey area, type **n** in the Key field, and check the Alt box in the Modifiers group below. You should see the following message just below the radio buttons:

   ```
   "Alt-n" is assigned to: nothing.
   ```

   This means the key is available for use. (If it's not, try another key.)

3. Scroll to the bottom of the Categories list and select User—you will see that the Commands list is now empty, because there are no user-defined commands yet. In the bottom portion of the window, click the New button, and then in the Name field, type **Sphere** or something you find useful. In the Description field, enter something like the following:

   ```
   Make and move a sphere.
   ```

4. Then, in the Command field, type the following (you can also paste commands from the Script Editor):

   ```
   sphere -radius 4 -name ball -pivot 0 0 0 -ssw 0 -esw 360;
   move -relative 0 5 0;
   ```

Figure 20.9

The Hotkey Editor

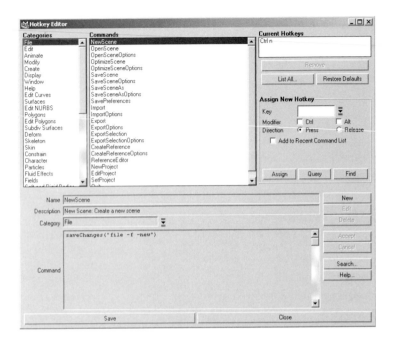

Click the Accept button. The Commands list is updated, and you'll see your command text listed in the Command field.

5. In the Assign New Hotkey section, Alt+n should still be enabled (if not, type **n** in the Key field, and select Alt). Now select the Press radio button, and click Assign. The Current Hotkeys pane is updated, reflecting that your command has now been turned into a hotkey.

6. Click the Save button and close this window.

7. Now hold down the Alt key and press **n**. If you did everything right, you should see a sphere sitting in your window called "ball" and resting 5 units up from the grid on the Y axis.

Congratulations! You have now written some MEL commands and made them work simply by pressing a key!

If you don't get what you expected, check the Script Editor to see if there was an error. If so, go back to the Hotkey Editor and edit the command to make it work. If the Script Editor doesn't show anything happening at all, verify that you mapped the command to the Alt+n key combination. If you're still having trouble, try typing the sphere commands in the Script Editor, get them to work properly, and then copy them into the Command field.

If you now want to delete this command, simply select it in the Hotkey Editor and click the Delete button (near the bottom right).

Placing Objects Using a Marking Menu

So far you have seen how to record MEL commands and make them into a button on a shelf, and you've seen how to issue MEL commands in text form and turn them into a hotkey. Now you will learn how to create a marking menu that performs any of several MEL commands.

Let's say that you want to move a selected object (or objects) around in different directions simply by selecting an item from a GUI list. This is the perfect situation in which to use a Maya marking menu.

1. First, create a new NURBS sphere (or cone or whatever) at the origin of the grid. Now, in the Script Editor, type the following:

   ```
   move -r 0 5 0;
   ```

2. When you execute this command, the ball (or other object) should move 5 units up the Y axis (remember, -r stands for relative in this case, meaning that the object moves relative to its current position along the Y axis). To move the ball back to 0, type:

   ```
   move -r 0 -5 0;
   ```

   The ball moves 5 units down and goes back to 0.

3. Now open the Marking Menus window by choosing Window → Settings/Preferences → Marking Menus to open the Marking Menus window, as shown in Figure 20.10.

   The top pane lists marking menus built into Maya (most are related to the Hotbox). But of course you can build your own as well.

4. Click Create Marking Menu to open the Create Marking Menu window, shown in Figure 20.11, in which you can build a menu of your own.

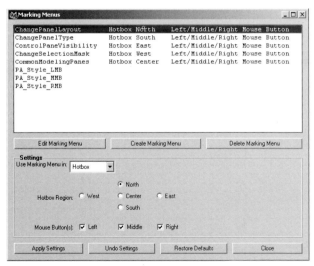

Figure 20.10

The Marking Menus window

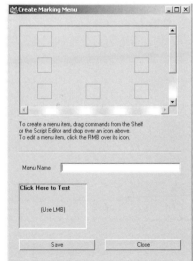

Figure 20.11

The Create Marking Menu window

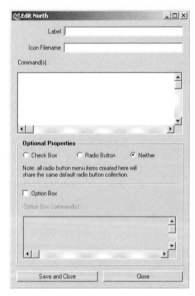

Figure 20.12

The Edit North window

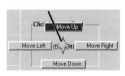

Figure 20.13

**Testing the complete
marking menu for
Move Object**

5. In the Menu Name field, type **MoveObject**. Now RM click the top-center yellowish button in the upper pane and select Edit Menu Item (shown to the left) to open the Edit North window, as shown in Figure 20.12.

In addition to the eight main marking menu positions (North, Northeast, East, and so on), a ninth position is at the bottom-left of the window and is called the "overflow" menu item. If you add a command to this item, another is created just below it, allowing you to make the menu as large as you wish. Also, all menu items can have submenus, giving you even greater flexibility in building a marking menu.

6. In the Label field, type **Move Up**, and leave the Icon Filename field blank. (You can specify a path for an image that will appear in this position when the marking menu is accessed.) In the Command(s) field, type:

        move -r 0 5 0;

7. Leave Optional Properties set at Neither, leave the Option Box blank, and click Save And Close.

   What you have just done is to create a marking menu item that moves a selected object up by 5 units.

8. To test this action, select an object in your scene and then click the LM button in the Click Here To Test area. Whatever you selected should move up by 5 units when you select the command.

9. Now, edit the East, West, and South marking menu buttons to the following, respectively:

        move -r 5 0 0;
        move -r -5 0 0;
        move -r 0 -5 0;

10. Give them appropriate titles and test that they work as they should (see Figure 20.13).

11. Once you're happy with how the menu buttons work, click the Save button and return to the Marking Menus window.

12. At the bottom of the list, you'll now see MoveObject listed. With this item selected, in the Settings pane, select Hotkey Editor in the Use Marking Menu In drop-down list. (This allows you to make a hotkey for the menu you just made.) Click the Apply Settings button and close the window.

Figure 20.14

The `moveObject_Release` command selected

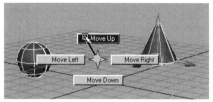

Figure 20.15

The moveObject marking menu at the ready

13. Now, to use the new marking menu, you must go back to the Hotkey Editor (Window → Settings/Preferences → Hotkeys) and make a hotkey for the menu.

14. Scroll to the bottom of the Categories list and click the User Marking Menus option. You'll see two new items in the Commands list: MoveObject_Press and MoveObject_Release. By mapping these two items, we will create a hotkey that will display our new marking menu. (If the release key is not mapped for marking menus, the menu will continue to display even after the hotkey is released!)

15. Query the Alt+o key to see if it's mapped. (If it is, try another one; you might need to try the key in the Assign New Hotkey area to get Maya to check the key.)

16. Select the MoveObject_Press item in the Commands list, and click the Assign button. Maya asks whether you want to assign the release key as well (a nice time-saver), so click Yes in the dialog box that pops up. The MoveObject item should be updated to show that Alt+o is its new hotkey, as shown in Figure 20.14, and both press and release should be properly mapped. (Click the `MoveObject_Release` command to verify that this has indeed happened.)

17. Click the Save button and close the Hotkey Editor window.

18. Let's test our new marking menu: select an object in the scene window, press and hold the Alt and o keys, and press the mouse button. You should see your marking menu, similar to Figure 20.15, ready for action!

19. Move the object(s) you selected around the screen to see how the new menu works.

Figure 20.16

The Expression Editor window.

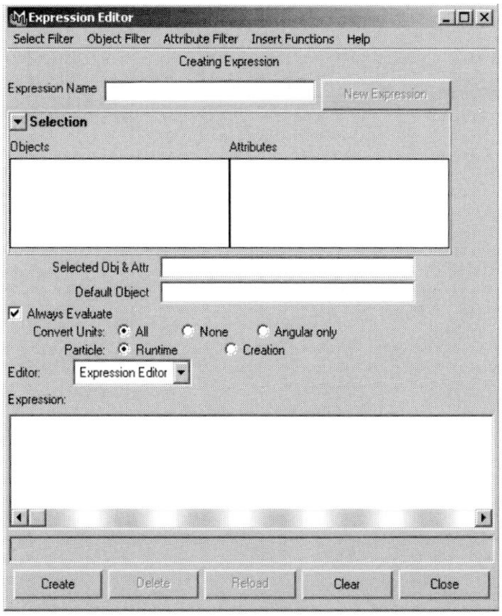

You can reuse these steps to create marking menus to do anything you like. For example, if you create several lighting setups, you can create a marking menu to allow you to select any of these light setups quickly and intuitively.

You've seen how to record or type simple commands and place them on the shelf, in a hotkey, or even in a marking menu. Now let's take a closer look at how MEL can work with the attributes of any object in a scene.

Using Expressions with MEL

Expressions are a specialized subset of the MEL scripting language that are designed to execute through time, not just when the command or script is called. Although MEL is evaluated only when the script or macro is run (except in special cases), expressions are evaluated at every frame or after each interaction on screen (like moving an object). Expressions deal primarily with changing an object's attributes based on time, the current frame, or another attribute. Thus, expressions are well suited to calculating particle properties (see Chapter 23, "Using Particle Expressions, Ramps, and Volumes") or to creating relationships between scene objects in Maya. Unlike MEL, you do not need to use a `setAttr` or `getAttr` statement in expressions, which allows their syntax to be somewhat simpler and makes them powerful aids to creating complex behaviors in your Maya animations. You can also embed expressions in MEL scripts, which allows you to create time-based expressions directly through MEL scripting.

In this section, you'll find three exercises that give you an opportunity to try out the Expression Editor. In the first, you'll make a cone move up and down by moving a sphere back and forth. In the second, you'll make a ball move back and forth in rhythm as time elapses. In the last, you'll use an expression to make a wheel "stick" to the pavement so it doesn't slip.

The expressions we'll deal with here are fairly simple; however, if this kind of thing appeals to you, and especially if you like to work with particles and dynamics, you'll want to peruse a more advanced discussion on the use of expressions with dynamics in Chapter 23.

Transforming a Cone

Let's begin with a simple example: we're going to make a cone move up and down by moving a sphere back and forth on the Z axis.

1. Make a new scene and create a sphere and a cone (call the sphere "ball" and the cone "cone"). Select the cone, and, as shown in Figure 20.16, open the Expression Editor (Window → Animation Editors → Expression Editor).

2. In the Expression Name field, type **moveCone**.

3. In the Expression field at the bottom, type the following:

```
translateY = ball.translateZ;
//to save time, you could also just type:
//ty = ball.tz;
```

Because the cone is selected, Maya knows to apply the `transateY` command to the cone. (If the object is not selected, simply type **cone.ty = ball.tz;**.) Click the Create button. If you enter the information correctly, the feedback line (or the Script Editor's history pane) displays the following:

```
Result: moveCone
```

If not, you will see an error message.

4. Once the expression is accepted, move the ball back and forth in the Z axis, and watch the cone move up and down.

Although this is a simple example, it indicates how you can solve some complex interactions between objects more efficiently by using an expression instead of keyframing.

Rock the Boat

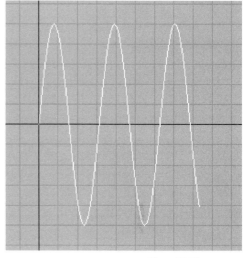

Figure 20.17

The sine function curve

Now we're going to dust off those ancient memories of high-school math class and put them to practical use—bet you thought you'd never hear that one! Using the sine function, we're going to get our favorite object, a sphere, to move back and forth over time.

1. Make a new scene in Maya, and add a NURBS sphere (called "ball").

2. In the Expression Editor, type the following:

```
ball.tx = 5 * sin (time);
```

3. Set your time slider to about 400 frames and play the animation.

You should see the ball moving back and forth in rhythm as time (frames divided by frames-per-second, or the number of seconds that have elapsed) progresses. The sine function takes an input number (the time of the animation) and converts it to a wave that goes back and forth between –1 and 1. Multiplying the sine function by 5 just makes it bigger (increases the amplitude). Starting from 0, Figure 20.17 shows what the sine function itself looks like.

The X component of the sphere's motion just moves up and down (or back and forth) from –5 to 5 as time passes. We can also make the ball go back and forth more quickly by typing the following (and clicking Edit) in the Expression Editor:

```
ball.tx = 5 * sin (2 * time);
```

Here, the ball will go back and forth twice as fast, since time is being multiplied by 2. In general, you can alter the sine function's amplitude and frequency as follows:

amplitude × sine (frequency × value)

The frequency component adjusts how fast the ball goes back and forth, while the amplitude adjusts how big the motion is. You can also put the frame number into the expression as well as time:

```
ball.tx = 5 * sin (frame);
```

When you play back this expression, the ball travels back and forth far more quickly than before, because the number of the current frame increases much more rapidly than does the time.

Now let's make the ball do something a bit more interesting, such as move in a circle. Once again, edit the expression on the ball, this time to the following:

```
ball.tx = 5 * sin (time);
ball.tz = 5 * cos (time);
```

Here, the ball's X position is controlled by the sine function, while the ball's Z position is controlled by the cosine function. (Remember that the cosine is perfectly "out of phase" with the sine function. In other words, it begins at a value of 1 rather than 0.) When you play back the animation, the ball should move around in a perfect circle. How would you make the circle "squashed" (an ellipse)? Try changing one of the amplitude multipliers to 2 instead of 5. What happens when you increase the frequency of one of the positions? Try making `ball.tz` equal to 5 * cos (2 * time) and see what happens. What if the frequency number is 3 or 5? You can quickly see how you can create some complex motion with relatively simple expressions.

As a further exercise in using expressions, try making the ball move around a three-dimensional circle instead of just on the X–Z plane.

Wheels That Stick

As a last example of expressions, let's create something that can really come in handy: a wheel (in this case, our famous ball) that "sticks" to the pavement so as not to slip. If you've ever tried to keyframe a non-slipping wheel, you know what a pain it is; but with a simple expression, Maya will do it for you!

1. In an empty scene, create a sphere (or cylinder, if you prefer) with a radius of 1 unit and name it "tire."

2. Create a plane and scale it "big."

3. Now move the ball up by 1 on the Y axis so that it just rests on the plane. (If you think you're ready, try making the plane and sphere and then moving the sphere, all using MEL commands in the Script Editor.)

4. Select the tire ball and open the Expression Editor. Name the expression stickyTires and then, in the Expression window, type the following:

```
tire.rz = - (tire.tx * (360.0 / (2 * 3.1415)));
```

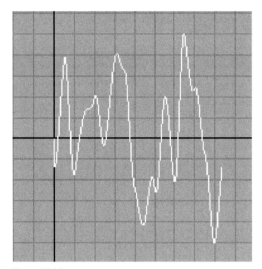

Figure 20.18

The noise function

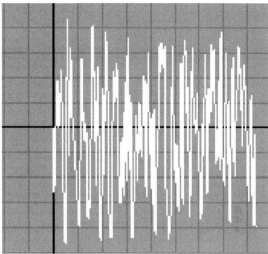

Figure 20.19

The rand function

This expression takes the `translateX` component of tire and turns it into an angle for the `rotateZ` component. The negative sign ensures that the tire actually rotates the proper direction when the wheel is moved. The parenthetical expression just converts degrees to radians so that the two numbers will match.

5. In the scene window, move the ball back and forth in the X direction and watch how the ball always rolls just the right amount to keep up with how far it moves.

As a further exercise, can you make the ball roll properly as it's moved in the Z direction (be sure to set the X, Y, and Z positions back to 0 before you do this)? This is tougher than it sounds, so be forewarned!

Finally, let's use a nice little built-in MEL function called `noise` to make the tire move back and forth in the X direction, as it sticks to the ground. The noise function creates a random, but connected, motion path (as opposed to the `rand` function, which goes all over the place). Compare the two motion paths shown in Figures 20.18 and 20.19.

Although the `noise` function is a random motion, it moves from point to point in a smooth path. The `rand` function, however, is chaotic. There are cases in which each has an advantage; here, we need to use the `noise` function to make the tire move smoothly back and forth. In the Expression Editor, type the following to edit the expression you've already been working on:

```
tire.tx = 5 * noise (time);
tire.rz = - (tire.tx * (360.0 / (2 * 3.1415)));
```

As time increases, `noise` generates a new number for each new time, but each number is connected to the old one in such a way as to keep them relatively close together. When you play back the new tire animation, the wheel moves back and forth on the X axis, all the while "sticking" to the ground as it rolls. Considering how simple this expression is, it produces some complex motion that would be difficult to reproduce in timely fashion using keyframes.

Learning from the Masters

No matter how much you learn in this chapter, space and time simply aren't sufficient here for you to learn everything MEL has to offer. One of the best ways to continue learning MEL is, quite simply, to look at (and copy from) other people's scripts. If you can go through each line of a script and figure out what it does, you will learn a great deal. Better yet, if you can grab some code someone else wrote and modify it to do what you want it to, you can really start to put together some neat and useful scripts to solve your everyday work bottlenecks.

To begin your journey of discovery, take a look at the sample scripts on the CD that comes with this book. So that you get used to reading commented scripts, all comments about the scripts are *inside* the scripts, rather than in a separate text file.

Summary

In this chapter, you learned what MEL is and how Maya is constructed on it, and you gained hands-on experience with some basic (yet powerful) ways to take advantage of scripting. We worked with variables, loops, and conditional branches. You learned how to make custom GUIs for any purpose. You also learned how to make your scripts quickly available as buttons, hotkeys, or marking menus. Finally, you learned the difference between MEL commands and expressions, and you learned how to create some basic expressions that do neat things. (If you are interested in further exploring expressions and how they are used in dynamics, see Chapter 24, "Dynamics of Soft Bodies.")

CHAPTER 21

Particle Basics

This chapter introduces Maya's built-in particle dynamics engine, which you can use to simulate everything from dust motes in the air to hordes of rocket ships battling in space. This tool both simulates the physics of the real world and can handle huge volumes of particles; even millions of particles can be simulated. As a result, it is one of the most powerful tools in Maya for producing exciting and visually appealing work.

We will begin with elementary particle systems and work our way up to more complex simulations, including particle interaction with rigid bodies. If you have not read Chapter 15, "Working with Rigid Body Dynamics," do that before reading this chapter. Because particles and rigid bodies share many underlying features, understanding one can help with understanding the other. Although we use relatively simple examples to demonstrate working with particles, this area is difficult for most animators to grasp. Be prepared to spend some time working through the examples in this chapter and experimenting on your own. Topics include:

- **The Particle tool**
- **Particle emitters**
- **Fields as forces on particles**
- **Particle collision collections and events**
- **Particle lifespan**
- **Particle and rigid body interactions**

What Are Particles?

Essentially, particles are little points (like dust or confetti) that you can place in your animations manually or have emitted by a particle emitter. Particles, like rigid bodies, are physics simulations, not animation in the traditional sense; so you cannot manipulate them directly. To control particles, you must adjust their attributes (or the attributes of their emitters) in the Channel Box or Attribute Editor. Particles can be affected by collisions and fields, and their attributes can be altered by expressions. You can render particles in many ways, including simply as points, and they can even make up collective bodies (called soft bodies).

> This chapter covers using collisions and fields with particles. Expressions, rendering, and soft bodies are discussed in the next chapters.

Like (active) rigid bodies, particles themselves cannot be keyframed (although their parent emitter objects can). If particles cannot be keyframed and you need to use numbers to alter their behavior, why bother? As you will see, using particles is a great way to create random or large-scale behavior that would be nearly impossible to produce using traditional keyframing. Using particles, you can simulate items ranging from rocket exhaust, to leaves, to human hair. If you need a plasma cannon or a fountain (our first two projects), particles come to the rescue.

Because particles (like active rigid bodies) depend solely on their attributes, you need to bring along a sense of adventure to your work with particles. The best way to get to know how to do things with particles is to play (and play and play) with the numbers in the Channel Box or Attribute Editor. Oddly enough, although particle simulation is based on science, getting the particles to do what you want is really an art.

Creating Particles

Before we begin making things with particles, let's figure out how to create the particles themselves. You can do so in a couple of basic ways: you can simply draw them in the scene using the Particle tool, or you can create an emitter to shoot them into the scene. In the brief examples in the following sections, you'll try both methods.

Drawing Particles in a Scene

To draw a particle in a scene, create a new scene in Maya and choose Particles → Particle Tool ❐ from the Dynamics menu set to open the Particle tool's Tool Settings window, as shown in Figure 21.1.

This window includes settings for creating single particles, multiple particles, random particles, and particles in grids. To see how they work, follow these steps:

Figure 21.1

Particle Tool options window

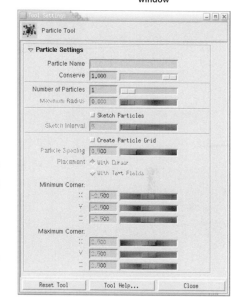

1. Leave the Particle tool at its default settings and LM click anywhere in the scene. You should see a red cross (a little bigger than a dot) indicating where you have just created a particle. Click a few more times to create several particles in the scene; you can rotate your view to get the particles in different places. Press Enter to turn this bunch of particles into a group. Particles in a group all live on the same node and share the same fields, collisions, and render types.

2. Let's create clumps of particles instead of individual ones when we click. Delete all the particles you just created, and choose Particles → Particle Tool ❑. In the Particle Options section, set Number Of Particles to 10 and Maximum Radius to 5. Click in the scene. You see a clump of 10 particles created in an imaginary sphere 5 units in radius, as shown in Figure 21.2. If you continue to click, the new clumps will be part of your current particle node. If you press Enter between clicks (and then **y** to return to the Particle tool), you will create a new particle node each time.

The easiest way to delete particles is to LM drag over them using the Select tool (Q on the keyboard or the arrow in the menu) and then press Delete. You can also RM choose Select All and delete them, but the particles must be *un*selected first.

3. Now try sketching particles in a line. Delete your particles once again and press **y** to open the Particle tool's window again. Click the Reset Tool button to return to the default Particle tool settings. Then click the Sketch Particles check box. In your scene window, LM drag to create a line of particles, as in Figure 21.3. Next, open the Particle tool window and reset Number Of Particles to 10 and Maximum Radius to 5. Sketch in the window again. You see a kind of "tube" of particles, created with a radius of 5. If you don't press Enter, both the curve and the tube of particles will share the same particle node, so the same forces affect them.

Figure 21.2

A clump of new particles

Figure 21.3

A curve of sketched particles

4. Finally, let's have Maya create a grid of particles for us. Delete the old particles and reset the Particle tool. Check the Create Particle Grid check box. (You can adjust the spacing between particles here as well, if you want.) LM click once in the scene window, where the lower-left corner of the imaginary box around your grid should be, click again in the upper-right corner, and then press Enter. You'll get a two-dimensional grid

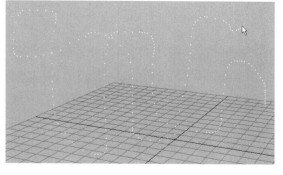

like the one shown in Figure 21.4. If you would rather have a 3D "box" of particles, shown in Figure 21.5, choose a view panel (click in the Perspective view, for instance), click the With Text Fields radio button in the Create Particle Grid section of the Particle Tool Settings window, and enter the coordinates of the corners in XYZ space. Press Enter.

You now know how to create groups of particles by placing them with the Particle tool. The other technique for dispersing particles uses an emitter, as described in the next section.

To see the difference between one particle of many parts and several smaller particle groups, try selecting one particle only. If you created one giant particle node, all the particles in the scene are highlighted. If you created several smaller particle nodes, only those in that particle's group are highlighted.

Figure 21.4

A grid of particles

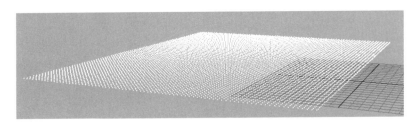

Figure 21.5

A 3D box of particles

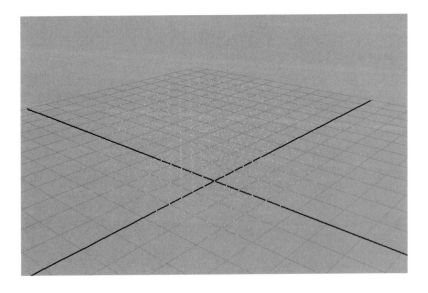

Emitting Particles

Now let's see what a particle emitter does. But before you begin: In order for more complex dynamics animations to play back properly, you need to set Maya's playback rate to Play Every Frame. To do so, click the Animation Options button (at the far right end of the Range Slider bar) or choose Window → Settings/Preferences → Preferences and choose the Settings/ Timeline category. Then, in the Playback section, set Playback Speed to Play Every Frame.

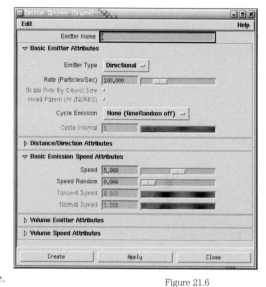

Figure 21.6

The Emitter Options (Create) window

1. Clear your scene again and choose Particles → Create Emitter ❏ to open the window shown in Figure 21.6.

2. In the Basic Emitter Attributes section, select Directional for Emitter Type. In the Distance/Direction Attributes section, change DirectionX (the direction in which the particles will be emitted) to –1. In the Basic Emission Speed Attributes section, increase the Speed setting to 5, and then click Create.

3. You'll see a small ball in the scene window and attribute options listed in the Channel Box. Play back the animation. You should see a purple line extending out from the particle emitter, as shown in Figure 21.7.

To play back an animation, use the VCR-like controls at the bottom-right of the screen, or press Alt+V to play (and stop) the animation. But remember that you must *always* rewind your animation before playing it when dynamics are involved. Because all dynamics simulations are calculated based on information from the last frame, failing to rewind will result in bizarre playback behavior (as will scrubbing through the animation). To fix this, simply rewind and play the animation from the beginning. Click the Rewind button on the Playback bar or press Alt+Shift+V to rewind the animation.

4. To see the individual particles a bit more clearly, try turning down the Rate attribute in the Channel Box from its default 100 to about 10 or so. Now you should see little peas shooting off into the distance.

Now that you've tried both methods for creating particles, let's see how to use them in your projects.

Figure 21.7

A particle emitter emitting a line of particles

Working with Particles

As we've done throughout this book, we'll introduce you to the basics of particles by going through a couple of examples. In the following sections, we will build a plasma cannon and a fountain.

Making a Plasma Cannon

Every good science-fiction battle game needs at least one plasma cannon. This weapon of mass destruction shoots a blast of plasma—a collection of charged particles—toward the bad guys. Although a plasma cannon is not something you want to have pointed at you, it's a good introductory workout for Maya's particle dynamics engine.

1. If you don't have an emitter from the previous example, create one with emission DirectionX set at –1, Rate at 10, and Speed at 5.

2. To make our cannon, we're going to keyframe the emitter on and off, making the particle stream "pulse," rather than emit particles continuously. Set Rate to 0 in the Channel Box (or Attribute Editor), and be sure you are at the first frame in the Timeline.

3. With the word *rate* (to the left of the number field) selected in the Channel Box, RM choose Key Selected to set the first key for the rate (at a rate of 0, which means it emits nothing). Move to about frame 10, and key another frame at rate 0.

4. At frame 11, set a keyframe for the rate at 50 (or more, if you want a thicker stream). At frame 18, set another keyframe at 50. At frame 19, set a keyframe at 0 again (turning off the emitter again).

If you turn on the Auto Key function (click the keylike button at the lower-right corner of your screen so that it turns red), Maya automatically creates the keys for you as you go—after you manually create the first keyframe.

5. Rewind and play back the animation. You should see a pulse of particles move away from the emitter.

6. To make the cannon pulse on and off, select all the keyframes you have made and copy them down the Timeline several times. To copy keyframes, Shift+select the keyframes in the Time Slider, and then RM choose Copy. Move the Timeline to another frame (like 25 in this case), and RM choose Paste → Paste. You should see a pulsed stream of particles, as shown in Figure 21.8. (If you don't see the particles playing back properly, remember to set your playback speed to Play Every Frame in the Animation Preferences dialog box.)

7. Let's give these pulses a bit of spread so that they're not all lined up perfectly. With the emitter still selected, set the spread attribute to 0.05 (a spread of 0 is a straight line; a spread of 1 is a 180-degree half-sphere around the emitter). You might also want to increase the rate of particle emission for your keyframes to make a thicker cloud. (Just be sure to set all your nonzero keyframes to the larger number.) Now when you play back the animation, the particles should look more spread out, as in Figure 21.9.

The easiest way to change several keyframes at once is to use the Graph Editor (Window → Animation Editors → Graph Editor). With the emitter selected, you can select all the nonzero keyframes and type a new value for the rate (or interactively move the values up or down). See Chapter 9, "Animating in Maya," for more about using the Graph Editor.

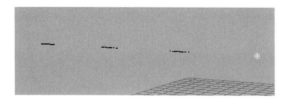

Figure 21.8

A pulsed stream of particles

Figure 21.9

The pulsed stream of particles with spread

8. You will notice (if your window is large enough and if your frames are set high enough) that the particles appear to go on forever. As any true science fiction fan knows, a plasma cannon creates blasts with limited range (in other words, the particles must die off after a certain time). To make this happen, you must select the particle shape node itself (not the emitter). Play back your animation for a few seconds, until you see particles. Now select the particles themselves, as shown in Figure 21.10.

Figure 21.10

The pulsed particles selected

9. With the particle shape selected, open the Attribute Editor. In the Lifespan Attributes section, change the Lifespan Mode from Live Forever to Random Range, set the Lifespan to 3 (seconds), and change the Lifespan Random from 0 to 1. Now the particles will all die off in a range from 2 seconds (3 minus 1) to 4 seconds (3 plus 1) after they are emitted from the "gun," as shown in Figure 21.11.

Figure 21.11

Emitted particles with random lifespan; the first group of particles has only half its original particles.

10. Although we have created a fully functional plasma cannon, let's improve it by having it emit streaks of light rather than just particle specks. Select the particles (not the emitter) and open the Attribute Editor. Near the center of the window is a Render Attributes section that allows you to select how you want your particles rendered. Choose MultiStreak from the pop-up window (Figure 21.12), which makes each particle a clump of streaks instead of a single point.

Figure 21.12

Choose MultiStreak from the Particle Render Type pop-up menu.

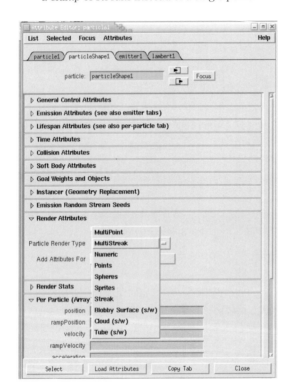

11. In the Current Render Attributes section of the Attribute Editor, click the Current Render Type button to add controls for new attributes associated with the MultiStreak particle type. Adjust these numbers to get a satisfactory-looking streak of particles. The settings that produced Figure 21.13 are Line Width = 2, Multi-Count = 12, Multi-Radius = 0.165, Normal Dir = 2, Tail Fade = –0.5, and Tail Size = 10.5.

Figure 21.13

The plasma canon with multistreak particles

12. Save this project (name it `plasmaCannon1`). We will use it again in the next chapter.

As you saw in step 10, there are many choices for particle styles. We will use some other types in the next examples. For a full discussion of the various types, see Chapter 22, "Particle Rendering."

Adding Motion to Particles with Fields

In Chapter 15, you learned how to use fields with rigid bodies. You can also use fields with particles; they simulate forces affecting the motion of particles. To demonstrate how this works, we will build a fountain using particles and fields. Follow these steps:

Figure 21.14

A shower of particles shooting straight up

1. Create a new scene in Maya. Create an emitter. In the Emitter Options window, Channel Box, or Attribute Editor, make the emitter Directional, set the emitter's Rate to 500, DirectionX to 0, DirectionY to 1, Spread to 0.3, and Speed to 10. When you play back the animation, you should see something like the image shown in Figure 21.14.

2. You will notice that this image lacks an important element to make it look even remotely like a fountain: gravity. To add this element, choose Fields → Gravity. Then select Window → Relationship Editors → Dynamic Relationships. In the Dynamic Relationships Editor, select particle1 on the left and highlight Gravity on the right. Now when you play back the animation, the particles will fall, as in Figure 21.15.

If you select the particles (not the emitter) before creating gravity, the two will be connected automatically, and you can skip the extra step of connecting them through the Dynamic Relationships Editor.

3. Add a plane and scale it across the grid. You'll see something like a fountain in a pool of water. (OK, it's rough right now—we'll make it look better over the next few chapters!) To get a slightly better look for the water, change the render type of the particles to spheres. (Select the particles, open the Attribute Editor, and choose Spheres from the Particle Render Type pop-up menu in the Render Attributes section.) Click the Current Render Type button, and then change the radius of the spheres to about 0.25 (so the spheres are smaller).

Figure 21.15

The particle shower with gravity

4. This is looking better, but everything is too smooth. To fix this, let's add a turbulence field to the fountain. Select the particles (spheres)—just grab any of the particles to select all of them—and then choose Fields → Turbulence.

5. With the Turbulence Field selected, in the Channel Box or Attribute Editor set Magnitude to 30, Attenuation to 0.5, and Frequency to 60. Now when you play back the animation, the spheres should move in a more random pattern, as in Figure 21.16.

Figure 21.16

The particle shower with spheres and turbulence

In this example, we've set three of the attributes for the Turbulence field:

- Magnitude sets the power of the field.

- Attenuation sets the falloff of the turbulence field as particles get farther from it.

- Frequency sets how often the irregularities change.

Experiment with the settings for these attributes and discover how changing each one affects the playback.

Save your file (call it `fountain`) for later use.

Using Collisions to Make a Splash

In the example we just finished, you probably noticed that the spheres pass right through the plane, which makes the fountain seem a bit unreal. We need some splashing of water as our fountain operates. Fortunately, Maya comes to the rescue again, by providing particle collisions. To see how to make particles collide, follow these steps:

1. Move the emitter (not the particle shape node) just a bit above the surface of the plane. (Otherwise, the spheres will be "trapped" in the plane and will not emit properly.)

2. Now select the particles (not the emitter) and Shift+select the plane. Choose Particles → Make Collide ❑. Set the Resilience (bounciness) to 0.9, and set the Friction to 0.1; then click the Create button to create a collision connection between the particles and the plane. (In the Dynamic Relationships Editor, you can see this connection under the Collisions radio button—and you could break it if you wanted to.) Play back the animation. The spheres should bounce off the plane now.

3. We have a collision, but we need something more interesting for our splashes. We need to create a bunch of smaller "splash" particles. Choose Particles → Particle Collision Events. As shown in Figure 21.17, select particle1, set All Collisions on, Type to Emit, Random # Particles on, Num Particles to 5, Spread to 0.5, Inherit Velocity to 0.5, and Original Particle Dies on. Then click the Create Event button.

4. We now have a second group of particles, called particles2, that will "emit" when the first particles hit the plane (between 1 and 5 will be created per collision). Now set the second particle group's Render Type to Sphere, and set its Scale to 0.12 or so (so these particles are smaller than the spheres in group 1). Connect the gravity and turbulence fields to the second group of particles (see step 2 in the previous section).

5. When you play back the animation, you will see the second group of particles created, but they will simply fall through the plane, just as particle1 did at first. We need to create a collision event between these particles and the plane as well. We could use the same method as in step 2, but let's try another way: open the Dynamic Relationships Editor, select the second group of particles on the left, click the Collisions radio button, and highlight the plane in the right window.

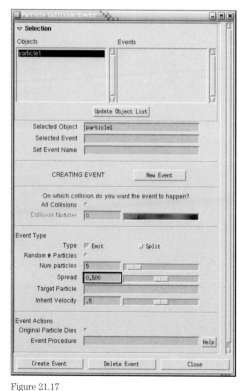

Figure 21.17

The Particle Collision Events option window for particle1

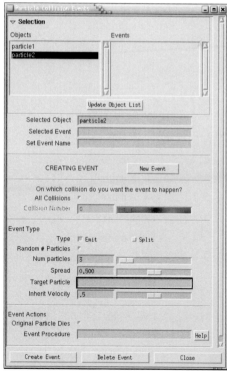

Figure 21.18

The Particle Collision Events window for particle2

6. Once you have connected the collision, go back to the Particle Collision Events dialog box and set the particle2 event (be sure particle2 is highlighted) as shown in Figure 21.18. Most options are set as they were for the first particle group, but the number of particles will only be 3 this time.

7. Return to the Dynamic Relationships Editor and connect the new particles you've just created (the particle3 group) to gravity, turbulence, and the collision with the plane. Here we can leave the render type as Point—these are the little splashes.

8. You could continue adding collisions and new particles, but you've probably noticed by now that playback is getting slow because of all the calculations Maya needs to do for so many particles. Let's just make one more collision event to "kill" all the particles in group 3 when they collide with the plane. In the Particle Collision Events dialog box, select particle3 and check the Original Particle Dies box in the Event Actions section at the bottom. At the top of the Event Type section, turn off both Emit and Split (this ensures that no more particles are created). When you play back the animation, it should look something like the picture shown in Figure 21.19.

9. Save this project (as `fountain1.ma`). In the next chapter, we'll make the particles look a lot more like water.

This example should give you a basic idea of how to create effects with particle collisions. Just keep in mind that we used multiple collisions and did the following for *each* collision:

- Connected the particles to the collision surface (the plane)
- Connected the particles to our fields (gravity and turbulence)
- Created a collision event that created new particles and/or killed the old ones

As long as you take these steps one at a time, it's amazingly simple to create complex simulations with particles. As usual, play with the settings in the Particle Collision Events dialog box and watch what happens in your scene.

Figure 21.19

The fountain with three sets of particles

TIPS ON SPEEDING UP PLAYBACK

It probably became apparent in our fountain example that playback can get really bogged down as you add elements, especially those requiring calculations. You might want to increase playback speed, even if it sacrifices some degree of accuracy. The most obvious way to speed up the playback of our fountain example is to change all the render types to simple points. (You can change it back to whatever shape you want just before you do a render.) This will save a great deal of time, because Maya doesn't need to calculate the shapes of the particles.

Short of changing the particle render type, you can do a few other things to speed up playback. If you want your fountain going full force at the beginning of the animation, play it back until it is at full volume, stop it, and type that frame number in the Animation Start Time text field in the far-left corner of the screen (below the time slider). When you rewind and play now, you do not need to wait to see the fountain "run up" to its full-volume state. However, you do need to start your animation at that frame.

To set the state of the objects at the current frame so that you can rewind to the beginning of the animation and they will retain their state, choose Solvers → Initial State → Set For All Dynamic. This sets the current state of all dynamic objects to their initial values when you rewind the animation to frame 1. The one problem with this method is that you can't undo it.

A better solution—especially for scrubbing—is to enable scene caching (Solvers → Memory Caching → Enable). It may take a while to cache the frames, but once they are cached, you can scrub back and forth in the Timeline and play back the animation at much faster speeds. This solution is especially useful if there are other elements in the animation. For example, if the fountain is a background element in a character animation, not having Maya calculating the fountain's state at every frame can be a real time-saver.

In the particleShape1 tab in the Attribute Editor, you can also decrease the Max Count and Level Of Detail to reduce the number of particles being emitted. A Max Count of 100, for example, limits the number of particles emitted to 100. (The emitter ceases to emit particles until the number in the particle group falls below 100.) A Max Count of –1 (the default) means there is no limit to the number of particles in a group. The Level Of Detail setting randomly removes particles based on the percentage you enter in the box (a number between 0 and 1). If, for example, you emit 100 particles per second and set the Level Of Detail to 0.3, the emitter emits about 30 particles per second. These two settings are a great way to lower particle counts, but be sure to reset them to default levels before rendering if you want the render to contain the original number of particles.

You can also temporarily disable all dynamics calculations in a scene, thereby speeding up playback of other scene elements. Simply select the particle object you want to disable and turn isDynamic off in either the Channel Box or the Attribute Editor.

If you want to see your spheres flowing, but don't want to wait for the slow speed of Maya's playback, you can try to adjust the tessellation factor to speed up playback. Select any particle shape, and then select the GeoConnector1 tab in the Attribute Editor. Change the tessellation factor from its default of 200 to something low, such as 10, and see if it makes any difference in your playback speed.

Adding Particles to Objects: Plop, Plop, Fizz, Fizz

So far, we've painted particles into the scene and used emitters to make our particles for us. Another technique is to add particle emitters to objects. When you create a stand-alone emitter, it is just a point that sprays out particles; when you add a particle emitter to an object, you can tell the emitter to emit the particles from the actual surface of the object. To examine how to do this, let's re-create an image from a famous ad for a fizzy antacid: a tablet dropping in water and then bubbling.

Creating the Objects and Bubbles

We won't worry too much about our models right now—we just want to get the feel here.

1. Create a new scene in Maya. Create a large cylinder (the water glass) and a smaller, squashed one (the tablet). For the glass and tablet cylinders, choose Create → Nurbs Primitives → Cylinder ❐. To cap the ends of the cylinder for the tablet, click the Cap Both radio button. For the glass, click the Cap Bottom button.

2. You can make the glass bluish and the tablet white if you want. At the least, set X-ray mode on by choosing Shading → Shade Options → Xray. (For information about texturing objects, see Chapter 17, "Shading and Texturing Surfaces.") Your two objects should look like those shown in Figure 21.20.

3. Before we add our bubbles, let's animate the tablet falling into the water. Place the tablet a distance above the glass and keyframe all translate and rotate channels. At frame 15 or so, place the tablet just where the water starts (or at the top of the glass) and keyframe all values again. At about frame 55, place the tablet near the bottom of the glass and rotate it about. Feel free to tweak this animation as much as you want, but at least get this basic motion. (For information about how to create a keyframed animation, see Chapter 9.)

   If you don't want to bother with this animation, you can get an already animated file (`22glassAnimated.mb`) on the CD that accompanies this book.

4. Now we'll *add* (instead of create) a particle emitter to the top surface of the tablet. In the Hypergraph or Outliner, be sure Show Shapes is enabled (Options → Display → Shape Nodes in the Hypergraph), and then, from the shape nodes below the tablet shape, select the revolveTopCap2 node and choose Particles → Emit From Object ❐. In the Emitter Options window (see Figure 21.21), change the Emitter Type to Surface, the Rate to 100, the Speed to 1, the Speed Random to 0.3, the Normal Speed to 1, and the Tangent Speed to 1.3, as shown in Figure 21.21. Then create the emitter and close the window.

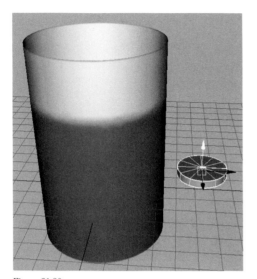

Figure 21.20

A basic glass and antacid tablet

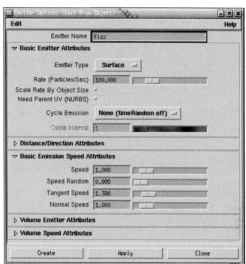

Figure 21.21

The Emitter Options window

5. Because we've added an emitter to the top of the cylinder and set its emitter type to Surface, the entire surface of the top of the tablet will act as an emitter. When you make the tangent speed of the surface emitter greater than 0 (1.3 in this case), the surface emits particles parallel to the tablet's surface, rather than just straight out from it. (Try playing with the settings in the Channel Box, and watch the results.)

6. Select the particles and open the Attribute Editor. Click the particleShape1 tab. Select Spheres as the particle Render type, with a Radius of about 0.1 (for small bubbles).

You can add emitters to the side and bottom of the tablet as well. However, for this example, emitting from only the top surface will suffice. To add emitters to all surfaces at once, you can drag-select all the tablet's surfaces and add particle emitters to them by choosing Particles → Emit From Object.

7. If you have already played back the animation, you probably noticed that the particles emit slowly and mostly just hang around. To make them rise a bit faster (as if they were air bubbles escaping from water), we'll create a weak gravity field that actually pulls the particles up instead of down. Choose Fields → Gravity ❑. Set its strength (Magnitude) to 1 or 2 instead of 9.8, and make its Y direction +1 instead of –1 so that it pulls the particles up instead of dragging them down. Then assign the gravity field to the bubble particles in the Dynamic Relationships Editor.

Adjusting the Particles' Lifespan

We have a couple of other problems with our particles: they start emitting immediately, and they don't die! You can handle both problems by keyframing either the rate or the lifespan of the particles. If you get stuck, take a look at a finished version of this scene on the CD-ROM that accompanies this book, (`21glassComplete`).

1. Before we adjust the particles' lifespan, let's make sure we start emitting the particles after the tablet has fallen into the water. Select the emitter (not the particles), and set a keyframe on its rate to 0 at the start frame. Create another keyframe a little after the tablet enters the water and set it to 0 as well. (We don't want the particles to begin emitting just at the frame where the tablet enters the water—the tablet needs time to begin dissolving.) Then, at frame 35 or 40, set the rate to about 100, so the tablet is bubbling at full strength by then.

2. If you play back the animation now, you will see the particles begin emitting at the right time. However, they come shooting out of and around the glass (see Figure 21.22)! First, let's take care of those pesky bubbles that are escaping from the sides of the glass by making a collision between the glass and bubbles. Create a collision link between the particles and the glass, as described in the "Using Collisions to Make a Splash" section earlier in this chapter.

Figure 21.22

Particles passing through the glass

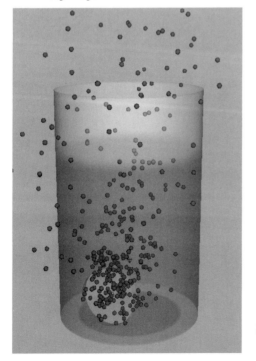

3. By creating a collision connection, we keep the bubbles inside the sides of the glass. However, they bubble right out of the top of the glass—talk about a head on your root beer! To keep the bubbles from popping out of the glass, we need to keyframe the lifespan of the particles. Because the lifespan of the particle controls how long it lives, adjusting the lifespan will change how far the particles can rise before they disappear. Getting the lifespan keyframed just right will take a bit of doing. First, change the Lifespan Mode of the particles (under Lifespan Attributes in the Attribute Editor) to Constant. Then try keying the resultant Lifespan attribute as follows:

AT THIS FRAME...	LIFESPAN IS...
19	0
20	0.5
35	1
50	2
85	2.5

Unless you copied everything exactly, your mileage will vary, and you'll need to adjust your keyframes to get a good result.

4. Save this animation (as `glass`) for use in the next two chapters.

After you finish adjusting the lifespan of the bubble particles, you should have a fairly nice animation, although it's by no means perfect yet. Fear not, however; over the course of the next two chapters, we'll turn our fizzing antacid tablet into a really nice-looking sequence.

Colliding with Rigid Bodies

You might wonder whether rigid bodies can react to particles, in addition to particles reacting to other scene objects. Because all these objects are dynamic, they can interact to produce interesting and useful behavior. To examine how particles and rigid bodies interact, let's create a simple plane rigid body and turn a fire hose of particles loose on it. Follow these steps:

1. In a new scene, make a plane, scale it out to about grid size, and rotate it 90 in the Z axis (so it stands upright).

2. Create an emitter that is directional, with a speed of about 10 and a spread of about 0.2. When you play back the animation, it should look something like Figure 21.23. It doesn't look much like a hose, but it's good enough for our purposes. After the work we've already done, it's a good idea to reset the options on the emitter when you create it. Just choose Particles → Create Emitter ❒ and then choose Edit → Reset Settings to reset the emitter.

3. Make the plane a rigid body (select it and choose Soft/Rigid Bodies → Create Active Rigid Body). When you play back the animation, it still won't show any interaction between the plane and the particles. That's because you must also create a collision event (just as in the fountain example) before the two will interact.

4. Select the particles (not the emitter) and then the plane, and choose Particles → Make Collide. During playback, you now see the particles ricochet off the rigid body. This would be great, except that the rigid body isn't moving.

Figure 21.23

Emitted particles shooting at a plane

To see the plane and particles better, you can adjust the plane's color (in the Hypershade) to white, and you can change the particles' color to black by creating a per-object Color attribute in the Attribute Editor. You will learn more about particle render properties in the next chapter.

5. We need to throw one last "switch" before the rigid body will react to the particles. In the Channel Box (with the plane selected), open the Rigid Body section and set Particle Collision on. When you play back the animation now, the plane goes shooting off with the first particle.

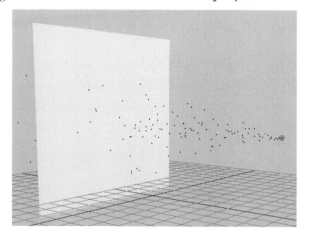

6. To reduce the motion of the plane, we need to do a few things: reduce the number of particles emitted, reduce the emitter's speed, and increase the mass of the rigid body. In the Channel Box for the emitter, reduce the speed 1 or 2, and reduce the rate to 40. With the plane selected, change the mass to 1000 to make it heavier. Play back the animation, and you will see that the plane rotates but does not move away as quickly, as in Figure 21.24. Because playback of these animations can be slow, try using playblast to see your work in real time (choose Window → Playblast).

Figure 21.24

Particles colliding with the plane

As you can imagine, in addition to creating something like a fire hose, particle/rigid body collisions also can be useful for many other simulations—for example, space ships reacting to fire or meteors striking buildings (the buildings being made up of many smaller rigid bodies). We will use particle-to-rigid-body collisions again in Chapter 24, "Dynamics of Soft Bodies."

As an exercise, try to balance a ball on a fountain of water (remember to include gravity). It's no easy task! To make things less difficult, try setting the initial state of the fountain after it's running at full volume.

Attaching Fields to Objects

As a final example of basic particles (if there is such a thing), let's try attaching a field to a scene object and then have that object affect particles in the scene. Specifically, we'll make a UFO kick up some dust on a dry desert floor. (If you don't want to build and animate this scene, just load 22UFOAnimated from the CD-ROM that accompanies this book.) To attach a field to an object, follow these steps:

1. In a new scene, create a cone, flip it on its side, and squash it a bit (or use any UFO model you have handy). Next, place a plane a little beneath the UFO, as in Figure 21.25.

2. Animate the UFO to make a flight path across the plane. For good measure, throw in a loop and a few up-and-down moves.

Figure 21.25

A simple UFO model and ground plane

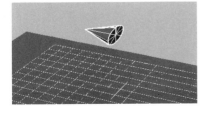

3. Create a grid of particles that will be blown around by the UFO's speedy rush through the desert. Open the Particle tool's option window (choose Particles → Particle Tool ❏), check the Create Particle Grid box, and set Particle Spacing to 10. (Adding any more particles slows down playback later.)

4. Choose the top scene view and scale out so that you can see the whole plane. Click the lower-left and upper-right corners of the plane and press Enter. You should get a grid of particle points across the plane.

5. In the Attribute Editor, click the Current Render Type button and set the point size to 10 (so the particles are easily visible), and then move the particle grid up on the Y axis until the particles are a bit above the plane.

   If you have a fast computer, you can increase the density of particles in your grid. Be aware, however, that very dense grids can choke Maya, so save a backup copy of your scene file.

6. Now we have our UFO and particles. All we need to do is make a field to help the two interact. Select the UFO and choose Fields → Air ❑.

7. In the Air Options window, click the Wake button, and then try the settings shown in Figure 21.26. Setting Direction X, Y, and Z to 1 enables the UFO to interact with the particles in all directions. Turning on Inherit Rotation allows the curving motion of the UFO to "suck up" particles. Decreasing the Magnitude to 0 means that only the motion of the UFO will affect the particles, not any constant "wind" force created by the field. Increasing Max Distance to 25 allows the field to displace particles farther from it. (The Max Distance setting is actually not necessary when a volume field type is chosen, as in step 8. However, it will not cause any problems in the simulation, and for completeness' sake we've included it here.)

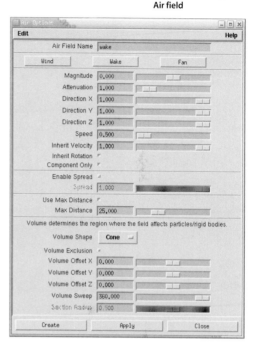

Figure 21.26

The options window for creating a wake type Air field

8. We will now create a volume area in which field forces are applied. In the bottom section of the Air Options window, set the volume shape to Cone, and leave the other settings as-is. Click Create to create the field. As always, try playing with these numbers to see what happens.

9. Now, let's connect the new field to our UFO, using another technique. Select the Wake field, and then (in the Hypergraph or Outliner) select the NurbsConeShape node and choose Fields → Use Selected As Source Of Field. You will see the cone attach itself to the UFO, as in Figure 21.27.

10. Deselect everything in your scene, select the wake cone (so you don't move the UFO at the same time), and then rotate and scale the cone until it shoots out from the back of the UFO like an exhaust plume, as Figure 21.28 illustrates.

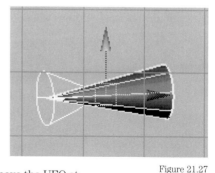

Figure 21.27

The cone of the Wake field is attached to the UFO.

Figure 21.28

The cone, adjusted

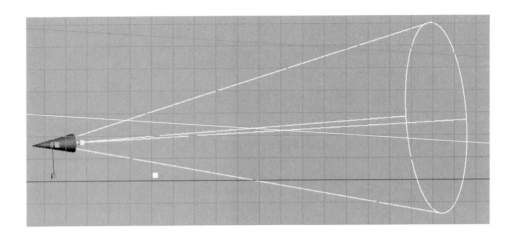

11. To connect the field to the particles, use the Dynamic Relationships Editor as described earlier in the chapter. Then play back the animation, and the dust particles should move around after the UFO.

12. To make this simulation look a bit more realistic (or at least appear as realistic as giant blocks moving around can), we need to add a gravity field and allow collisions between the particles and the plane so that they don't just fall through it. Select the particles, and then choose Fields → Gravity. (Be sure Gravity is in the negative Y direction for this example.) You will need to drastically reduce the effect of gravity here so that the particles float back to earth as if they were light. Try setting Gravity to 2 and see what happens.

13. Select the particles, and then Shift+select the plane. Choose Particles → Make Collide ❑, and set resilience (or bounciness) to 0.2 and friction to 0.5. The frictional force will make the particles stop moving when they collide with the ground. If all worked well, you should see the dust whirl after the UFO as it passes by, as seen in Figure 21.29.

> Finding the proper settings for gravity and collision forces took quite a lot of tweaking. Try experimenting with the numbers and see what happens. (Remember to save a clean version of the project first.)

14. Save your project (as UFO) for more work in the next chapter.

If you notice that the particles are bouncing off the desert floor and then settling, you might want to set the initial condition for the particles to be their state after coming to rest on the plane. First, turn off the Air field (set its Speed to 0), and then run the animation until the particles have settled onto the plane. Then select the particles and choose Solvers → Initial State → Set For Selected.

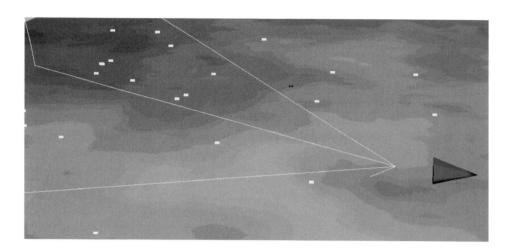

If you want the dust to look better, try setting the render type to MultiStreak, increasing the number of particles (the Multi Count), and increasing the Multi Radius. The neat thing about streaks is that they exist only when they are in motion, which means that they disappear back into the desert when they collide with the floor. This can make for a much nicer animation, although it's a bit hard to see. (This effect is too subtle to be seen as reproduced in print; to see the flying dust in action, check out `22UFO.mov` on the accompanying CD-ROM.)

As an exercise, try making a jet trail of particles for your UFO. Will it be affected by wind and gravity? How fast will it go? Will it be constant or pulsing?

It is often useful to create sparsely packed particles that are big and blocky. This saves a great deal of time in setting up an animation. When you are ready to render the particles, simply increase the particle density and make them look more presentable.

Summary

In this chapter, we worked with particle dynamics, getting to know how to create and emit particles. You learned how to change the look and lifespan of particles, how to get them to interact with fields, how to get them to collide with objects—either standard objects or rigid bodies—and, finally, how to attach fields to objects that then affect particles.

At this point, you know most of the basic elements for creating and using particles in your work. Over the next two chapters, you will take the work we started here (plus some other examples) and learn the intricacies of rendering them, as well as how to add expressions to them. So save your work and get ready to go—it just gets better from here!

CHAPTER 22

Particle Rendering

This chapter continues the work we started in the preceding chapter. We will examine several ways to render particles; specifically, we will look at how hardware rendering and software rendering differ. We will also discuss situations in which various types of rendering are appropriate.

Because of the special nature of hardware-rendered particles, this chapter also touches lightly on compositing techniques. If you have not read Chapter 21, you should be familiar with creating and using particles in a variety of situations before proceeding with this chapter. Also, if you are not acquainted with basic rendering using Maya, read Chapter 16 before getting into this chapter.

This chapter covers the following topics:

- **Hardware rendering**
- **Hardware rendering and compositing**
- **Software rendering**
- **Using sprite particles in particle rendering**
- **Fine-tuning your particle rendering**

Particle Rendering in Maya

When you work in Maya's workspace, you use your computer's built-in OpenGL graphics card, which supports flat shading in real time. When you tell Maya to render into a new window (Render → Render Current Frame) or to batch render (Render → Batch Render), you are launching a separate program that renders shadows, reflections, and refractions and generally produces a smoother, more realistic image. But all this is at the cost of lengthier rendering times. In general terms, unless you are a game producer, you work in Maya's workspace and then produce your final images via Maya's rendering program (or an alternative rendering program such as RenderMan).

In the preceding chapter, we examined how to create particles in the Maya workspace. Here we will take particles to the next stage: creating images suitable as final products.

Keep in mind throughout this chapter that rendering is truly in the eye of the beholder. Always tweak your materials until you get a rendering you are satisfied with—even if it is quite different from our suggested material. What pleases our collective eye may not please yours and vice versa.

And in This Corner: Hardware versus Software Rendering

If you previously used Maya particles for production work, you already know that one of the most confusing aspects of Maya's implementation of particles is the issue of hardware rendering versus software rendering. In the Render Attributes section of the Attribute Editor for a particle shape, one of the available options is to set Particle Render Type to Blobby Surface (s/w), Cloud (s/w), or Tube (s/w). That "s/w" indicates that the corresponding particles are software rendered. Other particle types (such as Point and MultiStreak) are hardware rendered.

What does it mean that some particles are hardware rendered and some are software rendered? Isn't all rendering part hardware and part software? If these questions seem confusing, take comfort—there is a reasonably simple explanation. *Software rendering* is the type of final rendering you are already familiar with (that is, rendering with the full power of Maya's rendering engine). *Hardware rendering,* on the other hand, uses the power of your computer's OpenGL graphics card to quickly create flat-shaded images of your particles. Perhaps the main obstacle to understanding hardware rendering is its name, because you don't use only hardware to render the particles. Rather, you use a combination of Maya's and OpenGL's software, along with the processing power of your graphics card to create the images. It might be easier for you to think of this type of rendering as *hybrid rendering.* It's a bit of a cross between the default shading you see in your workspace and the images produced by Maya's batch-rendering module.

To do hardware rendering, Maya first creates a flat-shaded image of your particles (taking into account your preferences for rendering) and then actually performs a screen capture to "grab" the image just created. Because of this nifty trick, hardware-rendered particles can often be rendered in near real time. Software-rendered particles, in contrast, can take a long time to render.

> Because hardware rendering uses a type of screen capture to create its images, you *must not* allow anything to come in front of the render window (including a screen saver). Be sure not to move any windows in front of the render window, and remember to turn off your screen saver if you are about to start a potentially long hardware rendering.

The primary difficulty with hardware rendering is that you need to know and use a *compositing program* (such as Alias|Wavefront's own Composer for IRIX, or Shake or After Effects for other platforms) to combine software and hardware renderings. This can also be a big advantage, however, because you can control the look of your particles independently from the way the rest of the scene works. Indeed, compositing is such an effective and time-saving way of working with 3D animation that many animators render software particles separately from their scenes. Some basic compositing techniques are discussed later in this chapter (see "Hardware Rendering and Compositing") to give you some insight into the power of this technique.

Hardware Rendering

Let's now take a closer look at hardware rendering, using as an example the handy plasma cannon that you created in the last chapter. If you don't have a finished copy of the plasma cannon from Chapter 21, "Particle Basics," you can use 21plasmaCannon on the CD-ROM that accompanies this book.

Figure 22.1

The Hardware Render Buffer window

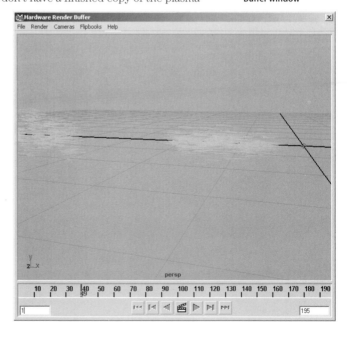

Open your saved project (or the one on the CD-ROM), and play the animation until it reaches a frame where you can see some of the particles. Now choose Window → Rendering Editors → Hardware Render Buffer to open the Hardware Render Buffer window. This window, shown in Figure 22.1, opens with the current frame from the workspace loaded. You have at your disposal several menus from which to adjust render options. The Render menu has options for test and final renderings; the Cameras menu lets you render from any camera in the scene (including an orthographic camera); and the Flipbooks menu lets you choose or clear any flipbooks you create.

A *flipbook* is Maya's term for a sequence of hardware-rendered images that are created in the *projectName*\images directory by default. Remember to set up your project before you begin rendering images; otherwise, you won't know where they're going as they are rendered. See Chapter 1, "The Maya Interface," for more on creating and setting projects.

Give the hardware renderer a whirl:

1. Choose Render → Test Render (or click the clapper board icon below the Time Slider). You should see your particles against a black background.

2. Now let's adjust the render attributes for the Hardware Render Buffer. Choose Render → Attributes to open the Attribute Editor, which includes several options for modifying your hardware rendering.

For now, we will only look at the first section of the Attribute Editor: Image Output Files, shown in Figure 22.2. Here, just as in the Render Globals window for software rendering, you can set the filename, extension numbering (including the number of zeros in the name), start and end frames, image file type, and resolution. You can also set alpha channel information here. In the Alpha Source list box, you can choose None (for no alpha channel), Hardware Alpha, Luminance, and any of the RGB channels. (See the "Alpha Channels" sidebar for more information.)

3. Leave Alpha Source set to Off (the default), but keep in mind that you'll need to turn it on (that is, use Hardware Alpha or Luminance or one of the other settings) for final renderings that you want to composite later.

4. Before you leave the Image Output Files section, be sure to set your start and end frames to the start and end frames of your animation, and give your rendering a filename.

You can also write the Z depth (or the distance of each object from the camera) into your images. You can use this information to help you composite the image, but the method is somewhat complex and beyond the scope of this book. See your compositing program's user manual for information about whether it supports Z depth compositing and how it works.

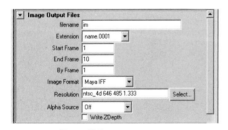

Figure 22.2

The Image Output Files section of the Attribute Editor

5. To see your particle animation run in the scene portion of the window, choose Render → Render Sequence from the Hardware Render Buffer window.

6. After the sequence is rendered, you can play back the animation in a separate (Fcheck) window by choosing Flipbooks from the Hardware Render Buffer window and then selecting your animation name. (See Chapter 16, "Rendering Basics," for a look at the Fcheck utility.)

If you want to stop the hardware rendering before it is complete, simply press the Esc key.

ALPHA CHANNELS

An *alpha channel* (also known as a *mask* or *matte channel*) is an outline of the rendered elements of your scene. Everything within the outline is visible in the final image; everything outside it is invisible. (In addition, there are semitransparent parts at the edges of the outline, which partially show those pixels.) Think of an alpha channel as a cookie cutter that slices out the rendered pixels of an image, allowing you to place the cut image on top of another image in a compositing program. You can learn more about alpha channels from your compositing program's documentation.

If you can, use Hardware Alpha as the alpha channel setting for your renderings. In the Hardware Render Buffer window (Window → Rendering Editors → Hardware Render Buffer), choose Render→ Attributes and set Alpha Source to Hardware Alpha. If your graphics card doesn't support Hardware Alpha, you will see an error message in the feedback line when you try to select this option. In that case, you will generally want to set Alpha Source to Luminance to create your alpha channel.

When you watch the animation, you might discover that the particles are the wrong color or that they are moving too slowly or too quickly. To remedy these problems, tweak your animation for speed, tail size, and color. When the particles are moving too slowly, select the emitter and change the speed to something like 20 instead of 5. To compensate, shorten the particle's tail size a bit by selecting the particles, changing to the Attribute Editor, and set-

Figure 22.3

A hardware rendering of the updated plasma cannon particles

ting the tail size to, say, 2. So far, so good; the particles should now have a bit more zip to them. You can try rerendering in the Hardware Render Buffer for verification of your work and, of course, tweak it some more if you are not happy with the results.

With speed and tail size under control, you can now modify the color to your liking. Make sure the particles are still selected. In the Attribute Editor for the particle shape, click the Color button in the Add Dynamic Attributes section, and select the Add Per Object Attribute option in the Particle Color dialog box—this option is grayed out if you have previously adjusted the particle color. After you add your per-object color, you will see the following listed in the Render Attributes section of the Attribute

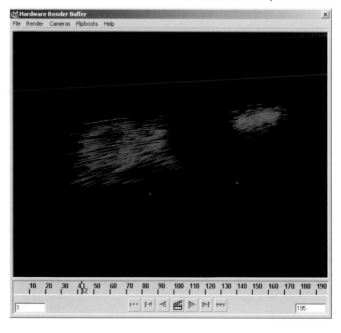

Editor: Color Red, Color Green, and Color Blue, along with the other attributes that pertain to the currently selected Particle Render Type. Try changing the color boxes (Red/Green/-Blue) to suit your tastes. We've done this in Figure 22.3, which you can find in the Color Gallery on the CD. We used a fiery orange, with values of 0.9, 0.2, and 0.1, respectively. You can then rerender the sequence to see if you like what you have done.

> If you keep your image sequence name the same when rendering, Maya writes over your last sequence for you, saving disk space. If you want to keep a sequence for later use, rename your rendering in the Attribute Editor.

You might have noticed when you did the test render that you did not need a light in the scene to make these particles show up. If you do not have any lights, Maya provides a default light to emphasize the particles—thus, they appear in your scene even if you haven't yet placed a light in it. (Of course, you might prefer to use your own.) From the Hardware Render Buffer window, choose Render → Attributes. In the Attribute Editor's Render Modes section, you can set Lighting Mode to Default Light, All Lights, or Selected Lights. Feel free to play with some lighting setups now and see how they affect the plasma cannon's appearance. (You might find that the choice of lights used with a particular particle or streak-rendering type makes no difference.)

Save your rendering of the plasma cannon for use in the next chapter.

Hardware Rendering and Compositing

Now that you have a good feeling for the basics of hardware rendering, let's create an example in which we can composite the particles on top of a software-rendered scene. Open your UFO project from Chapter 21, and add a few lights to the scene (if you haven't already).

If you didn't complete or save the UFO project in the preceding chapter, use `21UFOComplete` from the CD-ROM.

1. If your particles in the UFO project are still large blocks, select them. In the Attribute Editor, change their type to MultiStreak in the Render Attributes section.

2. Click the Current Render Type button, and set the render attributes. Aim for something similar to the following: ColorRed 0.8, ColorGreen 0.6, ColorBlue 0.2, Line Width 2, Multi Count 20, Multi Radius 1, Normal Direction 2, Tail Fade 0, and Tail Size 1. You can choose to turn on Use Lighting, but you will need to reduce the colors on your particles, or they will appear almost white. Feel free to experiment until you have the look you want.

3. Open the hardware rendering window (Window → Rendering Editors → Hardware Render Buffer). Specify a filename for the image sequence in the Attribute Editor, set your beginning and ending frames, and choose to use All Lights in the Render Modes section.

4. Run a test sequence, and you will get an image sequence that essentially looks like a clean playblast rendering. (If your geometry is not included in the rendering, be sure the Geometry Mask check box is not highlighted.)

In this situation, it is best to have a software rendering of the geometry (the plane and UFO) rather than a hardware rendering of the entire scene. To do this, you will have to render out two individual sequences for the animation—a hardware rendering of the particles only, and a software rendering of the rest of the scene—and then composite them. If you do not have a compositing software package, you can still follow along until the last step.

5. If you've closed the Attribute Editor, open it again (in the Hardware Render Buffer window, choose Render → Attributes). Set the default globals for hardware render.

6. In the Image Output Files section, set your alpha channel (Alpha Source) to either Hardware Alpha (if your graphics card supports this) or Luminance.

7. To mask out the geometry (so that you can use a software rendering for it), check the Geometry Mask box in the Render Modes section.

8. Render the sequence again in the Hardware Render Buffer window, and the geometry will no longer appear. You'll see only the particles.

Although it might not be obvious in this sequence, the geometry of the plane still masks the particles even though it does not appear in the rendering. If, for example, the particles pass beneath the plane in this scene, they will be blocked out and not rendered. This feature is useful for later compositing.

Adding Multi-Pass Render and Motion Blur

One thing you might have noticed previously in testing particle- and streak-rendering types is that the particles and streaks are sharply defined. For the desert dust being blown around by our UFO, a slightly more diffuse look to the particles would be better. Fortunately, Maya has two features that can help here: Multi-Pass Render and Motion Blur.

When Maya does multi-pass rendering, it renders out a number of frames *in between* the frames of the animation, based on the number you select. If, for example, you select 3, the Hardware Render Buffer renders three "in-between" images for each frame and then averages them together. This makes for a much smoother and subtler particle rendering—but it also takes much longer to render (three times as long for three rendering passes, five times as long for five, and so on). See Figure 22.4 for a comparison of particles rendered with single and multi-pass hardware rendering.

Figure 22.4

Comparison of single (on the left) and multi-pass rendering (on the right; set to 5 render passes).

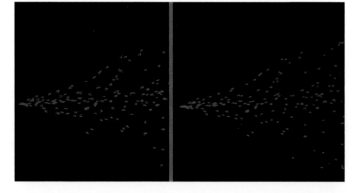

Motion Blur simulates the period of time a camera shutter is open during a picture's exposure, producing a blurring of quickly moving objects. The larger the Motion Blur number (between 0 and 1), the more blur. It is often useful to keep this number small when rendering and then add a bit more motion blur when compositing.

To try out these two options, go to the Multi-Pass Render Options section of the Attribute Editor. Click the Multi-Pass Rendering check box. Below it, a pop-up menu with a number (3, by default) will be enabled, allowing you to select how many render passes to make for each frame. Choose a fairly low number here (5, for instance). You can also add a bit of motion blur (say, 0.1 or 0.2).

Render the sequence again, and this time you might find the dust effect too subtle (that is, indiscernible). To make the dust stand out more, you can adjust the number of passes, the color of the dust, the transparency of the dust, or the motion blur factor. Or you can make these adjustments in your compositing package—a much faster and more versatile way to tweak your rendering.

When working with composited layers, you'll often have to rework render settings to make elements a bit bolder in their rendered look, in order to provide more choices when it comes time to composite. You can easily *reduce* the visibility of a layer in a compositing package, but it is extremely difficult to make a layer *more* visible.

When your test renders look good, choose Render → Render Sequence to render an image sequence out to your images folder. You can then import these images into your compositing package and combine them with your software-rendered sequence. (If you need help with the process of software rendering, see "Software Rendering" later in this chapter. Also, see Chapter 16, "Rendering Basics.")

Once your hardware-rendered sequence is finished, you need to render your geometry out in a separate, software-rendered image sequence. Open the Render Globals window (for software renderings, choose Window → Rendering Editors → Render Globals). Set your start/end frames, and set the image format to be the same as your particle-rendered sequence—Maya IFF (.iff) is the default. Then batch-render the sequence.

> Watch out—do not give your geometry render sequence the same name as your particle render sequence. If you do, the geometry rendering will erase the particle-rendered image sequence.

To reduce render times, you can render out the UFO ship and ground plane in separate passes, taking just one "still" image of the ground plane, because it doesn't change throughout the render. See the following section for more on how to do this.

Once you complete your hardware and software render sequences, import them into your compositing package, and be sure to place the particle layer (with its alpha channel) as the top layer of your composition. Then, in the compositing package, adjust the brightness, opacity, and/or transform mode of the particles (and geometry) to get a high-quality final product, as illustrated in Figure 22.5. (A color version of this shot is available on the CD-ROM.) Save your Maya project (as UFOParticles, perhaps) for use in the next chapter.

For a finished example of this UFO sequence, see 22UFO.mov on the CD-ROM. (Due to the small movie size, the dust has been somewhat exaggerated for visibility's sake.)

Figure 22.5

A shot of the UFO kicking up dust

Hardware Rendering and Compositing, Take Two

Before we leave the subject of hardware rendering and compositing, let's quickly revisit our antacid tablet project from Chapter 21. The particle-rendering techniques we've just discussed allow us to create much more subtle, realistic bubbles for our tablet.

Open your saved file from that project (or use the 21glassComplete file on the book's CD-ROM). Recall that we used the sphere-rendering type for our bubble particles. The sphere type, because it's hardware rendered, doesn't support transparency, but we can make the bubbles transparent in the compositing package since they are being rendered separately. We will render all three elements (glass, tablet, and bubbles) in turn. Then we will composite the bubbles with a still shot of the glass (instead of rendering out many frames of the same shot of the glass—a nifty, time-saving trick), plus the animated tablet.

Instead of the sphere-rendering type, you can also use the cloud-rendering (software) type. If you're curious, you can experiment with the cloud type to see how it compares with sphere.

Rendering the glass, tablet, and bubbles is a bit more complex than what we did with the UFO project, because the glass is supposed to be semitransparent; thus, using the geometry mask will not work. Fortunately, we need to add only one extra step to this process to make it work properly: We hide the geometry selectively.

Before doing that, let's first perform a little trick to save some time in the rendering process.

1. Rewind to the first frame of the animation, select the tablet, and choose Display → Hide → Hide Selection (to hide the tablet).

2. Change your render globals to whatever you intend to use for your tablet rendering. For example, in the Resolution section, set Render Resolution to 320×240 (the default); under Anti-aliasing Quality, set Edge Anti-aliasing to Medium Quality; and turn Motion Blur on. Then set your start and end render frames to 1.

3. Now batch-render the "sequence" (actually just one frame), naming it something like `glass`. By rendering only one frame with the glass (which doesn't move during the animation and which takes a relatively long time to render), we save both time and disk space for this element of the tablet sequence.

4. Now we can take up the process of hiding geometry selectively. Reopen the Render Globals window, and leave everything the same except for the end frame. Set that to the final frame in your animation. Close this window.

5. Choose Display → Show → Show Last Hidden to display your tablet again. Then highlight and hide the glass by selecting the glass and choosing Display → Hide → Hide Selection.

6. With only the tablet now showing, render out the complete animation, calling it something like `tablet`. You now have your software-rendered sequences, and it's time for the bubbles.

7. From the Hardware Render Buffer window, choose Render → Attributes. In the Image Output Files section, set Alpha Source to Hardware Alpha (if your computer supports it) or Luminance. Name the sequence something like `bubbles`. In the Multi-Pass Render Options section, turn on Multi-Pass Rendering. (Creating a multi-pass rendering smooths out the bubbles just a bit.)

8. Render the sequence.

Once the rendering is finished, import all three pieces of your project (glass, bubbles, and tablet) into your compositing package. Here, you have many options for combining the pieces. We chose to place two copies of the glass in our composition—one on top, set to low opacity and with some color adjustments; and one on the bottom, a more opaque version of the glass that makes it look solid in the final composite. We then sandwiched the bubbles and the tablet between the glasses, with the bubbles above the tablet so they're visible. You can reduce the bubbles' opacity (or visibility) to give them a "see-through" look. You can also create an opacity ramp for the bubbles so that they fade out as they rise through the water.

Figure 22.6 (in color on the CD-ROM) shows a still from the animation sequence. A finished version of the animation is available as `22glass.mov` on the CD-ROM.

Some Compositing Guidelines

When you work with Maya in conjunction with your compositing package, you will surely encounter a number of problems—both artistic and technical. It is difficult in the context of this book to be specific about compositing Maya renderings because a number of software packages perform this function, and all of them work a little differently. Nevertheless, we can offer you a few rules of thumb:

Figure 22.6

A still shot from the glass animation, showing compositing techniques in action

- Do early testing of single frames of your animation in the compositing package. This way, you only have to render one frame for each composition layer to see whether the composition will work, saving you time in renderings.

- Always use alpha channels, even for layers that you expect won't need them. It's better to be prepared than to have to rerender.

- Render particles to be highly visible in Maya rather than going for the subtler look you intend to get in the end. Having more data (visibility) to work with can only help in the long run, and it's easy to blur or reduce the opacity of particles in your compositing package as a last step.

- Be sure to test-render some images in the resolution of your final project. Often you'll get excellent results at 320 × 240 pixels, only to get an inferior product when you do your final compositing at 640 × 480.

- Don't be afraid to try new ways of combining layers in your compositing package. Just as in Maya, you might discover a much more interesting look by doing a bit of experimentation.

Never move your render camera! If you move the camera between renderings, your particles and geometry will not match, and the results will be awful. It is often a good idea to create a separate camera (not the default perspective camera) to use for renderings. Using a separate camera reduces the chance of accidentally moving the camera as you work. This camera can then be keyed or locked to preserve the position.

Although multiple renderings and compositing might at first seem a confusing waste of time, stick with it. Once you begin to see how creatively (and often easily) you can alter the look of a particle-rendered sequence, using Maya plus a compositing package for particle sequences (and in general) will likely become your preferred method of working.

Save this project (as `glassFizz2`, perhaps) for use in the next chapter.

Software Rendering

Now that we've covered hardware rendering, let's take a look at Maya software-rendered particles and see where they might be useful. In general, Maya uses hardware rendering for speed when rendering simple points and shapes. When it comes to complex render types, however, such as clouds, water, or fire effects, Maya sacrifices speed for the power of the software renderer. The result is a photorealistic image.

Software rendering can be slow. While doing the work for this section, you might want to reduce the quality and size of your renderings to keep waiting time reasonable. Temporarily reducing the number of particles emitted, while adjusting particle properties, can also be useful. Working with just a few particles will give a good suggestion of the final product, without forcing you to endure overlong rendering times.

The three types of software rendering are Tube, Blobby Surface, and Cloud.

- *Tubes* are, of course, tubes—they can have beginning and ending radii that differ, and they can be rendered with several special effects added. Tubes are useful for everything from hair to laser beams, similar to Figure 22.7.

- *Blobby surfaces* are known as metaballs, spheres that blob together like drops of mercury. Blobbies can be used for water, lava, or a range of other liquid materials (see Figure 22.8 for one example).

- The *Cloud* type, as illustrated in Figure 22.9, is a blobby surface that is blurred or semitransparent. Clouds are useful for airy effects such as fire, smoke, and real clouds.

> Remember that IPR renders (discussed in Chapter 16) do *not* at present work with particles, even software particles. You must rerender each image (or section thereof) manually while adjusting the look of software-rendered particles.

Figures 22.7, 22.8, and 22.9, which demonstrate the software render types, all have images with similar effects available in the Color Gallery on the CD.

As an exercise, let's see how blobby surfaces can be used to create the effect of water.

1. Either open your fountain project from Chapter 21, or use the `21fountain` project on the CD.

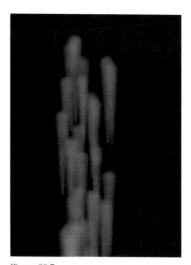

Figure 22.7

Some Tube particles

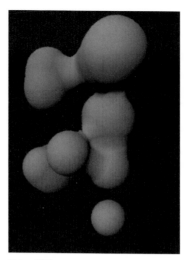

Figure 22.8

Blobby Surface particles

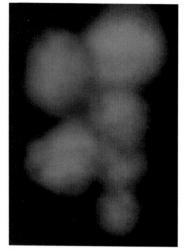

Figure 22.9

Cloud particles

2. Depending on the speed of your computer, you might want to reduce the number of particles (currently spheres) being emitted by the fountain emitter, because blobby surfaces render slowly with even a few particles. We found a rate of about 200 to be sufficient for the purposes of experimentation, although using more particles allows for a smaller radius for each particle and increases the watery look. Choose whatever you find is a good compromise between speed and final quality.

3. After adjusting the particle emitter, select the particles emitted (the particle1 group, which the emitter directly emits). In the Attribute Editor or Channel Box, change the render type to Blobby Surface. In the Render Attributes section of the Attribute Editor for the particle shape (particleShape1), set Particle Render Type to Blobby Surface (s/w).

4. Click the Current Render Type button to display attributes for the blobby surface render type. You can set two controls over blobby surfaces: the Radius attribute (the size of each individual surface) and the Threshold attribute (which controls how the spheres blob together). The two controls work complementarily. As you increase the threshold from 0 (no interaction—the spheres just act like spheres) to 1 (complete meshing—spheres that are not connected will disappear), you will need to increase the radius because the apparent size of the particles will decrease.

Setting the threshold of blobby surfaces to 0 is a good way to produce software-rendered spheres, allowing you to adjust materials and transparency much more carefully than with hardware-rendered spheres. Longer rendering time is the price you pay for software-rendered spheres.

Like almost all other areas of Maya dynamics, a good deal of experimentation is required to get the right effect for blobby surfaces. After some tweaking, we were satisfied with a radius setting of 0.6 and a threshold of 0.9 for the particles. Your tastes might differ, of course, so try some alternate settings yourself. You will need to render test images as you go, so be sure to add a light or two to the scene so you can see your results.

Another element of blobby surfaces (like any geometry) that greatly affects the quality of the rendering is the surface type. To get something approaching a watery appearance, we used a phongE shading group, made it a very unsaturated blue and transparent, and gave it a small but bright specular highlight. A version of the project with this texture is on the CD-ROM (22fountain).

Let's see if we can adjust the properties of the second set of particles produced by the fountain (the ones that appear after the first particle group's collision event). With the particles selected, open the Attribute Editor, click the Current Render Type button, and set the render type to Blobby Surface (s/w). For starters, try a radius of 0.5 and a threshold of 0.8 for these particles. You can then take the same material you created for the first set of particles and use it for the second one—or make up a new material if you prefer.

Recall that we set the third group of particles (those emitted when the second group collides with the plane) to be points. You can either leave them like this and composite them in later, change their type to Blobby Surface and then render them all together, or even leave them out entirely. We found the smallish splashes created by a multipoint particle to be a nice contrast to the blobbies of the other two-particle types, so we composited them into the final rendering, producing the 22fountain.mov movie on the CD-ROM. A still from this animation is shown in Figure 22.10 (and the color version is on the CD-ROM).

Figure 22.10

The fountain with blobby surfaces for water

As an exercise, try redoing your plasma cannon project using a Particle Render Type setting of Tube (s/w). Adjust the radii (that is, the Radius0 and Radius1 attributes, which are added after you click the Current Render Type button) to make the blasts grow in size as they move away from the emitter.

As with hardware rendering, you can tweak and perfect software rendering in countless ways. Although you can achieve decent results with software-rendered particles quickly, getting just the right look with them can be a tricky and time-consuming affair—especially if you don't have much experience creating them. You probably already know, from attempting the fountain example, that even minor changes to a particle's attributes or an emitter rate often result in highly altered renderings. Additionally, the interaction of textures, particle types, emitter rates, and so forth create a complex chain of interrelated variables that can prove frustrating to even an experienced user.

Apply two rules to get your software particles to do what you want:

- Be a perfectionist. "Close enough" is usually not.

- Be patient. You want the best results, so give yourself the time and freedom to make mistakes.

With a critical eye and some practice, you can get excellent results with Maya's software particles. Experiment with the Cloud and Tube render types, now that you have an understanding of what software particle rendering can do. Try creating a fuzzy beam of light with Tube or a dissipating puff of smoke with Cloud. If you have difficulty understanding any of the settings, don't forget that Maya's electronic documentation (especially Chapter 14 of the *Dynamics* manual) is an excellent source of information.

Save this project (as `fountain3`, perhaps) for use in Chapter 23, "Using Particle Expressions, Ramps, and Volumes."

Don't forget: It's often useful to render software particles in a separate pass, just as must be done for hardware particles. It gives you a great deal of control over how the particles interact with the rest of the scene.

Pictures from Outside: Using Sprite Particles

Before moving on, we'll discuss a particle rendering type that falls somewhere between hardware and software rendering: the *sprite*. Sprites are simply placeholders for an image you create somewhere else—it can be another 3D rendering, a computer-based image, or a scanned photograph. The image is mapped onto a two-dimensional rectangle (the sprite), and, for each particle, an instance of the image is created in the hardware renderer. Although sprites are 2D images, they are always oriented toward the camera, so they appear to have depth. You can also choose to use either one image or several images in a sequence (or animation) to map onto your sprites. (We will discuss mapping of image sequences to sprites in Chapter 23.)

As an example of how to use sprites, we'll revisit the UFO project—this time changing our streak particles to sprite images of leaves that the UFO can blow around.

1. To begin, open your UFO project (or 22UFO from the CD-ROM). In the Hypergraph, select the particle group. In the Render Attributes section of the Attribute Editor, change the Particle Render Type to Sprites.

2. The Sprite render type has several attributes, accessed by clicking the Current Render Type button in the Attribute Editor. For our purposes, check Use Lighting, and then set the Sprite Twist (or rotation about the Z axis) to 90. This will lay the leaves on their sides. If you desire, you can also change the Sprite Scale X and Sprite Scale Y values, altering the size of the sprites in the scene.

3. The sprites now look like little boxes, so we need to create a texture for them. First, create a Lambert shader group. (Because Lambert shaders have no specularity—or shine—to them, they work well for sprites.) To create a Lambert shader in the Hypershade, open the Hypershade window (Window →Rendering Editors → Hypershade), and from the menu bar (or RM choose), choose Create → Materials → Lambert (alternatively, click the Lambert icon from the Create Bar panel).

4. Select the Lambert materials group from either the Work Area tab or the Materials tab, and open the Attribute Editor (Ctrl+A). In the Common Material Attributes section, click the button that looks like a checkerboard to the right of the Color swatch and slider.

5. In the Create Render Node window, on the Textures tab (the default), make sure the type "normal" is selected and click the File button in the 2D Textures section. This creates a texture that places an image you specify on whatever object the material is applied to. Close this window.

> You can also create your own image(s) for the file texture. Just be sure you include an alpha channel in your image in order to cut it out from the background. If you don't, you will be able to see the edges of the sprite rectangle when you apply the Lambert shader to the sprite. When creating alpha channels, keep in mind that for hardware rendering the white regions are opaque and the black regions are transparent, while the opposite is true for software rendering.

6. The Attribute Editor is now focused on the file1 texture, with an Image Name text field and a Browse folder icon under the File Attributes section. Click this folder icon, find the 22leaf.tif file on the CD, and choose it for your file texture. You should see something like Figure 22.11 in your Attribute Editor.

It is a good idea to transfer any images into your *scene*/source images folder, where Maya will look for them by default.

7. Now that you have a shader and a sprite, you need to connect the two. In the scene window (or Hypergraph), select the particle group. Then, in the Hypershade, RM over the Lambert shader you just made and choose Assign Material To Selection. If all went well, you should now see Figure 22.12: a bunch of leaves spread across your desert floor. Figure 22.12 is in the Color Gallery on the CD.

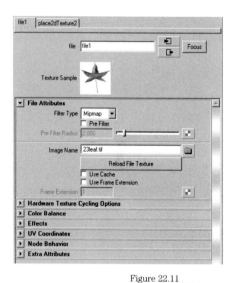

If you now play back the animation (or if you just look at the first frame, depending on how high you have placed your particles), you will see that the leaves fall halfway through the plane before they stop. This is because the sprites detect a collision with the plane only when their *center points* hit the plane (that is, when they are halfway through it). To get around this problem, we need a bit of trickery.

8. Select the plane that is the current floor, and duplicate it (Edit → Duplicate).

Figure 22.11

A leaf texture mapped to a file texture for the particle sprites

9. In the front or side view, move the original plane up until it just covers the top edges of the leaves.

10. Now deselect the plane and select the leaves, and move the leaves up until their middles are just above the original plane.

11. Finally, select the original plane and hide it (Display → Hide → Hide Selection), revealing the duplicate plane below. The leaves will now collide with the original (invisible) plane and thus will stay above the visible plane.

Figure 22.12

Sprite leaves on the desert floor

12. Save your project for use in the next chapter.

> You might have noticed this same problem when rendering the Sphere particle type for the tablet-and-glass animation. The same solution will work for that situation, as well.

To add a bit more turbulence to this version of the animation (these are leaves blowing around, after all!), we altered the Magnitude and Direction attributes of the Wake field (attached to the UFO). We set the Magnitude to –7 and the X, Y, and Z directions (the way the force is directed) to 0.5, 1, and –0.5, respectively. For even more fun, you can try adding a turbulence field to the animation, forcing the leaves to rock as they travel through the air.

When you now run your animation, the leaves should blow around in the wake of the passing UFO. You can either render this project out in hardware or just create a hardware rendering of the leaves blowing. (In the Hardware Render Buffer window, select Render Attributes. In the Image Output Files section, be sure Alpha Source is set to Hardware Alpha or Luminance, not to Off. In the Render Modes section, be sure Geometry Mask is on.) You can use this new image sequence with your *old* UFO software rendering to make a new animation, saving the time and disk space of another rendering. A final composite movie is available on the CD-ROM as `22UFOSprite.mov`. Figure 22.13 shows a still from this animation.

> Can you use sprites for the antacid tablet project? Try to create an image of a bubble (with alpha channel), and map this to your particles. Does this method work better for this animation?

Figure 22.13

A still from the UFO sprite animation

Fine-Tuning Particle Rendering

While rendering the UFO leaf animation in the preceding section, you might have noticed that the leaves lacked a realistic twirling motion as they were blown around by the UFO. This is because the sprites are always pointed at the camera. To get around this problem, you can use Maya's Particle Instancer feature (Particles → Instancer) to replace your particles with one or more geometric shapes (see *Dynamics,* Chapter 15 of the Maya reference manuals, for details). You can then create a box or rectangle, map onto it an image of a leaf, and use the script to replace the particles with that geometry and shading group. The leaves will blow around more naturally.

> If you want, you can also use a nifty little script, the `particleReplacer.mel` script, which is available from Alias|Wavefront's website (`http://www.aliaswavefront.com`) or from a number of other websites (such as `www.highend3D.com`). Since this script replicates, for the most part, the Particle Instancer feature, you might find it easier now just to use Maya's built-in feature. If you are not familiar with using MEL scripts, refer to Chapter 20.

When dealing with small particles such as points, you probably ran into a problem when you tried to composite them on top of your software-rendered sequence, especially if you used the Luminance alpha channel: the particles were probably close to invisible in your composition. This trouble occurs because Luminance alpha takes as its alpha value the brightness (or luminance) of each particle. This is fine when the particles are bright, but when they are darker, the alpha channel will be mostly dark too, making the particles dim. Although it's a bit of a pain, there is an old and effective trick that solves this problem. First, make a new copy of your scene so you won't mess up your good version. Next, create a new (Lambert) shading group, and assign it to all your hardware-rendered particle groups. In the Attribute Editor, change the Lambert group's color to pure white, and increase its incandescence to full. The sample should show all white.

If you are using sprites, create a file texture for the sprites with the alpha channel copied into the RGB channels of the image. (Call this `spriteImageWhite.tif` or something similar.) This step, combined with the complete incandescence of the shading group, will produce a good alpha channel for a sprite group.

The particles assigned to the new shading group should now all be pure white. When you do a new hardware rendering, using Luminance to create the alpha channel, you will get a version with white particles in exactly the same places as your colored particles from before. (Be sure to name the two sequences with different names!) Finally, in your compositing package, use the newly rendered sequence as an alpha matte for your other, colored particle layer. (See your compositing software's manuals for more on how to do this.) You will now have a much more visible set of particles to work with!

Summary

In this chapter, we took the first steps toward creating finished animations using particles. Using either hardware or software particles and employing many different techniques (and a few tricks), we were able to produce high-quality renderings. We also used multiple renders for hardware and software particles to separate the elements of an animation, so that we could then combine them in a compositing package. Although certainly not exhaustive on the subject, this chapter gives you a good start into the difficult but rewarding area of particle renderings.

In the next chapter, you will learn how to use expressions and ramp generators to create complex per-particle (rather than group-level) effects. So make sure you've saved your work from this chapter, and let's move on!

CHAPTER 23

Using Particle Expressions, Ramps, and Volumes

In Chapters 21 and 22, we created, tweaked, and rendered Maya's dynamics particles. For the most part, however, we only worked with these particles as entire groups. Now it's time to dig a little deeper into the power of Maya's dynamics and learn how to control Maya particles in specific ways—as individual particles as well as intact groups. The tools for particle manipulation are *expressions, ramps, volume emitters,* and *volume fields.*

This chapter covers the following topics:

- **Using volume emitters**

- **How expressions and ramps work in Maya's particle dynamics**

- **Changing the color, lifespan, and radius of particles**

- **Moving particles around in a volume field and with expressions**

- **Employing collision events and expressions**

- **Using transparency ramps**

- **Creating emitter expressions**

- **Changing opacity and rotation with motion**

Particle Manipulation in Maya

You've worked briefly with all the particle manipulation tools in earlier chapters, and here in this chapter you'll see much more of what you can accomplish by developing your skill with these tools. As we began exploring MEL in Chapter 20, "MEL," you got a glimpse of how the Expression Editor helps define the mathematical formulae that control object behavior. Ramps, introduced in Chapter 17, "Shading and Texturing Surfaces," are akin to the gradients you might have created in a program such as Adobe Photoshop. And in the UFO project from Chapters 21 ("Particle Basics") and 22 ("Particle Rendering"), you worked with a volumetric wake field. The particle manipulation tools overlap somewhat in functionality, but each has its own strengths, as you will see during the course of this chapter.

After a general introduction to volume emitters, particle expressions, and ramps, we'll try out various modifications of expressions and ramps. Then we'll explore some new opportunities for emitting and affecting particles, provided by volumetric emitters and fields. Although the complexity of particle manipulation tools can at times be daunting, the power and control they bring to particle systems make mastering these tools truly worth your effort.

Volume Emitters

Using volume emitters is an effective way to emit particles from a volume of space, rather than from a single point or from the surface of an object. Volume fields give you substantial control over and visual feedback for the effects of a field. Setting volume fields is often far quicker and more intuitive than trying to adjust the Displacement and Max Distance attributes of a field.

Emitting particles from a volume lets you produce particle groups with true depth. That's because volume emitters, as opposed to surface emitters, create particles throughout the entire body of the emitter, not just on the surface. For example, volume emitters are excellent for creating moving star clusters, antibody cells in an animation of a human artery, or even the appearance of blood drops "sweating" from a knife (see the "Bloody Knife" image in the color insert). As with most elements of Maya, what you can produce with this type of emitter is limited only by your imagination.

Volume emitters come in five shapes: Cube, Sphere, Cylinder, Cone, and Torus. You cannot create any arbitrary volume shape for an emitter, but you can scale and rotate all five primitive shapes. You'll be able to achieve a variety of looks, giving you great freedom in setting the form your emitter will take.

> We're going to work through these next examples rather briskly. If you aren't comfortable with the steps for particle creation, you might want to go back and work through Chapter 21 before you continue with this chapter.

For a quick look at the effects of volume emitters, let's create a simple disk-type galaxy using the Torus-shaped emitter.

1. Open a new scene in Maya, and choose Particles → Create Emitter ❑.

2. Set the following for your emitter:

   - Under Basic Emitter Attributes, set the Emitter Type to Volume, and set the rate to about 500.

   - Under Distance/Direction Attributes, set Direction X, Y, and Z to 0 (this reduces the linear velocity of the particles to 0).

   - Under Basic Emission Speed Attributes, set Speed Random to 0.7.

   - In the Volume Emitter Attributes section, set the volume type to Torus, and set the section radius (the thickness of the torus) to about 0.3.

   - In the Volume Speed Attributes section, set Away From Axis to 0, Along Axis to 1, Around Axis to 0.5, and Random Direction to 0.2.

3. Click Create. The settings you've just made adjust the particles' circulation around the torus emitter—feel free to play with the settings and watch how the particle attributes change. Then scale the torus emitter shape outward until it looks something like Figure 23.1.

4. Select the particles, choose Fields → Newton ❑, and set the following attributes: Magnitude = 2, Attenuation = 0.2, and Use Max Distance turned Off. Click Create and click Play, and you should get a disk of particles that spiral in on the origin, similar to a galaxy or a spiraling dust cloud. See Figure 23.2.

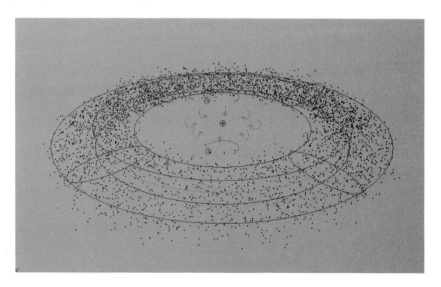

Figure 23.1

The scaled torus emitter, with particles

Figure 23.2

A disk of particles

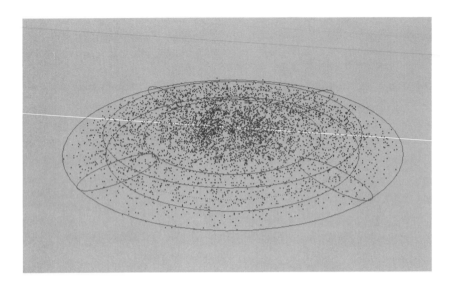

This is a simple example, but consider how difficult it would be to create the same effect using point or surface emitters. Volume emitters have a valuable place in the dynamics animator's toolbox, because they can turn out effects that would be problematic for traditional emitter types.

Later in this chapter, we will work with volume fields, another useful tool for working with particles.

A Simple Expression and a Simple Ramp

To explore how expressions and ramps work in Maya's particle dynamics, let's begin with a very simple example of each. Start by creating a default directional point emitter that shoots point particles straight up, give it a bit of spread (say, 0.3), and set a fairly slow speed with a high degree of speed randomness. To create an emitter:

1. Select Particles → Create Emitter ❑ .

2. In the Emitter Options (Create) window, set Emitter Type to Directional.

3. In the Distance/Direction Attributes section, set Spread to 0.3, directionY to 1, and both directionX and directionZ to 0. With these settings, the particles will shoot straight up along the Y axis of the workspace.

4. In the Basic Emission Speed Attributes section, set Speed to 1 or 2 for a fairly slow speed, and set Speed Random to about 3.

Now, to make our emitter a little more interesting, we will vary the particles' lifespan using an expression based on their initial speed (which has been randomized by the Speed Random setting). Then we will vary the particles' subsequent velocity in an unusual manner by using a ramp.

Particle Expressions: Controlling Lifespan

Maya gives you substantial control over random ranges for the life of
particles (their *lifespan*)—without having to resort to expressions. By
setting the Lifespan Attributes' Lifespan Mode to Random Range, you
can control how long particles live, with a minimum and maximum
particle life. If, for example, you set the Lifespan to 2 seconds and the
Lifespan Random to 1 second, you get particles that live between 1 (2
– 1) and 3 (2 + 1) seconds. (See Chapter 21 for more on creating particles with random lifespans.) You can also set a constant lifespan for
all particles (by choosing Constant from the Lifespan Mode menu, or
just setting the Random Range to 0). Or you can have the particles
live forever (the default state).

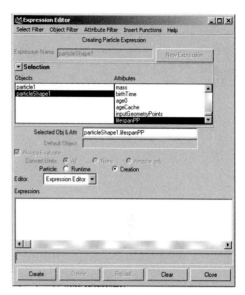

Figure 23.3

The Expression Editor,
with particleShape1
lifespanPP loaded

Sometimes, however, using expressions gives you the most exact
control over the lifespan of particles, far more exact than working
with the basic random lifespan settings. In our example here, we will
control the lifespan of each particle based on its initial speed as it is emitted.

> Be sure you have set your emitter's Speed Random (in the Basic Emission Attributes section)
> to a high number relative to its Speed setting. Otherwise, you will have a hard time seeing
> the effects of the expression you create in this exercise.

Before you can use an expression to control how a particle lives and dies, you need to tell
Maya that you want to control the lifespan attribute yourself. You might have noticed a setting in the Lifespan Mode menu called LifespanPP Only (PP stands for Per Particle). Select
this option now, and your particles will live forever, since we have not yet defined their lifespans using an expression. (You can test this by playing back your animation and noting that
the particles never die.)

> You can switch lifespan settings at any time by choosing another Lifespan Mode setting.

Now that you have control over your particles' lifespans, let's get to
work creating an expression for them. With the particles still selected,
scroll down to the Per Particle (Array) Attributes section. With your
mouse in the LifespanPP text field, RM choose Creation Expression to
open the Expression Editor (Figure 23.3), ready for you to create an
expression to control the lifespan of each particle.

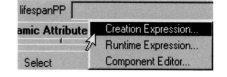

CREATION VERSUS RUNTIME

What's the difference between a creation expression and a runtime expression? A creation expression runs once for each particle (on its birth frame). A runtime expression runs for every frame (except the birth frame) for each particle.

- When a particle is first created (when its age is 0 frames—that is, at its creation frame), you can have an expression that will execute once for each particle, but *only* for that frame. In other words, if a particle is created at frame 21 (the particle's frame 0 or birth frame) and you have a creation expression for it, the creation expression will run *for that one frame*. Then the particle will go on its merry way.

- If you make a runtime expression, it will execute for that particle for each frame *except* the birth frame. It will execute starting at frame 1 for the particle, or frame 22 in our example.

In some cases, as in setting particles' lifespans, it is better to just run the expression once at the particle's birth (so it just has one lifespan value). In other cases, it is better to use a runtime expression. In yet other situations, you must use *both* a creation and a runtime expression. As you proceed through the chapter, you will see more of how these two types of expressions work together.

Context-sensitivity is a convenient feature you might not have noticed when you worked with the Expression Editor in Chapter 20. Here in this exercise, because we're launching the Expression Editor from the particle array section of the Attribute Editor, it automatically loads the proper object (particleShape1) in the Objects window, as shown in Figure 23.3.

Also notice that the Expression Editor has two radio buttons for particle expressions that allow you to select either creation or runtime expressions. You therefore don't need to close and reopen the Expression Editor to create each type of expression.

In the Expression area at the bottom of the Expression Editor window, type the following equation

```
lifespanPP = 2 * velocity;
```

and then click the Create button. If you entered the expression correctly, you will see the following message in the feedback line (or Script Editor): `Result: particleShape1`. If you see an error message instead, examine your expression for errors. The `velocity` is a Per Particle attribute (even though it does not have the PP moniker at the end), and the expression simply assigns each particle (as it is created) a lifespan equal to its velocity, times two.

When you now play back the animation, you can see that the more rapidly moving particles live longer than the slower ones, as in Figure 23.4. (You might need to look carefully or make the particles' Point Size bigger to see them.)

For a bit more fun, try changing the expression to

```
lifespanPP = 2/velocity;
```

Now the slower particles will live longer than those with a quick initial velocity. Figure 23.5 shows how the particle fountain looks slightly different with the new settings (notice that the top area of this figure is filled with more particles than in Figure 23.4). Additionally, the fountain will now appear to move much more slowly than it did with the former expression, since the bulk of visible particles are now moving at low, rather than high speed.

> To edit an expression, just retype it and click the Edit button. If you do not see your expression in the editing window, choose Select Filter → By Expression Name from the Expression Editor menu, and click the particleShape1 name under the expressions list.

When you reopen the Expression Editor after creating your expression, you will see that Maya has updated the expression to read as follows:

```
particleShape1.lifespanPP = 2/particleShape1.velocity;
```

Because you previously selected the particleShape1 node before opening the Expression Editor, Maya knew to apply the lifespanPP expression to this node. Had you not selected the particleShape1 node first, you could still create the expression, but you would have to use the full name of the attribute (such as `particleShape1.lifespanPP`).

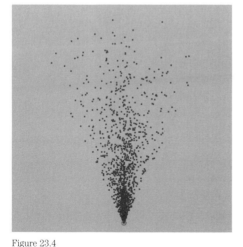

Figure 23.4

Particles with lifespan set to their initial velocities

Figure 23.5

Particles with lifespan set to the inverse of their initial velocities

Particle Ramps: Controlling the Velocity

Pretty neat stuff—using a simple formula, we quickly and (almost) painlessly made our particles die off after a time determined by their initial velocity. Next, instead of using velocity as an input in an expression, let's create a ramp to control the velocity of the particles, making them move around in a circle. (Because velocity is simply position-per-unit time, controlling particle velocity controls the particle's position in space at any given time.)

1. First, we need to get rid of the expression that's currently controlling the lifespan so that the lifespan per object will control how long the particles live. Reopen the Expression Editor, select the expression, and click the Delete button. Alternatively, you can select the particles and choose Constant from the Lifespan Mode menu; set the lifespan to somewhere around five seconds.

2. Now return to the Attribute Editor. In the rampVelocity text field, in the Per Particle (Array) Attributes section, RM select Create Ramp ❐, as shown in Figure 23.6. In the Create Ramp Options window that pops up, you can control how and where the ramp is applied (see Figure 23.7). We'll use the default options here: Input U set to None, Input V set to Particle's Age, and Map To set to New Ramp. (You should get familiar with these options, in case you want to map the ramp to a different set of attributes.) After checking these settings, close the window by clicking OK.

3. Return to the Attribute Editor, and, from the rampVelocity text field, RM select ArrayMapper1.outColorPP → ArrayMapper1.outColorPP → Edit Ramp. This focuses the Attribute Editor on the ramp you just created, as in Figure 23.8.

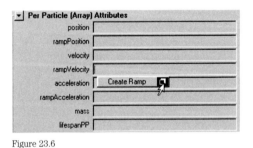

Figure 23.6

Choosing the Create Ramp option

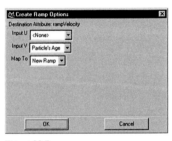

Figure 23.7

The Create Ramp Options window

In the top section of the Ramp section of the Attribute Editor (not shown in Figure 23.8) is the name of the ramp (currently ramp1), along with a texture swatch that is updated as you change the values in the section below. The swatch is set to a ramp between red, green, and blue. For velocity, position, and acceleration values, don't think of red, green, and blue as colors, but as values on a given axis: red is the X direction/velocity/acceleration, green is the Y value, and blue is the Z value. (The scene window uses these colors to represent the X,

Y, and Z axes.) As the particles age, their velocity values move up the ramp, going from red (out the X axis) to green (up the Y axis) to blue (out the Z axis). If you play back the animation right now, the particles move to the right, then up, then toward you, and finally die. (This is based on the Constant lifespan you assigned in step 1. To change the speed at which all this happens, set the lifespan value to a greater or lesser value.)

> If you have Lifespan Mode set to Forever, you will not get correct behavior out of your ramp. You must have a per-object or per-particle lifespan set in order for particles to "age" properly and thus move up the ramp.

To make the particles travel in a circle, you need to change the default ramp. But first you must remap the array because currently no particle can travel less than velocity 0 (no negative values). In order for the particles to travel in a circle, they must be able to go in a negative as well as a positive direction.

4. The array mapper is the part of the ramp group that tells Maya how to interpret the gradient. To focus on the array mapper, click the right-arrow box next to the Focus button at the top of the Attribute Editor.

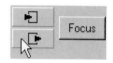

- The Min Value field tells Maya what the minimum value for the ramp will be. For our purposes, let's make this value –1, so the particles will travel at a velocity of –1 when a certain ramp color value is 0.

- Leave the Max Value set to 1, so the particles will travel at a velocity of 1 when a color value is 1.

Because of this remapping, a value of 0.5 for any color will translate into a velocity of 0, which is halfway between –1 and 1. This remapping might be a bit confusing, but stay with it here; things will get a bit clearer when we edit the ramp. If you want, try playing back the animation now and notice that the particles travel in a different path.

5. Now that the ramp has been remapped, it's time to edit the ramp. From the Attribute Editor's menu, choose Focus → ramp1 (or just click the Ramp tab) to return to the ramp. Set the first color swatch to RGB values of 0.5, 1, 0.5. To do this, first click the red dot at the bottom-left of the gradient, and then click the red box to the right of Selected Color to display the color picker. In the color picker under Sliders, change to RGB mode.. Finally, enter the values 0.5, 1, 0.5 in the R, G, and B channels. The particles will now start life moving straight up the Y axis— remember that 0.5 on the color ramp equates to a 0 velocity, so there will be no motion in the X or Z directions.

Figure 23.8

The Attribute Editor showing the default ramp

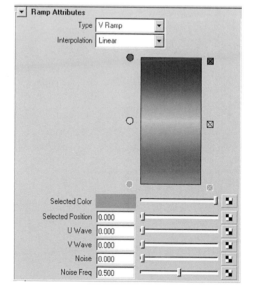

6. To make a circle, we need five points on our ramp:

- Somewhere between the bottom and middle points, click in the ramp to create a new point. With the new point selected, change the Selected Position to 0.25 (one-fourth of the way up the ramp). Then change the R, G, and B values of this point to 0, 0.5, 0.5, respectively. At this point (one-fourth of the way through the particle's life), the particle will be traveling in the negative X direction.

- Now click the middle point, be sure its Selected Position is set at 0.5, and set its RGB colors to 0.5, 0, 0.5 (traveling straight down).

- Next, click above the middle point in the ramp to create a new point, set its Selected Position to 0.75, and set its RGB values to 1, 0.5, 0.5.

- Finally, select the top point and set its RGB values to 0.5, 1, 0.5.

When finished, your ramp should look like Figure 23.9.

Now when you play back the animation, the particles will travel around in a circle, as in Figure 23.10—a pretty neat effect! (A color version of this image is on the CD.) You can, of course, play with the ramp values to get different effects. Also, try randomizing the lifespanPP values so that all particles do not have the same age (such as `particleShape1.lifespanPP = rand(2,6);`). As you can see, the ramp mapper allows you to create some interesting graphical effects.

To delete a point on the ramp, uncheck its box on the right side of the ramp.

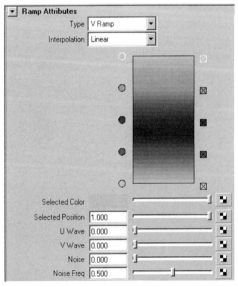

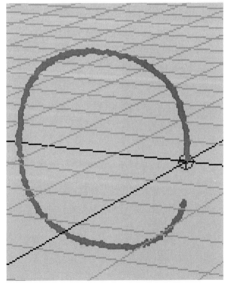

Figure 23.9

The ramp, used to make particles move in a circle

Figure 23.10

Particles traveling in a circle

With this introduction to volume emitters, particle expressions, and ramps under our belts, we'll devote the rest of the chapter to trying various modifications of these basic techniques. Sometimes we'll use one technique or another, but often we'll use two together. The common thread in all these exercises is that we'll be using the power of Maya to achieve more realistic—or at least more interesting—animation. This chapter's samples are meant only as an introduction, however, to the range of possibilities available with these controls. As you work through the examples, consider what other effects you might be able to produce with similar techniques. Then—using what's in this chapter as a guide—try to create what you envision.

Moving Particles Around in a Volume Field

Volume fields are a useful, interactive way to visualize the fields you create and use with particles and rigid bodies. Unless you plan to employ a universal force that applies evenly everywhere (such as a gravity field), you will likely find a volume field more intuitive than setting the range of a field's effects using only the maximum distance settings. Volume fields can also produce special effects not easily done with traditional fields. Let's take a look at two effects we can create using volume fields and the new Volume Axis field.

The Volume Axis field pushes, pulls, and rotates particles (and rigid bodies) within its volume area, allowing effects such as particle obstacles and tornadoes (the two examples we will create), as well as a number of other possibilities. First, let's force a stream of particles to flow around a volume field.

1. Create a directional particle emitter that emits in the X direction, with a rate of 100, a spread of 0.3, and a speed of about 2.

2. Begin the animation, select the particles, and then create a Volume Axis field (Fields → Volume Axis ❑). Use the following settings: Magnitude = 3, Attenuation = 0.1, Volume Shape = Torus, Away From Axis = 1; set everything else to 0 and click Create.

3. Move the torus a bit to the right, scale it outward some, and rotate it so it is partially in the path of the particle stream, as in Figure 23.11.

The Magnitude of the Volume Axis field sets the amount of force applied by the field. Attenuation sets how rapidly this force decreases away

Figure 23.11

Particles dividing around a toroidal Volume Axis field

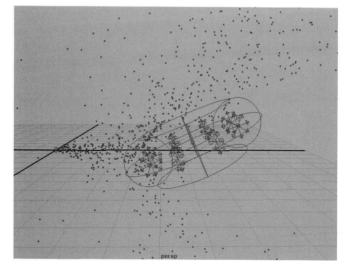

persp

from the center ring of the torus (slowly, in this case). The Away From Axis setting is the speed the force is applied on an axis radiating from the torus—notice the arrows in Figure 23.11 that point out from the center of the torus. You also have controls for circulating particles around the axis and along the axis; additionally, you can add a constant force in one or more directions using the Directional Speed and Direction (X, Y, Z) attributes. Try playing with the different settings to see how your altered settings change the particle's motion.

With the settings you've just arranged for the Volume Axis field, the particles in this scene move partway through the torus before they are "pushed" out and away from the center ring. To create more force, you can alter the magnitude of the entire Volume Axis field, reduce the attenuation so the field is applied out toward the edge of the torus, or increase the Away From Axis value. This last way to increase the Volume Axis force is useful, because you can control the field's force specifically in the Away, Along, and Around Axis directions.

Now let's create a tornado effect using the Volume Axis field.

> It is a good idea to reset Maya's settings when creating new emitters or fields. Choose Edit → Reset Settings in the appropriate options window.

Create a new scene, and make a volume emitter of type Cylinder with a rate of about 1000, a directionY of 1, and an Along Axis speed of 5. Scale this to be a good size for the bottom of your tornado. Then run the animation forward and select the particles. (Notice that they all run straight up the Y axis and out of the cylinder.) Choose Fields → Volume Axis ❏, and set Magnitude to 50, Attenuation to 1, Shape to Cylinder, Around Axis to 0.75, Along Axis to 0.5, and Away From Axis to –4; then check the Invert Attenuation box.

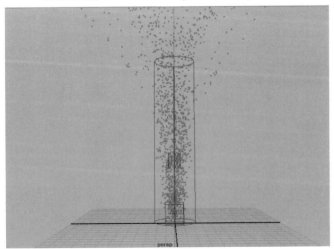

Figure 23.12

Whirling particles in a tornado within a Volume Axis field

These settings pull the particles up the axis (Along Axis), spin them around (Around Axis), and pull them back into the cylinder (Away From Axis with a negative setting). Enabling the Invert Attenuation option makes all these forces more extreme at the edges of the cylinder, rather than in the center. (You'll immediately see the difference if you try running the animation with Invert Attenuation turned off.) When you finish, you should end up with an effect similar to Figure 23.12.

The settings we achieved in Figure 23.12 took quite a lot of tweaking to get right. You are welcome to play with the settings, but you will find it is fairly difficult to keep the particles trapped within the cylinder.

Obviously, you can achieve any number of effects using volume fields. As an exercise, try creating a mushroom cloud using the Volume Axis field in a sphere shape. You'll need to place the emitter inside the sphere and turn on Invert Attenuation to get the right look.

Changing Color and Lifespan per Particle

Our next technique uses expressions and ramps. We'll make the blasts from the plasma cannon we've been working on in the last two chapters more realistic (or, at least, more visually appealing) by modifying the lifespan and the color of the plasma.

Open your saved plasma cannon project from Chapter 22, or use the `22plasmaCannon` project from the CD-ROM.

If you have not previously set the plasma particles to have a random lifespan, or if you want to give the `rand` function a try, you can use an expression to control the lifespan. Only one thing is missing from our cannon to produce the perfect blast: the color of the particles should fade from a bright blue-white to a duller orange as the energy of each blast lessens. Using a ramp is a good way to accomplish this.

With the particles selected, click the Color button in the Attribute Editor. Check the Add Per Particle Attribute check box, and add the attribute. Next, create a ramp for the newly created rgbPP attribute at the bottom of the Per Particle (Array) Attributes section. Then edit the resulting default ramp. (Follow the earlier steps in the "Particle Ramps: Controlling the Velocity" section if you get lost.)

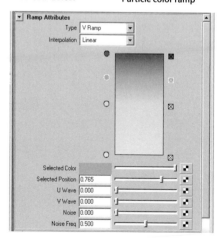

Figure 23.13

Particle color ramp

Now let's change the colors, starting at the bottom. First, click the round red button to the left of the gradient; then click the red color swatch below it to open the color picker. Choose a nearly-white blue (or whatever color you want) for your first color. Choose the next point up, and make it a yellowish color; then make the top color a darker red/orange. One point is still missing—add a point between the yellow and red points (by clicking in the gradient), and make it an orange that's less saturated than the top color. When you are finished, you should have something resembling Figure 23.13 (see the Color Gallery on the CD for a color view).

Play back your animation. You should see the particles change color as they shoot across the screen, as in Figure 23.14 (also in color on the CD).

Figure 23.14

The plasma cannon with changing colors for the blast

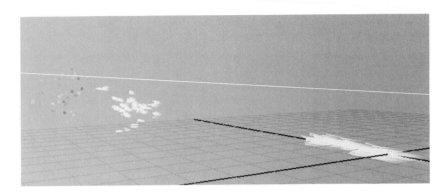

FORCING A COMPLETE RAMP CYCLE

Advanced Maya users might be aware that, because particle lifespans are random, many of the particles will not cycle through a complete color ramp. To force all particles, regardless of their lifespan, to go through a complete color range, you can change the lifespan mode to lifespanPP Only and then use the following expressions. In the creation expression, enter the following:

```
lifespanPP=0.5+rand(2);
$howOld = smoothstep (0, particleShape1.lifespanPP, particleShape1.age);
particleShape1.rgbPP = <<1.5 - $howOld, $howOld/1.2, $howOld/1.5>>;
```

and in the runtime expression, enter:

```
$howOld = smoothstep (0, particleShape1.lifespanPP, particleShape1.age);
particleShape1.rgbPP = <<1.5 - $howOld, $howOld/1.2, $howOld/1.5>>;
```

The smoothstep function creates a smooth ramp from 0 (at time 0) to 1 (at time lifespan) for each particle. The rgbPP components (red, green, blue) are then assigned values between 1 (1.5, actually) and 0, based on the particle's age compared to its full life expectancy. The numbers (1.5, 1.2, and 1.5) are just ways of adjusting the colors to make for a nice transition, as shown here and in the Color Gallery on the CD.

Changing Radius by Position

Now let's see how we can change particle shape by using expressions. Create a directional emitter that shoots particles up in the air with a speed of 2 or 3, and then assign the particles a Sphere render type. Next, keyframe the emitter to move from 0 up to about 10 on the Y axis over about 200 frames—we'll use this motion to change the particles' radii. If you want, give the particles a random lifespan between 4 and 10.

We are now going to create an expression that ties the radius of each particle to the birth position of the emitter. First, we need to create a radiusPP attribute for the particles. To create the radiusPP attribute, click the General button in the Add Dynamic Attributes section of the Attribute Editor for your particles, as shown in Figure 23.15. In the window that pops up after you click the Particles tab, select radiusPP, click Add, and close the window.

Now open the Expression Editor window by RM choosing Creation Expression from the radiusPP field. In the creation expression, type the following:

```
particleShape1.radiusPP = emitter1.ty/10;
```

This simple expression gives each particle a radius based on where the emitter is at the moment of creation. (The radius equals the Y position of the emitter, divided by 10.) When you play back the animation, you should get something like Figure 23.16.

To see the difference between creation and runtime expressions, cut your script (Ctrl+X) from the creation expression click the edit button, and then click the radio button to select Runtime instead of Creation. Then just paste the line you cut from the other expression into this new one, and click the Create button. Play back the animation again, and you will see the radii of all particles increase as the emitter moves up the Y axis (see Figure 23.17). Because the runtime expression is evaluated at *every* frame (except the first one), the particles' radii will constantly increase—in sync, no less—as the emitter rises.

Figure 23.15

Adding the radiusPP attribute

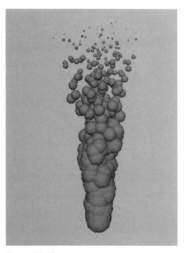

Figure 23.16

Particles with varying radii

Figure 23.17

Particles with the same increasing radius

Moving Particles Upward in a Spiral

If you're familiar with *Using Maya: Expressions* in the old Maya 2 manual, you might recall seeing a picture of particles rising in a spiral from the ground. This might appear to be a complex effect, but we're going to create it here with a fairly straightforward runtime expression. We'll use the sine function to place particles into a loop and push them up at the same time, so they form a spiral.

> If you are unfamiliar with the sine function, see Chapter 20 (or a trigonometry book) for more information on what it is and how it works. (The Maya help documentation also contains an explanation and examples of the sine function.)

First, create an emitter that emits roughly five particles per second (about one for each five frames) and set the speed to 0. Make the render type Sphere. Using an expression, we're going to place the spheres in a position based on their age, and, by virtue of the sine function's properties, the position of the particles will form a moving spiral. In the Attribute Editor (with the particle shape selected), RM choose Runtime Expression in the Position field. Copy the following expression into the editing window.

```
$pX = 15 * sin(particleShape1.age);
$pZ = 15 * cos(particleShape1.age);
particleShape1.position = <<$pX, particleShape1.age, $pZ>>;
```

This expression first declares the variables *$pX* and *$pZ* (for position X and Z) and then assigns them a value based on the sine of their age (which starts at 0 when they are born, increasing from there). (For more on variables, see Chapter 20.)

Because sine function values range only between –1 and 1, we multiplied the function by 15 to get a wider range (from –15 to 15). Note that *$pZ* uses the cosine function instead of the sine function. This is because the cosine is perfectly out of phase with the sine function (that is, it is 0 when the sine is 1 and vice versa), and when the two are combined this way, they make the particle travel in a circle on the X-Z plane.

The final statement of the expression does all the real work: It assigns to the X, Y, and Z positions of each particle the value of *$pX*, the age of the particle (forcing the spheres up in the Y direction as they age), and *$pZ*. As all these values change on every frame, the particles move in a nice spiral, shown in Figure 23.18.

You might notice a flickering at the origin as you play your animation. This is the sphere being created (at 0, 0, 0) on its first frame of life because the runtime expression does not work for a particle's birth frame. To get rid of this annoying problem, simply cut and paste the runtime expression into the Creation Expression window (switch over to the Creation Expression window using the Creation/Runtime radio buttons in the Expression Editor).

As a last step, see if you can figure out how to make the spheres' colors change as they spiral up, as shown in Figure 23.19 (and in color on the CD). You can use the same sine (and cosine) function to alter colors as well.

If you get stuck, try looking at this code to help you out:

```
$pX = 15 * sin(particleShape1.age);
$pZ = 15 * cos(particleShape1.age);
$R = (1+($pX/15))/2;
$G = .65;
$B = (1+($pZ/15))/2;
particleShape1.position = <<$pX, particleShape1.age, $pZ>>;
particleShape1.rgbPP=<<$R, $G, $B>>;
```

The new variables (*$R* and *$B*) reset (more properly, they "renormalize") the *$pX* and *$pZ* variables to between 0 and 1. (They originally ranged from –15 to 15.) The rgbPP statement just assigns these variables (plus *$G* for green) to the spheres' red and blue color channels.

Here, with just a few lines of code, you have created an animation that would be next to impossible using traditional keyframe methods.

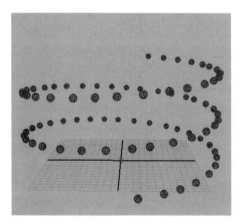

Figure 23.18

Particles in a spiral

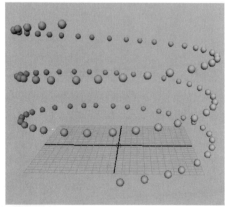

Figure 23.19

Spiral particles with color

Collision Events and Expressions

For particles, not only does Maya keep track of color, age, and other attributes, it also tracks events such as the number of collisions a particle has experienced.

Create a new scene with a fountain shooting spheres up in the air. Add gravity, create a plane, and create a collision plane. (If you don't want to go to the trouble of setting this up, just open the 23collide project on the CD-ROM.) Now let's create a runtime expression that will change each particle's color based on the number of times it has collided with the plane.

We will use the event attribute (which is a per-particle attribute, even though it doesn't end in PP) to determine how many collisions each particle has been through. Then we'll use an if – else if – else statement to assign a particular color to the particle, depending on how many collisions it has been through. To add the event attribute, you have to create a particle collision event. Select the particles—not the emitter—and choose Particles → Particle Collision Events. Click the Create Event button. Several new channels will be added to the particleShape1 node, and the event attribute will be listed in the Expression Editor's Attributes box. (If you are not familiar with if – then statements, see Chapter 20 of this book or a basic programming text.)

Create a per-particle color Attribute (if none exists yet), and RM select a runtime expression for the rgbPP of the particles. Type the following expression into the Expression Editor, and click the Create button when you are finished:

```
if (event == 0)
    rgbPP = <<0,1,0>>;
else if (event == 1)
    rgbPP = <<1,0,0>>;
else if (event == 2)
    rgbPP = <<0,0,1>>;
else rgbPP = <<1,1,1>>;
```

This expression executes on every frame (except the birth frame), checking the number of collisions of each particle. If the number is 0 (no collisions), the expression assigns a green color to the sphere. If the number of collisions is 1 (after the first bounce), it assigns the color red to the sphere. If the number is 2 (after the second bounce), it assigns the color blue to the spheres. In all other cases (when the particle has bounced more than twice), the expression assigns a white color (all 1s) to the sphere.

> The test condition is specified by a *double* equal sign (event == 0), not a single equal sign. A single equal sign tells Maya to assign a value to the left side of an equation (as in rgbPP = X); a double equal sign tells Maya to test whether the two sides of the equation are equivalent.

You can also use a switch command in expressions like the previous one, rather than if – then – else. A switch and an if – else statement perform the same function but in a slightly different way. For more information about the switch command, see the *Using Maya: Expressions* manual.

Play back the animation and watch each sphere; you will see that the individual particles change color each time they bounce, ending with a white color after they have bounced more than twice, as shown in Figure 23.20. You might also notice that the spheres are emitted as completely black objects—this is (again) because a runtime expression is not evaluated on the birth frame of the particles. To solve this problem, simply copy and paste the expression into a creation expression for the rgbPP of the spheres.

Figure 23.20

Colored bouncing particles

In the Maya documentation, see *Using Maya: Dynamics* for more information about creating particle collision events (Chapter 4, "Particle Collisions") and the event attribute (Chapter 15, "Advanced Particle Topics").

Transparency Ramps: Disappearing Bubbles

One problem with our antacid tablet from Chapters 21 and 22 is that the bubbles rising from the tablet all have the same size. Let's take care of that deficiency in Maya, using a transparency ramp and particles with blobby surfaces.

First, open your antacid project from the last chapter or open the 22glass file on the CD-ROM. For a little different look, let's change the bubbles to software-rendered ones. In the Attribute Editor, set the particle type to Blobby Surface, and set the threshold to 0; click Add Attribute if the Threshold setting does not exist. (Remember that setting the threshold of a blobby surface to 0 makes the spheres noninteractive and, thus, just spheres. For bubbles, this is exactly what we're after.) With particles selected, add a per-particle radius attribute to the bubbles, and then create and edit the ramp of radiusPP to look something like Figure 23.21.

You'll probably find that the bubbles created with this ramp range in size too much, overall, so remap their sizes using the Array Mapper (RM choose radiusPP → arrayMapper1.outvaluePP → arrayMapper1.outvaluePP → Edit

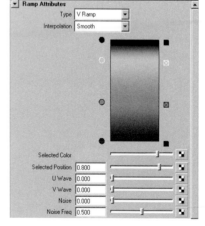

Figure 23.21

A radius ramp for the bubbles

Array Mapper). A minimum value of 0.1 and a maximum of about 0.3 give a much subtler effect, as shown in Figure 23.22.

The bubbles in this image have a material attached to them—a phongE material with high specularity and low opacity. This, of course, improves the look of the bubbles tremendously.

Figure 23.22

A glass with bubbles of varying radii

Emitter Expressions

So far, we have created several ramps and expressions for particles, but we have yet to create expressions for particle emitters. You can either create a default emitter for this example, or reopen your fountain project from Chapter 22 (or `22fountain` on the CD). Because it's easier to see the effects of this particular expression in a simpler project, it might be advisable to first create a simple emitter. Then, after you see how the expression works, you can copy it into the fountain project.

Although emitters are random in their particle output, they tend to produce a "constant" randomness (a kind of even spread) over time. To get the emitter to create a widely varying number of particles and a wide range of spread, we could keyframe these values—or we could simply create a two-line expression using the `noise` function.

> We could also use the rand function, but `noise` produces a more connected randomness (as opposed to the rand function's jumping from value to value). With `noise`, the look is more like the varying water pressure we might see in a fountain. For more on the `noise` function, see Chapter 20.

With the emitter (not the particles) selected, open the Expression Editor and type the following expression.

```
emitter1.rate = ((noise (time) + 1) * 200) + 20;
emitter1.spread = ((noise (time) + 1)/4) + 0.1;
emitter1.speed = ((noise (time) +1) * 5) + 3;
```

In essence, each line of this little expression tells the emitter to vary its rate (or spread amount) according to a random amount as defined by the noise function, which uses time as its input to create its numbers. The other numbers in the script are simply to get the value output by noise into a good range for each attribute. Because noise varies between –1 and 1, we added 1 to both lines so the result would vary between 0 and 2. For the rate, we wanted the value to range between 20 and 420, so we multiplied the results of noise by 200 (giving a range of 0 to 400) and added 20. For the spread, a good range seemed to fall between about 0.1 and 0.6, so we divided by 4 (giving a range of 0 to 0.5) and added 0.1. Finally, we adjusted the speed of the emitted particles, as well, multiplying the noise function by 5 and adding 3 to the results. As your results should show, the noise function is a powerful way to create a more "live" look to your particles.

The result of this expression applied to the fountain project is on your CD-ROM as 23fountain.mov. If you compare this with the previous fountain movie (22fountain.mov), you'll see the fountain's dramatically improved realism (like one of those shooting fountains).

Changing Opacity with Motion

We're now going to create a nice little effect using expressions: increasing the opacity of a particle based on its motion—in other words, the more it moves, the more opaque it is. To test this out, open your UFO project from Chapter 22 (or use 22UFO on the CD-ROM).

With the particles selected, change their render type to MultiPoint, reduce the point size to 2, and increase the Multi Radius to about 2. Next, create a per-particle opacity attribute (Add Dynamic Attributes: Opacity). Then open the Expression Editor and type the following simple runtime expression.

```
if (particleShape1.velocity != 0)
    particleShape1.opacityPP = (particleShape1.velocity / 2.0);
else
particleShape1.opacityPP = 0;
```

All we're doing here is testing whether the velocity is not 0 (the ! sign preceding a comparison operator means "not"). If the particle is moving, its opacity is based on its speed. We divided by 2 to get a more gradual fade-up of opacity—you can try other numbers if you like. If the particle is at rest (the else statement), its opacity is defined as 0, or invisible.

Thus, the "dust" is invisible when it is resting on our desert floor. As the UFO picks it up and moves it around, the dust becomes visible; then, as it falls back to the ground, it disappears again.

A movie of this new UFO sequence is on the CD-ROM, `23UFOFade.mov`, and Figure 23.23 shows a still from this movie.

Figure 23.23

The UFO and semi-opaque dust

Changing Rotation with Motion

Now that we have dust appearing and disappearing, it seems only natural to visit the UFO project we did in the last chapter with sprites. This time, instead of simply pulling the leaf sprites along in the UFO's wake, we'll make them rotate based on their motion (so they aren't just sliding across the desert floor).

Either open your UFO sprite project, or use the one on the CD-ROM (`22UFOSprite`). With the particles selected, add a spriteTwistPP attribute (click the General button in the Attribute Editor, scroll down to spriteTwistPP, highlight it, and click the Add button). In the text field next to the new spriteTwistPP attribute, RM choose New Expression; and in the Expression Editor, type the following runtime expression:

```
float $speed = particleShape1.velocity;
if (particleShape1.velocity != 0)
    particleShape1.spriteTwistPP = particleShape1.spriteTwistPP
    + ($speed * noise(time) * 2);
```

The essence of this expression is the same as the one for changing opacity in the preceding section. If the velocity isn't 0, we rotate the leaves. Some of the details have changed, however.

- First, we created a variable (notice that it is a **float**) called *$speed*, which receives the *magnitude* of the particle's velocity.

- The second line checks to see if the sprite's velocity is *not* 0; if that's the case, the spriteTwistPP of the particle is changed by the value of *$speed*. The multipliers (`noise` and `2`) are there to make the motion of each leaf different from the others. Essentially, the value of *$speed* is multiplied by a randomly changing number between –2 and 2, making the leaves spin in both directions by varying amounts. You will notice that there is no `else` statement here—if the leaf isn't moving, its rotation should just stay where it is, not suddenly jump back to some other number (such as 90 degrees).

Figure 23.24

The UFO with spinning leaves trailing

Figure 23.24 shows a still from a movie of the leaves, which can be seen as `23UFOSpriteSpin.mov` on the CD.

More Expressions: Animated Sprites

As one last example of using expressions, let's create a more interesting, animated array of plant life for our UFO to pass over. The leaves in our desert were rather boring, so let's remedy that situation and make them less flat-looking. Open the `23UFOSprite` project (or your saved one). You can use the one we just worked on, too, although the results will be a bit harder to see with all that spinning.

Select the Lambert shader that controls the sprite shape (the one with the leaf on it). In the Attribute Editor, click the Focus button next to the Color attribute (the triangle in a square) to display the file1 attributes. Now you need to open the `LeafSequence` subdirectory. (You will see about 50 files in the sequence.) You can get this from the CD or the directory on your hard disk where you've saved the `Working_Files` directories, or you can copy the `LeafSequence` folder to your project's `sourceimages` folder. Choose any file from `LeafSequence`; then be sure to check the Use Frame Extension box below the Reload File Texture button. This assigns the first leaf in the sequence to the shader.

CONVERTING DATA TYPES IN MEL

The *velocity* variable is a vector quantity (with X,Y,Z values), but *$speed* is a scalar (just one number). When Maya sees an assignment operator (a single equal sign), Maya always forces the value on the right to fit that on the left if it can. In the case of a vector's being converted to a float, Maya takes the magnitude of the vector (the square root of each element squared and added together), which is a single number, and assigns that number to *$speed*. Whew— enough math for one day!

Hardware texture cycling is *extremely* picky about your numbering and tagging of the files you want to use. You must *not* use any frame padding (that is, leading 0s), and you *cannot* have an .xxx extension at the end of your filename. This is especially challenging in the Windows world, where the filename extension is usually hidden from view. To get around these traps, it's generally best to use a good file-naming utility (such as SiliWin for Windows).

Now, in the Hardware Texture Cycling Options, check Use Hardware Texture Cycling. Set the Start Cycle Extension to 1, the End Cycle Extension to 50 (for 23leaves.1 and 23leaves.50, respectively), and the By Cycle Increment to 1.

The By Cycle Increment controls how many images are skipped before the next one is shown. For an animation (of, say, a bird flying, or a rendered animation sequence you've made previously), set the increment to 1. For a choppier look (skipping some of the images, thus producing a "stop motion" look as the sequence plays), an increment of 2 or 3 would work.

You might be realizing at this point that sprite sequences can be extremely useful. For instance, you can play back a movie (saved as an image sequence) in sprites, creating a dazzling array of moving images in your final scene.

If you play back the animation now, you won't see anything different. That's because we have to write an expression to alter the look of each sprite. First, add a new attribute: spriteNumPP (click the General button in the Attribute Editor and add it). Then RM choose a new runtime expression and type the following:

```
particleShape1.spriteNumPP = ((frame/10) % 50) + 1;
```

The % is the modulus (or remainder) function—whatever number remains from dividing one-tenth of the frame number by 50 is returned (plus 1 so that the number is never 0, for which no sprite is defined). The division by 10 simply ensures that the leaves change color more slowly. For example, on frame 1, 1 % 50 returns 1 (the remainder of 1 / 50), the second frame returns 2, and so on. At each frame, a different spriteNumPP is defined. We could also write a noise function to get each sprite to randomly change colors, instead of having all of them changing in synch. Either way, we get to see all the fall colors in short order!

Figure 23.25 (in color on the CD) shows a still from the movie, UFOSpriteColors.mov (also on the CD).

As an exercise, try creating a new emitter that produces leaves of different colors that then stay the same color for the rest of their lives. You'll need to use a creation expression this time, instead of a runtime expression.

Figure 23.25

The UFO trailing colored leaves

Summary

In this chapter, you have discovered how to unlock the power of particle dynamics by using volume emitters and fields, ramps, and expressions. With volume emitters and fields, you gain fine control over particle emission as well as the interaction of forces with particles in space. Using ramps, you can produce large-scale effects—opacity, color, or even velocity— that occur over the lifetime of each particle. In contrast, expressions are best at breaking groups of particles into their constituents, and you learned how an expression allows you to control each particle in a different but related manner. None of the expressions you studied were more than a couple of lines long, yet they produced impressive results, ranging from positioning particles based on the sine curve to varying opacity based on the particles' rate of movement.

If you have a fairly good grasp of the techniques covered in Chapters 21 through 23, you are now ready to create some sophisticated effects in (most important!) a relatively short time. The next chapter, on soft bodies, is the final chapter on particle dynamics. You'll see that the term *soft bodies* is a slight misnomer—they are actually collections of particles that act as bodies. And these past three chapters are just the primer you need for creating these complex and challenging objects. When you're ready, turn the page to begin exploring soft bodies!

CHAPTER 24

Dynamics of Soft Bodies

In this chapter, you'll learn what soft bodies are, how to use them, and where you can use them to create amazing special effects. Along the way, you'll revisit two projects begun earlier: the boy's head, improving the appearance of the hair; and the fountain, this time concentrating on the plane below the fountain. You'll also have a chance to work through an advanced use of soft bodies to create an effect similar to the famous "water head" scene in the film, *The Abyss*. In these and other exercises, you will see how soft bodies are the culmination of Maya's particle dynamics and how they allow you, the animator, to create a whole new realm of animation. Many animation effects you have avoided in the past because of their difficulty are now within easy grasp. The ability to use soft bodies to create flexible, fluid objects is indeed one of Maya's most powerful features. Topics include:

- **Creating a basic soft body**
- **Adjusting goal weights**
- **Using goal weights to create fluid motion**
- **Adding springs to soft bodies**
- **Faking a bounce**
- **Denting soft bodies**
- **Hands On: Painting goal weights on hair**
- **Advanced Hands On: Adding ripples to the fountain project**
- **Advanced Hands On: Creating a watery body and face**

What Are Soft Bodies?

At heart, *soft bodies* are simply collections of particles linked to a corresponding piece of geometry. The key characteristic is that these soft-body particles are attached to the geometry to form the soft-body object. This symbiotic relationship creates a special effect: a solid piece of geometry that reacts as if it were a bunch of particles reacting to forces or motions applied to them. The particles each control one vertex or CV of the geometry and, with their motion, deform the geometry to create fluidic surface movements and clothlike motion. Although working with them can be quite complex, creating soft bodies in Maya is easy: you simply select your model and tell Maya to make a soft body out of it.

Creating a Basic Soft Body

To begin working with soft bodies, create a basic NURBS sphere in a new scene. Then take the following steps:

1. From the Dynamics menu set, choose Soft/Rigid Bodies → Create Soft Body ❒ to open the Soft Options dialog box, which contains options for creating a soft body.

2. Be sure that Make Soft (the default option) is selected from the Creation Options drop-down menu, as shown in Figure 24.1.

3. Click Create, and then click Close.

Don't try adding or subtracting spans or faces after you begin animating. You will end up with bizarre, uncontrollable soft-body effects!

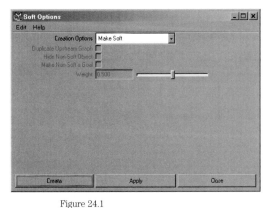

Figure 24.1

Select Make Soft from the drop-down menu.

That's about it! You have just converted your original geometry (the sphere) into a soft body. You will see your original sphere now surrounded by points (or particles) that take up positions at each CV of the shape. The number of isoparms (or polygon faces) in your original geometry determines the number of particle points. If you want more points (for higher-resolution effects), create your original shape with more isoparms. To see how this works, select the makeNurbSphere1 node before you create the soft body and change the number of spans (or sections) to 8. You will see the number of soft-body particles change to match when you create the new soft body.

Understanding the Structure of the Soft Body

Before we actually use this soft body, let's take a quick look at its structure in the Hypergraph.

1. Open the Hypergraph and choose Options → Display → Shape Nodes. Your Hypergraph window should show something like Figure 24.2.

2. The highlighted nodes (nurbsSphere1Particle and nurbsSphere1ParticleShape) are your new soft-body transform and shape nodes that have been attached to your old sphere (and replace it). If you highlight the nurbsSphere1ParticleShape node and look in the Channel Box (or Attribute Editor), you will see that the attributes listed there—shown in Figure 24.3—exactly match the attributes you'd find if you created a standard particle shape. When you finish examining the structure of your soft body, close the Hypergraph.

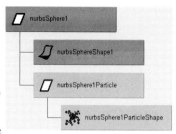

Figure 24.2

The Hypergraph representation of a soft body

Using a Soft Body

Now that we have created a soft body, what can we do with it? First, let's create a gravity field to affect it. Follow these steps:

1. Select the sphere and then choose Fields → Gravity. Notice the gravity field now displayed in the center of the workspace. When you play back the animation, the ball drops under the influence of gravity (just as a rigid body would).

2. Rewind the animation, move the ball up, and add a plane to the scene (be sure to scale it large enough so that the ball will fall on it). Remember that you always have to rewind a particle animation before playing it back. If you do not, you will see bizarre actions when you play back your animation.

3. Select the sphere, Shift+select the plane, and then choose Particles → Make Collide. Now, as gravity forces the soft body to fall, the *particles that make up the soft body* will collide with the plane. When you play back the animation, you should see something like Figure 24.4.

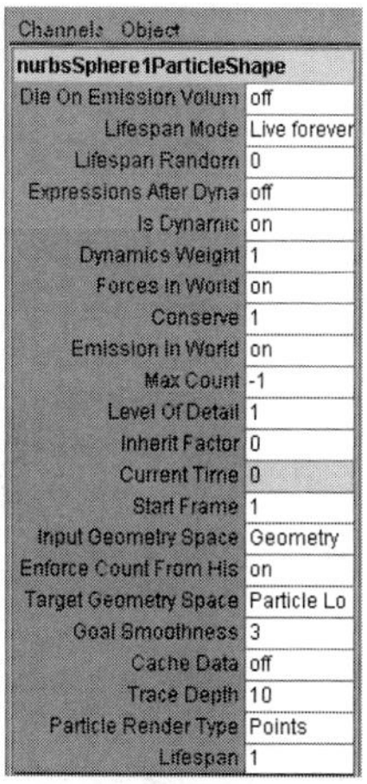

You can see that the soft-body collision is different from a rigid-body collision. First, rigid bodies (assuming they use the same rigid solver) automatically collide with one another. Since soft bodies are controlled more or less by their particles, you have to define the collision with the soft-body particle object, as you do with standard particle groups. Second, since the collisions occur on a per particle basis, each particle—not the solid surface as a whole—collides with the plane at a different time, giving rise to the sphere's distortion.

Figure 24.3

The particle shape node of a soft body

Figure 24.4

A soft-body ball collides with a plane

As when you created standard particle collisions (in Chapter 21, "Particle Basics"), you have control over how the soft body collides with the plane. Both the soft-body shape and the plane (in its geoConnector node) have controls for resilience (bounciness) and friction (how much the objects "stick" when they collide at an angle) for the collision. You cannot adjust the soft body's resilience and friction apart from the plane's: they are constrained to be the same values via the geoConnector. To see how the soft body reacts with these attributes, try the following:

1. To see how resilience works, try changing the plane's Resilience attribute to a number larger than 1 (such as 1.2). When you play back the animation, the particles will bounce higher and higher (because, on each bounce, they rise 120 percent of their last height—impossible in our world, but not in Maya's). If you decrease resilience to 0, the particles simply stick to the plane when they strike it.

Maya also supports negative resilience. With a negative value, your soft body will move through the plane and then bounce back toward it from underneath. If you use this feature with gravity, however, the particle will continue to fall (because gravity continues to pull on the object). To counteract this problem, you can keyframe gravity to change directions.

2. Now move Resilience back to 0.8 or so, and be sure that the friction value is 0.6 or so. If there is no sideways movement to the particle (no movement tangent to the plane), you will see the friction value make no difference.

3. Try, however, adding a bit of shear to your gravity; set the directionX value of gravity at 0.2 or so (select the gravity node at the center of the Maya grid or in the Hypergraph, and set directionX to about 0.2). When you play back the animation, you will see the ball move sideways under "gravity"; then, as it collides with the plane, it will slow on each collision. If the ball slides off the plane, just make the plane bigger (or enjoy the spill!). If you set the friction of the plane to a large value, such as 4, the ball particles will actually bounce *backward* when you play back the animation because friction is greater than 100% (which is, again, impossible in the real world). If you make friction negative, the ball particles will be pulled forward on each collision.

If you try to keyframe the ball's motion, you can potentially run into a nasty little problem called *double transforms*. Because each point is being transformed twice what it ought to be, you will see the particles jump out ahead of the ball shape. To counteract this problem, simply group the soft body to itself (select the shape, and then press Ctrl+G), and keyframe the position of the ball using this new node (called group1 by default).

Adjusting Goal Weights

Now that we've created a soft body, let's make one that isn't so squishy. Goal weights are a way to control how closely a soft body mimics its original shape (the shape you used to create the soft body). The closer a goal weight is to 1, the more closely the soft body maintains the original shape, whereas if the weight is 0, the soft body does not follow the original shape at all. Adjusting goal weights properly can create everything from gelatin-like jiggles to pouring water. In the following steps, we'll create a soft body sphere and assign a goal shape:

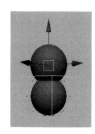

Figure 24.5

The soft body sphere tries to retain its original shape via its goal.

1. Create a new scene like the last one—a sphere above a plane.

2. Open the Create Soft Body options window (choose Soft/Rigid Bodies → Create Soft Body ❑). Choose Duplicate, Make Copy Soft from the drop-down menu, check Make Non-Soft A Goal, and create the object. (Notice that there is a slider for an attribute, Goal Weight, that is now enabled—be sure this is set to about 0.5.) Generally, here you want to hide the original geometry (by selecting that check box in the Create Soft Body options window). For this example, we're leaving it visible so that we can see how the soft body and original geometry interact. Next, highlight the soft-body sphere, and create gravity. If you look in the Hypergraph now, you will see the original geometry (nubsSphere1) and the duplicate soft body (copyOfnubsSphere1 plus the particle node). Be sure to turn collisions on again by selecting the particles and the plane and choosing Particles → Make Collide once you create your soft body. We'll need this turned on for later.

3. Play back the animation. You should see the soft-body sphere "sag" a little bit and quickly try to bounce back to its original location and shape. The soft-body particles are being pulled down by gravity, but they have a "goal" to stay as close as possible to their original shape—the original sphere. To exaggerate this point, select the particle node (you may need to do this in the Outliner or Hypergraph), set your goal weight to 0.2, and play back the scene. The sphere should look as it does in Figure 24.5. We can alter how strongly attracted to its original shape a particle is simply by adjusting its goal weight.

4. Select the particle node, and find the goalWeight[0] and goalActive[0] attributes listed there. They should be set to 0.2 (or 20%) and "on" settings, respectively. If you turn the goalActive attribute to "off" (by typing **off** or entering in a value of 0 in the text field), the soft body will fall away from the sphere and bounce off the plane when you play the animation, just as in our first example. Why? Because turning that attribute off tells Maya to pay no further attention to the goal weight.

5. Now turn goalActive[0] back on (you can type **on** or enter 1).

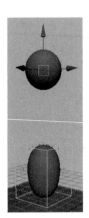

Figure 24.6

The soft body with a higher Goal Smoothness bounces off the floor and deforms.

GoalActive[0] can be keyframed, meaning that you can animate whether the soft body will attempt to match its original shape or simply follow the forces applied to it. The [0] for goalActive and goalWeight is a note that these attributes are for the first element in the particle array (they thus apply to the whole group).

As you can see, by adjusting the goalWeight[0] from its default 0.5, you will gain much more subtle control over goal weights. If you turn the goal weight up to 1, the soft body will no longer sag; it will now perfectly match the original shape. If you turn the goal weight down to 0, the soft body will fall away from the sphere; this is the same as turning off the goalActive attribute. Low numbers make the soft body react strongly to gravity; high numbers make it hold its original shape well. Try changing goalWeight's numbers, and then see how this changes playback.

Now, try changing the Goal Smoothness attribute. This affects how smoothly and quickly the soft body attempts to reach its goal shape and position. The higher this number, the smoother or "bouncier" the animation of the soft body as it reaches its goal. It will also take longer to achieve that shape. Select the sphere, try entering a Goal Smoothness of 2 from the default of 3, and notice how the ball snaps into its place rather quickly after sagging only a little bit. Now try a higher number such as 3.5, and you'll notice the ball sag all the way to the ground plane and bounce up and down, deforming itself. The deformations occur when the soft body hits the plane, which causes the particles to bounce up, turning the sphere inside and out. If your soft-body sphere does not reach the floor, increase the Goal Smoothness value (see Figure 24.6).

Changing the Shape of a Soft Body

Now let's try changing the original shape and see how the soft body reacts. Follow these steps:

1. Be sure your goal weight is about 0.3.

2. Be sure you select the original shape (nurbsSphere1—not nurbsSphere1Copy!), and scale this shape out in the X axis. When you play back the animation, you will see the soft body stretch to fit the new shape of the sphere; it will overextend, however (as its goal weight isn't 1), and will "jiggle" back and forth until it finally nears the sphere's new shape, as shown in Figure 24.7.

3. Change the scale of the original shape back to 1, and then keyframe a Z rotation to the original sphere (try rotating it about 500 degrees in 40 frames). Now, as the animation plays back, the soft-body shape will "balloon" out, as shown in Figure 24.8, because each particle is being driven away from the original shape by centrifugal force. When the original sphere stops rotating, the soft-body shape will oscillate until it adjusts back to the goal shape.

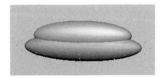

Figure 24.7

A soft body (below) trying to match the shape of a distorted sphere

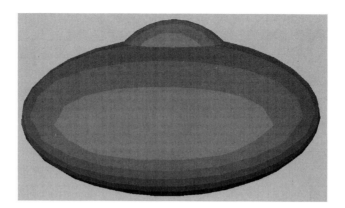

Figure 24.8

A soft body (below) ballooning out from a spinning sphere

If you think this image looks like a UFO and want to save the soft body (and original sphere) as a model, simply select the sphere and soft body, choose Edit → Duplicate ❑, make sure the Duplicate Upstream Graph option is *not* on, and duplicate the object. There's more on how to model using soft bodies later in the chapter.

By now, you should start to see what a fun and powerful tool soft bodies can be, so let's kick things up a notch. Not only can you adjust the soft body's goal weight as a whole, you can do so on a per-particle basis.

First, set your object goal weight (goalWeight[0]) to 1. With the particle node selected, in the Attribute Editor's Per Particle (Array) Attributes section, you will see a new per-particle attribute called goalPP. This attribute controls the goal weight of each particle individually, just as the other per-particle attributes do.

Now you need to set your object goal weight to 1 because the object goal weight is multiplied by the particle goal weight (if a particle goal weight is 0.5 and the object goal weight is 0.6, the final goal weight of the particle will be 0.3). If the object goal weight is not 1, there will be some "play" in the entire object, and you will not see the results pictured in the next section.

Adjusting Goal Weights Using the Component Editor

Let's explore how to adjust goal weights using the Component Editor with our spherical soft body. Follow these steps:

1. First, select the particle node again if it's not already selected (click copyOfnurbs-Sphere1Particle in the Outliner or Hypergraph). Then, in the Per Particle (Array) Attributes section in the Attribute Editor, RM click in the text field next to the goalPP attribute and choose Component Editor. (You can also open this editor by choosing Window → General Editors → Component Editor.) A window pops up that lets you control the value of any selected attributes.

2. With the Component Editor open, move back into the scene window, and then switch to Select By Component mode and turn off all components but points.

To change to Select By Component Type, click the Component Type button on the top toolbar (a cube with an arrow pointing at it), or press the F8 key. To turn off all types but points, choose All Components Off in the pop-up menu next to the button, and then click the Points button next to the menu (the black square), or RM on the sphere for the marking menu and choose Particle.

3. Your sphere should now have a cloud of blue-purple points around it. Select half the points on the sphere (the top, say), and, in the Particles tab, select the entire goalPP column (Shift+click the top and bottom entries), and change all entries to a value such as 0.2, as shown in Figure 24.9. When you play your animation, the top half should spin away from the original sphere while the bottom half stays put, as in Figure 24.10.

As an exercise, try using what you learned in the previous chapter to create an expression that randomizes the goal weight. If you can't figure it out, keep reading.

Using Goal Weights to Create Fluid Motion

One of the primary benefits of using soft bodies is the ability to create realistic flexion in objects. Rather than have to keyframe individual points on a model to get this illusion, you can simply manipulate the goal weights of a soft body to do so. Let's put aside our sphere test project for a moment and create a new one, but save the sphere project for use later in the chapter. Follow these steps:

1. In a new scene, create a nice, long, skinny cylinder without end caps (a tentacle, if you will), make sure it's standing on its end and that it has about 20 spans, and animate it to move side to side on the X axis. (Try to make the motions occur at different speeds, including some very rapid motions.) Then make the cylinder a soft body, this time hiding the original object and setting the Goal Weight to 1. You should end up with something that looks like Figure 24.11.

Figure 24.9

The goal weights adjusted for selected particle points

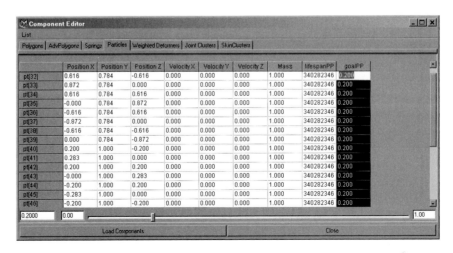

Figure 24.10

The top half of the soft body (with lower goal weights) balloons out, while the lower half (with high goal weights) stays fixed on the original sphere.

2. When you play the animation, the (invisible) cylinder will move, forcing the soft body to follow. Because the soft body's Goal Weight is currently 1, it will move in perfect synch with the original shape—not very exciting yet. Now let's create an expression to alter the goal weights based on where each particle is. Select the particle object and open the Attribute Editor. RM choose Creation Expression in the text field next to the particle's goalPP attribute.

3. In the Expression Editor, type the following:

```
float $scaling = 0.9;
float $offset = 0.1;

vector $pos = copyOfnurbsCylinder1ParticleShape.position;
float $posY = $pos.y;

copyOfnurbsCylinder1ParticleShape.goalPP =
    ((($posY + 1) / 2) * $scaling) + $offset;
```

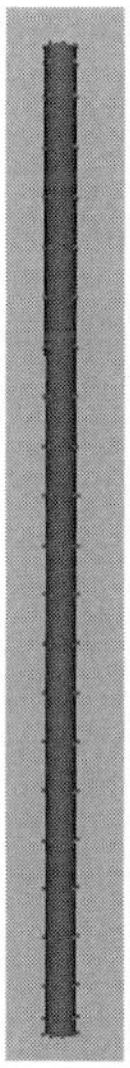

Figure 24.11

A soft-body tentacle

Most of the components of this expression are simply variable definitions. The one line that actually does something (the last line) tells Maya to assign each particle its goal weight based on how far to the right it is on the cylinder. The first two lines define a scaling and an offset constant. These variables adjust the range of values that the bottom equation will produce (in this case, 0.9 adjusts the range of goal weights to 0–0.9 instead of 0–1) and the offset of the values (in this case, the range will be 0.1–1.0 instead of 0–0.9). The next two lines read the (vector) particle position into a variable, *$pos*. This variable's Y component is then read into another variable, *$posY*. The reason we read in the cylinder's Y position instead of its X position is that, although the cylinder is lying on its side, its Y axis is still along its long axis, and thus the Y axis of the cylinder is the X axis in world space.

> You cannot directly read a single element (such as the Y component) of a vector attribute (such as position) into a scalar (float) variable. Thus, you must first read the value into a vector variable and then take that variable's Y component and read it into another, scalar, variable.

The final line of the equation grabs the relative position of each particle (which is always between –1 and 1) and renormalizes it to a range of 0 to 1. The scaling and offset values are then used to further refine the range of goal weight values. When you run the animation, on the first frame, each particle is assigned a goal weight between 0.1 and 1, and then, depending on your cylinder's animation characteristics, the tentacle or "tail" will waggle more the farther to the right you go on the cylinder, as in Figure 24.12.

4. If your Component Editor is still open, you can look at the value of each particle by highlighting it (in Component mode), selecting the Particles tab, and reading the goalPP value in the last column.

We could, of course, have manually adjusted all the goal weights using the Component Editor, but it's sometimes nice to have Maya do the math for us. In this case, it would probably be just as fast to use the Component Editor to change the goal weights, but our expression gives us the ability (via the *$scaling* and *$offset* variables) to quickly play with the numbers to get the characteristics we want. Additionally, given a more complex shape with more points that are closer together, the previous expression is far faster than adjusting goal weights by hand. In short, use whichever way will prove faster and more flexible for your situation.

In addition, you can paint goal weights directly onto objects such as this tail using Artisan's Paint Attribute tool. For more information on this tool, see Chapter 7, "Working with Artisan," or the advanced tutorial on hair at the end of this chapter. Also, for more on expressions, see Chapter 23, "Using Particle Expressions, Ramps, and Volumes."

Figure 24.12

A soft-body cylinder with variable goal weights

Adding Springs to Soft Bodies

If you created violent motion on your cylinder in the last section, you probably noticed that, when you played back the animation, the right end of your "tentacle" looked more like a flimsy piece of clay than a tail or an octopus arm, because it stretched all over the place. In more formal terms, the soft body did not maintain its length or overall volume; it didn't have a kind of "bone" structure inside it, helping it to maintain these two properties. Even more obvious, each part of the tentacle looked separate; what was going on at the bottom had no effect on the middle or the top—not a good simulation of a tail! This is where Maya *springs* come in. They act (for the most part) just like little springs between each particle, helping them to maintain their shape better under the stress of violent motion and allowing the motion of one particle to affect the motion of others.

Use your project from the last section (or, if you're not happy with that project, open the `24tentacle` file on the CD-ROM), and follow these steps

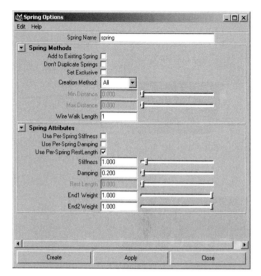

Figure 24.13

The Spring Options dialog box

1. Select your soft-body shape in the scene window, and then choose Soft/Rigid Bodies → Create Springs ❑ to open the Spring Options dialog box, shown in Figure 24.13.

2. In the Spring Methods section, set Creation Method to All (all particles are connected). You can leave all the other areas of this dialog box in their default state. Click the Create button, and then close the window.

3. You will see a huge mess of dark dots (springs) covering your cylinder. As you play the animation, you will see the springs stretching and contracting to keep the cylinder moving in a more natural, connected motion, as in Figure 24.14. Once you see how the springs work, you might want to hide them to prevent screen clutter.

You can create per-spring (PS) attributes for Stiffness, Damping, Rest Length, and End Weights. If you don't create per-spring attributes, Maya uses per-object attributes, just as with particles. Although we won't discuss modifying springs on a per-spring basis, the method is the same as for per-particle attributes, and the results can be extremely subtle and beautiful.

With springs selected, you can (in the Channel Box or Attribute Editor) adjust the stiffness of the springs (how resistant to bending they are) and their damping (how quickly they come back to rest after they've been moved). Although very low stiffness and damping values make the tail play back as if no springs are attached, increasing stiffness and damping can often create the rigidity that makes an object such as ours appear to have a constant length.

4. Try moving the Damping up to about 0.4, and set the Stiffness to 1 or a bit higher to get the tentacle to bend a bit more stiffly and not stretch as much. If you're lucky, you'll see your animation play back as it should. If not, you'll see the simulation go out of control, as in Figure 24.15.

This bizarre behavior occurs because Maya can't calculate the solution given its sampling rate (once per frame is the default). The solution, if you want to keep the current damping and stiffness settings, is to increase the sampling rate to allow Maya to better calculate the motion of the springs.

Figure 24.14

A soft-body cylinder with springs

Figure 24.15

A soft-body cylinder with misbehaving springs

702 ■ CHAPTER 24: DYNAMICS OF SOFT BODIES

4. From the Dynamics menu set, choose Solvers → Edit Oversampling or Cache Settings. The Attribute Editor opens with one option: Oversampling Rate (which should currently be set to 1). Try setting this number to 2 and see if that fixes the simulation. If not, move up to 3, and so on. Once you have an animation that doesn't break, try playblasting it to see how much like a tentacle your cylinder looks. But be careful to increase the oversampling rate slowly—it will affect your playback times! Although Maya appears to work much more quickly with high sampling rates, the number you enter in the field is still related to how many times longer the simulation will take to play than if the rate were set to 1. So first increase by 1, and see if the simulation works; if not, increase it again by 1, and so on. Generally, very high values for Stiffness and Damping are not desirable anyway, so alter these numbers slowly as well.

As you can see, springs can really contribute to more realistic motion for soft bodies, so keep them in mind when your soft bodies look a bit too much like stretched clay!

The All creation method in springs creates a spring relationship between every particle in the soft body. Although this method seems the best way to go for a uniform structure—since each particle's movement will affect the movement of all the other particles in the soft body—using Wireframe or Min Max can yield similar results with far fewer calculations, resulting in faster scene playback and higher interactivity.

The Wireframe method sets up a spring relationship between particles along the wireframe mesh of the soft-body object. This creation method is controlled by the wire walk length attribute, which controls how far a spring extends from one particle to the others. A walk length of 1 sets springs to each particle's first closest neighbor on all sides. A walk length of 2 sets springs between the two closest neighbors on all sides. At higher settings, the object will have more structure, but there will be an added calculation cost because of the higher number of springs.

The Min Max creation method creates a distance range in which the selected particles are connected together.

Faking a Bounce

Although you can use rigid body objects as goals for soft bodies, at times, for control and accuracy (not to mention playback speed!), creating a bit of keyframed "dynamics" on your own can be advantageous.

1. Create a new scene with a ball and a plane, and then type the following expression for motion into the Expression Editor (or just use the 24bouncingBall file on the CD).

```
NurbsSphere1.translateY =
    1 + (10 * (1 - linstep(0, 300, frame)) * abs(cos(time)));
```

This equation makes the ball bounce (using the Cosine function) lower and lower, until the ball comes to rest (using the linstep function).

The method for creating a soft body with a rigid body goal is the same as the one described earlier for normal geometry, except that you have to check the Duplicate Upstream Graph check box in the Create Soft Body Options dialog box. If you don't do this, the soft body will just go along for the ride, as if it had a goal weight of 1.

The `linstep` function in the expression (and the similar `smoothstep`) is handy. You give it a starting and ending value (the start and end frame) and the "unit" it will be using (frames), and then the function moves between 0 and 1 over that range. In this example, the value output by `linstep` increases from 0 to 1 over the range of 0 to 300 frames.

Now we have a bouncing-ball motion. Let's add a soft body, adjust its goal weights, add some springs, and see what happens.

2. Add a soft body to the sphere (use the Duplicate, Make Copy Soft, Make Non-soft A Goal Object, and Hide Non-Soft Object options) and set its Weight to 1. We're making the copy a soft-body object as opposed to the original because the original has the input connections of the bouncing animation. Making the original the goal object will make the soft-body object bounce like the original, but also deform as a soft body.

3. Using the Component Editor (or the expression for goal weights given earlier), set the top points of the sphere to have a goal weight near 0.9, set the middle points to about 0.6, and set the bottom points to have a goal weight near 0.4. Keep playing with the values until you get a look something like Figure 24.16.

In playing back the animation, you should see the ball (the bottom especially) jiggle quite a bit as the ball falls to the ground, stretching up and down as it goes. Although this could be a useful effect in itself, let's add some springs to it to give the whole ball a more connected look.

4. Select the soft-body sphere and add springs to it using the wireframe creation option. Start with the wire walk length of 1, and play back the results. Then try increasing the wire walk length by 1 until you give it enough structure to bounce well.

When the ball bounces now, it reacts more connectedly, its sides moving in as the ball bounces away from the plane (thus imitating real-life squash and stretch by preserving volume), as shown in Figure 24.17. Additionally, the ball now wiggles much less, because the spring dampens the extra motion—of course, you can adjust setting using the Damping and Stiffness controls. The bottom of the ball is still rather jiggly though.

Now delete the existing springs and re-create them using the All option. Notice the ball still behaves relatively the same, but the playback runs slightly slower than before. Using a wireframe creation method with a wire walk length of about 2 or 3 gives us the desired results, but a little more efficiently.

One last thing to check out with these springs is using the Rest Length setting (in the Channel Box or the Attribute Editor). First, be sure the restLengthPS check box is set to off,

Figure 24.16

A deformed bouncing ball

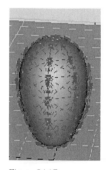

Figure 24.17

A deformed bouncing ball with springs

and then try adjusting the rest length. If you set the number to 0, the ball will shrink dramatically; whereas if you set the value to 5 or 6, the ball will expand. The rest length tells the springs how far apart they should be when "resting" (in other words, when they're not being moved by forces or collisions), so the larger the number in the field, the bigger the distance between springs (and thus points), and thus the larger the sphere.

One great feature of springs is that you can place them between standard particles (not just soft bodies). You can connect a stream of emitter particles to form an interacting group, enabling you to produce anything from a simulation of molecules in a room to a "blob" that can shoot across the screen. For more information on adding springs to standard particles, see the "Springs" topic in the Maya online reference. You can also look at an animation of particles connected by springs on the CD: 24cloudSprings.mov.

Denting Soft Bodies

To see how you can use soft bodies for modeling as well as animation, we're going to look at two ways to create an asteroid: first by using a Turbulence field to distort a sphere, and then by using an emitter to bombard the sphere with particles. Follow these steps:

1. Open a new scene and create a sphere with about 32 spans and sections (so that the soft body will have lots of points on it). If you want, you can stretch the sphere up a bit, as shown in Figure 24.18, since no one ever heard of a perfectly round asteroid!

Save this project now as a separate file, because we'll use the sphere again when we create the asteroid using a particle emitter.

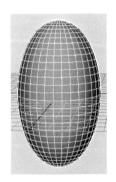

Figure 24.18

A scaled sphere with 32 spans

2. With the sphere selected, choose Soft/Rigid Bodies → Create Soft Body □. In the Soft Options dialog box, set the Creation Options to Make Soft and create the body. Choosing Make Soft tells Maya to convert the original object to a soft body (there will no longer be any original geometry). Because there is no goal object, there is no goal weighting for this type of soft body.

3. Now, with the new soft body selected, choose Fields → Turbulence □. Reset the defaults (choose Edit → Reset Settings), set Magnitude (the force of the turbulence) to about 5 and Frequency (the number of "waves" of turbulence) to about 20, and create the field. As you play the animation, you will see the sphere distort under the influence of the Turbulence field. Since there is no goal weight to bring the sphere back, the sphere will distort too much if the animation plays back too long. Try a few settings for magnitude and frequency, and stop the animation at a frame where you like the look of your new asteroid, as in Figure 24.19.

4. Now that you have the shape, getting it to be a permanent model is as easy as duplicating the object. With the soft body selected, choose Edit → Duplicate ❐. In the option window, reset the default values, making sure Duplicate Upstream Graph is *off*, and then duplicate the object by clicking the Duplicate button. Voilà, one ready-built asteroid!

If you were to duplicate the upstream graph (the input connections), Maya would create another soft body that would then change with the Turbulence field. By turning this option off, you create the model as a standard node with no history. If you see a group of points when you move your duplicate copy (the duplicate soft-body points), you can simply delete them.

5. You can now either delete the original shape or alter its shape and the magnitude and frequency of the Turbulence field to make a few more asteroids.

Now that we've used a field to create an asteroid, let's try using an emitter plus a field (emulating lots of little meteorite collisions) to do the same thing. Follow these steps:

1. Open your original sphere, and make it a soft body, using the Duplicate, Make Copy Soft option, checking the Make Non-Soft A Goal box, and setting the goal weight to 0 (or some low number such as 0.2).

2. Create an emitter that shoots particles at a rate of about 50 toward the sphere. Figure 24.20 shows the particles being shot at the sphere.

3. Deselect any objects and choose Fields → Air ❐. In the options window, click the Wind button, and then set the Magnitude to 20, the Directions X, Y, and Z to –1, –0.1, –0.1, respectively. Be sure Use Max Distance is on, set it to 1; then click Create.

4. With the field still selected, Shift+select the particles (not the emitter) and choose Fields → Use Selected As Source Of Field. Next, select the sphere soft body, open the Dynamic Relationships Editor (Window → Relationship Editors → Dynamic Relationships) and highlight the Air field, connecting it with the particles. You will now have an Air field that is owned by the particle group (the icon will move along with the particles if you play the animation). However, if you now play back the animation, you will notice that the Air field affects only the particles on the sphere as the actual fan icon passes by, which is not what we're after here.

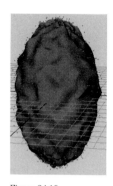

Figure 24.19

A sphere distorted by turbulence

USING LATTICES AS SOFT BODIES

You can also turn lattices into soft bodies as opposed to using the object's geometry. As an exercise, try adding a lattice shape to your original sphere, turning the lattice into a soft body and then adding a Turbulence field to the lattice. How does this alter the way the distorted sphere looks? You might like the results better. Using a lattice also makes it easier to calculate the deformations, since not as many points as the original geometry are used for the soft bodies.

Figure 24.20

Emitter shooting particles at a sphere

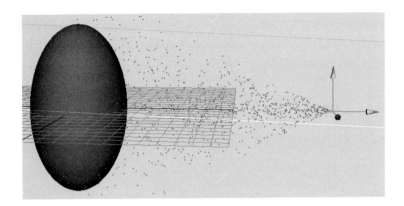

5. To alter this behavior, select the Air field, and, in the Attribute Editor, open the Special Effects section and check the Apply Per Vertex option, which now attaches the wind to each particle, rather than to the particle group as a whole. Because the Use Max Distance setting is on and because the distance is only 1 unit, each particle will create a little "ball" of wind around it that will affect any object connected to it.

Because the particles now strike the sphere, it will distort—probably more than you want it to! Never fear; we can use random goal weights to fix that problem.

6. With the soft body's particle node (copyOfnurbsSphere1Particle) selected, open the Attribute Editor. Under Per Particle (Array) Attributes, RM click the text field next to goalPP, choose Create Expression, and type the following expression. (Try adjusting the numbers in this code for different effects.)

```
goalPP = rand (0.3, 0.6);
```

This expression simply sets the goal weights of the soft body's particles to a random number between 0.3 and 0.6. Now, as the particles (plus their Air field) pass through the sphere, different parts of the sphere will react in differing amounts to the Air field, creating a more interesting look to the distortion. But you will need to set the Goal Weight[0] to 1 for this effect to work properly. Also, you will need to increase the Magnitude of the Air field to about 500 to see results.

7. To get an even spread of dents, try rotating the sphere around its Y axis twice (720 degrees) over about 200 frames (select the sphere, and then key its Y rotation value between 0 and 720).

One last adjustment we can make is to force the particles to collide with the sphere. You might have noticed that, now, the particles pass through the sphere and dent it outward on the far side of the object—not what a meteorite collision would do!

8. Select the emitted particles first, Shift-select the original sphere (nurbsSphere1, not copyOfnurbsSphere1), and then choose Particles → Make Collide. Now, when the particles strike the sphere, they bounce off, creating only dents, not stretches in the sphere.

> You can make a couple of adjustments to fine-tune your collisions: (1) try increasing the magnitude of the wind force to about 1000; (2) change the value of the resilience for the collision, and see what different values produce. A low resilience will keep the particles around the sphere longer, creating deeper pits.

Although playback can be a bit slow with fields and collisions turned on, you can do millions of years of damage to your asteroid in just minutes! Figure 24.21 shows a banged-up asteroid.

To create a permanent model from your new asteroid, simply stop on a frame you like and duplicate the object, as we did earlier. As you can see, using soft bodies can be a fast way to create organic, or beat-up, shapes.

Hands On: Painting Goal Weights on Hair

In earlier chapters of this book, we created a head complete with locks of hair. As you might have noticed, however, this hair did not move around realistically if you moved the head about. To solve this problem, we're going to create soft bodies out of all the strands of hair and then paint appropriate goal weights on each strand to get the ends to flow around as the head moves. Follow these steps:

Figure 24.21

An asteroid dented by particles

1. Open your head project file, or open `24hair` off the CD-ROM. If you open your own project, make sure all the elements of the head are children of the main head node and then animate the head so it rotates around a couple of axes. (We'll use this motion to see how our hair reacts as we adjust it.) If you use the CD project file, some animation is already included—feel free to alter this.

2. Rather than create and paint each soft-body strand of hair separately, we're going to save some time by working with the whole head at once. Using the Hypergraph, select all the hair on the left side of the model (all the nodes beneath the hair1 node), as in Figure 24.22. Do *not* just select the hair1 node, or you will not be allowed to create a soft body.

3. Now Shift+select the hair strands on the other side of the head, and then choose Soft/Rigid Bodies → Create Soft Body ❐. Select the Duplicate, Make Copy Soft option, make the non-soft object a goal, hide the original geometry, and set the goal weight to 1. You will see a mess of bounding boxes, as shown in Figure 24.23. Maya has created a soft body for each hair strand.

4. With all the soft bodies still selected, choose Deform → Create Cluster from the Animation menu set, creating a cluster that contains all the soft-body particles.

5. Now return to the Hypergraph and drag-select all the soft bodies. Once you have all the elements selected, choose Soft/Rigid Bodies → Paint Soft Body Weights Tool ❑ to open Artisan's options for the paint soft bodies tool (Figure 24.24).

6. If the boy's hair turns white, you are almost ready to begin painting on goal weights. If not, choose the Display section, turn Show Wireframe off, and turn on Color Feedback (also be sure the Min and Max Colors are set to 0 and 1 respectively). If all the hair objects are still not turning white, you're in for a little bit of tedium, but it's necessary. Under the Paint Attributes section of the Soft Body Weights Tool Settings window, you'll see a bar button with the name of one of the hair objects selected. Click that bar to display Particle > and then a context menu with a listing of all the selected hair objects GoalPP value attributes. As you select each one down the list, it should turn white in your work window, making it ready for painting. This issue may or may not arise depending on your video card. By selecting each of the goalPPs from the menu, you force Maya to display their goalPP weight, thereby turning them white. Now you can interactively paint all the hair objects together.

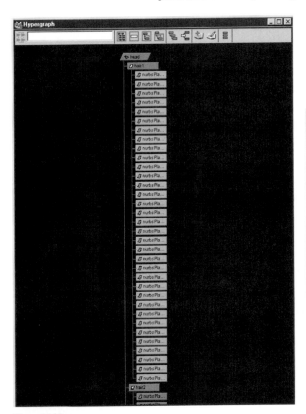

Figure 24.22

Selecting hair strands

Figure 24.23

The hair, converted into soft bodies

A tablet can be useful for painting weights. If you have one, set the Stylus Pressure to Both (radius and opacity) in the Stroke tab.

7. We're almost ready here! Set the opacity of the brush to a low value such as 0.4, set the Value to about 0.7, and set the Paint Operation to Replace. When you paint now, your brush will (slowly, because of the opacity setting) change the particle goal weights from 1 (solid white) to a minimum of 0.7 (a light gray). A goal weight of 0.7 is still fairly high, so the hair will not flop around greatly. You can, of course, go back and set Value lower (or higher) and repaint to get the effect you're after.

8. Go to the scene window now, and paint a darker color (lower goalPP value) on to the tips of the hair strands around the boy's head, as shown in Figure 24.25. If, after you have painted around the head, you discover that you have trouble getting to a hair that's underneath others, you can deselect the group of soft bodies, select only the hair you want (plus the cluster node), and paint that strand of hair. Remember that you're going for subtlety here: you don't want big chunks of hair that are a very dark color, or they will fly off the head and stretch in odd ways. Just a little gray (lower goalPP values) goes a long way toward making effective hair. Remember to test-animate and repaint hair as necessary.

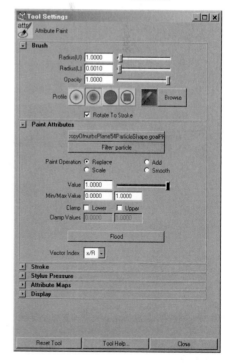

Figure 24.24

Modify the soft body attributes.

If you start deselecting and reselecting soft bodies, you are likely to run into a "feature" of the Paint Attributes tool: the attribute being painted (in this case, the goalPP attribute) becomes deselected when you switch the objects you paint on. You need to reselect the goalPP attribute for each strand before you can return to painting.

If you are happy with the hair you have working now, feel free to leave the project as it is. If you want to try a few more tricks to get even better hair, you can add gravity to the scene (be sure the soft bodies are selected first) to make the hair fall toward the ground. You can also create a collision between the head and strands of hair, so the hair won't pene-trate the head. Finally, you can add springs to the hair, which will give each strand more structure—you may find you need to paint on lower goal weights when springs are applied. Also, bear in mind that adding collision detection and springs will substantially increase the calculations required and thus slow down playback. The best advice (as always) is to try the simpler methods first and add more complex elements such as collisions and springs only as needed.

You can check out a render of the boy and hair (including springs, collisions, and gravity) on the CD: 24hair.mov.

Figure 24.25

The boy's hair, with goal weights painted on

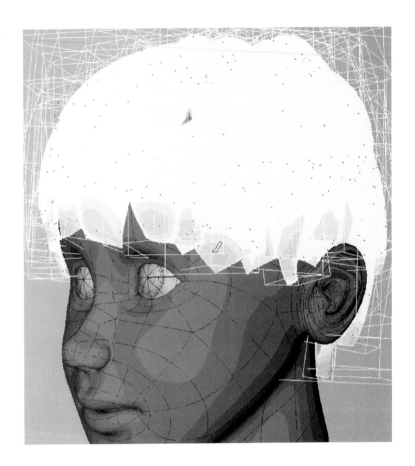

Advanced Hands On: Adding Ripples to the Fountain Project

If you thought we were finished with the fountain project after the previous three chapters, guess again. We have been leaving out an important part of our animation: the plane that the water drops strike. In real life, of course, the water in a fountain is agitated from the water that constantly falls on it—not like our flat and unassuming plane at all. To correct this, we'll make the plane a soft body and let the particles "collide" with it by having them carry an Air field with them, just as we did earlier with the asteroid.

1. Open your fountain project from the previous chapter (or use `23fountain` on the CD-ROM). Select the plane, go to makeNurbsPlane1, and then increase the U and V patches to about 50 so there will be more points for the soft body you will create, as in Figure 24.26. For a more accurate simulation, you can increase this number, but remember that Maya will slow to a crawl on all but the fastest computers, even at this setting. It's going to have to do a ton of calculations for each point on the grid!

Creating the large number of particle collisions in this project can be time-consuming. If you don't have a fast computer, you might want to just read through this section—or attach an Air field to the first group of particles.

2. Once your plane is subdivided, make a soft body out of it, using the Duplicate, Make Copy Soft option and setting the Goal Weight to 0.4. Once the plane is a soft body, you need to add an Air field to particles 1 and 2. Select the soft body particle group, create an Air field to affect them, and then do it again to create a second air field to affect them, as well. Set the Magnitude of these fields to about 500, the X and Z directions to 0.5, and the Y direction to –1. Select each field, make sure Apply Per Vertex is on as well as the Use Max Distance in the Channel Box or Attribute Editor, and then set the Max Distance for the first field to about 1; set the Max Distance for the second field to about 0.5 so that these particles make smaller "splashes." Once the Air fields are created, you will make the existing water particles become the emitters of these fields. Select the first Air field and then particle1, and choose Fields → Use Selected As Source Of Field. Select the second field and particle2, and do the same. The fields now become children of their respective particle objects. See Figure 24.27.

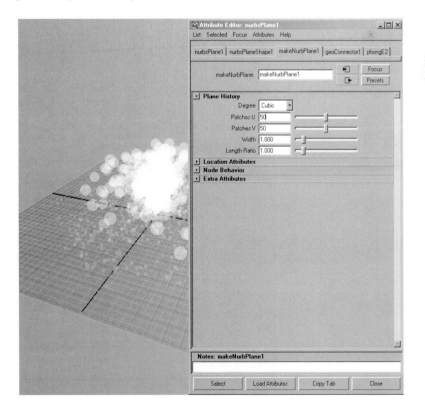

Figure 24.26

Increasing the U and V patches to increase surface density for the splashes

3. You can now play back your animation. You may find, however, that the playback speed is so slow that it is difficult to see the motion of the particles and waves. To compensate for this, either playblast (choose Windows ➜ Playblast) or hardware-render the scene.

4. When you can view the motion of the plane, you should see reasonably good results as in Figure 24.28. Each collision "dent," however, simply exists on its own; the waves don't connect and move. To solve this, we need—you guessed it—springs (as if playback weren't slow enough already!). Here is where the real compromises begin. It would be ideal to create springs between all particles; however, unless you have a beastly computer with lots of RAM, this will not be possible, because the process of creating springs will generate a memory error (there is not enough memory to create all the springs needed). Instead, try creating springs with the wireframe creation setting and a walk length of 1 or 2 (so that each particle is connected only to its nearest neighbor or two). If you have a fast computer with lots of RAM (512MB or so), try using a Min/Max setting, with a minimum spacing of about 0.1 (or just 0) and a max of about 2. This will produce better results, because more particles are connected, but it will be slower than the wireframe choice.

5. The waves will not propagate outward fully now, but the effect will still be better than it was. Set the Damping value of the springs very low (at 0.05 or lower) so that the waves continue moving after the collision, and set the Stiffness to a middle value such as 0.6. When you look at your playblast or hardware render of the scene, notice how the waves interact with one another and with the particles. If they don't look good enough to you, try adjusting the springs' stiffness and damping, as well as Air field Magnitude and Max Distance. With some patience and experimentation, it is possible to get some good-looking results.

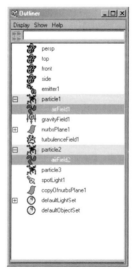

Figure 24.27

Particle objects set as sources for the air fields

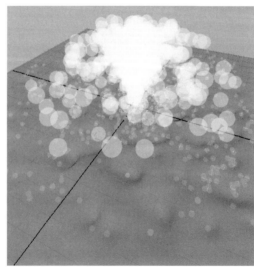

Figure 24.28

Dents in the water caused by air fields emitted from the water droplets

A final render of this scene, complete with Paint Effects trees and rocks, is available on the CD-ROM (`24fountain.mov`), and a still frame of this shot is included in the color section.

When creating complex dynamics simulations involving soft bodies—and especially springs—the art of a successful project often lies in compromising between the best settings and those that aren't quite as accurate but get the job done on deadline. If, for example, this fountain was a background element of your scene, it would make no sense to create such a time-consuming, accurate simulation. Simply make the plane a soft body, and add a Turbulence field to simulate ripples. By contrast, if the fountain will be the center of attention, it is probably worth the effort to create this effect, because the inaccuracy of a simple Turbulence field will call attention to itself. You, the artist, must decide where perfection and efficiency meet in these situations.

Advanced Hands On: Creating a Watery Body and Face

For this tutorial, we're going to use a long neck with a face attached to the end of it. In the steps that follow, we're going to make this figure a soft body and then animate the face and goal weights, creating an effect similar to the ground-breaking effect in the film, *The Abyss*. The techniques we use here are a culmination of many of the particle and soft-body lessons you have learned throughout the past four chapters, and you can apply them in a number of similar animation scenarios.

1. Open the file `24abyssDeformed` on the CD-ROM. If you play back this scene, you will see the "pseudopod" move in a bending path toward you, the face finally looking at you.

2. Let's now use some blend shapes to alter the face's expressions (two blend shapes are built into the CD-ROM file). As the face moves through the tube, shut its eyes, and give it a neutral expression. When it stops (after about frame 160), have it go through two or three more expressions, and then return it to neutral by the end of the animation (about 400 frames).

> If you want your file complete with blend shapes and lighting, use the `24abyssBlended` file on the CD-ROM.

3. Now for the soft-body stuff. We're going to turn the whole pseudopod into a soft body, adjust the goal weights on it, add a Turbulence field to it, and then animate the goal weights to make the face pop out of the pseudopod. First, drag a selection marquee around the entire body without the deformer; then make it a soft body with Duplicate, Make Copy Soft, and give it a Goal Weight of 1 (we'll adjust individual goal weights later—if you opened `24abyssBlended`, this step is done for you already). Test the soft body to be sure it animates properly. (If not, go back to the saved version and try again.) Because the Goal Weight is currently set to 1, the animation should look the same as before.

4. This is where things get tricky (it's an advanced tutorial, after all). Because the head is constructed of several (eight, to be exact) objects and because we need to vary the goal weight, we need to control all of them via an expression that we'll cut and paste into each particle shape's goalPP attribute. First, however, find the two cylinder pieces, and change their global Goal Weight values to 0.5. They will be at this goal weight constantly, so we don't need to do anything further with them.

5. Now, type the following in the Expression Editor, and copy it so that you can paste it into all eight `goalPP` runtime expressions.

```
float $goalStart = 0.6;
float $goalUp = (0.6 * smoothstep (181, 190, frame)) + 0.25;
float $goalDown = (0.6 * (1 - smoothstep (361, 385, frame))) + 0.25;

if (frame <=180)
   {
   goalPP = $goalStart;
   }
else if ((frame >180) && (frame <=360))
   {
   goalPP = $goalUp;
   }
else goalPP = $goalDown;
```

This expression sets the goal weight of each particle based on the current frame. Early in the animation (during the pseudopod's motion), the goal weight is lower. In the middle, during the facial expressions, the weight is higher, rising using a `smoothstep` function. At the end, again, the weight is lowered back down using a `smoothstep` function.

> You could also control the goal weight for each segment of the face by keying the per-object goal weight. This technique is more intuitive, but it requires keyframing eight objects. Use the method that seems easier to you.

6. Now that the goal weights are animated, let's add a bit of turbulence. Drag-select all the soft bodies, and then choose Fields → Turbulence ❐. Set Magnitude to about 60, Attenuation to 0, Frequency to a high number such as 100 or so (this will make for smaller waves), leave Phase at 0, and set Use Max Distance to off. As a final touch, we parented the Air field to one of the head soft bodies so that the turbulence would travel along with the form. You might like the turbulence to stay in one place while the figure moves through it; try both ways and see which you prefer.

7. If you like your animation, all that's really left is to create and apply a water texture. Try creating a PhongE shader with a pale blue color (almost white), slightly roughened, but tight and bright specular colors, and a good deal of transparency (only the highlights of water really show well). You might also add a background image or geometry and set the shader to have a refraction and reflection so that it looks more like water.

A finished movie is available on the CD-ROM as `24waterHead.mov`, and you can see a rendered still in the color section of this book.

> For more on how to create materials, see Chapter 16, "Rendering Basics."

This animation (like the fountain we developed earlier) should take you a good deal of time to get right. These projects are the culmination of your understanding of the entire Maya dynamics package, so, when you finish, congratulate yourself on a job well done!

Summary

In this chapter, you learned what soft bodies are, how to create them, and how to use them for everything from simple animation effects, to modeling, to adding the final touches to complex projects. As a group of particles that act as a whole, soft bodies are a unique blend of form and motion, allowing us to create effects that would otherwise be so difficult to do correctly that we probably wouldn't even try. Although this chapter has only begun to reveal the power of Maya dynamics, we hope that you now have enough knowledge and the confidence to continue experimenting and working on your own. Think of something you always wanted to animate that has clouds of dust or jiggling, organic figures in it. Now go on and create that animation!

CHAPTER 25

Fluid Effects

Fluid Effects, which is new for Maya 4.5 Unlimited, is a striking combination of the insanely complex and the sublimely simple. At its heart, Fluid Effects (except for the Ocean Effects portion) is based on the famous Navier-Stokes equation for viscous fluid flow, one of the most complex formulas from nineteenth-century classical physics. This complexity, however, is wrapped in a "drag-and-drop" package that is so simple to use, just about anyone can create jaw-dropping effects with no effort by using Maya's built-in presets. If, however, you want to go beyond the presets and start playing with Fluid Effects' attributes, you will quickly run up against 400+ adjustable parameters, which can be quite overwhelming if you don't know where to start.

That is where this chapter comes in. Although Fluid Effects is far too large to cover in detail in just one chapter, with some knowledge of which attributes to alter to get different effects, you will soon be able to create or modify Fluid Effects to your specifications with a solid understanding of what you're doing and why. Maya's research engineers have spent a great deal of time creating this package and making it simple to use, so get ready to put flowing fluids and ocean surfaces on your demo reel!

This chapter includes:

- **Introduction to fluids**

- **Drag-and-drop Fluid Effects**

- **Creating and editing a simple 2D fluid, a simple 3D fluid, and a simple ocean effect**

- **Hands on: creating a coffee cup with 2D and 3D fluids**

What Is a Fluid (and What Isn't It)?

Maya Fluid Effects actually comprises two independent entities: 2D/3D Fluids and Ocean Effects. The 2D/3D Fluids entity runs a simulation engine, similar to Maya's particles engine, to find fluid flow, but Ocean Effects is actually a combination of displacement mapping and complex texturing, plus particles, to simulate the surface of an ocean or other large body of water. Thus, although 2D/3D Fluids is a fluid simulator, Ocean Effects is not. While Ocean Effects is not simulated, you can still do quasi-simulated effects such as floating objects on the ocean's surface, moving objects around like boats, and even raising and sinking objects (using buoyancy) through the surface.

In order for Fluid Effects to actually run the simulation engine, you must set at least Density and Velocity to Dynamic in the Fluid Effects Attributes section of the Attribute Editor. If these attributes are set to Static, the engine calculates them once (for the initial state) and never again.

Fluid Effects, on the other hand, is an actual simulator. Thus you can fully simulate the motion of gases and fluids (such as lava), collide the fluids with objects, and alter their properties by adding heat, fuel, and other elements. To control the massive computational work it takes to simulate fluid flow, Fluid Effects only exists in a space defined by the fluid container (as shown in Figure 25.1)—a rectangle for 2D fluids or a box for 3D fluids.

Figure 25.1

A 2D fluid container (left) and a 3D fluid container (right)

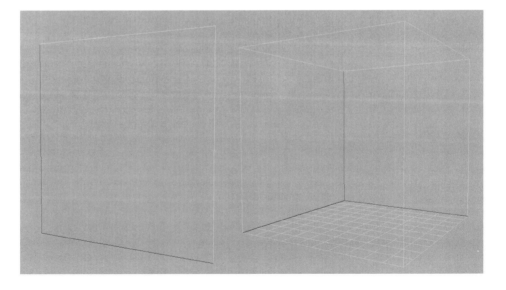

The rectangle or box is then subdivided into a grid (like a checkerboard for the 2D fluid) in which each square (2D fluids) or cube (3D fluids) defines what is known as a *voxel,* or volume pixel. The more voxels you set for your fluid simulation space, the more detailed your simulation—but the slower it will run, because more voxels require more calculations per frame for the simulation. In a 2D fluid, if you double the grid defining the voxels in both directions, you quadruple the number of calculations that have to be performed (2^2); in a 3D fluid, if you double the grid in each direction, you increase the calculations by a factor of 8 (2^3). Obviously, then, creating an adequate simulation with the minimum number of voxels is important in order to save computation time. Fortunately, Fluid Effects, especially for 2D fluids, is very fast, allowing fairly complex systems to be simulated in near real time.

Although you might assume that a 2D fluid would not be particularly useful for 3D rendering, in actuality a 2D fluid container is simply a 3D fluid container that is around one voxel thick. Thus, 2D fluids actually have some depth, allowing for self-shadowing and other 3D effects. While the illusion of depth breaks down if the camera rotates around the container, for many effects in which the camera is still or merely zooming straight in or out, a 2D fluid works well indeed and is much faster to interact with and render than a 3D fluid.

So what can a 2D or 3D fluid simulate? Any single-fluid motion you wish! Clouds, explosions, smoke, fire, fog, lava, and mixing paint colors are just some of the things you can simulate—and with Maya's built-in presets, a generic version of most of these simulations is just a drag away, as discussed later in this chapter. In essence, Fluid Effects allows you to view and render out the density gradient of a set of fluid particles over time as they interact with one another, react to velocity, temperature, density, and other fields, and collide off surfaces and/or the container itself. You can view and render the results either as cloudlike volume renders, which can be texture mapped to taste, or as more substantial polygonal meshes that render as anything you want to texture them (water or lava, for example).

What Fluid Effects will not simulate (with "this version," according to Alias|Wavefront's documentation, indicating this may be possible with a later iteration of this package) are two or more fluid simulations. A situation such as water pouring into a glass, for example, is two-fluid simulations in which water (fluid 1) and air (fluid 2) interact. Because Fluid Effects currently allows simulation of only one fluid, a simulation like this is not possible, though with some "cheating" of the density gradient, you can fake the effect using a steep drop-off from one density (the "water") to the other (the "air"), similar to the way a fire effect is created. (See the Hands On section later in this chapter, specifically how the creamer is created, to find out how to do this.) Even with the single fluid restriction, Fluid Effects is remarkably useful for a range of effects, as noted earlier, and thus deserves a place in any animator's arsenal.

Finally, fluids are different from Maya's particles. While they both use some of the same kinds of simulation elements (for example, gravity, turbulence, and collisions), particles are calculated as separate points in space and thus do not interact with other particles, nor do they render as single objects (with the exception of blobby surfaces and clouds render types, which blend particles together when they are close together). Although particles are quick to calculate, they are poorly suited for viscous fluid simulations because they don't interact with one another; each particle behaving independently of all the others. Fluids in Fluid Effects, on the other hand, behave in more uniform large-scale ways because they are controlled by velocity (and other) gradients. Thus, Fluid Effects, while being slower to compute, are far better suited for situations (such as fire, water, or lava) in which the elements need to interact.

Particles actually can be influenced by fluids in a fluid container. Thus, particles can become part of a Fluid Effects simulation.

Here is a quick run-down of some of the most important fluid properties:

Density, which represents the material property of the fluid. You can think of density as fluid geometry.

Velocity, which affects the behavior of dynamic fluids, moving Density, Temperature, Fuel, and Color values. Velocity is required for dynamic fluid simulations. It has both magnitude and direction. For dynamic simulations, Velocity values are based on the forces you apply to the simulation. You can also use Velocity as a fixed force.

Temperature, which affects the behavior of a dynamic fluid via a gradient of temperatures in the container.

Fuel, which, combined with Density, creates a situation in which a reaction can take place. Density values represent the material, and Fuel values determine the state of the reaction. Temperature can "ignite" the Fuel to start a reaction (such as in an explosion). As the reaction unfolds, the Density and Fuel values dissipate until the reaction is over.

Color, which appears in a container only in which there is Density. You can apply color in two ways:

- Using the built-in ramp slider. A shader that is part of the fluid object makes it relatively simple to color your fluids object.
- Using a grid. A grid lets you control where color shows up in each voxel. Colors can behave dynamically so that they can mix.

We will cover all these fluid properties in more detail throughout this chapter.

Drag-and-Drop Fluids

The simplest way to create a Fluid Effect is to drop it into a scene from the Visor. In such cases, you get a pre-made simulation that runs well and looks good for any number of purposes without any work at all.

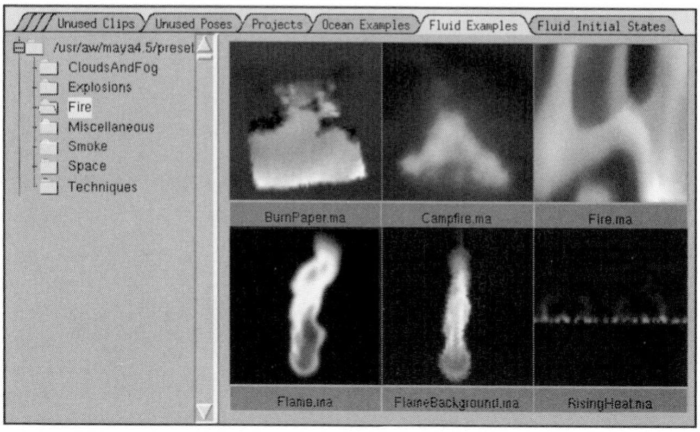

Figure 25.2

The Visor, showing various fire effects

To create a 2D fire effect, take the following steps.

1. Open a new scene in Maya.

2. Open the Visor (choose Windows → General Editors → Visor), or, alternatively, from the Dynamics menu set choose Fluid Effects → Get Fluid Example.

3. Select the Fluid Examples tab in the Visor (if it's not already highlighted), and click the Fire folder icon at the left (see Figure 25.2).

4. MM drag the `Campfire.ma` icon onto your scene window, and play forward several frames into the animation. You should see something similar to the left image in Figure 25.3.

5. Render out a test image (as shown on the right in Figure 25.3) to see your instant campfire!

This is a 2D fluid example, so if you rotate the camera around to the side, the illusion of depth will break down. From the front, however, this is a pretty convincing effect!

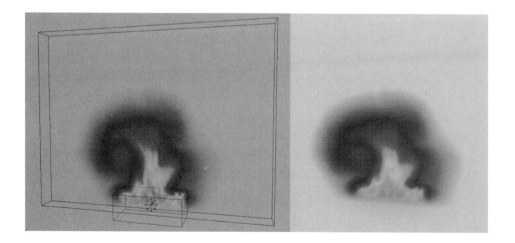

Figure 25.3

The campfire simulation shown in the Maya scene window (left) and in a final render (right)

To create a stormy ocean, take the following steps.

1. Open a new scene in Maya

2. Open the Visor (choose Windows → General Editors → Visor), or, alternatively, from the Dynamics menu set choose Fluid Effects → Get Ocean Shader Example.

3. Select the Ocean Examples tab in the Visor (if it's not already highlighted) to display the various ocean presets (shown in Figure 25.4).

Figure 25.4

The Visor, showing various Ocean Shader examples

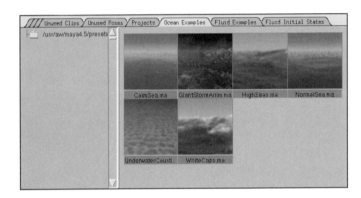

4. MM drag the `HighSeas.ma` file into your scene, and play the animation in your scene window. You should see something that looks like the left side of Figure 25.5.

5. Render out a test image from your animation to see a stormy ocean, complete with distance fog, displaced waves, and variable surface texturing, as shown on the right in Figure 25.5. If you have the time, try rendering out several frames to see the ocean swells in action.

Ocean Effects and 3D Fluid Effects simulations can take a long time to render due to the complex nature of their simulation, so be prepared to wait on renders, especially if you want to render at high quality or large size.

Figure 25.5

The High Seas ocean shader scene shown in the Maya scene window (left) and in a final render (right)

As you should be able to tell from these two simple examples, it is extremely easy to create highly realistic ocean and fluid simulations. Try dragging other example files into Maya to see what they do. If you select the fluid container (for Fluid Effects) or ocean surface (for Ocean Effects) and open the Attribute Editor, you can experiment with the parameters of these preset scenes.

When you've finished playing around with these scenes, proceed on to the following sections, in which we'll start from scratch instead of using a preset and show you how to create your own scenes. We'll also describe some of the more important attributes you can change to modify your scenes (or the included presets) to your specific needs.

Creating and Editing Fluids

Creating a 2D or 3D fluid from scratch actually isn't much more difficult than dragging a prebuilt scene in from the Visor. You have two basic options when creating a new container: creating an empty container or creating one with an emitter. If you want a fluid container with an emitter in it, it is obviously much easier to create one with the emitter already inside, though, as you will see, adding an emitter is not at all difficult.

Creating a 2D Fluid

In a new Maya scene, choose (from the Dynamics menu set) Fluid Effects → Create 2D Container With Emitter. This will create a new container (named fluid1 by default) with an emitter built in, as shown in Figure 25.6. Set your view to smooth shaded (press the 6 key on the keyboard), rewind the animation, and play it back to show a white gaslike substance being released by the emitter into the container, as shown on the right in the figure.

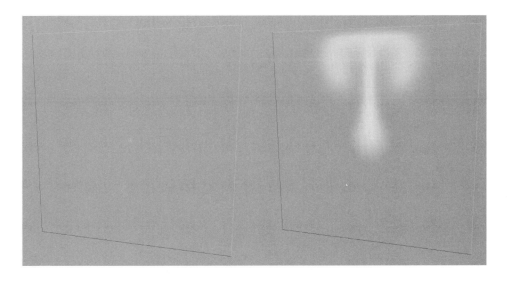

Figure 25.6

A 2D fluid container with included fluid emitter (left) and the emitter emitting fluids into the container (right)

Be sure that you have your animation playback set to play every frame, or the simulation will break down. Choose Window → Settings/Preferences → Preferences, and then Choose Settings: Timeline.

To add a second emitter to your fluid container, choose Fluid Effects → Add/Edit Contents → Emitter. Although a second emitter has been created, you will not see it in the scene because it is in the same location as the first emitter. To see the new emitter, with it still selected, move the emitter to a new location in X or Y. Once you have moved the second emitter, play back the animation again. You should see both emitters working and the fluids from both intermingling, as in Figure 25.7.

Be sure not to move your emitter on the Z axis. If the emitter leaves the fluid container, it will not emit a fluid any longer. (You can try this to see for yourself.) The need for the emitter to remain within the fluid container is one important difference between fluid and particle emitters.

Fluid Interaction with Other Objects

To make a simulation a little more interesting, you can create any type of geometric primitive or particle and, placing it in the fluid container, let it interact with the fluid itself. To demonstrate this, use your basic 2D fluid from earlier (or create a new 2D fluid container with an emitter), and then create a NURBS torus (choose Create → NURBS Primitives → Torus).

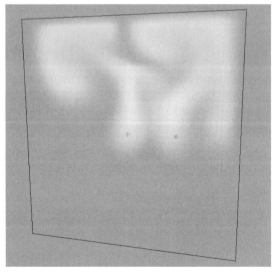

Figure 25.7

Two fluid emitters in the 2D container. Note that the fluids from both emitters interact with each other.

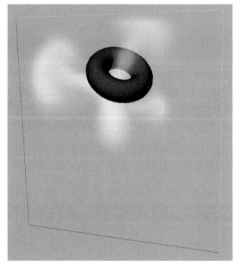

Figure 25.8

A 2D fluid interacting with a torus primitive

Stretch or deform the torus if you want, and then place it inside the fluid container. (Only a portion of the torus will fit within the container, of course, because it is 2D.) If you play back the animation now, the fluid will ignore the torus because the fluid and the torus have not yet been made to interact with each other. To make the two scene elements "see" each other, select the torus, Shift-select the fluid container, and choose Fluid Effects ➔ Make Collide. Now play back the simulation, and you should see the fluid wrap around the torus, as in Figure 25.8.

> The process of making fluids interact with geometry is analogous to that of making fluids interact with particles.

Creating a 3D Fluid

Creating a basic 3D fluid is essentially the same as creating a 2D fluid, and the options in the Attribute Editor are much the same as well—which all makes good sense since 2D fluids are just a special (1-voxel-thick) case of 3D fluids. On the other hand, 3D fluids are generally much slower to interact with, due to the added computational challenges of a third dimension. Thus, although 3D fluids can be used for all cases when a fluid is needed, it is often wise to ask whether a 2D fluid can be used instead. For many purposes, a 2D fluid will work adequately and will simulate (and render) much faster; for other cases a 3D fluid is a must.

To create a 3D fluid with an included emitter, choose (from the Dynamics menu set) Fluid Effects ➔ Create 3D Container With Emitter. You will get a cube with an included fluid emitter, which, if you play back the animation, will produce a 3D volume of gaslike fluid (see Figure 25.9).

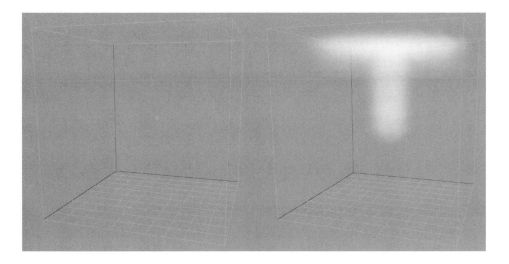

Figure 25.9

A 3D fluid container with emitter (left) and the emitter emitting fluids into the container (right)

Because 2D and 3D containers are essentially the same, as far as attributes are concerned, we'll now examine fluid and container attributes using a default 2D fluid as a test case.

Editing Fluid Attributes

Now let's take a look at some of the attributes you can adjust to change the behavior of your fluid. First, create a default 2D fluid container with an emitter. Then select the container and open the Attribute Editor. You should see the fluidShape1 tab selected at the top, some sections (hidden behind twirl-down arrows) of attributes you can adjust, and a Notes section at the bottom of the window (see Figure 25.10). The Notes section at the bottom of the window is an area into which either you or anyone else can write notes about the current fluid. This is a great way for you to write down the specifics of a particular fluid you've built or for you to read about a fluid someone else has created. If, for example, you open one of the preset fluids from the Visor and look at it in the Attribute Editor, you will see several sentences describing the particular preset and some suggested methods for modifying it.

Figure 25.10

The Attribute Editor for fluid1

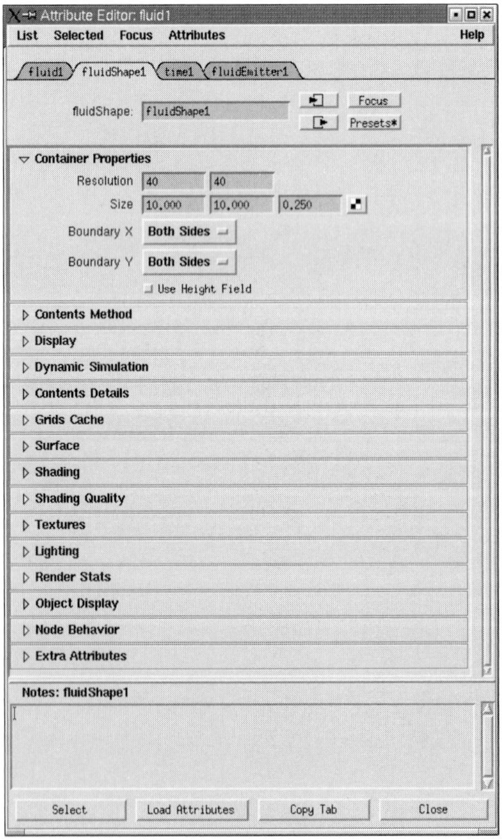

The rest of the Attribute Editor obviously contains a multitude of settings you can adjust to alter the behavior of either the fluid itself or the container in which it exists.

Although we don't have the space to discuss every attribute, we will point out some of the most useful ones here. As always with dynamics simulations, a bit of experimentation is a great way to get to know all the attributes of a fluid, so feel free to play with settings.

Container Properties

Starting at the top, let's first look at the Container Properties section of the Attribute Editor, which adjusts the resolution and behavior of the fluid container itself. The Resolution settings (set to 40 in X and Y by default) control how many voxels are in the container. A larger number (such as 100 in each direction) means a finer fluid simulation, but one that runs slower due to the greater number of calculations that must be performed with more voxels. The Size attributes (set to 10 in X and Y and 0.25 in Z by default) control the size of the fluid container. (You can also use the Scale tool to interactively change the container's size.) The 2D fluid container is actually three-dimensional, having a Z depth, but the depth is small, making the fluid behave like a 2D fluid.

The Boundary X and Y attributes control how the container deals with fluids that reach container walls. By default, these are set to Both Sides, indicating that the fluid will react to all four walls (both sides in X and Y) and thus behave as if it's in a "room" from which it cannot escape. If, on the other hand, you wanted the fluid to interact with only one wall, wrap (come up from the bottom of the container when it reaches the top), or simply not interact with the walls at all, you could choose the appropriate condition from the pop-up menu. Figure 25.11 shows a higher resolution (100 × 100) fluid simulation running with Boundary X and Y set to None. The fluid passes through the boundary of the container (and thus disappears). This might be a more desirable behavior if, say, you wanted to create an outdoor campfire and didn't want the smoke from the fire to wrap back around to the ground once it reached the top of the container.

> When a fluid passes outside the boundaries of its container (which is possible when Boundary conditions are set so that fluids can pass through them), it disappears completely from the scene. Thus, you will not generally want to show the boundary of a container that allows fluids to pass through it, because it will reveal a harsh break between the simulated fluid and nothing.

Contents Method

In the Contents Method section (below the Container Properties) are several pop-up controls that determine how the fluid behaves within the container. For the default 2D fluid case, Density and Velocity are set to Dynamic Grid, Temperature and Fuel are set to Off, and the Color Method is set to Use Shading Color. A dynamic grid updates its conditions over time, which allows the simulation to run. If you turn either Density or Velocity to Static Grid instead (causing the simulation not to update on each frame), the fluid will simply collect around the emitter instead of rising up and filling the container.

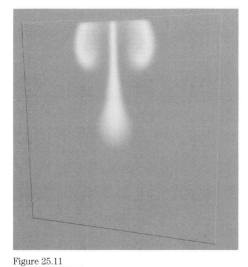

Figure 25.11

A finer simulation (100 × 100 voxels) with Boundary conditions set to None

Figure 25.12

Using an X Gradient velocity (rather than Dynamic Grid) on a fluid

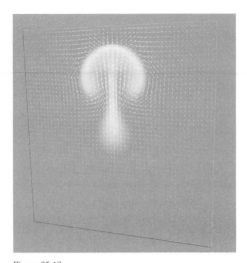

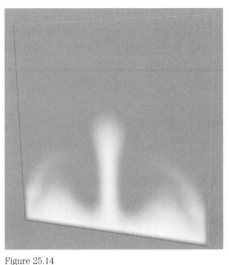

Figure 25.13

A fluid simulation with Velocity Draw indicating the speed and direction of fluid motion at each point in the container

Figure 25.14

A fluid simulation with negative gravity, medium viscosity, and high friction settings

Turning Velocity to Gradient mode instead and setting the Velocity Gradient to an X Gradient causes all the emitted fluid to rise at a 45-degree angle away from the emitter, as in Figure 25.12. (Other Gradient options cause motion in different directions.) Changing the Temperature settings to Gradient and X Gradient causes a temperature gradient in the X direction to "heat" the fluid, causing it to rise more quickly and at an angle in the X direction. (This effect is more easily seen if you first reset the Velocity method back to Dynamic Grid.) Without fuel in the scene (see the next section for more on creating fuel), the Fuel setting has no effect on this simulation. Finally, Color Method controls how fluid color is calculated. The Use Shading Color option (selected by default) uses settings from the Shading section of the Attribute Editor to control color. Static and Dynamic Grid allow specific control over color (statically or dynamically as indicated), which you emit or paint into a container. (Use the Contents Details: Color section to control color in this case; see the later section "Painting into Containers" for more on that subject.)

Display

In the Display section of the Attribute Editor are controls for interactive shading of the fluid within Maya itself (as opposed to the Render controls, which control how it looks when rendered). You can display the rendered version of the fluid when in shaded mode (the default), you can set the display to None, or you can set it to density, color, temperature, and the like. You can also turn on display of the internal grid within the container or set it to Outline (the default) or Bounding Box. You can turn on a Numeric Display of each fluid voxel's density, temperature, or fuel. In addition, you can enable display of the velocity of all points in the container by choosing the Velocity Draw option; once this is enabled, you can adjust the Draw Skip (reducing the number of arrows on the screen) and/or the length of each arrow. Figure 25.13 shows our basic simulation with velocity arrows drawn in.

Dynamic Simulation

The Dynamic Simulation section of the Attribute Editor allows control over the physical simulation of fluids in a container. The basic control Gravity determines how a fluid is "pulled" in the scene. At default (9.8), gravity pulls the fluid upward toward the top of the container at a sedate speed. If Gravity is made negative, it will pull the fluid downward instead; its magnitude determines how rapidly the fluid will rise or fall within the container. Viscosity determines how much each fluid particle "sticks" to its neighbors. A value of 0 means that they slide over each other freely; a value of 1 means that they all stick together (and thus don't move from the emitter). Meantime, Friction determines how the fluid will react with the boundaries of the container (or objects with which it collides): a value of 0 means there is no friction, and a value of 1 means that all fluid cells that strike the container (or object) will stick to them completely. Figure 25.14 shows a fluid simulation with negative gravity, viscosity set to 0.3, and friction set to 1.

Grid Interpolation determines how finely a simulation is run: a Linear interpolation is coarser than a Hermite one, but runs faster. Start Frame determines when the simulation begins running, the Simulation Rate Scale scales the simulation larger or smaller than default, and Disable Evaluation turns off the fluid calculations altogether. The Conserve Mass, Use Collisions, Emission, and Fields check boxes allow individual elements of the simulation to be turned on or off as work progresses on a scene.

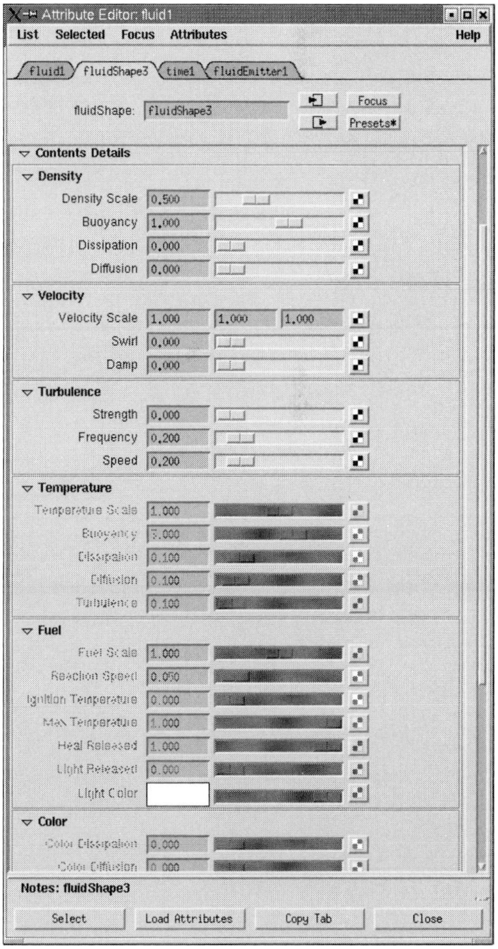

Contents Details

In the Contents Details section of the Attribute Editor (shown in Figure 25.15) are subsections dealing with Density, Velocity, Turbulence, Temperature, Fuel, and Color, all of which are used to refine the behavior of the fluid itself. Some of the more

Figure 25.15

The Contents Details section of the Attribute Editor

interesting controls in this section are discussed here. Under Density are Buoyancy, which controls how positively or negatively buoyant the fluid is (negative buoyancy causes a fluid to drop instead of rise), Diffusion, and Dissipation. A Diffusion larger than 0 causes the fluid to scatter about the container rather than hanging together, and a nonzero Dissipation causes the fluid to disappear back into the normal (uncolored) state of the container.

Swirl and Damp (under Velocity) control how many vortices are created in a fluid and how rapidly motion is damped out, respectively. Figure 25.16 shows a fluid with a Swirl of 8 and a Damping of 0.1. Turbulence Strength, Frequency, and Speed control how much a turbulence field will affect the fluid system. High values for all these settings produces something like Figure 25.17.

Under Fuel (which is disabled until you set the Fuel Contents Method to Dynamic or Static Grid) are controls for Reaction Speed (how fast the fuel burns), Ignition Temperature (when the fuel is ignited), and Heat and Light Released from the fuel burn. If fuel and temperature are painted into the container (see the next section), the fluid simulation will look similar to Figure 25.18. In this image, the visible fluid has been pushed around by the temperature variation from the burning fuel, and (in its final rendered state) it will take on the color of the burning fuel as set in the Light Released settings.

Grids Cache

The Grids Cache section of the Attribute Editor allows control over which portions of a fluid cache (used to speed up playback) will be read as a scene is played back.

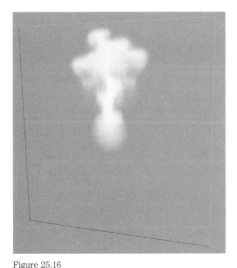

Figure 25.16

A fluid with high Swirl and medium velocity damping settings

Figure 25.17

A fluid influenced by a high Turbulence field

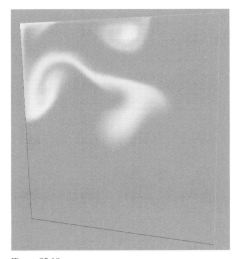

Figure 25.18

A fluid distorted by (invisible) burning fuel

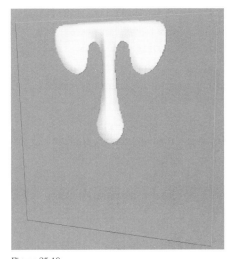

Figure 25.19

The fluid simulation displayed as a surface rather than as a volume

Surface

In the Surface section are controls for how the fluid itself is rendered. The two types are Volume (checked by default) and Surface (shown in Figure 25.19), which creates a more solid-looking fluid, which can represent anything from water to lava. The Hard Surface option makes the fluid look more solid (and blocky), and the Soft Surface option makes the surface look more amorphous. Surface Threshold controls where the surface begins and ends: a low threshold includes most of the fluid effect (and density which is above ambient), and a high threshold includes only the densest sections of the fluid. The other attributes in this section control how the surface looks (and refracts) once it is rendered.

Shading

In the Shading section (shown in Figure 25.20) are controls for how the fluid is rendered. Most of these are similar to shading options you would come across in a shader network (see Chapter 17, "Shading and Texturing Surfaces," for more on shading networks), but several options are unique to fluids. As an example, set the Dropoff Shape and Edge Dropoff options to Cube and a small number (such as 0.05), respectively, and play the simulation back to see how the fluid reacts now. Dropoff Shape controls how the fluid's boundaries are computed. Cubic dropoff shape creates an invisible cube around the object, causing the fluid to fade out when it comes in contact with the cube. A Sphere or Cone shape (two other options) creates a spherical or conic boundary. The Edge Dropoff setting controls how tightly the boundary shape is wrapped around the fluid object. The easiest way to see how these settings work is to run the simulation until you have fluid visible; then select a Dropoff Shape and slide the Edge Dropoff slider back and forth to see how the boundary of the fluid changes.

The Color section allows control over the color of the fluid and which properties are mapped to color. You can choose a single value for color (the default condition) or, by clicking in the ramp slider at the right side of the Selected Color swatch, create a ramp of colors (click the Selected Color swatch to set individual colors on the ramp). The Color Input controls which aspect of the fluid is being colored (and thus displayed and rendered), and the Input Bias moves all the ramp colors either up or down in case the default ramp settings are not set quite right. Figure 25.21 shows color settings and the results in the 2D container. The Incandescence settings work in just the same way as color, but they multiply their effects with the color settings, creating an incandescent effect when rendered.

Finally, the Opacity settings control which property of the fluid to map to opacity (the Opacity Input) and how it is mapped (the Opacity ramp). The default linear ramp from 0 (transparent) at left to 1 (fully opaque) at right produces the effects we are used to seeing. If, on the other hand, you use Density as the Opacity Input and move the left ramp point up to 1, the entire scene becomes opaque (at the color set at the far left end of the Color ramp). This is because the entire fluid is *one* fluid; only the density changes are being displayed in this single fluid. Thus, if the entire fluid is made opaque, you can see that the container is filled with this fluid. By clicking within the Opacity ramp, you can add and change the curve, and by changing the Interpolation method (Linear by default), you can change how the ramp transitions from one opacity to another.

One other point worth mentioning here is that each color, incandescence, or opacity value in each ramp can be mapped with a file or procedural texture simply by clicking the checkerboard button next to the Selected Color (or Selected Value) button when that point is selected in the ramp.

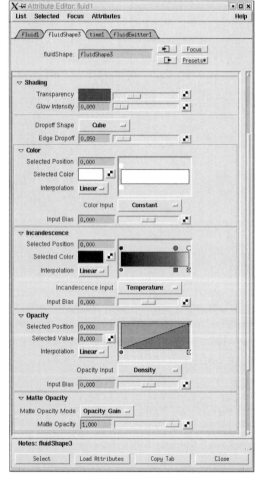

Figure 25.20

The Shading section of the Attribute Editor

Shading Quality

The Shading Quality section controls how finely the fluid image will be rendered. The most important settings here are Quality (higher quality looks better but takes longer to render) and Sample Method, which can help get rid of bands using Jittered or Adaptive Jittered, but at the cost of some noise in the final image. Using a higher-quality setting reduces the noise problem, but with increased render times.

Textures

In the Textures section of the Attribute Editor (shown in Figure 25.22) are controls allowing you to remap a given fluid in more refined ways than with simple coloring. What's more, these textures can be moving, giving the illusion of 3D motion to an otherwise static simulation. Thus, you can create, say, a 3D cloud simulation with a static grid (thus avoiding the computation involved in dynamically solving a large 3D grid) and just map the fluid with a moving texture, making it appear to be in motion. This is, in fact, how the stormyClouds preset is created. (All contents methods for this preset are turned off.)

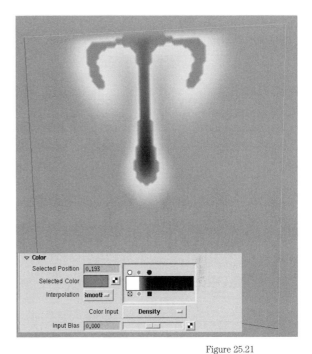

Figure 25.21

Fluid Color settings and the resultant display of the fluid

Texture Opacity is the most obvious control (Color and Incandescence are controlled in similar fashion); after turning on Texture Opacity, selecting an option such as Billow from the Texture Type pop-up menu alters the basic look of the fluid into one that is more broken up, cloudlike, or billowy. At this point, altering the Threshold, Amplitude, Ratio, and so on control the basic properties of the Billow (or other) texture type; playing around with the Texture Type and these settings will create any number of different looks. Billow (and Waves) also has a series of special controls at the bottom of the Textures section. By altering the Billow Density, Spottiness, Size Rand, and Randomness, you can alter the basic look of the Billow texture to suit your taste.

The Implode controls allow the texture to look as if it's imploding inward (with a controllable center of implosion). Finally, the Texture Time, Frequency, Scale, and Origin controls allow you to adjust elements such as the scale and frequency of the texture, and, using the Texture Time control, you can move through the texture (by sliding the slider) to find the moment in texture time when the texture looks right to you.

Figure 25.23 shows our basic 2D fluid with a Billow texture and a higher than default frequency. As with most other attributes for Fluids, most in the Textures section can be texture mapped by selecting the checkerboard icon at the right of the control.

If you play back your textured animation, you will likely notice that the texture stays in place while the fluid flows, which looks unnatural. By keyframing Texture Time (and many of the other attributes), however, you can make the texture animate over time, giving the illusion that it is moving. For example, if you play your animation back to a frame you like, select Fluid Effects → Set Initial State (to set the current frame to the fluid's initial condition), set Velocity (under Contents Method) to 0, and then keyframe the Texture Time attribute (RM choose Set Key with the mouse over the Texture Time words) to different values over time, the fluid will appear to evolve over time even though it is now static—a fact that can be observed if you play back the animation past your last keyframe. By combining dynamic simulations and moving textures (or just moving textures by themselves), you can create convincing effects that simulate quickly and render fast.

Figure 25.22

The Textures section of the Attribute Editor

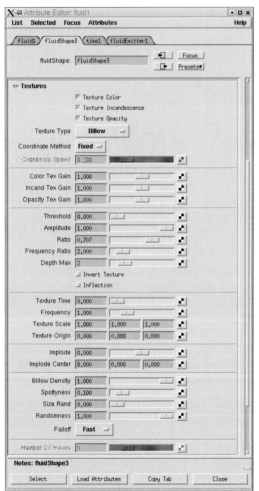

Lighting

The final section of the Attribute Editor that is unique to Fluid Effects is the Lighting section. Here there are a few controls over how the fluid itself is lit: self-shadowing and use of a built-in or real lighting. Choosing the Self Shadow option allows the fluid to shadow itself (and clicking the Hardware Shadow check box allows you to see this shadowing in the Maya scene window). With self-shadowing on, volumetric fluids such as clouds will appear much more real than if they do not shadow themselves. If the Real Lights check box is off, Fluids uses a default directional light (whose position you can control via the Directional Light X, Y, and Z number fields); if you select Real Lights, the actual lights in the scene are used to calculate self-shadowing. Using real lights can be a better option, but it is much more computationally intensive than using the default light, so be prepared for slower renders.

Figure 25.23

The 2D fluid with a Billow texture on it

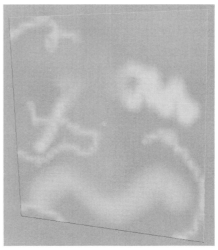

Figure 25.24

Some density strokes painted into a 2D fluid container

Painting into Containers

Now that you have a good sense of how the various attributes of a fluid control its behavior and appearance, let's look at how to actually paint properties into a container. First, create a basic 2D fluid with *no* emitter attached. Next, choose Fluid Effects → Add/Edit Contents → Paint Fluids Tool □. In the Paint Attributes section, be sure the Paintable Attributes pop-up menu is set to Density, and then use your mouse to paint some fluid density into your scene. If you have a tablet, you can set the pressure of the stylus to change the amount of density (whiteness) of the fluid you're painting; otherwise, change the Value (Paint Attributes section) and Radius U and L values (Brush section) to alter the density and size of your strokes. After some strokes at different values and brush sizes, you should have something like Figure 25.24. If you then play back your animation, you will see the fluid move and swirl around under the influence of the default gravity and collisions with the container itself.

The Paint Fluids tool is actually one of the tools in the Artisan plug-in (see Chapter 7 for more on Artisan brush tools).

Now that you know how to paint density, let's see what happens when we paint other properties into the container. Follow these steps:

1. Set Gravity to 0 in the Dynamic Simulation section of the Attribute Editor. (You can check to see that your fluid now no longer moves from its initial position.)

2. In the Paint Fluids tool, erase the contents of your container by setting the Value (in Paint Attributes) to 0 and clicking the Flood button.

3. Reset the Value to 1 and paint a circle of density near the middle of the container, as in Figure 25.25. If you play back the animation, it should not move, because gravity is no longer influencing it.

4. Set the Paintable Attributes pop-up to Temperature instead of Density. You should get a warning that you need to set the Temperature grid to Dynamic so the simulation will run properly. Click the Set To Dynamic button to allow this. You will notice that the container is now empty again: while the density you painted on is still present, you can no longer see it as you are now in temperature "mode."

5. Paint several strokes of high temperature (white) at the bottom-right corner of the container, as in Figure 25.26.

Figure 25.25

Painted density in the 2D fluid

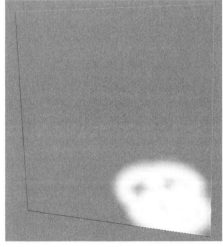

Figure 25.26

Temperature strokes painted into the 2D container

6. Switch back to Density on the Paintable Attributes pop-up, and play back the animation. You should see the density of the fluid swirled around due to the high temperature of the bottom-right of the container (Figure 25.27).

You can paint other properties into the container, including velocity fields (which will shove the density field around) and fuel, which, when burned by temperature fields above a threshold temperature (set in the Attribute Editor), will ignite, giving off heat and light and thus altering the look and position of the fluid density in the container. Try using the previous scene, but paint in some fuel across the bottom of the container that touches the temperature area you painted on before (when you are asked, be sure to set the Fuel grid to dynamic). If you leave the display set to Fuel, you can play back the animation

Figure 25.27

Density of the fluid influenced by the (invisible) painted temperature

and watch the fuel being consumed as it burns (as in the left image of Figure 25.28); if you set the display to Density, you will see the fluid density affected by the burning fuel (on the right in Figure 25.28).

Figure 25.28

Fuel being consumed as it burns (left) and the fluid density affected by this burning fuel (right)

Creating an Ocean Effect

Creating an Ocean Effect from scratch is fairly similar to creating a Fluid Effect. From the Dynamics menu set, choose Fluid Effects → Ocean → Create Ocean to display a distorted, circular NURBS patch called oceanPlane1 in your scene, like the one in Figure 25.29. If you render the scene out, you will see a basic set of waves against a blue background.

If you play back the animation in the scene window, you will notice that nothing happens. This is because Ocean Effects, not being true fluid simulations, create their ocean appearance and wave motion via texture mapping and displacement mapping, respectively. If you do a quick render of your scene at frame 1 and then re-render a section of your previous render at a new frame, you will see that the waves on the surface actually do move in the render, producing the appropriate illusion of a large body of water (see Figure 25.30).

Figure 25.29

A long-distance view of the NURBS patch that contains the ocean shader

Figure 25.30

The basic ocean simulation rendered at frame 1 (on the left) and at frame 50 (on the right). The waves do not match up between frames, showing that the displacement map creating the wave effect is in motion.

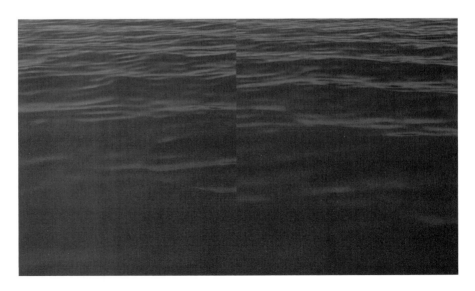

You will discover that rendering ocean surfaces is a long process, especially if you set anti-aliasing to a high quality, which occurs because the displacement and texturing process behind this kind of effect is computationally expensive. One way to mitigate this trouble is to use low-resolution, low-quality anti-aliasing on your test renders until you are happy with your results.

Within the Attribute Editor, in similar fashion to Fluid Effects, are controls over the Ocean Effect itself, including wave height, turbulence, coloring, and so forth. None of these controls actually effect any kind of simulation; they simply control texturing and displacement.

To see how some of these controls work, select your ocean surface and open the Ocean Attributes section of the Attribute Editor (see Figure 25.31). First, notice that at the top, the Type of shader is set to Ocean Shader, which enables the controls below. In the blocks directly below the Type pop-up menu, some of the more important attributes are Time (which controls the animation of the effect and should be keyframed by default), Scale (which controls the scale of the simulation), Wind (which controls the wind speed, that in turn affects the wave height and motion), and Observer Speed (which sets the observer in motion relative to the waves). Most of the other controls in the top two blocks of the Ocean Attributes section are fairly self-explanatory, and a bit of quick experimentation should get you familiar with how they affect the ocean.

Figure 25.31

The Attribute Editor, showing part of the Ocean Attributes section

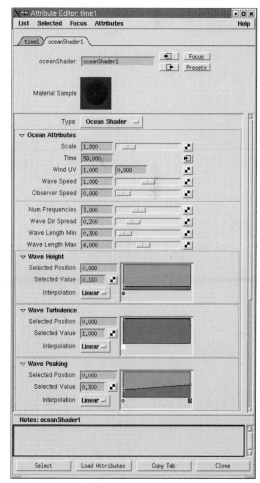

The next three blocks—Wave Height, Turbulence, and Peaking—use a ramp metaphor similar to those in the Fluid Effects Attributes. Wave Height, for example, uses the ramp to determine the size of the waves based on their wavelength. On the left side of the ramp are the smallest wavelength waves, and on the right side are the longest; adding or moving points on the ramp, then, controls the height of the waves for each sized wave. (A flat-line ramp makes all the waves the same size.) If, for example, you set the left side of the ramp to 1 and the right side to 0, the shortest, highest frequency waves will be very large, and the longer waves will have no height at all, creating a ripple effect and causing the water to look more like a bathtub than an ocean. Doing the opposite (setting 0 and 1 respectively) makes for large, long-wavelength waves with no fine detail, producing a look that is too smooth for natural water. Experimenting with different values (usually above 0 across the board) produces much more satisfying results.

The wavelength of a wave, which is the inverse of its frequency, is the distance between two troughs (or peaks) of a wave. The two are related by the equation $\lambda = (\kappa / f)$, in which λ is wavelength, f is frequency, and κ is a constant representing the wave speed. Long wavelength waves, then, have a long distance between each wave and thus look like large ocean swells—these would be the waves you would see crashing to the shore or on which people surf. Short wavelength waves, on the other hand, have a short distance between troughs, producing the detailed rippling of waves that exist on top of (or superimposed on) the larger waves. Thus, in general, you want your short wavelength waves to have equal or smaller height than your long wavelength waves.

Wave Turbulence, which is controlled in the same fashion as Wave Height, controls the turbulence (or random motion) of the waves. If Wave Turbulence is set to 0 across the frequency spectrum, all the waves line up perfectly, creating a smooth, unnatural look. Wave Peaking, which only functions if Wave Turbulence is greater than 0, creates a side-to-side (rather than up-down) motion to the waves so that they jitter back and forth over time. Again, setting this to a value greater than 0 creates a more random, dynamic-looking water surface, though at the expense of additional render time, because Wave Peaking is computationally intensive.

At the bottom of the Ocean Attributes section are the Foam Emission, Threshold, and Offset values, which allow generation of foam at the tops of larger waves (the size of "large" waves being set by the Threshold value). You can create stormier ocean scenes by adding this foamy white-cap effect into the mix (see Figure 25.32).

Figure 25.32

The basic ocean scene with the addition of white-capped foamy waves

Finally, under the Common Material Attributes section are controls for the actual color of the water itself. Here you can adjust water and foam color, incandescence, translucence, and the refractive index of the water, allowing you to create anything from highly photorealistic water to the unearthly pink oceans of some alien planet.

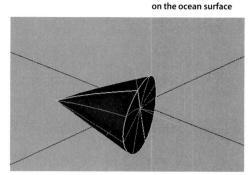

Figure 25.33

A cone "boat" floating on the ocean surface

One other important aspect of Ocean Effects is your ability to float any number of objects on the ocean surface itself. Because the surface is calculated through displacement mapping, you must use an expression that determines the displacement of any point on the surface to figure out how an object will float, but, fortunately (again), Alias|Wavefront has made the process mostly transparent to the user. Choose Fluid Effects → Ocean to display options for floating objects on your ocean surface, including floating locators (to which you can later attach a camera or an object), Buoy (a locator with a sphere attached), and the option to float any geometric object (Float Selected Objects) or create an unpowered or powered boat (Make Boat and Make Motor Boat, respectively).

These floating objects all work in similar ways (with varying options), so we'll just use Make Boat as an example. Into your basic ocean scene (or just create a new one), create some geometric primitive such as a NURBS cone, or add any model you want. With the object selected, choose Fluid Effects → Ocean → Make Boats. You should see your object now attached to a locator, which keeps track of floating the object. If you play back the animation, you will see the "boat" rocking up and down on the (invisible) ocean surface, as in Figure 25.33. Creating a boat allows 3D motion of the object you create. If you use Float Object, the object will bounce up and down, but won't rotate around to stay on the surface.

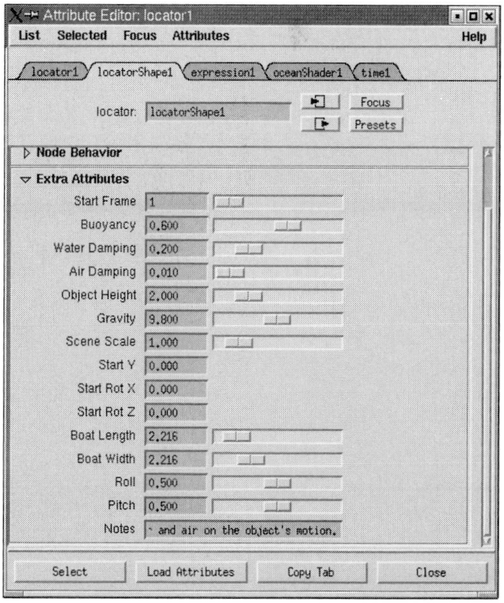

Figure 25.34

The Attribute Editor, showing extra attributes for an ocean-going boat

If you look in the Expression Editor (sort by expression name), you will see, under expression1, a long expression that actually does the dirty work of floating your object on top of the ocean. Fortunately you don't have to deal with this expression (unless you want to—in that case, have fun!). You can just open the Attribute Editor for locatorShape1 and twirl down the Extra Attributes section to display controls for the boat (see Figure 25.34), all of which relate to variables in the expression you just viewed. After working through this chapter, most of these settings should be easy to understand. As an example, you can choose to alter the buoyancy from its default 0.6. If you make the object less buoyant (like, say, 0.2), it will sink into the ocean; whereas if you increase buoyancy, it will float like a beach ball just touching the waves. (You will likely have to increase Air

Damping in this case, or the boat will jiggle around like crazy.) If you set the buoyancy to less than zero, the boat will sink like a stone. Thus, by keyframing buoyancy, you can cause the boat to rise up to the surface, bounce around on it, and then sink back down under the water again.

One unfortunate consequence of Ocean Effects being a displacement simulation is that the wake from a boat or other floating object is not calculated. Thus, while a boat floats on the surface of the water, it will not properly interact with the ocean, creating foam or waves as it floats or moves around the surface.

Hands On: Creating Coffee and Cream with 2D and 3D Fluids

Now that we have covered the basics of fluids, here is a more complex example of how to create, solve, and edit the look of a cup of coffee as creamer is poured in and steam is coming off the coffee surface. The first effect is a 2D fluid rendered as a solid surface. The objective is to create the look of a cup of coffee as the creamer mixes in with the coffee. The second effect adds a little steam coming off the coffee surface. The last effect shows you how to simulate a stream of creamer pouring into a cup.

Coffee Surface

Start by creating a 2D fluid container with an emitter: choose Fluid Effects → Create 2D Container With Emitter. Play your simulation (be sure to press the 5 or 6 key to smooth shade the fluid). Next you will have to create a behavior and a look that is more consistent with cream being introduced into a cup of coffee. Follow these steps:

1. Select the fluid container.

2. Open the Attribute Editor and in the Dynamic Simulation section set Gravity to 0.

3. Under the Contents Details portion of the Attribute Editor, in the Density section, set Density Scale to 0.4, decreasing the density overall. (This setting simply multiplies the density values within the fluid container by the scale value.)

4. In the Velocity section, set Swirl to 12.

5. In the Turbulence section, set Strength to 1, and set Frequency to 0.2.

6. Click the Play button to preview. You can see that the behavior has changed quite a bit. If you like, you can play the simulation as you are changing dynamic simulation values in the Attribute Editor so that you can watch them update dynamically on your fluid object (see Figure 25.35).

If you want to simulate a liquid in a horizontal plane, all you have to do is rotate your fluid in place. Select only the container (not the emitter) and rotate it –90 degrees around the X axis.

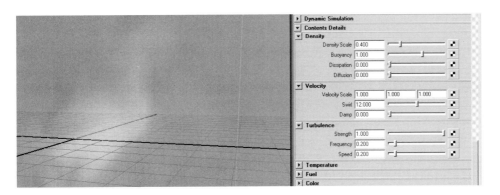

Figure 25.35

Interactively changing attributes of the fluid

To get better visual feedback on your fluid object in space, you can modify the container resolution and the way it is displayed. In the Display section of the Attribute Editor, set Boundary Draw to Bounding Box. This way you get a visual representation of the height of the volume within which the coffee surface will occur. Now, under Container Properties in the Attribute Editor, modify the container size (the three Size fields) to 10, 10, and 1 (see Figure 25.36).

Turn on the Use Height Field option to see what your fluid looks like rendered. By default, in hardware rendering the fluid container shows you the fluid object as a transparent object in which there is no density. Only the density renders by default. The Use Height Field option will render the entire fluid object for which height is a function of density rather than opacity.

Figure 25.36

The newly resized 2D fluid container

To give the coffee a "surface," you can turn on surface rendering as opposed to volume rendering. Open the Surface tab in the Attribute Editor, and turn on Surface Render. This will show your fluid with an apparent relief as a result of the way it is shaded, thus making your fluid object look like a surface. There is still some transparency on this object, which is set by default under the Shading tab. Although you can control the transparency of a surface-rendered fluid, the density no longer controls opacity. Feel free to play with the opacity graph and watch how it updates the height of your fluid. Just make sure you set this graph back to its default values before you proceed (open the Shading tab in the Attribute Editor and set Transparency to black).

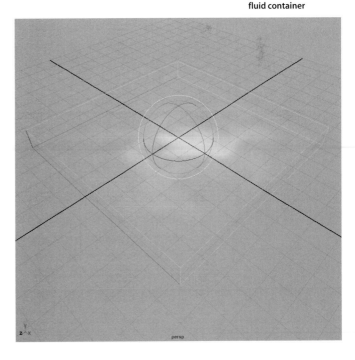

In the Shading section, under the Color tab in the Attribute Editor, you need to specify a color for the coffee and the creamer. You can base color on the density of a fluid object for instance. Low density will be assigned the color of the handle on the left side of your ramp slider, and high density will receive the color of the handle on the right side of your ramp slider. By moving these sliders and inserting/deleting points, you can modify the transition between any number of colors, or you can set Interpolation to another preset, modifying the way it interpolates between handles. (The Interpolation control works on a per handle basis, just like the color swatches.)

1. In the Color tab, introduce a second and a third handle into the ramp slider for the color attribute by LM clicking in the slider itself.

2. Place these sliders at the respective positions of 0, 0.1, and 0.5.

3. Change their colors to whatever you want coffee and creamer to look like, or you can use the following values. The first one (left) corresponds with coffee (HSV in the color editor: H = 31.0, S = 1.0, V = 0.18). The second simulates creamer that is visible but has not broken the surface yet (32.0, 0.41, 0.65), and the third handle represents the color of creamer at the surface (34.2, 0.16, 1). Figure 25.37 shows the new color ramp plus the resultant look of the fluid.

4. Switch the Color input to Density, and play your simulation to see what you have.

Figure 25.37

The Attribute Editor color ramp settings, and the resultant colors shown in the fluid itself

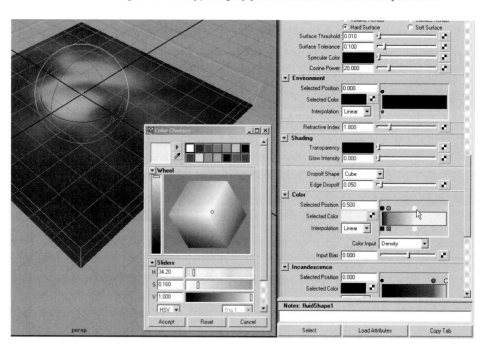

To make sure your color is not contaminated by incandescence, make your incandescence black by deleting any handles with color in the incandescence ramp slider. In the Incandescence tab, delete the handles that show a default orange and yellow by clicking the little color boxes below the ramp slider.

Next comes the opacity. In the opacity graph, horizontally you have your opacity input values, and vertically you find the actual opacity values with which your fluid is rendered. Density is the default opacity input, so in a default graph your opacity goes up as your density goes up. Since opacity now affects height (Use Height is turned on), reversing your graph gives you lowest height at highest density and creates height at lowest density. This way, if you were to animate a spoon stirring the creamer into the coffee, you would get a mini-vortex at the center of your coffee. In the opacity graph, move your left handle up vertically to a Selected Value of 1. Move your right handle to 0, effectively reversing the displacement between the coffee and the creamer, as shown in Figure 25.38. Notice how that affects your displayed scene.

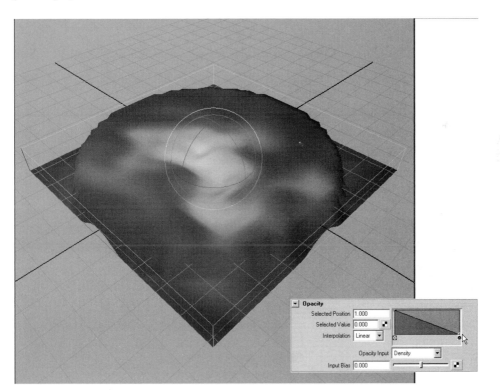

Figure 25.38

Altering the Opacity ramp of the coffee/creamer fluid

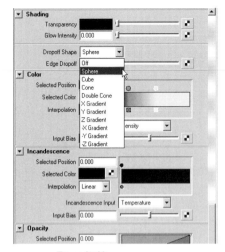

Figure 25.39

**Selecting a Sphere
Edge Dropoff shape**

Experiment with this graph by inserting multiple handles and modifying the shape of the curve and interpolation. When you're finished experimenting, make sure you reset the graph to the settings described earlier before you continue.

If you software render the current scene, you will see that the fluid surface is still showing up in the shape of a plane. You can use a Dropoff Shape preset (in the Shading tab of the Attribute Editor) such as Sphere (see Figure 25.39) to render your fluid object as a circular fluid shape. Later this will be where the cup wall hits the coffee surface. In the Shading tab, select Sphere as your Dropoff Shape.

> If you are hardware rendering a sequence and you want your fluid to render as a circular boundary, you must turn off the Use Height Field option.

As a final touch, lets add some specular value to our coffee and cream. Follow these steps:

1. In the Surface tab of the Attribute Editor, drag Specular Color to whichever value you like, or specify a color numerically. You can also modify Cosine Power; larger values give you smaller specular highlights.

2. Create a light to test the look of your coffee.

Once your coffee surface is finished, it is time to build the cup and make your fluid fit the inside of your cup. Follow these steps:

1. Build a basic double-walled cup, like the one in Figure 25.40, by revolving a curve around the Y axis. If you don't want to build the cup yourself, you can grab the `emptyCup` file off the CD-ROM.

2. Make sure the diameter of the cup fits the circular portion of your 2D fluid object that is displaced by drawing your curve as such or by scaling your cup once you finish modeling it.

3. Assign a new shader to the cup so you can texture it, or just give it some nice specular values and a ceramic coloration. If you make the cup's specular fairly bright, later, if you raytrace the scene, you will get some nice reflections of the coffee surface onto the cup.

You can have fluid objects collide with either NURBS or polygonal geometry. On collision, you can have the fluid react to the geometry, you can have the geometry react to the fluid, or both. In the case of your coffee cup, you can collide the creamer fluid with the wall of the coffee cup. Select both the container and the cup (the order in which you select them

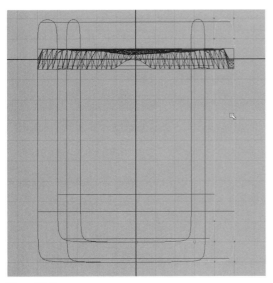

Figure 25.40

Building the coffee cup

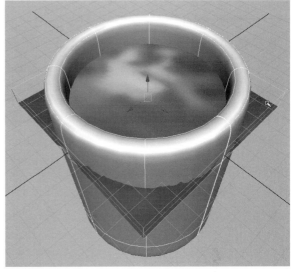

Figure 25.41

Selecting the cup and fluid before making them collide

doesn't matter), as shown in Figure 25.41, and choose Fluid Effects → Make Collide. This adds a geoConnector node to the fluid container from which you can modify Resilience, Friction, and Tesselation Factor. In the case of NURBS geometry, it is a good idea to increase Tesselation Factor so that the fluid collides more accurately with the object.

Save your file. The cup and fluid should now resemble Figure 25.42 when it is rendered.

> Increasing tessellation creates more collision surfaces for the cup, thus allowing the fluid to "see" a more smoothly rounded surface with which to collide.

Steam Volume

The next effect is some steam coming off the hot coffee. This time you will use a 3D fluid object to create a more volumetric look. Later the steam will start at the surface of the coffee, so don't forget that once the creamer starts mixing in, the coffee will displace downward: it essentially creates a vortex in the center of the cup. Thus,

Figure 25.42

A render of the coffee cup and coffee/creamer fluid

you will want to move your steam fluid emitter a bit below the surface of the coffee fluid so there's no gap when the simulation gets going.

1. Create a new scene.

2. Create a 3D fluid by choosing Fluid Effects → Create 3D Container (without emitter).

3. In the Attribute Editor, modify the resolution and size of the container to 10, 15, and 10.

4. Set Boundary Y to -Y Side to ensure that the fluid will not collide with the ceiling of the container. It will simply appear to bleed through the top of the container.

5. Create a simple NURBS primitive circle, and move it so that it resides just above the bottom of the 3D container. Also scale it so it is roughly half the width of your 3D container.

6. Select the 3D container and the circle, and open the Emit From Object Options window (see Figure 25.43) by choosing Fluid Effects → Add/Edit Contents → Emit From Object ❐.

7. Set the Emitter Type to Curve, and click Apply And Close.

8. In the Outliner, select the curve's fluid emitter and open the Attribute Editor. In the Fluid Attributes section, change the emission rate (Density/Voxel/Sec) to 0.01 (see Figure 25.44). At this point you should have a curve emitter emitting steam from below the coffee surface. To get a look similar to steam, you need make the 3D fluid effect as wispy as you can.

9. Select the container, and in the Attribute Editor, change Density Scale to 0.2, Swirl to 40, and Turbulence Strength to 0.5. The results are shown in Figure 25.45.

10. Set Transparency to 0.25, and select the Cube dropoff shape, so that the steam starts slightly above the coffee.

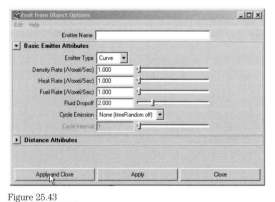

Figure 25.43

The Emit From Object Options window

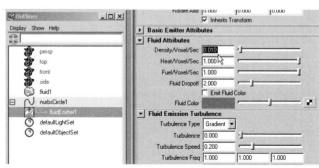

Figure 25.44

Altering the Density/Voxel/Sec emission rate

11. You can use the Edge Dropoff attribute to control how much your density drops off within your dropoff shape. Set the Edge Dropoff attribute to 0.8.

12. Play your simulation and save your file.

Liquid Creamer Surface

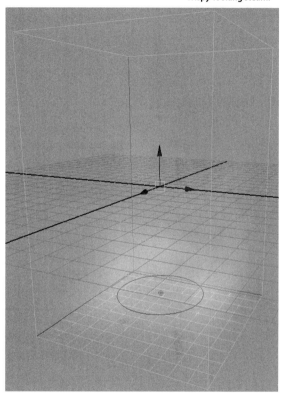

Figure 25.45

Wispy-looking steam.

To create an effect of liquid creamer streaming into a cup of coffee (a bit of a cheat, as you can have only one fluid in a container at a time), you can use a 2D fluid object that produces a sharp contrast between low- and high-density sections, thus giving the illusion that two fluids are being rendered. Follow these steps:

1. Create a new file.

2. Choose Fluid Effects → Create 2D Container With Emitter. Make sure you move the emitter toward the top of the container.

3. In the Attribute Editor, in the Display section, turn on Bounding Box.

4. In Container Properties, make the container size 10, 10, and 2, and set Boundary Y to -Y Side. This makes the liquid disregard the bottom of the container.

5. Turn on Use Height Field and turn on shaded mode. Also, in Contents Details set Buoyancy to –1, Swirl to 1, and Damping to 0.1.

6. In the Surface section, set the Render Type to Surface Render.

7. In the Shading tab, set Transparency to black, and make the color of your creamer the same as the color of the creamer in the coffee (HSV = 34.2, 0.16, 1).

8. Next, set the left handle of the opacity graph to a position of 0.4 and a value of 0 (see Figure 25.46).

9. Finally, to apply some additional noise to the liquid, in the Textures tab turn on Texture Opacity. Leave the preset set to Perlin Noise. Reduce Ratio to 0.4, softening the noise; turn on Inflection; and set Texture Scale to 1, 4, and 1, stretching the noise in the Y direction (see Figure 25.47). This will break up the liquid stream shape a bit. By modifying texture parameters, you can control surface noise.

You may find that the edges of your creamer are "noisy" (there are little bits of grain around the edges where the creamer stream disappears). To alleviate this problem, you will need to adjust the settings in the Render Globals window. Open the window, turn on raytracing, and in the Anti-Aliasing Quality section, set Shading and Max Shading to higher values (for example, 4 and 16 respectively). While adjusting these settings will reduce edge noise, it increases render times by a great deal, so adjust these values up slowly. Also, keep in mind that these settings will effect your entire render including the cup, coffee, steam, and surface, as well as the creamer.

10. Save your file.

Figure 25.46

Setting the creamer opacity and color

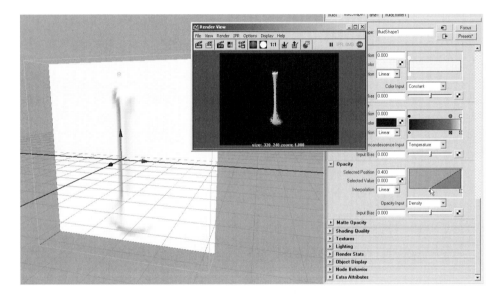

Combining the Effects

Finally you need to combine all the effects into one file. Open the file with your coffee surface in it, and import the liquid creamer file. Move the liquid creamer container with its emitter so that the base of the pouring container is somewhat submerged in the coffee. Next, import your steam file, and move both the container and the circle emitter so that the circle emitter is slightly submerged below the coffee surface.

Now play your simulation, and notice that you need to start the creamer/coffee mixing later. The liquid creamer enters the coffee about frame 170. Start the simulation for the coffee surface at about frame 170—in the Dynamic Simulation section, set Start Frame to 170 (as in Figure 25.48). This turns off the dynamic simulation of the mixing coffee and cream until the poured cream reaches the surface of the coffee.

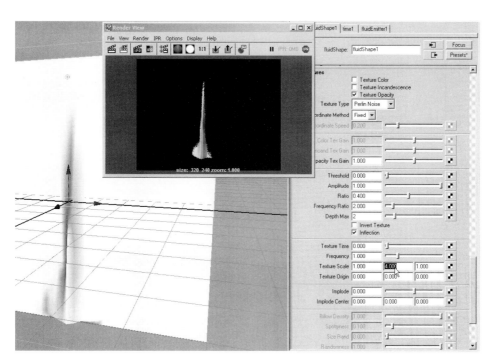

Figure 25.47

Adjusting the texture and inflection value of the creamer

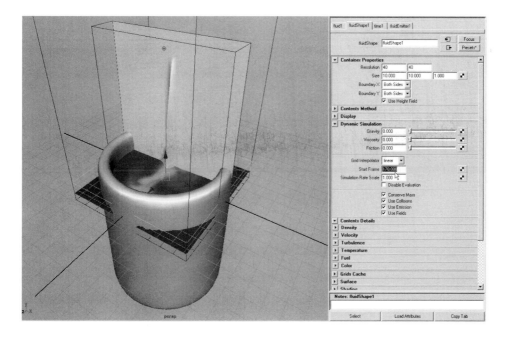

Figure 25.48

Adjusting Start Frame for the coffee/creamer simulation

Rendering Your Coffee

You can software render any frame or sequence of frames the same way you render objects. Fluids at this point will have to be rendered in the Maya renderer. The good news is that rendering frames of Fluid Objects is multiprocessed, so if you have a fast multiprocessor machine, things will move along.

As far as casting shadows, Maya can have fluid objects cast shadows onto geometry using raytracing. Maya can also render depth maps or raytraced shadows of geometry onto fluid objects. Self-shadowing of fluid objects does not require you to raytrace.

To render shadows of the cup onto the coffee surface, simply turn on Use Depth Map Shadows on a light. You can increase the value of Shadow Color to obtain lighter and more transparent-looking depth maps. If you are raytracing, you can turn on Use Ray Trace Shadows.

To render a reflection of the coffee surface onto the inside of the cup, make sure you are raytracing, select the coffee fluid object, and in the Render Stats tab in the Attribute Editor, turn on Visible In Reflections.

If you want the creamer stream to cast a shadow onto other fluid objects as well as geometry, you have to turn on Use Ray Trace Shadows for the light and make sure that the Cast Shadows option for the fluid object is turned on (by default it is on). Due to the computation involved, this will be quite slow. Run the entire simulation up to frame 265 or so, and render out a frame to see what the final result looks like; it should be similar to Figure 25.49. If you

Figure 25.49

A final render of the coffee, creamer, and steam simulation

would like to see how we created this project, you can load the `CompleteCoffee` scene from the accompanying CD. Also, there is an animation of the creamer and coffee, `CreamandCoffee.mov`, available on the CD (note that this movie is not raytraced due to time considerations).

> If you turn on Use Ray Trace Shadows (and Ray Tracing in Render Globals), the Maya renderer has to calculate huge numbers of ray paths through the volumes of fluids in the scene, so your render times and memory usage will shoot up dramatically. If you don't have enough RAM (more than 1GB) on your system, this could lead to render crashes. To alleviate this trouble, as well as to speed up preview renders, turn off Use Ray Trace Shadows, or turn off Ray Tracing altogether, at least until you are ready to try for a final render.

Summary

Although fluids are obviously an extremely complex type of simulation, this chapter has shown how easy it is to create rich, natural-looking effects with them—without you having to delve into the complexities of the simulation itself. By adjusting various elements of a basic simulation, you can get any number of different smoke, fire, cloud, water, and ocean effects— or, if you want to start with something prebuilt for you, you can simply drag a 2D or 3D fluid or ocean effect directly into your scene.

We hope the new Fluid Effects plug-in for Maya Unlimited will inspire you to create wonderful natural (or supernatural) images and animations on your own. With a little practice and a solid knowledge of what fluid and ocean effects can do for you, you should be set to create all sorts of misty, smoky, and wet environments for your animations!

Interviews

Interview with Jill Ramsay

Alias|Wavefront's Jill Ramsay is the director of Brush-based technologies and a Maya Product Manager. She has, over the years, spent a lot of time on the discussion groups answering questions from the Maya community after hours, earning her "hero" status among users of Maya. She is Product Manager of Fluid Effects, the new Maya 4.5 Unlimited module that allows the creation of fluids, oceans, smoke, and so on. She spoke with us about the creation of the product, how it has evolved, and gave us some insight into the way functionality gets added to Maya.

Perry Harovas Please give us some background about how Fluid Effects came into being in its present form.

Jill Ramsay Jos Stam has been sort of playing around with various fluid solvers for, I would say, quite a number of years. I saw some 2D fluid solver technology being prototyped by Jos and the rest of the research department at least two and a half years ago. He started with just a touch screen prototype in 2D where you could swirl an image around in a fluidic manner using the 2D fluid solver. So, we decided when we were planning Maya 4, that this was something we would like to investigate. We started working on it as a product before Maya 4 shipped, actually, but we continued through the Maya 4 process into the next release of Maya, version 4.5, to actually bring that out as a product working with Duncan Brinsmead, who of course is taking care of the rendering side of things for us.

Perry Harovas I've been very interested in fluid dynamics for years, and in the last six months or so I've read everything that Jos has published. What I've garnered is that he's taken something that was very "researchy," if that's a word, and figured how to kind of stabilize it so that you can use it in a production environment.

Jill Ramsay That sounds correct to me. Yeah, certainly one of the hardest challenges in fluids is to keep the solvers stable and to have them not, you know, freak out and go beyond their limits. Although Fluid Effects is physically based and to a certain extent the simulations are physically accurate, that is not the most important thing when you're working in the production environment. True physical accuracy is not necessarily what's required—it's simulation of something that looks good and feels good and can be calculated in a reasonable amount of time. So it does, as you say, take that from a pure research and scientific topic into something that is useful for a production environment.

Perry Harovas And, you know, if it looks right, it is right, basically.

Jill Ramsay Exactly, for *us*. Whereas, if you're making aircraft wings, it can't just look right; it has to be right, or somebody's going to crash.

Perry Harovas How does Fluid Effects work so quickly? Is it because it's not 100% real-world dynamics based? Or did Jos have to sacrifice a few small animals?

Jill Ramsay (laughs) Well, we have two Navier-Stokes solvers within Fluid Effects. We have a 2D solver, which is very, very fast, and of course in real life there's no such thing as a 2D fluid. So, yes, in that sense we get a lot more speed because it's not truly realistic. And we have the 3D solver, which is a lot slower to simulate. It's still much faster than what's been done in the past in true Navier-Stokes simulation. And that is down to sacrificing small animals and having incredibly brilliant people working for us, which is wonderful!

Perry Harovas That actually leads me to another question which is, what is the memory hit for rendering Fluid Effects? Is really going to tax an animator's computer?

Jill Ramsay Well, yes, it will, unfortunately. We have this concept of grids—if you can imagine a grid of voxels which hold the data—and for every sort of fluid attribute that you want to simulate dynamically, such as density, velocity, temperature, and so on, you need a grid of voxels in memory. That is quite computationally intense and quite memory intensive. So, yeah, you're going to need a decent system to run fluids on.

Perry Harovas And that brings me very nicely to another question, which is: Can Fluid Effects be used fairly interactively on a G-Force card, or are we going to need something heavier?

Jill Ramsay I haven't personally tried it on a G-Force card, but I don't believe that it's particularly dependent on overlay planes or anything like that, which is the only area in which G-Force cards tend to fall down. So I should imagine you'd be absolutely fine with a G-Force card. But that is something we need to try.

Perry Harovas I will be trying it very shortly. And as a side note, which has nothing to do with the interview, I feel like I'm going to get the shakes if I don't get the Maya 4.5 beta soon!

Jill Ramsay I know, I'm sorry! I must say as well, this is totally normal. This is what happens with beta. I mean, what happened today is that we were just about to send the thing out the door and we found a really nasty crash. So that means that the bug has to be found, the code has to be either backed out from what was causing it or fixed, and then the betas have to be re-released and then re-verified by QA. So that immediately puts another two days on the schedule.

Perry Harovas Well, that's preferable than having everybody crash immediately.

Jill Ramsay Well, the thing is, it's beta, so there will be problems, but we don't want a problem that is going to stop people from beta testing, from getting anything done. That's not helpful. Actually the bug has nothing to do with fluids; it's something else. But you know it's a piece of code, and we have to make it reasonably usable in beta.

Perry Harovas Right, which actually is a good lead-in for the next question, and this is something I think to all our readers has been kind of misunderstood and ethereal, as it certainly has been to me: How does a major new module get added to Maya? Considering Maya's size already, how do you go about actually creating a way for a user to interact with a new module and than hook up all the things that module needs to access? It seems to me that you do all these things, everything has a ripple effect, and you have to go back and decide "was that a good move or not a good move." It seems like it's quite an involved process.

Jill Ramsay You're absolutely right; it is a difficult thing to do. And one of the things that we try to do within Maya is to have the various parts of the software work well together with other parts of the software, and that's, as you say, increasingly difficult the larger the software gets. So, for example, with Fluid Effects, we'd start off with a prototype—and the prototype would generally not even be within Maya. And, for example, Jos's work was not done in Maya; it was a stand-alone prototype. Then we have to get someone to build it into Maya. What usually happens is, it starts off with some incredibly rudimentary and rather bad UI, and we then put it in front of our in-house user community. We have product specialists working on the team who first of all sit down and try to play with it, and then, basically, it's weeks and months of trying to refine the UI and come up with concepts.

For example, you'll see when you get the code, we came up with the concept of having a container and then the fluid stuff that goes inside it, and that wasn't originally there in the UI. We were having a terrible problem in getting the concepts of what was the fluid and what was the space around it sort of thing. Finally, over a period of time, we had several trials and meetings with the user community, and we suddenly hit on this: well, what if that outside thing was called the container and then we sort of talked about different ways of filling the container? And suddenly it all fell into place, and then the UI was developed around that. And when we'd done that, we found that users who were exposed to it for the first time were much more able to grasp what was going on.

So, it's really a sort of trial-and-error thing. And we're still not done of course. Next we send it out to people like yourself in the beta community and see how they get along with it. Because we become familiar with the concepts over a period of time, it's not easy for us to see how hard that is for a first-time user. You know, we need to constantly expose the product to fresh blood to see how users react. But Fluid Effects particularly was very, very difficult because it is a difficult concept to understand in real life. So, yeah, a lot of what we do is trying to get that right. It's a difficult process.

Perry Harovas You said that the next stage is sending it out to beta teams, although in many ways it sounds to me like your hands are tied because you've had to feature lock before you send it out. And so anything that's fundamentally wrong with it that is found by the beta team is an integral part of it now.

Jill Ramsay Well, you've got a good point. If it would require an entire rewrite, it's not going to happen, and we have to rely on the fact that our own internal user base would've found something that was that bad. But if we find that our beta sites don't understand this term or this concept, we can try to fix the UI to make that better, and we certainly will do that.

Perry Harovas OK, geek question, now: Can we finally do pyroclastic clouds? And more important probably, can we fly through them in a nice, smooth way?

Jill Ramsay Yes! There are certain Fluid Effects that we won't be able to do with the first release, and people will be disappointed about that I'm sure, like pouring water and that kind of thing. That's not something we'll be doing in the first release. But atmospherics, clouds, really nice pyroclastic effects are exactly what we will be able to do, and Duncan's already done some interesting renders and tests. I must warn you that render times are not going to be super fast on this, though, and that's one thing that we validated with some customers before we began this project. We asked if it was it okay if render time was going to be fairly significant, and the feedback we got was: it's okay as long as I can get some good interactive feedback of the motion and what's going on before I send it off to the render farm.

Perry Harovas With Alias|Wavefront opening up basically unlimited licenses and with hardware being so cheap, that's less important. I concur, basically, it's less important than interactivity in production.

Jill Ramsay Right, that's what we were told. So, yes, I think you'll be very pleased with the pyroclastic sort of effects that you can get.

Perry Harovas I think that's been kind of the hallmark for Maya since day one, because I was a PowerAnimator user before I was a Maya user. I really struggled for quite a long time with slow updates of IK and things that weren't the fault of Alias|Wavefront, or actually at that point Alias. At that point the code was 10 or 11 years old. It was code piled on top of code, and when Maya came out and the speed and interactivity of every element of it was apparent, that was the thing that drew me to it and drew a lot of people to it. And it looks like you're keeping that up and that's remained a focus.

Jill Ramsay Certainly. And we're doing everything we can in that respect. It is tough. I heard that there are some people who sit in a room waiting for computational fluid dynamics to solve with their industrial software at the rate of a day a frame. So, anything we can do that is two seconds a frame is certainly a great advance there. Our 2D solver is great. It's more or less real time, but 3D is slower. I'm not going to pretend to you that it's not. And you may well have some frustration with that. But it's all on a relative scale of what you're looking at in the outside world to do this kind of thing.

Perry Harovas How does Fluid Effects differ from some of the other fluid plug-ins for Maya, such as Arete and RealFlow?

Jill Ramsay It's a matter of integration, really. With Fluid Effects, if you want your fluid to drive the particles in your scene, you can have that happen. If you want it to affect soft bodies, you can have that happen. If you want your character to walk through and disturb fluid, you can have that happen.

Perry Harovas Is the rendering of the fluids an embedded renderer within the normal Maya renderer, or is it one that's maybe been optimized for volumes? Or is it just an extension of Maya's native renderer?

Jill Ramsay I would say that it's an extension of Maya's renderer.

Perry Harovas It's not a post effect?

Jill Ramsay Not a post effect, no. It's within 3D there.

Perry Harovas I can hear people cheering right now that it's not a post effect.

Jill Ramsay Me too!

Perry Harovas Even though they're both fantastic for what they can do, their limits, I think, drive people a little nuts.

Jill Ramsay I'm sure they do.

Perry Harovas But I think unreasonably so in a lot of ways, because people are given this great technology, and Alias doesn't make any false promises as to what it is or what it isn't. They just say this is a new technology, this is a way that we found to do it, and here are the workarounds to doing it. And then immediately a lot of the response is, "Well, how come it can't do A, B, and C?" And I think part of why this new technology is so cool, if we're talking about for instance Paint FX, is it's a new way of doing something that enables us to do something we could never do before, and we have to make certain sacrifices to be able to do it so quickly (or even at all).

Jill Ramsay I think that's true. And I also think that if we were to spend the time making it do what they want it to do, which would be, "Okay, you don't want any other features for 4.5 at all, we're just going to make Paint FX not be a post effect," we probably still couldn't even do it. But say we did. Many people would just say, "All right, thanks. So how come there aren't any other features?" That's what's really frustrating, because it's just… don't you get how long it takes for us to do that?

Perry Harovas Well, that was the response for Maya 4. People said it's basically a large bug fix.

Jill Ramsay Yes, despite the fact that what everybody asks us to do again and again and again was to fix the existing stuff.

Perry Harovas I'm probably going to be accused of being an employee of Alias|Wavefront, but I've always been—to the degree that I can be as a user of the software—sympathetic to the challenge that it must be to try to make everybody happy all the time, which is absolutely impossible.

Jill Ramsay Totally. I must say sometimes we do get a little fed up because we can't do anything right. If we lower the price, the people who just bought it complain that we've taken away their value. If we don't lower the price, we're gouging. Sometimes there's just nothing you can do. It's quite frustrating.

Perry Harovas I know there's a reason that Maya's used in so many production houses out there, and I really think that reason is the value it brings…you can get software cheaper, but can it do the same number of things? And is it as open? The answer is no. And developing technology like that is expensive. And that also takes time to develop. And I think if you own a CG facility, you're keenly aware of how long it takes to do things, what things cost, how much of a value you have to put on human beings that are working for you, and how long it takes those people to actually do something for you.

Jill Ramsay Absolutely.

Perry Harovas It's almost like a dynamic effect. I'm such a geek that I always relate it back to CGI, but the people that are working for you in a company, especially a company as massive as Alias|Wavefront, they kind of feed off each other. If one person does something that causes a ripple effect, everybody else is affected. And there's an ebb and a flow in a company like that, much like a particle (or fluid) system! Nobody works in a vacuum.

Jill Ramsay Absolutely. That's so true.

Perry Harovas Could you describe what the brush-based technologies division is, and also what it might be in the future? You know, what types of things you're looking at to try to bring that kind of paradigm to the rest of Maya.

Jill Ramsay Well, we have two types of brush technology in Maya at the moment. There's Artisan in all its various guises, and there's Paint FX. And in version 4 we re-architected Artisan, and we began to port over the tools to the new architecture. We were immediately able to see the benefit of that because we could now paint in fluids. One of the reasons for the port was that Artisan was written as a very NURBS-specific tool, and it was hard to extend it to work on other surface types. We expended a lot of effort to make it work on polys, and we started to expend an equivalent amount of effort making it work on SubD's, so we realized that wasn't the right thing to do. The right thing to do is to re-architect Artisan so it's surface independent, and so that's what we did. I sort of managed that whole process

Basically we see the brush-based paradigm of Artisan as just being part of Maya wherever you go. There are now something like 13 Artisan tools within Maya. People originally seemed to think it was just a sculpting tool. That was the one they grabbed hold of and they could get their head around. But that was just one of 13 tools in there. So whatever new feature we put in, like we put in fluids, the obvious way to paint velocity or to add velocity directions into your fluids is with a brush; so we have Artisan painting velocity within fluids now. You can paint down the temperature where you want the fluid to heat up, and we have that working quite nicely. The same with Fur. The way that we can comb the hair in Fur I think is one of the coolest things about Maya's particular fur implementation. And cloth—if you want to paint where the stiffer part of the material is, you can use the brush to do that. And it's a natural paradigm, something that we want to keep building on.

Perry Harovas Could you be more specific as to how Maya particles can interact with Fluid Effects, and does it really make particles obsolete?

Jill Ramsay No, it certainly doesn't make particles obsolete. What we can do is connect a fluid to a force, and then connect the particles to the fluid. So, what that allows you to do is to mix the two types—have the particles be carried along with the fluid or in fluids by the motions of the fluid.

Perry Harovas Could you tell me about the different ways to surface fluids, one of them being, I guess, the poly display, and how much is that tied into the rest of Maya? Meaning can you apply deformers to the poly fluid and do all the rest of the poly tools work on the poly version of the fluid, et cetera?

Jill Ramsay Well, if you convert to poly, it's simply a poly. So you can do anything you like with it at that stage. It's not a special type of poly; it's just a poly. You have three kinds of surface types inherent in the fluid itself. There's either a soft cloudlike volume with no surface—it's just a volume right through; then we have a hard surface, which is more like a blobby type of particle surface, for things like say mercury or ice or that kind of thing; and there's something called a cloud surface, which has a softness on the very edge so you don't get that sudden cut-off where a voxel is either on or off or full or not full.

Perry Harovas With regards to the poly fluid, what happens to the UVs as it's being created?

Jill Ramsay Now this is one area in which we do have a limitation right now. There are no UVs on the fluid. There are UVWs, and it's not super straightforward to extract UVs from that. So, the UVs—god knows what sort of UVs you get, you probably don't get anything on the fluid on the poly that comes out the other end. *[Jill tests the UV's on her computer.]* Yeah, there are no UVs. One of the nice things though with the fluid is you can actually simulate the UVs also. For example, if you've got a texture on say lava, you can pull the UVs along with the fluid so that they move naturally with the fluid, which is what you'd expect. If the

UV stays still, obviously the texture is going to sit there, and the fluid won't move through it, which wouldn't look realistic at all. Also, you can animate or move the texture node itself. You can texture the opacity, the color, and the incandescence of the fluid with a Perlin texture, which is one of the ways you get more detail in the fluid without upping the resolution usually.

Perry Harovas It's a Perlin noise texture, but it moves and flows along the fluid itself.

Jill Ramsay Yes, you can turn that on. The only issue with that is you can't move it too far because the UVs get stretched beyond all recognition from their original position, and then they start to get very stringy. If you want the texture to move a really long way, you also animate the position of the texture placement. You'd move that along with it rather than just try and move the UVs, because the stretching would be extreme.

Perry Harovas Can you use any texture on a fluid?

Jill Ramsay I know it's definitely a very bad idea, and I'm not sure whether we have made it impossible or just recommend that you don't do it. There are other ways to texture, though. You could use the fluid as a texture on something else. So the fluid could be a texture without actually being a fluid in both 2D and 3D, which is kind of nice.

Perry Harovas Oh wow.

Jill Ramsay So that's another very cool thing that you can do with this that I really love. It's the nonrealistic fluids, so things like…have a fluid go dripping around simulating and doing stuff and then use that as a texture on a logo or something for a company sign. Very cool. You can get some effects that just obviously you would never normally see. Some real "fluidy" motion going on, which is a lot of fun as well.

Perry Harovas How does that specifically work in 3D? Is there a conversion process?

Jill Ramsay It's a solid texture in that case. If you use a 3D fluid, it acts as a solid texture. If you use a 2D fluid, it acts as a 2D texture.

Perry Harovas And Maya takes care of slapping that texture on whatever you're putting it on?

Jill Ramsay Yes. You'll see in Hypershade that when you go into the 2D textures, there's a new texture type called 2D fluid, and if you go into the 3D textures, there's a new texture type called 3D fluid. Once you create that, a fluid appears in your scene, and you can do all the things you would normally do to it, but it gets applied only as a texture.

Perry Harovas Now for the obvious—I'll give you the history on the question. I did an effect for a film five or six years ago that I was never happy with. It was a tornado. This was right at the time *Twister* came out, and we were asked to basically combine a tornado and the Tasmanian devil. And having just read that, I'm sure anybody else would know that that's never going to come across as something interesting. It was a failed effects shot. So I'm of the mind to redo, every few years, some of the things that always annoyed me about my previous projects, and one of them is redoing this twister. To make my life easier, how many presets are you planning on shipping with the product, and are there any tornado presets? (laughs)

Jill Ramsay (laughs) The thing is, Duncan will do all the presets at the last minute—that's what happened with Paint FX. We all stressfully slaved away and managed to get two or three or five each, and then Duncan came along at the last minute and put 300 in. We're kind of hoping for a rerun of that, although it won't be 300—these are much more time-consuming to create than Paint FX brushes, which if you know what you're doing you can create in two minutes each. So I would hope that we can have at least 50. The other thing we're doing is, we're going to have them all available on the website, and hopefully we're going to have a link within Maya directly to the website to go and get them, which will be really fun.

Perry Harovas And I imagine that some of your presets are going to be things that if somebody wants an explosion, they have an explosion and it's ready, but other ones may be just instructive in nature.

Jill Ramsay That's absolutely correct. There are two reasons for the presets. One is to just get people started and give them some things to play with, and the second is to say, "Here's what we're doing here. This is the way that we've put this together." And the chances are you won't use that actual preset, but you'll learn from it how to do something on your own. There are a lot of really cool texturing tricks that only Duncan knows, so we have to make sure we get one of each of those in there at least.

Perry Harovas Speaking of Duncan, where did Jos leave off and Duncan start?

Jill Ramsay Well, Duncan has really done everything apart from the actual solver, the actual Navier-Stokes solver. So he's done everything else, even implementation within Maya. We have teams of people working on it. Julia Pakalns follows along behind and cleans up the mess after the geniuses. Julia is amazing. She's sort of a technical team lead and does all the grunt work, although she's fairly genius-like herself. Duncan and Julia have worked together to actually implement the stuff right within Maya. But Duncan really understands what's going on in there with the way these things appear in the render. Rendering is a big chunk of what fluids is all about. Lighting and rendering—he put the volume lights in so that they can interact nicely with the fluids. And all of the ramp shader stuff—which you saw in Siggraph I presume?

Perry Harovas Yes. Please elaborate, though.

Jill Ramsay The ramp shader stuff is just a way of defining attributes that Duncan has implemented. He did it for fluids, but as a result we have these things all over the place. We have a ramp shader on its own, which has nothing to do with fluids, that you can use for toon shading and all sorts of things, which is really cool.

Perry Harovas What is the Ocean Shader? The results look better than *The Perfect Storm* in many ways, which is amazing in its own right.

Jill Ramsay *The Perfect Storm* was a combination of many different effects—particles, shaders, all dynamics, and god knows what else. The Ocean Shader is purely a shader, so what you see in those effects is a plane and a shader. That's what's incredible about it. It's just really amazing.

Perry Harovas And I saw foam being generated. That's all part of the shader?

Jill Ramsay That's part of the shader, yeah.

Perry Harovas Has anybody checked his DNA to see if he's really human?

Jill Ramsay Oh, we know he's not human. We've known that for a long time! (laughs)

Perry Harovas Well, Jill, I want to thank you so much for talking to me, and the one thing I wanted to get across to you for a long time is this: I've read your posts—everybody has read your posts—and can't believe that *you* are actually human. Because you answer questions left and right when it seems that you should have gone to sleep long ago We all really appreciate the input into the Highend3D board and the listserv and things like that. It's just quite amazing. And you're definitely an asset to the whole Maya community.

Jill Ramsay Well, that's very kind of you, Perry. I really appreciate that, and it is nice to hear, because sometimes you only hear the bad news.

Perry Harovas I have a feeling that Maya 4.5 will change a lot of that!

Interview with Shai Hinitz

As of October 2002, those who purchase version 4.5 of Maya Complete and Maya Unlimited receive a free version of Mental Ray for Maya, a rendering plug-in from Mental Images. Alias|Wavefront and Mental Images also announced they would develop and integrate Mental Ray for Maya as a standard rendering feature in future versions of Maya.

In this interview with Perry Harovas, Maya Product Manager Shai Hinitz discusses the integration.

Perry Harovas In light of the announcement of Mental Ray for Maya being the default Maya renderer from now on, what is the fate of Maya's native renderer?

Shai Hinitz There is no change in the fate of Maya's renderer. We will continue to maintain it as a viable option for Maya customers. And one of the great benefits of this new arrangement is that Maya customers can choose between the Maya software renderer—if they've come to depend on it for whatever productions they're working on or however they've learned to use it and rely on a certain look—or Mental Ray for Maya to take advantage of all the productivity and advanced effects it can offer.

Perry Harovas Will it be improved or just maintained and bug-fixed?

Shai Hinitz We will look at those questions every release. We have a pile of things that we want to do every release and a pile of resources that we can apply to get it done, and then based on the business climate and the market conditions we make decisions on what resources to put on what development. If it gets a high priority, it will get done. So it's just another part of the application that needs to be prioritized like everything else.

Perry Harovas Thank you! So how long have you been with Alias|Wavefront?

Shai Hinitz It's going to be four years in the spring, so that's three and three-quarter years!

Perry Harovas And if I'm not mistaken, you were, prior to doing Mental Ray, heavily involved with Maya Fusion and the compositing end of things?

Shai Hinitz I've always been the Maya product manager focused on imaging, rendering, and compositing and anything to do with post-processes. I'm now also the product manager that's focused on animation as well.

Perry Harovas I'm interested you bring that up, and I'll just skip ahead to that question now. Are there plans to make the render engine that does post-process effects available to Mental Ray renders in Maya?

Shai Hinitz Yes. I think what you're asking me is, will Mental Ray for Maya support all the renderable features in Maya?

Perry Harovas Well, yes and no, because I realize that even Maya's renderer doesn't really render Paint Effects or Fur—they're a post-process. So I'm just wondering if the post-process engine that you guys are applying to your own renderer will be available to Mental Ray renders.

Shai Hinitz Well our goal is to make Mental Ray for Maya an equal citizen and render everything or launch other renderers—for example, Paint Effects—and composite those results the same way the Maya software renderer does.

Perry Harovas That's great!

Shai Hinitz But because of the robustness of Mental Ray, the core, there are a lot more opportunities to integrate things that were difficult or required significant investments to integrate in previous architectures.

Perry Harovas Oh really… That's cool, because I remember speaking with Duncan [Brinsmead, Alias|Wavefront principal scientist] about the difficulty of incorporating some things in Maya that were hard to put in the main renderer. He said it would require an entire rewrite of Maya's code to integrate those effects. Are those the types of things you're talking about?

Shai Hinitz Something like that…. That's what I'm hinting about.

Perry Harovas Do you have a time frame on things, or is it pretty much as you see fit?

Shai Hinitz We have a list of things, and once again we prioritize as things come up. Because Maya is not only rendering—the resources are shared among all the functionality that we do.

Perry Harovas What was the initiative that started this whole push to get Mental Ray integrated? What was the impetus that caused you guys to say you wanted to do this?

Shai Hinitz It's a combination of several things, I think, in no particular order: customers' requests and, you know, suggestions from them that we should have a look at this renderer. It's a serious renderer. It's got good features, and they'd like to see it "talk with" Maya. We recognized that Mental Images as a company dedicates 100 percent of their resources to rendering. Look at the advancements in rendering over the last couple of years. They have really been on top of them or even leading the way, and that's something that a company that produces a content creation application like Maya, which is modeling, animation, dynamics, effects, particles, Paint Effects, Fluid Effects, and rendering, can't do—we can't dedicate 100 percent of our attention to rendering. So it makes sense to partner with that type of company who can. It was another one of those investment/resource decisions we are constantly making.

Perry Harovas That is probably what I would have guessed. But in talking to some people about that, one of the concerns that came up was what happens if Mental Images closes their doors?

Shai Hinitz I'm sure we are all positioned for success, so there's no reason to be concerned about that. Well, the worst that could happen is that we continue to have what we have. In other words, we never lose anything. The plan is that Mental Images continues to develop the core, Mental Ray, and add new effects and push the envelope of CG imagery and rendering, and we continue to expose that stuff in Mental Ray for Maya. If things go bad, we keep what we have, and that doesn't go away.

Perry Harovas That's good, and probably another reason to keep the Maya renderer active and operational for each release. As a backup, not just because of the people who are currently using it and are happy with it.

Shai Hinitz And also for the customers that rely on universal rendering. We don't offer unlimited Mental Ray rendering licenses for free, but we still do with the native Maya software renderer and we will continue to provide that.

Perry Harovas Who are some of the key people on your team to create this plug-in and system?

Shai Hinitz Well, we have a team of engineers who are dedicated on our side to this product, to this effort, and that team grows and shrinks depending on, again, how much resource we dedicate to different parts of Maya. So obviously in the beginning, it's quite a big effort to get the architecture there, to get the workflow and the UI and everything, so it was a significant effort. There is an equal effort, an equal engineering team in Germany at Mental Images, that we work very, very closely with. We are constantly sending code back and forth and have weekly team meetings. So it's a big team effort. It sometimes feels like they are just down the hall—it's just a very, very *long* hall over to Germany!

Perry Harovas Is there a feeling that what they're doing with you guys and what they're doing with Softimage can be mutually beneficial or mutually exclusive?

Shai Hinitz From our point of view?

Perry Harovas Well, from their point of view since they're kind of in the middle between two competing companies that create content.

Shai Hinitz Well, I don't know for sure, but logic says that yes, from their point of view, they create once and repurpose for as many applications that they have partnerships with. The way that Mental Ray, the core, communicates with the applications, though it's not the same I suspect, and so there isn't a lot of overlap there.

Perry Harovas And that's actually a perfect segue into my next question, which is: The way XSI incorporates Mental Ray, from my limited understanding of it, is that it's basically part of the whole binary of XSI, and the way Maya does it is through translation in a plug-in, if I'm not incorrect. Are there any plans to change that so it's more part of the code?

Shai Hinitz Well, in Maya Unlimited, you use Fur or Cloth, and those are also plug-ins. When you use them, you don't even know that they're plug-ins because the workflow is so well integrated. Maya's architecture provides that ability to integrate plug-ins well.

Perry Harovas Well, I guess the reason I'm asking it is that the translation time that I've seen personally using Mental Ray for Maya and then doing the same thing in XSI seems to be longer in Maya than in XSI.

Shai Hinitz Well, I suspect what you're seeing is due to the fact that XSI has been developing their support for Mental Ray for some years now. They've been at it for about two or three years more than we have, and we're not as optimized as we can be. In practical terms, there is no such thing as *no* translation. Even the Maya software renderer, the native renderer, when you click the Render button, it looks at the scene and says, "Ooh, I've got a bunch of stuff to render. Okay, organize it this way, organize it that way, move some data around. These things need to get tessellated." That's what's happening when you click the Render button to Mental Ray as well. There is no export process. It's as if there's a scene database that's being stored all the time in memory, and as you make changes to your scene in Maya, those changes get updated into the Mental Ray for Maya database. And so when you click Render, it's not exporting anything per se. It's basically processing what you've asked it to render.

Perry Harovas Well, you know what? That's really good to know, because that is a giant misconception that I also bought into out in the CG community, that part of the advantage that XSI has is that they don't need to do this, what you're saying basically everybody needs to do, but they've optimized.

Shai Hinitz That's exactly correct. It is a huge misconception, partially because of history. Before Mental Images and Alias|Wavefront entered into a mutual agreement, I think Mental Images set out to create an exporter, which had a two-step process in which you had to first export your scene to another format and then render it in the stand-alone renderer. That effort was abandoned in favor of the integrated version, because it is a much more productive and a much more intuitive way of doing things. So the misconception might be partially due to history, but also partially due to people's desire to, I don't know, hang on to their old beliefs. It's hard for people to believe that we're moving so fast, giving this stuff away.

Perry Harovas Right. And some people look at that as a good thing, like myself, and some people look at that as a sure sign that you're going down the tubes because that's what they would like.

Shai Hinitz And to them I would say, how *can* we be going down the tubes if we're being so aggressive and so passionate in investing in so many things? Maya is more popular than ever.

Perry Harovas Speaking of the translation, scene translation, or databasing, that leads me to something else that I've been wondering about, which is: Is IPR (Interactive Photorealistic Renderer) on your roadmap?

Shai Hinitz Well, I can't really say what we are planning, but I can say that IPR, which is a specific thing that really makes sense to implement for the Maya software renderer, isn't in our plan. However, something that gives people capabilities similar to that of IPR is something we're looking at doing in a future version. Once again, we want Mental Ray for Maya to be an equal citizen.

Perry Harovas I remember using—and I'm going to date myself here—TDI and their version, the original version, of IPR. And it was doing raytracing! It's always been kind of a wonderment to me that it wasn't incorporated into Maya's IPR. I assumed because it was called IPR it was doing somewhat of the same thing, but of course it was totally different code. I guess it just wasn't possible in the architecture that was created for Maya's IPR?

Shai Hinitz It's a combination of things—that's one side of it. The other side of it was that, from what I understand, what you were really seeing in Explore's IPR wasn't raytracing; it was a simulation.

Perry Harovas Oh, really?

Shai Hinitz Yeah. And so people say, well, who cares, it was productive, it helped, whatever. But the issue is that the implementation of that method would have been more work than actually making raytracing happen for real in Maya's IPR.

Perry Harovas Hmmm… And are you going to support raytracing in this new thing?

Shai Hinitz It would be great to support everything that the renderer can do, but I can't really promise at this time.

Perry Harovas That would be fantastic. Much the same way that XSI seems to be able to support everything. It is the true renderer.

Shai Hinitz Yes, however, in XSI from what I'm told, the limitation is that the more complex your scene, and the more you're asking of the interactive rendering, the longer things will take. So the interactivity actually suffers. They may have nice ways of dealing with it, how they can dial down the quality very quickly. But I believe we can do better so that "price" won't be there. Again, I'm hesitant to say because we shouldn't talk about things that are not in the product yet.

Perry Harovas Understood. OK, here's a question that's still in the same category: Will Duncan [Brinsmead] eventually program things for Mental Ray?

Shai Hinitz Duncan is someone who surprises us all. We sometimes have no idea what he's doing, actually. I've spoken with Duncan about the Mental Ray core, and he's excited about it and understands some of the benefits that Maya can derive from the use of custom shaders for everything. But I don't know for sure. It's really up to him. He's one of the people here who really has some freedom to create anything, and he does come up with some pretty cool things.

Perry Harovas He's just a mad scientist.

Shai Hinitz He's a sweet mad scientist.

I think from my last conversation with him, there'll be some pretty interesting things for the next version of Maya that will be coming out of Duncan.

Perry Harovas Jill Ramsay mentioned to me when we spoke at Siggraph that the development cycle for Maya is going to shrink back again from the year that it went up to back to something a little less, maybe six months. Is that going to be accurate now that this has all happened?

Shai Hinitz Perhaps, and that goes back to how aggressive we are right now. We are making it our goal, to provide people with more than one upgrade a year. So that does shrink the cycle I suppose.

Perry Harovas That's great. So, here's the next question: are all the Mental Ray features currently available to users of Mental Ray for Maya even if they're hidden?

Shai Hinitz The short answer is yes, because you suffixed your question with the "even if they're hidden" part. So everything is available. Some things are not as easy to get at as others. Our goal in the first pass in this version—1.5 is still the first version in my eyes—is to make the functionality that Maya customers are accustomed to using available to them. So that they can derive the benefits of Mental Ray for Maya without having to switch anything in their workflow. That was really the goal. In addition to that there was a goal that says if you are a Mental Ray expert, you will be able to have access to the functionality that you want. And that's available in Mental Ray for Maya through two things: custom text and custom shader integration that we've added in 1.5.

Perry Harovas Such as the environment variable that you have to set in order to see the Create Mental Ray rendering nodes?

Shai Hinitz Right. We're midway through the exposure of that feature. So because we aren't finished and we're not sure if it's going to be where you see it now, we decided to make it hidden by default and say okay if you want to look and experiment with this stuff, here it is, here's how you get to it. We're not going to promise it's going to stay that way, so just beware. It may change. And that's part of the stuff that lets you get at the functionality that isn't specifically exposed by Mental Ray for Maya UI.

Perry Harovas I'm wondering, when you guys started doing this, did you find anything interesting when you were doing one-to-one tests between Maya's and Mental Ray's renderer? Anything of note?

Shai Hinitz The things that Mental Ray is really good for are where we saw the differences. So, for example, displacement mapping, the subpixel displacement mapping is really superb in Mental Ray, and even though feature-based displacement is nice in Maya, you sometimes have to raise the tessellation, and then you might run into memory-usage problems. That stuff all goes away with Mental Ray. Displacement is fantastic. The whole concept of parallelism (parallel rendering across the network) is just amazing. You have to experience it. It's amazing! You open the verbose window of how it's communicating with all the other render slaves, and it's just sending the tasks, and you see the results coming back, and it's just perfectly scalable. So if you have ten stand-alone render nodes connected to your interactive render, it seems like you speed up your interactive render by ten.

Perry Harovas What are your thoughts about all the criticism that's been leveled at Maya's renderer?

Shai Hinitz My thoughts? I'm very passionate about the renderer. I mean, it's my baby, right? I think that it gets a bad rap unfairly, but again perhaps because of history. And you know, in the days of Maya 1, it was difficult to get pretty images out. The subsequent releases received significant investment in improving the quality, improving stability, and improving usability. And it seems like those things get noticed for a very brief period of time, and then it goes back to the negative perception that seems to be out there in the community. So I think that negative perception today is mostly unfair and that rendering in general is not a simple thing. It's difficult, and getting things to look just right is an art. If you have the patience to learn how to do that in any renderer, whether it be the one that is most popular like, let's say, Renderman, you can achieve similar results in the Maya renderer.

That said, I go back to the original question that you asked, which was, why did we enter into this new arrangement with Mental Images? As I mentioned, they are focusing 100 percent of their efforts on rendering. And some of the things that have become the new standards like global illumination, like secondary blur of elements—that is, reflections, , refractions, and shadows—are not features that are in the Maya renderer and would require investment to implement. It's not that it would be difficult, but it's work. And so then the question is, is that going to be beneficial to the Maya community more so than putting that investment in something else?

That's the product management game that we play. That's exactly what my job is with my colleagues and fellow product managers on Maya. We go and talk to our customers and talk to our sales people and get the feedback from everyone we can. We then try to decide where we're going to get the biggest bang for the buck—to really look out for the users' best interest—users new and existing. In that research, we talk to a lot of customers and roughly about 75 percent of them tell us they use the Maya renderer every day, successfully make money, and produce stunning images. So I think the negative comments we hear come mostly from a noisy minority. Not to say there is no room for improvement, but I think the reputation is unfair.

Perry Harovas But I'm assuming you didn't make such a momentous decision based on what 25 percent of the people said.

Shai Hinitz No, the decision is based on many factors and, in the long run, on what we feel is best for Maya and its users. Let's put it this way: the decision was not based solely on the perception of Maya's renderer.

Perry Harovas Look, I have a love/hate relationship with Maya's renderer myself. I was one of the biggest supporters of Maya's renderer for quite a long time until actually just recently. It's never been publicly stated that I was starting to get unhappy with it, but it's funny because I actually go completely opposite of what the curve is. I'm starting to have more and more trouble with Maya's renderer as time goes on and not less and less, and the issues are tending to be stability and grain, which is one of the reasons I was so excited about Mental Ray. I did some one-to-one tests, and using Mental Ray immediately fixed my problems. I'm not saying it's impossible to get the same quality in Maya's renderer. I've found myself running out of time to fix some of those things when I was heavily into production, and it seemed like I got a better result faster by just using Mental Ray.

Shai Hinitz It sounds to me like what you are communicating is the lack of quality default settings, because if you look at some of the pictures that Duncan renders, or some of our customers, or expert users, you think to yourself, "My God, that's stunning and beautiful," and they are impressive. But when you try to do that yourself without knowing how, you can't, and you can't explain why. The reason is that some of the default settings that are present in Maya today are there for either historical reasons or for the wrong reasons. Meaning they were taken from another place that was not applicable or determined by chance.

And that really goes hand in hand with the question of how many resources a company should put on a specific area. Creating meaningful and applicable default settings is an important thing. You know, it's like Maya's Paint Effects. In a way, it's a bunch of settings. That's not fair. I'm belittling it somewhat, but the point I'm trying to make is if you go in and try to touch those settings without knowing what's going on, you find yourself in a mess pretty quickly. But there are probably 400 or 500 brush settings now that you can use that are radically different from one another. And the difference between them is "just" settings. Fluid Effects are similar. With Fluid Effects, you can get goopy tar or cloudy skies. And it's the same technology, "just" different settings.

Perry Harovas Right. In that regard, I will completely agree. Because I found that I had to up the settings, the shading sample settings, in Maya's production quality default setting because it wasn't good enough. It wasn't giving me the detail I needed and the clean rendered image that I needed, but if I upped it, I got a much better render out of it right off the bat. And so I can see where you're coming from in terms of defaults. Let me just move on. And I appreciate your candor. Here's one you may not know. Can you render with external XSI shaders if they were recompiled?

Shai Hinitz It's a tricky question. Mental ray has this concept of custom shaders, which is basically a set of commands that Mental Ray understands and knows what to do with. The beauty of Mental Ray for Maya is that you can write those custom shaders in the correct syntax that the renderer supports and bring them into Maya, and they become a rendering node, like a shading node, just like any other shading node. Then you can hook them up and make connections and so on and so forth and change attributes and move sliders if you program them that way. So what you're asking me is, if someone creates a custom shader in another program and attempts to bring them into Maya, what will happen?

Perry Harovas Right.

Shai Hinitz If that person provides you with the libraries that those shaders rely on, and you can put them into Maya or put them into the place where they can be accessible when you try to load them into Maya, they should work.

Perry Harovas Okay.

Shai Hinitz However, it has a lot to do with, how they've been written and how the attributes have been exposed and so on. So it can get tricky.

Perry Harovas Okay, thank you. What sort of API would be available to people? Is there going to be an API specific to Mental Ray for Maya that they'll need to use?

Shai Hinitz The answer is divided into a few parts. If what they want to access is the Mental Ray core functionality, they would go through Mental Ray's API. If what they want to get at is the Mental Ray for Maya access to Mental Ray, they go through Maya, and we've extended the API for Maya 4.5 and will be adding more to the next version of Maya that lets people do that. Actually, by doing so, we're opening up the rendering architecture to this sort of "plug-in whatever renderer you want" possibility. So customers who want to use a different renderer can take advantage of these hooks and can technically get similar integration benefits that we have in Mental Ray for Maya.

Perry Harovas That's very interesting, because you're basically saying, if I understand you, that you're opening up Maya and exposing it to not just Mental Ray but any renderer that wants to become a standard default Maya renderer.

Shai Hinitz Right. And that philosophy started awhile ago when I came on board with the compositing agenda, because what we found was that people are pretty picky about what they want to use, and they really hate when companies force them to use a specific application. The whole "our company provides the entire pipeline from concept to finished product" slogan is not what most people want, I find. Because one guy likes working in a layered paradigm in a compositor, and the other guy likes a procedural paradigm in a compositor, and that guy likes using Photoshop for his 2D, and this guy likes using Painter or whatever else they use. And so rather than fight that and force people buy our software for their entire production pipeline—we decided that we'd open stuff up to derive the benefit of integration outside Maya. It started with compositing when we retired our compositing product, and we had this open compositing philosophy that meant customers can choose whichever compositor they like to use and still have productivity and integration with Maya. I met with and talked to all the compositing vendors and made sure that they knew how to integrate with Maya and knew how to get the data from the scene that they needed and so on and so forth. Some of them have taken advantage of that. and when you see the workflow. it's fantastic. Like Shake and Fusion and After Effects have done.

That lent itself as a great model for rendering as well. As soon as you decide that it's not a competitive issue but an embracing issue, it's like a complete 180-degree turn. You then start embracing everybody, and it's great because you say, okay look, Renderman is great, Mental Ray is great, Brazil is great, ART is great, Embedded Light Flow is great, and so on. You say to your customers, choose whichever one your project needs, you know. If your project needs the things that renderer X offers, by all means go use that and use it with Maya, and we're happy to be there for you. We are very, very serious about the change, and we're very serious about making customers realize that we're serious about this change.

Perry Harovas In terms of rendering layers, one of the things that bothered me about rendering in layers in Maya that I don't know about in Mental Ray, is it would give a separate render pass for each render. In Lightwave's renderer, it seems to hold things in buffers and then split them out at the end so that it's only one render, one frame, with lots of information. Is that possible in Mental Ray, or is it still the same paradigm of rendering different passes for each thing you want?

Shai Hinitz It's a simple question but has a complex answer. It is possible that multiple things get rendered in one process. It's difficult to do that because it takes away a lot of the freedom and arbitrariness of the whole concept of shading and texturing and lighting. Each tiny little thing produces a different result. And when you want those multiple results coming out in one process, you have to make a lot of assumptions. Like for example, sometimes people want the pure diffuse component or the pure specular component of the image that they're rendering. And if we know that, we can do that. We can do the pure components like diffuse, specular, and so on that contribute to the final result all in one process and just split them out into different files. The problem is that on most occasions, they don't just want the pure specular component; they want it a bit hotter so that they can then tune it down in a compositor later. You know, things like that.

When you try to make something an arbitrary solution that will sort of be general and apply to everything, it's harder to make those assumptions, and therefore it's harder to make those optimizations. So, the answer to your question is probably that some things will be able to happen that way, and probably some things won't. My advice to the reviewer is to be careful about what companies claim they're doing. For example, another package claims to do the render layers all in one process. But really what they're doing is doing the preprocessing, like tessellation and preparing things into groups and putting data into memory and writing a bunch of information out, and then running the final part of it which is the "what color is this pixel supposed to be in this pass" part of it, the number of times they need to do that. *And* keep the first part there. Does that make sense?

Perry Harovas Yup.

Shai Hinitz And so those kinds of optimizations are definitely things that we want to do, and they're already there for many cases, like shadow maps, for example. It's just a matter of are those the most important things that we need to do based on all the things that we have to do. And that's how they get done.

Perry Harovas There are some renderers that do anti-aliased z depth passes. Does Mental Ray?

Shai Hinitz I love this question. If it's called z depth, it shouldn't be anti-aliased. So they may have this other data channel, but it's not what computer graphics calls depth. Graphics defines depth as a single per-pixel value.

Perry Harovas So the solution would be to basically do what we do now and apply a shader rendered in RGB and then use the RGB as your depth channel.

Shai Hinitz Well, again, you're doing something else. It's not depth.

Perry Harovas Well, no. But in terms of taking it into a compositor and not having ragged edges …

Shai Hinitz The compositor will look at a single value per pixel, because that's what it's told depth is. One thing to do is to scale everything up and render really large-resolution images, and then once you're done compositing using depth, which is aliased, you scale it back down. And by that you interpolate things a little, and some things look a bit cleaner.

Perry Harovas Or do another render pass using a black-to-white shader, like the UU depth shader that's on Highend3D, and then you get an anti-aliased RGB image that you can use as your depth.

Shai Hinitz Right … but …

Perry Harovas It's not depth. But it's giving you black-to-white and gray values that are anti-aliased that you can do the same thing with. To a degree.

Shai Hinitz Maybe it looks better, but the answer is when you composite it, the compositing application does the following: "Okay, I've got two pixels. One is this depth, and one is the other depth. Which one is in front of which?" Right, you can't blend. What you want to accomplish though is blend the color. You're looking at the edge of the object, and it's not fully covering the pixel. How much of this object is contributing to the final color of the composited pixel? Let's take that much of its color versus the thing that's behind it, which is the remaining object that's covering the pixel and its color. That means you've got two values there. And depth just can't do that. Compositing using depth is a bad thing. It's a misleading way to work, especially when you have intersecting and overlapping objects. If you want to get the results cleanly, you've got to render things out in layers and manage objects going over and under manually.

Perry Harovas Well that makes, sense, though. And it's never really been explained to me in that way. Well, that's all we have time for. I appreciate your candor and your passion about what you do. It's infectious! Thank you very much, Shai.

Index

Note to the Reader: Throughout this index **boldfaced** page numbers indicate primary discussions of a topic. *Italicized* page numbers indicate illustrations.

Want to Learn More?

Alias|Wavefront publishes a variety of self-study learning materials that can help you improve your skills.

Visit

www.aliaswavefrontstore.com

and check out our books and training materials.

CAN YOU IMAGINE™

What's on the CD

The *Maya 4.5 Savvy* CD-ROM that accompanies this book provides all the sample images, movies, code, and files that you need to work through the projects in the book, as well as Maya Personal Learning Edition 4.5.

Chapter Files You can access files from the CD interface by clicking the Chapter Files button. In the chapter folders, you'll find images and source documents used in the book's step-by-step procedures and Hands On tutorials.

You get a variety of Maya binary files, Quick-Time movies, still images and textures, as well as MEL scripting code.

These files are for practice use only and cannot be used or reproduced for any other purpose. Copyright remains with the original copyright holder. Please delete practice files from your computer when you're done using them.

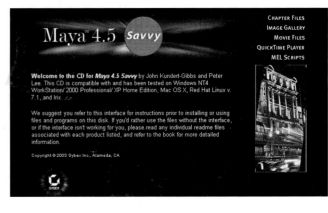

Maya Personal Learning Edition 4.5 If you don't already have Maya 4.5, you may want to install the Maya Personal Learning Edition 4.5 software, which is a special version of Maya that gives you free access to Maya Complete for non-commercial use. Maya PLE 4.5 works on Windows 2000/XP Professional and Mac OS X and allows you to work in wireframe mode without watermarks, as well as open native Maya ASCII and binary files.

Maya Personal Learning Edition 4.5 includes the following features, which will allow you to perform most of the tutorials in the book:

- Modeling & Animation
  - Polygon Modeling
  - NURBS Modeling
  - Subdivision Surface Modeling
  - General Animation
  - Character Animation
  - Deformers
- Integration and Expandability
  - Rendering

- Maya Embedded Language (MEL)
  - Integration and I/O
- Dynamics
  - Rigid and Soft-Body Dynamics
  - Particles and Fields
- 2D and 3D Paint
  - Maya Artisan
  - Maya Paint Effects (2D and 3D)
  - 3D Paint

QuickTime 6 If you don't already have QuickTime on your computer, we've included an installer in the `QuickTime6` folder on the CD.

Sybex strives to keep you supplied with the latest tools and information you need for your work. Please check www.sybex.com for additional content and updates that supplement this book and CD.
